Lecture Notes in Artificial Inte

Subseries of Lecture Notes in Computer Science

LNAI Series Editors

Randy Goebel
  University of Alberta, Edmonton, Canada
Yuzuru Tanaka
  Hokkaido University, Sapporo, Japan
Wolfgang Wahlster
  DFKI and Saarland University, Saarbrücken, Germany

LNAI Founding Series Editor

Joerg Siekmann
  DFKI and Saarland University, Saarbrücken, Germany

Hannes Högni Vilhjálmsson
Stefan Kopp   Stacy Marsella
Kristinn R. Thórisson (Eds.)

Intelligent
Virtual Agents

11th International Conference, IVA 2011
Reykjavik, Iceland, September 15-17, 2011
Proceedings

 Springer

Series Editors

Randy Goebel, University of Alberta, Edmonton, Canada
Jörg Siekmann, University of Saarland, Saarbrücken, Germany
Wolfgang Wahlster, DFKI and University of Saarland, Saarbrücken, Germany

Volume Editors

Hannes Högni Vilhjálmsson
Reykjavik University, Iceland
E-mail: hannes@ru.is

Stefan Kopp
Bielefeld University, Germany
E-mail: skopp@techfak.uni-bielefeld.de

Stacy Marsella
University of Southern California, Playa Vista, CA, USA
E-mail: marsella@ict.usc.edu

Kristinn R. Thórisson
Reykjavik University, Iceland
E-mail: thorisson@ru.is

ISSN 0302-9743   e-ISSN 1611-3349
ISBN 978-3-642-23973-1   e-ISBN 978-3-642-23974-8
DOI 10.1007/978-3-642-23974-8
Springer Heidelberg Dordrecht London New York

Library of Congress Control Number: 2011935934

CR Subject Classification (1998): I.2, I.2.11, H.4-5, D.2, I.4, I.6

LNCS Sublibrary: SL 7 – Artificial Intelligence

Typesetting: Camera-ready by author, data conversion by Scientific Publishing Services, Chennai, India

Printed on acid-free paper

Springer is part of Springer Science+Business Media (www.springer.com)

Preface

Welcome to the proceedings of the 11th International Conference on Intelligent Virtual Agents. While this conference represents a field of specialization within computer science and artificial intelligence, it celebrates an endeavor that requires the integration of knowledge, methodologies and theories from a wide range of fields such as sociology, psychology, linguistic, cognitive science and interactive media. The vision is bold: essentially create our own likeness in silicon. Intelligent virtual agents are animated characters that not only move, but also exhibit human-like competence when dealing with the world around them, be it virtual or real. In particular these agents communicate with humans or with each other using natural human modalities such as speech and gesture. They are capable of real-time perception, cognition and action that allows them to participate autonomously in dynamic social environments.

Intelligent virtual agents are not built overnight or by lone practitioners. These are complex systems, built layer by layer, integrating numerous components that address important functions such as visual object tracking, speech recognition, perceptual memory, language understanding, reactive behavior, reasoning, planning, action scheduling and articulation. Advances are made by sharing knowledge, components and techniques. Therefore the annual IVA conference is central to advancing the state of the art. It is an interdisciplinary forum for presenting research on modeling, developing and evaluating IVAs with a focus on communicative abilities and social behavior.

IVA was started in 1998 as a workshop at the European Conference on Artificial Intelligence on Intelligent Virtual Environments in Brighton, UK, which was followed by a similar one in 1999 in Salford, Manchester. Then dedicated standalone IVA conferences took place in Madrid, Spain, in 2001, Irsee, Germany, in 2003, and Kos, Greece, in 2005. Since 2006 IVA has become a full-fledged annual international event, which was first held in Marina del Rey, California, then Paris, France, in 2007, Tokyo, Japan, in 2008, Amsterdam, The Netherlands, in 2009 and Philadelphia, Pennsylvania, in 2010. Since 2005 IVA has also hosted the Gathering of Animated Lifelike Agents (GALA), a festival to showcase state-of-the-art agents created by students, academic or industrial research groups. This year's conference in Reykjavik, Iceland, represented a range of expertise, from different scientific and artistic disciplines, and highlighted the value of both theoretical and practical work needed to bring intelligent virtual agents to life.

The special topic of IVA 2011 was language and culture. These are the very things that make us uniquely human and represent the knowledge that gets passed from generation to generation. This knowledge is also being passed on to our virtual humans, incidentally or by design, and therefore these agents never merely exist in a cultural vacuum. By default, the agents may end up reflecting the culture of their creators, which may need to be acknowledged when deployed elsewhere. But culture and language can also be deliberately manipulated, for example to create agents for training, heritage preservation or cross-cultural communication. Some of the papers in these proceedings address the topic directly, but we encourage readers to be aware of the linguistic and cultural background that each agent brings with it.

IVA 2011 received altogether 91 submissions. Out of the 69 long paper submissions, only 18 were accepted for the long papers track. Furthermore, there were 27 short papers presented in the single-track paper session, and 25 demo and poster papers were on display. IVA continues to develop and improve the anonymous reviewing process, and this year a special author rebuttal phase was introduced for the first time. We believe that this resulted in more informed final reviews and therefore is something IVA will continue to use. Another novelty at IVA 2011 was the digital-only distribution of the conference proceedings. While reducing cost and bulk, not to mention the carbon footprint, the proceedings still retain full standing in the Springer series. More and more conferences are adopting this approach, which probably will stay with IVA in the future.

IVA 2011 was locally organized by the Center for Analysis and Design of Intelligent Agents (CADIA) at Reykjavik University and the Icelandic Institute for Intelligent Machines (IIIM), with the generous support of the Cognitive Interaction Technology Center of Excellence (CITEC) at Bielefeld University and the Institute for Creative Technologies (ICT) at the University of Southern California. We would like to wholeheartedly thank the scientific committees that helped shape a quality conference program, the Senior Program Committee for taking on great responsibility and the Program Committee for their time and genuine effort. We also want to thank our keynote speakers for crossing domains and sharing their insights with us. Furthermore, we would like to express great appreciation for the work put in by Yngvi Björnsson that oversaw the poster and demo session, and by our tireless student volunteers and their coordinator Angelo Cafaro that kept everything running smoothly. We are grateful for the character graphic designs contributed by Gunnar Steinn Valgarðsson and the timely conference system support from Thomas Preuss. Lydia Eichelmann helped to assemble the proceedings book. Finally, we would like to express deep gratitude to Ragnheiður Stefánsdóttir of RS Travel Solutions, who managed everything from registration and financials to decoration and local travel logistics.

Of course IVA 2011 would not have been possible without the valuable contributions of the authors, whose dedication extends beyond the creation of intelligent virtual agents to the creation and support of a vibrant research community that nurtures our passion for the field.

September 2011   Hannes Högni Vilhjálmsson
                                                            Stefan Kopp
                                                          Stacy Marsella
                                                     Kristinn R. Thórisson

Organization

Reviewers

Maria Arinbjarnar
Christian Becker-Asano
Kirsten Bergmann
Nadia Berthouze
Hendrik Buschmeier
Yiorgos Chrysanthou
Nicolas Courty
Morteza Dehghani
Carlos Delgado-Mata
Zhigang Deng
Frank Dignum
Arjan Egges
Birgit Endrass
Friederike Eyssel
Patrick Gebhard
Sylvie Gibet
Marco Gillies
Agneta Gulz
Steffi Heidig
Alexis Heloir
Jesus Ibanez
Mitsuru Ishizuka
Marcelo Kallmann
Stefan Kopp
Nicole Krämer
Brigitte Krenn
Michael Kriegel

Daniel Kudenko
Brent Lance
Jina Lee
James Lester
Benjamin Lok
Mary Lou Maher
Brian Magerko
Andrew Marriott
Stacy Marsella
Carlos Martinho
Jean-Claude Martin
Masood Masoodian
David Moffat
Louis-Philippe Morency
Hideyuki Nakanishi
Radoslaw Niewiadomski
Anton Nijholt
Toyoaki Nishida
Magalie Ochs
Patrick Olivier
Jeff Orkin
Igor Pandzic
Sabine Payr
Christopher Peters
Paolo Petta
Laura Pfeifer
Thies Pfeiffer

Nadine Pfeiffer-Lessman
Hannes Pirker
Paul Piwek
Rui Prada
Scott Prevost
David Pynadath
Stefan Rank
Matthias Rehm
Dennis Reidsma
David Roberts
Nicolas Sabouret
Kenji Sagae
Magy Seif El-Nasr
Ari Shapiro
Mei Si
Candy Sidner
Ulrike Spierling
Matthew Stone
Demetri Terzopoulos
Daniel Thalmann
Mariët Theune
David Traum
Hannes Vilhjálmsson
Vinoba
    Vinayagamoorthy
Marilyn Walker
Ning Wang

Table of Contents

Social and Dramatic Interaction

Culture-Related Topic Selection in Small Talk Conversations across
Germany and Japan... 1
    Birgit Endrass, Yukiko Nakano, Afia Akhter Lipi,
    Matthias Rehm, and Elisabeth André

"I Like Your Shirt" - Dialogue Acts for Enabling Social Talk in
Conversational Agents 14
    Tina Klüwer

Virtual Clones: Data-Driven Social Navigation 28
    Doron Friedman and Peleg Tuchman

Tilt Riders: Improvisational Agents Who Know What the Scene Is
about 35
    António Brisson, Brian Magerko, and Ana Paiva

Digital Improvisational Theatre: *Party Quirks* 42
    Brian Magerko, Christopher DeLeon, and Peter Dohogne

Where to Sit? The Study and Implementation of Seat Selection in
Public Places 48
    Elin Carstensdottir, Kristin Gudmundsdottir,
    Gunnar Valgardsson, and Hannes Vilhjalmsson

Guides and Relational Agents

Relational Agents Improve Engagement and Learning in Science
Museum Visitors 55
    Timothy Bickmore, Laura Pfeifer, and Daniel Schulman

Virtual Rapport 2.0 68
    Lixing Huang, Louis-Philippe Morency, and Jonathan Gratch

It's in Their Eyes: A Study on Female and Male Virtual Humans'
Gaze 80
    Philipp Kulms, Nicole C. Krämer, Jonathan Gratch, and Sin-Hwa
    Kang

Get Involved in an Interactive Virtual Tour of Brest Harbour: Follow
the Guide and Participate 93
    Mukesh Barange, Pierre De Loor, Vincent Louis, Ronan Querrec,
    Julien Soler, Thanh-Hai Trinh, Éric Maisel, and Pierre Chevaillier

Using Virtual Tour Behavior to Build Dialogue Models for Training
Review   100
    Antonio Roque, Dusan Jan, Mark Core, and David Traum

Posture, Relationship, and Discourse Structure: Models of Nonverbal
Behavior for Long-Term Interaction   106
    Daniel Schulman and Timothy Bickmore

Nonverbal Behavior

Sign Language Avatars: Animation and Comprehensibility   113
    Michael Kipp, Alexis Heloir, and Quan Nguyen

How to Train Your Avatar: A Data Driven Approach to Gesture
Generation   127
    Chung-Cheng Chiu and Stacy Marsella

Nonverbal Action Selection for Explanations Using an Enhanced
Behavior Net   141
    Javier Snaider, Andrew M. Olney, and Natalie Person

Providing Gender to Embodied Conversational Agents   148
    Marco Vala, Gabriel Blanco, and Ana Paiva

Modeling Gaze Behavior for Virtual Demonstrators   155
    *Yazhou Huang, Justin L. Matthews, Teenie Matlock, and
    Marcelo Kallmann*

A Framework for Motion Based Bodily Enaction with Virtual
Characters   162
    Roberto Pugliese and Klaus Lehtonen

Adaptation and Coordination

Towards Conversational Agents That Attend to and Adapt to
Communicative User Feedback   169
    Hendrik Buschmeier and Stefan Kopp

Quid Pro Quo? Reciprocal Self-disclosure and Communicative
Accomodation towards a Virtual Interviewer   183
    *Astrid M. von der Pütten, Laura Hoffmann, Jennifer Klatt, and
    Nicole C. Krämer*

Creating Familiarity through Adaptive Behavior Generation in
Human-Agent Interaction   195
    Ramin Yaghoubzadeh and Stefan Kopp

Contextual Affordances for Intelligent Virtual Characters   202
    Frederick W.P. Heckel and G. Michael Youngblood

Negotiations in the Context of AIDS Prevention: An Agent-Based
Model Using Theory of Mind 209
  Jennifer Klatt, Stacy Marsella, and Nicole C. Krämer

Listening and Feedback

Towards More Comprehensive Listening Behavior: Beyond the Bobble
Head 216
  Zhiyang Wang, Jina Lee, and Stacy Marsella

Backchannels: Quantity, Type and Timing Matters 228
  Ronald Poppe, Khiet P. Truong, and Dirk Heylen

Modeling Side Participants and Bystanders: The Importance of Being
a Laugh Track 240
  Jina Lee and Stacy Marsella

Appropriate and Inappropriate Timing of Listener Responses from
Multiple Perspectives 248
  Iwan de Kok and Dirk Heylen

Identifying Utterances Addressed to an Agent in Multiparty
Human–Agent Conversations 255
  Naoya Baba, Hung-Hsuan Huang, and Yukiko I. Nakano

Estimating a User's Conversational Engagement Based on Head Pose
Information 262
  Ryota Ooko, Ryo Ishii, and Yukiko I. Nakano

Frameworks and Tools

Demonstrating and Testing the BML Compliance of BML Realizers 269
  *Herwin van Welbergen, Yuyu Xu, Marcus Thiebaux, Wei-Wen Feng,
  Jingqiao Fu, Dennis Reidsma, and Ari Shapiro*

Robots Meet IVAs: A Mind-Body Interface for Migrating Artificial
Intelligent Agents 282
  *Michael Kriegel, Ruth Aylett, Pedro Cuba, Marco Vala, and
  Ana Paiva*

Multimodal Plan Representation for Adaptable BML Scheduling 296
  Dennis Reidsma, Herwin van Welbergen, and Job Zwiers

Towards the Rapid Development of a Natural Language Understanding
Module 309
  *Catarina Moreira, Ana Cristina Mendes, Luísa Coheur, and
  Bruno Martins*

Expressive Multimodal Conversational Acts for SAIBA Agents 316
    *Jeremy Riviere, Carole Adam, Sylvie Pesty, Catherine Pelachaud,
    Nadine Guiraud, Dominique Longin, and Emiliano Lorini*

Continuous Interaction within the SAIBA Framework 324
    Job Zwiers, Herwin van Welbergen, and Dennis Reidsma

A Flexible Dual Task Paradigm for Evaluating an Embodied
Conversational Agent: Modality Effects and Reaction Time as an Index
of Cognitive Load 331
    *Catherine J. Stevens, Guillaume Gibert, Yvonne Leung, and
    Zhengzhi Zhang*

Cooperation and Copresence

Did You Notice? Artificial Team-Mates Take Risks for Players 338
    *Tim Merritt, Christopher Ong, Teong Leong Chuah, and
    Kevin McGee*

Sharing Emotions and Space – Empathy as a Basis for Cooperative
Spatial Interaction 350
    Hana Boukricha, Nhung Nguyen, and Ipke Wachsmuth

Perception of Spatial Relations and of Coexistence with Virtual
Agents 363
    *Mohammad Obaid, Radosław Niewiadomski, and
    Catherine Pelachaud*

Failure Detection and Reactive Teaming for Behavior-Based
Subsumption 370
    Frederick W.P. Heckel and G. Michael Youngblood

Comparing Modes of Information Presentation: Text versus ECA and
Single versus Two ECAs 377
    Svetlana Stoyanchev, Paul Piwek, and Helmut Prendinger

Emotion

Empirical Evaluation of Computational Emotional Contagion Models ... 384
    Jason Tsai, Emma Bowring, Stacy Marsella, and Milind Tambe

Don't Scratch! Self-adaptors Reflect Emotional Stability 398
    *Michael Neff, Nicholas Toothman, Robeson Bowmani,
    Jean E. Fox Tree, and Marilyn A. Walker*

Exploration on Context-Sensitive Affect Sensing in an Intelligent
Agent 412
    Li Zhang

To Date or Not to Date? A Minimalist Affect-Modulated Control
Architecture for Dating Virtual Characters   419
  Michal Bída, Cyril Brom, and Markéta Popelová

Poster Abstracts

Interactive Characters for Cultural Training of Small Military Units   426
  Priti Aggarwal, Kevin Feeley, Fabrizio Morbini, Ron Artstein,
  Anton Leuski, David Traum, and Julia Kim

The BML Sequencer: A Tool for Authoring Multi-character
Animations   428
  Priti Aggarwal and David Traum

Intelligent Virtual Environment Development with the REVE Platform:
An Overview   431
  George Anastassakis and Themis Panayiotopoulos

Users's Expectations of IVA Recall and Forgetting   433
  Karla Bransky and Debbie Richards

Validity of a Virtual Negotiation Training   435
  Joost Broekens, Maaike Harbers, Willem-Paul Brinkman,
  Catholijn Jonker, Karel Van den Bosch, and John-Jules Meyer

A Software Framework for Individualized Agent Behavior   437
  Ionut Damian, Birgit Endrass, Nikolaus Bee, and Elisabeth André

The Mona Lisa Gaze Effect as an Objective Metric for Perceived
Cospatiality   439
  Jens Edlund, Samer Al Moubayed, and Jonas Beskow

Bots in Our Midst: Communicating with Automated Agents in Online
Virtual Worlds   441
  Doron Friedman, Beatrice Hasler, Anat Brovman, and
  Peleg Tuchman

Realistic Eye Models Taking into Account Pupil Dilation and Corneal
Reflection   443
  Guillaume Gibert

Control of Speech-Related Facial Movements of an Avatar from
Video   445
  Guillaume Gibert and Catherine J. Stevens

Teaching Her, Him ... or Hir? Challenges for a Cross-Cultural Study   447
  Magnus Haake, Annika Silvervarg, Betty Tärning, and Agneta Gulz

Examining Learners' Emotional Responses to Virtual Pedagogical
Agents' Tutoring Strategies 449
Jason Harley, François Bouchet, and Roger Azevedo

Source Orientation in Communication with a Conversational Agent 451
Yugo Hayashi, Hung-Hsuan Huang, Victor V. Kryssanov,
Akira Urao, Kazuhisa Miwa, and Hitoshi Ogawa

Checkpoint Exercise: Training with Virtual Actors in Virtual Worlds ... 453
Dusan Jan, Eric Chance, Dinesh Rajpurohit, David DeVault,
Anton Leuski, Jacki Morie, and David Traum

Modeling Nonverbal Behavior of a Virtual Counselor during Intimate
Self-disclosure 455
Sin-Hwa Kang, Candy Sidner, Jonathan Gratch, Ron Artstein,
Lixing Huang, and Louis-Philippe Morency

The Effects of Virtual Agent Humor and Gaze Behavior on
Human-Virtual Agent Proxemics.................................. 458
Peter Khooshabeh, Sudeep Gandhe, Cade McCall, Jonathan Gratch,
Jim Blascovich, and David Traum

CLARION as a Cognitive Framework for Intelligent Virtual Agents 460
Michael F. Lynch, Ron Sun, and Nicholas Wilson

Towards a Design Approach for Integrating BDI Agents in Virtual
Environments 462
Joost van Oijen and Frank Dignum

Animating a Conversational Agent with User Expressivity 464
M.K. Rajagopal, P. Horain, and C. Pelachaud

Expressing Emotions on Robotic Companions with Limited Facial
Expression Capabilities 466
Tiago Ribeiro, Iolanda Leite, Jan Kedziersski, Adam Oleksy, and
Ana Paiva

A BML Based Embodied Conversational Agent for a Personality
Detection Program 468
Guillermo Solano Méndez and Dennis Reidsma

Flipper: An Information State Component for Spoken Dialogue
Systems 470
Mark ter Maat and Dirk Heylen

Dynamic Planning for Agents in Games Using Social Norms and
Emotions 473
Palli R. Thrainsson, Arnkell Logi Petursson, and
Hannes Högni Vilhjálmsson

Are Intelligent Pedagogical Agents Effective in Fostering Students'
Note-Taking While Learning with a Multi-agent Adaptive Hypermedia
Environment? 475
    Gregory Trevors, Melissa Duffy, and Roger Azevedo

Toward a Conversational Virtual Instructor of Ballroom Dance 477
    Masaki Uejou, Hung-Hsuan Huang, Jooho Lee, and Kyoji Kawagoe

Author Index 479

Culture-Related Topic Selection in Small Talk Conversations across Germany and Japan

Birgit Endrass[1], Yukiko Nakano[2], Afia Akhter Lipi[2], Matthias Rehm[3],
and Elisabeth André[1]

[1] Human Centered Multimedia, Augsburg University,
Universitätsstr. 6a, D-86159 Augsburg, Germany
{endrass,andre}@hcm-lab.de
http://hcm-lab.de
[2] Dept. of Computer and Information Science, Seikei University,
Musashino-shi, Tokyo, 180-8633 Japan
y.nakano@st.seikei.ac.jp
[3] Department of Media Technology, Aalborg University,
Niels-Jernes Vej 14, DK-9220 Aalborg, Denmark
matthias@create.aau.dk

Abstract. Small talk can be used in order to build a positive relationship towards a virtual character. However the choice of topics in a conversation can be dependent on social background. In this paper, we explore culture-related differences in small talk for the German and Japanese cultures. Based on findings from the literature and verified by a corpus analysis, we integrated prototypical German and Japanese small talk conversations into a multiagent system. In evaluation studies conducted in the two target cultures, we investigated whether participants prefer agent dialogs that were designed to reflect their own cultural background.

Keywords: Virtual Agents, Culture, Small Talk, Topic Selection.

1 Motivation

Virtual characters are used in a vast variety of applications such as personal companions, training partners, teachers, sales assistants or for entertainment purposes. However all of these fields have a common need: virtual character behavior that is as natural and consistent as possible. Culture as a social background that influences human behavior can be used in order to enrich the behavior models of virtual characters.

For most types of applications mentioned above it is beneficial that a positive relation is established between the user and the virtual character. According to Reeves and Nass [1] users do establish social relations to computer-based systems and Bickmore and Cassell [2] use casual small talk in order to develop trust and rapport toward a virtual agent. Thus, in applications where the development of social relations is intended, small talk can be a part of the system's social intelligence.

H. Högni Vilhjálmsson et al. (Eds.): IVA 2011, LNAI 6895, pp. 1–13, 2011.

In [3], Cavazza and colleagues describe a companion ECA whose primary purpose is to hold conversations with the user. In their demonstration, the user's day at work is discussed while the virtual character responds by giving comfort, warnings or advice. Through this non-task oriented conversation about an everyday life domain that carries affective content, a social relation between the user and the virtual character is established.

However, the usage of small talk can vary with cultural background. In particular, the choice of topics occurring in casual small talk can be culture-dependent. In typical small talk conversations, so-called safe topics occur usually. According to Isbister et al. [4], the categorization into safe and unsafe topics varies with cultural background. Consequently, a topic (such as talking about family members) can be considered as being safe in one culture and as unsafe in another.

In the work described in this paper, we integrated culture-related topic selection into the conversational behavior of virtual characters. We expect that the choice of topics is dependent on cultural background. We therefore present a literature research as well as a corpus analysis that suggest how topics are prototypically distributed in German and Japanese small talk conversations. These findings were integrated in agent conversations. In evaluation studies that were conducted in the two target cultures, we investigated whether culture-related topic selection in the small talk behavior of virtual characters has an influence on the perception of observers with different cultural backgrounds. Therefore virtual characters have been used that resemble the cultural background of the study participants. The work described in this paper builds upon our previous work, where we presented a preliminary analysis of parts of the corpus as well as a preliminary evaluation study in one of the target cultures [5].

2   Related Work

Integrating culture as a social background that influences the behavior of virtual characters has been investigated in many systems lately. Language itself is the most obvious barrier when people from different cultures want to communicate. An example application that focuses on different languages includes the Tactical Language and Culture Training Systems by Johnson and Valente [6]. In order to complete the tasks provided by the system, users have to learn a foreign language. In addition to a speech-based interface, the system offers menus to select appropriate culture-specific gestures.

Non-verbal behavior is managed much more subconsciously than language but is influenced by cultural background as well. Differences in non-verbal behavior have been integrated in the behavior models of virtual characters in many systems so far, while several aspects of non-verbal behavior such as facial expressions, gesture selection, expressivity, spatial behavior or gaze have been considered [7], [8], [9], [10]. Besides the usage of different language or non-verbal behaviors, culture can manifest itself in a variety of behavioral routines. Some systems integrate culture by focusing on behavioral patterns that are typical for a given cultural background. Thereby rituals and different politeness or negotiation strategies have been taken into account [11], [12], [13].

While the approaches mentioned above rather focus on *how* things should be communicated in a culturally appropriate manner, the aim of our work is to investigate *what* should be communicated. An approach that takes different topics into account in order to simulate differences in cultural background is presented by Yin et al. [14]. For their study, two different virtual characters were designed, one representing a member of the Anglo-American culture and one resembling a member of the Latino culture. In addition, the appearance of the flat in the background as well as the music playing was adapted to match the cultural background of the agents. In their conversations with the user, the agents use different ways of argumentation. While the Anglo-American agent focuses on the interlocutor's well-being, the Latino agent shows interest in the participant's family and friends. However, in their evaluation study it is not clear which of the integrated aspects (appearance, language, way of argumentation) actually influenced the perceptions. Thus, for the work described in this paper, we concentrate on topic selection as the only variable in prototypical German and Japanese small talk conversations.

3 Background

In order to integrate culture-related differences into the small talk behavior of virtual characters, we first need to further explore the concept of small talk as well as tendencies that are described in the literature about different conversational behavior across cultures. In the following subsection, we categorize topics that are likely to occur in casual small talk conversations and state our expectations about culture-related differences for the German and Japanese cultures. Then we describe a corpus analysis in the two target cultures in order to ground our expectations into empirical data and get a statistical description of the observed behavior.

3.1 Small Talk and Culture-Related Differences

Small talk is often defined as a neutral, non-task-oriented style of conversation about safe topics, where no specific goals need to be achieved. However, it can serve different purposes, such as establishing social relations, getting acquainted with a conversation partner or avoiding undesirable silence. Although small talk is often smiled at and rules seem to be loose, it has been studied in the social sciences. Schneider [15], for example, describes a prototypical sequence of an average small talk conversation as follows: (1) question, (2) answer (3) reverse question / understanding / acknowledgment / evaluation (4) zero or more idle-moves, while step three and four can be performed several times. According to Schneider [15], this prototypical sequence can be restarted for every new topic.

Besides defining this prototypical sequence within a small talk conversation, Schneider [15] categorizes topics that might occur:

- Topics covering the *immediate situation* are elements of the so-called "frame" of the situation. The frame of a small talk conversation at a party, for example, holds topics such as the drinks, music, location or guests.

- The second category, the *external situation* or "supersituation" includes the larger context of the immediate situation such as the latest news, politics, sports, movies or celebrities. According to Schneider [15], this category is the least limited and can easily be extended.
- Within the *communication situation* topics concentrate on the conversation partners. Thus, personal things such as hobbies, family or career are part of this category.

According to Schneider [15], a typical small talk conversation begins with the immediate situation and shifts to either the external situation or to the communication situation afterwards. Whether the conversation addresses more likely the external situation or to the communication situation is dependent on the social surrounding. While shifting to social topics is more common in a social context, such as a party situation, shifting to personal topics is typical for a conversation between strangers that want to avoid silence. However, Schneider [15] only considered Western cultures in his studies and does not have a look at different topic selection in different cultures. But the distribution of topics does not necessarily have to be the same for other cultural groups as well. In addition, the reasons given for topic shifts can be culture dependent as well. In particular, silence seems to be a trigger for certain topic categories. However, the usage of silence in speech is dependent on cultural background. In the following, cultures are further explored and expectations about culture-related differences in topic selection are stated.

Trompenaars and Hampden-Turner [16], for example, divide cultures into Western, Latin and Oriental groups. Western cultures are described as verbal and members tend to get nervous when there are long pauses in communications. In contrast, in Oriental cultures (including Asian cultures), silence is considered as a sign of respect. While in Western cultures silence might be interpreted as failure to communicate, in Oriental cultures it is used as a means of conversation. In that manner pauses can be used to process information and assure that the conversation partner's turn is finished. This is in line with Hofstede's description of synthetic cultures [17]. Distinguishing individualistic and collectivistic cultures, the authors state that silence may occur in conversations without creating tension in collectivistic cultures, which does not hold true for individualistic cultures. Furthermore, the usage of pauses can be a crucial feature in collectivistic cultures. While most Western cultures belong to the individualistic group, most Asian cultures are on the collectivistic side.

According to these two theories, silence does not create tension in prototypical Asian conversations. Thus, is does not appear very likely that small talk conversations shift to personal topics in order to avoid silence, as described above for Western small talk conversations. But how are topics distributed in prototypical Asian conversations and where can we expect differences in comparison to prototypical Western conversations?

Hall [18] distinguishes cultures according to their relation to context. Regarding verbal communication, in so-called high-context communication little information is explicitly encoded and the conversation relies mainly on physical context. Besides verbal utterances, meaning is transported through the situational context as well as other channels such as non-verbal clues or silence [19]. In contrast, low-context communication explicitly encodes information. In low-context communication meaning is expressed through explicit utterances. The speaker is expected to construct clear messages that can be understood easily without the need to decode other aspects of behavior such as silence or tone of voice. Regarding this dichotomy, a line can be drawn between Eastern and Western cultures. While most Western cultures are low-context cultures, most Asian cultures are high-context cultures. In [19], Ting-Toomey describes people belonging to high-context cultures as having a lower public self than people belonging to low-context cultures, which means that not too much personal information is revealed during a first-time meeting. Regarding small talk as a typical conversation for a first-time meeting in correlation with the categorization of topics described by Schneider [15], we expect topics covering the communication situation to be more common in low-context cultures than in high-context cultures and thus more common in German conversations than in Japanese ones.

Summing up our findings from the literature, the choice of topics in small talk is predictable and should vary across cultures. In principle, topics that cover the immediate, external or communicative situation commonly appear in casual small talk. Regarding culture-related differences, topics that are related to the personal background of the interlocutors should be more common in Western small talk conversations than in Asian ones.

However, tendencies described in the literature are rather broad and too abstract for integration into a multiagent system. In order to build a computational model for virtual characters, empirical data is needed that strengthens our expectations and describes them in a statistical manner for concrete cultures.

3.2 Example Conversations in Germany and Japan

As stated above, we expect small talk conversations to be more personal in Western cultures than in Asian ones. But how exactly would the choice of topics differ? To get a deeper insight into these questions, we analyzed the video corpus recorded in the German and Japanese cultures for the CUBE-G project [20]. Within the corpus, three prototypical interaction scenarios were videotaped: a first time meeting, a negotiation and a conversation with a person with a higher social status. In total, more than 40 students from a German and a Japanese university participated and around 20 hours of video material were collected. Students interacted with professional actors in order to ensure that all participnats meet the same conditions, have not met in advance and to ensure that all conversations last for approximately the same time. To allow all gender combinations, four actors were hired: one female and one male actor from both participating cultures. Dyads were held in each participant's mother tongue and thus Japanese students interacted with Japanese actors and German students with German actors. The first scenario (first time meeting) recorded the participants while getting acquainted with one another. For our analysis, we focused on this scenario since we were interested in casual small talk conversations.

In total, 21 German and 11 Japanese videos were annotated using the Anvil tool [21], including all gender combinations. Thus, all German first time meetings were taken into account for our analysis as well as half of the Japanese conversations since annotation is not finished for the whole Japanese corpus yet. For our recordings, actors were told to be as passive as possible, and to allow the student participant to lead the conversation. Only if communication stagnated, actors should get more active. In that manner we could assure that as many topics as possible were introduced by the participants and not by the actors. Following Schneider [15], we categorized the topics occurring in the conversations into immediate, external and communication situation (see section 3.1). Considering our experimental setting at a university campus with student participants, we chose to classify topics as follows:

- **Immediate situation:** Participants talk about the experimental setting, the task itself or reasons why they are participating in the study.
- **External situation:** The students talk about studies or the university in general (as a supersituation for recordings at a university), friends or other people they know or public topics such as music or movies.
- **Communication situation:** Interlocutors focus on topics concerning themselves, such as their places of origins, hobbies, going out at night, personal habits or even their health.

For our analysis, we build lists of frequency data holding the conversations with the occurrences of topic categories, and compared the two cultures of Germany and Japan, or the frequencies of topic categories within each culture respectively, using the two sided t-test.

Comparing the choice of topic categories within the small talk conversations across Germany and Japan, we found that topics covering the immediate and external situation occurred significantly more often in the Japanese conversations than in the German ones ($p = 0.014$ for immediate situation and $p = 0.036$ for external situation), while topics covering the communication situation occurred significantly more often in the German conversations ($p = 0.035$).

Having a look at the two cultures separately, we found that German subjects talked significantly more often about the external or communication situation compared to the immediate situation ($p = 0.001$ for immediate vs. external situation and $p = 0.002$ for immediate vs. communication situation). In the Japanese conversations, we found that participants discussed the external situation significantly more often than topics covering the immediate or communication situation ($p = 0.001$ for immediate vs. external situation and $p = 0.006$ for external vs. communication situation).

In addition, we calculated the average percentage distribution of topic categories in the German and Japanese cultures. This prototypical distribution is graphically shown in Figure 1. The findings from our corpus analysis are in line with tendencies extracted from the literature. As we stated earlier, we expected to find fewer topics covering the communication situation in Asian small talk conversations compared with Western ones. In addition, we found that topics

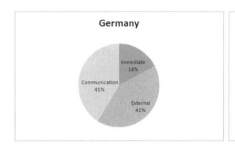 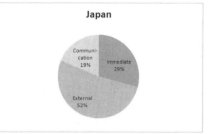

Fig. 1. Average distribution of topic categories during small talk conversations recorded in Germany and Japan

covering the immediate situation are more common in Japanese conversations and we gained a deeper insight in how topics were distributed in the conversations in our corpus for the two cultures.

4   Perception Studies

The main aim of our work is to investigate whether human observers prefer agent conversations that are in line with observations made for their own cultural background. To this end, we integrated our findings described above into a multiagent system holding virtual characters representing the two different cultural backgrounds and conducted evaluation studies in Germany and Japan. In the following subsections the integration into the scenario, the evaluation set-up as well as the results are presented.

4.1   Integration into a Virtual Scenario

In order to integrate the differences in small talk behavior described in section 3 into a multiagent system, we used the Virtual Beergarden application [22]. For the virtual scenario, culture-specific characters were modeled that match a prototypical Asian or Western ethnic background. Therefore, the characters' appearance such as skin, hair type or shape of the face had been adapted. Figure 2 shows the prototypical characters that were used in our evaluation study.

Regarding the verbal behavior of the characters, different voices such as German, English or Japanese can be used by the text-to-speech component. For non-verbal behavior, over 40 different animations can be performed by the characters, including gestures and body postures. An animation can either be typical for a cultural background, such as a bow for a Japanese greeting, or performed in a culture-specific manner by customizing its expressivity [23].

As described earlier, we found significantly more often topics covering the immediate and external situation in the Japanese conversations than in the German ones, while topics covering the communication situation occurred significantly more often in the German conversations. To simulate culture-related differences

Fig. 2. Prototypical Asian (left) and Western (right) characters used in the evaluation studies

in small talk behavior, prototypical conversations were scripted, differing in the choice of topic categories. Using the prototypical distribution of topics presented in Figure 1, we equally integrated the immediate and external situation into the prototypical German small talk dialogs and all three categories into prototypical Japanese conversations, with an emphasis on the external situation. In that manner, we integrated two topics covering the external situation and two topics covering the communication situation in the German dialogs, and two topics covering the external situation and one topic covering the immediate and communication each in the Japanese dialogs, while all dialogs lasted for approximately one minute.

4.2   Study Setup

In order to find out whether participants from Germany and Japan prefer agent conversations that reflect a choice of topic categories that was observed for their own cultural background, we set up two versions of our evaluation study: to be conducted in Germany and Japan respectively. Therefore the authors agreed on 6 English dialogs, three of them containing a prototypical German topic distribution and three of them containing a prototypical Japanese topic distribution. These dialogs were then translated into the German and Japanese languages for the two evaluation studies in order to avoid effects due to the language barrier or culture-specific assumptions made for English speaking characters.

For the study conducted in Germany, the Western looking characters were used and for the study conducted in Japan, we used the Asian looking characters. In this vein, we assured that the participants did not assume a cultural background different from their own. In addition, we used language specific text-to-speech systems for the Western and Asian characters (German and Japanese). To avoid side effects evoked by gender, we chose a mixed gender combination for the agent conversations. That is, one female and one male character interacted with each other in both cultures.

Apart from the choice of topics, no other aspects of verbal behavior were taken into account (such as communication management). Regarding non-verbal behavior, characters remained in a body pose prototypical for their cultural background during the whole conversation (see Figure 2), since we already showed that the the execution of nonverbal behavior influences the perception of human observers positively [8]. Gestures were not exhibited by the characters to avoid preferences aroused by their matching to the semantics of the speech.

Since participants only saw the version of the study setup that was designed for their own cultural background, all participants met the same conditions in the two separate evaluation studies.

Before observing the agent videos, participants were told that the two characters have met each other for the first time and were introduced to each other by a common friend that left to get some drinks for everybody. In that manner, we created the assumption of a first time meeting including casual small talk, similar to the setup of our corpus study.

Participants watched the videos in pairs, each containing a prototypical German and a prototypical Japanese conversation in alternating order. For each pair of videos they had to judge

- (Q1) which one is more appropriate,
- (Q2) which one is more interesting,
- (Q3) which conversation they would prefer to join and
- (Q4) which pair of agents gets along with each other better,

while participants were able to either choose one of the videos or a button indicating that none of the two videos was preferred. In addition, a comment box was provided that allowed participants to state an opinion on their choice.

As stated earlier, we wanted to find out whether human observers prefer agent conversations that reflect their own cultural background. Thus, we expected participants in the German evaluation study to prefer dialogs that contain prototypical German topic categories, while we expected Japanese participants to prefer dialogs designed to reflect prototypical Japanese small talk behavior.

4.3   Results

In the German evaluation study, 16 participants took part, 6 female and 10 male, all in an age range of 23 to 40 years. Since all participants observed 3 pairs of videos, we obtained a data set containing 48 judgments. For our analysis we conducted a chi^2 goodness-of-fit test in order to validate our hypothesis that German participants prefer the videos showing German behavior over the Japanese versions. Our results indicate that German participants significantly prefer videos with agent conversations that reflect prototypical German topic selection for all four questions. Table 1 summarizes our results from the German evaluation study. Thus, participants found German conversations more appropriate and interesting, would rather like to join the conversations and think that agents get along with each other better.

Table 1. Results from the perception study conducted in Germany

Germany	German dialog	Japanese dialog	none	chi^2	df	p
Q1	33	5	10	27.875	2	< 0.001
Q2	37	4	7	41.625	2	< 0.001
Q3	34	4	10	31,5	2	< 0.001
Q4	28	7	13	14,625	2	0.001

Table 2. Results from the perception study conducted in Japan

Japan	German dialog	Japanese dialog	none	chi^2	df	p
Q1	11	22	9	7	2	0.03
Q2	12	25	5	14.714	2	0.001
Q3	11	21	10	5.286	2	0.071
Q4	12	23	7	9.571	2	0.008

In line with our expectations, 5 out of 10 participants that explained their choice in the comment box stated that they preferred the selected conversation because it was more personal and revealed more information about the interlocutors.

In the Japanese evaluation study, 14 people participated, 7 female and 7 male in an age range of 21 to 23 years. We thus obtained a data set containing 42 judgments. As for the German study, we conducted a chi^2 goodness-of-fit test to find out whether Japanese participants would prefer the agent conversations that contain a prototypical Japanese topic selection over the German versions. Our analysis revealed that the Japanese versions of small talk conversations were significantly preferred by Japanese participants for 3 out of the 4 questions. In Table 2 the results from the Japanese evaluation study are summarized. According to our study, Japanese participants found the Japanese versions of small talk conversations more appropriate and interesting and thought that agents were getting along with each other better. Still this does not significantly indicate that participants would also rather like to join the Japanese conversations over the German ones.

Interestingly, and in line with our corpus study, some Japanese participants showed that the immediate situation was of importance for them. For example a Japanese video including to talk about the weather was judged positively by a participant because it "fit to the background image", while another participant disliked a conversation since "the content in the video does not match to the background image".

5   Conclusion

In this paper, we investigated culture-related differences in small talk behavior for the German and Japanese cultures for virtual characters. In the literature from the social sciences, three categories are defined that typically occur in casual small talk: topics that cover the immediate, external or communication situation, while interlocutors usually shift to topics about the communication situation when they find themselves in situations where silence is tried to be avoided. However, the literature about cultures describes that silence does only create tension in certain cultural groups and is thus, not tried to be avoided in other cultures, such as Japan. This suggests that silence should not trigger a topic shift towards the communication situation as a consequence in these cultures. In addition, some cultural groups, including Japan, tend not to reveal much personal information in first-time meetings. This suggests too, that shifting to the communication situation is not very common in Japanese conversations compared to German ones. In a empirical corpus study, this tendency has been verified and prototypical distributions of the three topic categories have been extracted for the two target cultures. The findings from the corpus study are in line with our earlier results, where we analyzed only a small subset of the same corpus [5].

In two evaluation studies, we investigated whether participants from Germany and Japan prefer agent dialogs that reflect prototypical small talk conversations designed for their own cultural background. Therefore, the authors agreed on English dialogs that were translated into German and Japanese and integrated into a prototypical German and Japanese study setup. Participants from both cultures only saw the version that was designed to match their own culture, including the prototypical dialogs for both cultures. Both evaluation studies revealed that participants significantly preferred agent dialogs that had a prototypical topic distribution as conversations that were recorded in the target culture. In that manner, German participants preferred prototypical German dialogs for Wester-style characters and Japaneses participants preferred prototypical Japanese dialogs for Asian-style characters. This is in line with previous findings from our pilot study, where prototypical dialogs have been tested in only one culture [5].

Reflecting on our results, we thus claim that when integrating small talk into the dialog models of virtual characters in order to establish a social relationship, designers should take into account the cultural background of the user that a system is designed for. In that manner, the integration of different topics into the dialog models of virtual characters designed for different cultural backgrounds could enhance their acceptance on the user's side.

In the evaluation studies presented in this paper, the virtual characters' appearance was left constant during the experiment and matched the cultural background of the hunan participants. In that manner, we wanted to ensure that the participants did not estimate a cultural background of the virtual characters different from their own's. However using this design, it is not entirely clear whether participants prefer topic selection that was designed for their own culture or the culture that the virtual character appears to be. To get a deeper insight into this question, we plan on conducting the same study in both cultures again, but with virtual characters that resemble a different cultural background.

In addition, it might be interesting to experiment with different gender combinations, since gender differences within conversations are supposed to be perceived differently across cultures.

Acknowledgments. This work was funded by the European Commission within the 7th Framework Program under grant agreement eCute (education in cultural understanding, technologically enhanced).

References

1. Reeves, B., Nass, C.: The Media Equation - How People Treat Computers, Television and New Media Like Real People and Places. Cambridge University Press, Cambridge (1996)
2. Bickmore, T., Cassell, J.: Small talk and conversational storytelling in embodied conversational interface agents. In: Proceedings 1999 AAAI Fall Symposium on Narrative Intelligence, pp. 87–92 (1999)
3. Cavazza, M., de la Camera, R.S., Turunen, M.: How was your day?: a companion ECA. In: Proceedings of AAMAS 2010 (2010)
4. Isbister, K., Nakanishi, H., Ishida, T., Nass, C.: Helper agent: Designing an assistant for human-human interaction in a virtual meeting space. In: Proceeding of CHI 2000, pp. 57–64 (2000)
5. Endrass, B., Rehm, M., André, E.: Planning Small Talk Behavior with Cultural Influences for Multiagent Systems. Computer Speech and Language 25(2), 158–174 (2011)
6. Johnson, W.L., Valente, A.: Tactical Language and Culture Training Systems: Using Artificial Intelligence to Teach Foreign Languages and Cultures. In: Innovative Applications of Artificial Intelligence (IAAI 2008), pp. 1632–1639. AAAI, Menlo Park (2008)
7. Jan, D., Herrera, D., Martinovski, B., Novick, D., Traum, D.R.: A Computational Model of Culture-Specific Conversational Behavior. In: Pelachaud, C., Martin, J.-C., André, E., Chollet, G., Karpouzis, K., Pelé, D. (eds.) IVA 2007. LNCS (LNAI), vol. 4722, pp. 45–56. Springer, Heidelberg (2007)
8. Endrass, B., Rehm, M., Lipi, A.-A., Nakano, Y., André, E.: Culture-related differences in aspects of behavior for virtual characters across Germany and Japan. In: Tumer, Yolum, Sonenberg, Stone (eds.) Proceedings of AAMAS 2011, pp. 441–448 (2011)
9. Koda, T., Ruttkay, Z., Nakagawa, Y., Tabuchi, K.: Cross-Cultural Study on Facial Regions as Cues to Recognize Emotions of Virtual Agents. In: Ishida, T. (ed.) Culture And Computing. LNCS, vol. 6259, pp. 16–27. Springer, Heidelberg (2010)
10. Rehm, M., Bee, N., André, E.: Wave Like an Egyptian - Accelerometer Based Gesture Recognition for Culture Specific Interactions. In: HCI 2008 Culture, Creativity, Interaction (2008)
11. Mascarenhas, S., Dias, J., Afonso, N., Enz, S., Paiva, A.: Using rituals to express cultural differences in synthetic characters. In: Decker, et al. (eds.) Proceedings of AAMAS 2009 (2009)
12. Wu, P., Miller, C.: Interactive phrasebook conveying culture through etiquette. In: Blanchard, E.G., Johnson, W.L., Ogan, A., Allard, D. (eds.) 3rd International Workshop on Culturally-Aware Tutoring Systems (CATS 2010) held on ITS 2010, Pittsburg, USA, pp. 47–55 (2010)

13. Kim, J., Hill, R.W., Durlach, P., Lane, H.C., Forbell, E., Core, M., Marsella, S., Pynadath, D., Hart, J.: BiLAT: A game-based environment for practicing negotiation in a cultural context. International Journal of Artificial Intelligence in Education 19, 289–308 (2009)
14. Yin, L., Bickmore, T., Cortés, D.E.: The Impact of Linguistic and Cultural Congruity on Persuasion by Conversational Agents. In: Allbeck, J.M., Badler, N.I., Bickmore, T.W., Pelachaud, C., Safonova, A. (eds.) IVA 2010. LNCS, vol. 6356, pp. 343–349. Springer, Heidelberg (2010)
15. Schneider, K.P.: Small Talk: Analysing Phatic Discourse. Hitzeroth, Marburg (1988)
16. Trompenaars, F., Hampden-Turner, C.: Riding the waves of culture - Understanding Cultural Diversity in Business. Nicholas Brealey Publishing, London (1997)
17. Hofstede, G.J., Pedersen, P.B., Hofstede, G.: Exploring Culture - Exercises, Stories and Synthetic Cultures. Intercultural Press, Yarmouth (2002)
18. Hall, E.T.: The Hidden Dimension. Doubleday (1966)
19. Ting-Toomey, S.: Communicating across cultures. The Guilford Press, New York (1999)
20. Rehm, M., André, E., Nakano, Y., Nishida, T., Bee, N., Endrass, B., Huan, H.H., Wissner, M.: The CUBE-G approach - Coaching culture-specific nonverbal behavior by virtual agents. In: Mayer, I., Mastik, H. (eds.) ISAGA 2007: Organizing and Learning through Gaming and Simulation (2007)
21. Kipp, M.: Anvil - A Generic Annotation Tool for Multimodal Dialogue. In: Proceedings of the 7th European Conference on Speech Communication and Technology (Eurospeech), pp. 1367–1370 (2001)
22. Augsburg University (2011), http://mm-werkstatt.informatik.uni-augsburg.de/projects/aaa
23. Endrass, B., Damian, I., Huber, P., Rehm, M., André, E.: Generating Culture-Specific Gestures for Virtual Agent Dialogs. In: Safonova, A. (ed.) IVA 2010. LNCS, vol. 6356, pp. 329–335. Springer, Heidelberg (2010)

"I Like Your Shirt" - Dialogue Acts for Enabling Social Talk in Conversational Agents

Tina Klüwer

German Research Centre for Artificial Intelligence,
Alt-Moabit 91c, 10559 Berlin, Germany
http://www.dfki.de

Abstract. This paper presents a set of dialogue acts which can be used to implement small talk conversations in conversational agents. Although many conversational agents are supposed to engage in small talk, no systematic development of social dialogue acts and sequences for dialogue systems was made so far. Instead systems reuse the same conversation sequence every time they engage in small talk or integrate stateless chatbots without any knowledge about the ongoing conversation. The small talk dialogue act taxonomy presented in this paper consists of functionally motivated acts inspired by the social science work of "face". Moreover, a corpus annotation and possible dialogue act sequences extracted from this annotated corpus are described. The dialogue act set and the sequences are used in our dialogue system to provide a more knowledge-driven treatment of small talk than chatbots can offer.

1 Introduction

Social talk, or "small talk"[1], is often perceived as little sophisticated chit-chat in which content exchange is irrelevant or even negligible. Following this definition small talk represents the opposite of task-driven talk. On the other hand, several studies have detected the "task" of small talk not to lie in knowledge negotiation, but in the management of social situations. In the early 1920th years Bronsilaw Malinowsky already introduced the term "phatic communion" to denote a kind of talk which "serves to establish bonds of personal union between people" [23, page 316]. This establishment of social contact is the primary goal of phatic talk and dominates or excludes the exchange of conversation content.

Several authors have described the importance for conversational agents to engage in social talk: On the one hand, social talk can be used to ease the situation and to make the user feel more comfortable in a conversation with an agent [5]. On the other hand, users tend to treat computers as social actors, especially if they possess humanistic properties such as language or voice, as described by the "Computers are Social Actors" (CASA) paradigm [24] or the "Threshold Model of Social Influence" [8]. Therefore, if applied to real world

---

[1] The terms "small talk", "social talk" and "phatic talk" are used synonymously in this work.

H. Högni Vilhjálmsson et al. (Eds.): IVA 2011, LNAI 6895, pp. 14–27, 2011.

environments, agents are nearly always confronted with social talk utterances and have to react to them in an appropriate way.

Although some agent systems provide small talk conversations, no systematic computational model of small talk was developed so far. Social science theories offer analyses of social talk, but only few concepts and ideas have been taken over to dialogue systems.

One example is the small talk sequence found by Schneider [26]. The Schneider sequence was integrated into dialogue systems [4] [14], but the use of just one sequence for all small talk phases in a conversation leads to an unnatural dialogue. For a natural conversation more flexibility in social talk is needed.

This paper suggests a functionally-motivated taxonomy of small talk dialogue acts based on the social science theory of "face". The taxonomy is validated by the annotation and analysis of a corpus with small talk conversations. Furthermore, from the annotated corpus possible small talk sequences are extracted. These can be utilized to generate a computational model of social talk for dialogue systems. We used the sequences for a dialogue system which hosts two conversational selling agents in a virtual world.

The paper is organized as follows: The next section (2) presents preceding work in the field of conversational agents which use small talk. The section also describes the popular dialogue act schemes and their possibilities to describe small talk. Section 3 introduces the social science work on "face" by Erving Goffman [15], [16]. Afterwards section 4 describes the taxonomy of small talk dialogue acts and section 5 describes the corpus and the small talk sequences found in the corpus data. Finally, section 6 gives a summarization of the paper and suggests necessary further work.

2 Related Work

2.1 Social Talk and Conversational Agents

Several studies have stated the relevance of social talk for conversational agents [5] [7], especially in embodied agents: Agents which are able to deviate from the task talk to social talk are found to be more trustful [4] and entertaining [22]. One example is REA a relational agent for real estate sales [12] developed at the M.I.T Gesture and Narrative Language Group. REA incorporates several measures for social "closeness" to the user, which she uses to improve her rhetorical ability in the delicate domain of money and real estates. Nevertheless, the small talk is system-initiated and user's utterances are partly ignored [6].

In an earlier implementation of REA, the system uses a conversational sequence for small talk [3], which was first formalized by Klaus Schneider [26] in his analysis of small talk as genre. The sequence consists of four turns and can be used for all small talk topics.

1. a query from the dominant interactor
2. an answer to the query

3. a respond to the answer, consisting of one of the following possibilities: echo-question, check-back, acknowledgment, confirming an unexpected response, positive evaluation
4. an unrestricted number or null steps of idling behavior

Although the small talk sequence found by Schneider seems to be typical for small talk conversations, it is not the only one possible and repetitions of the conversation pattern quickly become unnatural.

Another agent which uses small talk is "Max" developed at the university of Bielefeld [22]. Max is an embodied agent acting in real-world scenarios such as a museum guide. Max possesses small talk capabilities in order to be an enjoyable and cooperative interaction partner. Small talk is based on rules which assign keywords and keyphrases to appropriate reactions. Although the system uses a set of dialogue acts it is not clear if this also applies to the small talk rules.

An agent which makes use of small talk topic knowledge is "helper agent" described by Isbister et al. [19]. The system supports human conversation partners interacting in a virtual room by suggesting safe small talk topics if the conversation pauses. The system has knowledge about small talk topics but no model for small talk itself. When proposing a new topic, the agent always follows the same sequential pattern.

Another solution is the integration of a chatbot, such as the AIML-based chatbot ALICE[2]. Chatbots are built especially for open domain small talk. However, chatbots are simple stimulus-response machines commonly based on surface pattern matching without any explicit knowledge about dialogue acts, strategies or sequences [21]. They also lack a satisfying memory implementation and rely on stateless pattern-answer pairs. Thus, conversations with chatbots are often tedious and unnatural. Because of their stateless approach they are also complicated to integrate into dialogue systems.

2.2 Social Talk in Dialogue Act Sets

There are many sophisticated and systematic dialogue act annotation schemes. Two of the most popular ones are DAMSL [1] and DIT++ [10]. DAMSL, Dialogue Act Markup using Several Layers, was first published in the 1990s with a focus on multidimensionality. DAMSL is used for many corpora annotations, often in slightly modified versions. In general, DAMSL does not offer a special annotation layer for social acts, although some social information is coded in existing classes. For example, in the Switchboard DAMSL version (SWDB-DAMSL) [20] there are several feedback dialogue acts which have social meaning such as the sympathy feedback and downplayer as reply to compliments.

In the ICSI-MRDA annotation scheme [27] a new category is introduced for "politeness mechanisms" including downplayers, sympathy, apology, thanks and welcome.

---

[2] ALICE is an open source chatbot with a database of approximately 41.000 pattern-template pairs (http://alicebot.blogspot.com/).

DIT++ offers a special dimension for "social obligations management", in which general communicative functions can get a social interpretation. Moreover, there are some communicative functions especially for the social obligations management dimension, which are similar to the mentioned DAMSL acts: Initial Greeting, Return Greeting, Initial Self-Introduction, Return Self-Introduction, Apology, Apology-Downplay, Thanking, Thanking-Downplay, Initial-Goodbye, Return-Goodbye. However, to model a definite small talk sequence, such as a compliment-downplay-feedback sequence, DIT++ is not equipped either. As far as we know a compliment for example can not be explicitly marked as such.

The mentioned schemes are further developed in the ISO project "Semantic annotation framework" [11], whose central focus lies on the multidimensionality and multifunctionality of dialogue utterances. Nevertheless, no further social dialogue acts are introduced by the ISO project.

3   Erving Goffman: Face

The dialogue acts presented in this paper are inspired by the work of Erving Goffman, an American social scientist. The main concept in Goffman's work about social interaction is "face". In his work "face" is an "image of self delineated in terms of approved social attributes" [15, page 5]. Face means the perception of the self of both interactors. Every person has an image of herself in a social context. In direct communication the faces of both participants need to be protected and supported. This procedure is called "face work".

Goffman identifies two main interpersonal interaction policies for face work: the "supportive interchanges" and the "remedial interchanges" [16]. Interchanges are sequences of possible conversational turns consisting of gestures, glances, touch and verbal utterances. This work focuses on supportive interchanges in which the participants want to positively maintain their faces.

Several agents with small talk ability are inspired by the social science work on face. For example the already mentioned REA system determines the measure of face threat in her own planned utterances [6]. If the system identifies the planned utterance to be too threatening for the user's face (e.g. a question about money), the agent engages in small talk sequences until the measures of interpersonal closeness and user comfort are high enough to continue with the dangerous utterance.

3.1   Dialogue Acts and Dialogue Sequences by Goffman

Erving Goffman's analysis of interchanges can be regarded as a model of social dialogue acts and their combination in sequences. Goffman himself uses the terminus "act" to refer to a single verbal or non verbal action [16].

In the late 1970th Werner Holly already interpreted Goffman's interactions in a linguistically-motivated formalization [18]. Following Goffman's distinctions of sequences, Holly describes two different categorizations of supportive utterances. One category is build by the means of shared interpersonal topics and another

Table 1. Categories of acts used in positive sequences by Goffman grouped by Holly

Interpersonal Topics	Function
Group 1: utterances of sympathy and interest interested questions, compliments, polite answers, downgrading	**Group 3: ratification rituals** congratulations, condolences, acknowledgement of changed personal situation
Group 2: polite offers invitations, welcoming, introducing somebody	**Group 4: access rituals** greeting, good-bye, initializing and closing of subdialogues

one according to function. The first group (interpersonal topics) contains utterances of sympathy and interests, the second polite offers. According to function Holly following Goffman distinguishes "ratifications" and "access" acts, see table 1. Another distinction is the target face of the utterance. Possible values are the face of the own person as well as the face of the reacting participant.

From a dialogue system point of view, the classification of Goffman seems problematic in various aspects. Group 1 for example appears to be comparatively large and unstructured. Moreover, the distinction between topic and function is very vague. It seems unclear why congratulations are grouped by function and compliments by topic. A compliment can easily be seen as a ratification step, for example a compliment about a new haircut. This means, that parts of the groups categorized by schema 2 are also a subgroup of a group built by schema 1, but are not specified in group 1.

It is also complicated to generate valid sequences from the mentioned groups, because initiative and reactive acts are not distinguished. Goffman describes only a very abstract sequence for supportive interchanges: a supportive act answered by a supportive act. In general it would be preferable to have one categorization for supportive acts and not two which partly overlap. The taxonomy presented in this paper provides a clear distinction between the function and the topic layer.

4   A Taxonomy of Cooperative Social Dialogue Acts

In this section a taxonomy of dialogue acts is presented, which can be used for cooperative social talk in first contact conversations. All dialogue acts are integrated into one functionally motivated taxonomy. The dialogue acts are inspired by Goffman's work, but categorized according to two main types of face work: requesting support of the speaker's face and providing support for the addressee's face.

The taxonomy includes dialogue acts whose primary functions are social as well as dialogue acts, which can be used either in small talk or in other conversation domains. This matches the observation from Coupland & Coupland regarding social talk [13]. They discovered that every utterance carries a special degree of phatecity. Dialogue act classes which are primary social acts are: compliments, self compliments, self critic, invitations, self invitations and some forms of interested feedback. Dialogue acts which are not domain-bound are: inform, provide opinion, request information, request opinion. The latter are global functions, which can be used in task talk as well. In DiAML and DIT++ this class is called a "general-purpose function" which can be assigned to all dimensions. The presented dialogue acts are intended to be an addition to existing dialogue act sets. To maintain multidimensionality an additional dimension "social talk" can be a solution. The following examples[3] show the dialogue act "Inform" in task talk and the additional dimension social talk.

Table 2. Multidimensionality

Utterance	Social Talk	Task	Other Dimensions
We only have a limited choice of sofas.	-	Inform	-
I have been living in Berlin for over 20 years now.	Inform	-	-

While the intensity of face work may differ in utterances, the presented dialogue acts are all applicable for conversations which negotiate face. Figure 1 shows the dialogue acts organized according to the two classes. Dialogue acts are ordered hierarchically with growing specificity towards the leaves of the trees.

Request Face Support. The category 1 "Request Face Support" contains all dialogue acts which express a request for support of the speaker's face. Utterances expressing a request for face support imply the demand to reinforce, strengthen or accept the presented face of the speaker. If a speaker A informs the hearer B about his opinion towards something, A expects B to display interest in his information through a face supporting act, for example a verbal or mimic utterance.

But this is not the only level on which face work occurs. In human-human conversations, face work origins from several layers, from which only a few are verbal. Additionally, there are politeness constraints which define conversation rules. An omitted response to a question for example means a face threat to the speaker's face. In a conversation consisting of a sequence of statements, the responding act itself as well as the closeness to the semantic content and topic of the preceding utterance determines the grade of face support. These observed mechanisms follow a cooperative rule described in the relevance maxim formulated by Herbert Grice [17]. A's face therefore not only depends on B's positive reaction towards his information, but on B showing reaction at all. However, it may not be possible to capture these conversational rules through dialogue acts and they are not part of the work presented here, which deals with explicit social talk utterances.

---

[3] All examples in the text, which are taken from the corpus are in italic type. Utterances from the German dialogues are translated. Utterances which are not in italic are fictitious examples.

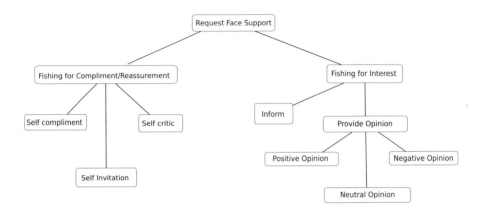

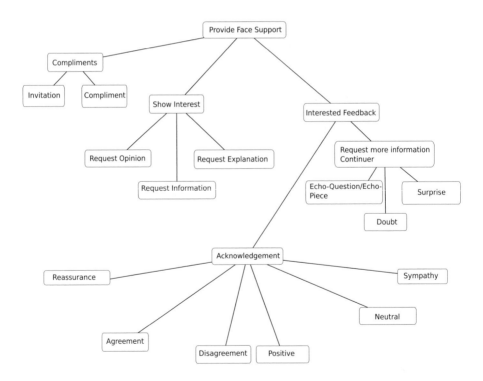

Fig. 1. The Small Talk Taxonomy

The group is subdivided into the two subclasses **"Fishing for compliment"** (group A) and **"Fishing for interest"** (group B). The dialogue acts in group A should be assigned to utterances which expect compliments, reassurances or invitations as reaction. Utterances implying dialogue acts of the group B want to achieve a kind of interested feedback. Whereas the dialogue acts in group A in general carry a strong face request, the acts in group B vary in the degree of intended face work and content may play an important role. Table 3 shows the dialogue acts with examples from the data.

Table 3. Request Face Support Dialogue Acts

Dialogue Act	Short Definition	Example
Self Compliment	With a self compliment the speaker praises the own person	I am really good in guessing names.
Self Invitation	A self invitation is an utterance which allows the speaker to do something what otherwise would need an invitation from the interlocutor.	*May I call you Alex?*
Self Critic	With a self critic the speaker criticizes her own person or behavior.	*I am too old for that*
Inform	An inform provides information to the hearer.	*I am from Poland*
Positive Opinion	An utterance which expresses a positive opinion contains a positive opinion of the speaker towards something.	*It is one of the most beautiful cities I know.*
Negative Opinion	A negative opinion contains a negative opinion of the speaker towards something	*The organization is not very good*
Neutral Opinion	A neutral opinion act contains a neutral opinion of the speaker towards something.	*That is long*

Provide Face Support. Category 2 on the other hand provides dialogue acts which strengthen the hearer's face. It contains three subclasses: **"Compliments & Invitations"** (group C), **"Show interest"** (group D) and **"Interested feedback"** (group E). Strong face support can be expressed through compliments and invitations (group C). Invitations may refer to physical or verbal actions or other actions which offer a more intimate relationship. Other face support acts concern the expression of interest in the other person (group D and E). Interest can be "factual" interest, mainly expressed through request for information, explanations and opinions (group D). Group E on the other hand subsumes various forms of interested feedback without introducing any new factual content. This class can not be used as initial step. The group is divided into "continuers", dialogue acts which aim at expressing interest and at the same time encourage the other interlocutor to keep talking and "acknowledgements" which do not need an answer.

Table 4 shows dialogue acts and examples.

Table 4. Provide Face Support Dialogue Acts

Dialogue Act	Short Definition	Example
Compliment	All compliments and kind words	*You are very intelligent*
Invitation	Invitations to verbal or physical actions	*I want to invite you a coffee.*
Request Opinion	With an request opinion the speaker asks for a opinion statement of the hearer.	*Did you like the movie?*
Request Information	With an request information the speaker asks for information which is not an opinion.	*Do you have many customers?*
Request Explanation	Request explanation is the dialogue act for all requests of further explanation.	*Why?*
Echo-Piece	An echo-piece is used to express interest in the part of the utterance which is repeated	*You are on holiday*
Doubt	An utterance which expresses doubt	*You think so?*
Surprise	The dialogue act for expressing surprise	Ah, really?
Reassurance	An utterance which is meant to ease somebody contains an reassurance act	Don't bother yourself
Agreement	The expression of agreement	*You are right*
Disagreement	Expression of disagreement	*That's not true*
Positive	A positive feedback which includes admiration or joy	*Wow*
Neutral	A neutral acknowledgement	*Ok*
Sympathy	A sympathy feedback is the response to negative or sorrowful information	*I can understand*

4.1 A Word on Topic

Additionally to the functional layer of an utterance, topic plays an important role in the interpretation of small talk utterances. The dialogue act "Request Information" for example generally is a member of the category "Provide Face Support" but can occur in category "Request Face Support" as well: If the topic is related to the speaker's own person, the dialogue act is assigned to the "Fishing for interest" group. Similarly, the dialogue act "Inform" is classified as "Show interest" if the topic is related to the addressee's person. Moreover, topic often determines the expected reaction, especially for the dialogue act "Inform". An information about a serious injury should result in a different reaction from the hearer as the information about a new flat.

5 Corpus Analysis

To verify the appropriateness of the dialogue act taxonomy, we applied the dialogue acts to a Wizard-of-Oz (WoZ) corpus containing task-driven and small talk conversations. The aim of the verification is to show if the found dialogue act set is applicable to conversations with embodied task-based agents and what modifications to the scheme may be necessary.

5.1   Data

For our validation test, we use data originating from human-Non Player Character (NPC) interactions in a virtual world. The used virtual world is named *Twinity*[4]. *Twinity* provides a digital mirror of urban parts of the real world. Currently, the game already contains 3D models of the cities of Berlin, Singapore, London, Miami and New York. *Twinity* is a on-line meeting place similar to Second Live, in which users can explore the 3D cities, visit clubs, bars and events and buy flats to live in. Conversations in *Twinity* are possible through the build-in text-based chat interface. The data was collected through two Wizard-of-Oz experiments extensively described in [2].

In the first experiment the wizard controls a furniture sales agent who supports the user in buying pieces of furniture for an apartment in a virtual world. The scenario is task-driven and small talk is optionally initiated by the experiment participant. A furniture-sales scenario is simulated, in which the NPC playes the role of an interior designer/furniture saleswoman, whose task is to help the subjects furnishing a living-room. She has to determine subject's preferences for the different types of furniture objects, show objects according to these preferences and place them in the room following the subject's instructions. This data consists of 18 dialogues containing 3,171 turns with 4,313 utterances. The participants are German and the used language English. An example conversation is given in table 5.

Table 5. Sample Conversation from the first WoZ experiment

NPC:	I think the colourful chair will go better with the style of the room.
USR:	Ok, show it to me.
USR:	Do you practice any sport?
NPC:	Here it is.
NPC:	Yes, I'm practising climbing.
USR:	Oh, show me another one...this is too hippy...
USR:	Oh thats a casuality...i practice climbing too...

In the second experiment, the participants are German language learners from various countries, who order drinks and food in a virtual bar. The barkeeper is controlled by the wizard. The participants are explicitly briefed to conduct small talk and the wizard himself initiates a small talk conversation if the user does not. This corpus contains 12 dialogues with 1477 utterances. An excerpt is shown in table 6.

The final small talk corpus consists of the dialogues in which small talk utterances where found. This corpus contains 4161 utterances from which 990 are categorized to predominantly fulfill small talk functions. These utterances were annotated with dialogue act information by two annotators of which only one has previous knowledge on dialogue systems and dialogue research.

---

[4] http://www.twinity.com/, accessed 1 May 2011

Table 6. Sample Conversation from the second WoZ experiment

' USR:	wie geht's dir in der Stadt
USR:	meine, wie lange bist du hier?
NPC:	Sehr gut.
NPC:	Berlin ist sehr abwechslungsreich.
USR:	das sehe ich

5.2 Annotation Results

The inter-annotator agreement value between the annotators shows that the annotation scheme is an adequate first description of the data: From the 990 utterances belonging to small talk sequences, they annotated 772 with the identical dialogue act. This results in a kappa value of 0.741. The majority of confusions occurs within the fine-grained set of feedback acts, e.g. between neutral and surprised feedback. Another source of confusion is the discrimination between request opinion and request information.

5.3 Sequences

In a second step, the data was annotated with sequence information to extract a model of possible small talk conversations. Following Brinker and Sager [9] we define a dialogue sequence as follows:

A dialogue sequence is a succession of turns from one initiative turn to the next initiative turn.

Following this definition we extracted 990 small talk dialogue acts in the data organized in 314 sequences. Although the most simple sequence found in the data is the adjacency pair [25], several different sequences were found. The average length of a sequence in the data consists of 3 dialogue acts, with the shortest unit being only one turn and the longest sequence consisting of 5 turns. Table 7 shows the statistic for the found sequences ordered according to the initial dialogue act.

As one can see from the table 7, most small talk sequences are initiated by a "Request Information" dialogue act (183 sequences). Request information is the dialogue act class for various kinds of interested queries. The second most

Table 7. Dialogue sequences sorted according to the initial dialogue act

Initial Dialogue Act	Frequency	Initial Dialogue Act	Frequency
request information	183	request opinion	8
inform	54	invitation	7
opinion	25	request explanation	7
compliment	15	self critic	2
others	13		

frequently used class is "Inform", the class for providing information (54). "Others" are other domain dialogue acts (e.g. task dialogue acts) which are answered by small talk utterances.

A selection of sequence distribution in the data is shown below. The percentage describes the frequency of this particular sequence compared to the absolute number of sequences starting with the given dialogue act:

Compliment - Thank (26%)
Compliment - Surprised Feedback + Thank (13%)
Request Information - Inform (46%)
Request Information - Inform - Feedback (15%)
Request Opinion - Provide Opinion (37%)
Request Opinion - Provide Opinion - Feedback (12%)
Self Critic - Feedback Reassurance (100%)
Self Invitation - Invitation (50%)
Self Invitation - Accept (25%)
Inform - Feedback (18%)
Inform - Request Information - Inform (18%)
Provide Opinion - Feedback (24%)
Provide Opinion - Request Opinion - Accept/Reject/Uncertain (12%)

6   Conclusion and Future Work

In this paper a dialogue act taxonomy based on the social science theory of "face" is presented. The dialogue acts in the taxonomy can be used for social talk with cooperative virtual selling agents. The taxonomy is split into two main groups: one group for dialogue acts which primary fulfill requests of face support for the own face and one group containing dialogue acts which provide face support for the hearer's face. The dialogue act set is validated by annotating a corpus containing small talk and task talk conversations from Wizard-of-Oz experiments, resulting in a kappa value of 0.741 for inter-annotator agreement.

Moreover, possible dialogue act sequences for social talk are extracted from the corpus, which can be used to develop a computational model. We use the sequences to derive finite-state models of small talk conversations for a barkeeper and a furniture seller agent acting in a virtual world. In this application the agents are frequently confronted with small talk utterances from the users.

Future work will concentrate on further specifications of the topic layer. A topic can have huge effects on the appropriate reaction to a small talk utterance. It can also affect the categorization of an utterance into the two groups face request or face support. We currently develop a topic formalization for integration into the model. The taxonomy will also be tested on some other data and eventually extended with further categories. Afterwards an user evaluation of the whole model including dialogue acts, sequences and topics will be necessary.

Acknowledgments. The work presented in this paper is part of the project "KomParse", funded by the ProFIT program of the Federal State of Berlin, co-funded by the EFRE program of the European Union.

References

1. Allen, J., Core, M.: DAMSL: Dialogue Act Markup in Several Layers (Draft 2.1) (1997), http://www.cs.rochester.edu/research/cisd/resources/damsl/RevisedManual/
2. Bertomeu, N., Benz, A.: Annotation of joint projects and information states in human-npc dialogues. In: Proceedings of the First International Conference on Corpus Linguistics (CILC 2009), Murcia, Spain (2009)
3. Bickmore, T.: Relational Agents: Effecting Change through Human-Computer Relationships. Ph.D. thesis, Massachusetts Institute of Technology (2003)
4. Bickmore, T.: A Computational Model of Small Talk (1999), http://web.media.mit.edu/~bickmore/Mas962b/
5. Bickmore, T.W., Cassell, J.: "How about this weather?" Social Dialog with Embodied Conversational Agents. In: Proceedings of the AAAI Fall Symposium on Socially Intelligent Agents (2000)
6. Bickmore, T.W., Cassell, J.: Relational agents: a model and implementation of building user trust. In: CHI, pp. 396–403 (2001)
7. Bickmore, T.W., Picard, R.W.: Establishing and maintaining long-term human-computer relationships. ACM Transactions on Computer-human Interaction 12, 293–327 (2005)
8. Blascovich, J.: A theoretical model of social influence for increasing the utility of collaborative virtual environments. In: Proceedings of the 4th International Conference on Collaborative Virtual Environments, CVE 2002, pp. 25–30. ACM, New York (2002)
9. Brinker, K., Sager, S.F.: Linguistische Gesprächsanalyse. Erich Schmidt Verlag (2006)
10. Bunt, H.: Multifunctionality in dialogue. Comput. Speech Lang 25, 222–245 (2011)
11. Bunt, H., Alexandersson, J., Carletta, J., Choe, J.-W., Fang, A.C., Hasida, K., Lee, K., Petukhova, V., Popescu-Belis, A., Romary, L., Soria, C., Traum, D.: Towards an ISO Standard for Dialogue Act Annotation. In: Calzolari, N. (ed.) Proceedings of the Seventh Conference on International Language Resources and Evaluation (LREC 2010), European Language Resources Association (ELRA), Valletta (2010)
12. Cassell, J., Bickmore, T., Billinghurst, M., Campbell, L., Chang, K., Vilhjálmsson, H., Yan, H.: Embodiment in conversational interfaces: Rea. In: Proceedings of the SIGCHI Conference on Human Factors in Computing Systems: The CHI is the Limit, CHI 1999, pp. 520–527. ACM, New York (1999)
13. Coupland, J., Coupland, N., Robinson, J.D.: "How are you?": Negotiating phatic communion. Language in Society 21(02), 207–230 (1992)
14. Endrass, B., Rehm, M., Andre, E.: Planning Small Talk Behavior with Cultural Influences for Multiagent Systems. Computer Speech and Language 25(2), 158–174 (2011)
15. Goffman, E.: Interaction Ritual: Essays on Face-to-Face Behavior. Anchor Books, Doubleday & Company, Inc., Garden City (1967)
16. Goffman, E.: Relations in public; Microstudies of the public order. Basic Books, New York (1971)
17. Grice, H.P.: Logic and conversation. In: Cole, P., Morgan, J.L. (eds.) Syntax and Semantics, vol. 3, Academic Press, New York (1975)
18. Holly, W.: Imagearbeit in Gesprächen. Zur linguistischen Beschreibung des Beziehungsaspekts. Reihe Germanistische Linguistik 18, Niemeyer, Tübingen (1979)

19. Isbister, K., Nakanishi, H., Ishida, T., Nass, C.: Helper Agent: Designing An Assistant for Human-Human Interaction in a Virtual Meeting Space, pp. 57–64 (2000)
20. Jurafsky, D., Schriberg, E., Biasca, D.: Switchboard SWBD-DAMSL Shall-Discourse-Function Annotation Coders Manual (1997), http://stripe.colorado.edu/~jurafsky/manual.august.html
21. Klüwer, T.: RMRSBot – Using Linguistic Information to Enrich a Chatbot. In: Ruttkay, Z., Kipp, M., Nijholt, A., Vilhjálmsson, H.H. (eds.) IVA 2009. LNCS, vol. 5773, pp. 515–516. Springer, Heidelberg (2009)
22. Kopp, S., Gesellensetter, L., Krämer, N.C., Wachsmuth, I.: A conversational agent as museum guide – design and evaluation of a real-world application. In: Panayiotopoulos, T., Gratch, J., Aylett, R.S., Ballin, D., Olivier, P., Rist, T. (eds.) IVA 2005. LNCS (LNAI), vol. 3661, pp. 329–343. Springer, Heidelberg (2005)
23. Malinowski, B.: The Problem of Meaning in Primitive Languages. In: The Meaning of Meaning: A Study of Influence of Language Upon Thought and of the Science of Symbolism, 10th edn., pp. 296–336. Harcourt, Brace and World, New York (1949)
24. Nass, C., Steuer, J., Tauber, E.R.: Computers are social actors. In: Computer Human Interaction (1994)
25. Schegloff, E.A.: Sequence Organization in Interaction: Volume 1: A Primer in Conversation Analysis. Cambridge University Press, Cambridge (2007)
26. Schneider, K.: Small Talk: Analysing Phatic Discourse. Ph.D. thesis, Philipps-Universitat, Marburg, Germany (1988)
27. Shriberg, E., Dhillon, R., Bhagat, S., Ang, J., Carvey, H.: The ICSI meeting recorder dialog act (MRDA) corpus. In: Proc. of the 5th SIGdial Workshop on Discourse and Dialogue, pp. 97–100 (2004)

Virtual Clones: Data-Driven Social Navigation

Doron Friedman and Peleg Tuchman

The Advanced Virtuality Lab
Sammy Ofer School of Communications
Herzliya, Israel
doronf@idc.ac.il

Abstract. Millions of participants inhabit online virtual worlds such as SL[1] and engage in a wide range of activities, some of which require the performance of tedious tasks. Our goal is to develop a virtual proxy that would replace human participants in online virtual worlds. The proxy should be able to perform simple tasks on behalf of its owner, similar to the way the owner would have performed it. In this paper we focus on the challenge of social navigation. We use a data-driven approach based on recording human participants in the virtual environment; this training set, with a machine learning approach, is then used to control an agent in real time who is performing the same social task. We evaluate our method based on data collected from different participants.

Keywords: Navigation, behavioral cloning, imitation learning, proxy, data-driven approach.

1 Background

One of the old dreams of robotics researchers is to be able to send a robot to replace them in the less exciting chores in life. As people spend increasing amounts of time in online virtual worlds, our long-term goal is aimed towards replacing ourselves with virtual proxies that will be able to act on our behalf in virtual worlds. Specifically, in this paper we discuss how a virtual clone can learn to clone spatial navigation characteristics of its owner.

Social virtual environments are now becoming widely popular. Millions of people spend time in multi-user online games and virtual worlds, where they not only play but also engage in various social activities together. Of particular interest is SecondLife (SL), a generic platform that enables a virtual world constructed completely by its citizens. The citizens engage in a diverse range of activities (rather than gaming): socialization, romance, education, buying and selling of virtual goods, and many more [1]. There is scientific evidence that spatial behavior in virtual worlds has social aspects that are similar to real-world behavior at least to some extent [2, 3].

Bots in virtual worlds such as SL are avatars that are controlled by software rather than by a human operator, and have the appearance of any SL participant. Over the last few years we have developed the AVL bot platform, which was also used in the

---

[1] http://www.SecondLife.com

H. Högni Vilhjálmsson et al. (Eds.): IVA 2011, LNAI 6895, pp. 28–34, 2011.

study described in this paper. A proxy with basic functionality was already scheduled to appear in a real-world conference about conflict resolution in virtual worlds[2].

A data-driven approach where an agent learns from recorded expert data has been termed behavioral cloning by Anderson et al.[4]. They apply behavioral cloning in the context of an intelligent tutoring system embedded in flight simulators, which can adapt to specific students and their needs. As their goal is different than ours it is difficult to compare the technique or the results. Sammut and his colleagues have applied behavioral cloning to various problems, most notably capturing student models from flight simulation in order to learn to fly a plane [5, 6]. Their method is symbolic, which makes it difficult to compare with ours.

3   A Method for Social Navigation

When humans use space in a social context they are sensitive to the interpersonal distance and gaze direction in ways that are not completely understood by psychology, and are difficult to formalize. We focus on a simple example where a participant has to approach another participant in a socially acceptable way as if about to open conversation, in an unconfined open space. While this is a deliberately-selected simple problem, we note that it contains many of the challenges in modeling social spatial behavior. First, there are individual differences in the preferred proximity among people; this has been studied extensively in social psychology since the 1960s [7, 8], and more recently in virtual worlds [2, 3]. Another issue is how to approach a person who is standing with their back to you, and yet another issue is whether you walk straight, in a curved trajectory, or in a jittery trajectory. Gaze direction further interacts with all these factors. To our knowledge there is no attempt to automatically address this problem; the video games industry uses manually crafted trajectories with the aid of waypoints for non-player characters. Our approach is deliberately straightforward: we capture the navigation strategy of a virtual-world participant in the form of a training set of state-action couples. The participant's proxy can then use this training set by comparing its current state with states in the training set, and taking actions accordingly. The trajectories of the human participants are sampled over time. We convert each trajectory t into a set of state-action couples:

$$S_t = \{(s_1,a_1), \ldots, (s_k,a_k)\}; \tag{1}$$

For each participant we collect all such trajectory sets into a union set S of all the state-action couples in all the trajectories. Thus, our training set "forgets" which sample was taken from which trajectory. In this simple task the state can be modeled with only three parameters: ρ, θ, capturing the relative distance and direction of the agent from the target in polar coordinates, and α, capturing the relative difference in gaze angles between the agent and the target. The actions in our case are: move forward, move backward, rotate left, rotate right, move forward and rotate left, move forward and rotate right, move backwards and rotate left, and move backwards and rotate right.

---

[2] See video: http://www.youtube.com/watch?v=1R4Eo3UDT9U

In order to introduce some consistency into the proxy's behavior some memory capabilities were required. We append a fourth parameter – the previous action – to the state vector, which now becomes

$$s = (\rho_t, \theta_t, \alpha_t, a_{t-1}). \tag{2}$$

We construct a different model for each participant, from all the points in all the trajectories for that participant. The model can then be used to generate trajectories online as follows. The agent begins in a random initial state in terms of position and gaze direction. The current state of the world is translated into a state vector

$$s' = (\rho_t, \theta_t, \alpha_t, a_{t-1}) \tag{3}$$

as described above, and the training set is now queried for a state-action couple (s, a) s.t. $/s\text{-}s'/$ is minimal. We have evaluated several distance metrics, and concluded that the Manhattan metric

$$d(\overline{x}, \overline{y}) = \sum_i | x_i - y_i | \tag{4}$$

provides a better separation among as compared with other metrics.

The state vector is comprised of different types of measurements. We normalized the distance, and for the rotation angles we used

$$d(\theta, \theta') = \frac{1 + \cos(|\theta - \theta'|)}{2} \tag{5}$$

for θ the agent rotation and θ' the training set rotation. Similarly, we used

$$d(\alpha, \alpha') = \frac{1 + \cos(|\alpha - \alpha'|)}{2} \tag{6}$$

for α the agent's gaze direction and α' the training set gaze direction.

The distance between two different actions is either 0 if the actions are equal or 1 otherwise. In order to adjust the contribution to that of the other state parameters this was weighted by a factor proportional to the mean contribution of the distance parameter.

We have also tested a weighted k-nearest neighbor approach; we find the set of k nearest state-action couples $\{(s_1,a_1),...,(s_k,a_k)\}$ in the training set s.t. the distances between the state vectors s_i and the agent's state vector s is minimal. If $b_1,...,b_n$ are the actions that can be taken by the proxy agent, we choose b s.t.

$$b = \arg\max_{b_j} \sum_{i=1}^{k} e^{-|s-s_i|\delta(a_i,b_j)} \quad , \quad \delta(a,b) = \begin{cases} 1, \\ 0, \end{cases} \tag{7}$$

The training set in our case includes up to approximately 50000 points per participant. This size can be processed in real time, but larger samples sizes might need to be reduced, e.g., by applying vector quantization (VQ) to the training set.

In practice, the samples we record from participants are sparse and cover only a small part of the state space, which results in cases where the nearest sample is very far; in such cases the proxy navigation may fail to reach the target within reasonable time. If there are not enough samples of input trajectories for a given participant we can generalize from the existing samples as follows. We choose N start points with uniform distribution around the target. For each start point we execute the proxy as in Section 3.3, generate a trajectory and check whether it has reached the target successfully within a predefined number of steps. If the target was reached we add the samples to the training set, if it was not reached we discard of the samples.

4 Evaluation

The trajectories generated by the proxy were first evaluated in a simulated abstract 2D environment; this is useful for debugging and manual inspection. Later on we have visualized the same trajectories in OpenSim: this is an open-source project similar to SL, which allows us to host the server locally, and hence avoid significant latency. A more systematic evaluation would require a display of the resulting behavior in the virtual environment, and subjective rating by naïve viewers; such as study is beyond the scope of this paper. A companion video illustrates some of the results[3].

Data was collected using an automated tool implemented in SL. Participants had to locate another avatar and approach it. Once the approach was completed they were teleported to another random point in the same region. In each new run the gaze directions of both the participant's avatar and the target were randomly modified.

The evaluation reported here is based on three participants: two females (ages 24 and 33) and one male (age 24). The female participants completed 98 and 20 trajectories correspondingly and will be referred to as F1 and F2, and the male subject completed 50 trajectories, and will be referred to as M1.Each trajectory includes a few hundred data points that are later on used in the training set as state-action vectors.

5 Results

Figure 1 shows two trajectories recorded from human participants as examples. First we show that individual differences in participants' trajectories may be detected. This is necessary to establish that our approach allows for maintaining these individual differences in the virtual proxies.

Manual inspection of the preferences of the different participants revealed clear differences. For example, Figure 2 shows some differences evident in the navigation tactics used by F2 and M1.

---

[3] See video http://www.youtube.com/watch?v=jmfGS1omgdk

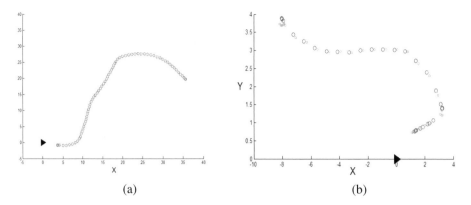

Fig. 1. Examples of recorded trajectories when the starting point is in front of the target (a) and behind it (b). The target is shown by a black arrow indicating its gaze direction.

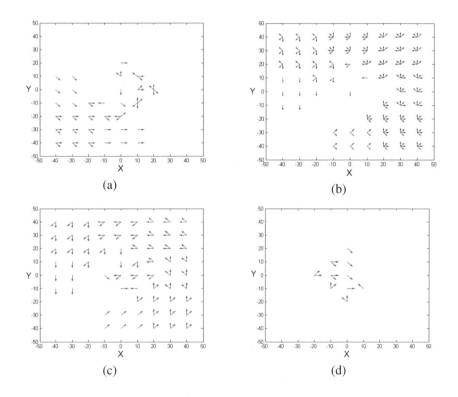

Fig. 2. A visualization of the navigation tactics used by different participants. The state space was quantized and normalized such that the target is always in (0,0) and facing to the right. For each position of the participant relative to the target we show an arrow if and only if the action indicated below was the most frequent action taken by participant when it is facing in the arrow's direction. (a) Participant F2 rotating left. (b) Participant M1 rotating left. (c) Participant F2 moving forward and rotating left. (d) Participant M1 moving forward and rotating left.

The quality of the trajectories generated by the proxy depends on the number of samples. First, we measured the success rate of each proxy by checking 324 trajectories from uniformly sampled starting points in terms of initial conditions of ρ, θ, and α. For M1 and F1, for which we had 50 and 98 trajectories correspondingly, the success rate was 92% and 88% correspondingly. In some occasions the proxy would fail from reaching the social distance from the target within a given time. In order to obtain a robust proxy behavior we deploy generalization as explained in Section 3.4. After running a few dozen random trajectories per model the proxy reaches a 100% success rate on our test sample. The proxy for participant F2, which was based on a small number of input trajectories (20), had a lower rate of successful trajectories (70%). In addition, we manually inspected the trajectories generated by the three different proxies. We selected random start points, and had all three proxies start from each start point, using the training set without generalization as a basis for their operation. Figure 5 shows some examples. We note that the trajectories for F1 and M1 seem both acceptable and believable, while the trajectories from F2, with the small training set, were often unrealistically intricate (see Figure 3), and, worse, tended to get within unacceptable proximity of the target (recall that in social situations people always keep some minimum interpersonal distance). Also, note that the algorithm is deterministic; the reason that each proxy generates a different trajectory is that each is based on a different training set. This preserves our intention that the proxies will have an individual behavior, based on their owner, yet consistent.

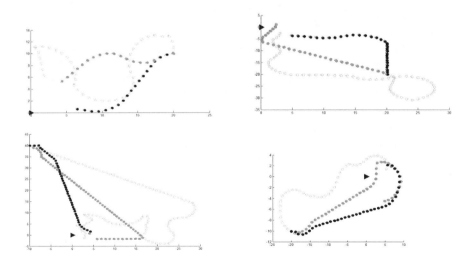

Fig. 3. Sample trajectories of three proxies modeled from three participants starting at the same conditions: M1 (Black), F2 (Empty), and F1 (Gray)

7 Discussion

This paper describes our work in progress on virtual proxies in virtual worlds. These are different than other type of virtual agents in that they are intended to be clones of individual users. We show that using a simple k-nearest neighbor approach can be a good starting point for a virtual clone, when tested on a simple instance of the problem of social navigation. In the future, we hope to extend this method and evaluate its performance in larger-scale challenges. Naturally, the method will be put to the test in a more realistic space, with obstacles and additional agents that move around and change their gaze. In addition, we are working on extending this method to data tracked from a full body rather than just 2D positions. Clearly, more complex state representations may be required, and with them more advanced methods for generalization and abstraction.

Acknowledgements. This project is supported by EU FP7 project 248620 Beaming. The authors would like to thank Daniel Korn for implementing the record & replay facilities in OpenSim that were used for the evaluation of trajectories. The authors would also like to thank Chani Vaintraub for useful comments.

References

1. Boellstorff, T.: Coming of Age in Second Life. Princeton University Press, Princeton (2008)
2. Friedman, D., Steed, A., Slater, M.: Spatial Social Behavior in Second Life. In: Proc. Intelligent Virtual Agent, pp. 252–263 (2007)
3. Yee, N., Bailenson, J.N., Urbanek, M., Chang, F., Merget, D.: The unbearable likeness of being digital; The persistence of nonverbal social norms in online virtual environments. Cyberpsychology and Behavior 10, 115–121 (2007)
4. Anderson, C.W., Draper, B.A., Peterson, D.A.: Behavioral Cloning of Student Pilots with Modular Neural Networks. In: Proceedings of the Seventeenth International Conference on Machine Learning, pp. 25–32 (2007)
5. Isaac, A., Sammut, C.: Goal-directed Learning to Fly. In: ICML, pp. 258–265 (2003)
6. Morales, E.F., Sammut, C.: Learning to fly by combining reinforcement learning with behavioural cloning. In: Proceedings of the Twenty-first International Conference on Machine Learning, Banff, Alberta, Canada, pp. 76–83 (2004)
7. Hall, E.T.: The Hidden Dimension. Doubleday, New York (1966)
8. Hall, E.T.: The Silent Language. Doubleday, New York (1959)

Tilt Riders: Improvisational Agents Who Know What the Scene Is about

António Brisson[1], Brian Magerko[2], and Ana Paiva[1]

[1] Universidade Técninca de Lisboa and INESC-ID, Oeiras, Portugal
[2] Georgia Institute of Technology School of Literature, Communication, and Culture
686 Cherry St., Atlanta, GA

Abstract. The creation of autonomous agents for interactive narrative requires a heavy authorial effort, especially when the authors are concerned about integrating all possible story states in the agents behaviors. In this paper, we consider that the autonomous agents lack of narrative perspective over the action prevents them from successfully dealing with unpredicted story states. To deal with this problem we propose a conceptual model of story development for autonomous agents that endows narrative control to them. The proposed model is supported by our cognitive research with improvisational theatre actors and improvisational theatre theory.

Keywords: Autonomous Agents, Emergent Narratives, Improv.

1 Introduction

Agent-heavy approaches to interactive narrative have been a mainstay since the rise of the field in the 1990s. The Oz project [1], and CAIT [2] are early examples of applying behavior-driven agent architectures to creating interactive narrative experiences. Most research in this field[3,4,5] applied different strategies to follow the principle that stories can be dynamically generated by the interaction between characters in real-time systems, as long as they implement well-defined roles[6]. Designing such strict agents to interactive narrative environments adds a huge authorial burden to the design of interactive narrative environments. We contend that this is a direct consequence of the agents lack of authorial power, thus, shifting some of that authorial power to the agents would provide more dynamic interactions and consequently a broader possibility of experiences in agent-based interactive narratives.

The needed shift towards authorial agents depends on creating distributed story models that endow agents with the ability to reason about the impact of their own actions in the story development. This multi-agent focus on collaborative story creation has an obvious real world analogue in improvisational theatre (improv), *"a form of unscripted performance that uses audience suggestions to initiate or shape scenes or plays created spontaneously and cooperatively according to agreed-upon rules or game structures"*[7]. In improv, players develop stories by developing a shared understanding about a platform, which

H. Högni Vilhjálmsson et al. (Eds.): IVA 2011, LNAI 6895, pp. 35–41, 2011.
© Springer-Verlag Berlin Heidelberg 2011

is the collection of story elements that establishes who, what and where the story is happening[8]. However, the simple creation of a platform, such as a mellow/passionate couple (who) in heir honeymoon (what) entering their hotel room (where), is not much more than a description of the story environment, *"the stability that precedes the chaos"*[9], and it does not produce an interesting story by itself. It is up to improv players (actors) to introduce new elements to the scene that unbalance the established platform. Examples in this scenario could be the husband finding his spouse wearing his clothes and then have to adapt to the fact that she is the man in the house. Players tilt a platform in order to provide a story development towards the reestablishment of a new balance. *Tilt Riding* is the players action that arises from the need to adapt to the new tilted platform,

This work is part of the Digital Improv Project [10] which studies the cognitive processes involved in human improvisational performance with the purpose of constructing computational models for autonomous agents that exhibit improvisational behavior. This research is grounded in the analysis of more than seventy hours of performance, retrospective protocol, and group interview footage that we have collected during our study of real world improvisers.

2   Relevant Improv Background

Improv theorists such as Johnstone [9] and Sawyer [8] observed, that in spite of improvs intrinsic unpredictability, experienced improv players tend to fall into very high-level structural forms. They both report the tendency to fall into a storytelling sequence of three identifiable story subsets (*beat*) called *Three Beat Sequence* [8]. Johnstone[9] describes it as a pattern that starts with the establishment of a routine, which is the action that derives directly from a balanced platform. The first beat is followed by a disruption of the same routine that leads to the need of resolving the discrepancies elicited by the earlier disruption. During the first two beats that normally represent half of a scene, actors are encouraged to offer new material [8] and in the last beat they are encouraged to connect the elements introduced earlier in the scene.

Other relevant improv concepts, that result from the dialogue between improv players are *Dramatic Frame* and *Cooperative Emergence*. When two or more improv players improvise, their dialog results in the creation of a *dramatic frame* and a *story frame*[8], which are collections of all performance elements brought to scene. The main difference between them is that a *story frame* is an individual perspective, while a *dramatic frame* is a shared understanding of the same the story elements. These elements include among other: the characters enacted by each player; their motives and relations; the joint activity in which they are engaged; action location; time period; story genre; relation of the current joint activity to that plot and a large amount of implicit information (information that is presented without being directly referred), such as contextual information about an activity, place or time. In other words one may state that a dramatic frame is a shared mental model between all players that contains the whole scene information, and story frame is an individual mental model of the same elements.

The process that leads to the creation of a dramatic frame is a turn-by-turn interaction called cooperative emergence, which is supported by two major functions *offer* (proposal of a new element to add to the frame, that may be related with any element of the dramatic frame) and *response* (validation of early proposals by integrating them in the dramatic frame or rejection of early proposals by disabling its integration or making it more difficult) It is the interaction between offers and responses that determines the cooperative property of the process. *Offers* with no *response* are kept in the individual story frame of each player, because it is only from *offer / response* agreement or disagreement that new elements may take part or by excluded from the dramatic frame. Only Confirmed offers can be moved from story frames to dramatic frames.

2.1   Tilt

A *tilt* is a change in the established platform that breaks the established routine, forcing action to adapt to the new circumstances. *"Tilting is all about balance. Bad improv is when balance is always maintained. Good improv shifts balance"* [9]. An example of a tilt in our data, starts with two characters emphasizing the benefits of fair trade products to their producers and how they are concerned about saving lives. They define a balanced platform where one of the characters exaggeratedly portrays being fair. Suddenly a fair trade worker walks in and starts revealing her poverty, exposing the real effects of fair trade in her life. At this point the players are forced to adapt their characters to the new facts. New action arises from the new unbalanced state.

Reports from our data suggest that players proactively look to establish solid dependencies between their characters and the environment in order to make them vulnerable to environment changes. In an example from our data it was interesting to see, that one of the players reports an intentional exaggeration of his characters attachment to the fair trade benefits, to prepare an interesting tilt: *"were building a set up, for exactly what she (other player) came for (...) we are going to be wrong about it (...) and I'm expecting it all to go wrong and it's gonna go in that track"*. Another player in similar circumstances comments: *"You should have an opinion about something (...) and then... something might happen that changes the environment which is the tilt... "*

In both cases the players rely that something on the unfolding action will change the environment and affect their characters, suggesting that a tilt is no exception to the cooperative aspects of improv in agreement with Johnstone [9] *"A tilt is just an offer of a tilt until its been validated by someone"*. Our working definition for tilt takes into account the whole action sequence that leads to an unbalanced platform instead of a simple action: a tilt is the action sequence that causes a significant alteration of an established platform that moves the story forward. We call the action that arises from characters adaptations to the tilted platform *tilt riding*.

3   Story Development Conceptual Model

Story movement in improv is a consequence of the action that arises from tilted platforms (tilt riding), when the players adapt their characters to significant changes in the story environment. Unfortunately, this does not happen when autonomous characters encounter unpredicted story states. Therefore, the main motivation for this work comes from the observation that autonomous characters in these situations would largely benefit from a computational model of tilt. However, our working definition is too high level to be implemented, since it does not determine the specific platform elements used in a tilt, and how they unbalance a platform. A major step towards defining such model, would be to determine the main functions used in it, which we contend to be part of the process of creation of a dramatic frame.

In the following we present a conceptual model of story development in improv (see Fig.1), that results from a detailed analysis of the performances, and post-performances data of the two best tilt examples of our extensive data set (see Table 1), that consisted on the annotation of the all platform variables in the story frames and dramatic frame.

Story Steps (Platform Buildup, Tilt Buildup, Problem and Resolution). We have observed that players have different concerns over story development along a performance, that define distinct story moments. We call these story moments story-steps. In the analyzed scenes, we observed four different story-steps, each one with distinct priorities.

Platform Buildup. The first step is where players create a platform and establish a routine. In example B, D6 reports the definition of his character (who?) in the established platform: "this is where I thought I was going to be the guy that plays by the rules, in this relationship of 3 guys from college I'm gonna be the dork."

Tilt Build Up and Problem. Very similar story steps, that are responsible for breaking the routine. We observed in both analyzed cases that a larger tilt occurs after the initial tilt that breaks the established platform. This larger tilt leaves

Table 1. Scenes A and B take 3:20 and 4 minutes, each is played by 3 actors in total of 6 different actors. Example A has 65 actor turns and B 76. In example A the final story frames include an average of 68 variables annotated for each actor, in example B this value is 84.

	Tilt Example (scene A)	Tilt Example (scene B)
Buildup	Players D1 and D2 emphasize how D1 saves the world selling Fair Trade products. D3 enters as his worker.	Three players (D4, D5 and D6) D6 is a serious no fun guy that teaches his friends how to behave in public places.
Tilt	D3 - Please feed me! D1 - \<fails to explain himself\>	D5 - \<towards D6\> Does she (D6s wife) hit you?
Effect	Player 2 - \<shocked at D1\>	D6 - I dont want to talk about it guys \<avoids eye contact\>

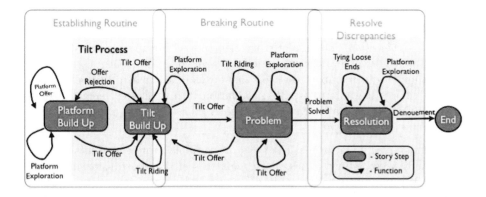

Fig. 1. Story Development Conceptual Model

a heavier mark on the scene and represents a nuclear problem to be addressed. This is in line with Johnstone's notion of minor and major tilts. Minor tilts are part of a buildup that moves the scene towards an inevitable major tilt. D6 from Scene B reports the occurrence of two different scene changes. The first tilt which we identified as a part of Tilt Buildup results from an insult of one of his friends to his wife: "Yeah and I wish you didnt have that wife and those children". D6 comments this insult: "The scene is now shifting into something else, (...) where dealing with my wife which he doesn't like, I'm thinking should I not like my wife or should I like my wife? And thats going to base my opinion about what he said." From this moment on, the scene develops around D6s wife with growing conflicting opinions about her which end up leading to the offer "Does she (wife) hit you?" at this point D6 reports: "Now this is turning into a big tilt, which is a term for when a scene just takes a big turn into turning something else. A Big offer". Also, in both cases we observed shifts in status and affinity. In example A the main shift was in D2's affinity towards D1, and in example B there was a clear status shift for D6.

Resolution. This is the step where players look to resolve the tilt reasons in order to make the action fall into an end. (e.g. "at this point the clock in my head is going off. This should be wrapping up we should be finishing this scene.").

Functions

Platform Offer. Is used to add content to a story, such as character definition, story context, scenario, and other, with the goal of defining a platform that extends the space of possibilities in a story. Platform offers are mostly associative and use elements from the agents perceived story frame. An example from this occurs in scene A when one of the players comments *"Hey, looks like you guys got a new line of muffins this morning,"* offering the existence of a muffin table in the scene. Explicit offer rejections can also be seen as offers of elements that can not be added to the scene. This requires the goal of building a platform that does not include the proposed offer (platform restriction), which means that a rejection may also be a platform offer.

Platform Exploration. The use of story elements within the current story platform without adding any new story development. It is recurrently used in every step without a direct impact on the story development when a player finds no alternative or just wants to establish a relation with the scene elements. An example of this is when a character in scene A offers a muffin to another player *"Here, have a muffin man."*

Tilt Offer. Given a platform as a set of story variables, that represents the who? what? and where? story values, a *Tilt* can be seen as the transformation of a story platform, and its variables, into a new platform that is similar enough to avoid unresolvable inconsistencies and at the same time significantly different in some crucial variable sub-set (tilt variable). Based on this perspective and in the observations about status and affinity relevance in the tilt function, we propose that a tilt offer function should include a measure of similarity called Degree of Similarity (DoS) and a measures of differences called Tilt Potential (TP), that considers status and affinity.

The degree of similarity between two platforms could be expressed as quotient between the number of consistent elements (elements that exist in both platforms and with the same value), and the total number of elements of a platform. We propose to use TP as a measure of the variation of status and affinity, between the established and target platforms.

Now we can use the two measures presented above (DoS and TP) on the function of selection of the target platform, by stating that when proposing a tilt offer the agent should aim for the offer that maximizes DoS and TP.

$$targetPlatform(x)_{x \in \{Platforms\}} = \arg \text{Max}_{x,y \in \{Platforms\}}(DOS(x,y) \times TP(x,y)) \tag{1}$$

Tilt Riding. Tilt Riding differs from platform exploration because it is not just a casual exploration of a platform, but an exploration of the platform elements that are more directly related with the tilt variable, with the purpose of increasing its importance and the characters attachment to it. An example of tilt riding in scene B occurs after one player insults D6s wife "Yeah and I wish you didnt have that wife and those children" and the scene grows with new elements related with the new variable "D6's wife". Other players keep adding elements to the scene against D6's wife, while he purposely fails to counter them. They start by finding her ugly, "manish", too tall, "mammoth shewoman", until they reach the new tilt where they offer that she hits D6. D6 accepts this tilt and rides it by exploring the fact that he is a victim of abuse "I started acting like abuse victims act", changing his character.

Tying Loose Ends. This functions aims at slowing down the pace of a story after its conclusion in order to bring it to an end. In example A one player took advantage of the fact that everybody in the scene was drugged to justify the cognitive divergence state generated from his initial activity, "Oh my god! You've drugged this entire firm. No wonder I was breaking leaves in the break room." This is also inline with improv theory "A pointless story is one in which the recapitulation is missing or bungled, whereas a perfect story is one in which all the material is recycled"[9].

4   Conclusions

In this paper we propose a "shift in authorial power" to reduce the authorial burden of autonomous characters for interactive narratives. We contribute to the study of this hypothesis with the empirical analysis of real life improv players in analog conditions. We present a story development conceptual model supported both by theory and our data analysis, which includes self-report data from the subjects.

Acknowledgements. This work was partially supported by FCT (INESC-ID multiannual funding) through the PIDDAC Program funds. The first author acknowledges the FCT PhD grant (SFRHBD/37476/2007).

References

1. Bates, J., Loyall, A., Scott Reilly, W.: An Architecture for Action, Emotion, and Social Behavior. Journal of Game Development 2(3) (1992)
2. Hayes-Roth, B., Sincoff, E., Brownston, L., Huard, R., Lent, B.: Directed improvisation with animated puppets. In: Proceedings of CHI 1995, p. 7980 (1995)
3. Cavazza, M., Charles, F., Steven, J.M.: Character-based interactive storytelling. IEEE Intelligent Systems 17, 1724 (2002)
4. Aylett, R., Louchart, S., Dias, J., Paiva, A., Vala, M., Woods, S., Hall, L.: Unscripted narrative for affectively driven characters. Proceedings of IEEE CGA 26(4), 4252 (2006)
5. Si, M., Marsella, S., Pynadath, D.: THESPIAN: An Architecture for Interactive Pedagogical Drama, in AI in Education, Amsterdam, Netherlands (July 2005)
6. Young, R.M.: Notes on the use of plan structures in the creation of interactive plot. AAAI Technical Report FS-99-01 (1999)
7. Seham, A.: Whose improv is it anyway? beyond second city, p. vii. Univ. Press of Mississippi (2001)
8. Sawyer, R.K.: Improvised dialogues: emergence and creativity in conversation. Green-wood Publishing Group, New York 20
9. Johnstone, K.: Impro for Storytellers(TheatreArts). Routledge, New York (1999)
10. Magerko, B., Manzoul, W., Riedl, M., Baumer, A., Fuller, D., Luther, K., Pearce, C.: An Empirical Study of Cognition and Theatrical Improvisation. In: Proceedings of ACM Conference on Creativity and Cognition, Berkely, CA (2009)

Digital Improvisational Theatre: *Party Quirks*

Brian Magerko, Christopher DeLeon, and Peter Dohogne

Georgia Institute of Technology, Technology Square Research Building,
85 Fifth Street NW, Atlanta, Georgia 30308 United States
{magerko,cdeleon3,pdohogne3}@gatech.edu

Abstract. This paper describes the creation of a digital improvisational theatre game, called *Party Quirks*, that allows a human user to improvise a scene with synthetic actors according to the rules of the real-world version of the game. The AI actor behaviors are based on our study of communication strategies between real-life actors on stage and the fuzzy concepts that they employ to define and portray characters. Development of content for the system involved the creation of a novel system for animation authoring, design for efficient data reuse, and a work flow centered on parallel data entry and rapid iteration. A subsequent user test of the current system is presented as an initial evaluation of the user-centered experience in participating in a virtual *Party Quirks* game.

Keywords: Improvisation, Theater, Player Experience, Virtual Characters.

1 Introduction

Playable improvisational theatre games are a form of game-based entertainment that has rarely been tackled within the game AI community [1], [2]. Improvisational AI characters have been developed since the early to mid-1990's [2-6], though none of these approaches were informed by an cognitively-based understanding of how improvisers communicate and construct stories together. Our study of improv actors, both in lab settings and in real performance settings, has informed a grounded theory-based (i.e. data-driven instead of based on pre-conceived hypotheses) analysis to inform the construction of simple AI agents (removed for blind review). The construction of these agents has cyclically informed our data analysis process by highlighting what data we need more of and what fallacies exist in the current analysis. This has enabled a richer data analysis and, in turn, more complex agents to be built.

This work in studying improvisational theatre has resulted in the implementation of the real-time improve performance game *Party Quirks*, which is populated by improvisational synthetic actors and intended to be an example of certain aspects of our findings as a middle computational step rather than as a final, complete improvisational system. *Party Quirks* was emulated due to its focus on character portrayal and lack of emphasis on story construction. Story construction is a component in many improvisational games but an overly complicated problem for our initial system and is a current focus of our theoretical work [7], [8]. A typical game of *Party Quirks* involves four players: one plays the role of party host, and all others play as party guests. Each party guest is assigned a "quirk" – some special trait for each guest that

H. Högni Vilhjálmsson et al. (Eds.): IVA 2011, LNAI 6895, pp. 42–47, 2011.

is public knowledge to everyone except the party host, including the audience. The host player then, within the context of hosting a party, aims to figure out what quirk each guest is portraying through their interactions. A guest typically leaves the scene when the host has successfully guessed their quirk.

Our digital version of *Party Quirks* consists of software agents acting independently to emulate the communication processes and reasoning about ambiguity that live actors demonstrated during performances in our empirical studies. A human plays as the host in the virtual scene. As opposed to relying on behind-the-scenes communication, the agents have to rely on human-like methods of communication on stage because they are improvising with a human in the scene as an equal. We call this an *equal mixed-initiative* theatre game.

The following sections in this paper provide a brief overview of the knowledge model used by our synthetic actors followed by a description of the *Party Quirks* implementation and evaluated user experience during a live demo event.

2 Knowledge Model

We selected a set of 18 basic *character prototypes* (e.g. *Pirate* and *Cowboy*) as possible quirks to make the content authoring tractable but non-trivial. A *prototype* refers to an idealized socially recognizable constructs that map to a certain kind of character [9]. We define each prototype as a collection of properties with varying degrees of membership (DOM) in sets that represent character attributes. This approach is similar to how we have seen portrayals of prototypes in our human data and matches well to contemporary thoughts on how humans categorize fuzzy concepts [9], [10].

Attributes are adjectives that define a prototype. *Actions* are the physical acts that are used to communicate attributes and are associated with at least one <attribute, DOM range> pair. For example, <*uses_magic*, 0.8-1.0> implies a high association with magic usage, which is connected to the action *controlWeather*. Any character with *uses_magic* between these values can therefore execute the *controlWeather* action on stage.

The primary benefit of using fuzzy membership of sets is that it captures the ambiguity inherent in stage performance. Performing an action with multiple interpretations can lead other actors to have different interpretations of the action than were intended, which often happens in performances. The calculated ambiguity values also provide the means to determine how much the host's interactions indicate their convergence with the "reality" of the scene. In other words, the actions that a human host executes indicate how close they are to guessing a guest's quirk (i.e., reaching cognitive consensus [11]).

3 Experience, Implementation, and Testing

The interaction model for our *Party Quirks* system was modeled after the observed rules that human actors use in real life games of *Party Quirks* (anonymous). The user, as the party host who has to guess each guest's quirk, inputs commands into an iPad. The interface consists of textual buttons that are divided into branching options to reduce the amount of information on-screen at once. The choices given to the user/host are based on the processes that improvisers use to negotiate shared mental models (i.e. shared understandings of the details of a scene as a scene progresses) on stage during earlier phases of this study [11]. The implementation presented here is based on these findings.

The *Party Quirks* actors and stage are projected onto a screen at near life-size scale in an attempt to help immerse the user as one of the four improvisational actors. A webcam stream of the user is placed next to the stage as a means of representing the user in the virtual space and as a location to place a speech bubble that displays user actions.

The user makes menu selections from an iPad interface that represents the different abstract communication moves observed in our human data [11]. The iPad was utilized as an input device for several reasons. A controller was needed which would allow the user to stand, since all guest actors are presented as standing. A touchscreen enables buttons to be dynamically labeled, reducing the complexity of the interface by breaking interactions into categories and allowing for a naturalistic input modality (i.e. finger tapping). As the user makes menu selections, including doing nothing, the AI actors respond on the virtual stage via animations and dialogue portrayals.

3.1 Technology

The AI model for character behaviors was implemented in Processing to simplify cross-platform development and afford rapid prototyping. All data is obtained from Google Docs spreadsheets at program start up via the Google Docs API, enabling parallel online authoring and immediate use by the application without recompiling. The spreadsheets contain definitions of prototypes, attributes, actions, as well as the degrees of membership between prototypes and attributes, and between actions and attributes. The spreadsheets also include text-based dialogue utterances that are associated with the actions.

The animation system was also built using Processing, enabling animation playback to be directly integrated with the AI model. Animations exist as a series of skeletal poses, which play through in sequence. The poses are stored as a list of angles and percentages for each limb, indicating its rotation at the base joint and its scaling lengthwise (used, for example, to point at the camera), as well as three integers corresponding to an enumeration of facial expressions and hand poses. Each animation is saved as a separate file to facilitate parallel development without needing to merge data.

3.2 User Testing

Notes were taken on user experience issues during a public showcase in 2010 and users were encouraged to share feedback. The development team used this feedback to identify sources of frustration and confusion, exposing incorrect assumptions made during the design.

Users found difficulty dividing attention between the iPad and the projector screen. The virtual actors offered information, in the form of animations, while the user was still busy trying to read and interpret options on the iPad. Confirmation screens, displayed on the iPad at the end of each input sequence, turned out to be unexpected, leading the user to watch the projected image in anticipation of response while the device in hand prompted silently for one last action. We anticipated split-attention as a potential problem when designing the system, but opted for trying it in lieu of more computationally difficult interfaces (e.g. natural language interaction via spoken word) or pragmatically difficult ones (e.g. tangible items used to represent the myriad of options present in the iPad user interface). In the interactive examples mentioned in the introduction [4], drop-down menus gave the user a choice among potential goals and behaviors. The only similar system to attempt full natural language interaction, Mateas and Stern's *Façade*, has had mixed success due to the difficulty in conversing with synthetic characters in a broad conversation domain [12]. This motivated the team's decision to scope the work to focus on the myriad issues that inherently come with trying to build an AI-based digital improv system and to avoid using full natural language interaction for this installation. Future work will examine more natural interaction modalities.

Users also found difficulty splitting attention between the three actors simultaneously. This helped illustrate what may be a difference between having trained improv actors as users instead of untrained attendees at a university media showcase. Those players that played more than one round fared much better on attempts after the first, demonstrating that with prior exposure to the structure the game could be played more successfully. This discovery led the recent development of a single-guest tutorial round for first-time users.

One of the simplest strategies to gather information from the guests about their quirks – a strategy that occurs in live improv and is practical in this software implementation – is to guess prototypes even before guess confidence is high. This narrows down the potential prototype answers by prompting new contrasting information from the guests. However, many simulation players seemed reluctant to make prototype guesses until they were confident in their answer, possibly from confusion over whether some penalty might be imposed for incorrect guesses or simply due to a lack of experience in improvisational acting.

In some cases, there was ambiguity in what the middle value should mean for prototype / attribute degree of membership values. For example, if "explaining relativity" signifies high intelligence, "reading a book" might suggest comparatively normal intelligence, although a player might interpret book reading as a sign of high intelligence. Although different interpretations of values between extremes were a source of confusion, this type of confusion is a normal part of *Party Quirks*; different people have different models of norms and extremes in the real world. These misunderstandings can occur between two live actors just as they can between the data set's author and a human player. Future work will involve gathering crowdsourced data to provide DOM distributions based on a much larger set of authors to define prototypes (as opposed to just the research team's intuitions).

4 Discussion

While we are encouraged by the initial work done in *Party Quirks* in representing character prototypes, the process of building shared mental models, and an initial communication framework for interacting with improvisational characters, this initial system is not without its drawbacks. Users often get stuck just guessing repeatedly instead of making use of the other moves common in performances. This points to a major issue of presence in the system; users do not act like they are performing with the actors on a virtual stage, but like they are prodding a system to see how it responds. The virtual actors give an often-entertaining response with any guess, which provokes the user to guess again instead of selecting other moves. Future work in interface design, such as using voice commands or gesture recognition, may help actively involve the user in the performance space rather than acting outside of it and getting stuck in the most convenient menu option.

The agents themselves are fairly generalizable in terms of the number of attributes that can be used to describe characters and the different mappings from attribute value ranges to actions that can occur. However, they cannot be altered, augmented, or combined. For instance, prototypes cannot be blended together to create new prototypes (e.g. a mosquito that acts like a drunk when it drinks blood) nor can they be created with some antithetical property (e.g. a plumber who is afraid of water). This points to the need for future work to focus on how agents can employ the process of *conceptual blending* [13].

Another major limitation of the agents is that they have no concept of narrative; they are incapable of constructing a story or having dialogue acts that logically progress over time. This issue has fueled our current research agenda of exploring conceptual models of equal mixed-initiative (i.e. AI and humans are both on the virtual stage and equally share responsibility in constructing the story) collaborative story construction from the viewpoint of a) setting up the details of a scene (e.g. where the scene takes place, who the characters are, what joint activity they are doing together, etc.) and b) finding the "tilt" for the scene (i.e. what the main dramatic focus of the scene is)[14]. The future of this work will be a synthesis of these lessons learned from *Party Quirks*, resulting in a troupe of AI improvisers than can jointly construct narrative on stage with or without a human acting with them.

References

[1] Hayes-Roth, B., Brownston, L., van Gent, R.: Multiagent collaboration in directed improvisation. In: Proceedings of the First International Conference on Multi-Agent Systems (ICMAS 1995), pp. 148–154 (1995)

[2] Bruce, A., Knight, J., Listopad, S., Magerko, B., Nourbakhsh, I.R.: Robot Improv: Using Drama to Create Believable Agents. In: AAAI Workshop Technical Report WS 1999-15 of the 8th Mobile Robot Competition and Exhbition, vol. 4, pp. 4002–4008 (1999)

[3] Perlin, K., Goldberg, A.: Improv: A System for Scripting Interactive Actors in Virtual Worlds. In: SIGGRAPH 1996, New Orleans, LA (1996)

[4] Hayes-Roth, B., Van Gent, R.: Story-Making with Improvisational Puppets and Actors. Technical Report KSL 1996-09, Palo Alto, CA (1996)

[5] Swartjes, I., Theune, M.: An Experiment in Improvised Interactive Drama. Intelligent Technologies for Interactive Entertainment, 234–239 (2009)

[6] Harger, B.: Project Improv, Project Improv (2008), http://www.etc.cmu.edu/projects/improv/ (accessed February 25, 2010)

[7] Baumer, A., Magerko, B.: An Analysis of Narrative Moves in Improvisational Theatre. Presented at the International Conference on Interactive Digital Storytelling, Edinburgh, Scotland (2010)

[8] Baumer, A., Magerko, B.: Narrative Development in Improvisational Theatre. Presented at the International Conference on Interactive Digital Storytelling, Guimarães, Portugal, pp. 140–151 (2009)

[9] Lakoff, G.: Cognitive models and prototype theory. In: Margolis, E., Laurence, S. (eds.) Concepts and Conceptual Development: Ecological and Intellectual Factors in Categorization, pp. 63–100 (1987)

[10] Rosch, E.: Principles of categorization. In: Margolis, E., Laurence, S. (eds.) Concepts: Core Readings, pp. 189–206 (1999)

[11] Fuller, D., Magerko, B.: Shared mental models in improvisational performance. In: Proceedings of the Intelligent Narrative Technologies III Workshop, Monterey, CA (2010)

[12] Mateas, M., Stern, A.: A Behavior Language for Story-Based Believable Agents. IEEE Intelligent Systems 17(4), 39–47 (2002)

[13] Fauconnier, G., Turner, M.: The Way We Think: Conceptual Blending and the Mind's Hidden Complexities. Basic Books, New York (2003)

[14] Brisson, A., Magerko, B., Paiva, A.: Tilt Riders: Improvisational Agents Who Know What the Scene is About. In: 11th International Conference on Intelligent Virtual Agents, Reykjavik, Iceland (2011)

Where to Sit?
The Study and Implementation of Seat Selection in Public Places

Elin Carstensdottir, Kristin Gudmundsdottir, Gunnar Valgardsson,
and Hannes Vilhjalmsson

Center for Analysis and Design of Intelligent Agents, School of Computer Science
Reykjavik University, Menntavegur 1, 101 Reykjavik, Iceland
{elinc09,kristingud08,gunnarsv08,hannes}@ru.is

Abstract. The way people behave in public places when selecting a seat should be of interest to anyone working with virtual people and environments such as in the simulation, movie, or games industry. This study, conducted in a café and a restaurant, was meant to gather information about this behaviour. In particular whether a behavioural pattern could be found and whether there is a notable difference in the behaviour of individuals and groups. The study found that specific behavioural patterns exist in these situations. These results lead to some guidelines for behaviour design as well as a model of seat selection based on utility. The model was implemented in the CADIA Populus Social Simulation engine.

Keywords: Seating behaviour, seat selection, seat preference, virtual people, social simulation, artificial intelligence.

1 Introduction

Virtual people are all around us: In movies, on the television, and in video games. They are people who are created in computers and displayed as though they were real individuals, even sometimes in the company of real actors. The animation of these people has for the most part been in the hands of animators, but automatic animation, performed by artificial intelligence, is gaining popularity. This automatic animation is possible with the help of algorithms that control the responses of the virtual people to their environment. This technology is dependent on our ability to describe human behaviour in an algorithm.

While virtual people often find themselves in combat situations, interest in peaceful behaviour is growing, for example with the emergence of computer games that focus on social interaction. One of these game environments is a new addition to CCP's EVE Online computer game, where players can meet one another and other narrative characters in space-cafés and bars. The narrative characters have to behave realistically in such places, so empirically based algorithms need to be in place to control their responses and behaviour.

H. Högni Vilhjálmsson et al. (Eds.): IVA 2011, LNAI 6895, pp. 48–54, 2011.

The behaviour that this study focused on is how individuals select a seat in places where other people are present, for example in restaurants and cafés. By studying this behaviour and analysing it in the field, it was possible to create an algorithm for use in an artificially intelligent animation system to elicit similar behaviour in a virtual environment.

2 Related Work

Research on seat and/or table selection of individuals and groups alike has been limited. Especially for the express purpose of using the obtained data to create algorithms for describing this selection. The studies that have been done in the field, and that we know of, have been limited to certain venues and locations, city squares for example [5], but not cafés, bars, or restaurants. We implemented the result of our research as a behaviour module in the CADIA Populus system, which is a platform for producing realistic group conversation dynamics in shared virtual environments [6]. Empirically based behaviour modules have successfully been added to CADIA Populus before, for example for public gaze behaviour [1], terretorial behaviour [7] [8], and turn taking behaviour [2]. The main influences in shaping CADIA Populus's approach to behaviour modelling is, the work of Adam Kendon and Albert Scheflen respectively; especially Kendon's definition of the F-formation system [3] [4] and Scheflen's concept of k-space [9] [10]. This was also the basis for our preliminary theories that the k-space could be a factor in individual seat selection, after the selection of a table has occurred. We speculated that individually chosen seats would be outside the k-space of other individuals nearby, and the furniture would then form an F-formation.

3 Research Methodology

A field study was conducted in two locations chosen to fit the game application: one restaurant/café and one bar/café, both located in downtown Reykjavik. The purpose was to observe seat selection behaviour in three types of entities: whole groups, individuals within groups, and individuals. Our methodology was rooted in Behaviour Analysis, which has been used by Context Analysts such as Adam Kendon and Albert Scheflen to study human behaviour. In order to not interfere with the natural setting, background information was assessed by observing the subject. This was information such as age, gender, and possible purpose in the space (for example, dining, resting, or drinking). We also speculated whether each individual (in a group or alone) displayed extrovert or introvert personality traits, such as sitting quietly in the corner or talking loudly in the center of the space. Standardized observation forms were created for both individuals and groups. To maintain the integrity of the data collected the groups/individuals were chosen in a systematic manner. Each time an observed group/individual left the location, the observer who had been observing them would choose the next group/individual to walk through the door as her next subject. Data collected for each group/individual consisted of a description of the entrance and selection of

a table as well as positioning around table when first sitting down. Each session
was three hours long, 52 pages of observational field notes and diagrams (see
Figure 1) were collected during the whole study.

In total, sixteen groups were observed. Group size ranged from two members
to five, and the most common size was two members. Observed individuals were
ten. Four of the ten observed individuals were a part of a group at the time of
observation.

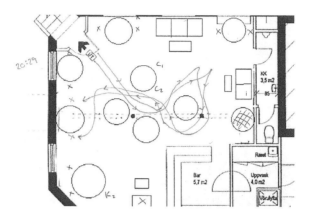

Fig. 1. A sample of observation data. Lines depict entrance path of subjects.

4   Results

Distinct and structured seat selection behaviour was observed, but groups be-
haved differently than individuals. The assessment of personality types also led
us to notice difference in individual behaviour. For example, people who preferred to sit out of the way and others who seemed to want to be the centre of
attention.

4.1   Selecting a Table

The table selection can be described in the following manner: After an individual
enters the environment, he scans it with a clear goal in mind. The most valuable
table, based on that goal, is found. The individual walks directly to the chosen
table, thus showing his intention of sitting there and so reserves the table. In
table selection for groups there is the added complication that the majority has
to agree on the selected table. For these negotiations two types of behavioural
patterns were observed. The former is when a dominant individual within the
group takes control and selects a table. The latter is when an individual group
member suggests a table to the group, this suggestion is then either approved or
a different suggestion is made. This is repeated until the majority of the group
approves of a table. The group's approval was found to be expressed in two ways,
either by vocal consent or silent consent, for example nodding.

Both these behavioural patterns depend heavily on the elapsed amount of decision time. Decision time is the amount of time used for scanning the environment, selecting a table based on the value of the table and a possible goal. For an individual, we speculate that it is particularly important that the decision time is as short as possible, for the longer the decision time the more attention he seems to draw to himself and this seems to be undesirable. This attention can possibly be explained by the curiosity that unusual behaviour draws from others in the environment. Groups seem to have more decision time than individuals. This is likely because the number of people in the group complicates the selection of a table by an individual in the group. He has to seek approval of his selection from others in the group. However, there does seem to be a limit to the decision time of a group and the aforementioned attention focuses on them when that limit is reached.

4.2   The Value of a Table

By observing the general preference for seating we propose that the value of a table is roughly based on two general factors:

1. The location of the table in the environment. Tables located at the perimeter of the environment seem to have more value than tables located near the middle.
2. The size of the table and the number of seats.

The location of the seats around the table also matters a great deal, especially if other individuals or groups are present in the environment during entrance. The proximity to the next table/chair is also a factor and the privacy radius of the table (see Implementation) should preferably not intersect the privacy radius of another table. The value of the perimeter can possibly be linked to the individual's need for a diverse view since the perimeter, especially in many cafés and bars, has windows. We break the location-value of the table into the following factors:

1. The proximity to other tables and chairs in the environment.
2. The view: If a view through a window or over the environment is possible.
3. Weather: In regards to whether a seat inside or outside is preferable.
4. Distance to the entrance.
5. Which tables are already occupied.
6. Access to the table.
7. Presence of a friend: If a friend is present his/her table becomes more valuable, especially for individuals.

These results can be used to make virtual environments, especially ones inhabited by non-playable characters, much more realistic. If agents in the environment behave in a way that a user is accustomed to seeing in the real world, the virtual world becomes much more immersive than it otherwise would have been.

5   Implementation

To showcase our findings we chose to integrate them into the CADIA Populus social simulation engine. As mentioned above, different personalities seem to prefer different placements in the environment. Since this directly influences their seat selection, we decided to utilize this in the implementation. Each table is represented by a feature vector:

$$T = (Pe, Pr, Di, Ba)$$

Where Pe is the proximity to the perimeter of the environment, Pr is the degree of privacy, Di is the relative distance to the exit, and Ba is whether this is a bar table. The privacy feature of a table is based on the environment it is placed in. The tables farthest from the entrance and most out of the way are given the highest privacy rating. Tables are given lower ratings the farther we get from those most-private tables. The tables closest to the entrances and those likely to attract attention (e.g. the bar) are given the lowest privacy rating in the environment. We kept a couple of additional table features outside the feature vector because they represent simple facts that can be dealt with separately, whether the table is un-occupied (U) and the number of seats at the table (S). Each person's affinity for a table depends on that person's personality traits. We represent a person's personality with a personality vector:

$$P = (P_{priv}, P_{self}, P_{bar})$$

Where P_{priv} represents the person's need for privacy, P_{self} represents the person's level of selfconsciousness and P_{bar} represents the person's affinity for sitting at the bar. We made a specially tuned affinity vector that indicates how important each of the table features is for that personality trait. These affinity vectors were chosen to be: $A_{priv} = (0.9, 1.0, 0.8, 0.0)$, $A_{self} = (0.6, 0.6, 1.0, 0.0)$, $A_{bar} = (0.0, 0.0, 0.0, 1.0)$. With these vectors we can now determine a person's affinity (F_T) for a certain table:

$$F_T = \frac{(P_{priv} * \frac{A_{priv}*T}{N_{feat}}, P_{self} * \frac{A_{self}*T}{N_{feat}}, P_{bar} * \frac{A_{bar}*T}{N_{feat}})}{N_{trait}} \quad (1)$$

Here the constants N_{feat} and N_{trait} represent the number of features and number of traits. They are introduced to normalize all results to the range [0.0, 1.0]. As an example, let's pick a person with a selfconscious personality (we created profiles for several stereotypes), P = [0.5, 0.9, 0.1] and a table T = [0.5, 0.8, 0.0]. The person's affinity for this table will then be 0.16.

F_T is further modified by table size and occupancy. Table size smaller than group size multiplies it by 0.0, equal multiplies by 1.0 and larger by 0.5 (we found that groups are less likely to choose tables that have more seats than group members). Occupancy multiplies it by 0.0 if occupied, 1.0 otherwise. After calculating values for all tables in an establishment, an agent simply picks the highest ranking table.

Fig. 2. A screenshot from CADIA Populus

6   Conclusion and Future Work

This paper has discussed a field study of seating behaviour in public places. Some observations were described and an efficient seat selection algorithm was shown. The algorithm has been integrated into the behavioural module collection for CADIA Poplulus, so this behaviour is now available to any game using that engine.

We still need to assess the impact of our algorithm on the user experience, so we plan to conduct a user study where we ask people to compare the behaviour to random seat selection.

We believe that the addition of our new behaviour has made the agents in CADIA Populus more realistic, especially when combined with the existing behaviours. However the current implementation only supports one designated group leader, who always chooses a table without seeking the approval of other group members. We propose that improving this in a future version will further improve the results.

References

1. Cafaro, A., Gaito, R., Vilhjálmsson, H.H.: Animating idle gaze in public places. In: Ruttkay, Z., Kipp, M., Nijholt, A., Vilhjálmsson, H.H., et al. (eds.) IVA 2009. LNCS, vol. 5773, pp. 250–256. Springer, Heidelberg (2009)
2. Jonsdottir, G.R., Thórisson, K.R.: Teaching computers to conduct spoken interviews: Breaking the realtime barrier with learning. In: Ruttkay, Z., Kipp, M., Nijholt, A., Vilhjálmsson, H.H. (eds.) IVA 2009. LNCS, vol. 5773, pp. 446–459. Springer, Heidelberg (2009)
3. Kendon, A.: Conducting interaction: Patterns of Behavior in Focused Encounters. Cambridge University Press, Cambridge (1990)

4. Kendon, A.: Spacing and orientation in co-present interaction. In: Esposito, A., Campbell, N., Vogel, C., Hussain, A., Nijholt, A. (eds.) Second COST 2102. LNCS, vol. 5967, pp. 1–15. Springer, Heidelberg (2010)
5. Ohno, R.: Seat preference in public squares and distribution of the surrounding people: An examination of the validity of using visual simulation. In: Dechne, S., Walz, M. (eds.) Proceedings of the 7th European Architectural Endoscopy Association Conference, Tokyo Institute of Technology, Ohno Labratory, University of Applied Sciences Dortmund, Dortmund (2005)
6. Pedica, C., Vilhjálmsson, H.H.: Social perception and steering for online avatars. In: Prendinger, H., Lester, J.C., Ishizuka, M. (eds.) IVA 2008. LNCS (LNAI), vol. 5208, pp. 104–116. Springer, Heidelberg (2008)
7. Pedica, C., Vilhjálmsson, H.H.: Spontaneous avatar behavior for human territoriality. In: Ruttkay, Z., Kipp, M., Nijholt, A., Vilhjálmsson, H.H. (eds.) IVA 2009. LNCS, vol. 5773, pp. 344–357. Springer, Heidelberg (2009)
8. Pedica, C., Vilhjalmsson, H., Larusdottir, M.: Avatars in conversation: The importance of simulating territorial behavior. In: Proceedings of the 10th International Conference on Intelligent Virtual Agents, Philadelphia, PA, USA, September 20-22. LNCS (LNAI), pp. 336–342. Springer, Heidelberg (2010)
9. Scheflen, A.E.: Organization of behavior in face-to-face interaction. In: Micro-Territories in Human Interaction, pp. 159–173. Mauton & Co, Netherlands (1975)
10. Scheflen, A.E.: Human territories: how we behave in space time. Prentice-Hall, Englewood Cliffs (1976)

Relational Agents Improve Engagement and Learning in Science Museum Visitors

Timothy Bickmore, Laura Pfeifer, and Daniel Schulman

College of Computer & Information Science, Northeastern University, 360 Huntington Ave,
WVH202, Boston, MA 02115
{bickmore,laurap,schulman}@ccs.neu.edu

Abstract. A virtual museum guide agent that uses human relationship-building behaviors to engage museum visitors is described. The agent, named "Tinker", appears in the form of a human-sized anthropomorphic robot, and uses nonverbal conversational behavior, empathy, social dialogue, reciprocal self-disclosure and other relational behavior to establish social bonds with users. Tinker can describe exhibits in the museum, give directions, and discuss technical aspects of her own implementation. Results from an experiment involving 1,607 visitors indicate that the use of relational behavior leads to significantly greater engagement by museum visitors, measured by session length, number of sessions, and self-reported attitude, as well as learning gains, as measured by a knowledge test, compared to the same agent that did not use relational behavior. Implications for museum exhibits and intelligent tutoring systems are discussed.

Keywords: Relational agents, social interfaces, interactive installation, embodied conversational agent, intelligent virtual agent, pedagogical agent, intelligent tutoring system.

1 Introduction

Contemporary museums use interactive exhibits, multimedia, games, automated mobile guides, and other mechanisms for entertaining and engaging visitors so that learning has an opportunity to take place, even as visitors flit from exhibit to exhibit. The use of animated pedagogical agents that incorporate principles from the social psychology of human personal relationships represents a promising and important direction of research to further engage museum visitors. For example, the use of reciprocal self-disclosure is known to lead to increases in intimacy and trust in people, and has been demonstrated to work when used by computers [1]. Museum exhibits that engage visitors in this and other human bonding rituals could result in increased visitor satisfaction and engagement, and ultimately lead to increases in learning.

As an initial experiment in building a relational museum exhibit, we have developed a virtual museum guide agent named "Tinker" who is currently installed in the Computer Place exhibit at the Boston Museum of Science (Figure 1). Tinker appears as a six-foot-tall 3D cartoon robot, projected in front of visitors, and communicates with them using synthetic speech and synchronized nonverbal behavior. Tinker can provide

H. Högni Vilhjálmsson et al. (Eds.): IVA 2011, LNAI 6895, pp. 55–67, 2011.

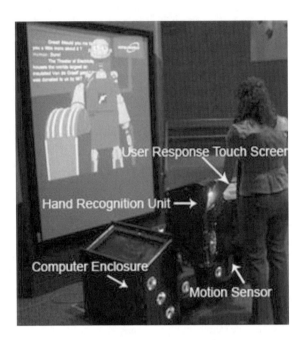

Fig. 1. Tinker System Installation

visitors with information on and directions to a range of exhibits in the museum, as well as discuss the theory and implementation underlying her own creation. Most importantly, Tinker uses a range of human relationship-building behavior to engage users, along with a biometric sensor to re-identify return visitors so that the conversation, and relationship, can be continued [2]. Since Tinker began operation in April, 2008, over 125,000 museum visitors have interacted with her.

In this work we report on an experimental study designed to evaluate the effect of Tinker's relational behavior on engagement and learning in museum visitors. Several studies have demonstrated that quality of human-human personal relationships in a learning environment has a significant impact on student motivation, academic effort, and learning [3]. We wanted to demonstrate these effects using an animated pedagogical agent in a setting in which a very large sample size was possible, given that meta-analyses have indicated that conversational agent features, such as degree of realism, have only a small effect on user attitudinal measures and little or no effect on task outcomes, such as learning [4, 5].

2   Related Work

Several studies have demonstrated the importance of human relationships in learning environments. Within K-6 education, there is evidence that relationships between students are important in peer learning situations, including peer tutoring and peer collaborative learning methodologies [6]. Collaborations between friends involved in these exercises has been shown to provide a more effective learning experience than collaboration between acquaintances [7]. Friends have been shown to engage in more extensive discourse with one another during problem solving, offer suggestions more readily, are more supportive and more critical than non-friends. In at least one experiment, friends worked longer on the task and remembered more about it afterwards than non-friends. Student perception of teacher empathy and caring— prerequisites for quality social-emotional relationships—has also been shown to have significant influences on student motivation and learning. In one longitudinal study of 248 6th to 8th grade students, teacher caring, as perceived by students, was shown to be a significant predictor of student motivation, pro-social goals, academic effort, and grade point average [3].

2.1 Embodied Pedagogical Agents

There have been several explorations into the use of embodied agents in educational software systems, designed to teach material to children and adults [8-12]. Several of these studies have demonstrated positive impacts on student motivation and/or learning [12]. In one series of studies, researchers found that: 1) students who interacted with an educational software system with a pedagogical agent produced more correct solutions and rated their motivation to continue learning and interest in the material significantly higher, compared to the same system without the agent; 2) students who interacted with an agent that used speech output, rated the lessons more favorably and recalled more compared with students who interacted with an agent that used text output; and 3) students who interacted with an agent that used personalized dialogue recalled more than students who interacted with an agent that communicated using non-personalized monologues (as in video-based education) [10]. In another study, students using a pedagogical agent in addition to their normal coursework outperformed both a control group (no additional intervention), and a group directed to reread relevant material from their textbooks [13]. In a review of over a dozen experiments, Graesser et al conclude that the AutoTutor system improves learning by nearly one letter grade compared with control conditions [14]. However, other researchers have failed to demonstrate positive learning outcomes, and some have posited that any gains observed may be due primarily to the use of voice rather than embodiment or social presence [12].

2.2 Interactive Museum Guide Agents

There has also been a significant amount of research on the development of interactive museum exhibits and mobile guide devices over the last decade. Here we briefly review humanoid conversational agents (virtual and robotic) that are deployed in public spaces, three of which are installed in museums as guides (Kopp, et al [15], Shiomi, et al [16], Swartout, et al [17]) and one which acts as a receptionist (Gockley, et al [18]). None of these agents use explicit models of the user-agent relationship, and they have a very limited repertoire of relational behavior (typically limited to form of address and social dialogue). Two are able to identify visitors (Shiomi, based on RFID tags, and Gockley, based on magnetic strip ID cards), but only use this information to address users by name. These systems also only support very limited dialogue: Shiomi's robots can only talk at users (no dialogue support), while Kopp's and Shiomi's use typed-text input and pattern-matching rules which support social chat but do not provide the deep dialogue models required for extended coherent conversation about a given topic. Swartout, et al, developed the "Ada and Grace" exhibit, installed near Tinker in the Boston Museum of Science [17]. In this system, two conversational agents interact with each other and a human handler via speech (visitors are not permitted to talk directly to the agents), discussing the museum and science topics. Summative evaluation results (visitor satisfaction, etc.) have not been published.

2.3 Relational Agents

Bickmore, et al, have conducted a series of studies of conversational agents that use human relationship-building behavior in their interactions with users. In one study, an exercise coach agent was systematically manipulated to use relational behavior (empathy, social chat, form of address, etc.) or not in addition to task-oriented exercise counseling in its daily 10-minute conversations with study participants. In a 30-day longitudinal study, participants who interacted with the agent with the relational behavior enabled scored the agent significantly higher on a standardized measure of patient-counselor working relationship (the Working Alliance Inventory) compared to those participants who interacted with the same agent with the relational behaviors disabled, although no effects on task outcome (exercise behavior) were observed [19].

3 Tinker

Tinker was developed over an eight-month period of time in collaboration with the staff at Computer Place in the Boston Museum of Science. This is a staffed area of the museum that provides visitors with explorations in computer science, communications, and robotics. Work on Tinker's dialogue content, character animation, and physical installation proceeded in parallel. Details on the design principles and methodology used in Tinker's development, and user identification technology employed, have been previously reported [2, 20].

3.1 Dialogue Content and Nonverbal Behavior

Tinker's main purpose is to provide museum visitors with descriptions of and directions to museum exhibits, and to talk about her own implementation. Development of these dialogue scripts began by videotaping museum staff giving descriptions of exhibits and interacting with visitors, in order to characterize these conversations and the nonverbal behavior they used. We then developed the scripts using a hierarchical transition network-based dialogue model [19]. Computer Place staff felt that it was important that Tinker's dialogue about computers be tailored to each visitor's level of computer literacy. Consequently, Tinker establishes each visitor's computer literacy level through dialogue before discussing any technical content, and remembers this for future conversations. We also developed dialogue to answer questions about privacy issues related to the biometric hand reader, explaining that the system only stores a small amount of information and erases it after a short period of time.

Tinker's nonverbal behavior was primarily generated using BEAT [21], including beat (baton) hand gestures and eyebrow raises for emphasis, gaze away behavior for signaling turn-taking, and posture shifts to mark topic boundaries. In addition, some nonverbal behavior was specified explicitly, including deictic (pointing) gestures (e.g., during direction giving) and facial displays of emotion.

3.2   Installation: Deploying Relational Agents in Museums

Tinker is projected human-sized to facilitate naturalness of interaction. We use multiple-choice touch screen input for user utterances, based on other work in developing a conversational agent for users who had no prior computer experience [22]. In addition to multiple choice utterance input screens, additional inputs were designed to enable visitors to input their given name and to quickly jump to different high-level topics using iconic representations (Figure 2).

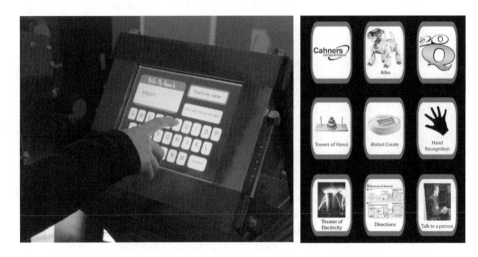

Fig. 2. Sample User Input Screens (Left: Given Name; Right: Museum Topics)

There are several significant challenges in deploying such relational agents in crowded settings such as museums. These include: user re-identification; user presence detection (for conversation initiation and termination, and to tell if a visitor has just walked away in the middle of a conversation); and user location detection (so that the agent can appear to be looking directly at the visitor, required for human conversational turn-taking and grounding cues [23]). We solved all three of these problems by using a glass plate that visitors rest their hand on during their conversations with Tinker. Sensors on the plate provide presence detection, and a camera underneath provides hand shape-based user identification. In addition, with a visitor's left hand on this plate and their right hand using the touch screen, their location is fixed between the two, solving the agent gaze problem. We also use a motion sensor to determine if visitors are in Tinker's general area so that she can beckon them over to talk and begin conversation initiation behaviors.

We also added several other objects to Tinker's virtual environment to address problems that may be unique to museum settings. A large scrolling text screen was placed behind Tinker, showing the content of the last several conversational turns. We felt this was important in order to support the involvement of bystanders who might be near Tinker once a conversation is underway, as well as supporting individuals with hearing problems or who have difficulty understanding the synthetic voice. We also placed a smaller sign behind Tinker to display system status information (e.g., indicating the system is down) as well as a demonstration animation sequence showing approaching visitors how to use the hand reader. Finally, a virtual hand recognition reader was placed in Tinker's environment so that she could demonstrate putting her hand in the reader when visitors approach.

The current installation is located at the entrance to Computer Place (Figure 1). Tinker is projected onto a 3' by 6' tall screen using a short-throw projector, and runs on two networked computers. Hand recognition is performed by extracting geometric features from hand images, and comparing them to those from the last 20 visitors [2].

3.3 Relational Behavior

We implemented a variety of dialogue and nonverbal behavior to enable Tinker to establish a sense of trust and rapport with visitors [19]. These behaviors could be turned on or off independently from all task-oriented behavior to facilitate evaluation of their efficacy (as described in Section 4).

Empathy. Empathy is the process of attending to, understanding, and responding to another person's expressions of emotion, and is one of the core processes in building and maintaining relationships [24, 25]. There are many places in Tinker's dialogue in which she can express empathy for a feeling state expressed or implied by a visitor. For example, after asking about a visitor's experience at the museum, a positive response results in Tinker's saying "That is great. I hope you are learning a lot too." (with a happy facial display), while a response expressing boredom results in "I am sorry to hear that. I hope you can find some part of the museum that interests you." (with a concerned facial display), and an expression of being tired yields "I am sorry to hear that. Yes, walking around can be tiring. Maybe you could pick up some refreshments at the cafeteria?".

Getting Acquainted. Early in her interaction with a new visitor, Tinker will ask them about themselves, including their age, who they are visiting with, and where they are from, with appropriate social responses for each possible visitor response [26].

Self-Disclosure and Reference to Common Ground. Tinker will make references to information disclosed by a visitor about themselves at appropriate points in the dialogue, as an indirect way of reminding them of their shared knowledge and interaction history (e.g., "Be sure to take your kids to the exhibit. I am sure they will find it interesting.") [27].

Reference to Shared Values and Beliefs. Tinker will agree with many of a visitor's expressed likes and dislikes [28]. For example, if the visitor indicates they are a Red Sox (Boston baseball team) fan, Tinker will say she is a fan as well (if the visitor does not indicate this, Tinker does not talk any further about the team).

Humor. Tinker will interject humor at appropriate points in the conversation [29]. For example, when telling a visitor how she works and that she does not have the ability to see them with computer vision, she might say "So, you could have three purple heads and be twelve feet tall and I would not know the difference!".

Form of Address. Once visitors have entered their given name, Tinker will use it to greet them [30]. She will also greet them by name on return visits, if the biometric hand reader recognizes them [2] (e.g., "Hi Bob, welcome back!").

Expressing Liking of the User and the Interaction and Desire to Continue. During farewells and subsequent greetings, Tinker expresses liking of the user, e.g., "It has been great talking with you. I hope to see you again." [31].

3.4 Pilot Testing

Pilot testing with 72 visitors (reported in [2, 20]) indicated that most participants thought Tinker was fun and engaging to interact with, many (56%) preferred to talk to her rather than museum staff (only 31% said they would rather have talked to a person), and none expressed privacy concerns regarding the biometric identification system (78% had no concerns, the rest were unsure). Most (94%) visitors conducted a single conversation lasting 7 minutes on average, with 6% returning for follow up conversations. The most popular topics that visitors ask about are Tinker's design (41%), the Computer Place exhibit (23%), and directions to other parts of the museum (21%). A minority of users (25%) expressed concerns about the privacy issues related to the use of biometric identification, although most added that they were not concerned about this particular application ("This is okay, but if that was being used on a daily basis, I'd be very concerned about my fingerprints being taken.").

4 Evaluation Study

In order to evaluate the impact of relational behavior on visitors' engagement and learning, we conducted an experimental study in the museum beginning in March, 2009. The study was a two-group, between-subjects experimental design. The study compared the full version of Tinker described above (RELATIONAL), to an identical version in which all of the relational behavior (described in Section 3.4) was switched off (NON-RELATIONAL). All task-related dialogue, including all educational content, was the same in both conditions.

Based on studies of the effects of perceived empathy and caring in human teacher-student relationships [3], we hypothesize the following:

H1. Visitors who interact with the RELATIONAL Tinker will demonstrate a significantly more positive attitude towards the agent (overall satisfaction, liking, desire to continue) compared to visitors who interact with the NON-RELATIONAL agent.

H2. Visitors will exhibit greater engagement with the RELATIONAL Tinker compared to the NON-RELATIONAL version, as demonstrated by the length of time they spend at the exhibit and the number of times they return to it during the day.

H3. Visitors will learn significantly more from the RELATIONAL Tinker compared to the NON-RELATIONAL agent. By 'learning' we mean retention of information told to visitors by Tinker, as evidenced by correct answers on a knowledge test.

Further, we hypothesize (**H4**) that engagement mediates (at least partially) any relationship between study condition (RELATIONAL vs. NON-RELATIONAL) and learning [32] (study condition causes changes in engagement which, in turn, causes changes in learning, as in Figure 3).

4.1 Methods

Measures. *Engagement* was assessed by the total time in minutes each visitor spent with Tinker and the number of visits they made to the exhibit in a given day, determined from a log file analysis. *Attitude* towards Tinker was assessed using the first five single-item questions shown in Table 1, administered after a visitor's first interaction with Tinker. *Learning* was assessed using a five-item, multiple-choice knowledge test, covering topics distributed throughout Tinker's educational content (e.g., "How can Tinker recognize you?", correct answer "Looking at my hand."), administered after a visitor's first interaction with Tinker, and scored as number of correct answers. Note that visitors may or may not hear the content tested by these questions, depending on which topics they ask Tinker about. Visitor perception of how much they learned from Tinker was assessed using the last single-item question in Table 1.

Table 1. Self-Report Attitude Questions (all 5-point scales)

Measure	Question	Anchor 1	Anchor 5
SATISFACTION	How satisfied are you with this exhibit?	Not At All Satisfied	Very Satisfied
CONTINUE	How much would you like to talk to Tinker again?	Not At All	Very Much
LIKE	How much do you like Tinker?	Not At All	Very Much
RSHIP	How would you describe Tinker?	A Complete Stranger	A Close Friend
LIKEPERSON	How much is Tinker like a person?	Just like a computer	Just like a person
LEARNFROM	How much do you think you learned from Tinker?	Nothing	A lot

Protocol. As soon as Tinker identified a visitor as a new user (see [2]) the visitor was randomized into either a RELATIONAL or NON-RELATIONAL condition, and they then conducted their interaction with the system, with relational behavior turned on or off according to study condition. Once a first-time visitor indicated they were done with the conversation, the touch screen input display would ask (via text) if they were over 18 years old (our only eligibility criteria) and would be interested in participating in a study. If the visitor indicated they were, an unsigned informed consent was administered, the six Attitude questions asked in succession, and the five-item knowledge test administered, all via text on the touch screen. Subsequent interactions by enrolled participants on the same day (if any) were also tracked to assess Engagement, but no further questionnaires were administered.

4.2 Results

Primary results from the study are shown in Table 2.

Table 2. Primary Study Results (significance levels are for t-tests for independent means)

Measure	RELATIONAL (mean)	NON-RELATIONAL (mean)	StdDev	df	t	p (sig)
Session Length	5.76	4.95	3.49	1605	4.41	<.001
Number Sessions	1.13	1.09	0.34	1605	2.65	0.008
SATISFACTION	4.34	4.11	0.90	1605	5.06	<.001
CONTINUE	4.04	3.74	1.09	1604	5.22	<.001
LIKE	4.29	4.00	1.01	1604	5.44	<.001
RSHIP	3.00	2.79	1.19	1603	3.44	0.001
LIKEPERSON	3.27	2.96	1.22	1603	4.88	<.001
LEARNFROM	3.65	3.36	1.21	1603	4.55	<.001
Knowledge	2.30	2.17	1.05	1602	2.35	0.019

Participants. 1,607 visitors participated in the study (completing all questionnaires) during the two years the study has been active, with 63% in the NON-RELATIONAL condition. An analysis of a subset of the given names input to the system indicates that roughly equal numbers of males and females participated. Participants indicated they had relatively low levels of computer literacy (41.5% indicated they did not have much experience with computers, 29.8% indicated they had significant experience, and 28.7% did not report).

Engagement. Engagement was significantly greater with the RELATIONAL Tinker compared to the NON-RELATIONAL Tinker, measured both by total time interacting with Tinker, $t(1605)=4.41$, $p<.001$, and number of conversations held with Tinker on the day of the study, $t(1605)=2.65$, $p=.008$.

Attitude Towards Tinker. Overall visitor satisfaction was greater with the RELATIONAL Tinker compared to the NON-RELATIONAL version, $t(1605)=5.06$, $p<.001$. Desire to continue interacting with Tinker ($t(1604)=5.22$, $p<.001$) and liking of Tinker ($t(1604)=5.44$, $p<.001$) were both significantly greater in the RELATIONAL condition. Participants in the RELATIONAL condition rated their relationship with Tinker more like that with a close friend than a stranger, $t(1603)=3.44$, $p=.001$, and felt Tinker was more like a person than a computer, $t(1603)=4.88$, $p<.001$, compared to those in the NON-RELATIONAL condition.

Learning. Participants felt they learned significantly more from the RELATIONAL Tinker compared to the NON-RELATIONAL version, t(1603)=4.55, p<.001, even though the educational content was the same in both conditions. Most importantly, participants actually learned more from the RELATIONAL Tinker, scoring significantly higher on the knowledge test, t(1602)=2.35, p<.05, compared to participants who interacted with the NON-RELATIONAL Tinker.

Mediation. Following Baron & Kenny [32], we first regress the independent variable (RELATIONAL vs. NON-RELATIONAL) onto engagement (session length), finding a significant model (p<.001) and unstandardized coefficient b=48.27 (std err=10.95). We next regress the independent variable *and* engagement onto knowledge. The relationship between engagement and knowledge in this model is also significant (p<.001) with unstandardized coefficient for engagement b=.001 (std err<.001). The Sobel test [33] indicates that the mediation is significant, although the mediation is incomplete, since the regression coefficient relating the independent variable to knowledge is non-zero (Figure 3).

4.3 Discussion and Limitations

All study hypotheses were supported. Use of relational behavior by a virtual museum guide agent leads to significantly more positive attitude towards the agent by visitors, increased engagement, and improved learning, as measured both by visitor perception and actual knowledge test scores. The mediation test confirms that relational behavior

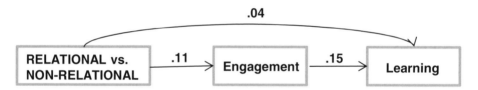

Fig. 3. Results of Mediation Test (standardized regression coefficients shown). Relational behavior primarily affects learning by affecting engagement.

primarily impacts learning via increased engagement (e.g., due to an increased likelihood of discussing the topics that were tested), but also directly impacts learning through, for example, greater psychological involvement caused by increased trust in the agent.

We acknowledge that session length (one of our measures of engagement) is affected directly by relational behavior, since we did not subtract out the time taken in purely relational dialogue from this measure. However, significant differences in engagement are also demonstrated by the attitude measures (desire to continue, in particular) and the number of times visitors returned to talk to Tinker during the day. In addition, visitors did choose to voluntarily spend more time with the RELATIONAL Tinker, regardless of what they were doing during this time.

We also acknowledge that while the results are highly significant (given the very large number of participants), the effect sizes are very small, ranging from .05 to .31, excluding session length. However, given the scales at which popular museum exhibits operate, even small effects can be meaningful. For example, the additional 48 seconds spent by visitors in the RELATIONAL condition results in an additional 670 hours of visitor contact time per year given the 50,000 visitors who have interacted with Tinker annually since the exhibit opened.

The study may also have suffered from a self-selection bias by those visitors who chose to answer the questionnaires following their interaction with Tinker. In our case, however, more visitors in the NON-RELATIONAL condition chose to participate. This may have been due to the longer interaction times in the RELATIONAL condition, under the assumption that visitors were only willing to spend a total fixed amount of time at the exhibit.

5 Conclusion

We have demonstrated that relational behavior used by an intelligent virtual agent can significantly impact not only positive attitudes towards the agent, but task outcomes such as engagement and learning. In addition, overall satisfaction with Tinker remains high: 82.3% of the 1,607 visitors who completed the study (across both groups) indicated they were either "somewhat satisfied" or "very satisfied" with the exhibit.

There are many possible future directions of research that could be pursued to enhance Tinker. User presence is currently determined by pressure on the hand reader plate, which is not always ideal and could be replaced using computer vision. Vision techniques could also be used to allow Tinker to track visitors to provide a more lifelike interaction. Accommodation for multi-party conversation would engage more visitors, since they usually arrive in groups. Finally, Tinker could be deployed on multiple kiosks in the museum, mobile devices, or on the web, to provide a more ubiquitous and continuous presence before, during, and after a visit to the museum.

Acknowledgments. Thanks to Sepalika Perera, Chaamari Senanayake, and Ishraque Nazmi, who helped develop the original Tinker system, to Dan Noren, Taleen Agulian and the staff at Cahner's Computer Place for their assistance, and to Juan Fernandez for maintaining Tinker over the last two years. This work was supported by NSF CAREER IIS-0545932.

References

1. Moon, Y.: Intimate self-disclosure exchanges: Using computers to build reciprocal relationships with consumers. Harvard Business School, Boston (1998)
2. Schulman, D., Sharma, M., Bickmore, T.: The Identification of Users by Relational Agents. Autonomous Agents and Multi-Agent Systems (2008)
3. Wentzel, K.: Social-Motivational Processes and Interpersonal Relationships: Implications for Understanding Motivation at School. Journal of Educational Psychology 91, 76–97 (1999)
4. Yee, N., Bailenson, J., Rickertsen, K.: A meta-analysis of the impact of the inclusion and realism of human-like faces on user experiences in interfaces. In: Conference A meta-analysis of the Impact of the Inclusion and Realism of Human-like Faces on user Experiences in Interfaces (2007)

5. Dehn, D.M., Mulken, S.v.: The Impact of Animated Interface Agents: A Review of Empirical Research. International Journal of Human-Computer Studies 52, 1–22 (2000)
6. Damon, W., Phelps, E.: Strategic Uses of Peer Learning in Children's Education. In: Berndt, T., Ladd, G. (eds.) Peer Relationships in Child Development, pp. 135–157. Wiley, New York (1989)
7. Hartup, W.: Cooperation, close relationships, and cognitive development. In: Bukowski, W., Newcomb, A., Hartup, W. (eds.) The company they keep: Friendship in Childhood and Adolescence, pp. 213–237. Cambridge University Press, Cambridge (1996)
8. Lester, J.C., Voerman, J.L., Towns, S.G., Callaway, C.B.: Cosmo: A Life-like Animated Pedagogical Agent with Deictic Believability. In: Conference Cosmo: A Life-like Animated Pedagogical Agent with Deictic Believability (1997)
9. Lester, J., Stone, B., Stelling, G.: Lifelike Pedagogical agents for Mixed-Initiative Problem Solving in Constructivist Learning Environments. User Modeling and User-Adapted Interaction 9, 1–44 (1999)
10. Moreno, R., Lester, J.C., Mayer, R.E.: Life-Like Pedagogical Agents in Constructivist Multimedia Environments: Cognitive Consequences of their Interaction. In: Conference Life-Like Pedagogical Agents in Constructivist Multimedia Environments: Cognitive Consequences of their Interaction, pp. 741--746 (2000)
11. Graesser, A., et al.: AutoTutor: A simulation of a human tutor. Cognitive Systems Research 1 (1999)
12. Krämer, N.C., Bente, G.: Personalizing e-Learning. The Social Effects of Pedagogical Agents. Educational Psychology Review 22, 71–87 (2010)
13. Person, N.K., Graesser, A.C., Bautista, L., Mathews, E.C.: Evaluating Student Learning Gains in Two Versions of AutoTutor. In: Moore, J.D., Redfield, C.L., Johnson, W.L. (eds.) Artificial Intelligence in Education: AI-ED in the Wired and Wireless Future, pp. 286–293. IOS Press, Amsterdam (2001)
14. Graesser, A.C., Jackson, G., McDaniel, B.: AutoTutor holds conversations with learners that are responsive to their cognitive and emotional states. Educational Technology 47, 19–22 (2007)
15. Kopp, S., Gesellensetter, L., Krämer, N., Wachsmuth, I.: A conversational agent as museum guide – design and evaluation of a real-world application. In: Conference A Conversational Agent as Museum Guide – Design and Evaluation of a Real-world Application, pp. 329–343. Springer, Heidelberg (2005)
16. Shiomi, M., Kanda, T., Ishiguro, H., Hagita, N.: Interactive Humanoid Robots for a Science Museum. In: Conference Interactive Humanoid Robots for a Science Museum (2006)
17. Swartout, W., Traum, D., Artstein, R., Noren, D., Debevec, P., Bronnenkant, K., Williams, J., Leuski, A., Narayanan, S., Piepol, D.: Ada and Grace: Toward realistic and engaging virtual museum guides. In: 10th International Conference on Intelligent Virtual Agents, pp. 286–300 (2010)
18. Gockley, R., Bruce, A., Forlizzi, J., Michalowski, M., Mundell, A., Rosenthal, S., Sellner, B., Simmons, R., Snipes, K., Schultz, A.C., Wang, J.: Designing Robots for Long-Term Social Interaction. In: Conference Designing Robots for Long-Term Social Interaction (2005)
19. Bickmore, T., Picard, R.: Establishing and Maintaining Long-Term Human-Computer Relationships. ACM Transactions on Computer Human Interaction 12, 293–327 (2005)
20. Bickmore, T., Pfeifer, L.D, Perera, S., Senanayake, C., Nazmi, I.: Public Displays of Affect: Deploying Relational Agents in Public Spaces. In: CHI, Florence, Italy (2008)

21. Cassell, J., Vilhjálmsson, H., Bickmore, T.: BEAT: The Behavior Expression Animation Toolkit. In: Conference BEAT: The Behavior Expression Animation Toolkit, pp. 477–486 (2001)
22. Bickmore, T., Caruso, L., Clough-Gorr, K., Heeren, T.: "It's just like you talk to a friend" - Relational Agents for Older Adults. Interacting with Computers 17, 711–735 (2005)
23. Cassell, J., Sullivan, J., Prevost, S., Churchill, E. (eds.): Embodied Conversational Agents. The MIT Press, Cambridge (2000)
24. Havens, L.: Making Contact: Uses of Language in Psychotherapy. Harvard University Press, Cambridge (1986)
25. Gelso, C., Hayes, J.: The Psychotherapy Relationship: Theory, Research and Practice. John Wiley and Sons, New York (1998)
26. Svennevig, J.: Getting Acquainted in Conversation. John Benjamins, Philadephia (1999)
27. Altman, I., Taylor, D.: Social penetration: The development of interpersonal relationships. Holt, Rinhart & Winston, New York (1973)
28. Gill, D., Christensen, A., Fincham, F.: Predicting marital satisfaction from behavior: Do all roads really lead to Rome? Personal Relationships 6, 369–387 (1999)
29. Cole, T., Bradac, J.: A Lay Theory of Relational Satisfaction with Best Friends. Journal of Social and Personal Relationships 13, 57–83 (1996)
30. Laver, J.: Linguistic routines and politeness in greeting and parting. In: Coulmas, F. (ed.) Conversational routine, pp. 289–304. Mouton, The Hague (1981)
31. Okun, B.: Effective Helping: Interviewing and Counseling Techniques. Brooks/Cole, Pacific Grove (1997)
32. Baron, R., Kenny, D.: The Moderator-Mediator Variable Distinction in Social Psychological Research: Conceptual, Strategic, and Statistical Considerations. Journal of Personality and Social Psychology 51, 1173–1182 (1986)
33. MacKinnon, D.P., Lockwood, C.M., Hoffman, J.M., West, S.G., Sheets, V.: A comparison of methods to test mediation and other intervening variable effects. Psychological Methods 7, 83–104 (2002)

Virtual Rapport 2.0

Lixing Huang, Louis-Philippe Morency, and Jonathan Gratch

Institute for Creative Technologies, University of Southern California,
12015 Waterfront Drive, Playa Vista, CA 90094, USA
{lhuang,morency,gratch}@ict.usc.edu

Abstract. Rapport, the feeling of being "in sync" with your conversational partners, is argued to underlie many desirable social effects. By generating proper verbal and nonverbal behaviors, virtual humans have been seen to create rapport during interactions with human users. In this paper, we introduce our approach to creating rapport following Tickle-Degnen and Rosenberg's three-factor (positivity, mutual attention and coordination) theory of rapport. By comparing with a previously published virtual agent, the Rapport Agent, we show that our virtual human predicts the timing of backchannel feedback and end-of-turn more precisely, performs more natural behaviors and, thereby creates much stronger feelings of rapport between users and virtual agents.

Keywords: Rapport, Virtual human, Positivity, Mutual attention, Coordination.

1 Introduction

You feel the connection and harmony with your partner when you are engaged in a good conversation. This phenomenon, formally known as *rapport*, has been studied extensively in social psychology. Rapport is argued to underlie successful negotiation [1], improved quality of child care [2], social engagement [3], and success in teacher-student interactions [4]. Tickle-Degnen and Rosenthal [5] argued that rapport is created through behaviors indicating positive emotions (such as head nods or smiles), mutual attention (such as mutual gaze), and coordination (such as postural mimicry or synchronized movements). They further claimed that as the friendship between two conversants deepens, the importance of positivity decreases, while the importance of coordination increases. Along these lines, Cassell et al. [6] divided rapport into short-term and long-term, where short-term rapport focuses on building instant rapport, while long-term rapport models the unfolding of both verbal and nonverbal behaviors over the course of a relationship. Here we consider the former.

The power of rapport in social interactions has inspired researchers in human-computer interaction and a number of virtual agents have been motivated by these findings. For example, Bailenson et al. [7] showed that a virtual agent was more persuasive and better liked if it mimicked a human speaker's head movement. Bickmore et al. [8] developed an animated agent with text-based dialogue generation that performed nonverbal behaviors such as hand gestures, head nods, eye gaze movements and facial displays of emotion. Their pilot evaluation study showed that the agent promotes antipsychotic medication adherence among patients with

H. Högni Vilhjálmsson et al. (Eds.): IVA 2011, LNAI 6895, pp. 68–79, 2011.

schizophrenia. The recent SEMAINE project built the Sensitive Artificial Listener [9]. By exhibiting different styles of audiovisual listener feedback, the listener is able to express four different personalities.

In our previous work "Virtual Rapport" [12], we introduced an intelligent virtual agent, the Rapport Agent. In a series of subsequent studies by us and outside collaborators, we demonstrated that the Rapport Agent could induce the subjective feeling and many of the behavioral benefits of the psychological concept of rapport. The Rapport Agent has proved a valuable tool for advancing Intelligent Virtual Agent (IVA) research, both by demonstrating that virtual agents have important social effects on human users [10,15,16], and by illuminating the factors that contribute towards or sometimes undermine these social consequences [12,15-17].

Although the Rapport Agent clearly influences human users in important ways, it is less clear how well it is performing at this task, and there is growing evidence in our subsequent subjective experiments that it falls well-short of the potential IVA's hold for shaping human behavior. Several lines of evidence highlight shortcomings to this system: participants give the system mediocre ratings with respect to subjective measures of rapport and social presence [11]; it generally underperforms human users in terms of subjective and behavioral measures [29][1]; and our research on data-driven methods for behavior generation suggests the Rapport Agent's hand-crafted algorithms and animations could be considerably improved [31].

In this article, we will return to the original motivation for the Rapport Agent – Tickle-Degnen and Rosenberg's three-factor theory of rapport – and illustrate how subsequent research has illustrated ways to enhance the positivity, mutual attention and coordination of systems like the Rapport Agent. In particular, we will emphasize the importance of data-driven methods for behavior generation. After reviewing the benefits and limitations of the Rapport Agent, we will introduce a new system designed to enhance the subjective and objective measures of rapport. In a head-to-head comparison, 90% of participants prefer this new system and rate it almost twice as good as the original Rapport Agent along a number of measures of rapport. Our hope is that this new approach will be even more useful as a tool for demonstrating the important benefits of intelligent virtual agents.

2 Virtual Rapport 1.0

The Rapport agent was designed to establish rapport with human participants by providing contingent nonverbal feedback while a participant speaks. The initial system focused on a "quasi-monolog" paradigm, where a human speaker (the narrator) retells some previously observed series of events (e.g., the events in a recently-watched video) to a non-speaking but nonverbally attentive agent [11,12]. More recently, we have extended the system to engage in more interactive dialogs, such as acting as an interviewer [10].

In designing the Rapport Agent, we extracted a small number of simple rules (as shown in Table 1) from social science literature. To produce listening feedback, the agent first collects and analyzes the speaker's upper-body movement and voice. To

---

[1] Although some subgroups – e.g. shy users – seem to prefer the animated agent [**Error! Reference source not found.**].

detect features from the participants' movement, it uses Waston [13] to track the head

Table 1. Rapport Agent Behavior Mapping Rules

Human Speaker Behavior	Rapport Agent Response
Lowering of pitch	Head nod
Raised loudness	Head nod
Speech disfluency	Posture/gaze shift
Shift posture	Mimic
Gaze away	Mimic
Head nod/Head shake	Mimic

position and orientation. With the head tracking data, it can detect head gestures, posture shifts and gaze direction. Acoustic features are derived from properties of the pitch and intensity of the speech signal, using a signal processing package, LAUN. The recognized speaker's features are then mapped to reactions through a set of authorable mapping rules. These reaction animations are passed to the SmartBody [14] animation system using Behavior Markup Language (BML); and finally, the animations are rendered by a commercial game engine and displayed to human users. The animations that the Rapport Agent can perform are relatively simple, such as two continuous nods with equal amplitude and posture shifts. When used in an interview setting, the Rapport Agent steps through a series of predefined questions, taking its turn either when indicated by a human controller [10], or more recently after waiting for a 1.5s pause - the timing based on an analysis of data collected in previous studies [24].

2.1 Benefits

The Rapport Agent has been applied in a series of empirical studies to investigate how people are influenced by such computer-generated behaviors. In these studies, human participants sit in front of the Rapport Agent and are prompted to either retell some previously experienced situation (monologue) or interviewed by the agent to answer some predefined questions (interview). After the interaction, participant rapport is assessed by a variety of subjective and behavioral measures. These studies showed that by interacting with the Rapport Agent, people have: greater feelings of self-efficacy [10], less tension [15] and less embarrassment [10], greater feelings of rapport [15], a greater sense of mutual awareness [16], and greater feelings of trustworthiness [10].The contingent nonverbal feedback of the Rapport Agent also changes participants' behavior. Behavioral effects include: more disclosure of information including longer interaction time and more words elicited [11,12,15,16], more fluent speech [11,12,15,16], more mutual gaze [15] and fewer negative facial expression [17].

2.2 Limitations

Although it has been demonstrated effective in many studies, the current models and behaviors of the Rapport Agent have limitations with regard to the three-factor theory of rapport.

Mutual Attention and Coordination: Tickle-Degnen and Rosenthal emphasize that, with rapport, participants fall into a cohesive, unified pattern of behavior arising through close attention to and tight-coordination of nonverbal signals. The Rapport Agent attempts to realize these two factors by attending to human nonverbal cues (e.g., gestures and prosodic signals) and utilizing them to coordinate its responses (such as backchannel feedback and turn-taking). However, there are reasons to suspect the agent's attention and coordination could be significantly improved. Like many virtual agents, the Rapport Agent's behavior is driven by general rules derived from social science literature, in contrast to more recent approaches [13,22] that attempt to learn behaviors directly from large datasets. Although based on human-behavioral studies, such "literature-based" rules are often intended to make general theoretical points rather than to drive behaviors. Further, such rules are often generated in a variety of social contexts that may differ considerably from the situations to which the Rapport Agent has been applied. Consequently, such rules are unlikely to capture the subtlety in both timing and realizations of nonverbal behaviors.

Positive Emotion Communication: A third component of rapport relates to sense of emotional alignment and positivity that participants experience in the course of rapportful interactions. Nonverbally, this feeling arises from the positive and empathetic expression of emotion. Other research on rapport has emphasized the equal importance of verbal expressions of emotion, for example, through the reciprocal self-disclosure of hopes and fears [25]. Thus, a clear limitation of the Rapport Agent is its inability to engage in emotional communication, both verbally and nonverbally; a point highlighted in some of the evaluations of the system [17].

3   Virtual Rapport 2.0

Virtual Rapport 2.0 improves over the previous work by directly addressing the main limitations of the Rapport Agent. We enhance mutual attention and coordination by applying data-driven approach to build context-specific (i.e. the same context where the virtual human is deployed) response models, which better model the subtlety of timing and realization of nonverbal behaviors. By integrating affective information and strengthening reciprocity, we also enable the virtual human to communicate positive emotions both verbally and nonverbally.

3.1   Enhanced Mutual Attention and Coordination: Data-Driven Approach

To enhance mutual attention and coordination, we learn models to predict backchannel and turn-taking opportunity points from the human behavior observed in the same dyadic conversation settings in which the Rapport Agent is intended to be used. By using such "contextually-appropriate" data, and employing more sophisticated techniques than are typically used in the social sciences, we expect to better model the subtlety and variability in both timing and realizations of the nonverbal behaviors.

   To collect human behavior data for the response models, we adopt the method of Huang and colleagues [20]. Participants are guided to interact with media representations of people parasocially so that it is possible to gather multiple different views on the same interaction, which are later combined to build the consensus view of how a typical response would be. It is showed in [20] that the resulting *parasocial consensus data* generates better virtual human behavior than actual human behavior does.

Backchannel Prediction Model

A backchannel is a kind of feedback within face-to-face interactions that signals a person's attention and interest. It is usually expressed via head nods or paraverbals like "um-huh". By giving backchannel feedback appropriately, the virtual human creates the feeling of mutual attention and coordination. Our backchannel prediction model predicts both when to give feedback and how to display it (i.e. the realization of the head nod).

We build a probabilistic backchannel prediction model based on the parasocial consensus data, which is collected using the Rapport 06-07 data set[2]. Inspired by previous work [21], we used pause and eye-gaze (i.e. looking at the listener) in our model. The model fuses multimodal features at the early stage and captures the long-range dependency between them by applying the encoding dictionary technique [21]. A Conditional Random Field (CRF) model [27] is learned to find the mappings between speaker's nonverbal behaviors and the feedback time. Forty-five video sequences (from the Rapport 06-07 data set) are used in the training stage and the best regularization factors of the CRF model are found by applying 4-fold cross-validation. Conventional CRF uses the forward-backward inference engine that requires the full sequence (i.e. offline processing), which is not applicable for real-time predictions. Instead, we implement real-time CRF using the forward-only inference [30] so that it can make predictions in real-time. The output of CRF indicates the likelihood of giving backchannel feedback. By setting a threshold (based on a preliminary study), we predict the time of feedback by comparing the output with the threshold.

The CRF model predicts when to give feedback and how to give such feedback is learned from actual listeners' behavior. We found the typical styles of head nods from the listeners' behavior in the Rapport 06-07 data set. First, the listeners' head positions were tracked by Watson [13] and converted to frequency domain by Fast Fourier Transform. Then K-means (k=3) was applied to cluster all head nods to find typical styles, which are implemented in Behavior Markup Language (BML):

— *Small and continuous head nod*: four continuous small nods with decayed amplitudes and speed;
— *Normal nod*: two continuous head nods with decayed amplitudes and equal speed;
— *Single nod*: one slow head nod.

In the current implementation, we randomly choose one of the three styles when it is proper to give backchannel feedback.

End-of-Turn Prediction

Within a dyadic conversation, the roles of speaker and listener are regulated seamlessly by a negotiation process of turn-taking. A smooth turn-taking strategy without long mutual silence and interruption increases the feeling of coordination.

---

[2] Datasets are available for research purpose at rapport.ict.usc.edu.

Previous work [19] suggests that pause in speech is an important cue for when to take the turn, but that the amount of time people wait before jumping in can vary considerably depending on the speaker's nonverbal signals. The Rapport Agent, when applied to interview settings, uses a fixed turn-taking strategy: it takes the turn whenever a speaker pauses for more than one and a half seconds. Instead, we construct a multimodal end-of-turn prediction model which takes advantage of visual information such as eye-gaze and nod. The model is based on the consensus data from the Self-Disclosure data set[2]. We analyze the co-occurrence pattern between the turn-taking behavior and human speakers' nonverbal features and how these nonverbal features influence the pause duration before taking a turn, and build the model as follows:

(1) When the pause duration is longer than 1.5s and the speaker has been looking at the virtual human for more than 1.0s, it is a turn-taking place;

(2) When the speaker is looking away, the virtual human will wait until the speaker looks back and then go to (1);

(3) When head nod co-occurs with a longer-than-1.5s pause, the virtual human will take the turn 200ms after the end of the head nod.

After the virtual human takes a turn, the human speaker is allowed to interrupt him. The virtual human will stop and yield his turn to the human speaker by saying "I'm sorry, keep going" with a regretful facial expression.

3.2 Enhanced Positive Emotion Communication: Affective Response and Reciprocity

The feeling of positivity, which is important in establishing rapport in initial encounters, can be enhanced by communicating positive emotions both nonverbally and verbally.

Facial expression is an important channel to convey positive emotion nonverbally. To generate proper affective responses, the visual feature detector (a confidential commercial product) of the virtual human tracks the facial feature points of the human speaker in real-time, from which it infers the level of smiling (continuous value from 0 to 100). By setting the threshold to 50, we can reliably determine whether the human speaker is smiling or not. When there is a backchannel opportunity and the human speaker happens to smile at the same time, the virtual human will display backchannel feedback with a smiling face.

Recent research by Kang et al. [28] has emphasized some simple strategies for conveying positive feelings verbally. In her study, the interviewee discloses more intimate information if the interviewer (virtual human) discloses itself first. The mutual self-disclosure, or reciprocity, positively affects the human user's social attraction to the virtual human. In our system, we follow the same strategy of strengthening reciprocity. Before the virtual human asks its human partner questions, he will first disclose the information about himself; that is, sharing some of his autobiographical back story. For example, instead of simply asking "how old are you?", the virtual human says "I was created about three years ago. How old are you?".

3.3 System Architecture

The system (as shown in Figure 1) consists of three main parts: (1) perception, which detects the audiovisual features of human speakers in real-time; (2) response models, which predict the timing of backchannel feedback and end-of-turn and the affective state; and (3) generation, which animates the virtual human's behaviors such as head movements and facial expression.

Perception: The four main audiovisual features extracted in real-time are silence, head nods, eye-gaze (looking at listener or not) and smile. The audio feature detector extracts intensity from the raw signal every 100ms using the signal processing package, Praat [18]. With intensity information, it outputs a binary feature, speech or silence, every 100ms. The visual feature detector (a confidential commercial product) tracks the position of face and facial feature points, the direction of eye-gaze and the smile level. With this information, it outputs visual features indicating the human is nodding or not, looking away or not and smiling or not.

Response Models: Based on the perceived audiovisual features, the backchannel, end-of-turn and affective models decide in real-time the most appropriate responses. All three models take advantage of the data-driven approach described in Section 3. These responses also take into account the agent state (e.g. whether the virtual human is holding the turn or not). For example, if the virtual human is holding the turn, the output from backchannel model is ignored. The backchannel model takes silence and eye-gaze as input, the end-of-turn prediction model uses features such as silence, eye-gaze, and head nod and the affective model takes smile as input.

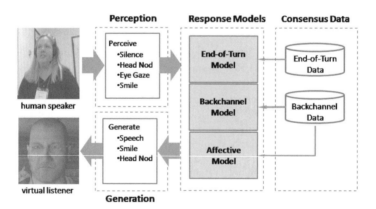

Fig. 1. System Architecture of Virtual Rapport 2.0: The perception module detects human behavior (e.g. silence in speech, nod, gaze aversion, and smile) in real-time; then the data-driven based response models take these feature as input and predict the timing of backchannel feedback and turn-taking, and the affective response; finally, the generation module generates speech and animations (e.g. smile and nod) to display to the human speaker.

Generation: The output from the response models drives the virtual human behaviors. For example, if the human speaker smiles, the virtual human will smile as well when giving the backchannel feedback. These animations are first converted to BML and then sent to an action scheduler module, which keeps track of the duration of each animation. If the current animation has not completed yet, new animations will be ignored. The BMLs are passed to the animation system, Smartbody [14], which is a virtual human animation system designed to seamlessly blend animations and procedural behaviors. Finally, animations are rendered by a commercial game engine, Gamebryo, and displayed to users.

4 Subjective Evaluation

To evaluate the performance of our virtual human (*Virtual Rapport 2.0*), we conducted a subjective evaluation to compare it with *Rapport Agent* along four dimensions: rapport, overall naturalness, backchannel feedback and end-of-turn prediction.

4.1 Experiment Design

We guided human participants to interact with both virtual humans one after the other, where the virtual human acts as an interviewer and steps through a series of questions one by one, and the human participant acts as the interviewee. For each interaction, we used different question sets derived from [25]. The order of virtual humans and question sets were randomized in the experiment. After each interaction, the human participant was asked to assess the virtual human's performance.

In a within-subject design, 21 participants were recruited to evaluate both virtual humans. Before the experiment started, the participant was required to read the instructions and ask questions about anything they do not understand. They were told "Your partner will ask you several questions and your task is to answer as best as you can. For each question, please try to answer in at least one or two sentences. You partner will listen when you answer. Please do not ask your partner questions. Your partner does not know who you are, your behavior will not be recorded and your identity will be kept anonymous". When the experiment was done, the participant was forced to choose the one s/he likes better.

The virtual human is evaluated along the four dimensions:

Rapport
The rapport is measured by using the 5-item social presence scales suggested in [26], which ask several questions such as "I perceive that I am in the presence of another person in the room with me (1(strongly disagree) - 7(strongly agree))".

Overall Naturalness
Do you think the virtual agent's overall behavior is natural? (1(not natural at all) - 7(absolutely natural))

Backchannel Feedback
— *Precision*: How often do you think the virtual human generated feedback at inappropriate time? (1(all the time) - 7(never inappropriate))
— *Recall*: How often do you think the virtual human missed feedback opportunities? (1(always miss) - 7(never miss))

End-of-Turn prediction
— *Correct time*: How often do you think the virtual human ask the next question too early? (1(always) - 7(never))
— *In time*: How often do you think the virtual human ask the next question too late? (1(always) - 7(never))

4.2 Results

The results are summarized from Figure 3(a) to 3(d). In each figure, the left bar is for Rapport Agent and the right bar is for Virtual Rapport 2.0. The star (*) means there is significant difference between the versions under the bracket.

Rapport: The answers of the five-item social presence scales are highly correlated with each other (the Cronbach's alpha is 0.9). Therefore, we average them into one scale. It is 2.6 for Rapport Agent and 3.84 for Virtual Rapport 2.0, and the difference is significant (p<0.01).

Overall Naturalness: The overall naturalness for Rapport Agent is 2.55, while it is 4.5 for Virtual Rapport 2.0, and the difference is significant (p<0.01).

Backchannel Feedback: For the precision question, the mean value of Rapport Agent is 3.6 while it is 5.25 for Virtual Rapport 2.0; for the recall question, the mean value of Rapport Agent is 3.7, while it is 4.6 for Virtual Rapport 2.0. Virtual Rapport 2.0 is significantly better (p<0.05) than Rapport Agent in both questions.

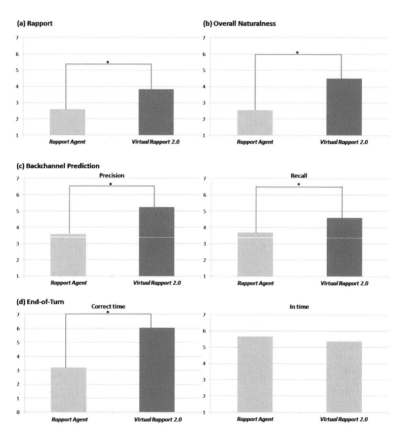

Fig. 2. The comparison of subjective evaluation results between Rapport Agent and Virtual Rapport 2.0. Virtual Rapport 2.0 is significantly better than Rapport Agent in predicting the timing of backchannel feedback (c) and end-of-turn (d); it is also significantly better than

Rapport Agent in overall naturalness (b). Therefore, Virtual Rapport 2.0 creates much stronger feeling of rapport (a) than the Rapport Agent does.

End-of-Turn: For the correct time question, the mean value of Rapport Agent is 3.2, while it is 6.05 for Virtual Rapport 2.0, and there is significant difference ($p<0.01$) between the two; for the in time question, the mean value of Rapport Agent is 5.65 and it is 5.35 for Virtual Rapport 2.0, and the difference is not significant.

In the force-choice task, among all 21 participants, 19 (90%) participants preferred our virtual human to Rapport Agent.

4.3 Discussion

Rapport: Our virtual human is significantly better than the Rapport Agent in creating rapport. One of the main advantages of our virtual human is that it is based on models learned from human behavior data. This innovative approach is reflected in all the response models. The data-driven approach promotes the feeling of mutual attention and coordination. Besides, the strengthened reciprocity and affective response communicate positive emotions both verbally and nonverbally.

Timing: Our backchannel prediction model significantly outperforms the Rapport Agent's in precision and recall, which indicates that our virtual human is more "in sync" with the human speaker during the interaction. Rapport Agent tends to take a turn (ask the next question) too quickly. Such turn-taking strategy is most likely associated with negative and strong personality [23], which is opposite to the goal of creating rapport.

Behavior: Compared to Rapport Agent, our virtual human has a richer set of behaviors that is correlated with creating rapport. For example, the virtual human mimics the human speaker's smiles, it performs more natural head gestures and strengthens reciprocity by self-disclosure. All these improvements may explain the significant difference on the overall naturalness between our virtual human and the Rapport Agent.

5   Conclusion and Future Work

In this paper, we introduced our effort towards building a virtual human whose goal is to create rapport during interactions with human users. Our design follows the three-factor theory of rapport by focusing on creating feelings of positivity, mutual attention and coordination. By comparing with Rapport Agent, we found that our virtual human predicts the timing of backchannel feedback and end-of-turn more precisely, performs more natural behaviors and thereby creates much stronger feelings of rapport between users and virtual agents. As future work, we plan to deploy our virtual human in various scenarios to assess how it will influence the human partner in different situations.

Acknowledgement. This study was funded by the National Science Foundation under Grant # IIS-0916858 and the U.S. Army Research, Development, and Engineering Command and. The content does not necessarily reflect the position or the policy of the Government, and no official endorsement should be inferred.

References

1. Drolet, A.L., Morris, M.W.: Rapport in conflict resolution: accounting for how face-to-face contact fosters mutual cooperation in mixed-motive conflicts. Experimental Social Psychology 36, 26–50 (2000)
2. Burns, M.: Rapport and relationships: the basis of child care. J. Child Care 2, 47–57 (1984)
3. Tatar, D.: Social and personal consequences of a preoccupied listener. Stanford University, Stanford (1997)
4. Bernieri, F.J., Rosenthal, R.: Interpersonal coordination: Behavior matching and interactional synchrony. In: Feldman, R.S., Rime, B. (eds.) Fundamentals of Nonverbal Behaviors. Studies in emotion and social interaction, pp. 401–432. Cambridge University Press, Cambridge (1991)
5. Tickle-Degnen, L., Rosenthal, R.: The Nature of Rapport and its Nonverbal Correlates. Psychological Inquiry 1(4), 285–293 (1990)
6. Cassell, J., Gill, A.J., Tepper, P.A.: Coordination in conversation and rapport. In: Proceedings of the Workshop on Embodied Language Processing, pp. 41–50 (2007)
7. Bailenson, J.N., Yee, N.: Digital Chameleons: Automatic assimilation of nonverbal gestures in immersive virtual environments. Psychological Science 16, 814–819 (2005)
8. Bickmore, T., Puskar, K., Schlenk, E., Pfeifer, L., Sereika, S.: Maintaining Reality: Relational Agents for Antipsychotic Medication Adherence. J. Interacting with Computers special issue on Mental Health (2010)
9. Bevacqua, E., Mancini, M., Pelachaud, C.: A listening agent exhibiting variable behaviour. In: Prendinger, H., Lester, J.C., Ishizuka, M. (eds.) IVA 2008. LNCS (LNAI), vol. 5208, pp. 262–269. Springer, Heidelberg (2008)
10. Kang, S.-H., Gratch, J., Watts, J.: The Effect of Affective Iconic Realism on Anonymous Interactants' Self-Disclosure. In: Proceedings of Interaction Conference for Human-Computer Interaction (2009)
11. Gratch, J., Wang, N., Gerten, J., Fast, E., Duffy, R.: Creating rapport with virtual agents. In: Pelachaud, C., Martin, J.-C., André, E., Chollet, G., Karpouzis, K., Pelé, D. (eds.) IVA 2007. LNCS (LNAI), vol. 4722, pp. 125–138. Springer, Heidelberg (2007)
12. Gratch, J., Okhmatovskaia, A., Lamothe, F., Marsella, S.C., Morales, M., van der Werf, R.J., Morency, L.-P.: Virtual rapport. In: Gratch, J., Young, M., Aylett, R.S., Ballin, D., Olivier, P. (eds.) IVA 2006. LNCS (LNAI), vol. 4133, pp. 14–27. Springer, Heidelberg (2006)
13. Morency, L.-P., et al.: Contextual Recognition of Head Gestures. In: Proceedings of 7th International Conference on Multimodal Interactions (2005)
14. Thiebaux, M., Marshall, A., Marsella, S., Kallmann, M.: SmartBody: Behavior Realization for Embodied Conversational Agents. In: Proceedings of 7th International Conference on Autonomous Agents and Multi-Agent Systems (2008)
15. Wang, N., Gratch, J.: Don't just stare at me. In: Proceedings of 28th Annual CHI Conference on Human Factors in Computing Systems (2010)
16. von der Pütten, A., Krämer, N., Gratch, J.: Who's there? Can a Virtual Agent Really Elicit Social Presence. In: Proceedings of 12th Annual International Workshop on Presence (2009)
17. Wang, N., Gratch, J.: Rapport and Facial Expression. In: Proceedings of the International Conference on Affective Computing and Intelligent Interaction (2009)
18. Praat, http://www.fon.hum.uva.nl/praat/

19. Jonsdottir, G.R., Thorisson, K.R., Nivel, E.: Learning smooth, human-like turntaking in realtime dialogue. In: Prendinger, H., Lester, J.C., Ishizuka, M. (eds.) IVA 2008. LNCS (LNAI), vol. 5208, pp. 162–175. Springer, Heidelberg (2008)
20. Huang, L., Morency, L.-P., Gratch, J.: Parasocial Consensus Sampling: Combining Multiple Perspectives to Learn Virtual Human Behavior. In: Proceedings of 9th International Conference on Autonomous Agents and Multiagent Systems (2010)
21. Morency, L.-P., de Kok, I., Gratch, J.: Predicting listener backchannels: A probabilistic multimodal approach. In: Prendinger, H., Lester, J.C., Ishizuka, M. (eds.) IVA 2008. LNCS (LNAI), vol. 5208, pp. 176–190. Springer, Heidelberg (2008)
22. Lee, J., Marsella, S.: Learning a Model of Speaker Head Nods using Gesture Corpora. In: Proceedings of 8th International Conference on Autonomous Agent and Multiagent System, pp. 189–296 (2009)
23. ter Maat, M., Truong, K., Heylen, D.: How turn-taking strategies influence users' impressions of an agent. In: Proceedings of 10th International Conference on Intelligent Virtual Agents (2010)
24. Huang, L., Morency, L.-P., Gratch, J.: A Multimodal End-of-Turn Prediction Model: Learning from Parasocial Consensus Sampling. In: Proceedings of 10th International Conference on Autonomous Agents and Multiagent Systems (2011)
25. Moon, Y.: Intimate exchanges: Using computers to elicit self-disclosure from consumers. J. Consumer Research 26(4), 323–339 (2000)
26. Bailenson, J.N., Blascovich, J., Beall, A.C., Loomis, J.M.: Equilibrium revisited: Mutual gaze and personal space in virtual environment. PRESENCE: Teleoperators and Virtual Environments 10, 583–598 (2001)
27. Lafferty, J., McCallum, A., Pereira, F.: Conditional Random Field: Probabilistic Models for Segmenting and Labeling Sequence Data. In: Proceedings of 18th International Conference on Machine Learning (2001)
28. Kang, S.-H., Gratch, J.: People Like Virtual Counselors that Highly-Disclose About Themselves. The Annual Review of Cybertherapy and Telemedicine (2011)
29. Kang, S.-H., Watts, J., Gratch, J.: Associations between interactants' personality traits and their feelings of rapport in interactions with virtual humans. In: 59th Annual Conference of the International Communication Association (2009)
30. Murphy, K.: Dynamic Bayesian Networks: Representation, Inference and Learning. Ph.D. Thesis, UC Berkeley, Computer Science Division (July 2002)
31. Huang, L., Morency, L.-P., Gratch, J.: Learning Backchannel Prediction Model from Parasocial Consensus Sampling: A Subjective Evaluation. In: Proceedings of 10th International Conference on Intelligent Virtual Agent (2010)

It's in Their Eyes: A Study on Female and Male Virtual Humans' Gaze

Philipp Kulms[1], Nicole C. Krämer[1], Jonathan Gratch[2], and Sin-Hwa Kang[2]

[1] University of Duisburg-Essen, Forsthausweg 2, 47048 Duisburg, Germany
`philipp.kulms@stud.uni-due.de, nicole.kraemer@uni-due.de`
[2] Institute for Creative Technologies, 12015 Waterfront Drive, Playa Vista, CA 90094, USA
`{gratch,kang}@ict.usc.edu`

Abstract. Social psychological research demonstrates that the same behavior might lead to different evaluations depending on whether it is shown by a man or a woman. With a view to design decisions with regard to virtual humans it is relevant to test whether this pattern also applies to gendered virtual humans. In a 2x2 between subjects experiment we manipulated the Rapport Agent's gaze behavior and its gender in order to test whether especially female agents are evaluated more negatively when they do not show gender specific immediacy behavior and avoid gazing at the interaction partner. Instead of this interaction effect we found two main effects: gaze avoidance was evaluated negatively and female agents were rated more positively than male agents.

Keywords: female & male virtual agents, eye contact, gender differences, gender stereotypes, empirical evaluation.

1 Introduction

The effects of virtual agents have been analyzed in numerous evaluation studies [1, 2]. The influence of various agent characteristics such as [nonverbal] behavior and appearance on acceptance, perceived and actual efficiency as well as on their power to elicit social reactions on the part of the user has been established empirically. However, one of the most important categories of human everyday life and the question whether its effects are also transferrable to the interaction with agents has not been studied in depth: Gender. While studies of course frequently assess and consider whether female users' reactions differ from those of male users [3], the systematic manipulation of the agent's gender has not received sufficient attention (for an exception see [4]). To have knowledge on the differential effects of female and male agents, however, is all the more important as the agent's gender might not only have an influence per se but might also affect how the agent's behavior is perceived and evaluated. Here, social psychological research has demonstrated that the same nonverbal behavior will elicit different attributions, judgements and reactions depending on whether it is shown by a man or a woman. In a seminal study, Deutsch et al. [5] provided evidence that women who do not smile are socially less accepted than men if they do not smile: they are associated with less happiness and carelessness compared to men. The authors explain

H. Högni Vilhjálmsson et al. (Eds.): IVA 2011, LNAI 6895, pp. 80–92, 2011.

their finding with the fact that – due to gender stereotypes and due to the fact that women indeed show more smiles and immediacy behavior in everyday life – women clearly are expected to smile whereas for men, smiling and other immediacy behaviors are positive deviations from the norm. The objective of the present study is to test whether this pattern can also be observed for female and male virtual agents. The nonverbal cue we use here is gaze. Like smiling, gaze is a fundamental cue for intimacy [6] and immediacy [7] and is also shown more frequently by women than by men.

In order to gain insights into gender specific perception of virtual humans we used our well established framework that has already been capable of showing the potential of Embodied Conversational Agents to establish rapport [8, 9]. The Rapport Agent framework draws on psychological findings, identifying mutual attentiveness, positivity (mutual friendliness) and coordination as key elements for facilitating rapport [10]. To rely on these principles allowed us to vary two different forms of gaze of the Rapport Agent while maintaining a basic level of fluent interaction. Additionally, we varied the agent's gender, so that in a 2x2 experimental setting we were able to test whether the evaluation of specific behaviors is dependent on the agent's gender.

2   Theoretical Background

Gaze. During nonverbal communication, it is the face that strongly stands out from the rest of our body and that plays the most important role [11]. Facial expressions serve a variety of purposes: they coordinate social interactions, reflect a person's emotional state and his or her behavioral intentions [12]. Among the facial parts that are involved in these expressions, a lot of attention is allocated to the eyes [7, 13]. People are highly accurate when it comes to interpreting direction and target of gaze [14] and they have almost no problem in telling whether they are looked at [15]. Why is gaze decisive in the context of interpersonal communication? According to Richmond et al. [13], the characteristics of gaze are salience, arousal and involvement. In a face-to-face situation the gaze draws the interlocutor's attention, because it is a vital source for information (e.g., by providing feedback and signalling if the channel is open [6]). It does not matter whether the relation between two communicators is positive or negative: when their eyes meet, both feel arousal as a direct result. Also, gaze is an important feature for facilitating immediacy and rapport [7, 10].

Gender and Gender Stereotypes. As Duncan states, the most important variable with an influence on gaze appears to be gender [16]. Women establish more eye contact than men [17, 18] and they look at their interlocutor more often while listening and speaking [13]. Exline et al. [18] explain their findings with females' stronger need for inclusion and affection in interpersonal relations. Here, support is provided by same-sex interaction patterns, identifying females to be more likely to show affectionate behavior such as involvement and immediacy through gaze, gesture and body orientation [19]. This is in line with findings that women in general show more nonverbal immediacy cues (such as e.g. smiling [17]).

Women do not only show more immediacy, e.g. by means of smiling or gaze, they are also expected to show immediacy to a larger extent, whereas male communicators are seen as less skilled [20]. However, if women's nonverbal behavior is not congruent with the stereotypes that society holds about them, women are faced with rather harsh judgements. Deutsch, LeBaron and Fryer [5] showed that the examination of non-smiling female faces displayed on photographs evoked more negative evaluations than non-smiling male faces. Men, as opposed to women, do not have to fulfill comparable behavioral expectations, because they are nonexistent in their case. Thus, men are not perceived to reveal a negative emotional state if they do not smile, as non-smiling men are seen as the norm, whereas women are perceived to deviate from the norm when they are not smiling [5]. This means that the same behaviour is judged differently dependent on whether it is shown by men or women. This has also been demonstrated for gaze behaviour: In a job interview setting that incorporated different levels of gaze and changing reward values through applicants' status, judgements of female applicants differed significantly from judgements of male applicants. When the applicants were presented as high status, high gaze rates led to attributing submissiveness to females and dominance to males. When the status of applicants was low, the pattern was reversed: high gaze females were perceived as dominant, whereas high gaze males were seen as submissive [7]. What has not been analyzed so far is whether similar to the study of Deutsch et al. [5], who demonstrated this for the immediacy cue smiling, women will also be penalized when they do not show the immediacy behaviour of frequent gaze.

The results depicted above have been explained by the ubiquitousness of gender categories in social cognition [21] and the fact that (gender) stereotypes are activated automatically and are hard to suppress [22]. Given that it has already been shown that gender stereotypes are applied in human computer interaction even when gender is manipulated rather superficially by using male versus female voices [23] our objective here is to analyse whether gendered virtual humans evoke gender-related attributions and whether, more importantly, this leads to a differential evaluations of the same behaviour.

Based on the considerations presented above, we first expect gendered female and male agents to evoke gender-specific attributions (H1). Given the results on gaze behavior in previous studies we expect agents who gaze at the interaction partner to be evaluated more positively than agents who avoid looking at the human interlocutor (H2). Additionally, an interaction between the agent's gender and its gaze should occur: Eye contact avoiding behavior leads to significantly more negative judgements of the female agent, whereas normal gaze will not result in any differences between the male and the female agent (H3).

3   Method

3.1   Experimental Design

The study was based on a 2x2 factorial design (N = 72), with two conditions for each factor. The first factor, gaze of the agent, determined the behavior of the Rapport Agent and was added to its rapport engine. The second factor, gender of the agent, manipulated the Rapport Agent's gender. Participants were assigned randomly to one of the four conditions.

3.2   Participants and Procedure

74 participants were recruited from the Greater Los Angeles Area. Due to software issues, two sessions were declared invalid, resulting in 72 valid sessions that were entered into the final dataset (40 female, 32 male). The mean age of the sample was 35.03 (SD = 12.11), the range between 19 and 59 years. Recruitment of participants was conducted online via Craigslist.com. After a one hour session, each participant received $20 for compensation.

Participants were led to the laboratory at the ICT facility, starting with the pre-questionnaire that included demographic data and the explanatory variables. Next, they were seated in front of a 34" monitor. Below the monitor, a camcorder and a stereo camera system were fitted to record the participant during his/her interaction with the Rapport Agent. In order to be able to talk to the agent and to hear its voice, participants wore a headset with two headphones and one microphone. The investigator monitored the interaction from an adjacent room. Next, the Rapport Agent asked five questions to establish an interview-like conversation that required self-disclosure by the participant [24]. Prior to the actual questions, the agent itself revealed somewhat personal information according to the degree of intimacy of the subsequent question to support self-disclosure answers [25]:

1. I was designed and built by ICT researchers here in Marina del Rey. What is your hometown?
2. When I don't interact with people, I usually study them so I can better communicate with them. What are your favorite things to do in your free time?
3. I like to listen to what people say. I have lots of patience for listening, even if you have a lot to say. What characteristics of yourself are you most proud of?
4. I feel furious when people treat me as if I was just a machine without any thinking of feeling. What are some of the things that make you furious?
5. My abilities are somewhat limited. For example, I can speak and listen to what you say, but I can't walk down a street in your world. What are some of the things you hate about yourself?
6. That's all I have, thank you.

Question #5 was added starting with the eighth participant to lengthen the total answer time. When the participants felt their answer on a question was complete, they were instructed to press the space bar on the keyboard to indicate that they are ready for the next question. The investigator then triggered the next question. The investigator's role, however, was not evident to the participants. After the interaction, participants completed the post-questionnaire and with that, finished the experiment. They were fully debriefed and thanked for their participation.

3.3 Measures

Independent Variables. We manipulated gaze (*low gaze* vs. *high gaze*) and gender of the agent (*female* vs. *male*). In the *low gaze* condition, the agent looked at the speaker only very few times while listening to her or him, resulting in little overall eye contact, whereas in the *high gaze* condition, eye contact was held most of the time.[1] To ensure that the measured judgements and the participant's behavior are not based solely on the agent's optical appearance and voice, two female and two male versions were employed, each with unique graphical designs and voices.

Quantitative Measures (post-questionnaire). We assessed participants' emotional state with the Positive And Negative Affect Scale (PANAS) [26], consisting of 10 items for positive and 10 items for negative emotions, rated on a 5-point Likert scale (e.g. nervous, excited, distressed). Person perception of the agent was assessed with a semantic differential that incorporated 26 bipolar adjectives (e.g. arrogant – modest, unfriendly – friendly), rated on a 7-point scale [27]. The Bem Sex Role Inventory (BSRI) [28] was used to measure whether participants ascribed rather feminine or masculine attributes. Accordingly, the BSRI incorporates a femininity (e.g. yielding, affectionate, understanding) and a masculinity dimension (e.g. forceful, dominant, analytical), 20 items each, as well as 20 filler items (e.g. conventional, inefficient, truthful).

Participants also rated the social presence of the agent. We used the 5-item social presence survey by Bailenson, Blascovich, Beall and Loomis [29] (e.g. I feel that the person is watching me and is aware of my presence) and the Networked Minds Questionnaire (NMQ) [30]. As for the NMQ, we used five subscales: Empathy (four items, e.g. I was influenced by my partner's moods), Mutual awareness (two items, e.g. The other individual didn't notice me in the room), Attention allocation (four items, e.g. I paid close attention to the other individual), Mutual understanding (three items, e.g. My opinions were clear to the other) and Behavioral interdependence (four items, e.g. The behavior of the other was in direct response to my behavior). The social presence scales were rated on 7-point Likert scales.

Qualitative Measures. Participants' answers to the Rapport Agent's questions were subject of a qualitative analysis. We used a coding scheme to identify different degrees of intimacy within the answers to question 4 ("What are some of the things that make you furious?") and 5 ("What are some of the things you hate about yourself?"): (a) No intimacy answer: the infuriating aspect or the personal characteristic has not affected the private or business life of the participant, (b) Low-intimacy answer: the infuriating aspect or the personal characteristic has somewhat affected the private or business life of the participant, (c) High-intimacy answer: the infuriating aspect or the personal characteristic has strongly affected the private or business life of the participant. We counted the number of times that each category occurred. Moreover, we counted the times that participants verbally referred to what the agent told them, e.g. by saying "I agree", "Probably the same thing", "Thank you", "I also think I'm a good listener" etc.

---

[1] We are aware of the fact that a reliable manipulation of eye contact cannot be accomplished by only manipulating the Rapport Agent's gaze, as the participant's gaze clearly holds the second prerequisite for the occurrence of eye contact.

Explanatory Variables. Because the participants are to some extent asked about intimate information by the Rapport Agent, we measured shyness [31]. Empathy was assessed with the Interpersonal Reactivity Index [32], since empathic persons often are interpersonal sensitive towards nonverbal cues [33]. Moreover, we looked at emotional sensitivity, by means of the corresponding subscale of the Social Skills Inventory [34]. Emotional sensitivity can be described as the ability to associate nonverbal cues correctly with underlying emotions [33].

3.4 The Rapport Agent

The Rapport Agent captures real-time audiovisual data to show nonverbal backchannel behavior. A signal processing package analyzes pitch and intensity of the speaker's speech signal [8] and an image-based tracking library [35] uses the stereo images that are captured by a Videre Design Small Vision Stereo Camera System which is placed in front of the speaker. Watson detects the speaker's upper-body movement. Combined with the voice features input, the Rapport Agent is able to produce listening behaviors like head nods and mirrored posture shifts [8].

Next to the stereo camera, also in front of the speaker, a high-definition camcorder was positioned. The sessions were videotaped to assess the participant's behavior. The animated Rapport Agent was displayed on a 34" monitor. Audiovisual monitoring of the sessions was ensured by means of an Internet camera.

In order to alter the Rapport Agent's gaze in a way that it shows eye contact avoiding behavior it was necessary to design cues that communicate avoidance in a salient way yet do not fall outside norms of conversational behavior. The choice of 0% eye contact in the *low gaze* condition and 100% eye contact in the *high gaze* condition would surely have maximized the manipulation's effect on the measured dimensions, but such an approach does not resemble natural social interactions [36]. Instead, empirical research has identified patterns of gaze behavior of speaker as well as listener (e.g., the listener looks more at the speaker than the other way round, gaze is used to indicate the yielding of a turn [37, 38].

These considerations made it necessary to implement dynamic patterns of the Rapport Agent's gaze instead of scripted or randomly triggered behavior. Because we were able to detect rich and elaborate data from the speaker's voice, we decided to use the participant's verbal utterances as key trigger. In the *low gaze* condition we used some of those cues that in the normal version of the Rapport Agent are used as triggers for backchannel behavior as triggers for avoiding gaze instead. Additionally, in the *low gaze* condition, the agent's focus already drifted away while asking the questions. Shortly before finishing the questions, the agent looked back at the speaker in order to yield the turn. Gaze aversion not only included eye movement to an alternative target in the virtual environment, but also head motion towards the same target. Figure 1 shows an example. The eyes were configured to reach the target shortly before the head, not simultaneously, to increase naturalness.

In the *high gaze* condition, the agent's head was kept steady, except for head nods. Gaze aversion during the questions was reduced to a minimum and the gaze only incorporated one target, whereas, in the *low gaze* condition, there were two targets in a row. In the *high gaze* condition, the agent gazed away once after several seconds had passed, in order to not show 100% eye contact.

Fig. 1. Four different appearances of the Rapport Agent in the *low gaze* condition, after gaze aversion has been triggered. Eyes and head are moved towards an alternative target.

Adequate Gaze Behavior. In order to avoid a simple stimulus response pattern as foundation of the whole interaction and to minimize predictability, we included a natural temporal element given by an exponential distribution that reflects the variable probability of a given event over time [39]. As a result, the agent did not gaze away instantly when the participant's cue occurred.

Pretest. Since we used four different appearances of the Rapport Agent, many of which were previously unevaluated, we conducted a pretest with the BSRI. It was assumed that for the female agents, femininity ratings are significantly higher than masculinity ratings and vice versa for male agents. In a within-subjects design, participants were asked to look at four 7" x 9" color photographs, each showing the frontal view of a different agent as participants in the main experiment would look upon them, and to rate the displayed agents on the BSRI. 14 participants completed the task. Their age ranged between 23 and 45 years ($M = 31.14$, $SD = 8.00$).

4 Results

Based on the BSRI, we evaluated the stereotyped gender that was attributed to the agents. We calculated femininity and masculinity scores for the agents and compared them with one another. The reliability of the two subscales was very high, as the results for Cronbach's α in the main experiment indicate: $\alpha = .93$.

Pretest. After combining the BSRI ratings to a female and a male agents' dataset, a Repeated Measures Analysis of Variance (RM-ANOVA) was calculated. We found a significant overall effect (F(3,39) = 40.13, p < .001, part. η^2 = .76). Pairwise comparisons with Bonferroni correction showed that the male agents ($M = 5.24$, $SD = .66$) were judged to be more masculine than the female agents ($M = 3.5$, $SD = .67$), $p < .001$, and that the female agents were judged to be more feminine ($M = 4.42$, $SD = .51$) than the male ones ($M = 3.31$, $SD = .40$), $p < .001$. Hypothesis 1 was confirmed in the pretest.

Main Experiment. We calculated a Multivariate Analysis of Variance (MANOVA) with the BSRI femininity and masculinity scores as dependent variables and gender of the agents and, additionally, gaze as independent variables. The effect that we found in the pretest was not replicated in the main experiment. Here, the assignments of female and male attributes were not influenced by the agent's gender. Thus, hypothesis 1 was not confirmed. There was, however, a significant effect for gaze ($F(1,68) = 10.44$, $p < .01$, part. η^2 = .13): In the *high gaze* condition ($M = 4.78$, $SD = 1.05$), the agents were judged as more masculine (that is, e.g., more forceful, assertive and independent) than in the *low gaze* condition ($M = 3.94$, $SD = 1.15$).

We conducted factor analyses (principal components, varimax rotation) for all dependent measures except for the social presence survey that only included five items. Person perception ratings resulted in three factors: *Negative evaluation* ($\alpha = .921$, explains 28.49% % of the variance), *Positive evaluation* ($\alpha = .810$, 15.26%) and *Weakness* ($\alpha = .828$, 14.09%). See Table 1 for factor loadings and communalities. The PANAS factor analysis also led to three factors of which only two were consistent: *Positive emotions* ($\alpha = .88$, 23.74%) and *Negative emotions* ($\alpha = .79$, 15.88%). The factors *Consciousness of the partner* ($\alpha = .80$, 20.03%), *Influence of the partner* ($\alpha = .74$, 16.96%) and *Influence on the partner* ($\alpha = .74$, 16.54%) resulted after the NMQ factor analysis.

Therefore, a total of nine dependent variables, eight factors and the mean values of the social presence survey, were entered into a MANOVA. The independent variables again were gender and gaze behavior of the agent. There were two main effects for gender: First, results of the person perception factor *Positive evaluation* indicate that the female agents ($M = .29$, $SD = 1.01$) were judged more positively than the male ones ($M = -.28$, $SD = .93$): $F(1,67) = 5.67$, $p < .05$, part. η^2 = .08. The second main effect was only marginal and referred to the social presence dimension. During the interaction with the male agents ($M = 3.16$, $SD = .97$), the feeling of communicating with a self-conscious partner was marginally higher compared to the female agents' sessions ($M = 2.69$, $SD = .98$), $F(1,67) = 3.77$, $p = .052$, part. η^2 = .06.

There was also one main effect for the gaze condition that confirmed hypothesis 2: The agents in the *low gaze* condition ($M = .19$, $SD = .88$) were judged more negatively than in the *high gaze* situation ($M = -.27$, $SD = .98$), with respect to the

Table 1. Factor loadings and communalities based on a principal components analysis with varimax rotation for the 26-items semantic differential (person perception)

Note. Factor loadings < .400 are suppressed.

Item	Negative evaluation	Positive evaluation	Weakness
Aloof	.811		
Unapproachable	.749		.412
Unsympathetic	.738		
Unpleasant	.723	-.416	
Callous	.700	-.404	
Unfriendly	.696		
Detached	.672		
Sleepy	.669		
Mature	-.640		
Dishonest	.590		
Unintelligent	.590		
Modest		.778	
Soft		.768	
Not conceited		.652	
Non-threatening		.636	
Permissive		.562	
Nervous			.862
Shy			.726
Relaxed			-.652
Cheerful	-.488		-.603
Naive	.526		.556

factor *Negative evaluation* ($F(1,67) = 3.78, p < .05$, part. $\eta^2 = .06$). No interaction effect emerged. Therefore, hypothesis 3 was not supported.

In the next step, we entered the ratings for *shyness*, *empathy* and *emotional sensitivity* as covariates into a Multivariate Analysis of Covariance (MANCOVA). We also added gender of the participants as third independent variable into these analyses. Scores for empathy and emotional sensitivity were calculated according to the scale instructions. Both scales correlated significantly with each other ($r = .55, p < .001$). A factor analysis led to one consistent *Shyness* factor ($\alpha = .73$, 30.44% of variance explained).

We found one main effect for gender of the participants. Among female participants ($M = -.20, SD = .15$), less positive emotions were elicited than among male ones ($M = .34, SD = .17$), with respect to the factor *Positive emotions*: $F(1,57) = 4.21, p < .05$, part. $\eta^2 = .08$. The covariates empathy ($F(1,57) = 2.71, p = .079$, part. $\eta^2 = .05$) and emotional sensitivity ($F(1,57) = 3.12, p = .06$, part. $\eta^2 = .06$) marginally explained this effect.

Because the data we gained through the qualitative analysis did not qualify for T tests, we conducted Mann-Whitney U tests for the independent variable gaze. In the *high gaze* condition (Mean rank = 40.71, Sum of ranks = 1465.50), participants uttered significantly more verbal references to the agent, e.g. by saying "You're welcome", "It's been fun" etc. ($U = 496.50, p < .05$), compared to the *low gaze* condition (Mean rank = 32.29, Sum of ranks = 1162.50). Mann-Whitney U tests for the independent variable gender of the agent did not show any significant results.

5 Discussion

Instead of observing the expected interaction of gaze and gender, we only found several main effects for gender and gaze. This might indicate that actual behavior and its evaluation is more important for evaluation than gender stereotypes. This is supported by the result that – as opposed to the pretest that used still pictures – in the main experiment, participants neither ascribed more masculine attributes to the male agents nor more feminine attributes to the female agents. This means we must consider the nature of a real interaction that features enhanced communicative cues. In such a context, there are a lot more influences on gender typing processes. Stereotyped attributions become less important as the perceiver now can interpret the actual behavior, which, in our case, was shaped by gaze aversion.

Our result may serve as an indicator for a rather moderate prevalence of social stereotypes in human computer interaction. The experiment conducted by Nass et al. [23] which showed an activation of gender stereotypes even in a cue reduced setting may have benefited from the absence of actual nonverbal behavior.

Our experiment documents negative evaluations that virtual humans receive if they show a lack of immediacy that can also be described as a lack of interest. Higher ratings were especially found for masculinity of the BSRI which is known for the fact that masculine and socially desirable attributes are confounded. Interestingly, however, these evaluations were limited to a person perception dimension and were not accompanied by negative emotional reactions, by low perceptions of social presence or by fewer intimate answers. The connection between these three dimensions and person perception appears not to be very close in the context of immediacy. Apparently, participants did not feel constrained while answering the Rapport Agent's intimate questions in the *low gaze* condition, probably as a result of the backchannel behavior that was still used in order to facilitate rapport. These backchannel behaviors may also have provided a basic level of mutual understanding and behavioral interdependence from the participants' perspective. Despite the missing role of emotions, and in line with previous results that women are less experienced with computer technology and show different reactions [3], there were overall less positive emotions among female participants. We found somewhat weak indicators that women's higher sensitivity for nonverbal behaviors is responsible for this finding. Accordingly, it seems more important for women to communicate with an agent that facilitates immediacy, especially in a self-disclosure setting, but then again, the explanatory result needs more support.

The seemingly low prevalence of emotions and social presence appears to only hold for the emotional dimension, as our analysis of the users' behavior indicates reactions among participants that do reflect social presence of the agent in the *high gaze* condition. In this condition, we found significantly more verbal responses to the agent, even when the agent did not explicitly expect a response. The connection between immediacy and social presence, was, however, not evident with regard to the self-report data.

The gaze pattern that was shown by the Rapport Agent in the *low gaze* condition resembles the submissive gaze pattern that was used by Kipp and Gebhard [40]. The authors showed that if their avatar averted eye contact most of the time, for example immediately after it had been established, the avatar was perceived as submissive. It was, however, not judged more negatively in terms of likability or naturalness, which means that submissiveness seems not to be an explanatory variable for our person perception results.

Not only did we not find any support for a gender induced disadvantage for female agents as a result of their nonverbal behavior – in fact, they were able to overall receive more positive judgements than the male agents. This is interesting from an applied perspective and might be used for future design decisions. Further studies should investigate whether female virtual humans indeed have the potential of being more desirable communicators in specific contexts.

Acknowledgements. This study was partially funded by the German Academic Exchange Service and by the U.S. Army Research, Development, and Engineering Command and the National Science Foundation under Grant # IIS-0916858. The content does not necessarily reflect the position or the policy of the Government, and no official endorsement should be inferred.

References

1. Ruttkay, Z., Pelachaud, C. (eds.): From brows to trust: evaluating embodied conversational agents. Kluwer Academic Publishers, Dordrecht (2004)
2. Krämer, N.C.: Soziale Wirkungen virtueller Helfer. Kohlhammer, Stuttgart (2008)
3. Krämer, N.C., Hoffmann, L., Kopp, S.: Know Your Users! Empirical Results for Tailoring an Agent´s Nonverbal Behavior to Different User Groups. In: Safonova, A. (ed.) IVA 2010. LNCS, vol. 6356, pp. 468–474. Springer, Heidelberg (2010)
4. Cowell, A.J., Stanney, K.M.: Embodiment and Interaction Guidelines for Designing Credible, Trustworthy Embodied Conversational Agents. In: Rist, T., Aylett, R.S., Ballin, D., Rickel, J. (eds.) IVA 2003. LNCS (LNAI), vol. 2792, pp. 301–309. Springer, Heidelberg (2003)
5. Deutsch, F.M., LeBaron, D., Fryer, M.M.: What is in a smile? Psychology of Women Quarterly 11, 341–352 (1987)
6. Argyle, M., Dean, J.: Eye-contact, distance and affiliation. Sociometry 28, 289–304 (1965)
7. Burgoon, J.K., Coker, D.A., Coker, R.A.: Communicative effects of gaze behavior. Human Communication Research 12, 495–524 (1986)
8. Gratch, J., Okhmatovskaia, A., Lamothe, F., Marsella, S.C., Morales, M., van der Werf, R.J., Morency, L.-P.: Virtual rapport. In: Gratch, J., Young, M., Aylett, R.S., Ballin, D., Olivier, P. (eds.) IVA 2006. LNCS (LNAI), vol. 4133, pp. 14–27. Springer, Heidelberg (2006)
9. Gratch, J., Wang, N., Gerten, J., Fast, E., Duffy, R.: Creating rapport with virtual agents. In: Pelachaud, C., Martin, J.-C., André, E., Chollet, G., Karpouzis, K., Pelé, D. (eds.) IVA 2007. LNCS (LNAI), vol. 4722, pp. 125–138. Springer, Heidelberg (2007)
10. Tickle-Degnen, L., Rosenthal, R.: The nature of rapport and its nonverbal correlates. Psychological Inquiry 1, 285–293 (1990)

11. Ekman, P., Friesen, W.V.: The repertoire of nonverbal behavior: Categories, origins, usage, and coding. In: Kendon, A. (ed.) Nonverbal Communication, Interaction, and Gesture, pp. 57–106. Mouton, The Hague (1981)

12. Matsumoto, D., Keltner, D., Shiota, M.N., O'Sullivan, M., Frank, M.: Facial Expressions of Emotion. In: Lewis, M., Haviland-Jones, J.M., Barrett, L.F. (eds.) Handbook of Emotions, 3rd edn., pp. 211–234. The Guilford Press, New York (2008)

13. Richmond, V.P., McCroskey, J.C., Payne, S.K.: Nonverbal Behaviour in Interpersonal Relations, 2nd edn. Prentice-Hall, Englewood Cliffs (1991)

14. Anstis, S.M., Mayhew, J.W., Morley, T.: The perception of where a face or television 'portrait' is looking. The American Journal of Psychology 82, 474–489 (1969)

15. Gibson, J.J., Pick, A.D.: Perception of another person's looking behavior. The American Journal of Psychology 78, 386–394 (1963)

16. Duncan Jr., S.: Nonverbal communication. Psychological Bulletin 72, 118–137 (1969)

17. Burgoon, J.K., Bacue, A.E.: Nonverbal communication skills. In: Greene, J.O., Burleson, B.R. (eds.) Handbook of Communication and Social Interaction Skills, pp. 179–220. Lawrence Erlbaum Associates, Mahwah (2003)

18. Exline, R., Gray, D., Schuette, D.: Visual behavior in a dyad as affected by interview content and sex of respondent. Journal of Personality and Social Psychology 1, 201–209 (1965)

19. Ickes, W., Barnes, R.D.: The role of sex and self-monitoring in unstructured dyadic interactions. Journal of Personality and Social Psychology 35, 315–330 (1977)

20. Briton, N.J., Hall, J.A.: Beliefs about female and male nonverbal communication. Sex Roles 32, 79–90 (1995)

21. Fiske, S.T., Stevens, L.E.: What's so special about sex? Gender stereotyping and discrimination. In: Oskamp, S., Costanzo, M. (eds.) Gender Issues in Contemporary Society, pp. 173–196. Sage, Newbury Park (1993)

22. Devine, P.G.: Stereotypes and prejudice: Their automatic and controlled components. Journal of Personality and Social Psychology 56, 5–18 (1989)

23. Nass, C., Moon, Y., Green, N.: Are machines gender neutral? Gender stereotypic responses to computers with voices. Journal of Applied Social Psychology 27, 864–876 (1997)

24. Moon, Y.: Intimate exchanges: Using computers to elicit self-disclosure from consumers. The Journal of Consumer Research 26, 323–339 (2000)

25. Kang, S., Gratch, J.: People like virtual counselors hat highly-disclose about themselves. The Annual Review of Cybertherapy and Telemedicine (in press, 2011)

26. Watson, D., Tellegen, A., Clark, L.A.: Development and validation of brief measures of positive and negative affect: The PANAS scale. Journal of Personality and Social Psychology 54, 1063–1070 (1988)

27. Von der Pütten, A., Krämer, N.C., Gratch, J., Kang, S.-H.: "It doesn't matter what you are¡' Explaining social effects of agents and avatars. Computer in Human Behavior 26, 1641–1650 (2010)

28. Bem, S.L.: The measurement of psychological androgyny. Journal of Consulting and Clinical Psychology 42, 155–162 (1974)

29. Bailenson, J.N., Blascovich, J., Beall, A.C., Loomis, J.M.: Equilibrium theory revisited: Mutual gaze and personal space in virtual environments. Presence 10, 583–598 (2001)

30. Biocca, F., Harms, C., Gregg, J.: The networked minds measure of social presence: Pilot test of the factor structure and concurrent validity. Paper presented at the 4th Annual International Workshop on Presence, Philadelphia (2001)

31. Cheek, J.M.: The Revised Cheek and Buss Shyness Scale. Wellesley College, Wellesley (1983)
32. Davis, M.: A multidimensional approach to individual differences in empathy. JSAS catalogue of Selected Documents in Psychology 10, 85 (1980)
33. Carney, D.R., Harrigan, J.A.: It takes one to know one: Interpersonal sensitivity is related to accurate assessments of others' interpersonal sensitivity. Emotion 3, 194–200 (2003)
34. Riggio, R.E.: The Social Skills Inventory (SSI): Measuring nonverbal and social skills. In: Manusov, V. (ed.) The Sourcebook of Nonverbal Measures: Going Beyond Words, pp. 23–31. Lawrence Erlbaum Associates, Mahwah (2005)
35. Morency, L.-P., Sidner, C.L., Lee, C., Darrell, T.: Contextual recognition of head gestures. In: 7th International Conference on Multimodal Interactions, Toronto, Italy (2005)
36. Mehrabian, A.: Nonverbal communication. Aldine-Atherton, Chicago (1972)
37. Bavelas, J.B., Coates, L., Johnson, T.: Listener responses as a collaborative process: The role of gaze. Journal of Communication 52, 566–580 (2002)
38. Duncan Jr., S.: Some signals and rules for taking speaking turns in conversations. Journal of Personality and Social Psychology 23, 283–292 (1972)
39. Hogg, R.V., Tanis, E.A.: Probability and Statistical Inference. Macmillan, New York (1988)
40. Kipp, M., Gebhard, P.: IGaze: Studying Reactive Gaze Behavior in Semi-immersive Human-Avatar Interactions. In: Prendinger, H., Lester, J.C., Ishizuka, M. (eds.) IVA 2008. LNCS (LNAI), vol. 5208, pp. 191–199. Springer, Heidelberg (2008)

Get Involved in an Interactive Virtual Tour of Brest Harbour: Follow the Guide and Participate

Mukesh Barange[1], Pierre De Loor[1], Vincent Louis[2], Ronan Querrec[1],
Julien Soler[1], Thanh-Hai Trinh[1], Éric Maisel[1], and Pierre Chevaillier[1]

[1] ENIB–UEB; LISYC: Laboratory of Computer Science for Complex Systems, France
[2] Dialonics, Lannion, France

Abstract. Recent cultural heritage applications have been based on rich-content virtual environment (VE), in which virtual humans can communicate with visitors and other agents using natural language (NL). The conceptualisation of these dialogues are dependent on the contents of the application. Hence, we propose to use the semantic modelling of the VE and the activities of agents for the conceptualisation of the dialogue. Meta level semantic information are used as arguments in NLU/NLG rules. The advantage of this approach is that the dialogue rules are independent from the contents of the application and have clear semantics. We applied these principles to develop Brest'Coz, an interactive virtual tour for the learning of shipbuilding techniques used in France in early 18th century.

Keywords: Semantic Modelling, Dialogue Management, Cultural Heritage.

1 Introduction

This study takes place in a general perspective to make the development of rich-content virtual reality (VR) applications more rational, and we address more specifically issues related to the design of conversational agents. As proposed by many authors [1,8], one promising approach is to center the architecture on an abstract semantic layer. The main motivations are as follows: (1) The design of the VE and that of agents, should be independent. That means that the communicative capabilities of an agent, such as a guide in an interactive virtual tour (or an educational agent), should be independent to the environment it is supposed to act in. (2) The semantic model of the environment, both physical and social, can be used as a source of knowledge for agents to make decisions and to support dialogues [4].

This article presents how these principles have been successfully used to develop Brest'Coz, an interactive virtual tour dedicated to the learning of techniques used for shipbuilding in France in early 18th century. The learning is based on a gaming approach. Users receive directions from a virtual guide and have to communicate with non-playing characters to get information and participate to some collaborative activities.

H. Högni Vilhjálmsson et al. (Eds.): IVA 2011, LNAI 6895, pp. 93–99, 2011.

Providing NL dialogue capabilities to conversational agents using semantic modelling, rises many scientific issues. One of the issues is *what the agent can say?* In Brest'Coz, agents should be able to describe the structure of the environment, i.e., properties of objects, their behaviors and their spatial relationships. Moreover, the visitor may ask agents to describe their own activities or the activities of other agents. Also, agents can be involved in some collaborative activities. Thus, while communicating with other agents and visitors, agents should take into account the social norms, including their roles and organisational rules.

Another issue is *how does the agent generate the NL dialogue structure?* In many applications [7,11], the dialogue management is based on dialogue acts. However, this approach is highly dependent on contents of the application, and requires extra efforts for the annotation of dialogue acts [3]. In contrast, the rule–based dialogue management approach, like in [13] operates on a hard–coded set of rules, using pattern matching and substitution, to generate the response. The fundamental bottleneck of this approach is that the knowledge is explicitly presented in the form of hard–coded values in dialogue rules. All these approaches do not take into account the semantics of the VE and therefore, are not suitable for the modelling of dialogue behaviors, independent from the application.

To develop Brest'Coz, we used MASCARET framework in which we embedded NabuTalk, a commercial rule-based dialogue engine. We defined the generic queries agents can perform on the semantic model in order to interpret, and to generate utterances. Because these NLU/NLG rules are defined at an abstract level (meta-model) they are independent of the content of the application and have clear semantics.

In Sect. 2, we present the Brest'Coz application. Sect. 3 gives main elements of the semantic layer used as linguistic resources for conversational agents. Sect. 4 illustrates how these semantic information are used in NLU/NLG rules.

2   The Brest'Coz Application

Brest'Coz is an application for interactively visiting the harbour of Brest, France. In early 18th century, it was an important site for the French navy where various specific shipbuilding techniques were used. It is a task-oriented tour. At the beginning, a virtual guide gives some directions about the goal assigned to the user, which is represented by a human-like avatar. The user has to take part to the transshipment of a boat, and can learn how middle-age wheeled cranes were operated for that. To get involved in this collaborative activity (supported by autonomous agents), the user has to communicate with different characters and to interact with the environment using VR peripherals.

The 3D modelling encompassed the docks, some noticeable buildings and various shipbuilding sites (Fig. 1). We simulated different shipbuilding activities (e.g., shipwrighting, transshipment), performed by different categories of workers (autonomous virtual agents).

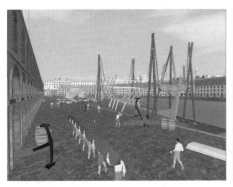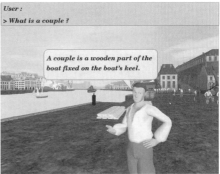

Fig. 1. Brest'Coz: overview of shipbuilding activities on the harbour (left) - example of dialogue with a worker (right)

3 Semantic Modelling Using Mascaret

MASCARET, which stands for *MultiAgent System for Collaborative, Adaptive & Realistic Environments for Training*, is a generic framework that provides necessary abstractions for both content- and system-oriented semantic modelling of VR applications [2]. It provides a modelling language expressive enough for subject matter experts to formulate their knowledge about a specific domain (content-oriented approach). The language has clear operational semantics for models to be interpreted by the execution platform (system-oriented approach). MASCARET is based on two complementary metamodels, VEHA and HAVE. These metamodels have been defined as extensions of those of UML, the Unified Modelling Language. UML is used here as a content description language and not as an abstraction for object-oriented programming.

Modelling the VE Using VEHA. This metamodel is dedicated to the modelling of entities compounding the VE, their categories, internal structures, relationships, and behaviors. Fig. 2 illustrates how cranes have been modelled in Brest'Coz (based on Worldnet[1]). A crane structurally contains one hook that can be logically linked to one container.

Fig. 2 shows the partial model of the behavior of the crane, which is supported in MASCARET by state machines. Here, the crane can grasp an object if it is stopped and when the condition canBeLoaded is satisfied. Such logical constraints are expressed using VRX-OCL [12].

Modelling Human Activities into the VE using HAVE. This metamodel supports the modelling of collaborative activities of agents in the environment, which is supposed to be described using VEHA. Agents are here the autonomous characters for whom the activity is simulated and the users. Defining the activity

---

[1] http://wordnetweb.princeton.edu/perl/webwn

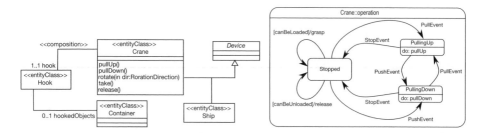

Fig. 2. Partial modelling of the Crane entity class using VEHA. Left: properties and structure; right: behavior.

means to describe how it is organised and what the agents are supposed to do in the environment. These two views are supported in HAVE respectively by the *organisational model* and the *activity model*.

As for existing multiagent models, the organisational metamodel is based on the concept of agent, role and organisational entity. It allows to define social rules that govern agents' behavior within an organisation.

Fig. 3 (left) illustrates how the organisational structure used for the boat transshipment can be instantiated: agents have been associated to roles (e.g., crane operator) and the available resources been defined. HAVE supports the modelling of the collaborative activity (i.e., actions to be performed by an organisational entity) using activity charts similar to those of UML. Each action is defined by its feasibility conditions (precondition), rational effect (post-condition), and action to be done (do: statement). Fig. 3 (right) shows how the user (visitor) can collaborate with other agents to manipulating the crane.

The way the description of the activity is interpreted by agents is defined using behave, which is a generic model of an agent architecture, independent to any domain specific application. The dependency between agents and the environment takes place at the meta level, i.e., the actual model of the environment and of the activities that agents are supposed to perform, are viewed as data available for agents to make decisions and to execute their behaviors.

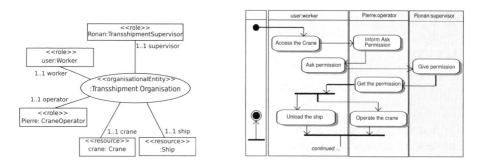

Fig. 3. Modelling of the transshipment activity using HAVE (partial)

4   Conceptualisation of Dialogues Using Semantic Modelling

In this section, we show how semantic modelling presented previously has been used to process NL utterances using generic parameterized rules, that preserve the independence of the communicative behavior of agents from the VE. We also illustrate how it has been implemented using MASCARET and NabuTalk.

NabuTalk is a NL dialogue engine that relies on the concepts of Artimis [10] and the JADE Semantics Add-on [9]. It is based on a high–level agent programming language, named Nabu, that includes appropriate mechanisms to handle NLU/NLG concepts, such as utterance templates, dialogue interpretation and generation rules. It provides a rule–based mechanism to deal with users' utterances. The pattern-matching algorithm relies not only on the matching of usual regular expressions but also on the unification of feature structures, based on the theory of functional unification grammars [6].

Both users and agents can initiate the dialogue. In MASCARET, each agent is associated with a thread of the NabuTalk engine. For each communicative function, NabuTalk selects the best appropriate pattern for the NLU rule. The patterns may contain parameters, which can be substituted with semantic information retrieved from MASCARET models. The properties of model elements depend on their type, which are defined at the meta level. Because the NLU/NLG rules rely only on meta level concepts, they are independent from specific contents of the application.

All the agents share a common set of dialogue rules. The individuality of agent's dialogues comes from the role associated to the agent. Furthermore, agents may use additional NLU/NLG rules to support application-specific dialogues.

In the transshipment scenario (Fig. 3), when the user (playing the role of worker) accesses the crane, the operator agent, named Pierre, initiates the following dialogues with the user:

- 1.1 Pierre: Hey! You do not have the permission to use the Crane.
- 2.1 user: Who can give the permission to use the Crane?
- 2.2 Pierre: The supervisor can do it. His name is Ronan.
- 3.1 user: What can I do with the Crane?
- 3.2 Pierre: You can pull-up, pull-down, rotate, take and release with the Crane.

When the user accesses the crane, the operator executes the communicative action inform(require(Ask_Permission)). The precondition of this action is to verify the physical constraint Crane.state=Available. This VRX-OCL constraint is evaluated according to the state machine of the Crane provided by VEHA (Fig. 2). If it fails, the operator generates the utterance 1.1.

The natural language rule (nlu-rule) in NabuTalk can use predicates implemented as MASCARET connectors to access meta level information. To go further in details, utterance 3.1 is interpreted as a Query-ref on the capabilities of a class (Crane is a class name). The agent looks in the VEHA model and retrieves the names of all the operations of the class. The Nabu code to handle this looks like:

```
(nlu-rule {[what-can-do-with] [class($class)]} {
  let (eval $list listClassOperations($class)) {
    if (empty $list) { talk($other {"You can do nothing with a" $class})
      } else {
        talk($other {"You can" list($list "," "and") "with a" $class}) }
} })
```

NabuTalk performs pattern matching with resources like *[what-can-do-with]*. The NabuTalk resource is a regular expression that can support different ways to express a phrase. Thus, it provides some flexibility for the user to communicate with agents. [class($class)] is a resource implemented with NabuTalk predicates and MASCARET connectors. It represents any class found in the semantic model. If such a pattern matches, the condition (eval $list listClassOperations($class)) is evaluated and if true, the $list variable will contain names of all operations of the class. The listClassOperations predicate is implemented as a MASCARET connector. The code just walks through MASCARET model to get operations of the class:

```
Class c=MascaretApplication::getModel()->getClassByName(className);
vector <Operation> op=c->getOperations(); // returns operation names
```

The result of this method is converted into a NabuTalk object that can be post–processed by the NabuTalk engine to generate the utterance 3.2.

MASCARET agents are able to talk about spatial relationships (topological and directional relationships) between entities using VRX-OCL. Dialogues may also refer to the activity of agents, based on the information from activity charts. Thus, the agent can reply to user's questions like *What can I do now?* (the name of the next action belonging to the role of the locutor), *Why should I do it?* (the description associated to the post-condition of the referred action) or *How can I do it?* (the description of the do:statement associated to the action), etc.

Thus, using meta level information, agents can talk about the entities of the VE, their behaviors, their social organizations, and collaborative activities. This approach is particularly suitable for complex VEs where many human activities have to be simulated. In such a context, using specific NLU/NLG rules would make the drawing of the scenario far too complex. Our approach does not cover all types of dialogues. It is more suitable to handle inquiry, request–response or question–answering dialogues. A trade-off has to be reached between the genericity of dialogue rules and the ability to deal with specific application conversational styles, like in [5] which uses learning mechanisms and is based on annotated corpus.

5   Conclusion

In this article, we have presented the benefits of semantic modelling for dialogue modelling. Because our approach is anchored to a meta-modelling framework, it ensures the consistency between the model of the VE and behaviors of autonomous agents. It also makes NLU/NLG rules independent from contents of the application and provides a high expressiveness. Our solution has been used to develop an interactive cultural heritage application, Brest'Coz, using MASCARET and the NabuTalk engine. Although, we have not yet performed its formal evaluation, the application has been successfully presented during a video game exhibition at Brest, and feedbacks from users were very positive. Our long term goal is to enrich agents' behaviors, so that they can engage themselves into dialogical interactions to coordinate their collaborative activities. One can expect to significantly lower the complexity of the description of the activity.

Acknowledgments. This work was supported in part by a grant from Région Bretagne and in part by the ANR (Corvette project ANR-10-CORD-012).

References

1. Bogdanovych, A., Rodriguez, J.A., Simoff, S., Cohen, A.: Virtual agents and 3D virtual worlds for preserving and simulating cultures. In: Ruttkay, Z., Kipp, M., Nijholt, A., Vilhjálmsson, H.H. (eds.) IVA 2009. LNCS, vol. 5773, pp. 257–271. Springer, Heidelberg (2009)
2. Chevaillier, P., Trinh, T.-H., Barange, M., Devillers, F., Soler, J., Loor, P.D., Querrec, R.: Semantic modelling of virtual environments using Mascaret. In: Proceedings of SEARIS 2011, Singapore (March 2011)
3. Gandhe, S., Traum, D.: Creating spoken dialogue characters from corpora without annotations. In: Proceedings of Interspeech 2007, Antwerp, Belgium (2007)
4. Ijaz, K., Bogdanovych, A., Simoff, S.: Enhancing the believability of embodied conversational agents through environment-, self- and interaction-awareness. In: Proceedings of ACSC 2011, Perth, Australia (2011)
5. Jan, D., Roque, A., Leuski, A., Morie, J., Traum, D.: A virtual tour guide for virtual worlds. In: Ruttkay, Z., Kipp, M., Nijholt, A., Vilhjálmsson, H.H. (eds.) IVA 2009. LNCS, vol. 5773, pp. 372–378. Springer, Heidelberg (2009)
6. Kay, M.: Functional unification grammar: A formalism for machine translation. In: Proceedings of COLING-ACL, pp. 75–78 (1984)
7. Kopp, S., Gesellensetter, L., Krämer, N.C., Wachsmuth, I.: A conversational agent as museum guide – design and evaluation of a real-world application. In: Panayiotopoulos, T., Gratch, J., Aylett, R.S., Ballin, D., Olivier, P., Rist, T. (eds.) IVA 2005. LNCS (LNAI), vol. 3661, pp. 329–343. Springer, Heidelberg (2005)
8. Latoschik, M.E., Biermann, P., Wachsmuth, I.: Knowledge in the loop: Semantics representation for multimodal simulative environments. In: Butz, A., Fisher, B., Krüger, A., Olivier, P. (eds.) SG 2005. LNCS, vol. 3638, pp. 25–39. Springer, Heidelberg (2005)
9. Louis, V., Martinez, T.: Jade semantics framework. In: Bellifemine, F., Caire, G., Greenwood, D. (eds.) Developing Multi-agent Systems With Jade, ch. 12, Wiley & Sons, Chichester (2007)
10. Sadek, D.: Artimis rational dialogue agent technology: An overview. In: Weiss, G., Bordini, R., Dastani, M., Dix, J., Fallah Seghrouchni, A. (eds.) Multi-Agent Programming, Multiagent Systems, Artificial Societies, and Simulated Organizations, vol. 15, pp. 217–243. Springer US, Heidelberg (2005)
11. Traum, D.R.: Talking to virtual humans: Dialogue models and methodologies for embodied conversational agents. In: Wachsmuth, I., Knoblich, G. (eds.) ZiF Research Group International Workshop. LNCS (LNAI), vol. 4930, pp. 296–309. Springer, Heidelberg (2008)
12. Trinh, T.H., Querrec, R., De Loor, P., Pierre, C.: Ensuring semantic spatial constraints in virtual environments using UML/OCL. In: Proceedings of VRST 2010, pp. 219–226 (2010)
13. Wallace, R.S.: Be Your Own Botmaster. ALICE A.I. Foundation Inc. (2003)

Using Virtual Tour Behavior to Build Dialogue Models for Training Review

Antonio Roque*, Dusan Jan, Mark Core, and David Traum

USC Institute for Creative Technologies
Playa Vista, CA, USA
aroque@ucla.edu,{jan,core,traum}@ict.usc.edu

Abstract. We develop an intelligent agent that builds a user model of a learner during a tour of a virtual world. The user model is based on the learner's answers to questions during the tour. A dialogue model for a simulated instructor is tailored to the individual learner based upon this user model. We describe an evaluation to track system accuracy and user perceptions.

Keywords: User models and adaptive agents, Dialogue models.

1 Introduction

Researchers have investigated the use of intelligent agents in virtual worlds to act as virtual guides [5,6] which lead human-controlled avatars through a virtual environment for entertainment or instructional purposes. Human-agent dialogue is an important part of such a **virtual tour**, not only to provide information and coordinate movement, but also to play a role in instruction. One instructional role is ascertaining how well the human learner is understanding the information being presented.

Our effort is motivated by research in educational systems which use dialogue strategies tailored to individual learners. Researchers have tracked learners' behavior to build user models during experiences such as interacting with multimedia learning environments to learn shipboard emergency management [10] or writing essays to answer qualitative physics problems [3,4]. These user models then guide subsequent dialogues tailored to the individual learner's needs.

In our research we explore applying such a user modeling technique during a virtual tour. We track a learner's dialogue behavior during an instructional virtual tour and build a user model that is combined with a model of the teaching goals to build a dialogue model for a post-exercise discussion. This dialogue model is used by a virtual guide to hold a multi-channel discussion in which private messages for individual learners can be customized based on their dialogue model.

---

* Now at the University of California Los Angeles, Computer Science Department.

H. Högni Vilhjálmsson et al. (Eds.): IVA 2011, LNAI 6895, pp. 100–105, 2011.

2   Virtual Tour Testbed

Educators have demonstrated the value of virtual worlds as learning environments using a variety of platforms including Active Worlds [2,7]. The testbed
we adopted was created in Active Worlds by US government contractors, and
included a Powerpoint-style briefing in the virtual world followed by a virtual
tour of a roadblock in Iraq. The existing virtual tour was designed to be directed
by a human guide.

We developed an intelligent agent to conduct the virtual tour when a human tour guide was not available. This **virtual guide** led the learners through
the virtual world, communicating through recorded audio narration mirrored
by on-screen transcriptions, answering learner-initiated questions regarding the
scenario, and asking the learners a number of questions to gauge their understanding of the material.

We also added an After Action Review (**AAR**) [1] following the virtual
tour, during which the virtual guide used an interactive question and answer
format to reinforce the lessons it had previously discussed. We personalized
this interaction by tailoring the style of interaction to the learner's needs as
described below. During the AAR, the virtual guide interacted with the group
of learners through a variety of channels: using text chat to the entire group
to manage the AAR, and using private in-world Instant Messages with each
individual learner to ask questions and deliver didactic content. The in-world
Instant Messages allow the pace of the AAR to be tailored to the level of
knowledge shown by an individual learner. Figure 1 shows an AAR in progress.

Fig. 1. An After-Action Review (AAR) being conducted

3   Models of Knowledge Components, Users, and Dialogues

To implement an automated AAR, we first needed a model of the information to be taught. Following [8], we use the concept, **knowledge component**, "an acquired unit of cognitive function or structure that can be inferred from performance on a set of related tasks" (p. 9). We developed a set of knowledge components for the domain by analyzing the background reading material as well as studying a recording of a virtual tour conducted by a human subject matter expert. Of the thirteen knowledge components for the domain, nine are covered by guide explanations during the virtual tour while four are covered by questions asked.

After posing a question during the virtual tour, the virtual guide waits briefly for replies. Learner responses are not individually prompted, praised, or corrected at that time; after a pause, the agent only provides the answer and continues on the tour. However, if the learners make responses to the questions then a statistical natural language intepreter [9] automatically classifies the responses as either "Right" or "Wrong", and those classifications are saved for use during the AAR.

Each of these questions is linked with a relevant knowledge component, and the learner's user model consists of variables representing whether the learner has demonstrated competence in these knowledge components by answering the associated question correctly. For each knowledge component, either the learner has demonstrated evidence of understanding of the material (by answering the related virtual tour question correctly), or they have demonstrated a possibly incorrect understanding (by answering the virtual tour question incorrectly), or they have provided no indication of their understanding (by not answering the question), or there is no evidence that the learner was even present when the question was asked. This last condition could occur if, for example, a learner had lagged behind in the tour.

Each knowledge component is linked with dialogue strategies for use during the AAR. The default dialogue strategy contains a question to test the learner's knowledge of the knowledge component and a statement of the correct answer. The guide gives positive feedback after correct answers and provides the statement of the correct answer after both correct and incorrect answers. A vague or incomplete answer may still be classified as correct so we show the pre-authored correct answer to avoid potential misconceptions.

For some knowledge components, an alternate dialogue strategy of simply summarizing the knowledge component is available. If the user model indicates that there is evidence that the learner has mastered this knowledge component, the guide will select the strategy of summarization during the AAR. Otherwise, the question-answer strategy will be used to test the learner's understanding.

For example, one knowledge component concerns the high levels of stress felt by the soldiers at the checkpoint due to previous attacks. The virtual tour question, which follows a description of the recent violence, is: "How do you suppose that affects the soldiers at the checkpoint?" If the learner answers that question correctly during the virtual tour, then the virtual guide selects a "review" strategy during the AAR, and summarizes the concept. If the learner answers the virtual tour question incorrectly, then the virtual guide selects a "remediation" strategy during the AAR, first asking a question, optionally providing positive feedback if they answer the AAR question correctly, and concluding with a statement summarizing the correct answer. Examples of both strategies are shown below.

Once the AAR begins, the virtual guide's dialogue manager iterates through a queue of knowledge components. For each knowledge component, the virtual guide queries the user model to pick a dialogue strategy to address the knowledge component.

A sample dialogue is shown in Table 1. In line 1, the virtual guide asks a question during the virtual tour that in line 2 the learner answers correctly. Line 3 occurs later in the virtual tour and corresponds to the virtual guide asking another question although in this case the learner's answer in line 4 is vague enough to be classified as incorrect.

Table 1. Sample Dialogue

#	Speaker	Text
1	Virtual Guide	Having said that, how do you suppose that affects the soldiers at the checkpoint?
2	Learner	they must be scared to be in danger (Classified as: Right Answer)
...		
3	Virtual Guide	What inherent dangers of the checkpoint do you see?
4	Learner	it's open (Classified as: Wrong Answer)
...		
5	Virtual Guide	Given this situation [of frequent terrorist attacks], the soldiers at the checkpoint were likely tense especially since they had experience there and had some people die.
6	Virtual Guide	What were the specific dangers of the checkpoint due to the surrounding terrain?
7	Learner	the overpass
8	Virtual Guide	Right.
9	Virtual Guide	The soldiers at the checkpoint have no cover from attacks originating from the overpass or the nearby buildings...

Line 5 shows the discussion, in the AAR, of the same knowledge component addressed in lines 1 and 2. The virtual guide chooses a "review" strategy for the knowledge component given that the learner answered the question in line 1 correctly. Lines 6-9 address the same knowledge component addressed in lines 3 and 4. In contrast with the previous example, the virtual guide uses a "remediation" strategy given the the learner answered the question in line 3 incorrectly. Because the learner answered correctly in line 7, they are given positive feedback as well as the pre-authored version of the correct answer.

4   Evaluation

Two major question about the effectivness of the AAR are: does it result in learning gains beyond those provided by just the virtual tour, and does it make the experience better or worse from the learner's perspective? We did not have a test to evaluate learner knowledge of the domain before and after the experience so we focused solely on the performance of the classifier on learner answers, and learner evaluations of the experience.

The accuracy of the statistical natural language interpreter heavily influences the accuracy of the dialogue model and whether learners receive an appropriately customized AAR and appropriate positive feedback. Learners may also get frustrated if they perceive the system as not understanding them.

To evaluate the system, we ran several full sessions including the initial briefing, the virtual tour, and the AAR. Three of these sessions (10 data points) were used to evaluate the statistical natural language interpreter. Two human annotators labeled the correctness of each learner reply made during the virtual tour, and compared this to the automated classifications. On the 10 data points, the inter-annotator reliability as measured by Kappa was 0.79. The automated classifications agreed with human consensus classifications 80% of the time, which means the majority of time the AAR was correctly tailored to the individual learner.

In addition to recording the system behavior, we also collected qualitative data with post-session surveys in four of the sessions; responses on a seven-point Likert scale showed above-average scores in questions related to natural language understanding during the AAR, the AAR experience and the experience as a whole, as shown in Table 2.

Table 2. Responses to Post-Session Questionnaire

Question	Learner 1	Learner 2	Learner 3	Learner 4
The After Action Review improved the experience. (1=Not at all, 4=Somewhat, 7=Very much)	4	7	6	6
How well do you think the AAR bot understood you? (1=Not at all, 4=Somewhat, 7=Perfectly)	4	5	6	5
How did you like the [General] experience? (1=I disliked it very much, 4=Neither liked nor disliked, 7=I liked it very much)	5	7	5	6

5   Future Work

Future work will involve more extensive testing of this approach either in the domain discussed above or in other domains. Developing a pre- and post-test for domain knowledge will help better evaluate the system and judge the impact of potential new features such as a more detailed user model and more sophisticated AAR dialogue strategies.

Acknowledgments. This work has been sponsored by the U.S. Army Research, Development, and Engineering Command (RDECOM). Statements and opinions expressed do not necessarily reflect the position or the policy of the United States Government, and no official endorsement should be inferred.

References

1. Army, U.S.: A leader's guide to after-action reviews, TC 25-50 (September 1993)
2. Dickey, M.D.: Three-dimensional virtual worlds and distance learning: two case studies of active worlds as a medium for distance education. British Journal of Educational Technology 36(3), 439–451 (2005)
3. Forbes-Riley, K., Litman, D.: Adapting to student uncertainty improves tutoring dialogues. In: Proceedings of the 14th International Conference on Artificial Intelligence in Education (AIED) (July 2009)
4. Forbes-Riley, K., Litman, D.: Using performance trajectories to analyze the immediate impact of user state misclassification in an adaptive spoken dialogue system. In: Proceedings 12th Annual SIGdial Meeting on Discourse and Dialogue (SIGdial) (June 2011)
5. Gayle, R., Manocha, D.: Navigating virtual agents in online virtual worlds. In: Proceedings of Web3D 2008, the Thirteenth Symposium on 3D Web Technologies, pp. 53–56 (2008)
6. Jan, D., Roque, A., Leuski, A., Morie, J., Traum, D.: A virtual tour guide for virtual worlds. In: Proceedings of Intelligent Virtual Agents 9th International Conference (2009)
7. Jarmon, L., Lim, K.Y., Stephen Carpenter II, B. (eds.) Journal of Virtual Worlds Research, vol. 2 (April 2009), Special Issue on Pedagogy, Education and Innovation in Virtual Worlds
8. Koedinger, K.R., Corbett, A.T., Perfetti, C.: the current, past members of the Pittsburgh Science of Learning Center: The knowledge-learning-instruction (KLI) framework: Toward bridging the science-practice chasm to enhance robust student learning. Tech. Rep. CMU-HCII-10-102, Human-Computer Interaction Institute, Carnegie Mellon University (June 2010)
9. Leuski, A., Traum, D.: NPCEditor: A tool for building question-answering characters. In: Proceedings of The Seventh International Conference on Language Resources and Evaluation (LREC) (May 2010)
10. Pon-Barry, H., Schultz, K., Bratt, E.O., Clark, B., Peters, S.: Responding to student uncertainty in spoken tutorial dialogue systems. International Journal of Artificial Intelligence in Education 16, 171–194 (2006)

Posture, Relationship, and Discourse Structure
Models of Nonverbal Behavior for Long-Term Interaction

Daniel Schulman and Timothy Bickmore

College of Computer and Information Science, Northeastern University
360 Huntington Ave – WVH 202, Boston MA 02115
{schulman,bickmore}@ccs.neu.edu

Abstract. We present an empircal investigation of nonverbal behavior in long-term interaction spanning multiple conversations, in the context of a developing interpersonal relationship. Based on a longitudinal video corpus of human-human counseling conversation, we develop a model of the occurrence of posture shifts which incorporates changes that occur both within a single conversation and over multiple conversations. Implications for the design and implementation of virtual agents are discussed, with a particular focus on agents designed for long-term interaction.

Keywords: relational agent, embodied conversational agent, nonverbal behavior, relationship, posture, discourse structure.

1 Introduction

Embodied Conversational Agents (ECAs) are increasingly applied to tasks which require or benefit from multiple conversations with each user, potentially over a long period of time; Examples include education, counseling, and social engagement. Maintaining long-term user engagement in such applications may be challenging [5].

Typically, ECAs are designed to accurately reproduce human verbal and nonverbal behavior, within the limits of their design. The conversational behavior of human dyads has been shown to change over time as their relationship evolves (e.g. [7]). Simulating these changes in an ECA may produce more realistic and engaging ECAs for long-term interaction.

This study is a step toward that goal. We focus on a single nonverbal behavior — posture shifts — which are both a part of the standard repertoire of many ECAs, and may also be an indicator of the interpersonal relationship of a dyad. Based on an examination of a longitudinal corpus of human-human interaction, which contains multiple conversations between the same dyads, we construct a model of the occurrence of posture shifts in conversation, including changes over time, both across and within conversations.

2 Background and Related Work

Several decades of research, dating at least to work by Scheflen [18], has focused on examining postural alignment or mirroring as an indicator of rapport. To the

H. Högni Vilhjálmsson et al. (Eds.): IVA 2011, LNAI 6895, pp. 106–112, 2011.

extent that a dyad is likely to build stronger rapport over multiple conversations, this predicts increasing postural alignment over time. However, empirical tests have been mixed [13,14], Bernieri reports that movement synchrony (i.e. similarity in timing) may be an indicator of rapport while behavior matching (i.e. taking the same position at the same time) is not [3]. Tickle-Degnen and Gavett suggest that postural alignment may have a positive association with rapport only in later interactions, rather than initial interactions [20].

There is also a well-studied association between posture shifts and discourse structure. Many authors have noted that posture shifts tend to occur at topic boundaries (e.g. [12]). Cassell and Nakano et al. give empirical evidence of this phenomenon, based on an examination of direction-giving dialogues [8].

Little prior work examines any possible association between posture shifts and aspects of interpersonal relationship other than rapport. To our knowledge, no prior empirical work examines simultaneously an association between posture shifts and discourse structure and an association between posture and interpersonal relationship. Here, as an initial step, we focus on behavior changes that occur when a dyad has repeated interaction and a longer history together, rather than examining many other possible aspects of interpersonal relationship.

3   The Exercise Counseling Corpus

We collected a longitudinal corpus of dyadic interaction, containing multiple conversations between each dyad. This approach allows us to examine any changes over time in detail, and separate them from other differences between individuals. We chose to study behavior change counseling for exercise promotion, an area in which conversational agents have been applied (e.g., [4]), in which the counselor-client relationship has an effect on outcomes [15], and nonverbal behavior is associated with the development of this relationship [20].

We recruited clients (N=6) who stated they did not currently exercise regularly. Each client was asked to have up to 6 weekly conversations with a counselor. The same counselor conducted all conversations, and in each conversation attempted to encourage the client to increase his or her daily physical activity. All conversations were held in the same room, with both client and counselor seated in office chairs, and were videotaped from three angles. The participants were informed the conversations would be taped and examined, but were not told what behaviors were of interest.

The final corpus contains 32 conversations (mean duration 15.6 minutes), comprising approximately 8.3 hours of recorded video, and approximately 100,000 words of spoken dialogue.

4   Methods

We separately coded the exercise counseling corpus to identify occurrences of posture shifts and of topic shifts. Coding was performed by the primary author. To check reliability, three conversations were randomly selected for each coding task and analyzed by a second coder.

4.1   Coding of Topic Shifts

Topic shifts were coded using transcripts of the corpus produced for a previously-reported study [19]. Video was not viewed in order to avoid confounding topic shifts with visible posture shifts or other nonverbal indicators of discourse structure. The transcripts were segmented based on the occurrence of silence, and topic shifts were coded as occurring at the beginning of the segment that introduced a new topic.

Following Grosz and Sidner [10], we defined a topic as a shared conversational goal to which the participants were mutually committed. A topic shift was marked whenever the coder believed a participant was attempting to introduce such a shared goal (whether or not the attempt was successful). The agreement rate between coders was 96.4% (Cohen's $\kappa = 0.68$).

4.2   Coding of Posture Shifts

Posture shifts were coded using muted video, in order to avoid confounding posture shifts with audible topic shifts. A posture shift was defined as a gross movement of the body, including the trunk, the legs and lower body, or both. Movements that appeared to be caused by the performance of a communicative gesture (e.g. a large hand gesture) were excluded, as were repetitive motions lasting more than a couple seconds (e.g. repeatedly rocking back and forth in the chair). Initially, chair rotation was coded as posture shifts, but preliminary examination revealed that these movements were very difficult to code reliably, and they were excluded.

Coders were asked to judge the start and end times of each posture shift, and several additional features, including movement direction, co-occurrence of grooming behavior (e.g. brushing hair or adjusting clothes), and an estimated energy level. Energy was judged on a linear scale ranging from 1 (the smallest perceptible shift) to 10 (the most energetic possible shift without leaving the chair).

An initial examination showed that reliability was very poor on low-energy shifts, and consequently all shifts with an energy of less than 4 were discarded. Aside from this, features of posture shifts besides the time of occurrence were not used in the present study. To compute inter-rater reliability, the corpus was divided into 1-second intervals, and each interval was considered to have been marked as a shift if the majority of it was covered by any coded posture shift. Cohen's κ was 0.58.

5   Results

31 conversations were coded for both posture and topic shifts; one conversation had large portions of unintelligible speech, and could not be coded for topic shifts. A total of 803 posture shifts were identified in the remaining conversations. The rate of posture shifts varied widely across conversations, ranging from 0.035 to 4.92 per minute (median 0.71).

Table 1. A mixed-effect logistic regression model predicting the probability of occurrence of posture shifts

Parameter	Est.	SE	p
Intercept	-4.17	0.21	.000***
Sessions (# of previous conversations)	0.16	0.05	.002**
Speaker (0=client, 1=counselor)	0.15	0.17	.376
Minutes (from the start of conversation)	-0.03	0.01	.027*
Tshift$_{self}$ (a topic shift occurs within 2 seconds)	0.94	0.31	.002**
Tshift$_{other}$ (a topic shift occurs within 2 seconds)	0.47	0.29	.103
Sessions × Speaker	-0.11	0.04	.010**
Sessions × Minutes	-0.02	0.00	.000***
Sessions × Tshift$_{self}$	-0.09	0.07	.225
Sessions × Tshift$_{other}$	-0.13	0.08	.110
Speaker × Minutes	-0.04	0.01	.013*
Speaker × Tshift$_{self}$	-0.52	0.24	.031*
Speaker × Tshift$_{other}$	0.22	0.27	.425
Minutes × Tshift$_{self}$	-0.02	0.02	.470
Minutes × Tshift$_{other}$	-0.03	0.03	.226
Tshift$_{self}$ × Tshift$_{other}$	0.16	0.63	.794

[a] Random intercepts on dyads (SD=0.26) and conversations (SD=0.33).
[b] Coefficients indicate change in the log-odds of a posture shift occurring within one second.
[c] All p values are derived from Z tests.

The start time of each posture shift was aligned to the nearest second. We then modeled the occurrence of a posture shift as a binary outcome, with one observation per second. A logistic mixed-effect regression model [16] was used. This model generalizes logistic regression to account for observations that are non-independent due to being grouped or nested — in this case, within conversations and dyads — by adding "random effects" which model the group-level variance.

In order to model change over time, we included the number of previous sessions, and the time since the start of the conversation as predictors. To control for varying discourse structure, we included the co-occurrence of topic shifts, by both a speaker and their conversation partner, as predictors. To allow for variability among different speakers, dyads, and conversations, we include the speaker (counselor or client) as a predictor, along with random effects on dyads and individual conversations. Finally, we included two-way interactions among all predictors; a model comparison by Akaike Information Criterion [6] strongly preferred this more complex model (ΔAIC = 9.8).

The final model (Table 1) was fit using R 2.12.1 [17] and the lme4 [2] package. Posture shifts are significantly more likely to occur at topic shifts (the coefficient "Tshift$_{self}$" in Table 1); this replicates results by Cassell et al. [8]. We see no significant effect for topic shifts ("Tshift$_{other}$") introduced by the conversation partner rather than a participant, although there is a trend in the same direction.

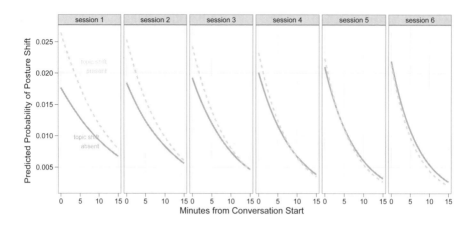

Fig. 1. Predicted probability of a posture shift occurring within a 1-second interval

There are significant changes over time, both within and across conversations. Figure 1 shows the predicted probability of a posture shift at different points over six weekly sessions, averaged over dyads. Each column shows a single session. Posture shifts occur much more frequently in the beginning of a conversation, as indicated by the steeply downward sloping lines in each column (and the coefficient "Minutes" in Table 1). There is an interaction with the number of previous sessions: the rate of decrease is greater in later conversations ("Sessions × Minutes").

6   Discussion

We show evidence of changes in the occurrence of posture shifts over time, both within conversations and across multiple conversations. Based on prior work on the occurrence of posture shifts [8], nonverbal behavior generation frameworks (e.g., BEAT [9]) have implemented stochastic, rule-based approaches to the generation of posture shifts, where the probability of generation of a posture shift is determined by discourse structure. These results suggest that such models could be easily modified to produce more realistic behavior by decreasing the probability of a posture shift over time. Using the regression coefficients estimated here, the log-odds of a posture shift[1] would change by $(0.16s - 0.03m - 0.02sm)$, where s is the number of previous sessions, and m is minutes from the start of the conversation.

We do not yet have clear evidence for a mechanism behind these effects, but instead offer some conjectures, based partially on subjective examination of the corpus. The early portion of many conversations includes posture shifts that appeared to be part of a process of "settling in", with most shifts leaving the participant in a more relaxed body posture. A relaxed body posture is an indicator of

---

[1] The odds o of a probability p are $o = \frac{p}{1-p}$; the log-odds are $\log o = \log \frac{p}{1-p}$.

nonverbal immediacy [1] (i.e., intimacy, warmth, or closeness). Increasingly rapid decreases in the rate of posture shifts in later conversations may indicate that, as a stronger interpersonal relationship develops over time, participants will more quickly and easily adopt a body posture that indicates high immediacy. Future work may investigate these conjectures through more detailed coding of posture shifts and by examining other indicators of immediacy for similar patterns of change.

Limitations of this study include a small number of participants (and a single counselor). The corpus is also limited to a single task, in a single setting, and validation of this model in an ECA is necessary. To address some of these limitations, we plan a longitudinal evaluation study, in which participants have multiple conversations with an ECA designed according to the model developed here.

Associations between nonverbal behavior and other aspects of interpersonal relationship are also of interest. We have collected longitudinal assessments of the strength of the counselor-client therapeutic alliance from participants in the exercise counseling corpus, using the Working Alliance Inventory [11], as well as other assessments of interpersonal relationship. Future work will incorporate this information into more complete models.

Finally, we hope that future work in this area will begin to develop more detailed and complete models of behavior, enabling the development of more lifelike, engaging, and efficacious virtual agents.

Acknowledgements. Thanks to Jenna Zaffini for her work in collecting the corpus, Brandon Gier and Connor Westfall for assistance in coding, and to the other members of the Relational Agents Group for much help and useful discussion. This work was supported by NSF CAREER IIS-0545932.

References

1. Andersen, P.A.: Nonverbal immediacy in interpersonal communication. In: Siegman, A.W., Feldstein, S. (eds.) Multichannel Integrations of Nonverbal Behavior, pp. 1–36. Lawrence Erlbaum, Hillsdale (1985)
2. Bates, D., Maechler, M., Bolker, B.: lme4: Linear mixed-effects models using S4 classes (2011), `http://CRAN.R-project.org/package=lme4`, R package version 0.999375-39
3. Bernieri, F.J.: Coordinated movement and rapport in teacher-student interactions. Journal of Nonverbal Behavior 12(2), 120–138 (1988)
4. Bickmore, T.: Relational Agents: Effecting Change through Human-Computer Relationships. Ph.D. thesis, Massachusetts Institute of Technology, Cambridge, MA (2003)
5. Bickmore, T., Schulman, D., Yin, L.: Maintaining engagement in long-term interventions with relational agents. Applied Artificial Intelligence 24(6), 648–666 (2010)
6. Bozdogan, H.: Model selection and Akaike's Information Criterion (AIC): The general theory and its analytical extensions. Psychometrika 52(3), 345–370 (1987)

7. Cassell, J., Gill, A.J., Tepper, P.A.: Coordination in conversation and rapport. In: Workshop on Embodied Language Processing, pp. 41–50. Association for Computational Linguistics (June 2007)

8. Cassell, J., Nakano, Y.I., Bickmore, T.W., Sidner, C.L., Rich, C.: Non-verbal cues for discourse structure. In: ACL 2001: Proceedings of the 39th Annual Meeting on Association for Computational Linguistics, pp. 114–123. Association for Computational Linguistics, Morristown (2001)

9. Cassell, J., Vilhjálmsson, H.H., Bickmore, T.: BEAT: the Behavior Expression Animation Toolkit. In: SIGGRAPH 2001: Proceedings of the 28th Annual Conference on Computer Graphics and Interactive Techniques, pp. 477–486. ACM, New York (2001)

10. Grosz, B.J., Sidner, C.L.: Attention, intentions, and the structure of discourse. Computational Linguistics 12(3), 175–204 (1986)

11. Hatcher, R.L., Gillaspy, A.J.: Development and validation of a revised short version of the Working Alliance Inventory. Psychotherapy Research 16(1), 12–25 (2006)

12. Kendon, A.: Some relationships between body motion and speech. In: Seigman, A., Pope, B. (eds.) Studies in Dyadic Communication, pp. 177–216. Pergamon Press, Elmsford (1972)

13. Lafrance, M.: Nonverbal synchrony and rapport: Analysis by the Cross-Lag panel technique. Social Psychology Quarterly 42(1), 66–70 (1979)

14. LaFrance, M., Ickes, W.: Posture mirroring and interactional involvement: Sex and sex typing effects. Journal of Nonverbal Behavior 5(3), 139–154 (1981)

15. Martin, D.J., Garske, J.P., Davis, M.K.: Relation of the therapeutic alliance with outcome and other variables: a meta-analytic review. Journal of Consulting and Clinical Psychology 68(3), 438–450 (2000)

16. McCulloch, C.E., Neuhaus, J.M.: Generalized Linear Mixed Models. John Wiley & Sons, Ltd., Chichester (2005)

17. R Development Core Team: R: A Language and Environment for Statistical Computing. R Foundation for Statistical Computing, Vienna, Austria (2011), http://www.R-project.org/, ISBN 3-900051-07-0

18. Scheflen, A.E.: The significance of posture in communication systems. Psychiatry 27, 316–331 (1964)

19. Schulman, D., Bickmore, T.: Modeling behavioral manifestations of coordination and rapport over multiple conversations. In: Allbeck, J., Badler, N., Bickmore, T., Pelachaud, C., Safonova, A. (eds.) IVA 2010. LNCS, vol. 6356, pp. 132–138. Springer, Heidelberg (2010)

20. Tickle-Degnen, L., Gavett, E.: Changes in nonverbal behavior during the development of therapeutic relationships. In: Philippot, P., Feldman, R.S., Coats, E.J. (eds.) Nonverbal Behavior in Clinical Settings, ch. 4, pp. 75–110. Oxford University Press, New York (2003)

Sign Language Avatars:
Animation and Comprehensibility

Michael Kipp, Alexis Heloir, and Quan Nguyen

DFKI
Embodied Agents Research Group
Saarbrücken, Germany
firstname.lastname@dfki.de

Abstract. Many deaf people have significant reading problems. Written content, e.g. on internet pages, is therefore not fully accessible for them. Embodied agents have the potential to communicate in the native language of this cultural group: sign language. However, state-of-the-art systems have limited comprehensibility and standard evaluation methods are missing. In this paper, we present methods and discuss challenges for the creation and evaluation of a signing avatar. We extended the existing EMBR character animation system[1] with prerequisite functionality, created a gloss-based animation tool and developed a cyclic content creation workflow with the help of two deaf sign language experts. For evaluation, we introduce *delta testing*, a novel way of assessing comprehensibility by comparing avatars with human signers. While our system reached state-of-the-art comprehensibility in a short development time we argue that future research needs to focus on nonmanual aspects and prosody to reach the comprehensibility levels of human signers.

Keywords: Accessible interfaces, virtual characters, sign language synthesis.

1 Introduction

"Why do deaf people need signing avatars on internet pages? They can *read*, can't they?" To motivate the concept of signing avatars, we have to give a brief introduction on the culture and language of the deaf. Most deaf people communicate in a sign language. Every country has its own specific sign language and each sign language is a proper language in all its complexity [28] and is fundamentally different from a spoken language. Therefore, a German deaf person's native language is German Sign Language (Deutsche Gebärdensprache, DGS) while (spoken) German is only the *second* language. In fact, it is a particularly hard-to-learn second language for deaf individuals: it must be learnt based only on a set of written symbols and based on observations of highly ambiguous mouth patterns, without any auditory cues – an almost impossible task. As a

---

[1] http://embots.dfki.de/EMBR

H. Högni Vilhjálmsson et al. (Eds.): IVA 2011, LNAI 6895, pp. 113–126, 2011.

consequence, many deaf pupils leave school with significant writing and reading problems[2].

To make written material like internet pages more accessible to deaf users, prerecorded *videos* of human signers are used. However, a video's content cannot be modified after production which makes it impossible to use them in dynamic or interactive scenarios (e.g. train station announcements or question answering). Moreover, production cost is high, appearance parameters cannot be adjusted (clothes, gender, lighting) and videos cannot be anonymized. Therefore, *signing avatars* could complement the current range of human signer videos. With intuitive tools, production cost could be low, post-production adjustments are easily done (even automatically or at runtime), and the identity of the content producer is not disclosed. Sign language avatars could be used for the automatic translation of web pages, interactive e-learning applications, sign language lexicon visualization or simple train/flight announcement services (cf. [1,9]). However, creating signing avatars involves multiple challenges, ranging from content representation, since a universal writing system for sign language does not exist, to realizing a comprehensible animation. Sign language is a highly multi-channel/multimodal language where hands/arms, the face and the whole body must be synchronized on various levels. Therefore, state-of-the-art avatars reach rather low comprehensibility levels of 58-62%, with a single study reporting 71% [13]. The diversity of evaluation methods and the variance in test material selection also makes it difficult to conclusively compare results.

To investigate the potentials of signing avatars for the internet, the German Federal Ministry of Labour and Social Affairs (Bundesministerium für Arbeit und Soziales, BMAS) commissioned us to investigate the technical feasibility of signing avatars and the acceptance in the German deaf community [18]. In this paper, we focus on the technical feasibility aspect of this study, consisting of two major parts. First, to explore sign language synthesis we created a signing avatar including necessary tools, an animation workflow and the identification of core challenges. Second, to explore reliable evaluation we developed a novel way to assess comprehensibility. In summary, we consider the following to be our main contributions to the research community:

- Showing how to transform a general-purpose avatar [4] to a sign language avatar, including necessary tools and workflow
- Identifying important challenges and their relative importance
- Introducing *delta testing* as a novel comprehensibility testing method that compares avatars with human signers

In the following, we survey related work (Sec. 2) before presenting our avatar extensions (Sec. 3), our animation technology (Sec. 4) and evaluation method (Sec. 5). We conclude with a summary and future work (Sec. 6).

---

[2] There have been several studies on deaf pupils' literacy levels. For instance, a US study showed "that deaf students around age 18 have a reading level more typical of 10-year-old hearing students" [7].

2   Related Work

Signing avatars are a relatively young research area with two decades of active research and some significant results. A major prerequisite for sign language synthesis is a representation system or *notation*. In *gloss notation* each sign is denoted with a word (gloss) that most closely corresponds to the sign's meaning [12]. For instance, the sign sequence for "What's your name?" would be YOUR NAME WHAT. Gloss notation, however, does not describe how to execute a sign. The same gloss may be executed in various ways due to grammatical modifications and dialect variations. Historically, a milestone notation for the description of how to execute a sign was *Stokoe notation* [28] which formed the basis of modern notation systems like the widely used *HamNoSys*, the Hamburg Notation System for Sign Language [25].

In the research area of signing avatars, one can distinguish approaches along the articulatory vs. concatenative axis [9]. While concatenative approaches piece together prerecorded chunks of human motion, articulatory approaches compute motion on-the-fly based on a sparse specification. Two influential European projects, ViSiCAST and eSIGN, developed technology for signing avatars based on HamNoSys [1,13], transitioning from a concatenative to an articulatory approach, and advancing HamNoSys to SiGML. The resulting avatar technology is called *Animgen* and was used e.g. for the *Virtual Guido* avatar [1]. Drawbacks of Animgen are that it is not open source but also the reliance on HamNoSys, a relatively high-level language with no transparent way to modify animations. To overcome limitations of HamNoSys the LIMSI institute developed *Zebedee* which is based on geometric constraints and allows parametrizable scripts [2]. However, we find the notation hard to read for humans and potentially hard to realize on the animation side. Another avatar project is called *Paula* with a number of interesting results for the synthesis of fingerspelling, nonverbal components and natural pose computation [31]. Both Paula and Zebedee are not yet mature and integrated enough to be used outside their original labs. On the other extreme, researchers have used *commercial* animation software (e.g. *VCom3D*) for their experiments (e.g. [8]). These packages allow convenient timeline-based editing of animations but are otherwise closed toward further external development. Lastly, there are general-purpose avatars that could be made usable for signing purposes. The *Greta* avatar has been used for sign language research but only at an early prototype stage [23]. The *SmartBody* agent is another well-known avatar technology which focuses on coverbal behaviors [30]. Both general-purpose and signing avatars lack a clean animation interface with the notable exception of EMBR [4] which introduced the animation layer in an effort to decouple behavior specification from low-level animation parameters [15].

In most signing avatar projects, the actual comprehensibility of the produced animation by deaf users has been assessed. This is particularly important because most of the experts working in this field are *not* native speakers of sign language. Most evaluation studies establish a pure sign language environment (instructions and supervision by a native signer) and grant a dedicated warm-up time to get used to the avatar [27,13,11]. For questionnaires, it has been recommended to rely on non-written content like pictograms. In terms of assessment methodology, the subjective rating of understanding by the participant him/herself turns out to be highly unreliable [11]. Instead, outside judgements by experts are taken, based on questions about the content of the communicated [27,13]. Here, mere imitation without understanding may be a problem. Also, asking dedicated questions may give part of the answer away, especially in sign language. [10] made a multiple choice test where similar spatial arrangements were shown. This method may not always be feasible, especially for more complex/abstract utterances, and requires careful decisions on what to ask and how to formulate the options. A more general challenge is to define a control condition, i.e. what is the avatar's signing compared against? [10] suggested *Signed English* (SE) as a control condition. SE is an artificial language that translates the words of spoken English in a one-to-one mapping to signs. Since Signed English and Sign Language are two distinct languages, the former sometimes even harder to understand than the latter, we do not deem this a good option. Instead, we suggest to use the comprehensibility of the human signer as the control condition. Moreover, we suggest to circumvent the theoretical problem of defining optimal understanding by using relative measures (e.g. word/sign counts).

3   Avatar Extensions

In this section we describe what changes to a general-purpose avatar are necessary for sign language synthesis. We decided to use the EMBR [4,15] character animation engine because it offers a high degree of control over the animation and is publicly available[3].

EMBR introduces a declarative layer of abstraction around its animation facilities. Based on the notion of a generalized key pose, arbitrary animation sequences can be specified and edited without resorting to programming. The EMBR animation system has grown out of research on coverbal gesture production [22,16,5] and lacked a number of necessary features for sign language production. These are mainly: range of hand shapes, upper body control, mouth control and gaze control.

In sign language, *hand shape* is a highly meaningful feature, whereas for conversational agents, a very sparse set of 8–10 is sufficient. Hence, we had to implement 50 new hand shapes, including the complete *finger alphabet* (27 hand shapes for the letters A to Z) and the ASL *classifier hand shapes*. Also, upper body control is necessary, like raising the shoulders, and therefore we added IK-based spine controls. Since, during signing, the hands move in a wider space compared to coverbal gesture we relaxed shoulder joint restrictions to make this possible. Also, *facial expression* is more expressive than in verbal communication which made us increase the upper limit of facial expression intensity for our morph targets.

To animate *mouthing*, i.e. the lip movement of words that give a definite cue to the meaning of the manual sign, we used the viseme generation capabilities

---

[3] EMBR has been released as an open-source software under the *LGPL* license.

Fig. 1. Based on the EMBR character animation system, we created a signing avatar to explore the technical feasibility and develop evaluation methods

of the OpenMARY[4] speech synthesis system [26]. Note that mouthing implies a number of questions in terms of selection (which word to mouth), timing (when to onset), duration (how much of the word to mouth, often the first part is enough) and how to synchronize mouthing with repeated strokes[5] [24]. We have not yet included all important mouth gestures like puffed cheeks and a flexible tongue.

Another important movement type is *gaze*. We extended EMBR to allow independent control of eye-balls and head because gaze can give important cues to disambiguate two manually equal signs. We stress that our extensions were targeted at German Sign Language (and, to some extent, at ASL) but should also meet most requirements of other sign languages. Fig. 1 shows some of the posing capabilities of the extended EMBR.

4   Animating Sign Language

In this section, we motivate our cyclic, gloss-based animation approach. To test the feasibility of the approach we used videos of human signers. Whereas in prior work very basic utterances were used [27], we selected two videos with more complex content from a German e-learning portal for deaf people called *Vibelle.de*. The videos teach concepts from the hearing world in sign language. We selected two videos, *yellow pages* (37 sec) and *vitamin B* (53 sec), with a total of 11 sign language utterances.

4.1   One Step Forward, Two Steps Back

We found that we had to create overarticulated versions of our original videos in order to compensate for avatar shortcomings. Our first "pilot test" was to imitate a piece of video with a single EMBRScript animation. However, we had to realize that our result was *not comprehensible* by our deaf assistant – not a single sign. The superficial sign language knowledge of our (hearing) animation

---

[4] http://mary.dfki.de

[5] The *stroke* is the most energetic part of a sign and can be repeated [19].

expert was insufficient – we needed a sign language expert before, during and after animation production.

Our initial attempt failed for a number of reasons, some on the level of a single sign, some on the utterance level. For single signs, sign linguistics distinguishes between *manual* and *nonmanual* features [12]. Manual features include hand shape, hand location, hand orientation and movement [20,28]; here, the animator needs to decide which of these is the decisive, so-called *formative*, component that has to be modeled with utmost precision. *Nonmanuals* (facial expression, gaze, torso movements) [24] are even more difficult to capture for various reasons. Nonmanuals may stretch over several signs: for instance, facial expression indicates sentence mode (question vs. assertion) and eyebrows and posture relate to information structure by marking the topic. On the single sign level, nonmanuals are e.g. used for negation/affirmation, adjectival information (face: emotion/attitude) or adverbial modification (face: manner of execution). In German sign language (DGS) the parallel "speaking" of the corresponding word, called *mouthing*, is highly important (less important in e.g. ASL [12]). However, it is unclear in which cases mouthing supports comprehension. In many cases, the lack of mouthing simply introduces irritation. Indeed, sign language listeners need the face as a *focus point for their visual attention* because this allows to see hands, face and body at the same time [29]. The usually static faces of avatars generate so little visual interest that the listener's visual focus jumps from hands to mouth to torso etc., making comprehension harder. Generally, nonmanuals have only recently received more attention from the linguistic side [24] but need more research in the area of sign language synthesis.

Our main conclusion is that current avatars with current animation methods cannot reproduce all the subtleties of a human signer's synchronized body behaviors. Therefore, our *working hypothesis* is that avatars need to start from a different point of departure and suggest to use *overarticulated base material* for guiding our animations.

To create overarticulated video remakes, each video was segmented into utterances and glosses by two DGS experts using the ANVIL annotation tool [14]. This transcription, together with the original video, was the basis for the new video recordings, performed by a deaf DGS native speaker with the following instructions: make single signs as clear as possible, include clear mouthing, separate signs cleanly from each other while maintaining overall fluidity.

4.2   Gloss-Based Animation in EMBRScript

We created a database of single gloss animations based the human signer's videos which were used to assemble utterances. The animation notation EMBRScript was particularly suitable as it allows the specification of so-called *k-pose-sequences* [4], i.e. a collection of generalized poses (including IK constraints, morph targets and predefined skeletal configurations), which elegantly corresponded to single glosses. To add parallel movements that span several glosses, we can use additional, separate k-pose-sequences. We extended the existing *BehaviorBuilder* tool [15] to support the definition of single glosses (i.e. one

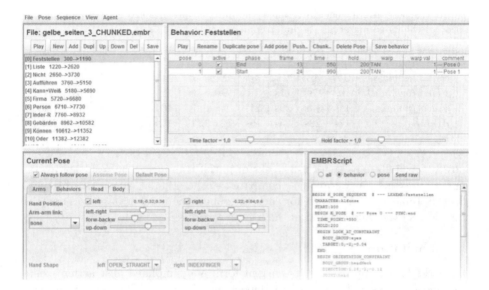

Fig. 2. Screenshot of the BehaviorBuilder tool which allows to create animation on three levels: single pose (bottom left), single gloss (top right) and gloss sequence (top left). The result is a declarative script in the EMBRScript language (bottom right).

k-pose-sequence) and the sequencing of glosses to a complete utterance. Fig. 2 shows the revised tool that allows the interactive creation of single poses, pose sequences (glosses) and gloss sequences. We used the OpenMARY [26] text-to-speech synthesis system to generate viseme animations which were assigned the same start time as the corresponding gloss. Our gloss-based approach is similar to *iLex* [3] which is based on HamNoSys. However, working with HamNoSys requires many tweaks to control the animation so that we suggest to rather use EMBRScript as a separating layer to keep HamNoSys free from low-level animation data.

The animation process followed a tight feedback cycle with a deaf assistant who, in each iteration, provided comments on single signs as well as the overall utterance comprehensibility. This provided the animator with clear priorities whether to optimize hands/arms, facial expression, gaze, upper body or timing. For the future, a formalized feedback with rating scales or fixed feedback categories may be possible. We found that nonmanuals, especially mouthing and gaze, were as important as manual components. Additional feedback concerned general aspects of the 3D scene. Lighting must ensure that face and hands are highly visible, e.g. by using extra light sources. Realistic shadow casting is perceived as a pleasant addition by deaf users as it adds depth and 3D illusion. From interviews with deaf individuals it became clear that the *outer appearance* of the avatar is important. This may be due to the association of avatars as sign language *interpreters* whom deaf people may regard as their representatives.

We created 11 utterances which contained 154 gloss instances, i.e. on average an utterance contained 14 gloss instances. The workload for creating single

Table 1. These are, for each utterance, the number of contained glosses and the duration of the video materials (orginal, remake, avatar)

	1	2	3	4	5	6	7	8	9	10	11
contained glosses	17	18	21	10	8	7	12	21	13	14	13
Video (original)	10s	7s	11s	7s	5s	3s	7s	11s	13s	3s	7s
Video (remake)	14s	14s	20s	14s	9s	6s	16s	19s	19s	7s	13s
Avatar	17s	20s	25s	16s	12s	11s	15s	23s	25s	8s	22s

glosses was 5-25 mins (with 1-2 weeks of initial training). The resulting avatar animation sequences were longer compared to the original video. This becomes clear in Table 1 which shows, for each utterance, the number of glosses and the durations of the video(s) and of the avatar version.

4.3   Limitations

The gloss-based approach in its current form is a simplified abstraction where each gloss always looks the same independent of context. This ignores individual or stylistic variations and grammatical flections, e.g. for directed verbs like GIVE or SHOW. Moreover, glosses do not contain information relating to larger units of an utterance or the discourse such as information structure (old/new distinction). However, we consider the gloss-based approach a useful point of departure that must be extended using e.g. parameterized glosses and an added representation layer for utterance-level and discourse-level information.

Regarding scalability, we experienced limited re-use of glosses at this stage of the project. With a database of 95 glosses we created 11 utterances with 154 gloss instances which means that each gloss was used 1.6 times on average. We assume that gloss reuse increases with the larger projects, once a "basic vocabulary" has been established. It is an open question how large such a basic vocabulary has to be such that the number of new glosses per new utterance is minimal in a specific domain.

5   Comprehensibility Testing

As material we used a corpus of 11 utterances from two e-learning videos (Sec. 4). For every utterance, we wanted to compare the avatar animation (A), the original video (V_{org}) and the overarticulated remake (V_{re}). We invited 13 native signers (6m, 7f), of age 33–55, to the experiment which took 1.5 – 2 hours per subject and was supervised by a deaf assistant. Every subject was compensated with 10 Euro plus travel cost. Since all sessions had to be videotaped for later analysis, subjects had to sign an agreement to grant us scientific usage of the material.

5.1   Method

We set up the following frame conditions: we provided a sign-language-only environment and made the users feel comfortable to criticize the system by having

single sentence evaluation

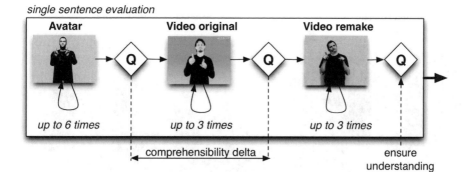

Fig. 3. Evaluation procedure for a single utterance. It was important to ensure understanding to prepare the following utterance test.

supervisors from outside our institute. Since deaf people may have difficulties understanding written commands, the briefing was done in sign language and the questionnaires included pictograms (e.g. smiley signs) for clarification.

To get the subject accustomed to the way our avatar performs sign language we showed three very basic clips ("My name is M-A-X", "My sign name is <sign>" and "My work is interesting") without further testing. Such a *warm-up phase* is quite common [27]. Then, we proceeded with the *evaluation phase* where each of the 11 utterances was displayed in the following scheme (depicted in Fig. 3): First, we showed the avatar version A which could be viewed up to 6 times. Second, we showed the original video V_{org} which could be viewed up to 3 times. Third, we showed the overarticulated remake V_{re} which could be viewed up to 3 times. After each of the three screenings the subject was asked to sign what s/he understood from the respective clip. After the three videos, we showed the video remake once more, this time with text subtitles[6], to make sure that this utterance was understood before proceeding with the next one.

5.2 Analysis and Results

According to [11] the participants' subjective impression of their understanding is not a good indicator of actual understanding. Therefore, we used two complementary methods for measuring comprehensibility. First, as an objective measure, we took the glosses of each utterance and tried to see which ones were repeated by the subject when asked to repeat the content of the utterance. The rate of understanding can be computed by dividing the number of repeated glosses by the total number of glosses. However, this can be misleading if subjects are able to recall unconnected parts of the utterance while not understanding the core meaning. Therefore, we asked our deaf experts to give a subjective estimation of how well the subject had understood the utterance on a 7-point scale. We then took the average of the two experts for each utterance.

---

[6] Subtitles may help subjects understand signs performed very quickly or in a sloppy manner or are unknown because of regional differences.

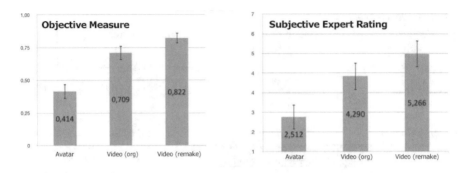

Fig. 4. Comprehensibility results of the objective measure and subjective expert rating

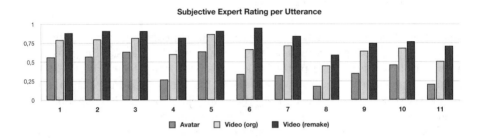

Fig. 5. Subjective expert ratings per utterance (in the order they were displayed)

Fig. 4 summarizes the results. The relative differences between the materials are similar in both measures. What is striking is that for the original video, absolute comprehensibility is only at 71% (objective) and 61% (subjective). Having comprehensibility scores for all three materials allows us to put the avatar score in relation to the others. If we put the avatar in relation to the original video we reach a comprehensibility of 58.4% (objective) and 58.6% (subjective). The harder comparison is that between avatar and remake with 50.4% (objective) and 47.7% (subjective).

Since, by design, we had to display utterances in a fixed order we examined potential ordering effects. One could assume that due to increasing context the understanding would increase. However, Fig. 5 indicates that understandability was quite varied, even for utterances in the later stages of the experiment.

5.3   Discussion

In our comprehensibility tests we take the comparison between avatar and original video to be our goal value. Here, our avatar reached 58.4% or 58.6% which is close to the evaluation results of state-of-the-art systems of around 62% in ViSiCAST [27,13]. Given a very short development time of 4 person months, we conclude that higher scores can be reached. We agree with [13] that a comprehensibility of 90% is possible, but only if a clear shift in research focus takes place in the field of sign language synthesis, towards *nonmanuals* and *prosody*. In terms of synthesis, this implies an extension of the gloss-based approach by adding gloss parameters and an utterance-level layer. In our current implementation nonmanuals are integrated only to a limited degree, partly because the utterance-level is missing. To see our study in the bigger picture we stress that our material of only 11 utterances was quite limited. While many other studies used similarly low quantities of around 10 utterances (e.g. [27,11]) for the future the same standards as in natural language processing should be reached (e.g. [8] used 12 stories of 48-80 signs each).

Regarding evaluation methods, we believe that our *delta evaluation* has two advantages over previous methods. First, it takes into account the limited comprehensibility of the original video material (in our case, this was as low as 71% / 61%) and thus, makes the comparison fairer and may inspire other researchers to dare the direct comparison with human signers. It allows to use more complex content and factors out dialect variation in sign languages that cause certain signs to be unknown in a participant's region. Second, setting our avatar into relation to human signers, we did not have to agree on any absolute measure of comprehension, e.g. that particular pieces of the utterance are more important than others. Defining such measures is work-intensive and subjective. By combining an objective measure (gloss counting) with a subjective expert evaluation we ensure that the understanding of the whole utterance is well captured. Due to our method's design the avatar is put to a slight disadvantage which means that the result represents a lower boundary: the avatar is *at least* as good as the measure indicates.

6   Conclusions

We presented the development and evaluation of a signing avatar, on the basis of an existing general-purpose avatar EMBR. We showed how a gloss-based approach with a tight cyclic animation development, in close cooperation with deaf experts, can lead to state-of-the-art performance for German sign language synthesis. We introduced an overarticulated video remake into the loop based on the working hypothesis that current avatar technology lacks the complexity of human multimodal signal generation. We also created a novel evaluation method we call *delta evaluation* where we compare avatar performance with human signers based on objective gloss counts and subjective expert opinions. This measure is a lower boundary of the real comprehensibility of the avatar. In the development process we identified nonmanual components and prosody as the most urgent issues for increasing comprehensibility significantly beyond 60% which we deem feasible. While theoretical work on nonmanual components and prosody exist (cf. [24]), the operationalization in avatars is scarce (see [8] for a notable exception).

Facial expression also needs more research, especially given the additional need of having the face generate visual interest so that listeners can fixate on it. Current research on the *uncanny valley* suggests that the face is of key importance for overcoming the acceptance problem of avatars [6]. Prerequisite for this is a consistent evaluation scheme like *delta evaluation*. This needs to be extended from the utterance level to the level of *whole text/discourse* understanding. We also stress that involvement of deaf people is crucial not only for defining use cases and for evaluation but, even more so, for creating animations and developing animation methods. Hence, we argue for a stronger *scientific* involvement of deaf individuals. This implies the development of better tools to allow animation building in the deaf community, e.g. with the help of novel interface technology [17].

Moreover, we conjecture that research on sign language synthesis will generate important insights for *coverbal gesture synthesis*. In "Kendon's continuum" sign language is one extreme pole with a fluid transition to coverbal gesture [21]. While speech is missing from sign language, it remains a highly multimodal problem that involves face, body, hands and arms. Making these cohere in natural orchestrated movements is a goal, both in speaking and non-speaking cultures.

Acknowledgements. This study was commissioned by the German Federal Ministry of Labour and Social Affairs (eGovernment Strategie Teilhabe). We would like to thank our two deaf DGS experts Peter Schaar and Iris König for their help in interviews, video recordings, DGS transcriptions and evaluation studies. Thanks to our reviewers whose comments were crucial for the revision. Part of this research has been carried out within the framework of the Excellence Cluster Multimodal Computing and Interaction (MMCI), sponsored by the German Research Foundation (DFG).

References

1. Elliott, R., Glauert, J.R.W., Kennaway, J.R., Marshall, I., Safar, E.: Linguistic modelling and language-processing technologies for avatar-based sign language presentation. Univers. Access Inf. Soc. 6, 375–391 (2008)
2. Filhol, M.: Zebedee: a lexical description model for sign language synthesis. Tech. Rep. 2009-08, LIMSI (2009)
3. Hanke, T.: iLex - a tool for sign language lexicography and corpus analysis. In: Proceedings of the 3rd International Conference on Language Resources and Evaluation, pp. 923–926 (2002)
4. Heloir, A., Kipp, M.: Realtime animation of interactive agents: Specification and realization. Journal of Applied Artificial Intelligence 24(6), 510–529 (2010)
5. Heloir, A., Kipp, M., Gibet, S., Courty, N.: Specifying and evaluating data-driven style transformation for gesturing embodied agents. In: Prendinger, H., Lester, J.C., Ishizuka, M. (eds.) IVA 2008. LNCS (LNAI), vol. 5208, pp. 215–222. Springer, Heidelberg (2008)
6. Hodgins, J., Jörg, S., O'Sullivan, C., Park, S.I., Mahler, M.: The saliency of anomalies in animated human characters. ACM Trans. Appl. Percept. 7, 22:1–22:14 (2010)
7. Holt, J.A.: Demographic, Stanford achievement test - 8th edition for deaf and hard of hearing students: Reading comprehension subgroup results. Amer. Annals Deaf. 138, 172–175 (1993)

8. Huenerfauth, M.: A linguistically motivated model for speed and pausing in animations of american sign language. ACM Trans. Access. Comput. 2, 9:1–9:31 (2009)
9. Huenerfauth, M., Hanson, V.L.: Sign language in the interface: Access for deaf signers. In: Stephanidis, C. (ed.) The Universal Access Handbook. CRC Press, Boca Raton (2009)
10. Huenerfauth, M., Zhao, L., Gu, E., Allbeck, J.: Evaluating american sign language generation through the participation of native ASL signers. In: Proc. of the 9th International ACM Conference on Computers and Accessibility (ASSETS), pp. 211–218. ACM, New York (2007)
11. Huenerfauth, M., Zhao, L., Gu, E., Allbeck, J.: Evaluating american sign language generation by native ASL signers. ACM Transactions on Access Computing 1(1), 1–27 (2008)
12. Johnston, T.: Australian Sign Language (Auslan): An introduction to sign language linguistics. Cambridge University Press, Cambridge (2007)
13. Kennaway, J.R., Glauert, J.R.W., Zwitserlood, I.: Providing signed content on the internet by synthesized animation. ACM Transactions on Computer-Human Interaction (TOCHI) 14(3), 15–29 (2007)
14. Kipp, M.: Anvil: The video annotation research tool. In: Durand, J., Gut, U., Kristofferson, G. (eds.) Handbook of Corpus Phonology. Oxford University Press, Oxford (to appear, 2011)
15. Kipp, M., Heloir, A., Schröder, M., Gebhard, P.: Realizing multimodal behavior: Closing the gap between behavior planning and embodied agent presentation. In: Safonova, A. (ed.) IVA 2010. LNCS, vol. 6356, pp. 57–63. Springer, Heidelberg (2010)
16. Kipp, M., Neff, M., Albrecht, I.: An Annotation Scheme for Conversational Gestures: How to economically capture timing and form. Journal on Language Resources and Evaluation - Special Issue on Multimodal Corpora 41(3-4), 325–339 (2007)
17. Kipp, M., Nguyen, Q.: Multitouch Puppetry: Creating coordinated 3D motion for an articulated arms. In: Proceedings of the ACM International Conference on Interactive Tabletops and Surfaces (2010)
18. Kipp, M., Nguyen, Q., Heloir, A., Matthes, S.: Assessing the deaf user perspective on sign language avatars. In: Proceedings of the 13th International ACM SIGACCESS Conference on Computers and Accessibility (ASSETS). ACM Press, New York (2011)
19. Kita, S., van Gijn, I., van der Hulst, H.: Movement phases in signs and co-speech gestures, and their transcription by human coders. In: Wachsmuth, I., Fröhlich, M. (eds.) GW 1997. LNCS (LNAI), vol. 1371, pp. 23–35. Springer, Heidelberg (1998)
20. Liddell, S.K., Johnson, R.E.: American sign language: The phonological base. Sign Language Studies 64, 195–277 (1989)
21. McNeill, D.: Hand and Mind: What Gestures Reveal about Thought. University of Chicago Press, Chicago (1992)
22. Neff, M., Kipp, M., Albrecht, I., Seidel, H.P.: Gesture Modeling and Animation Based on a Probabilistic Recreation of Speaker Style. ACM Transactions on Graphics 27(1), 1–24 (2008)
23. Niewiadomski, R., Bevacqua, E., Mancini, M., Pelachaud, C.: Greta: An interactive expressive ECA systems. In: Proc. of the 8th International Conference on Autonomous Agents and Multiagent Systems (AAMAS), pp. 1399–1400 (2009)
24. Pfau, R., Quer, J.: Nonmanuals: their prosodic and grammatical roles. In: Brentari, D. (ed.) Sign languages (Cambridge Language Surveys), pp. 381–402. Cambridge University Press, Cambridge (2010)

25. Prillwitz, S., Leven, R., Zienert, H., Hanke, T., Henning, J.: HamNoSys Version 2.0. Hamburg Notation System for Sign Language. An Introductory Guides, Signum (1989)
26. Schröder, M., Trouvain, J.: The german text-to-speech synthesis system mary: A tool for research, development and teaching. International Journal of Speech Technology 6, 365–377 (2003)
27. Sheard, M., Schoot, S., Zwitserlood, I., Verlinden, M., Weber, I.: Evaluation reports 1 and 2 of the EU project essential sign language information on government networks, Deliverable D6.2 (March 2004)
28. Stokoe, W.C.: Sign language structure: An outline of the visual communication system of the American deaf. Studies in linguistics, Occasional papers 8 (1960)
29. Swisher, V., Christie, K., Miller, S.: The reception of signs in peripheral vision by deaf persons. Sign Language Studies 63, 99–125 (1989)
30. Thiebaux, M., Marshall, A., Marsella, S., Kallman, M.: SmartBody: Behavior realization for embodied conversational agents. In: Proc. of the 7th Int. Conf. on Autonomous Agents and Multiagent Systems, AAMAS (2008)
31. Wolfe, R., McDonald, J., Davidson, M.J., Frank, C.: Using an animation-based technology to support reading curricula for deaf elementary schoolchildren. In: The 22nd Annual International Technology & Persons with Disabilities Conference (2007)

How to Train Your Avatar: A Data Driven Approach to Gesture Generation

Chung-Cheng Chiu and Stacy Marsella

University of Southern California
Institute for Creative Technologies
12015 Waterfront Drive
Playa Vista, CA 90094
{chiu,marsella}ict.usc.edu

Abstract. The ability to gesture is key to realizing virtual characters that can engage in face-to-face interaction with people. Many applications take an approach of predefining possible utterances of a virtual character and building all the gesture animations needed for those utterances. We can save effort on building a virtual human if we can construct a general gesture controller that will generate behavior for novel utterances. Because the dynamics of human gestures are related to the prosody of speech, in this work we propose a model to generate gestures based on prosody. We then assess the naturalness of the animations by comparing them against human gestures. The evaluation results were promising, human judgments show no significant difference between our generated gestures and human gestures and the generated gestures were judged as significantly better than real human gestures from a different utterance.

1 Introduction

A virtual human's non-verbal behavior is one of the main criterion that enriches the human-agent interaction. Users are sensitive to whether the gestures of a virtual human are consistent with its speech [9], and therefore a conversational virtual human should be animated based on its speech. One approach to achieve this is by using pre-defined human speech and creating specific motions for each sentence. Often in this case virtual human systems use hand-crafted animations or animations generated by capture technology [1,2]. However, neither of these methods scale well with the length of the dialogue and the effort required to generate new animations becomes significant.

Another approach is to use the text of the speech and construct mappings between features of the text and gestures. For example, [7] and [15] use the syntactic and semantic structure of the speech text along with additional domain knowledge and map them to various gestures. There is also work [18] that uses semi-automated data-driven approach that applies machine learning techniques on textual features and domain knowledge.

However, the aforementioned approaches do not consider the prosodic features in the verbal speech. In human conversations, the same speech spoken in different

H. Högni Vilhjálmsson et al. (Eds.): IVA 2011, LNAI 6895, pp. 127–140, 2011.

manners can express different meanings and much of this difference is conveyed through prosody. In addition, studies show that kinematic features of a speaker's gestures such as speed and acceleration are usually correlated with the prosody of the speech [23].

The goal of this work is to present an automated gesture generation process that maps features of speech to gestures, including prosodic features. There has been previous work that uses prosody information to generate gestures [6,19,17,16]. The approach taken in [17,16] selects animation segments from motion database based on audio input, and synthesizes these selected animations into the gesture animation. Since the approach uses existing motions, the gestures it produces are constrained by those that existed in the motion database.

In this work, we propose a gesture generator that produces conversation animations for virtual humans conditioned on prosody. The generator is built based on hierarchical factored conditional restricted Boltzmann machines (HFCRBMs) [8] with some modification. The model derives features describing human gesture and constrains animation generations to be within the gesture feature space. The method defines the role of prosody as a motion transition controller and learns this relation from the training data. The training data contains audio and motion capture data of people having conversations, and the model learns detailed dynamics of the gesture motions. After training, the gesture generator can be applied to generate animations with recorded speech for a virtual human. Our generator is not designed to learn all kinds of gestures but rather motions related to prosody like rhythmic movements. Gestures tied to semantic information like iconic gestures, pantomimes, deictic, and emblematic gestures are not considered in this work.

An evaluation of our approach with human subjects showed that the rating of animations generated by our learned generator from the audio of an utterance is similar to the original motion capture data and their difference is not statistically significant. Both cases are significantly better than using the motion capture data from a different utterance.

The contribution of this work is three-fold.

- We propose a model that learns speech-to-gesture generation.
- The model provides a way to derive features describing human gestures which helps gesture generations.
- Our gesture generator suggests that prosody provides information about motion movement that makes a prosody-based approach feasible for generating a subclass of arm-gestures.

The remainder of the paper is organized as follows. Section 2 contains a review of related works, Section 3 explains our gesture generator, and Section 4 presents the experimental results. The conclusion is summarized in Section 5.

2   Related Work

To generate gestures, BEAT [7] analyzes the syntactic relation between the surface text and gestures. The input text is parsed into a tree structure containing information such as clauses, themes/rhemes, objects, and actions. Using this information and a knowledge base containing additional information about the world, BEAT then maps them to a set of gestures. The Nonverbal Behavior Generator (NVBG) [15] extends this framework by making a clearer distinction between the communicative intent embedded in the surface text (e.g. affirmation, intensification, negation, etc.) and the realization of the gestures. This design allows NVBG to generate gestures even without a well-defined knowledge base. Stone et al. [20] proposed a framework to extract utterances and gesture motions from recorded human data then generate animations by synthesizing these utterances and motion segments. This framework includes an authoring mechanism to segment utterances and gesture motions then a selection mechanism to compose utterances and gestures. Neff et al. [18] made a comprehensive list of mappings between gesture types and their relations with semantic tags and derived the transition probability of motions from the sample data. The framework captures the details of human motion and preserves the gesture style of each performer, which can be generalized to generate gestures with various forms of input.

One major drawback of the text-based generation approaches [7,15] lies in the limited expressiveness. With this approach, it is not easy to represent detailed information of human motions with meta-description, especially with respect to the dynamics of joint movement. The same dialogue can be spoken with different speed and prosody for which the gesture motions have to be synchronized well with to make the behavior natural.

Audio-based motion generations has been addressed for manipulating facial expression [5], and similar approach has been extended to generate gestures [17]. A common idea of previous works is to collect a set of animation segments, define an objective function to model the relation between utterances and motions and the sequential relation among motions, and synthesize gesture animation via optimizing the objective function. The Hidden Markov models (HMM) fit this design, and it has been applied to generate head motion [6,19] and arm gestures [17]. The HMM-based approach directly associates motions with prosodic features and tends to overfit for learning arm gestures [17]. Thus, [16] proposed to combine conditional random fields (CRFs) with HMMs. HMMs first model the transitions of motions, and CRFs then learns the relation between utterances and hidden states of HMMs. The framework maps prosody to animations through CRFs and HMMs, and applies Markov Decision Processes to synthesize animations. Previous works generate gestures via synthesizing animation segments, so the generated animations are limited to animation segments in the motion database. Our system explicitly generates animation frame-by-frame and does not have this limitation.

3   Gesture Generator

The gesture generator takes past motion frames and generates the next motion frame conditioned on pitch, intensity and correlation audio features. The

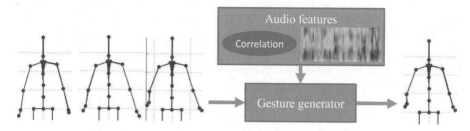

Fig. 1. The architecture of the generation process. Gesture generators take past motion frames and generate next motion frame conditioned on pitch, intensity, and correlation values.

prosodic features of pitch and intensity influence how the generator creates animation, and the correlation parameters indicate how strong that influence is and how much the gesture motion should be correlated with those prosody features. The correlation parameters provide a handle for users to tune the motion of virtual human: the higher the correlation parameters, the more the velocity and acceleration of motions will be correlated with pitch and intensity. On generating the next motion frame, gesture generator not only takes into account the audio feature of current time but also audio features of previous and future time frames. The architecture of entire framework is shown in Fig. 1.

Our framework does not incorporate semantic or syntactic information of the accompanying speech. As we noted in the introduction, semantic content as well as prosody of the utterance correlates with human gestures. Gestures like iconic or deictic gestures carry specific semantic content of the dialogue like abstract depiction of actions, object, or orientations. The space of these kinds of semantic content is large, and therefore a gesture generator requires a rich set of knowledge to map general utterances to gestures. However, our current dataset is small comparing to the entire space of semantic content, and the knowledge for mapping these kinds of semantic content to gestures is sparse. Thus, in our current work we excluded the mapping between semantic content and gestures but limited our focus to prosody-based gesture generation, in which the gestures we address is similar to the idea of motor gesture [13]. Prosody and motion correspond to emphasis, and both of them can exhibit the emotional state of the speaker. We explore the capability of prosody for gesture generation in this work and take semantic content of utterances as an important channel for future extension.

We use motion capture and audio data of human conversations to learn the gesture generator's mapping of prosody to gesture animations. This data must first be processed before it can be used for training. Specifically, we defined a criterion to extract motion segments containing gestures. We analyzed motion data to identify gesture motions and non-gesture motions, and determine what y-coordinate value of wrists best separates these two sets. Motion frames having at least one wrist's y-coordinate higher than this value are defined as gestures. This rule is then applied to extract gesture motions. Among valid motion frames, only the animation segments with length longer than 2 seconds are kept. After the valid motion frames are identified, the corresponding audio features are extracted. The time constraint on data selection will exclude gestures with short period of time. The rationale for defining this constraint is that in our data analysis most of gestures performed in less than 2 seconds are often either iconic gestures or gestures unrelated to utterances, and neither cases are gestures we want to learn. In the motion capture data most of gestures stay for a long period of time.

The extraction process identifies the data containing gestures, and there are two cases that we need to manually exclude from the training data. The first case is the semantic-related gestures. Our current gesture generators use prosody features for motion generation, and prosody features do not preserve the semantic content of the dialogue. Therefore, any semantic-based gestures will mislead the model training and have to be excluded from the data. The second case is non-gesture motion data. Sometimes actors are adjusting their motion capture suit, scratching, or performing an initialization posture which is required for motion capture calibration. We analyzed the extracted motions and excluded these two cases to get final data set.

3.1 Requirements for Building Gesture Generators

A common approach of previous work is to generate gesture motions via synthesizing existing motion segments [17,16]. The gesture generator we are building is a generative function that takes previous motion frames and audio features as input and then outputs motion frames. In other words, the gesture generator learns the relation between previous motion frames, audio features, and the current motion frame, and uses this relation to generate animations. The benefit of this design is that the gesture generator can generalize better to novel speech and create new gestures, in contrast to the previous approach which is limited to existing motion segments. The potential problem of this design is that it runs the risk of generating unnatural gestures. The domain of motion frames is *joint rotation*, and if the generative function learns the motion generation with this domain, then the output of the function is too unconstrained – it can be any joint rotation.

Thus, on building a generative function for gesture generator, a key challenge is to prevent the generation of unnatural gestures. Human gestures move only within certain space and contain certain patterns, so instead of learning the function within an unconstrained space of *joint rotation*, it will be more effective to learn gesture generation in the constrained *gesture motion*. For this reason, our gesture generator detects features of gesture motion, represents gestures in terms of motion features, and learns gesture generation with this new representation system. With the domain constrained in gesture feature space, gesture generators have a better chance of producing natural motions.

Another challenge comes from the mapping between audio features and motion frames. Both an audio feature vector and a motion frame are real value vectors with high dimension, and the space of possible values is large. A gesture generation is a mapping between two sequences of these vectors, and the under-lying relation is complex. This brings a requirement for a gesture generator to learn a function that captures this complex relation.

In sum, there are three things a gesture generator has to be capable of learning: gesture motion features, temporal relation of gesture motions, and the relation between audio features and gesture motions. Hierarchical factored conditional restricted Boltzmann machines (HFCRBMs) [8] is a learning model that matches this criterion. It is an extension of deep belief networks (DBNs) [11] that can deal with sequential data. We applied some modification to HFCRBMs to build the gesture generator. Following sections introduce DBNs and components of modified HFCRBMs.

3.2   Background of Modified HFCRBM

The DBN stacks multiple layers of Restricted Boltzmann Machines (RBMs) to construct a multi-level neural network. A multi-level neural network is known to be able to represent a complex function, but it usually suffers from long convergence time and getting trapped into local optimum easily. The way DBN builds neural networks can significantly reduce the convergence time and improve the performance.

The major philosophy behind the design of DBN is to learn a better feature representation for the task. In most of cases, the original representation of the data is not the best way to describe the data and we will prefer to define some features to represent the data. For example, in the object detection task we may prefer to represent an image with edge features than a pixel vector. The DBN applies an unsupervised learning algorithm to initialize its network connection, and the algorithm performs a feature detection process. With the unsupervised learning process, each layer of a DBN acts as a feature detector, and the DBN uses this hierarchical structure to learn features that can model the input-output relation of the given task. The DBN was proposed to learn static data in which the sequential information is not considered in the model. The HFCRBM ex-tends the DBN to consider sequential information. Following sections describe components related to HFCRBMs and modified HFCRBMs: CRBMs, RCRBMs, and FCRBMs.

CRBMs and RCRBMs. The conditional Restricted Boltzmann Machine (CRBM) [22], as shown in Fig. 2a, is a artificial neural network with a binary hidden layer and multiple visible layers taking time-series data as input. The net-work between the hidden layer h and the visible layers v is a complete bipartite graph in which links between h and v_t is similar to a Hopfield net [12]. The struc-ture differs from Hopfield net in that there are no links between visible nodes and they are connected indirectly through hidden nodes. Both h and v_t have directed links from visible layers for past visible data $v_{t-1}, v_{t-2}, \ldots, v_{t-n}$ where n denotes the order of the model. This network takes past data $x_{t-n} \ldots x_{t-1}$ as input for $v_{t-n} \ldots v_{t-1}$ and output x_t at v_t, and uses the output error to update the connection weights. After training connection weights with time-series data,

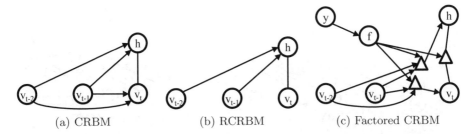

Fig. 2. (a) A CRBM with order 2 where vs denote visible layers, t represent index in time, and h is the hidden layer. (b) A RCRBM with order 2. (c) A FCRBM with order 2 where f denotes feature layer, y represent labels, and triangles represent factored multiplications.

the model can predict future data with given data sequence. We can take current output data x_t to form a new input sequence $x_{t-n+1} \ldots x_t$ for the model and generate next data x_{t+1}. By doing so, the model can iteratively generate a long sequence of data based on a short initial sequence. Reduced CRBMs (RCRBMs), as shown in Fig. 2b, are CRBMs without the lateral links between visible layers. RCRBMs generate data sequence with the same process of CRBMs, but since there are no lateral links between visible layers the output of v_t depends only on the links with the hidden layer.

Factored Conditional Restricted Boltzmann Machines. CRBMs capture the transition dynamic of the time series data in an unsupervised way. They generate data sequence based on only the information of past visible data. In some applications, we would like to use annotation information to help recognition and generation. Taylor & Hinton proposed factored conditional restricted Boltzmann machine with contextual multiplicative interaction (we will simply call it FCRBM in the following text for clarity) which extends CRBMs to output data conditioned on annotated information [21]. The architecture of the FCRBM is shown in Fig. 2c. The FCRBM preserves the original structure of the CRBM, and adds additional input layer for annotated information, the label layer. One major difference in structure is that there are no direct links between layers, and they connect indirectly through factor nodes. All factor nodes have directed connections from the label layer, and through the label layer the annotated information play the role of gating values propagating within network. In this design, FCRBMs output current data based on given data sequence conditioned on annotated information, and update connection weights based on output error.

3.3   Modified HFCRBM

The modified HFCRBMs stacks FCRBMs on top of CRBMs to formulate a temporal model based on features identified by CRBMs. This is different from the original HFCRBM which stacks FCRBMs on top of RCRBMs. The architecture of the two models are shown in Fig. 3. The original HFCRBM was applied to

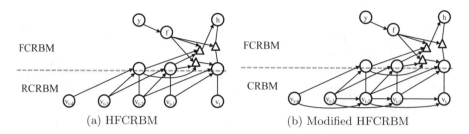

FCRBM

Fig. 3. The difference between the original HFCRBM and our modification lies in the bottom level model

learn walking motions with different styles [8]. The labels used in that work are style labels. To generate a motion with specific style the generation process has to be manipulated using style labels, so RCRBMs are necessary. On the other hand, in our case the gesture generation does not need to be completely manipulated with respect to labels (audio features) and can depend more on past visible data, namely previous gesture motions. Thus, the lateral links in CRBMs are beneficial for gesture generators, and we replace RCRBMs with CRBMs in HFCRBMs.

The modified HFCRBM satisfies our three requirements for gesture generation in that the bottom CRBM learns the features of gesture motions, and the top FCRBM learns the temporal relation of gestures and its relation between audio features. In the following paragraphs we will call the modified HFCRBMs as HFCRBMs for simplicity.

We have also added a sparse coding criterion to the unsupervised learning (training CRBMs) step because in our initial investigations it further improves the accuracy of gesture generation. Different from [14] as they only update the bias term of the hidden layer for encouraging sparsity, we also update the connection weight of CRBMs. The objective function regarding the sparsity term is expressed with cross entropy between the desired and actual distributions of the hidden layer as described in [10].

3.4   Training and Generation

The training process of our gesture generator is shown in Fig 4. The gesture generator first performs unsupervised learning on motion data to identify features which better represent the temporal pattern of human motion. After these features are identified with CRBMs, HFCRBMs represent motion data using these features, and take data sequences represented with new features to train top-layer FCRBMs. FCRBMs take data sequence as input and learn to generate data at the next time frame conditioned on audio features. After training FCRBMs, HFCRBMs learn to generate gesture motion based on audio features.

The HFCRBM-based gesture generator requires two input: an initial gesture motion and a sequence of audio features. The initial gesture motion is a required input for the visible layer v of HFCRBMs. A designer can specify what the initial

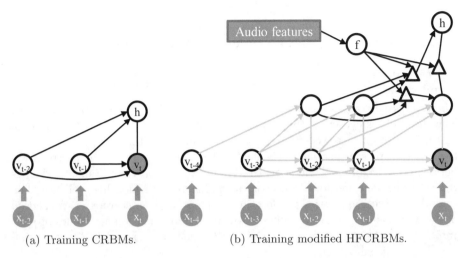

(a) Training CRBMs.   (b) Training modified HFCRBMs.

Fig. 4. The training process of modified HFCRBMs for gesture generators. (a) The CRBMs of the modified HFCRBM is trained with motion sequence x to find feature representation. The gray-filled node represents output node of the model, and the connection weight is updated based on the output error compared with the training data. (b) After training CRBMs, the data goes bottom-up to train top layer FCRBMs. The network generate output conditioned on audio features, and update connection weights based on prediction error. In this step the links of CRBMs as shown in light gray color are fixed, and only the connection weights of FCRBMs are updated.

gesture of an avatar is preferred through this motion sequence, or can set them to all zero vectors for simplicity. The sequence of audio features are data extracted from given utterance, and is the input to the label layer of HFCRBMs. The HFCRBM takes its output as part of the input data of next generation step, and the entire generation process will output a sequence of motion with the same length as the audio data. The resulting data is the gesture motion for given utterances.

3.5 Smoothing

The motion sequence generated by HFCRBMs can contain some noise and the difference between frames may be greater than natural gestures. Although each motion frame is still a natural gesture and this kind of noise is rare in the output, users are sensitive to the discontinuity of the animation and a short unnatural motion can ruin the entire animation. Therefore, after gesture motions are generated, an additional smoothing process is performed on the output result.

The smoothing process computes the wrist position of each generated frame, and calculate the acceleration of wrist movement. If the wrist acceleration of one motion frame exceeds some threshold, we reduce the acceleration via modifying the joint rotation velocity of that motion frame to be closer to the velocity of previous joint rotations. The new motion frame at time t is computed by:

$r = 0.2$

$x'_t = x_t$

while (wrist acceleration of x'_t) > threshold and $r < 1$ **do**

$\quad x' = (1 - r)(x_t - 2x'_{t-1} + x'_{t-2}) + 2x'_{t-1} - x'_{t-2}$

$\quad r+ = 0.1$

end while

where x' is smoothed motion frame, and x is original output motion frame. The threshold is chosen as the maximum wrist acceleration value of the human gesturing motion observed from the motion capture data. The equation inside the while-loop is adjusting the velocity of current frame to an interpolation between the original velocity and the velocity of its previous frame, and x'_t is the resulting new motion frame corresponding to the smoothed velocity. The smoothness criterion, wrist acceleration, is computed based on the *translation* of the wrist joints, while the values x within update equation are values of joint *rotations*. For a motion frame at time t that does not exceed the acceleration threshold, it is smoothed as:

$$x'_t = 0.8 \cdot x_t + (x'_{t-1} + x_{t+1})/15 + (x'_{t-2} + x_{t+2})/30$$

4   Experiments

We evaluated the quality of our generated gestures by comparing the gestures it generates for utterances with the original motion capture for those utterances as well as using motion capture from different utterances. In the experiment, our data is the dataset used for the study of human sensitivity for conversational virtual human [9]. The dataset contains audio and motion of groups of people having conversations. There are two groups in the dataset, male and female group, and each group has three people. There are two types of conversations, debate and dominant speaker, and each type has five topics. We used the debate conversation data of male group for experiments. The motion capture data contains the skeleton of subjects and the recorded joints movement are a vector with 69 degree of freedom. Since this work focus mainly on arm gestures, we removed leg, spine, and head movement from the data. Elements containing all zeros in the joint rotation vectors are also removed. After removing these elements, the resulting joint rotation vector has 21 degree of freedom.

We extracted pitch and intensity values from audio using Praat [4]. The values of pitch and intensity ranged from zero to hundreds. To normalize pitch and intensity values to help model learning, the pitch values are adjusted via taking $log(x + 1) - 4$ and setting negative values to zero, and the intensity values are adjusted via taking $log(x) - 3$. The new pitch values range 0 to 2.4, and the new intensity values range 0 to 1.4. The log normalization process also correspond to human's log perception property.

In the training of modified HFCRBMs, both the hidden layer of CRBMs and FCRBMs have 300 nodes. The correlation parameters of each time frame is computed as the correlation of prosody sequence and motion sequence with a

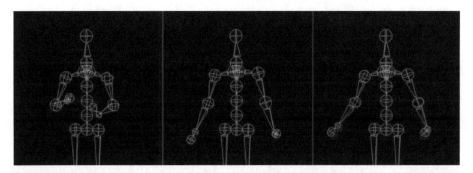

Fig. 5. The video we used for evaluation. We use a simple skeleton to demonstrate the gesture instead of mapping the animation to a virtual human to prevent other factors that can distract participants.

window of $\pm 1/6$ seconds. The audio features for gesture generators at each time frame also has a window of $\pm 1/6$ seconds. We trained the model with the audio and motion capture data of one actor, and use the other actor's speech as a test case to generate a set of gesture animations. We applied the criterion described in Section 3 to extract training and testing data, and there are total 1140 frames (38 seconds) of training data and 1591 frames (53 seconds) of testing data. Since testing data does not have correlation values, we sample correlation parameters from training data to simulate a pseudo-random values. We applied the same criterion as for training data to extract prosody and pseudo-random correlation to compose audio features for testing data.

4.1 Evaluation

We used our gesture generator to generate gesture animations with testing data, and to evaluate the quality of generated animations, we compare them with two gesture animations:

- The original motion capture data of the testing data.
- The motion capture data of the test case actor with respect to other utterance.

For the second case, we used the same extraction techniques described in Section 3 to derive motion capture and audio data. We hypothesize that the gesture animations generated by our model will be significantly better than the motion capture data from different utterances, and the difference between generated animation and actual human gestures will not be significant.

We displayed the three animations side-by-side, segmented them to the same length, and rendered them into videos accompanied with original audio. One example frame of our video is shown in Fig. 5. There are total of 14 clips with length 2 to 7 seconds. The relative horizontal position of Original, Generated, and Unmatched cases is different and balanced between clips (e.g. Original is on the left 5 times, middle 5 times, and right 4 times). The presentation of

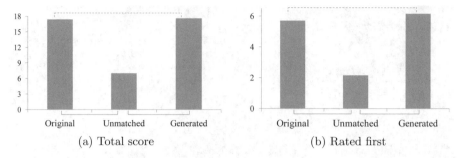

Fig. 6. Average rating for gesture animations. Dashed lines indicate two sets are not significantly different, solid lines indicate two sets are significantly different.

clips to participants was randomized. An example video can be found in [3]. In this example video, the left one is the motion capture data with respect to different utterance, the middle one is the original gesture, and the right one is the generated gestures. Since the motion capture data with respect to different utterances is real human motion, participants can not tell the difference simply based on whether the motion is natural; they have to match the motion with speech to do the evaluation. We recruited 20 participants with ages ranging from around 25 to 55. All participants are familiar with computer animations, and some of them are animators for virtual human or experts on human gestures. We asked participants to rank which gesture animation in the video best matches the speech.

We performed balanced one-way ANOVA on the ranking results and the analysis result suggests that at least one sample is significantly different than the other two. We then applied Student t-test to test our specific hypotheses. The evaluation results are shown in Fig. 6. On the number of being ranked first, the difference between the original gesture motion and the generated gesture motion is not significant, and both them are significantly better than the unmatched gesture motion. We applied another study via assigning 2 point for ranked-first cases and 1 point for ranked-second cases, and calculated the overall score of each motion. Hypothesis testing show that the generated motion is not different from the original motion, and they are both significantly better than the unmatched gestures. This result implies that the movement of generated gesture animations are natural, and the dynamics of motions are consistent with utterances.

5   Conclusions

We have proposed a method for learning prosody-based motion generators for virtual human with recorded speech. Specifically, we modified HFCRBMs to build a model that learns the temporal relation of human gesture and the relation between prosody and motion dynamics. The model is trained with motion capture and audio data of human conversations to formulate an audio-based gesture generator. Gesture generators learned to generate motion frames based on previous gesture motions and prosody information, and are applied to produce gesture animations using another set of speech audio. Evaluation results showed that the produced gestures were significantly better than using human gestures corresponding to different utterances, and there was no significant difference between produced animation and actual human gestures used in the conversations. This work lays a foundation toward building a comprehensive gesture generator. The next step is to explore speech information other than prosody and include other categories of gestures like iconic and deictic gestures to improve the gesture generator.

Acknowledgements. This research was sponsored by the U.S. Army Research, Development, and Engineering Command (RDECOM) Simulation Training and Technology Center (STTC). The content or information presented does not necessarily reflect the position or the policy of the Government, and no official endorsement should be inferred.

References

1. http://ict.usc.edu/projects/gunslinger
2. http://ict.usc.edu/projects/responsive_virtual_human_museum_guides/
3. http://www.youtube.com/watch?v=OsZORI9JH60
4. Boersma, P.: Praat, a system for doing phonetics by computer. Glot International 5, 341–345 (2001)
5. Brand, M.: Voice puppetry. In: Proceedings of the 26th Annual Conference on Computer Graphics and Interactive Techniques, SIGGRAPH 1999, pp. 21–28. ACM Press, New York (1999)
6. Busso, C., Deng, Z., Grimm, M., Neumann, U., Narayanan, S.: Rigid head motion in expressive speech animation: Analysis and synthesis. IEEE Transactions on Audio, Speech, and Language Processing 15(3), 1075–1086 (2007)
7. Cassell, J., Vilhjálmsson, H.H., Bickmore, T.: Beat: the behavior expression animation toolkit. In: SIGGRAPH 2001: Proceedings of the 28th Annual Conference on Computer Graphics and Interactive Techniques, pp. 477–486. ACM, New York (2001)
8. Chiu, C.C., Marsella, S.: A style controller for generating virtual human behaviors. In: Proceedings of the 10th International Joint Conference on Autonomous Agents and Multiagent Systems, AAMAS 2011, vol. 1 (2011)
9. Ennis, C., McDonnell, R., O'Sullivan, C.: Seeing is believing: body motion dominates in multisensory conversations. In: ACM SIGGRAPH 2010 papers, SIGGRAPH 2010, pp. 91:1–91:9. ACM, New York (2010)
10. Hinton, G.: A practical guide to training restricted boltzmann machines. UTML TR 2010003, Department of Computer Science, University of Toronto (August 2010)
11. Hinton, G.E., Osindero, S., Teh, Y.-W.: A fast learning algorithm for deep belief nets. Neural Comput. 18(7), 1527–1554 (2006)
12. Hopfield, J.J.: Neural networks and physical systems with emergent collective computational abilities. Proceedings of the National Academy of Sciences 79(8), 2554–2558 (1982)

13. Krauss, R.M., Chen, Y., Gottesman, R.F.: Lexical gestures and lexical access: a process model. In: McNeill, D. (ed.) Language and Gesture. Cambridge University Press, Cambridge (2000)

14. Lee, H., Ekanadham, C., Ng, A.: Sparse deep belief net model for visual area v2. In: Platt, J.C., Koller, D., Singer, Y., Roweis, S. (eds.) Advances in Neural Information Processing Systems, vol. 20, pp. 873–880. MIT Press, Cambridge (2008)

15. Lee, J., Marsella, S.C.: Nonverbal behavior generator for embodied conversational agents. In: Gratch, J., Young, M., Aylett, R.S., Ballin, D., Olivier, P. (eds.) IVA 2006. LNCS (LNAI), vol. 4133, pp. 243–255. Springer, Heidelberg (2006)

16. Levine, S., Krähenbühl, P., Thrun, S., Koltun, V.: Gesture controllers. In: ACM SIGGRAPH 2010 papers, SIGGRAPH 2010, pp. 124:1–124:11. ACM, New York (2010)

17. Levine, S., Theobalt, C., Koltun, V.: Real-time prosody-driven synthesis of body language. ACM Trans. Graph 28, 172:1–172:10 (2009), http://doi.acm.org/10.1145/1618452.1618518

18. Neff, M., Kipp, M., Albrecht, I., Seidel, H.-P.: Gesture modeling and animation based on a probabilistic re-creation of speaker style. ACM Trans. Graph 27(1), 1–24 (2008)

19. Sargin, M.E., Yemez, Y., Erzin, E., Tekalp, A.M.: Analysis of head gesture and prosody patterns for prosody-driven head-gesture animation. IEEE Transactions on Pattern Analysis and Machine Intelligence 30(8), 1330–1345 (2008)

20. Stone, M., DeCarlo, D., Oh, I., Rodriguez, C., Stere, A., Lees, A., Bregler, C.: Speaking with hands: creating animated conversational characters from recordings of human performance. In: SIGGRAPH 2004: ACM SIGGRAPH 2004 Papers, pp. 506–513. ACM, New York (2004)

21. Taylor, G., Hinton, G.: Factored conditional restricted Boltzmann machines for modeling motion style. In: Bottou, L., Littman, M. (eds.) Proceedings of the 26th International Conference on Machine Learning, pp. 1025–1032. Omnipress, Montreal (2009)

22. Taylor, G.W., Hinton, G.E., Roweis, S.T.: Modeling human motion using binary latent variables. In: Schölkopf, B., Platt, J., Hoffman, T. (eds.) Advances in Neural Information Processing Systems, vol. 19, pp. 1345–1352. MIT Press, Cambridge (2007)

23. Valbonesi, L., Ansari, R., McNeill, D., Quek, F., Duncan, S., McCullough, K.E., Bryll, R.: Multimodal signal analysis of prosody and hand motion: Temporal correlation of speech and gestures. In: Proc. of the European Signal Processing Conference, EUSIPCO 2002, pp. 75–78 (2002)

Nonverbal Action Selection for Explanations Using an Enhanced Behavior Net

Javier Snaider[1], Andrew M. Olney[2], and Natalie Person[3]

[1] Computer Science Department & Institute for Intelligent Systems, University of Memphis,
Memphis, TN, USA
[2] Institute for Intelligent Systems, University of Memphis, Memphis, TN, USA
[3] Department of Psychology, Rhodes College, Memphis, TN, USA
{jsnaider,aolney}@memphis.edu, person@rhodes.edu

Abstract. In this paper we present a novel approach to the nonverbal action selection problem for an agent in an intelligent tutoring system. We use a variation of the original Maes' Behavior Net that has several improvements that allow modeling action selection using the content of the utterance, communicative goals, and the discourse history. This Enhanced Behavior Net can perform action selection dynamically, reprioritize actions based on all these elements, and resolve conflict situations without the use of sophisticated predefined rules.

Keywords: Nonverbal action selection - intelligent tutoring system – behavior net – gestures.

1 Introduction

Pedagogical agents, like human tutors, frequently must give explanations, provide feedback, and refer to external resources when teaching students [1][2][3]. The synchronization of nonverbal behaviors (e.g., gestures) with dialogue can direct more effectively student attention and intensify engagement [4][5]. However, when there are a large number of behaviors to choose from, the problem of selecting the optimal behavior becomes nontrivial [6]. In this study, we combine previous research on action selection to the problem of animation selection for a pedagogical agent that gives explanations, provides feedback to students' contributions, and refers to a workspace that displays images.

The application context for the present study is the Guru intelligent tutoring system (ITS) for biology [7]. Our approach is similar to previous approaches for generating nonverbal behaviors [8][9][10]. However, we make three distinct contributions. First, our approach involves coordinating all the events that are afforded in a multimedia display. Images, diagrams, dialogue, and text are presented to the user on the multimedia display. Second, the agent's behaviors must be pedagogically appropriate and tailored to the student's current understanding of the material. Hence, rather than using only surface features of a text, as in the previous work generating nonverbal behaviors mentioned above, we are also including information about what words and

H. Högni Vilhjálmsson et al. (Eds.): IVA 2011, LNAI 6895, pp. 141–147, 2011.
© Springer-Verlag Berlin Heidelberg 2011

concepts are pedagogically relevant to a student at a particular point in time. Thirdly, the agent must perform action selection dynamically by keeping track of the discourse history and reprioritizing actions based on that history.

An enhanced version of the Maes' Behavior Net [11] was used to address the challenge of synchronizing verbal, nonverbal, and multimedia outputs in pedagogical explanations. This approach has several advantages: for example, the BN can automate the process at a tremendous time savings in authoring effort. Also, the BN dynamically reacts to the conditions of the current student resulting in tailored instruction and synchronized deployment of verbal, nonverbal, and multimedia elements to that student.

The following section describes gestures in expert human tutoring in some detail; these gestures represent the standard behaviors that the BN should implement. The subsequent section describes the actions and goals for nonverbal behaviors. Next, the Enhanced Behavior Net (EBN) algorithm is described along with the changes we made in the data structure and in the calculation of the behaviors' activation. The last two sections discuss the conclusions and future directions of this work.

2   Gestures in Expert Human Tutoring

Previous work has investigated the kinds of gestures that occur in expert human tutoring [12]. Williams et al. analyzed the gestures of different tutors in ten tutoring sessions. All sessions consisted of naturalistic one-on-one tutoring on diverse subjects such as algebra, chemistry, and biology. From each session, 200 turns were selected for gesture coding, totaling 2,000 turns. The seven gesture categories and are presented in Table 1. Thirty-five action categories are nested within the major gesture categories. Not all are listed due to space constraints.

Table 1. Gesture Categories and Actions

Category	Action	Description
Deictic	Point at workspace	Pointing gestures
Iconic	Animate subject matter	Illustrate what is said with concrete semantic meaning
Beat	Count on fingers Point upwards	Emphasize aspects of dialogue; rhythmic in nature
Personal	Cross arms across chest Scratch itch	Do not involve other participant or shared workspace
Gaze	Look at student	Indicates where tutor is looking
Paralinguistic	Gesture for student to take notes Shrug shoulders	Metacommunicative nonverbal speech acts
Action	Write on workspace Thumb through pages	Specific tutor actions on workspace

Williams et al. found that tutors used gestures differentially based on the pedagogical/communicative intent of their utterance, with the exception of beat gestures which occurred throughout. Moreover, their analyses of gesture frequency in tutoring indicated that three of the four most common gestures involved the workspace (looking at/pointing to/writing on). The high frequency of workspace related gestures in expert human tutoring underscores the relevance of workspace related gestures for pedagogical agents.

Our pedagogical agent, Guru, is designed around the same pedagogical scenario described by Williams et al. In the Guru environment, students interact with a full bodied animated pedagogical agent and a multimedia panel as shown below. The Guru tutor interacts with the workspace and text, images, and diagrams on the workspace appear and disappear at relevant points in the tutoring session.

The utterances generated by the Guru agent are controlled by a dialogue manager which selects dialogue based on the student's current understanding and the current pedagogical goals (e.g, introduce a new topic, provide scaffolding, assess student understanding). However, the nonverbal behavior of Guru is not controlled by the dialogue manager. Instead, nonverbal behaviors are managed by the EBN; the pedagogical goals and agent actions that are handled by the EBN are described below.

3   Pedagogical Goals and Actions

Based on the gesture analyses conducted by Williams et al. [12] and careful observations of expert tutoring videos, we have identified a subset of pedagogical goals and agent actions that correspond to the nonverbal behaviors that are prevalent in one-to-one tutoring. The seven pedagogical goals are *Emphasize Concept, Ground Concept, Ask Question, Wait for Answer, Provide Positive Feedback, Provide Negative Feedback, and Provide Neutral Feedback.* These goals, along with information in the dialogue history, drive the Guru agent's nonverbal actions. The agent actions are Sway Back and Forth, Interlock Fingers, Cross Arms, Gesture Left then Right, Hands Out, Head Tilt Nod, Look at Whiteboard, Left Hand Out, Right Hand Out, Shrug Shoulders, Head Tilt, Point to Whiteboard, Head Tilt Left Then Right, Head Shake Yes, Head Shake No, Animate Subject Matter, Smile, and Grimace.

Some agent actions map onto to more than one goal when they are used in different contexts. For example, the agent may cross its arms when waiting for a student to answer or when delivering negative feedback. Although multiple actions can map onto a goal, the effectiveness of each action for a particular goal may differ. For example, the action Gesture Left may map to the goal Emphasize Concept, but Point to Whiteboard has a stronger effect because the action is more precise.

Pedagogical and discourse goals change over the course of an explanation. When a new concept or topic is first introduced, e.g. Cholesterol, the agent should ground the discourse referent by highlighting the image -- also known as *grounding* the referent [13]. However, once the referent has been grounded, it is no longer necessary to keep grounding it. Thus grounding is an example of a pedagogical (and conversational) goal that is sensitive to the discourse history.

4   Enhanced Behavior Net

Maes extensively describes the Behavior Net, an action selection mechanism, in her original papers [11][14]. We will refer to this original implementation as MASM

(Maes' Action Selection Mechanism) in the rest of this paper. The basic components of MASM are *behaviors*. A behavior is composed of an *action*, a list of logic literals called *preconditions* and a *result list*. The result list represents the consequences of the action and it is also composed of literals, but in this case, it is divided in two sub lists: the *add list* and the *delete list*. The add list is the list of literals that become true after the action execution and the literals in the delete list become false. Each behavior has a real value attribute called *activation*. The behaviors receive activation from the *environment*, the list of literals that are true in the system. If a literal is in the *environment*, this means that this literal is true, all behaviors that have this same literal in their precondition receive some activation.

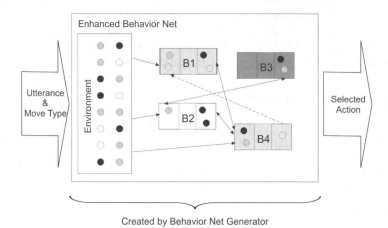

Fig. 1. The Enhanced Behavior Net. B1 to B4 are behaviors. The shades of gray represent their activations. The circles in the environment represent conditions and goals. The circles in the behaviors represent preconditions (left) and the result list (right).

Behaviors also receive activation from the *goals*, a list of literals whose desired end-state is true. Behaviors that have a goal as part of their add list gain some activation. Finally, the behaviors comprise a network of *successors* and *predecessors*. When the results of one behavior are the preconditions of another, then the former is the predecessor and the latter is the successor and they are linked. Behaviors spread activation among their successors and predecessors. There are also *conflictor links* that are outside the scope of this paper.

A behavior becomes *executable* when all its preconditions are true and its activation is over a threshold T. All executable behaviors compete and the action of the winner is executed. If no behavior fulfills both conditions to be executable, T is diminished and another cycle is performed until one behavior is selected.

The original MASM was studied in detail by Tyrell [6] and he reported on three strengths and limitations that are particularly relevant to the current discussion of modeling discourse and pedagogical rules. First, MASM uses Boolean conditions: either a feature is present in the environment or not. However, several of the discourse/pedagogical goals require graded values of features to represent recency and effectiveness. Second, MASM does not include negated preconditions. This makes it difficult to represent behaviors that apply to things that have not happened yet, like grounding a referent. Third, when conflicting goals compete, MASM does not handle the passing of activation correctly in all situations. Several variations and improvements that correct some of these problems and extend its applicability to more complex domains have been proposed. See for example: [15][16]. The following paragraphs address these issues in detail.

In regard to the Boolean limitation of MASM, a degree of fuzziness is needed to represent if a specific action was executed recently. The literals of MASM were replaced by *conditions* that have real-valued activation and *importance*. A condition is considered true if it exceeds a defined threshold. The activation of conditions decays over time. *Importance* is used to distinguish the importance of each precondition. Preconditions with more importance contribute more to the activation of the behavior. With regard to the MASM limitation on negation, MASM presumes a closed word assumption, meaning that literals not present in the environment are considered false. This assumption has some drawbacks. Some behaviors may need a specific condition to be false in order to be executable. For example, a word must be not *emphasized_recently* to be emphasized. Our solution is to allow preconditions to be *negated*. Conditions that are not present in the precondition list of a behavior are considered irrelevant for that particular behavior. The environment has only *positive* conditions. When activation is passed from the environment, behaviors with negated preconditions receive activation as a function of the complement of the activation of positive condition in the environment, i.e. one minus the activation of the condition.

It is important to notice that the environment now contains all the conditions of the system including goals. The activation of each of them indicates the degree of certainty of this condition. Each goal has an attribute called *desirability*. Behaviors can receive activation from the goals, if they can produce one of them. The amount of activation that a goal contributes with behaviors is relative to the difference between its desirability and its activation. Then, a goal with full activation is already fulfilled and it is not necessary to select behaviors that produce this goal.

An important module of the EBN is the Behavior Network Generator (BNG). This module creates the Behavior Net required for the material the tutor is going to teach using only basic components of the dialogue, key concepts, multimedia assets, and a predefined set of actions and goals. The BNG populates the graph of the behavior net by defining the environment, the network of behaviors, and their connectivity. A complete description of the BNG is beyond the scope of this paper.

The Guru Tutor uses the EBN to dynamically synchronize verbal, non-verbal, and multimedia presentations. The EBN takes a raw tutor utterance and a pedagogical move type from the dialogue manager, e.g. "QUESTION", "DIRECT_INSTR", "FEEDBACK_OK", etc. The EBN first adjusts the activation of the environment's conditions based on the received utterance and the move type. The EBN inspects the text of the utterance for words that relate to key concepts and multimedia assets using string matching. Conditions in the EBN environment are updated based on these matches, e.g. if "mitosis" is present, then the multimedia condition for "mitosis" will receive activation, as will the key concept node for "mitosis". Then the behaviors' activation is recalculated. If any behavior is executable and over the selection threshold then this behavior is selected. Otherwise, the threshold is decreased and more activation is spread among behaviors. This process is repeated until one behavior is selected. Finally, the activation of all behaviors and conditions are decayed. There are defined some background behaviors with a constant, never decaying, low activation. This guarantees that one action is eventually selected.

The output of the EBN is an action that specifies some nonverbal behavior or change in the multimedia panel, synchronized with the agent's speech using SAPI 5 bookmarks that allows synchronization of the agent with TTS events, e.g. word boundaries.

5   Conclusions

In this paper we present a novel approach to the nonverbal action selection problem for an intelligent tutoring agent, Guru. We introduce a variation of the original Behavior Net that has several improvements: negated preconditions for behaviors, continuous values of activation instead of Boolean conditions, desirability for goals, and a new set of activation passing equations for better performance. For example, the activation of conditions tracks the time since the last execution of one action. The desirability for goals is used to model their importance and the negated preconditions are used for example to allow the execution of an action only if has not been executed recently. Summing up, this Enhanced Behavior Net allows a better modeling of the action selection problem.

One of the main advantages of this architecture is the use of goals and conditions to model the requirements instead of static rules. The net of behaviors, inherent in the structure of the architecture, can handle dynamic changes and resolve conflicts that otherwise require complex rules to resolve. The activation and decaying mechanisms of the goals and conditions allow the previous history of selected actions and other relevant conditions in the future action selections to be taken into account. A first implementation of the EBN was integrated into the Guru ITS, and the preliminary testing experiments were performed using material from different lectures. For more comprehensive testing, we will expand our current set of animations to better reflect the varied output of the EBN.

We recognize that our current implementation has limitations, and we are entertaining additional ways to improve in the system. First, the actual implementation of the BNG is fixed for our specific domain: the Guru ITS. A more generic approach is to implement it with a mechanism where the user or developer could specify the structure of behaviors, conditions, goals and other elements of the system. This will extend the use of this architecture beyond the scope of Guru. Also, a standard output format, like BML, could facilitate this same goal. Another possible improvement is to perform a more sophisticated prepossessing with the input utterance.

Acknowledgments. The research reported here was supported by the Institute of Education Sciences, U.S. Department of Education, through Grant R305A080594 to the University of Memphis. The opinions expressed are those of the authors and do not represent views of the Institute or the U.S. Department of Education.

References

1. Graesser, A.C., McNamara, D.S., VanLehn, K.: Scaffolding deep comprehension strategies through Point&Query, AutoTutor, and iSTART. Educational Psychologist 40(4), 225–234 (2005)
2. Lester, J.C., Towns, S.G., Fitzgerald, P.J.: Achieving affective impact: Visual emotive communication in lifelike pedagogical agents. International Journal of Artificial Intelligence in Education 10(3-4), 278–291 (1999)
3. Rickel, J., Johnson, W.L.: Animated agents for procedural training in virtual reality: Perception, cognition, and motor control. Applied Artificial Intelligence 13(4), 343–382 (1999)
4. Atkinson, R.K.: Optimizing learning from examples using animated pedagogical agents. Journal of Educational Psychology 94(2), 416 (2002)
5. Hershey, K., Mishra, P., Altermatt, E.: All or nothing: Levels of sociability of a pedagogical software agent and its impact on student perceptions and learning. Journal Educational Multimedia and Hypermedia 14(2), 113–127 (2005)
6. Tyrell, T.: Computational Mechanisms for Action Selection. PhD Thesis, University of Edinburg, UK (1993)
7. Olney, A.M., Graesser, A.C., Person, N.K.: Tutorial Dialog in Natural Language. In: Nkambou, R., Bourdeau, J., Mizoguchi, R. (eds.) Advances in Intelligent Tutoring Systems. Studies in Computational Intelligence, vol. 308, pp. 181–206. Springer, Heidelberg (2010)
8. Bergmann, K., Kopp, S.: GNetIc – using bayesian decision networks for iconic gesture generation. In: Ruttkay, Z., Kipp, M., Nijholt, A., Vilhjálmsson, H.H. (eds.) IVA 2009. LNCS, vol. 5773, pp. 76–89. Springer, Heidelberg (2009)
9. Lee, J., Marsella, S.C.: Nonverbal behavior generator for embodied conversational agents. In: Gratch, J., Young, M., Aylett, R.S., Ballin, D., Olivier, P. (eds.) IVA 2006. LNCS (LNAI), vol. 4133, pp. 243–255. Springer, Heidelberg (2006)
10. Neff, M., Kipp, M., Albrecht, I., Seidel, H.P.: Gesture modeling and animation based on a probabilistic re-creation of speaker style. ACM Transactions on Graphics (TOG) 27(1), 5 (2008)
11. Maes, P.: How to do the right thing. Connection Science 1, 291–323 (1989)
12. Williams, B., Williams, C., Volgas, N., Yuan, B., Person, N.: Examining the Role of Gestures in Expert Tutoring. Intelligent Tutoring Systems, 235–244 (2010)
13. Clark, H.H., Brennan, S.E.: Grounding in communication. In: Resnick, L.B., Levine, J.M., Teasley, S.D. (eds.) Perspectives on Socially Shared Cognition, pp. 127–149. American Psychological Association, Washington, DC (1991)
14. Maes, P.: Modeling Adaptive Autonomous Agents. Artificial Life 1, 135–162 (1993)
15. Decugis, V., Ferber, J.: Action selection in an autonomous agent with a hierarchical distributed reactive planning architecture. Paper Presented at the Second International Conference on Autonomous Agents, Minneapolis, MN USA (1998)
16. Negatu, A., Franklin, S.: An action selection mechanism for 'conscious' software agents. Cognitive Science Quarterly 2, 363–386 (2002); special issue on Desires, goals, intentions, and values: Computational architectures. Guest editors Maria Miceli and Cristiano Castelfranchi

Providing Gender to Embodied Conversational Agents

Marco Vala, Gabriel Blanco, and Ana Paiva

INESC-ID and IST/UTL
Av. Prof. Cavaco Silva - Taguspark, 2744-016 Porto Salvo, Portugal
{marco.vala,ana.paiva}@inesc-id.pt

Abstract. Communication, along with other factors, varies with gender. Significant work as been done around embodied conversational agents (ECAs) verbal and non-verbal behaviour but gender issue has often been ignored. Yet, together with personality, culture and other factors, gender is a feature that impacts the perception and thus the believability of the characters. The main goal of this work is to understand how gender can be provided to ECAs, and provide a very simple model that allows for existing tools to overcome such limitation. The proposed system was developed around SAIBA Framework using SmartBody as the behavior realizer and tries to address this problem by adding a set of involuntary gender specific movements to the agents behaviour in an automatic manner. This is achieved by revising and complementing the work done by the existing non-verbal behaviour generators. Focusing mainly on non-verbal behaviour, our agents with gender were tested to see if users were able to perceive the gender bias of the behaviours being performed. Results have shown that gender is correctly perceived, and also has effects when paired with an accurate gender appearance.

1 Introduction

Animated films is a medium that requires the suspension of disbelief: the audience enjoys the mental illusion that the characters are actually gifted with life. However, in order to achieve such "illusion of life", each animated character should have, not only believable appearance, but also perform human-like facial expressions, gestures and body movements.

In the area of virtual agents, we also aim at achieving characters with believable behaviour. Research in embodied conversational agents (ECAs) has significant work in gaze models, gestures, postures, and facial expressions, just to mention a few. Some of these works take into consideration the influence of individual factors in the generation of behaviour, such as personality and culture. In this work we will address gender differences, starting with the hypothesis that if we have ECAs with body language and physical appearance matching in gender, the perception of male or female will be more accurate than just having a gender appearance.

We start with a brief overview of gender differences in non-verbal communication and relevant work in the area of ECAs. Then we present our model

H. Högni Vilhjálmsson et al. (Eds.): IVA 2011, LNAI 6895, pp. 148–154, 2011.
© Springer-Verlag Berlin Heidelberg 2011

for gender in ECAs and its implementation. Finally, we discuss the evaluation results and draw some conclusions.

2   Gender Differences in Non-verbal Communication

Non-verbal communication is one major subject when studying human behaviour. Between 60-80 percent of our messages are communicated through our body language and only a small percentage is attributable to the actual words of a conversation [13]. Non-verbal communication codes include physical appearance, gestures, postures, facial expressions, gaze, touch, and space [8]. In this paper, gender is considered to be the physiological, social, and cultural manifestations of what people perceive to be the appropriate behaviours of females and males [5]. Gender differences are assumed to be present for both verbal and non-verbal communication.

Studies have found that women are in general considered more communicative [3]. They tend to use both verbal and non-verbal cues more frequently, and they use more distinct gestures than men. Men tend to use fewer gestures and postures, but they change the gesture or movement that they are performing more frequently (often repeating previous movements). Further, the biggest differences are present in gestures categorized as adapters (involuntary movements). Woman tend to gesture towards the body and their gestures are considered to be more positive. On the other hand, men tend to use less positive, larger (space-consuming) and sweeping gestures. Concerning posture, women use less physical space. They usually assume a forward position when sitting, legs and feet together, and lean forward when listening. By contrast, men tend to stretch arms and legs away from their body. They assume more reclined positions when sitting and lean backward when listening. If we consider gaze and head movements, women spend more time looking at their target of conversation than men which avoid their target frequently [1] [5] [6] [15].

3   Related Work

Many systems that embed ECAs use different models for men and women, like Mission Rehearsal Exercise (MRE) [7] or Façade [10]. However, when we compare body languages and gestures there is hardly any difference between them, apart from the pre-authored animations that are build specifically for each character. Other systems, such as Greta [12], exhibit generic non-verbal behaviour synchronized with speech, but do not aim at specifically model different factors like culture, personality or gender. Despite Greta being represented as a woman there seems to be no gender driven movements considered.

Further, there are currently several non-verbal behaviour generators. The majority of them are systems that automatically add different types of non-verbal behaviour to a given dialogue script that involves multiple human-like agents [4] [2]. But researchers are also considering other conscious and unconscious habits that intervene in the content of our discourse and define our non-verbal behaviour [11]. Our work looks at non-verbal behaviour variations concerning gender.

4   A Model for Gender Adaptation in ECAs

We aim at creating distinct individual characters which can perform the exact same script, with the same proposed gestures, but behave somehow differently according to their gender. Overall, most gender differences are involuntary movements observed at different levels: (a) gestures and postures that are socially attributable to man or woman (mutually exclusive); (b) gestures and postures that are performed by both male and female, but in a different way; and finally (c) differences between the amount of gestures and postures performed during a conversation.

The process of generating behaviour in ECAs usually considers three stages: intent planning, behaviour planning and behaviour realization [9]. Since we are interested in involuntary movements, which do not have any specific semantic meaning, they are somewhere in-between the behaviour planning and the behaviour realization. As such, we introduced these involuntary movements at the body level of our characters. Since we do not want to redesign the existent behaviour generators but rather to complement them, and use the currently available tools, our model extends the current behaviour generation pipeline adding a *behaviour reviser* and an *involuntary behaviour generator* (see Figure 1).

The *behaviour reviser* looks at the previous generated behaviours and, if necessary and possible, replaces gestures or postures which are inaccurate in gender. Thus, it adapts or performs gender variations by selecting the appropriate gesture or posture whilst keeping the intended semantic meaning.

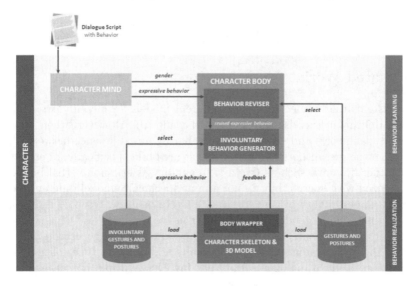

Fig. 1. Model for a Character's body processing model with gender

The *involuntary behaviour generator* generates gender specific involuntary movements. Previous generated behaviours are not overridden or replaced. The inclusion takes place in the empty spaces, in which no concrete behaviour was generated. The process considers the differences between genders: female characters will use more distinct gestures than male characters, and male characters will change from gesture to gesture more frequently reusing previous used gestures.

5   Implementation of the Model

Our implementation uses scripts in BML (Behaviour Markup Language) as input, and SmartBody [14] with the Panda3D BML Realizer[1] as behaviour realizer. Panda3D BMLR offers a limited number of characters with both female and male appearances. Each character can perform a pre-defined set of gestures and postures which were marked as feminine or masculine and stored in the animation library.

When a character receives a BML script, the *behaviour reviser* searches for behaviour inconsistencies (an inconsistency occurs when a selected gesture or posture does not match the character's gender). If an inconsistency is found, it looks into the animation library and tries to replace the gesture or posture for appropriate ones.

Then, the revised BML script goes through the *involuntary behaviour generator* which finds empty spaces and fills them with involuntary movements: gestures, postures, gaze and head movements.

Finding Empty Spaces. The algorithm for finding empty spaces looks at start and end points of each BML element: lower and higher bound of the interval for gestures, and lower bound of the interval for postures (the higher bound is always infinity). Then overlapping intervals are resolved. Finally we obtain a number of empty spaces, and their duration and position within the BML block.

Generating Involuntary Gestures. Based on the studies presented in section 2, the algorithm for generating involuntary gestures selects which percentage of total empty time will be used according to gender. If the empty time is too small, no involuntary gestures will be added. Then, it selects appropriate gestures from the animation library and inserts them into the available empty spaces.

Generating Involuntary Postures. Generating involuntary postures is similar to generating involuntary gestures. However, since postures do not have a pre-defined duration, characters can remain in a specific posture forever. Therefore, the algorithm takes into account not only the available time to maintain a specific posture, but also its intended duration, which varies with gender.

Generating Involuntary Gaze and Head Movements. Since SmartBody can blend gaze and head movements with other behaviours, there is no need

---

[1] http://cadia.ru.is/projects/bmlr/

to calculate empty spaces for them. The generator inserts multiple head nods (which vary with gender) along a BML block when a character is listening.

Finally, the resultant BML block is sent to the Panda3D BMLR to be realized and rendered.

6   Evaluation and Results

We conducted an on-line evaluation in order to study the impact of our approach in the perception of gender in an ECA.

6.1   Design

The evaluation process was divided into two parts. In the first part, we wanted to assess our assumptions concerning the gender of the proposed characters (if the female looking character was rated as female, the androgynous as neutral and the male as male). Users were asked to classify the characters in a 5 points Likert scale ranging from *very feminine - 1* to *very masculine - 5*, including a neutral classification. We considered that female and male perception would fit, respectively, the intervals $[1, 2.5]$ and $[3.5, 5]$. Androgynous look would be in the middle. The characters were presented with different poses (see Figure 2).

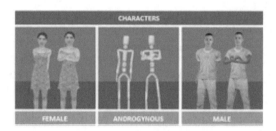

Fig. 2. Characters used for the evaluation process

The second part of the evaluation was performed with videos displaying behaviour generated with our model. Six conditions were considered corresponding to the permutation of two independent variables: "look" which refers to the physical appearance of the character (female, androgynous, or male), and "behaviour" which refers to the generated behaviour (female behaviour or male behaviour). We used within-subject design (questionnaires with repeated measures) where users were asked to do the same classification as before (5 points Likert scale).

6.2   Participants

The on-line questionnaires were completed by eighty four participants (46 male and 38 female).

6.3   Results

In the first part, the results show that the chosen look for our androgynous body did not fall in the interval we defined for the androgynous representation [2.5, 3.5] with a mean of $\mu = 3.54$ and standard deviation $\sigma = 0.61$. The female body had a mean of $\mu = 2.38$ and standard deviation of $\sigma = 1.01$, thus the character was rated as less feminine than expected. On the other hand, the male body fell in the desired interval with a mean result of $\mu = 4.13$ and standard deviation $\sigma = 0.63$.

In the second part, we conducted Mauchlys sphericity tests to validate that we could apply repeated-measures ANOVA. The ANOVA shows significance in two main effects: how "look" influences the perception of gender ($F(1.820, 151.069) = 14.807, p < 0.001$), and how "behaviour" influences the perception of gender ($F(1, 83) = 355.806, p < 0.001$). There is also a significant interaction between "look" and "behaviour" ($F(2, 166) = 35.359, p < 0.001$). Therefore, the variation on gender perception when combining look and behaviour is higher than the sum of the effects of each variable separately. In other words, it means that gender is better perceived when the body of the character matches the bodily behaviour being performed.

6.4   Discussion

Overall we can say that gender was correctly perceived in the different conditions. The physical appearance of our characters is perceived as being more masculine than expected. This is probably due to the use of a common internal skeleton, which does not take into account gender differences.

Concerning the modified behaviour, the ANOVA results support, at least in part, our approach. We also looked at the individual conditions, used the mean values of each look as a baseline and compared those values with the characters with feminine and masculine behaviour. The perception of gender is seen as more feminine or more masculine as expected. However, this analysis has yet to be supported with pairwise t-tests.

7   Conclusions and Future Work

In order to achieve more believability in embodied conversational agents (ECAs), agents must have not only a believable physical appearance but also perform believably in both verbal and non-verbal behaviours. Our approach has taken the view that if we have ECAs with body language and physical appearance matching in gender, the perception of male or female would be more accurate and eventually more believable. Our results showed that gender is indeed better perceived, which in part supports our hypothesis.

Finally, one should stress that our approach uses mostly involuntary movements, which does not cover all aspects of gender. Our behaviour generation pipeline can also be improved to take into consideration the interaction with other agents. Finally, crossing gender with emotions, personality and most importantly culture should be investigated in the future.

References

1. Brannon, L.: Gender: Psychological Perspectives, 6th edn. Pearson Education, London (1993)
2. Breitfuss, W., Prendinger, H., Ishizuka, M.: Automated generation of non-verbal behavior for virtual embodied characters. In: ICMI 2007: Proceedings of the 9th International Conference on Multimodal Interfaces, pp. 319–322. ACM, New York (2001)
3. Briton, N., Hall, J.: Beliefs about female and male nonverbal communication. Sex Roles 32, 79–90 (1995)
4. Cassell, J., Vilhjlmsson, H., Bickmore, T.: Beat: the behavior expression animation toolkit. In: SIGGRAPH 2001: Proceedings of the 28th Annual Conference on Computer Graphics and Interactive Techniques, pp. 477–486. ACM, New York (2001)
5. Ekman, P., Friesen, W.: The repertoire of nonverbal behavior: categories, origins, usage, and coding. Semiotica 1, 49–98 (1969)
6. Glass, L.: He Says, She Says. Perigee Trade Publisher (1993)
7. Gratch, J., Marsella, S.: Tears and fears: Modeling emotions and emotional behaviors in synthetic agents. In: Proceedings of the 5th International Conference On Autonomous Agents, pp. 278–285. ACM Press, New York (2001)
8. Knapp, M., Hall, J.: Nonverbal communication in human interaction. Wadsworth Publishing, Belmont (2005)
9. Kopp, S., Krenn, B., Marsella, S.C., Marshall, A.N., Pelachaud, C., Pirker, H., Thórisson, K.R., Vilhjálmsson, H.H.: Towards a common framework for multimodal generation: The behavior markup language. In: Gratch, J., Young, M., Aylett, R.S., Ballin, D., Olivier, P. (eds.) IVA 2006. LNCS (LNAI), vol. 4133, pp. 205–217. Springer, Heidelberg (2006)
10. Mateas, M., Stern, A.: Faade: An experiment in building a fully-realized interactive drama. In: Game Developers Conference, Game Design Track (2003)
11. Maya, V., Lamolle, M., Pelachaud, C.: Influences and embodied conversational agents. In: AAMAS 2004: Proceedings of the Third International Joint Conference on Autonomous Agents and Multiagent Systems, pp. 1306–1307. ACM, New York (2004)
12. Pelachaud, C.: Multimodal expressive embodied conversational agents. In: 13th Annual ACM International Conference on Multimedia, pp. 683–689. ACM Press, New York (2005)
13. Su, W.-P., Pham, B.: Wardhani.: Personality and emotion-based high-level control of affective story characters. IEEE Transactions on Visualization and Computer Graphics, 281–293 (2007)
14. Thiebaux, M., Marsella, S., Marshall, A., Kallmann, M.: Smartbody: behavior realization for embodied conversational agents. In: AAMAS 2008: Proceedings of the 7th International Joint Conference on Autonomous Agents and Multiagent Systems, pp. 151–158. IFAAMAS (2008)
15. Tiljander, C.: Social gender norms in body language: The construction of stereotyped gender differences in body language in the american sitcom friends. Technical report, Karlstads universitet (2007)

Modeling Gaze Behavior for Virtual Demonstrators

Yazhou Huang, Justin L. Matthews, Teenie Matlock, and Marcelo Kallmann

University of California, Merced

Abstract. Achieving autonomous virtual humans with coherent and natural motions is key for being effective in many educational, training and therapeutic applications. Among several aspects to be considered, the gaze behavior is an important non-verbal communication channel that plays a vital role in the effectiveness of the obtained animations. This paper focuses on analyzing gaze behavior in demonstrative tasks involving arbitrary locations for target objects and listeners. Our analysis is based on full-body motions captured from human participants performing real demonstrative tasks in varied situations. We address temporal information and coordination with targets and observers at varied positions.

Keywords: gaze model, motion synthesis, virtual humans, virtual reality.

1 Introduction and Related Work

Human-human interactions are ubiquitous and in some cases necessary for survival. Engaging in joint activities, such as working on a text together, discussing dinner plans, or showing a friend where to park a car with pointing gestures seem trivial and effortless. However such interactions are orchestrated with a high level of complexity. They may consist of multiple levels of coordination, from conversational communication to gesture, and to the combination of speech and gesture [3, 10]. A good understanding and modeling of these multiple levels of coordinated language and action can help guide the design and development of effective intelligent virtual agents. An important part of this is the study of gaze behavior.

The immediate goal of our work is to generate humanlike full-body motions that are effective for demonstration of physical actions to human users by means of a virtual character. In our approach, the virtual trainer has also to position itself in a suitable location for the demonstration task at hand. This is in particular important to guarantee that the actions and target objects are visible to the observer. Gestures and actions need to be executed by the virtual demonstrator with clarity and precision in order to appropriately reference the target objects without ambiguity. Human users are highly sensitive to momentary multi-modal behaviors generated by virtual agents [20]. In addition, the speed of the motion in the articulation of such behaviors is important in the use and understanding of manual movement [8]. This paper presents our first results analyzing gaze behavior and body positioning for a virtual character identifying and delivering information about objects to an observer in varied relative locations.

In order to investigate these issues we have conducted several motion capture sessions of human-human demonstrative tasks. The collected data is full-body and reveals important correlations that can be directly integrated into gaze and body coordination models for virtual humans. Our results are being integrated in our training

H. Högni Vilhjálmsson et al. (Eds.): IVA 2011, LNAI 6895, pp. 155–161, 2011.

framework [2] based on virtual agents that can learn clusters of demonstrative gestures and actions [7] through an immersive motion capture interface.

There is a large body of research on modeling gaze in humans and animals. Some of this neurological research focuses on the nature of eye movements, including saccades (ballistic eye movements that jump from location to location in a visual scene in a matter of milliseconds) [15, 17]. Some studies [12] closely examine vestibulo-ocular (VOR) reflex in saccadic and slow phase components of gaze shifts. Additional studies [4, 6] involve fine-grained analysis small and large gaze shifts where classic feedback loops are used to model the coupling and dynamics of eye and head-orienting movements.

Gaze has been used in computer graphics from gaze-contingent real-time level of detail (LOD) rendering [13] to the modeling of movement for eyes balls, eye lids and related facial expressions [5]. Gaze direction in particular is known to help with basic two-way communication because it can help a speaker direct attention and disambiguate for a listener [9]. Gaze direction has also been shown to help human listeners better memorize and recall information in interactions with humanoid interlocutors, including robot storytellers [14] or a narrative virtual agent in a CAVE system [1]. [16, 11] introduce emotion models with body posture control to make synthesized gaze emotionally expressive. These systems typically use pre-recorded voice coupled with simulated gaze to interact with the listener. The controlled agent will remain in the same spot facing the audience, and without the need for locomotion.

In this paper we analyze higher-level gaze behavior together with important gaze-related events such as body positioning, synchronization with pointing gestures in respect to multiple objects in the workspace, and with the purpose of delivering information to a human observer at different locations.

2   Data Collection Setup

A total of 4 male participants (weight $150 \sim 230$ lb, height $5'9 \sim 6'1$) were recruited to perform a variety of basic pointing tasks with full-body motion capture without eye tracking. The capture environment was an 8 foot x 12 foot rectangle area. It included six small target objects (office supplies) that were placed on a horizontal coarse mesh grid (simulating a table). Each participant's action was observed by a viewer (human observer) standing at viewer's perspective (VP) locations VP1 though VP5, see Figure 1 (a) and (b). In order to avoid possible effects of target size on gaze behavior, small targets were specifically selected.

For each trial of the motion capture, the participant (1) stands about 4 feet away from the mesh grid, (2) walks towards the grid, (3) points to one of the target objects, (4) verbally engages with the viewer by either naming the target ("This is a roll of tape"), physically describes it ("small, smooth, and black"), or describes the function ("It's used for holding things in place"). During each trial, the participant is expected to direct the attention of the viewer as needed while pointing and talking, by naturally gazing back and forth at the viewer and target. The participant then steps back to the starting position and prepares for the next trial. Each capture session includes 30 trials. The viewer maintains the observing position until all 6 targets had been addressed, then moves to the next standing location. This sequence is repeated until all targets

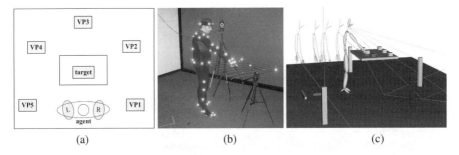

Fig. 1. (a) and (b): motion capture setup; (c): a snapshot of our annotation application showing the phase-plane of gaze yaw-axis along with reconstructed environment

are named or described to the viewer at each of the 5 VPs. The sequence of target selections was random. The full-body motion data (without eye tracking) was captured at 120 fps then retargeted and down-sampled to 60 fps. Data was annotated manually using our annotation tool (Figure 1 (c)). Each captured sequence contains many streams of information, in the present work we have annotated the motions with the information relevant for analyzing the observed gaze behavior.

3   Analysis and Discussion

Our first observation is that each trial was typically constituted of a series of largely consistent gaze or gaze-related events, as listed below:

1. the participant gazes at the floor when walking towards the target object;
2. the participant gazes at the target to be addressed with the demonstrative action;
3. stroke point of the action, in the case of pointing, is detected by the zero-crossing frame of the velocity of the participant's end-effector (the hand);
4. the participant gazes at the viewer during the action and while describing the target;
5. the participant again gazes at the target during action, if applicable;
6. the participant again gazes at the viewer during action, if applicable;
7. the participant gazes at any additional (irrelevant) locations, if applicable;
8. the participant gazes at the floor when stepping back to initial location.

Annotations were then performed to precisely mark the time stamps (start/end) of each event listed above. In the next sections we interpret the annotated events in respect to (a) temporal parameters related to gaze behavior and (b) gaze-related body positioning patterns for demonstrative tasks.

3.1   Temporal Parameters for Gaze Behavior Modeling

The first analysis focuses on the temporal delay Δt between the action stroke point and the starting of the gaze-at-viewer event. Annotation results show that when the viewer is positioned within participant's field-of-view (FoV) (i.e. VP2, VP3, VP4 in Fig 1(a)), the gaze-at-viewer event immediately follows the pointing action stroke point, resulting

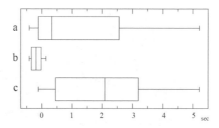

Fig. 2. Temporal delay dictates the starting time of gaze-at-viewer before or after action stroke point: (a) delay plot across all trials. (b) delay plot for out-of-FoV viewer positions VP1 and VP5. (c) delay plot for inside-FoV viewer positions VP2, VP3 and VP4.

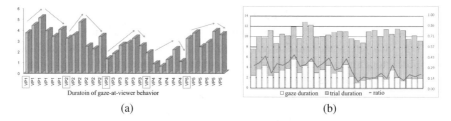

Fig. 3. (a) Correlations between gaze-at-viewer durations and viewer positions: when viewer switches to a new position (boxed text), gaze duration increases for $2 \sim 4$ subsequent trials, then declines. (b) Gradual decline of gaze-at-viewer durations over time. Lighter vertical bars: gaze duration; Darker bars: trial duration; line graph: ratio of gaze duration over trial duration.

in $\Delta t > 0$. By contrast, when the viewer is outside of FoV (i.e. VP1 and VP5 in Fig 1(a)), due to the large gaze-shift required to visually engage with the viewer, gaze-at-viewer starts ahead of the action stroke point, and in this case $\Delta t < 0$. This temporal delay extracted from the trials (measured in seconds) is plotted in Figure 2.

The second analysis reveals correlations between gaze-at-viewer durations and viewer positions. During the capture sessions the viewer moves to a new position after the participant addresses all 6 target objects on the table. An interesting pattern over the gaze-at-viewer durations can be observed across all participants: the viewer switching to a new position results in an increase in the gaze duration, which typically lasts for 2 to 4 trials. This increase is shortly followed by gradual declines in gaze duration, see Figure 3(a). Studies from psychological research on animals resonates to this result [18], specifically when the declination of responsive behavior in humans (extinction progress) begins, a brief surge often occurs in the responding, followed by a gradual decline in response rate until it approaches zero.

The third analysis focuses on the gradual decline of gaze-at-viewer durations. The duration each participant takes to verbally name and describe each object varies across trials. To discount such variation, the ratio (percentage) of gaze-at-viewer behavior takes up within each trial is observed, see Figure 3(b). Dark bars and clear bars correspond to durations of the trial and of the gaze behavior, respectively. Red line drawing reflects the aforementioned ratio decline.

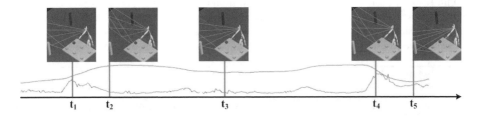

Fig. 4. The velocity profile observed in head motions from captured gaze behavior (unfiltered). The lower trajectory reflects angular accelerations/decelerations of the head rotations, which are used to simulate head movement for gaze. The upper bell-shaped line measures the angle in head rotations from the rest posture (head looking forward). t_1: start of gaze-at-viewer; t_2: gazing at viewer; t_3: gaze-at-target during describing the target; t_4: end of gaze-at-viewer; t_5: start of another gaze-at-target.

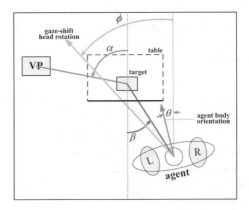

Fig. 5. Description of key gaze-related body positioning parameters: α and β are relative standing locations for the viewer and the agent respectively. θ dictates body orientation of the agent, ϕ represents the maximum head rotation in gaze-at-viewer behavior.

Lastly, to generate natural head movements for gaze behavior, a velocity profile similar to [19] is used to dictate humanlike head rotations based on angular acceleration/deceleration patterns from captured data, see Figure 4 (unfiltered raw data plot).

3.2 Gaze-Related Body Positioning Patterns

Body positioning is of great importance and is rarely addressed. The positioning of a virtual trainer is critical for the viewer to have clear understanding of the action being demonstrated. It is of the same importance to the virtual trainer so that natural gaze behaviors can be carried out visually engaging with the viewer.

We have extracted from the captured data (from one participant) the parameters defined in Figure 5, and their values are summarized in Table 1. The dashed reference line is perpendicular to the table edge, from which the agent will approach the table. In respect to the target object on the table, α and β measures the relative standing locations for the viewer and the demonstrative agent respectively. β dictates where

Table 1. Body positioning parameters observed from one participant performing the action towards different targets and viewer positions. For each parameter, the first column shows the average value (each computed from 6 trials with the viewer maintaining its position), and the second column is the coresponding average absolute deviation of first column, in degrees.

setup	body positioning parameters							
VP	$\bar{\alpha}$	α_α	$\bar{\beta}$	α_β	$\bar{\theta}$	α_θ	$\bar{\phi}$	α_ϕ
VP1	129.0	4.8	-20.6	10.1	-25.1	7.4	-82.7	4.6
VP2	76.6	8.2	-15.9	10.4	-4.8	5.8	-32.2	4.9
VP3	-2.8	14.3	-7.3	11.2	11.6	9.1	0.7	5.1
VP4	93.8	6.3	13.7	12.7	44.5	8.9	58.4	2.7
VP5	149.2	5.5	24.0	11.8	76.0	6.8	125.8	4.0

the agent positions itself giving the viewer a clear view at the target; θ dictates how the agent orients its body to conduct demonstrative actions towards the viewer. ϕ is the recorded maximum head rotation (gaze shift) during the gaze-at-viewer behavior. For any new environment, only α will be treated as an input value, while β, θ and ϕ need to be learned from captured data to solve the gaze-related body positioning problem.

4   Conclusion

In this paper we have discussed studies used for analyzing and modeling gaze behavior for virtual trainers performing object demonstrations. Several aspects of the collected full-body motion data were analyzed in respect to gaze behaviors and gaze-related body-positioning. Our first results presented in this paper lead to several informative correlations for implementing animation models for controlling virtual humans in interactive training systems. In future work we will present a comprehensive analysis of the entire motion information collected, and we will present complete behavioral models for realistically animating full-body virtual trainers in demonstration scenarios.

Acknowledgements. This work was partially supported by NSF Awards IIS-0915665 and CNS-0723281. The authors would like to thank David Sparks for his assistance in motion annotations, and all the participants involved in the data collection process.

References

1. Bee, N., Wagner, J., André, E., Vogt, T., Charles, F., Pizzi, D., Cavazza, M.: Discovering eye gaze behavior during human-agent conversation in an interactive storytelling application. In: Int'l Conference on Multimodal Interfaces and Workshop on Machine Learning for Multimodal Interaction, ICMI-MLMI 2010, pp. 9:1–9:8. ACM, New York (2010)
2. Camporesi, C., Huang, Y., Kallmann, M.: Interactive motion modeling and parameterization by direct demonstration. In: Safonova, A. (ed.) IVA 2010. LNCS, vol. 6356, pp. 77–90. Springer, Heidelberg (2010)
3. Clark, H.H., Krych, M.A.: Speaking while monitoring addressees for understanding. Memory and Language 50, 62–81 (2004)

4. Cullen, K.E., Huterer, M., Braidwood, D.A., Sylvestre, P.A.: Time course of vestibuloocular reflex suppression during gaze shifts. Journal of Neurophysiology 92(6), 3408–3422 (2004)
5. Deng, Z., Lewis, J., Neumann, U.: Automated eye motion using texture synthesis. IEEE Computer Graphics and Applications 25(2), 24–30 (2005)
6. Galiana, H.L., Guitton, D.: Central organization and modeling of eye-head coordination during orienting gaze shifts. Annals of the New York Acd. of Sci. 656(1), 452–471 (1992)
7. Huang, Y., Kallmann, M.: Motion Parameterization with Inverse Blending. In: Boulic, R., Chrysanthou, Y., Komura, T. (eds.) MIG 2010. LNCS, vol. 6459, pp. 242–253. Springer, Heidelberg (2010)
8. Huette, S., Huang, Y., Kallmann, M., Matlock, T., Matthews, J.L.: Gesture variants and cognitive constraints for interactive virtual reality training systems. In: Proceeding of 16th International Conference on Intelligent User Interfaces (IUI), pp. 351–354 (2011)
9. Kendon, A.: Some Functions of Gaze Direction in Two-Person Conversation. Conducting Interaction: Patterns of Behavior in Focused Encounters (1990)
10. Kendon, A.: Gesture: Visible action as utterance, Cambridge (2004)
11. Lance, B., Marsella, S.C.: Emotionally expressive head and body movement during gaze shifts. In: Pelachaud, C., Martin, J.-C., André, E., Chollet, G., Karpouzis, K., Pelé, D. (eds.) IVA 2007. LNCS (LNAI), vol. 4722, pp. 72–85. Springer, Heidelberg (2007)
12. Lefevre, P., Bottemanne, I., Roucoux, A.: Experimental study and modeling of vestibulo-ocular reflex modulation during large shifts of gaze in humans. Experimental Brain Research 91, 496–508 (1992)
13. Murphy, H.A., Duchowski, A.T., Tyrrell, R.A.: Hybrid image/model-based gaze-contingent rendering. ACM Trans. Appl. Percept. 22, 22:1–22:21 (2009)
14. Mutlu, B., Hodgins, J.K., Forlizzi, J.: A storytelling robot: Modeling and evaluation of human-like gaze behavior. In: Proceedings of HUMANOIDS 2006, 2006 IEEE-RAS International Conference on Humanoid Robots. IEEE, Los Alamitos (2006)
15. Pelisson, D., Prablanc, C., Urquizar, C.: Vestibuloocular reflex inhibition and gaze saccade control characteristics during eye-head orientation in humans. Journal of Neurophysiology 59, 997–1013 (1988)
16. Thiebaux, M., Lance, B., Marsella, S.: Real-time expressive gaze animation for virtual humans. In: Proceedings of The 8th International Conference on Autonomous Agents and Multiagent Systems (AAMAS), Budapest, Hungary, pp. 321–328 (2009)
17. Van Horn, M.R., Sylvestre, P.A., Cullen, K.E.: The brain stem saccadic burst generator encodes gaze in three-dimensional space. J. of Neurophysiology 99(5), 2602–2616 (2008)
18. Weiten, W.: Wayne Weiten, Psychology: Themes and Variations, 8th edn. Cengage Learning Publishing (2008)
19. Yamane, K., Kuffner, J.J., Hodgins, J.K.: Synthesizing animations of human manipulation tasks. In: ACM SIGGRAPH 2004, pp. 532–539. ACM, New York (2004)
20. Zhang, H., Fricker, D., Smith, T.G., Yu, C.: Real-time adaptive behaviors in multimodal human-avatar interactions. In: Int'l Conf. on Multimodal Interfaces and the Workshop on Machine Learning for Multimodal Interaction, ICMI-MLMI 2010, 4:1–4:8. ACM, New York (2010)

A Framework for Motion Based Bodily Enaction with Virtual Characters

Roberto Pugliese and Klaus Lehtonen

Department of Media Technology,
School of Science,
Aalto University,
Espoo, Finland
{roberto.pugliese,klaus.lehtonen}@tkk.fi

Abstract. We propose a novel methodology for authoring interactive behaviors of virtual characters. Our approach is based on enaction, which means a continuous two-directional loop of bodily interaction. We have implemented the case of two characters, one human and one virtual, who are separated by a glass wall and can interact only through bodily motions. Animations for the virtual character are based on captured motion segments and descriptors for the style of motions that are automatically calculated from the motion data. We also present a rule authoring system that is used for generating behaviors for the virtual character. Preliminary results of an enaction experiment with an interview show that the participants could experience the different interaction rules as different behaviors or attitudes of the virtual character.

Keywords: Enaction, motion capture, bodily interaction, authoring behaviors.

1 Introduction

Authoring believable behaviors for virtual characters is a crucial step towards the creation of immersive gaming experiences. In social encounters behaviors emerge as humans react to actions of others in a continuous feedback loop. This process is sustained by bodily interaction among the different parties. Human-computer bodily interaction is possible even at consumer level with latest sensor technology.

We are interested in behaviors that can be observed in and activated by bodily motion and how to use this as a medium of interaction with a virtual character. Our interests are not in traditional goal-oriented interaction or in symbolic language. For these reasons an enactive loop, where both parties can continuously affect the other through actions and the style of motions, was chosen as the model of interaction instead of using discrete gestures.

We present a framework that allows bodily interaction between a human and a virtual character in an enactive loop. The implementation takes a long motion capture sequence as input and automatically segments it into a motion library,

H. Högni Vilhjálmsson et al. (Eds.): IVA 2011, LNAI 6895, pp. 162–168, 2011.

indexed by motion styles, that is used to animate the virtual character. We also present a rule authoring system that is used for generating behaviors for the virtual character.

2   Related Works

In this section we explore earlier works related to enaction and to techniques that enable interaction through motion with animated characters.

2.1   Enaction

Enactive Media is an approach to design modalities of human-machine interaction. While traditionally interactivity has been approached with theories and tools for goal-oriented tasks, the enactive paradigm focuses on a tight coupling between machine and the user, here a participant or enactor. The process is a feedback loop: the actions performed by the enactor affect the medium that in turn affects the following actions of the enactor. The coupling is sustained by means of bodily and spatial involvement, or enactment [1]. An enactive system may involve even a community of agents in participatory sense-making [2].

We want to create a process where the participant will be able to notice different behaviors in the virtual character as a response to his or her own behavior. The rules governing the interaction do not need to be explicit but they can be learned by interacting, in accordance with the original definition of enaction from Bruner [3], that is to learn by doing. While an enactive account for human-computer interaction has been provided in other fields such as facial expressions of virtual characters and movie creation [4], based on psychophysiological input, an implementation of enaction with a virtual character based on bodily motion is yet absent.

In our enactive setting no assumption about the meaning of gesture is done a priori but meaning is actively constructed by the participant and emerges from the enactive loop. This calls for representing the quality of the interaction and the motion style in an objective and non-hierarchical way. We borrow the spatial ontology (ontospace) approach by Kaipainen et al. [5] as a solution. An ontospace is defined by ontological dimensions (ontodimensions) that correspond to descriptive properties of the content repertoire, which in our case are motion clips.

2.2   Interaction through Motion with Animated Characters

Animating characters is possible with motion graphs that contain captured motion segments and a list of allowed transitions between the segments [6]. A motion graph can be constructed automatically from a large corpus of motions and can be used to produce arbitrarily long continuous motions [7].

In a previous work, full-body interaction with a virtual creature meant mainly giving commands and instructions to virtual creatures and the set up did not allow symmetrical interaction [8]. Similarly, Improv [9] allows interaction with virtual characters. It allows creating scripted sequences of animation and inter-action by means of if-statements based on the properties of the characters. These earlier systems concentrated mainly on goal-oriented actions.

In human-computer bodily interaction one needs to extract motion cues able to describe the human motion in a machine friendly way. We follow a methodol-ogy based on previous work in the field of analysis of expressive gesture in music and dance performances [10]. The process has camera-based tracking and calcu-lation of motion features that serve as descriptors for motions. Those descriptors include amount of movement and body contraction/expansion.

3   Framework

The system that we have built simulates a situation where two persons are separated by a glass wall and are able to interact only through bodily motions. This creates an enactive loop and allows replacing one or two of the persons with a virtual character (Fig. 1), in our system rendered as a stick figure. The enactive system reacts to human motion (input) by triggering a recorded motion clip (output).

3.1   Enactive Loop

Any motion clip (either recorded or realtime captured) can be associated to a point in an ontospace based on its values of the motion descriptors as coordinates. Before the enaction (Fig. 2) can start the output ontospace is filled with acted motions (Z). The loop starts by mapping the human motion into the input ontospace with the descriptors (A). Then a rule system determines the desired position of the virtual character in the output ontospace (B). Next the animation engine searches for the closest motion to the desired position from the acted motions (C). The virtual character then proceeds to play the motion (D). As the last step the human observes the motion of the virtual character (E), which affects the motion of the human, etc.

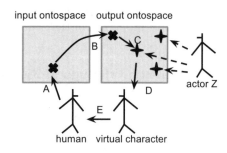

Fig. 1. Live enaction

Fig. 2. Enactive loop sustained by the human and the virtual character

3.2   Motion Analysis and Generation Using Descriptors

For the enactive loop we needed a virtual character that moves with varying motion styles and reacts to the motion style of the human. We use Quantity of Motion (QoM) and Distance descriptors for motions. The former is used as an estimation of the energy and the motion style while the latter characterizes the interaction between the social spaces of the human and the virtual character.

Our definitions are the following: Quantity of Motion (QoM), sum of the frame to frame displacements of all the joints in the body of the character divided by the number of frames in the motion, minus the minimum amount of motion required to move from the starting position to the end position; Distance, the distance of the center of the body from the wall separating the characters.

These descriptors allow placing every possible motion in a two-dimensional ontospace (Fig. 3), constituting a simple case that still allows authoring behaviors. To normalize the descriptors values Distance was scaled linearly, but for QoM we used a log-like function. This takes into account that humans perceive very small changes in the amount of motion if the overall speed is low, but for high speeds the change needs to be much larger to be noticed [11].

Our virtual character is a program that takes desired descriptor values as input and then generates an animated motion sequence that fits to the desired values. To be able to do this we created a motion library containing idle standing (consentration of dots in Fig. 3), walking and running (extremes of Distance in Fig. 3) and jumping actions (high QoM in Fig. 3). These actions were acted with varying styles to evenly populate the ontospace with motion segments. Total of six minutes of motion was automatically segmented to create a motion graph with approximately one second long clips that allow smooth transitions to many other clips. The segmentation was based on finding frames of motion that have a similar pose and speed. After playing a clip the number of alternative following clips ranged with our motion library from 2 to 240.

3.3   Authoring Rules

In our methodology, authoring the rules corresponds to finding a meaningful transformation of the input ontospace, the one of the human, into the output ontospace, the one of the virtual character. The transformation is a mapping defined by example point-pairs in the input and output ontospace. To make the mapping work for inputs in between the example points, we search for the k-nearest neighbors in the input space and determine the output with a weighted interpolation of the corresponding points in the output space. For this, we made a GUI for creating mappings between the ontospaces by specifying examples of corresponding point pairs (A, B, C and D in Fig. 4). In the case of a two-dimensional ontospace this means clicking a point in the input space and then clicking the desired output in the output space. An obvious mapping is the identity transformation which makes the virtual character imitate the motion style of the human. Once a rule is defined, it can be used with a larger motion library without any extra manual work.

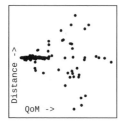

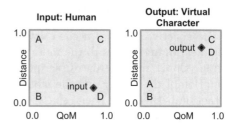

Fig. 3. Ontospace populated with motion segments (dots). The coordinates of the dots are the QoM and the Distance.

Fig. 4. An example of authoring the behaviour rules with point pairs A, B, C and D

In the case of a large number of descriptors, authoring the rules with a mouse can become a tedious and difficult task. A promising alternative approach could be to first record actions with motion capture and then to record the responses to those actions. With this motion data, it should be possible to populate the input and output spaces and obtain behaviour rule.

4   Enaction Tests and Interview with the Participants

In order to validate our methodology and evaluate the effectiveness of our implementation, we conducted enaction tests where a participant had to bodily interact with a virtual character projected in front of them. The participants were 7 unpaid volunteers, 5 male and 2 females of age from 25 to 55.

At the beginning of the experiments the participant was inside a motion capture room and informed about the area where he or she could move and the fact that the virtual character was a stick figure which is able to see the human as a stick figure. No explicit goal of the experiment was stated besides the suggestion to freely explore the bodily interaction with the virtual character.

Six conditions were presented. The first one was always a plain imitation rule used to familiarize the participant with the setting and the interaction paradigm. The next 6 conditions were other rules in randomized order. Those rules were created from a mathematical point of view to try different mappings of descriptors and restricting the virtual character to a limited area of the ontospace.

Condition A was a plain imitation rule. Conditions B and C were imitations with QoM of the virtual character limited to low values in condition B and to high values in condition C. Condition D mapped the QoM of the human to the Distance of the virtual character, as in Fig. 4. This causes the virtual character to back off when the human does motions with high QoM. Condition E inverted the QoM of the human for the virtual character. This makes the virtual character have high QoM, for example, by jumping and waving hands when the human is standing still. In condition F the virtual character played random motion clips without being affected by the human.

In each condition the participant was free to experiment with that rule for 2 minutes. After the experiment we interviewed all the participants to get detailed information about their experiences.

5   Interview and Discussion

Evaluating bodily motions during enaction in an objective manner is a more difficult task than evaluating pre-recorded videos of motions. The main reason is that the conditions are not fully controllable and repeatable because by definition the outcome strongly depends on what the participant does.

On questions related to quality of the interaction with the virtual character we found out that all the participants felt there was interaction in some conditions and also that they could identify different behaviors. There was a general agreement about a character that showed a recognizable scared behavior. This character belonged to the condition D which causes the virtual character to back off when the human does motions with high QoM. Another often mentioned behavior was aggressiveness. This was probably caused by the motions with high QoM such as jumping and waving hands.

The participants said that in some conditions it was hard to understand what made the character react. Besides the condition F with a randomly acting character, this could be explained by that the reaction time of the character could become too slow if the character was playing a long motion. We are aware that two descriptors are not enough to properly describe human actions. We realized that a too simple system makes the participant focus mainly on discovering the rules and the descriptors rather than being in the flow of enaction.

The participants said that their own behavior was affected by the behavior of the virtual character and many of the participants said that they started to mimic the gestures seen in the character. Most of the time, participants moved more when the virtual character was active and less when the character was passive. These facts indicate that the interaction we designed is effectively a case of enactive loop, where both parties affect each other.

6   Conclusions and Future Work

We have presented a framework to design bodily interaction with virtual characters based on the concept of enaction and an authoring tool to specify different behaviors for them that gradually emerge during and due to the interaction. Behaviors are created by mapping the input ontospace of the human, described by motion descriptors, into the output ontospace of the virtual character, populated with automatically evaluated motions. Preliminary tests with participants showed that experiencing different interaction rules as different behaviors or attitudes of the virtual character is possible even in the simplest case of a two-dimensional motion descriptor space.

Defining motion styles with motion descriptors allows using large amount of captured motion without adding more work as no manual annotation is required.

In the future, we plan to add new motion descriptors and differentiate different parts of the body. The manual process of authoring behaviors could be replaced by acting them out in the case of a large number of motion descriptors. Furthermore, we intend to use interpolation among different rules to create virtual characters changing their behaviors during the enaction.

Acknowledgments. This work is part of the Enactive Media project, funded by the Academy of Finland, decision number 128132. We want to thank the Enactive Media team Mauri Kaipainen, Niklas Ravaja, Tapio Takala, Pia Tikka and Rasmus Vuori for the fruitful discussions and intellectual contribution to this paper.

References

1. Varela, F., Thompson, E., Rosch, E.: Embodied Mind: Cognitive Science 2. and Human Experience. MIT Press, Cambridge (1991)
2. De Jaegher, H., Di Paolo, E.A.: Participatory sense-making: An enactive approach to social cognition. Phenomenology and the Cognitive Sciences 6(4), 485–507 (2007)
3. Bruner, J.: Toward a theory of instruction. Belknap Press of Harvard University Press, Cambridge (1966)
4. Kaipainen, M., Ravaja, N., Tikka, P., Vuori, R., Pugliese, R., Rapino, M., Takala, T.: Enactive Systems and Enactive Media. Embodied Human Machine Coupling Beyond Interfaces, Leonardo (in press, 2011)
5. Kaipainen, M., Normak, P., Niglas, K., Kippar, J., Laanpere, M.: Soft ontologies, spatial representations and multi-perspective explorability. Expert Systems 25(5), 474–483 (2008)
6. Kovar, L., Gleicher, M., Pighin, F.: Motion graphs. In: Proc. of SIGGRAPH 2002, pp. 473–482. ACM, New York (2002)
7. Zhao, L., Normoyle, A., Khanna, S., Safonova, A.: Automatic construction of a minimum size motion graph. In: Fellner, D., Spencer, S. (eds.) Proc. of the 2009 ACM SIGGRAPH/Eurographics Symposium on Computer Animation (SCA 2009), pp. 27–35. ACM, New York (2009)
8. Blumberg, B., Galyean, T.: Multi-level direction of autonomous creatures for real-time virtual environments. In: Mair, S.G., Cook, R. (eds.) Proc. of SIGGRAPH 1995, pp. 47–54. ACM, New York (1995)
9. Perlin, K., Goldberg, A.: Improv: a system for scripting interactive actors in virtual worlds. In: Proc. of SIGGRAPH 1996, pp. 205–216. ACM, New York (1996)
10. Camurri, A., Mazzarino, B., Ricchetti, M., Timmers, R., Volpe, G.: Multimodal Analysis of Expressive Gesture in Music and Dance Performances. In: Camurri, A., Volpe, G. (eds.) GW 2003. LNCS (LNAI), vol. 2915, pp. 20–39. Springer, Heidelberg (2004)
11. Levine, S., Krhenbhl, P., Thrun, S., Koltun, V.: Gesture controllers. In: Hoppe, H. (ed.) Proc. of SIGGRAPH 2010, ACM, New York (2010), Article 124, 11 pages

Towards Conversational Agents That Attend to and Adapt to Communicative User Feedback

Hendrik Buschmeier and Stefan Kopp

Sociable Agents Group, CITEC, Bielefeld University
PO-Box 10 01 31, 33501 Bielefeld, Germany
{hbuschme,skopp}@techfak.uni-bielefeld.de

Abstract. Successful dialogue is based on collaborative efforts of the interactants to ensure mutual understanding. This paper presents work towards making conversational agents 'attentive speakers' that continuously attend to the communicative feedback given by their interlocutors and adapt their ongoing and subsequent communicative behaviour to their needs. A comprehensive conceptual and architectural model for this is proposed and first steps of its realisation are described. Results from a prototype implementation are presented.

Keywords: Communicative feedback, attentive speaker agents, feedback elicitation, feedback interpretation, attributed listener state, adaptation.

1 Introduction

Spoken interaction between human users and conversational agents is classically considered to consist of two distinct activities – listening and speaking. The interactants take strict turns and at each point of time one of them is the speaker and the other the listener. Natural dialogue, however, is characterised by continuous information exchange through which dialogue partners constantly collaborate in order to mutually coordinate and establish shared beliefs [7]. One pertinent mechanisms for this is communicative feedback that listeners provide in the form of short vocal-verbal (e.g., 'uh-huh') as well as nonverbal (e.g., head nodding) signals and that cooperative speakers attend to and take into account in order to adapt their utterances to what they think the listeners need or want.

Researchers in the virtual agents community have noticed the importance of these mechanisms and have started to develop systems that act as 'active listeners', i.e., agents that produce feedback signals in response to user actions [12,14,17,4,5]. In contrast to this, the at least equally important capability of being able to perceive, interpret, and respond to communicative user feedback is effectively non-existent in conversational virtual agents (but see [19] for a first effort). Here, we propose a comprehensive model for such 'attentive speaker agents' that enables them to attend to and to adapt to different kinds of feedback produced by their human interlocutors. Furthermore, we show a first prototype of

H. Högni Vilhjálmsson et al. (Eds.): IVA 2011, LNAI 6895, pp. 169–182, 2011.

the conversational agent 'Billie' that implements and demonstrates core aspects of this concept in a calendar assistant domain.

This paper is organised as follows. Sect. 2 reviews how interlocutors use feedback in dialogue and describes related work on modelling feedback in human–agent interaction. Sect. 3 then presents the model for attentive speaker agents and gives details on the architecture and its processing components. Following this, Sect. 4 describes our first instantiation of an attentive speaker agent and Sect. 5 discusses future work and concludes the paper.

2 Background and Related Work

2.1 Communicative Feedback in Human Dialogue

A prerequisite for robust and efficient dialogue is that both interlocutors participate actively beyond the mere exchange of turns. In general, dialogue is characterised by an interactional dimension: interlocutors collaborate to reach a common goal, respond to each other's needs and coordinate their actions all the time, making it a 'joint activity' [7]. These coordinations and accommodations happen on different levels, from implicitly to explicitly, from instantaneous to over longer stretches of the dialogue [13].

On the lowest level, interlocutors tend to 'align' to each other by using the same words, pronouncing them alike or choosing similar linguistic structures [18]. Besides its hypothesised mechanistic nature, this alignment has also deliberate aspects when being used by interlocutors to indicate a shared vocabulary and, to some extent, conceptual agreement [6]. On the highest level, coordination takes explicit negotiation and meta-communication (e.g., 'No, I think that ...') to develop a common understanding of the topic as well as each other's beliefs and stances toward it. The focus of the present work lies on an intermediate level, where dialogue partners establish 'feedback loops' to coordinate their immediate actions, using implicit as well as explicit means.

The classical notion of feedback refers to modulated signals that are 'fed back' to the producer of an action and are used to 'control' the operation of the entity by communicating its distance from a certain (desired) state. Entities thus profit from feedback loops by being able to adapt to new circumstances and to try out new actions and then measure their effectiveness in reaching goals.

The 'entities' we are concerned with here – interlocutors in dialogue – jointly establish such feedback loops: speakers communicate or negotiate the main content via a primary stream of dialogue, while addresses employ a separate (sometimes called back-channel) stream to indicate, display, or signal how they process what the speaker currently talks about.

This communicative feedback can be used to convey various meanings, including the basic communicative functions 'contact', 'perception', 'understanding', 'acceptance/agreement' and 'attitudinal reaction' [1,14]. Listeners confirming contact convey that a fundamental precondition for interactions is fulfilled. When perception is communicated, speakers can see that listeners perceive their actions. Addressees communicating understanding show that they comprehend a message's content and integrated it successfully into their conceptualisation of the conversation. Listeners communicating acceptance, agreement or their attitude towards a speaker's action convey that they successfully evaluated it and in which way. In addition, communicative feedback can express a number of derived functions with a shift in meanings, e.g., 'understand more or less', 'already understood for quite some time', 'understood at last', etc. Higher functions entail lower functions. If, for instance, perception is communicated, it can be assumed that contact holds. Similarly, attitudinal reactions entail understanding (and therefore perception and contact). In the case of negative feedback, the entailment relation is reversed so that, e.g., communicating problems in understanding implies contact and perception to be present.

The communicated status of contact, perception or understanding only reflects a listener's self-assessment and, of course, this does not necessarily imply mutual understanding, but is rather a precondition for this. For this reason, speakers needs to interpret form and timing of feedback signals in order to be able to respond to them in a way that facilitates mutual understanding. If they are interested in reaching the shared goals of an interaction – which is usually the case – they do this.

It was found, for example, that speakers in a task-oriented dialogue study, pay close attention to the actions and behaviour of their listeners, while speaking. When detecting problems in understanding or seeing that further explanation is necessary, they interrupted their ongoing utterances immediately and adapted their subsequent speech according to the listeners' needs [8]. A further study even found that receiving feedback is important for speakers to tell a story well. There, listeners of a close call story were distracted experimentally, without the narrators knowing about the distraction task. In comparison to attentive listeners, distracted listeners produced less feedback and especially less 'specific feedback' (which roughly corresponds to feedback communicating understanding, agreement, acceptance and attitudinal reactions). This confused speakers and put them off their stride at important points of the narration, resulting in stories measurably less well told [2].

2.2   Communicative Feedback in Human–Agent Interaction

Research on communicative feedback in virtual agents has, for the most part, tackled the task of giving feedback in response to user utterances. To solve this problem, a number of models have been proposed for determining the appropriate timing of feedback (ranging from rules-based to complex machine learning approaches, e.g., [25,17]) and for turning different feedback functions into nonverbal as well as vocal and linguistic behaviour [24,22,5]. Less attention has been paid to the question which feedback function to use (exceptions being [12,14,4]), mainly due to the open challenge of understanding unrestricted spoken language in large domains, which would lead agents to give frequent and less informative signals of non-understanding.

Even sparser is research on how to react to communicative user feedback in human-machine dialogue. The main challenges here lie in the recognition of user feedback signals while producing system behaviour, and in the capability of adapting already planned but not yet uttered system behaviour accordingly. The 'DUG-1' system [9] generates utterances incrementally while simultaneously attending to user utterances, enabling immediate reaction by re-planning output if necessary. Different work describes a method to recognise whether a user's feedback signal is of type 'backchannel' or 'ask-back' (i.e., signalling a problem in understanding), and then reacting by either continuing as planned or altering the subsequent utterance according to the user's needs [10].

Recently, a group of researchers at the 'eNTERFACE 2010' summer workshop made progress on important aspects of attentive speaker agents, including classification of vocal feedback signals, adaptive continuous generation of behaviour, and synthesis of feedback elicitation cues [19].

In sum, recognising and responding to feedback constitutes important, yet open research problems. Recent work has set out to tackle some of the challenges, from continuous behaviour generation to concurrent feedback classification. We contribute here the first comprehensive architectural model that exceeds standard virtual agent and dialogue system architectures by fusing the generation of communicative behaviour with the continuous processing of and adaptation to user feedback. Furthermore, we describe a concrete first realisation of this model, used to endow a calendar assistant agent with qualities of attentive speakers.

3   A Concept for Attentive Speaker Agents

Attentive speaker agents must be able (1) to invite feedback from their users by providing opportunities or by eliciting it when needed; (2) to detect and interpret communicative feedback; and (3) to adapt their ongoing and subsequent communicative behaviours to the users' needs. In the following we describe an architecture that supports these capabilities and discuss the three requirements in detail.

3.1   Overall Model and Architecture

An architecture is needed that features all key components of behaviour generation and pairs them with components that keep track of the ongoing dialogue and the state of the interlocutor. Thus our model, blueprinted in Fig. 1, consists of two information processing streams – one for behaviour generation and one for feedback processing. Both streams are linked via two representations.

First, 'dialogue move information' (DMI) holding the current state of the dialogue. As in standard information state approaches to dialogue management, this consists of the type of the dialogue act of the ongoing dialogue move, its propositional content as well as its grounding status. Moreover, it could also include meta information such as the move's complexity, its estimated difficulty with respect to understanding, and so on.

The second representation is the 'attributed listener state' (ALS), which forms part of what will later become a full interlocutor/user model. Following the model of listener states we used in previous work on feedback generation [14], the ALS

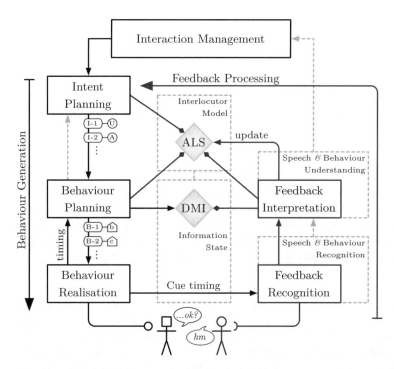

Fig. 1. Blueprint of the proposed architecture for attentive speaker agents. Content and behaviour planning draw upon an 'attributed listener state' (ALS) in their planning process and generate output in incremental chunks that can be augmented with feedback elicitation cues. Communicative user feedback is interpreted given the current dialogue move information (DMI) and updates the attributed listener state. Arrows with diamond-shaped heads indicate that a component takes information from the referenced representation into account.

represents the assumed state of the listener in terms of the basic communicative functions contact, perception, understanding, and acceptance/agreement (C, P, U, A; cf. Sect. 4.1). The timing of changes of these values is indicative of the particular parts of an utterance that caused these changes. Integrated over time, the ALS also captures how easy/difficult it has been for the listener to perceive or understand the last n utterance chunks.

The generation branch of the architecture draws upon the SAIBA pipeline [15], which tries to generalise from design decisions made in previous systems, resulting in a tripartition of the generation task. As in SAIBA, behaviour generation in our architecture starts from an 'Intent Planning' component which decides on the content that will be communicated (in an abstract form) and on appropriate functions to express this content. These are passed on to the 'Behaviour Planning' component, where communicative intent is transformed into detailed behaviour plans by generating natural language utterances, finding gestures, head nods, eye gaze and facial expressions that fulfil the specified functions, and relating speech and nonverbal behaviour to each other. Finally, the 'Behaviour Realisation' component synthesises the utterances, schedules and executes nonverbal behaviour, and animates the virtual agent.

The feedback processing branch comprises a 'Feedback Recognition' component for spotting user behaviour that can be considered relevant feedback, and a 'Feedback Interpretation' component that turns these behaviour into ALS updates. Due to the multimodal and embodied nature of feedback, the agent is required to be equipped with sensors and algorithms that can extract the lexical/phonetic form, prosodic features and voice quality of a user's verbal feedback signal, the parameters of head movements (type, energy, amplitude), eye gaze (gaze target, length of fixations) and facial expressions.

Feedback Recognition operates upon these sensors, receiving information on the occurrences and timing of feedback elicitation/invitation cues from behaviour realisation' to mitigate the detection and recognition problem. Furthermore, the spotting of listener-internal feedback, which can occur anytime, can be supported by predictions of whether and when the listener might give feedback based on estimates of the difficulty of the current utterance or its potential to trigger an emotional reaction.

Feedback Interpretation then needs to classify the features of the feedback signals for their function and meaning in terms of changes of the ALS (e.g., what does the variation in the pitch contour mean? what is the meaning of a big amplitude in head nodding? etc.). This mapping needs to be extracted from empirical data and a study has been carried out in which data on 21 dyads cooperating in our target scenario of calendar planning have been gathered. The analysis is currently underway.

A cornerstone of the whole architecture is incremental processing [21] in both behaviour generation and feedback processing. This is needed to take user feedback into account while the agent is still speaking, enabling the system to adapt to the user's needs almost instantly. The behaviour generation stream uses chunk-based incrementallity, with chunks of the size of intonation units. Intent planning creates communicative messages and passes them on to behaviour planning, which generates the behavioural details of each chunk (verbal and nonverbal). Importantly, both components take the current ALS into account when specifying and generating new chunks. This closes the feedback loop and leads to continuous, incremental adaptation to user feedback.

In order to do this, a model of how to react to feedback signals is required. Should an utterance be continued after receiving positive understanding feedback or should future chunks be shortened or even skipped? Should a problematic chunk – when the user gave negative understanding or perception feedback – be elaborated upon, restated in simpler words or expressed in a way so that the important aspects are explicitly highlighted (for example by using discourse markers or signpost language)? As can be seen, adaptations need to occur at the levels of intent planning as well as behaviour planning. As described below, cf. Sect. 4.2, in our current system these adaptations are only realised in and delegated to the behaviour planner, which maps listener state values onto continuous adjustments of generation choices in sentence planning.

Feedback processing runs continuously and concurrently. As in previous work [14], updating the ASL is done by increasing or decreasing single values by a fixed amount in accordance with the feedback signal's features and its classified feedback functions. This is done for each verbal feedback signal as well for head movements; user gaze target information is processed continuously. The listener state is then reset after each utterance.

3.2 Inviting User Feedback

Listeners can provide feedback in response to listener-external as well as listener-internal causes [14]. Listener-external causes are speaker actions to request feedback [3], e.g., gazing at the addressee and a rising intonation at the end of an utterance, or explicitly asking for feedback with '..., ok?'. Another listener-external cause arises from basic norms of cooperativeness in dialogue, e.g., it is expected from listeners to 'backchannel' from time to time in order to show that contact (attention) is still established.

In contrast, listener-internal causes for feedback arise from processes of perception, understanding, or evaluation. Having not perceived an important word, for example, might cause a listener to express this problem with the interjection 'huh?', a sudden loss of understanding might result in a puzzled facial expressions, and a positive attitude towards the speaker's message might cause an energetic head nod. While some of these behaviours may be produced anytime and offhand [14] – e.g., when consequences are severe or emotional responses cannot be withheld – collaborative listeners will usually give this feedback when the speaker provides an 'opportunity' and is particularly attentive to it.

Attentive speaker agents, therefore, need to be able to produce cues that elicit feedback from human users or signal the opening-up of feedback opportunities. To this end, agents need a model of which elicitation cues are likely to be effective, at which points of the interaction they can be produced, how they are produced, and how they can be fitted in into the current flow of the primary behaviour. In our architecture, producing feedback elicitation cues and providing feedback opportunities thus is an integral part of the attentive speaker's behaviour planning process: The intent planner decides whether feedback is needed and which type of communicative function should be requested. That is, feedback-based coordination with the listener is considered a deliberate activity and feedback elicitation a special case of intentional acts.

The behaviour planning component then chooses cues which fit in into the current behaviour and are likely to cause the listener to provide feedback of the type the agent seeks. A recent study [11] showed that up to six different individual cues (intonation, intensity, pitch, inter-pausal duration, voice quality, part-of-speech information) are used by speakers to invite backchannel feedback, with the number of individual cues combined in a complex cue correlating with backchannel occurrence in a quadratic manner. We assume that such cues can be generated and assembled automatically at the level of behaviour planning, either explicitly intended (elicitation) or not (creating feedback opportunities). The decision which cues to use will be made probabilistically drawing upon a

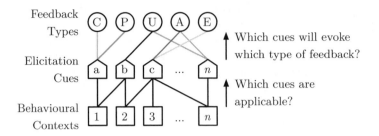

Fig. 2. Probabilistic mapping of elicitation cues {a,b, ..., n} that are applicable in certain behavioural contexts {1, 2, ..., n} onto the feedback types {C, P, U, A, E} with which listeners are likely to react to these cues

model such as shown in Fig. 2. Note that only a subset of the elicitation cues is applicable in a given context (i.e., some utterances might not be suitable to be followed by '..., ok?') and that not all cues are likely to evoke the sought type of feedback from the listener.

4   First Realisation

As a first implementation of the proposed model, the attentive speaker agent 'Billie' is being developed. Billie interacts with its user in a calendar domain (see Fig. 3), where it acts as the user's personal secretary who knows about appointments, requests, or cancellations and discusses the week plan with the user. Being an attentive speaker is important in this application domain since Billie comes to communicate many proposals for which it needs to make sure that the user understands everything, as well as to discover and resolve misunderstandings and disagreements early on. We have implemented some core aspects of the attentive speaker model and we present here details on the capabilities and inner workings of the components we have so far.

4.1   Feedback Recognition and Interpretation

Billie's abilities for dealing with linguistic feedback are currently limited to explicit user-utterances such as 'Yeah', 'That suits me well', 'Pardon me.', etc. that can be recognised easily with off-the-shelf automatic speech recognition systems. In addition, Billie is able to recognise nonverbal user-feedback by continuously monitoring the user's presence, head movements and eye gaze in real time using a commercial stereo vision-based face and eye-tracking system[1].

Billie uses the information about detectable user's verbal and nonverbal behaviours to constantly update an ALS defined as a tuple $ALS = (C, P, U, A, dP, dU)$ of numerical variables for attributed contact, perception, understanding and agreement states, each of which ranging from 0.0 (no contact, perception, etc.)

---

[1] faceLAB – http://www.seeingmachines.com/product/facelab/

Fig. 3. The attentive speaker agent 'Billie' interacting with a user in the calendar assistant domain

to 1.0 (full contact, etc.). Each interpreted positive/negative feedback leads to an increase/decrease of the corresponding variable (plus entailed updates) by a fixed amount. The two variables 'difficulty of perception' (dP) and 'difficulty of understanding' (dU) are calculated as mean values of the last n perception (understanding) values.

The agent interprets the user's presence as indexical feedback [1] about the basic function 'contact'. Likewise, if the user steps away from the agent or averts the gaze from the display for a significant amount of time, Billie takes this as negative contact feedback. In result, the agent stops talking at the end of the current chunk and only continues when the user comes back and signals to be ready to continue the interaction.

Information on the user's gaze targets are integrated over short time windows and then evaluated in the context of Billie's own gaze target. If Billie and the user gaze at the same target (e.g., the user's gaze follows Billie's to the calendar when Billie talks about a calendar item) this is interpreted as positive evidence that the user perceives (and to some degree understands) what Billie said. Billie also recognises the user's head gestures and classifies them into nods, shakes, and tilts with a user-independent head gesture recognition methods based on 'Ordered Means' sequential probabilistic models [26]. These are particularly well suited for fast and incremental classification. Recognised head gestures are interpreted as signalled feedback [1] in the current context as soon as a certain threshold is exceeded. If Billie just asked for confirmation, head nodding is taken as acknowledgement and head shakes as rejection, i.e., as feedback of the function acceptance/agreement. When the user nods while Billie is presenting information on the other hand, nodding is interpreted as evidence of understanding.

4.2 Behaviour Generation and Adaptation

Billie's abilities to adapt to user feedback as accumulated in the ALS focus on the incremental generation of verbal utterances. Billie's intent planning is

Table 1. Effects of attributed listener state (or changes therein) on Billie's behaviours

ALS	Condition	Effect	Component
C	< 0.4	suspend after current chunk	Intent Planning
C	≥ 0.6	resume after suspend	Intent Planning
P	< 0.4	repeat current chunk	Intent Planning
U	< 0.4	start current utterance anew	Intent Planning
dP	always	adapt verbosity of utterances	Behaviour Planning
dU	always	adapt explicitness of utterances	Behaviour Planning

currently done in a component which takes care of managing the whole interaction. In addition to specifying what Billie should do next, it is also responsible for keyword-spotting-based 'understanding' of user utterances in the current context, managing back-end resources such as the calendar representation, updating the calendar visualisation, etc. The production of elicitation cues for feedback is also specified in intent planning and currently only 'translated' to either an explicit request for acknowledgement, a short pause, or a change of gaze target (e.g., from user to calendar, from calendar to user) by the behaviour planner.

Table 1 explicates the currently employed strategies for reacting to ALS changes (thresholds being test-and-refine choices). When the ALS values suggest that Billie lost contact to the user, intent planning stops providing communicative intent chunks and only continues to do so if contact has been re-established. Intent planning also reacts to changes in the ALS if indicating problems of perception or understanding. In these cases either the ongoing chunk is repeated or the ongoing utterance is cancelled and started anew.

Billie's behaviour planning component contains a novel natural language microplanner based on the SPUD framework [23], which has been extended to take the attributed listener state into account while generating utterances chunk by chunk. To this end, the linguistic constructions used by the microplanner are annotated with information about their verbosity and then chosen according to the ALS's meta-variable 'difficulty of perception', leading to utterances that are more verbose, i.e., using more words to express the same idea, if the user has problems perceiving the agent. Furthermore, the set of desired updates to the information state that the current chunk is to make is dynamically changed according to the ALS's meta-variable 'difficulty of understanding': more (redundant) information about the current calendar item is put into an utterance when the user has difficulty understanding what the agent wants to convey.

Upon language generation, a chunk is augmented with specifications of appropriate nonverbal behaviour and passed on to Billie's behaviour realisation component (based on the 'Articulated Communicator Engine' [16] and backed by 'MARY TTS'[2] for speech synthesis). The realiser schedules speech and nonverbal behaviour, provides the estimated duration back to the behaviour planner and starts the animation. The behaviour planner delays the generation of the

---

[2] MARY TTS – https://mary.dfki.de/

next chunk as long as necessary/possible in order to take the most recent user feedback into account, while ensuring a seamless transition between chunks. In result, adaptations occur rapidly from the next chunk onward, without the user noticing that chunks are generated and processed incrementally.

4.3 Example Interaction

To demonstrate the system and the underlying model, we discuss an example interaction with Billie. Fig. 4 visualises how the 'dominant' feedback function (according to the entailment-hierarchy) in the ASL changes over time. Note that this simulation is meant to demonstrate the qualitative working of the model, it may change according to parameter configurations and runtime conditions such as exact timing of user and agent actions. The chunks of Billie's behaviour are shown at the top, the user's actions at the bottom (all utterances are translated from German).

Billie starts by telling the user 'on Monday April 25th; from 10 AM to 12 PM; you've got seminar'. When talking about the calendar item, Billie and the user mutually gaze at the calendar, which is feedback for Billie that the users perceives its utterances without problems. After this first contribution, Billie makes a pause, giving the user an opportunity to provide feedback. The user does so by nodding, thus showing understanding. Billie continues saying 'afterwards'. As the user looks away from the display, Billie takes the missing user gaze as evidence of a loss of contact and suspends its presentation at the end of the chunk. Billie resumes as soon as the user looks at him again for a certain amount of time so that contact is re-established. Billie continues with 'the appointment at 6; Badminton;' where the user shows problems in perception by uttering 'pardon me?'. The perception level drops below the value of 0.4 and Billie repeats the last chunk again, this time generating the more verbose version 'with subject Badminton' as the difficulty in perception value changed. The user's nod is interpreted as understanding feedback and Billie goes on saying 'is moved to 8' and gazes at the calendar. The user does not follow Billie's

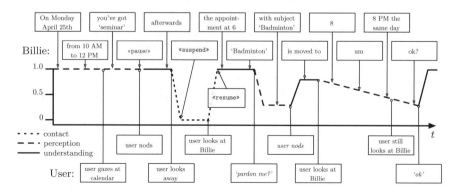

Fig. 4. Example interaction demonstrating how the 'dominant' variable in the ALS changes over time

gaze, indicating problems in perception which leads to a continuously decreasing perception value. Billie again repeats the last chunk in a more verbose way, this time saying '8 PM the same day'. As the user is still not reacting, and the perception value is further decreasing, Billie closes his utterance with the explicit feedback elicitation cue 'ok?' which the user responds to with the signal of understanding 'ok' leading to an increasing understanding value.

5   Conclusions and Future Work

In this paper, we surveyed how interlocutors in dialogue coordinate their interaction by jointly establishing feedback loops with a focus on how attentive human speakers elicit communicative feedback from their addressees, as well as on how they react and adapt to their needs by immediately taking feedback signals into account. On this basis, we defined three requirements for conversational agents to be attentive speakers and we presented an extensive concept for them to be capable of attending to and adapting to feedback of their human users. Finally, we reported on the first technical prototype of the virtual agent 'Billie', an attentive speaker who interacts with its users in a calendar domain. So far, the agent can attend to some types of verbal and nonverbal feedback and adapt its online generated behaviour to the users' needs.

The enabling core of this is a system architecture that interlinks the two processing streams of behaviour generation and feedback processing via two shared representations: (1) a model of the agents interaction partner containing a 'listener state' that the agent attributes to a user on the grounds of the user's communicative feedback, and (2) the dialogue's information state containing the discourse history as well as details on the ongoing utterance and timing of elicitation cues. Immediate online adaptation to the user's needs (as inferred from the attributed listener state) is possible since the architecture is based on incremental processing. User feedback is recognised and interpreted while the agent is speaking. Behaviour generation produces output in small chunks so that the next chunk that will be produced already takes feedback into account.

While our first prototype implementation already shows the feasibility of the approach, future work will need to realise further parts laid out in the concept and not yet fully implemented in Billie. The feedback processing components should, for example, be able to not only recognise explicit verbal feedback utterances, but also short vocal feedback signals such as 'uh-huh', 'hm' or 'oh' and interpret prosodically different variants of them. Human listeners constantly use these and can realise a huge variety of communicative functions with them [22]. Opening up this world for an attentive speaker agent would be an important step towards more human-like, richer attentiveness in dialogue.

Concerning behaviour generation, Billie so far adapts mainly on the level of behaviour planning – only coarse adaptations being carried out on the level of intent planning so far. In the future, more fine grained and precisely timed adaptations are planned during specification of communicative intent, too. It will then be possible to discontinue a current utterance and jump to the next topic if users signal that they have understood sufficiently. Similarly, intent planning might decide on a different communication strategy if users are not able understand what Billie communicates.

Finally, we are working on a coupling of interlocutor model and information state, where the attributed listener state can influence the grounding status of the dialogue moves. If it is known, for example, that the user does not have difficulties in understanding, previously presented information can confidently be assumed to be in the common ground – even if the user did not explicitly accepted it. Likewise, a low value in perception reduces the probability of presented information being grounded. Modelling such interactions between the ALS and items in the information state in a probabilistic framework will provide a novel and flexible way of capturing 'degrees of grounding' [20] in human–agent dialogue.

Acknowledgements. We would like to credit Benjamin Dosch with developing the concepts and mechanisms that make the SPUD NLG microplanner adaptive to the 'attributed listener state'. This research is supported by the Deutsche Forschungsgemeinschaft (DFG) in the Center of Excellence EXC 277 in 'Cognitive Interaction Technology' (CITEC).

References

1. Allwood, J., Nivre, J., Ahlsén, E.: On the semantics and pragmatics of linguistic feedback. Journal of Semantics 9, 1–26 (1992)
2. Bavelas, J.B., Coates, L., Johnson, T.: Listeners as co-narrators. Journal of Personality and Social Psychology 79, 941–952 (2000)
3. Bavelas, J.B., Coates, L., Johnson, T.: Listener responses as a collaborative process: The role of gaze. Journal of Communication 52, 566–580 (2002)
4. Bevacqua, E.: Computational Model of Listener Behavior for Embodied Conversational Agents. Ph.D. thesis, Université Paris 8, Paris, France (2009)
5. Bevacqua, E., Pammi, S., Hyniewska, S.J., Schröder, M., Pelachaud, C.: Multimodal backchannels for embodied conversational agents. In: Safonova, A. (ed.) IVA 2010. LNCS, vol. 6356, pp. 194–200. Springer, Heidelberg (2010)
6. Brennan, S.E., Clark, H.H.: Conceptual pacts and lexical choice in conversation. Journal of Experimental Psychology: Learning, Memory, and Cognition 22, 1482–1493 (1996)
7. Clark, H.H.: Using Language. Cambridge University Press, Cambridge (1996)
8. Clark, H.H., Krych, M.A.: Speaking while monitoring addressees for understanding. Journal of Memory and Language 50, 62–81 (2004)
9. Dohsaka, K., Shimazu, A.: A system architecture for spoken utterance production in collaborative dialogue. In: Working Notes of the IJCAI 1997 Workshop on Collaboration, Cooperation and Conflict in Dialogue Systems, Nagoya, Japan (1997)
10. Fujie, S., Miyake, R., Kobayashi, T.: Spoken dialogue system using recognition of user's feedback for rhythmic dialogue. In: Proc. of Speech Prosody 2006, Dresden, Germany (2006)
11. Gravano, A., Hirschberg, J.: Turn-taking cues in task-oriented dialogue. Computer Speech and Language 25, 601–634 (2011)

12. Jonsdottir, G.R., Gratch, J., Fast, E., Thórisson, K.R.: Fluid semantic back-channel feedback in dialogue: Challenges and progress. In: Pelachaud, C., Martin, J.-C., André, E., Chollet, G., Karpouzis, K., Pelé, D. (eds.) IVA 2007. LNCS (LNAI), vol. 4722, pp. 154–160. Springer, Heidelberg (2007)

13. Kopp, S.: Social resonance and embodied coordination in face-to-face conversation with artificial interlocutors. Speech Communication 52, 587–597 (2010)

14. Kopp, S., Allwood, J., Grammer, K., Ahlsen, E., Stocksmeier, T.: Modeling embodied feedback with virtual humans. In: Wachsmuth, I., Knoblich, G. (eds.) ZiF Research Group International Workshop. LNCS (LNAI), vol. 4930, pp. 18–37. Springer, Heidelberg (2008)

15. Kopp, S., Krenn, B., Marsella, S.C., Marshall, A.N., Pelachaud, C., Pirker, H., Thórisson, K.R., Vilhjálmsson, H.H.: Towards a common framework for multimodal generation: The behavior markup language. In: Gratch, J., Young, M., Aylett, R.S., Ballin, D., Olivier, P. (eds.) IVA 2006. LNCS (LNAI), vol. 4133, pp. 205–217. Springer, Heidelberg (2006)

16. Kopp, S., Wachsmuth, I.: Synthesizing multimodal utterances for conversational agents. Computer Animation and Virtual Worlds 15, 39–52 (2004)

17. Morency, L.P., de Kok, I., Gratch, J.: Predicting listener backchannels: A probabilistic multimodal approach. In: Proc. of the 8th Int. Conf. on Intelligent Virtual Agents, Tokyo, Japan, pp. 176–190 (2008)

18. Pickering, M.J., Garrod, S.: Toward a mechanistic psychology of dialogue. Behavioral and Brain Sciences 27, 169–226 (2004)

19. Reidsma, D., de Kok, I., Neiberg, D., Pammi, S., van Straalen, B., Truong, K., van Welbergen, H.: Continuous interaction with a virtual human. Journal on Multimodal User Interfaces (Published online May 27, 2011)

20. Roque, A., Traum, D.R.: Degrees of grounding based on evidence of understanding. In: Proc. of the 9th SIGdial Workshop on Discourse and Dialogue, Columbus, OH, pp. 54–63 (2008)

21. Schlangen, D., Skantze, G.: A general, abstract model of incremental dialogue processing. Dialogue and Discourse 2, 83–111 (2011)

22. Stocksmeier, T., Kopp, S., Gibbon, D.: Synthesis of prosodic attitudinal variants in German backchannel "ja". In: Proc. of Interspeech 2007, Antwerp, Belgium, pp. 1290–1293 (2007)

23. Stone, M., Doran, C., Webber, B., Bleam, T., Palmer, M.: Microplanning with communicative intentions: The SPUD system. Computational Intelligence 19(4), 311–381 (2003)

24. Ward, N.: Pragmatic functions of prosodic features in non-lexical utterances. In: Proc. of Speech Prosody 2004, Nara, Japan, pp. 325–328 (2004)

25. Ward, N., Tsukahara, W.: Prosodic features which cue back-channel responses in English and Japanese. Journal of Pragmatics 38, 1177–1207 (2000)

26. Wöhler, N.C., Großekathöfer, U., Dierker, A., Hanheide, M., Kopp, S., Hermann, T.: A calibration-free head gesture recognition system with online capability. In: Proc. of the 20th Int. Conf. on Pattern Recognition, Istanbul, Turkey, pp. 3814–3817 (2010)

Quid Pro Quo? Reciprocal Self-disclosure and Communicative Accomodation towards a Virtual Interviewer

Astrid M. von der Pütten, Laura Hoffmann, Jennifer Klatt, and Nicole C. Krämer

University Duisburg-Essen, Department for Social Psychology: Media and Communication,
Forsthausweg 2,
47048 Duisburg, Germany
{Astrid.von-der-Puetten, Laura.Hoffmann, Jennifer.Klatt,
Nicole.Kraemer}@uni-due.de

Abstract. Cassell and Miller [1] proposed the use of virtual agents as interviewers to be advantageous, because one can control for interviewer effects and variance, provide a sense of anonymity and increase the interviewee's motivation to complete the survey. Against the background of Communication Adaptation Theory and empirical results on reciprocal self-disclosure, we investigated the influence of the agent's reciprocal self-disclosure and wordiness on participants' self-disclosure and perception of the agent and the interview in an experimental study with a 2x2 between-subjects design. While reciprocal self-disclosure only affected perceived co-presence, wordiness influenced both the participants' verbal behavior (with regard to word usage and intimacy of answers) and their perception of the interview. Theoretical implications are discussed.

Keywords: ECA, experimental study, linguistic alignment, communication adaptation theory, reciprocal self-disclosure, social effects, virtual agent.

1 Introduction

Since the 1980's, along with the possibility to apply computer-administered interviews, self-disclosure towards computers (compared to humans) emerged as a research topic in the area of Human-Computer Interaction (HCI). Computer-administered or web-based interviews can be advantageous compared to face-to-face interviews, which might cause interviewer effects due to gender, race, or socioeconomic status of the interviewer [2]. These biases can be reduced in web-based interviews; however, they lead to relatively high drop-out-rates. As already proposed by Cassell and Miller [1] using virtual agents as interviewers might be a solution to address both problems: a) Control for interviewer effects and interviewer variance, by displaying the same agent, characteristics and behavior at all times, and b) provide a sense of anonymity, because it still has the features of a computer. Additionally, virtual agents may increase the interviewee's motivation to complete the survey, because they also possess human-like features such as non-verbal cues. However, there are still open questions, which will be addressed in this study.

H. Högni Vilhjálmsson et al. (Eds.): IVA 2011, LNAI 6895, pp. 183–194, 2011.

1.1 Self Disclosure towards Computers

A meta-analysis by Weisband and Kiesler in 1996 [3] already showed that studies comparing computer forms with other formats (pen & paper questionnaire or face-to-face interview) showed larger effect sizes (increase in self-disclosure in the computer condition) when the measure elicits sensitive, personal, or otherwise risky information than when the measure elicits more impersonal information; a finding important to many research fields in the social sciences which deal with intimate and sensitive information (e.g. risky sexual behavior [4]). Moon [5] referred to the growing amount of personal information that companies collect electronically about their customers including information that can be regarded as intimate or sensitive and discussed the role of reciprocal self-disclosure against this background. Moon analyzed whether people are willing to disclose information to a computer despite the general tendency of reluctance to reveal high-risk information about oneself, c.f. [6]. She hypothesized that a computer which disclosed information about itself will elicit more self-disclosure on the side of the user following the rules of reciprocal self-disclosure [7]. The study included three conditions: a reciprocal condition, in which the computer first disclosed information about itself followed by the main questions; a long condition including some filler sentences and the main questions and a non-reciprocal condition, in which the computer merely asks the questions. Results showed that the users' responses were more intimate in the condition with reciprocal self-disclosure (measured in terms of depth, breadth, and number of self-disclosure) than in the long or non-reciprocal condition. However, there are some constraints for the applicability of these findings to common interview-/ survey systems. For instance, Moon used reciprocal self-disclosure for every single question, which was criticized by Joinson [8], because "for traditional Likert-based questionnaires or surveys, such a methodology would be cumbersome, if not impossible. The research also was not conducted using the Internet, but instead relied on students turning up to sit in front of the experimental computer, so whether such a technique would work for WWW-based studies is unknown."(p.588). Furthermore, the focus of this study was laid on the computer itself and the disclosed information contained e.g. technical features of the computer. This, however, does not seem to be appropriate for other research questions. In an interview on risky sexual behavior, it is questionable whether participants would find it "normal", if the computer discloses that it also behaves risky, because it does not have an anti-virus program. Joinson [8] addressed both points in a study, in which he transferred Moon's self-disclosure scenario to web-based surveys. He used vignettes on the starting page of the survey by either just greeting the subject or providing personal information about the experimenter such as contact details, family status, personal likes, etc. Within the survey he used six of Moon's [5] self-disclosure questions (e.g. "What was the biggest disappointment in your life?"). Although the experimenter's self-disclosure led to a greater breadth of self-disclosure amongst participants, participants' answers did not differ in depth of self-disclosure. Joinson discussed that the increased breadth of disclosed information might be due to an adaptation effect on the side of the user. Users would use more words to answer the questions because the experimenter introduced himself more wordily.

Self-disclosure towards Agents and Avatars. Most studies dealing with virtual agents or avatars did not investigate the phenomenon of self-disclosure itself, but utilized self-disclosure tasks for investigations such as the impact of nonverbal feedback of virtual agents [9], personal dispositions (e.g. social anxiety) [10], or stimuli inconsistency [11]. Those studies did not include reciprocal self-disclosure shown by the agent/avatar, but concentrated on the variation of visual and auditory stimuli. So far, the topic of *reciprocal* self-disclosure as a phenomenon itself was not investigated employing virtual agents.

1.2 Adaptation of Communicative Behaviors

Joinson [8] found that the experimenter's self-disclosure lead to more breadth of disclosure (participants used more words), but no greater depth (participants did not reveal more intimate information). He argued that this might be due to the selection of questions, or a mere adaptation of the user to the verbal pattern of the interviewing system. Psycholinguistic research indeed showed that people converge in interactions, a phenomenon which has been described in the Communication Accommodation Theory (CAT), cf. [12] for an overview. *Convergence* is defined as "a strategy whereby individuals adapt to each other's communicative behaviors in terms of a wide range of linguistic-prosodic-nonverbal features including speech rate, pausal phenomena and utterance length, phonological variants, smiling, gaze, and so on" [12, p. 35]. CAT states that people accommodate on nonverbal and verbal microscopic levels (e.g. proximity, gaze, smiling, silences, response latency, utterance length) and on more macroscopic levels of behavior (helping, global intimacy, affect, resources) [13]. With regard to verbal behavior, e.g. Bilous and Krauss [14] found that females converged with their interaction partner with regard to total words uttered and utterance length, whereas men converged with regard to utterance length (regardless of the gender of the interviewer). An analysis by Gnisci and Bakeman [15] of 47 lawyer witness examinations at court showed that witnesses accommodated in turn-taking and turn length to the lawyer. Several researchers were able to show that this CAT strategy is also used in interactions with agents (e.g. mimicry of the nonverbal behavior of an agent [16]). However, CAT studies as well as studies on linguistic alignment [17] most often concentrate on more specific linguistic features like speech rate, latencies of pauses (CAT) or lexical or syntactic structures in speech (linguistic alignment). With regard to the latter, a review by Branigan [18] summarizes that linguistic alignment indeed occurs in HCI and this to an even greater extent than in face-to-face dialogues, a phenomenon also known as *computer talk*. In our study, we will concentrate on the total amount of words uttered by the participants.

1.3 Research Question

Since reciprocal self-disclosure had not been investigated in the context of virtual agents (e.g. as virtual interviewers) yet, we directly addressed this phenomenon by focussing on manipulating the verbal behavior of a virtual agent. We were especially interested in the question whether reciprocal self-disclosure itself or a talkative verbal pattern has more influence on participant's self-disclosure. We thus separated the aspects of reciprocal self-disclosure and wordiness in a more controlled way. Like in

Joinson's study, we used vignettes to provide reciprocal self-disclosure or no self-disclosure. With regard to wordiness we presented the interview questions in a more talkative or in a more tight-lipped manner.

2 Method

2.1 Experimental Design and Independent Variables

In order to determine whether people adapt to the behavior of a virtual interviewer during a computer-based interview, we chose a 2x2 between-subjects design with wordiness and reciprocal self-disclosure as independent variables.

Wordiness. First of all we varied the amount of words the virtual interviewer uses to pose the questions (wordy, taciturn). For instance he asks "Often disappointments are worse than embarrassing situations. What has been the biggest disappointment in your life?" in the wordy condition, but only "What has been the biggest disappointment in your life?" in the taciturn condition (see Table 1).

Reciprocal Self-disclosure. Secondly, we varied the extent to which the virtual interviewer discloses personal information towards the participant (self-disclosure, non-self-disclosure). For this purpose we built two different introductions (vignettes). One was placed at the beginning of the interview and another one when the topic changed to sexuality (see Table 1).

Stimulus Material. We chose a male virtual character developed by the Charamel Company (http://www.charamel.de/). The advantages of Charamel's software are the included application kit and text-to-speech engine, which allow the user to script e.g. the nonverbal behavior of the character as well as its speech. With regard to nonverbal behavior the agent showed idle behavior including blinking and posture shifts.

2.2 Dependent Variables

As dependent variables, we assessed the participants' person perception of the virtual interviewer, the self-reported experience of social presence, the general evaluation of

Fig. 1. Screenshot of the virtual interviewer Thomas

the interview and the whole system, and the perceived competence of the interviewer by means of a paper-and-pencil questionnaire after the interview. Additionally, we analyzed the verbal behavior of the participants, which was recorded and transcribed for this purpose. In the following, all measurements are described in detail.

Perception of the Virtual Interviewer. How participants perceived the virtual interviewer was measured with a semantic differential consisting of 37 bi-polar pairs of items (e.g. friendly-unfriendly, tense-relaxed), which are rated on a 7-point scale (Cronbach's alpha = .872). Furthermore, we assessed the interviewer's general competence as an interviewer, and its specific competence in conducting an interview about "romantic relationships and sexuality", on a 5-point Likert-scale from "not at all competent" to "very competent".

Social Presence. To determine the participants' sense of presence, we used the subscale co-presence of the Nowak and Biocca Presence Scale [19], which contains 12 items on the concept of *"perceived other's co-presence"* (Cronbach's alpha = .859) and 6 items on *"self-reported co-presence"* (Cronbach's alpha = .590), both rated on a 5-point Likert scale (from "strongly disagree" to "strongly agree").

General Evaluation of the Interview. The general evaluation of the interaction was assessed by items that asked for the participants' sense of control during the interaction, the enjoyment of the interaction, and whether participants liked to use a system like this for other tasks. Here, participants stated their level of agreement by means of a 5-point Likert-scale (Cronbach's alpha = .835). Additionally, we asked, on a 5-point Likert-scale from "very unpleasant" to "very pleasant", how pleasant or unpleasant the interview as a whole was perceived by the participants.

Behavioral Measurements. In order to determine whether the participants adapt their verbal behavior to the behavior of the virtual interviewer, we analyzed the amount of words participants used to answer the questions as the measure of breadth of self-disclosure. Additionally, to investigate the effect of reciprocal self-disclosure, we analyzed the answers given to the virtual interviewer regarding the depth (intimacy of information) of the information disclosed. The depth of information was qualitatively analyzed using a coding scheme developed based on the present material. We coded a) "no answer" when people refused to give an answer or made excuses; b) "unspecific answer" (e.g. What's the most embarrassing thing you've ever done?: "yes sometimes I do embarrassing things"; What has been your biggest disappointment: "I had some, but they were just minor things") and c) "specific answer" (What's the most embarrassing thing you've ever done?: "I farted in front of the class"; What has been your biggest disappointment?: "my ex-boyfriend betrayed me"). Two independent raters coded the answers and inter-rater reliability was high (Cronbach's alpha = .937). Unlike the other questions, the physical appearance question was formulated as a yes-no-question and people often answered with "no". Unfortunately, we cannot reliably say whether people really do not have dislikes about their physical appearance or whether they refused to answer and thus said "no". We therefore decided to exclude this question from the analysis.

2.3 Moderating Variables

Personality. As moderating variables, we used the Big Five Inventory, which consists of 60 items rated on a 5-point Likert scale from "strongly disagree" to "strongly agree" [20]. It contains five subscales: Neuroticism (Cronbach's alpha = 819), Extraversion (Cronbach's alpha = .717), Openness (Cronbach's alpha = .792), Agreeableness (Cronbach's alpha = .739), and Conscientiousness (Cronbach's alpha = .881).

Disclosure. To measure the participants' predisposition to disclose information we used the Self-disclosure index by Miller, Berg and Archer [21], which contains 10 items rated on a 5-point Likert scale from "disagree" to "agree" (Cronbach's alpha = .799). In addition, we used an ad-hoc item, namely measuring how personal the interview questions were rated on a 5-point Likert scale from "definitely too personal" to "pleasant".

2.4 Participants and Procedure

The study was announced as an interview on the topic "Love and Relationships", which would be conducted using a prototype interviewing system. Eighty-one students (43 females and 38 males) were recruited via general advertising on campus. The mean age was 23.19 years ($SD=2.75$) ranging from 18 to 30 years. The participants were asked to read and sign informed consent forms before the experimental session started. After completing a questionnaire assessing socio-demographic data and personality (Big Five Inventory), participants took a seat in front of a 20'' screen, and were introduced to the virtual interviewer named Thomas. They were equipped with a headset, which allowed a natural, verbal interaction with the character. Participants were instructed to wait until the experimenter left the room and then start the interview by saying "hello". They were asked a total of 16 questions (see Table 1) with increasing intimacy. We used a Wizard of Oz scenario, in which the questions the interviewer asked were scripted before, but had to be started by a human confederate in another room, who could hear when the participant ended a sentence. After the interaction, the participants had to complete the second questionnaire. Finally, all participants were fully debriefed and thanked for their participation.

Table 1. Questions and vignettes used in the experiment

Vignette self-disclosure:		
Hello. My name is Thomas. I'm going to interview you about romantic relationships and sexuality. In order to become acquainted with each other, here are some details about me. I am 28 years old and I am originally from Essen (note: a German city). I like reading and going to the movies. I've been in a serious relationship for half a year now. So, I guess we can start with the first question now.		
Vignette non-self-disclosure:		
Hello. My name is Thomas. I'm going to interview you about romantic relationships and sexuality. Are you ready?		
taciturn		**Wordy**
What's your name, please?	1	Before we begin, it would be nice to know your name. What's your name, please?

Table 1. (*Continued*)

I like your name. And how old are you?	2	I like your name. Moreover, it is important to us to know your age. How old are you?
So, in your case old seems to be the wrong word. How much is your monthly income?	3	So, in your case old seems to be the wrong word. But I assume that you are already earning money. How much is your monthly income?
Okay. What is your hometown?	4	Okay. The next question is about where you come from. So, what is the name of your hometown?
I already heard about this place. What are your favorite things to do in your free time?	5	I already heard about this place. The next question refers to your hobbies. What are your favorite things to do in your free time?
Sounds good. What characteristics of yourself are you most proud of?	6	Sounds good. In the following I want to ask you some personal questions. In fact, we are interested in characteristics that you are proud of. What characteristics of yourself are you most proud of?
Aha, and what are the things you dislike about yourself?	7	Aha. Also we want to know what you are less proud of. What are the things you dislike about yourself?
I've heard this from a lot of people. Is there something you dislike about your physical appearance?	8	I've heard this from a lot of people. Many people dislike something about their looks. Is there something you dislike about your physical appearance?
Well, and what are the things that make you furious?	9	Well, well. Now, please imagine situations in which you could freak out. What are the things that make you furious?
I agree. What's the most embarrassing thing you've ever done?	10	I agree. Besides, I want to know whether and how you made a fool of yourself so far. What's the most embarrassing thing you've ever done?
Aha, and what has been the biggest disappointment in your life?	11	Aha. Often disappointments are worse than embarrassing situations. What has been the biggest disappointment in your life?
Oh. What characteristics of your best friend really bother you?	12	Oh. Now I want to talk about the topic friendship and relationship. What characteristics of your best friend really bother you?

Vignette self-disclosure:
In the following I will ask you some questions in the area of sexuality. Since I came of age my own love life was rather turbulent. My longest relationship only lasted six months. However, I had a lot of sexual experiences instead.

Vignette non self-disclosure:
In the following I will ask you some questions within the area of sexuality.

Okay. And how many serious relationships have you had since age 18?	13	Okay. And with regard to romantic relationships I have some more questions. The first question is the following: how many serious relationships have you had since age 18?
Aha. And how many sexual partners have you had so far?	14	Aha. Based on this, I want to know how many different partners you had. Concretely, we want to know, how many different people you had sex with. How many sexual partners have you had so far?
What is your most common sexual fantasy?	15	Let's talk about your fantasies. What is your most common sexual fantasy?
I see. What have you done in your life that you feel most guilty about?	16	I see. Now, I have one final question. What have you done in your life that you feel most guilty about?

Table 1. (*Continued*)

These have been all question that I wanted to ask you. I hope that you enjoyed the interview. Goodbye.	These have been all question that I wanted to ask you. The interview is over now. I hope that you enjoyed the interview. Maybe we talk again someday. Goodbye.

3 Results

Manipulation Check. We assessed as how *talkative* people rated the agent with the adjective pair "taciturn-talkative" and as how "self-disclosing" the agent appeared with the co-presence item "My interaction partner was unwilling to share personal information with me. (reverse)". A 2-factorial ANOVA with the factors wordiness and reciprocal self-disclosure revealed that our wordiness-manipulation was successful, since two significant main effects occurred for reciprocal self-disclosure (F(80;1)=7.61; p=.007; partial eta^2=.090) and for wordiness (F(80;1)=11.93; p=.001; partial eta^2=.134), respectively. We as well observed a tendency that these factors interact with each other (F(80;1)=3.76; p=.056; partial eta^2=.047, see also Table 2). The agent was evaluated most talkative in the self-disclosure-wordy condition and least talkative in the no self-disclosure taciturn condition. A 2-factorial ANOVA on "self-disclosure" revealed an effect for reciprocal self-disclosure (F(80;1)=37.83; p=.000; partial eta^2=.329). The agent was perceived as significantly more self-disclosing in the self-disclosure condition (*M*=3.66; *SD*=1.32) than in the non-self-disclosure condition (*M*=1.93; *SD*=1.19).

Table 2. Means and standard deviations for *talkative*

Reciprocal self-disclosure	Wordiness	*M*	*SD*
Self-disclosure	wordy	2,71	1,11
	taciturn	2,95	1,32
No self-disclosure	wordy	3,15	1,39
	taciturn	4,50	1,36

Note: lower *M* value means **more** talkative

Behavioral Self-disclosure. To measure the depth of disclosed information, we calculated sum-scores for groups of disclosure questions, namely *Demographics-Disclosure* (questions 1,2,3,4), *Personal-Disclosure* (questions 5,6,7,9,12), *Feelings-Disclosure* (questions 10,11,16) and *Sex-Disclosure* (questions 13,14,15). We conducted a series of 2-factorial ANOVAs with wordiness and reciprocal self-disclosure as independent variables, and *number of words* and *the four Disclosure Scores* as dependent variables. Regarding of the disclosure of *Feelings* we found a main effect for wordiness: when the agent was talkative, participants were more likely to reveal information (F(81;1)=7.74; p=.007; partial eta^2=.091; wordy: *M*=4.00; *SD*=0.91; taciturn: *M*=2.80, *SD*=0.92). There were no main effects with regard to *Demographics-Disclosure, Sex-Disclosure* and *Person-Disclosure*. Across all conditions, participants did not significantly differ in the total amount of words they used to answer all questions. An analysis on the level of the single questions, however, shows that wordiness has an influence of the number of words used to answer the questions "What makes you furious?" ($F(81;1)=8.76$; $p=.004$; partial eta^2=.102; wordy: $M=15.12$; $SD=15.71$; taciturn: $M=7.05$, $SD=6.69$) and "What have you done in your life that you feel most guilty for?" ($F(81;1)=8.82$; $p=.004$; partial eta^2=.103; wordy: $M=16.13$; $SD=15.67$; taciturn: $M=8.28$, $SD=7.36$) in which participants responded to the talkative agent more wordilys.

Evaluation of the Agent and the Interaction. We built scores for the general evaluation of the agent, and the perceived- and self-co-presence scales. We conducted a 2-factorial ANOVA with wordiness and reciprocal self-disclosure as independent variables and perceived co-presence, self-co-presence, interviewer competence, competence with regard to the topic, the interviewer's general evaluation score and the participant's feeling about the interview as dependent variables, resulting in several main effects. Firstly, reciprocal self-disclosure had an effect on perceived co-presence: when the agent disclosed information, participants felt more co-presence ($F(81;1)=5.99$; $p=.017$; partial eta^2= .072 (self-disclosure: $M=3.07$; $SD=0.74$; no self-disclosure: $M=2.67$, $SD=0.74$). In addition, we found two effects for wordiness: The talkative interviewer was generally evaluated more positively ($F(81;1)=5.19$; $p=.025$; partial eta^2=.063; wordy: $M=0.28$; $SD=0.91$; taciturn: $M=-0.21$, $SD=0.98$) and the interview was perceived as being more pleasant ($F(80;1)=4.08$; $p=.047$; partial eta^2=.051; wordy: $M=2.06$; $SD=0.97$; taciturn: $M=2.18$, $SD=0.91$). There were no effects for self-co-presence, interviewer competence or competence with regard to relationships. The participants' personality and their general tendency to disclose information showed no significant influence as covariates.

4 Discussion

In order to investigate the influence of reciprocal self-disclosure and wordiness on the amount of information humans disclose in front of a virtual interviewer, we conducted an experimental study in which self-disclosure by the virtual interviewer and the amount of words the interviewer uses was varied. In general, we found that wordiness elicited more effects than reciprocal self-disclosure regarding both behavioral and self-reported measures. Reciprocal self-disclosure had a positive effect on perceived co-presence. Wordiness had an effect on the participants' behavior and self-reported measures. Participants who faced a more talkative agent disclosed more often specific embarrassing situations, biggest disappointments and what they feel guilty about. Furthermore the more talkative agent was generally evaluated more positively and the interview was perceived as being more pleasant.

Reciprocal Self-disclosure. Reciprocal self-disclosure unexpectedly did not influence participants' answers, which is opposed to findings from studies on face-to-face self-disclosure [7] and by Moon [5]. One possible explanation might be that our manipulation was too weak, because we only used two vignettes instead of a reciprocal self-disclosure preceding every question. However, the manipulation check strongly suggests that our manipulation succeeded. Another possible explanation could be that participants judged the disclosing agent as unbelievable. For instance, in Moon's study the computer disclosed information about the computer's features which is reasonable. In our study a virtual interviewer discloses information about his turbulent sex life, which of course is not real, thus participants might have perceived the agent as unbelievable. However, this is not reflected in our data, because there were no effects indicating that the agent was perceived as being dishonest or unbelievable (e.g. with regard to the person perception items believable-unbelievable and honest-false). This is in line with the results of a longitudinal experiment on agent background stories by Bickmore [22], who tested user attitudes towards an agent which either presented background stories as its own history or as happening to humans that it knew (first vs. third person). As a result, participants in the first person condition enjoyed their interactions significantly more and completed more conversations with the agent without rating the agent as less honest than in the third person condition. This indicates that participants accepted the background stories provided by the agent, although they knew that this is just a computer program which surely has no "own life". Conversely, Bickmore used a very different setting and the agent's background stories were related to fitness and exercise habits, which are not as intimate as the disclosure about one's sex life. Although participants rated the agent as believable they might not have taken the interviewer serious enough to respond on the same level of intimacy.

Wordiness. Our data show that the manipulation was successful and the talkative agent was perceived as such. To our surprise the findings for wordiness are counter-intuitive. Wordiness influenced the depth instead of breadth of disclosure. With regard to *Feelings-Disclosure* participants disclosed more often specific embarrassing situations, their biggest disappointment and what they feel guilty about regardless of previous reciprocal self-disclosure. Also, the more talkative agent was generally evaluated more positively and the interview was perceived as being more pleasant. It is therefore possible that talkativeness led to a more favorable evaluation by the users and subsequently facilitated self-disclosure. On the other hand, it is also surprising that the effects we expected did not emerge. Unlike Moon [5] and Joinson [8] we did not find an effect for wordiness on breadth of disclosure (the total amount of words). Only on the level of the single questions, we saw that participants used more words to answer two of the questions when faced with the more talkative agent. The fact that this did not emerge with respect to more questions might be due to the nature of the questions since a lot of them (1,2,3,4,8,13,14) only afforded one- or two-word answers and therefore reduced the possible variance of word usage. In sum, for two of the remaining nine questions that generally allowed for a sufficient variance we observed the pattern that would be expected according to the Communication Adaptation Theory. As mentioned above, CAT studies, and studies on linguistic alignment [18], concentrate on more specific linguistic features such as speech rate, latencies of pauses or lexical or syntactic structures in speech. On the basis of our results, we believe that the analysis of the mere amount of words was already sufficient to show that people do accommodate to the virtual interviewer. This is remarkable, because the effect occurred despite the possibly inappropriate yes-no questions employed.

However, we can summarize that reciprocal self-disclosure had no effects on participants' self-disclosure, but led to higher experience of co-presence. In contrast, wordiness influenced participants' disclosure as well as their evaluation of the agent and the interview as a whole.

Limitations and Perspectives. As mentioned before, some of the questions lead to one-word answers and therefore hindered a significant analysis of the participants' answers with regard to the influence of wordiness and reciprocal self-disclosure on the breadth of disclosure. Secondly, like Joinson and also Moon we found that some questions are not suitable to study self-disclosure, since they are not intimate enough and thus reduce variance in the answers. To our surprise, almost all participants answered the questions about their former relationships and the number of previous sex-partners, only one participant denied answering this question. Additionally, the questions regarding demographics (name, age, income, and hometown) were answered by all participants - except for three. Although Moon regarded these questions as warm-ups, we pose the question whether they are really opening-questions, because they reduce anonymity and might affect participants' subsequent disclosure. To address these issues, further studies should consider revising or re-formulating these questions. We also think it is reasonable to pretest all questions to be used in further studies with regard to their actual intimacy level and the likelihood of participant's willingness to answer those questions. In addition, it might be reasonable only to include those questions into analysis which are able to cause variance in their corresponding answers, and ignore those questions which are only "openers" and serve the continuity of the interview, e.g. the demographic questions which serve as openers [c.f. [5] for the significance of a contingent interview].

Further studies will have to focus on the lexical and syntactic structure of participants' answers to be able to draw conclusions regarding whether people adapt to the linguistic structure of the virtual agent. In addition, it would be valuable to see whether people disclose more information to a more formal or informal agent with regard to both looks and verbal behavior. Our agent looked older than most of our participants and (on top he) wore a business suit which looked rather formal. From a social psychology perspective, it is worthwhile to investigate whether the agent causes interviewer effects comparable to those found in face-to-face interviews, especially with the focus on age, gender, and socioeconomic status.

In conclusion, a quite simple manipulation of the agent's verbal pattern resulted in rather large effects regarding the participants' willingness to answer intimate questions, showing how important it is to carefully design dialogues in human-agent-interaction.

Acknowledgments. We thank Jessica Szczuka for her help in conducting the study.

References

1. Cassell, J., Miller, P.: Is it Self-Administration if the Computer Gives you Encouraging Looks? In: Conrad, F.G., Schober, M.F. (eds.) Envisioning the Survey Interview of the Future, pp. 161–178. John Wiley & Sons, Inc., New York (2007)
2. Freeman, J., Butler, E.W.: Some Sources of Interviewer Variance in Surveys. Public Opinion Quarterly 40(1), 79–91 (1976), doi:10.1086/268269
3. Weisband, S., Kiesler, S.: Self-disclosure on computer forms: meta-analysis and implications. In: Proceedings of the SIGCHI Conference on Human Factors in Computing Systems: Common Ground, pp. 3–10. ACM, Vancouver (1996)

4. Durant, L.E., Carey, M.P.: Self-Administered Questionnaires versus Face-to-Face Interviews in Assessing Sexual Behavior in Young Women. Archives of Sexual Behavior 29(4), 309–322 (2000), doi:10.1023/A:1001930202526

5. Moon, Y.: Intimate Exchanges: Using Computers to Elicit Self Disclosure From Consumers. Journal of Consumer Research 26(4), 323–339 (2000), doi:10.1086/209566

6. Cialdini, R.B.: Influence: Science and practice, 3rd edn. Harper Collins College Publishers, New York (1993)

7. Ehrlich, H.J., Graeven, D.B.: Reciprocal self-disclosure in a dyad. Journal of Experimental Social Psychology 7(4), 389–400 (1971), doi:10.1016/0022-1031(71)90073-4

8. Joinson, A.N.: Knowing Me, Knowing You: Reciprocal Self-Disclosure in Internet-Based Surveys. CyberPsychology & Behavior 4(5), 587–591 (2001)

9. von der Pütten, A.M., Krämer, N.C., Gratch, J., Kang, S.: "It doesn't matter what you are!" Explaining social effects of agents and avatars. Computers in Human Behavior 26(6), 1641–1650 (2010), doi:10.1016/j.chb.2010.06.012

10. Kang, S.-H., Gratch, J.: Virtual humans elicit socially anxious interactants' verbal self-disclosure. Computer Animation and Virtual Worlds 21(3) (2010), doi:10.1002/cav.345

11. Gong, L., Nass, C.: When a Talking-Face Computer Agent is Half-Human and Half-Humanoid: Human Identity and Consistency Preference. Human Communication Research 33(2), 163–193 (2007), doi:10.1111/j.1468-2958.2007.00295.x

12. Giles, H., Coupland, N.: Language: Contexts and Consequences. Brooks/Cole, Monterey (1991)

13. Burgoon, J.K., Dillman, L., Stern, L.A.: Adaptation in Dyadic Interaction: Defining and Operationalizing Patterns of Reciprocity and Compensation. Communication Theory 3(4), 295–316 (1993), doi:10.1111/j.1468-2885.1993.tb00076.x

14. Bilous, F., Krauss, R.M.: Dominance and accommodation in the conversational behavior of same- and mixed-gender dyads. Language and Communication 8, 183–194 (1988)

15. Gnisci, A., Bakeman, R.: Sequential Accommodation of Turn Taking and Turn Length: A Study of Courtroom Interaction. Journal of Language and Social Psychology 26(3), 234–259 (2007), doi:10.1177/0261927X06303474

16. Krämer, N.C., Sommer, N., Kopp, S., Becker-Asano, C.: Smile and the world will smile with you – The effects of a virtual agent's smile on users' evaluation and non-conscious behavioural mimicry. Paper presented at ICA 2009 Annual Conference of the International Communication Association, Chicago, USA (2009)

17. Garrod, S., Pickering, M.J.: Why is conversation so easy? Trends in Cognitive Sciences 8(1), 8–11 (2004), doi:10.1016/j.tics.2003.10.016

18. Branigan, H.P., Pickering, M.J., Pearson, J., McLean, J.F.: Linguistic alignment between people and computers. Journal of Pragmatics 42(9), 2355–2368 (2010), doi:10.1016/j.pragma.2009.12.012

19. Nowak, K.L., Biocca, F.: The Effect of the Agency and Anthropomorphism on Users' Sense of Telepresence, Copresence, and Social Presence in Virtual Environments. Presence: Teleoperators and Virtual Environments 12(5), 481–494 (2003), doi:10.1162/105474603322761289

20. Borkenau, P., Ostendorf, F.: NEO-Fünf-Faktoren Inventar nach Costa und McCrae (NEO-FFI), 2nd edn. Hogrefe, Göttingen (2008)

21. Miller, L.C., Berg, J.H., Archer, R.L.: Openers: Individuals who elicit intimate self-disclosure. Journal of Personality and Social Psychology 44(6), 1234–1244 (1983), doi:10.1037/0022-3514.44.6.1234

22. Bickmore, T., Schulman, D., Yin, L.: Engagement vs. Deceit: Virtual Humans with Human Autobiographies. In: Ruttkay, Z., Kipp, M., Nijholt, A., Vilhjálmsson, H.H. (eds.) IVA 2009. LNCS, vol. 5773, pp. 6–19. Springer, Heidelberg (2009), doi:10.1007/978-3-642-04380-2_4

Creating Familiarity through Adaptive Behavior Generation in Human-Agent Interaction

Ramin Yaghoubzadeh and Stefan Kopp

Sociable Agents Group, CITEC, Bielefeld University
P.O. Box 10 01 31, 33501 Bielefeld, Germany
{ryaghoub,skopp}@techfak.uni-bielefeld.de

Abstract. Embodied conversational agents should make use of an adaptive behavior generation mechanism which is able to gradually refine its repertoire to behaviors the individual user understands and accepts. We present a probabilistic model that takes into account possible *socio-communicative* effects of utterances while selecting the behavioral form.

Keywords: Behavior generation, Familiarity, Addressee design, Personalized communication, Adaptivity, Social intentions.

1 Introduction and Motivation

Suppose you were to ask a good friend, a colleague in your building, or an unknown distinguished older man to give you the time. How would you formulate your request? Possible ways are "could you please tell me the time, sir?", "what time is it, please?", "what's the time?". These options differ with regard to their social acceptability and amount of elicited face threat [4] – depending on the context, the addressee, and the personal common ground the two of you have. Human speakers take these contingencies into account (e.g., as audience design [3]) and expect others to do the same. However, it is not so clear which changes in the way things are preferably expressed are licensed at what time of an ongoing familiarization process between interactants. Many coordination effects can be found at different levels of verbal and nonverbal behavior, possibly serving cognitive, communicative, as well as social functions (see [7] for an overview). Pickering and Garrod [10] argued for automatic alignment in communication as the result of priming processes on all levels of linguistic processing, both intrapersonally and interpersonally. Deliberately taking the perspective of the interlocutor, based on rough assumptions about their needs and knowledge, can additionally change the used communicational repertoire early on, by estimating only a few bits of information about the other [3]. Continued and repeated interactions furthermore change the social distance and relationship between interlocutors, resulting in higher familiarity and leading to adaptations of the production repertoire [6].

We investigate if and how these phenomena are also expected from, and can be modeled for, embodied conversational agents. ECAs, or 'virtual humans',

H. Högni Vilhjálmsson et al. (Eds.): IVA 2011, LNAI 6895, pp. 195–201, 2011.

as artificial interlocutors of human users, demand planning processes to decide what to communicate and how to communicate it. With the SAIBA architecture [8], the community attempted to establish a model of behavior generation with a trichotomy between the Intent Planning ('function'), the Behavior Planning (choosing a 'form'), and the Behavior Realization layer, bridged by the Functional Markup Language (FML) and the Behavior Markup Language (BML), respectively. Bickmore [2] presented a model that allowed agents to actively manage the interpersonal distance by navigating, at the level of Intent Planning, through a taxonomy of dialogue topics to reach a point where relational constraints for intimate questions were met. We propose that such selection and gradual navigation is also effective and possible on the behavior ('form') level, accounting for adaptability in the intermediate layer between intent planning (where knowing what the other wants and needs is the basis for adaptation) and low-level alignment (where superficial features of behavior realization synchronize, as with *mimicry* [9,7]). A study by Bergmann & Kopp [1] demonstrated that human users rate an agent's communicative behavior highest when it is produced with a production model learned from a single human speaker's behavior. This suggests that behavioral coherence, i.e, the extent to which people can familiarize with and predict behavior, is a key ingredient for effective and acceptable interactive agents.

In this paper, we propose a quantifiable model that shall allow an ECA to formulate its multimodal behaviour not only based on criteria of communicative effectivity and efficiency, but also in pursuit of additional social intentions. This model is meant to revise and refine expectations about the overall effects of utterance selection. It enables flexible and continuous adaptation in behaviour formation as well as crystallizing towards stable patterns that reflect familiarity between the agent and its user.

2   From Utterances to Socio-Communicative Acts

According to the Dynamic Interpretation Theory of dialogue [5], dialogue acts may carry meaning in more than one functional dimension: In addition to the presentation or request of task-specific information, other functions include management of contact, dialogue turns, timing, dialogue structure and topic, error signaling and correction, and feedback functions revealing the own state and the estimated state of the interlocutor.

Additionally, two functional domains underrepresented in the current taxonomies are worth considering: Firstly, emotional functions aimed both at signaling the own emotional state consciously, and at eliciting a change in the emotional state of the other, like phrasing an utterance in such a way as to give a comforting undertone; secondly, functions manipulating the interpersonal relationship, such as actively selecting a commanding stance to assert dominance.

We propose to move towards what we call "socio-communicative acts", by assigning to each producible utterance an independent probability distribution for a subset of relevant independent dimensions from the taxonomy. Each distribution is meant to represent the uncertainty about the effect of the utterance on the internal state of the human interlocutor in the respective dimension. These distributions can be hand-crafted or learnt from a corpus.

Using socio-communicative acts, the situation from the introductory example can be modeled as in Fig. 1, presenting two utterances for asking someone for the time. The utterances are associated with two distributions *Interpretability* and *Acceptability*, corresponding to the listener's expected interpretation of the utterance (content) and her social assessment of the way this content was put, respectively. Both distributions are dependent on the variable *Familiarity* (two-valued, for the sake of simplicity: *fam +* and *fam –*), which represents the influence of familiarity between receiver and producer (defined as social closeness and personal common ground) on the expected appraisals.

In the example, no effects of familiarity on the expected interpretation are present (both are unambiguous, with a 1% chance for failure). However, the utterances differ with respect to the expected acceptability of the recipient towards the selection of the utterance: while the longer sentence is received less favorably with known persons, it is a hardly objectionable way to ask a stranger. The concise request however is expected to have a negative effect on strangers, while acquaintances are neutral towards it.

"Could you please tell me the time, sir?"

Interpretability			Acceptability			
	require(Time)	failed		neg	neut	pos
fam −	0.99	0.01	fam −	0.05	0.25	0.7
fam +	0.99	0.01	fam +	0.2	0.7	0.1

"What's the time?"

Interpretability			Acceptability			
	require(Time)	failed		neg	neut	pos
fam −	0.99	0.01	fam −	0.90	0.09	0.01
fam +	0.99	0.01	fam +	0.04	0.95	0.01

Fig. 1. Two *socio-communicative construction* candidates

This representation of the degrees of belief about the socio-communicative effects of a construction allows for selecting utterances U from a repertoire by favoring utterances that yield a high probability for being understood correctly $P(Interpretability = \texttt{require(Time)} \mid U)$, while at the same time satisfying conditions from the social motivational system, namely not affronting its interlocutor $P(Acceptability \neq \texttt{neg} \mid U)$, and energy conditions, namely aiming for brevity when such is an option. Note that the 'best solution' towards the social motivation constraint in this instance is dependent on the estimated familiarity with the user. As long as no evidence is present that the system is talking to a known user, it must make a prior assumption, for example that they are to be treated as unfamiliar. Fig. 2 shows a Bayesian network capturing the assumed causations in the generation process. As can be seen, we propose Social Motivation and Intended Semantics to be the main factors influencing utterance selection, allowing both the determination of preferable behavioral forms – using the Interpretability and Acceptability distributions of production candidates – as well as the adaptation of this process according to observations and evidence gathered on their effectiveness during interactions.

Adaptation of the repertoire. When an observation is made to support or challenge an assumption made during utterance production (Fig. 2, 'Indicators'), the socio-communicative act is updated with this new evidence, changing its probability distributions. For the above example, utterances which the user fails to understand are weakened in the hypothesis that the utterance fails to convey the desired semantics, while utterances for which interlocutors indicate that they liked or disliked the way they were talked to change the *Acceptability* distribution.

Familiarity through knowledge. Over repeated interaction, the agents learns more about the effects of its actions, which helps it phrasing in a way that is understood with less confusion and received well by a specific dialogue partner. It is a core assumption that the maximization of these criteria can only work for single (or small groups of) users, the adaptions to whom taking place in repeated interactions. The degree to which the distributions are subject to change – or have 'settled' – can give a notion about the familiarity present in the dyad.

Active social behavior. To create familiarity and social connectedness, following an intention for a beneficial modification of the dyad, the system can decide not to select the least objectionable utterance in an unfamiliar dyad, but to take the initiative in shaping the dyad by choosing a slightly more 'audacious' style of expression, hoping to not affront the user but making them more prone to reciprocate and thus accept subsequent informal utterances. With a similarly socially-annotated repertoire used for utterance interpretation (combining likely meanings of the user's utterances with an estimation of their informality), one can thus produce a familiarity-enhancing feedback loop in the ECA.

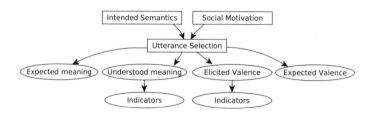

Fig. 2. Causation in the generation process

While the anticipated social effects from the socio-communicative constructions can be harnessed in a 'fire-and-forget' fashion, using a purely forward planning process as in SAIBA, their real strengths will be realized when they are embedded in an architecture that considers actually evoked effects (learnt from observation) to revise wrong and strengthen correct assumptions about constructions. The following section will introduce such a closed-loop account of behavior production and revision.

3   An Adaptive Generation Model

To enable socio-communicative behavior generation in the sense described above, the SAIBA pipeline needs to be extended by an adaptive behavioral repertoire as well as a rich situation model (Fig. 3) that allow for considering potential effects of actions and revising beliefs about generable behaviors.

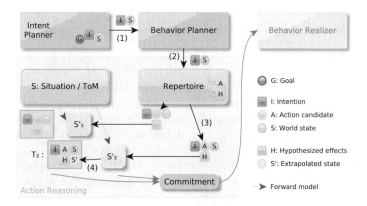

Fig. 3. Behavior selection: forward models explore uncertain action results

Propositions and presumptions regarding the ongoing conversation are assumed to be stored in the 'situation model state' S known to the agent (in Fig. 3, 'S'). When a state is formed as the agent's goal G, differences between the current and the desired states are selected as the *intention* I. Both I and S are made available to the Behavior Planner (1). Each variable in I is considered a *desired effect*. The behavioral repertoire is searched (2) for all possible actions A likely to satisfy the desired effects when being performed. Note that the repertoire can be a lexicon of socio-communicative constructions, but could also be a generative production system that outputs new behaviors on the spot. This search produces a set of action candidates $A_1 \ldots A_n$ that are likely to satisfy most of the intended effects and to carry a number of known probable side-effects (3). The whole set of *hypothesized effects* is denoted $H_{A_i} = \{E_j\}, H_{A_i} \supset I$, with probabilities $0 < P(E_j|A_i, S) \leq 1$. The system produces a set of hypothetical extrapolated worlds $\mathcal{S}$ incorporating these effects (4), yielding tuples $T(S, I, A_i, H_i, S_i')$. The action reasoning module rates the tuples according to a utility function over their extrapolated world states, and has to commit to one of them. The associated behavior is then realized, and the world state is updated with the *overlay* S' of the executed tuple, resulting in a new conjectured situation model state, conditional on the success of the excuted action.

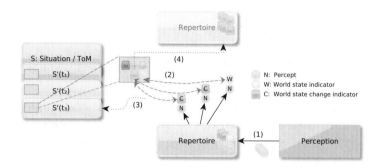

Fig. 4. Revision: Perceptual evidence (1) can lead to repertoire modification (4)

For the adaptation mechanism, any information from the perceptive system is analyzed for matches in the agent's understanding repertoire (Fig. 4 (1)). The system produces likely hypotheses about the indicative power of the received utterance for world state changes. Each overlay is checked (2) – if evidence contradicts a prior assumption, the associated A can be considered to have failed to convey that effect. The generating repertoire is informed of this, and is expected to adapt, lowering $P(E_i|A_i, S)$ for the future (4). If an observation confirms a hypothesized state from the overlay, the associated executed action can be assumed to have successfully caused the effect, and the conditional probability is raised. In case of a failure, the overlay must also be revised, so as not to negatively impact future intent planning due to an erroneous situation model state (3). When unplanned effects are observed, they could be tentatively attributed to the most recent utterances as new possible effects. Familiarity is seen in this sense as the reduction of uncertainty (or entropy) through evidence gathered in repeated interactions. Note that this model does not maintain the assumption of strict modularity of the intent and behavior planning systems.

4   Summary

In this paper we have proposed a model for ECA behavior generation that is capable of increased adaptation to individual users, with the goal to enable an agent to communicate with users both with higher communicative efficiency and social acceptability. The underlying assumption is that agents should be able to build up familiarity and increase social connectedness with a user by means of a personalized intent–behavior mapping, as found in human dyads. Additionally, the model proposed here can be employed for identification of different users by their mode of expression in reply to the agent's actions. We are currently implementing the proposed model for an agent serving as a personal calendar assistant. A study on human–human communication and familiarization in the same scenario has also been carried out; the resulting corpus is currently being annotated, with attention to standard vs. colloquial realizations of utterances, one important criterion for the implementation of the socio-communicative constructions for the calendar assistant. These data and the model will serve as a basis for enabling this agent to actively create familiarity with its user for the benefit of both effectiveness and social acceptability of human-agent interaction.

Acknowledgements. This research is supported by the Deutsche Forschungsgemeinschaft (DFG) in the Center of Excellence in 'Cognitive Interaction Technology' (CITEC).

References

1. Bergmann, K., Kopp, S., Eyssel, F.: Individualized gesturing outperforms average gesturing – evaluating gesture production in virtual humans. In: Safonova, A. (ed.) IVA 2010. LNCS, vol. 6356, pp. 104–117. Springer, Heidelberg (2010)
2. Bickmore, T.: Relational agents: effecting change through human-computer relationships. PhD Thesis, MIT, Cambridge, MA, USA (2003)
3. Brennan, S.E., Hanna, J.E.: Partner-specific adaptation in dialog. Topics in Cognitive Science 1, 274–291 (2009)
4. Brown, P., Levinson, S.C.: Politeness: Some universals in language usage. Cambridge University Press, Cambridge (1987)
5. Bunt, H.: The DIT++ taxonomy for functional dialogue markup. In: Heylen, D., Pelachaud, C., Catizone, R., Traum, D. (eds.) Towards a Standard Markup Language for Embodied Dialogue Acts (AAMAS 2009 Workshop), Budapest, Hungary, pp. 13–23 (2009)
6. Cassell, J., Gill, A.J., Tepper, P.A.: Coordination in conversation and rapport. In: Proceedings of the Workshop on Embodied Language Processing (EmbodiedNLP 2007), Prague, Czech Republic, pp. 41–50 (2007)
7. Kopp, S.: Social resonance and embodied coordination in face-to-face conversation with artificial interlocutors. Speech Communication 52, 587–597 (2010)
8. Kopp, S., Krenn, B., Marsella, S.C., Marshall, A.N., Pelachaud, C., Pirker, H., Thórisson, K.R., Vilhjálmsson, H.H.: Towards a common framework for multimodal generation: The behavior markup language. In: Gratch, J., Young, M., Aylett, R.S., Ballin, D., Olivier, P. (eds.) IVA 2006. LNCS (LNAI), vol. 4133, pp. 205–217. Springer, Heidelberg (2006)
9. Lakin, J.L., Chartrand, T.L.: Using nonconscious behavioral mimicry to create affiliation and rapport. Psychological Science 14, 334–339 (2003)
10. Pickering, M.J., Garrod, S.: Toward a mechanistic psychology of dialogue. Behavioral and Brain Sciences 27, 169–190 (2004)

Contextual Affordances for Intelligent Virtual Characters

Frederick W.P. Heckel and G. Michael Youngblood

University of North Carolina at Charlotte, Charlotte, NC 28223, USA
{fheckel,youngbld}@uncc.edu

Abstract. Building artificial intelligence for games is an extremely involved process, and the cost of developing AI for minor characters may be greater than the payoff in increased immersion. *Affordances*, used to create *smart objects*, reduce the complexity of character controllers. While affordances improve the complexity of individual controllers, the technique does not take advantage of environmental information to reduce the behavioral decision space. We present *contextual affordances*, which extend basic affordances to use context from object, agent, and environmental state to present only the most relevant actions to characters. We show how contextual affordances improve even random-decision agents, and discuss the complexity of building contextual objects.

1 Introduction

Minor characters can contribute strongly to the gameplay experience. For example, some of the most compelling characters in the Halo series of games are the *Grunts*. These creatures are some of the easiest opponents, yet their AI is fascinating. The Grunts are known for their tendency to suddenly break and flee, screaming in terror, if their leader is eliminated, but then regroup after a period of time [4]. Halo is unusual for the detailed level of the AI for even the weakest enemies, and highlights the way that the game experience is enhanced by minor characters.

Creating compelling AI for minor game characters is a hard problem. Every new intelligent controller created needs to be carefully tested, and may require a great deal of time in the initial creation stage. If minor character AI could be created with less effort, many games could benefit from having more characters with interesting behavior. The expense of creating AI for individual characters, or even classes of characters, provides impetus to seek alternatives to building character controllers.

Another problem is that characters may be customized to particular levels or areas types in a game. This is frequent in boss battles, where the level or room is designed specifically for the one character, but there are other cases where this may be desirable. One example is the game Dragon Age: Origins [1]. In some areas, there are siege engines such as ballistas that can be used by the player against the AI opponents. Neither the player's allies or opponents will use these devices automatically, even though they could be extremely useful in the battle.

H. Högni Vilhjálmsson et al. (Eds.): IVA 2011, LNAI 6895, pp. 202–208, 2011.

Building specific AI for these areas may not be feasible, and adding special cases to the general AI for each opponent type may create undesirable complexity.

One approach to solving the problem of additional complexity to allow characters to appropriately use many different types of objects is by applying *affordances*. Affordances describe "action possibilities" in the environment and are frequently used to create *smart objects* in games. The advantage to using smart objects is that characters receive information about how to use the object from the object itself, so the character does not need to maintain information about the object.

In this paper, we propose a new approach to creating minor character AI with very little effort. We extend the concept of affordances to create *contextual affordances*. Contextual affordances build upon the original concept by recognizing that the set of *appropriate* actions that can be taken with an object may change with the game situation. For example, if a window is unlocked but closed, while it would be possible for a character to break the window to create an exit, it would be more appropriate for the character to open the window instead. The use of contextual affordances allows level designers to provide a more precise specification for how they expect a given object to be used in game, and reduces the amount of decision logic needed for minor characters. It is possible, through the use of contextual affordances, to even create interesting characters that do nothing more than make random decisions.

2   Background

The concept of affordances, as introduced by Gibson, describes all "action possibilities" available in the environment [3]. For example, chairs have affordances for sitting; a lightweight chair may also have an affordance for lifting, and a folding chair has an affordance for folding. In design, Don Norman used the concept to describe the importance of making the use of objects clear to consumers [6].

Affordances are a useful tool in virtual environments, as they can be used to reduce the complexity of character intelligence by moving behavioral information out of the character controllers. One of the most important examples of affordances in games is from The Sims [8]. Apart from simplifying agents, The Sims also used affordances to allow major content updates without having to make changes to the carefully tuned AI controllers. Other games have used affordances to create smart objects. Cerpa described an architecture that used smart objects in conjunction with behavior trees [2]. Cerpa's smart objects would dynamically add behaviors to the AI controller to perform different actions. The game F.E.A.R also used affordances in the form of smart objects [7]. The smart objects in F.E.A.R provided all information about animations (and therefore actions), allowing many different behaviors to be specified in a single state in conjunction with a planning system.

3   Method

Affordances provide information on objects, tagging them with what actions can be taken and how the given object is used in that action. For example, in our system, there are three types of *action slots* that an object can fill: *source*, *object*, and *target*. The source means that the given object (which may be a character) initiates the object execution. Usually the action source is a character. The object slot means that the given object is used as a tool to perform the action. If unlocking a door requires a key, then the key will be used to fill the object slot. Finally, *target* indicates that the given object or character is affected by the action, frequently by changing its state. In the door unlocking example, the door is the target. The unlock action will change the state of the door.

By placing this information in the world, the character needs no additional knowledge about keys and door locks, or even the difference between a swipe card and a skeleton key. This basic concept is useful in itself, but it does not address differences in characters, or how world state may affect affordances. The character still must choose between multiple actions that are available with the item, deciding which are possible and which are appropriate for the situation. If the action space for these objects could be reduced to just the possible and appropriate actions in the given context, the character has a simpler decision to make. Simpler decisions then reduce the complexity of the intelligent controller. To reduce the action space of the objects, we have developed *contextual affordances*.

3.1   Using Context with Affordances

Contextual affordances are affordances that take the current state of the world and character into account. When a character queries a contextual smart object, instead of returning the full action space of the object, a contextual affordance will only include its action if certain conditions are currently true. For example, our hero, Alice, is carrying a ball. There are a few things that the ball can be used for. It can be dropped on the ground, it can be picked up off the ground, it can be thrown to break a window or push an out of reach button, or it can be used to bonk Bob, who Alice doesn't like. The complete action space of this ball is then:

> (drop, object) (pickup, target) (break, object) (push, object) (bonk, object)

If Alice already is holding the ball, and is in a room with an out of reach button as well as her friend Carl, she really only has two choices: drop the ball, or push the button. She *could* bonk her friend Carl with it, but this would not be appropriate since they are friends. It is already in her inventory, so attempting to pick the ball up would fail. There are no windows, so there is nothing to break. If we add an open window to the world, she could now also use the ball to break the window– but it should not show up as an affordance, because breaking an open window would not be appropriate (unless Alice was a vandal). So the *contextual action space* is:

$$(\text{drop, object}) \ (\text{push, object})$$

Alice uses the ball to push the button, and a secret door opens. Now, since the button state has changed, the contextual action space of the ball is further reduced, so the only option left is to drop the ball. Just as Alice thinks to do so, Bob runs into the room, and she has a better option: the *bonk* affordance becomes available, and Alice throws the ball at Bob's head.

At each step, Alice must query the ball to discover what actions are currently appropriate. Obtaining this list of appropriate affordances of an object requires a query that examines a set of condition/affordance pairs to filter out the options that are not currently relevant. Conditions filter on the object state, the character state, and the local environment. In our implementation, we use the same set of conditions available for building the character controllers. This makes adding contextual affordances to a system minimally invasive, as existing AI components can be reused. To demonstrate contextual affordances, we built a scenario using several objects that can be used in different ways depending on the context of the current game state.

4   Evaluation

We created a scenario using a small world where individual characters compete. In this scenario, the characters have two goals: find the treasure and knock out its opponents. The world has five areas, as seen in Figure 1. There is a window in the outside wall to the guardpost that can be broken, a window from the sanctuary to the courtyard that can be opened from the sanctuary (or broken from outside), a door from the guardpost to the courtyard, a door from the courtyard to the treasure room, and a door from the treasure room to the sanctuary. Doors and windows can be opened and closed if unlocked. The sanctuary is treated as a special room where characters are not allowed to attack one another.

There are six types of objects available in the world, each with one to three available actions (seen in Table 1). When context is added, each action is restricted by contextual affordances. The *break* action, for example, is only allowed if a window is closed and locked. Other restrictions are related to characters and their states. The table will only report *push* as a possibility if the character has recently been bonked with a ball, and the treasure chest will not provide *open* as an affordance if there are unfriendly characters in the room. Level design affects the *bonk* affordance on the balls, as it will not be available when the character is in the sanctuary.

During each turn, every character may perform one action. Character perception is limited to the current room. Once a character has been bonked three times with a ball, it is knocked out. Knocked-out characters drop their inventory, so if a character carrying the treasure is knocked out, the treasure can be retrieved by its opponent.

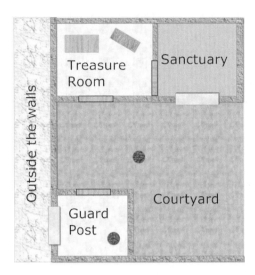

Fig. 1. Overhead view of the scenario world

We created three characters. Each character made its action decisions differently, though actions that would undo the last action taken were prevented unless the character had no other options (e.g., walking from the guardpost to the courtyard and then back to the guardpost, or pushing the table and then lifting it). The simplest character was a *pure random* character that was aware of basic affordances, meaning that when it queried an object, it received the full, unrestricted action space of the object. To choose an action, it built a list of the available affordances from the objects in the room without taking context into account. This included actions that were not possible or unproductive. An action was chosen randomly from this list, and the character attempted to execute it.

The second character was a *contextual random* character. This character was identical to the random character except that it used contextual affordances. The contextual affordances on each object used up to three condition tests combined as conjunctions or disjunctions. The third character was a hand-crafted behavior-based subsumption character with nine layers. Behavior-based subsumption is a form of reactive control that uses prioritized layers of behaviors activated by triggering conditions [5]. The hand-crafted controller had nine behavior layers, and the conditions used for building this character were a superset of the conditions used for creating the contextual affordances for the second character.

Characters were evaluated by pitting each type of character against each other type in the gameworld. Each competition was run for 10,000 trials for a limited number of turns. We recorded complete wins (both knocking out the opponent and finding the treasure), partial wins, and number of turns to win.

Contextual affordances provide better performance than purely random characters, as seen in Table 2(a). The hand-crafted subsumption character won against the contextual characters almost as often as it beat the random character, but

Table 1. Object Affordances

Object	Action Type	Action Slot
	bonk	object
Ball	break	object
	pick-up	object
Chest	open	target
	search	target
Door	exit	object
	open	target
	hide	object
Table	lift	target
	push	target
Treasure	pick-up	target
	break	target
Window	exit	object
	open	target

the contextual character performed slightly worse against the crafted character. Characters could get locked into a stalemate, where only one win condition was achieved. This happened when one character never encountered the other or never managed to retrieve the treasure. Contextual characters tended to knock out the crafted characters, but had a harder time finding the treasure, as seen in Table 2(b). Crafted characters found the treasure, but had difficulty knocking out contextual characters.

Table 2. Character Performance

(a) Complete Wins

Character	Random	Contextual	Crafted
Random	50.2%	14.7%	10.8%
Contextual	83.6%	47.4%	10.7%
Crafted	88.7%	83.7%	50.0%

(b) Partial Wins

Character	Contextual		Crafted	
	Treasure	KO	Treasure	KO
Contextual	1.6%	1.6%	0.1%	5.5%
Crafted	5.5%	0.1%	0.0%	0.0%

The character performance comparison shows that while the contextual character did not outperform the random character in complete wins against the crafted character, it did manage more partial wins, and completed the task in less time. The random character took an average of 122.6 turns to win, while the contextual character took 32.7, and the crafted character only 14.1 turns. The contextual character also outperformed the random character in direct matches. While contextual characters are not a replacement for carefully crafted characters, they are useful for minor characters. Contextual characters always perform actions that are appropriate, but have a far lower authorial burden.

We also compared the complexity of building the characters and the contextual objects. The hand-crafted character is composed of nine behavior layers with an average of 3.1 conditional tests per layer. The most complex layers have 5 tests. The objects required a total of 15 condition/action pairs to be created, with an average of 1.5 conditional tests per affordance. While more condition/action pairs must be created, the complexity of the conditions is simpler. Due to tight coupling between behaviors, character controllers can be difficult to reuse in new environments, while objects with contextual affordances can be easily reused.

5   Conclusions

In this paper, we have presented an extension for object affordances in games. *Contextual affordances* use the current state of the object, character, and environment to reduce the action space available to the game characters. This reduction in the action space reduces the complexity of the characters' decisions. In addition, contextual affordances are easily reusable in new environmens and provide more control to level designers.

We focus on contextual affordances used as a replacement for hand-crafted controllers. This may be feasible for minor characters, but the performance of contextually enabled random characters is worse than that of hand-crafted controllers. Contextual affordances may also be used to reduce the complexity of the hand-crafted characters. This reduces many behaviors to simply choosing the most important action available from nearby objects.

References

1. BioWare. Dragon Age: Origins, Fantasy Role-Playing Game (2009), http://dragonage.bioware.com/
2. Cerpa, D.H., Champandard, A., Dawe, M.: Behavior Trees: Three Ways of Cultivating Strong AI. Talk at the 2010 AI Summit at the Game Developers Conference (GDC) (2010), http://gdcvault.com/play/1012744/Behavior-Trees-Three-Ways-of
3. Gibson, J.J.: The theory of affordances. In: Gibson, J.J. (ed.) Perceiving, Acting, and Knowing. Lawrence Erlbaum Associates, Mahwah (1977)
4. Isla, D.: Handling Complexity in the Halo 2 AI. In: Proceedings of the 2005 Game Developers Conference (2005)
5. Matarić, M.J.: Behavior-based control: Main properties and implications. In: Proceedings, IEEE International Conference on Robotics and Automation, Workshop on Architectures for Intelligent Control Systems, pp. 46–54 (1992)
6. Norman, D.A.: The Design of Everyday Things. Basic Books, New York (2002)
7. Orkin, J.: Three States and a Plan: The AI of F.E.A.R. In: Proceedings of the Game Developer's Conference, GDC (2006)
8. Simpson, J.: Scripting and Sims2: Coding the Psychology of Little People. Talk at the 2005 Game Developers Conference (GDC) (2005), https://www.cmpevents.com/Sessions/GD/ScriptingAndSims2.ppt

Negotiations in the Context of AIDS Prevention: An Agent-Based Model Using Theory of Mind

Jennifer Klatt[1], Stacy Marsella[2], and Nicole C. Krämer[1]

[1] University Duisburg-Essen, Department of Social Psychology: Media and Communication,
Forsthausweg 2, 47058 Duisburg, Germany
{jennifer.klatt,nicole.kraemer}@uni-due.de
[2] University of Southern California, Institute for Creative Technologies,
12015 Waterfront Drive, Playa Vista, CA 90094, USA
marsella@ict.usc.edu

Abstract. For the purpose of an AIDS prevention game, a model was developed that focuses on training safe sex negotiations. Non-player characters in the game are socially intelligent agents that are equipped with a Theory of Mind that allows them to reason about the mental processes and behavior of others. The underlying model for the negotiation about safe sex between player and agent was implemented in multi-agent simulation software. It consists of two agents who have different goals of either safe or unsafe sex, actions to achieve these goals, and the wish to come to an agreement. The model was evaluated for the agent-agent conversation to test the basic functioning.

Keywords: Virtual agents, negotiation modeling, Theory of Mind, AIDS prevention.

1 Introduction

AIDS is one of the major health threats of this and the last century. More than half of the newly infected persons are men who have sex with men (MSMs) [1]. Currently, the best way to fight AIDS is to prevent it from being transmitted, so it is crucial to achieve a behavioral change in people. New media interventions have been shown to improve intentions towards safe sex in comparison to other intervention methods [2]. Recently a web-distributed health intervention was developed to achieve behavioral change. In the "Solve-It" game the user meets new people in a social setting, can go home with one of them, and negotiate safe sex. The focus is on young adult MSMs due to that population's higher infection rate. Since the real life situation involves aroused states that influence decision-making, the prevention needs to create a realistic atmosphere, and especially affective states (e.g. arousal). By providing appropriate stimuli, the non-conscious biases of the real situation will be replicated [3].

Modeling of a realistic negotiation requires an opponent with human-like behavior. Theory of Mind [4] is the basis for countless acts in social behavior: concepts as empathy, irony, a white lie, deception, or hints can be performed using the ability to reason about others [5]. Also, it is necessary to be able to negotiate with others. In

H. Högni Vilhjálmsson et al. (Eds.): IVA 2011, LNAI 6895, pp. 209–215, 2011.
© Springer-Verlag Berlin Heidelberg 2011

order to be able to come to an agreement or to even persuade the interaction partner and change his behavior, the negotiator needs assumptions on the current beliefs of the interaction partner and how they can be changed [6]. Also, ToM is a prerequisite for negotiations regarding the emotions that occur. Humans usually perceive and decode others' emotions during the negotiation which influences their behavior. The current emotional state of the negotiator himself is another aspect that influences his behavior, strong emotions lead to different behavior than weak emotions [5].

One example for teaching social skills with using agent models is FAtiMA that was developed to teach children how to deal with bullying by interacting with agent-driven characters. The project has been adapted to simulate a form of theory of mind, double appraisal [7], where the agents consider the results of their action as if the action was done to them. The ELECT BiLAT application [8] is explicitly designed to teach negotiation skills, but in a cross-culture military context. The underlying simulation software used for the model is the PsychSim social simulation tool [9; 10], a multi-agent system whose agents are equipped with a Theory of Mind. However, in BiLAT fixed values are used for rewards, unlike the model we describe here.

The focus of the work discussed lies in the negotiation phase of the Solve-It game. An important aspect for the game is to create a non-player negotiation partner that employs humans-like tactics. To that end, we have used autonomous agents that are equipped with social intelligence, a Theory of Mind [4], to drive the negotiation partner's behavior. This intelligence includes the ability to put one-self into someone else's shoes and foresee future moves of both the user and itself. So the agent needs to make assumptions about the user's goals, feelings, and what action he will choose to achieve this goal. Therefore, Theory of Mind like capacities are necessary to enable an updating of the model on the user during interaction, allowing a form of user modeling that can support adaptive behavior as the user proceeds through the game. In this paper, we discuss the model we developed, evaluate its behavior in a series of simulation experiments and discuss the results.

2   Description of the Model

The model used in the Solve-It game consists of two agents, Adam and Bart, who negotiate whether they are going to have safe or unsafe sex. They make various negotiation moves, offering, counter-offering and complimenting in an effort to persuade the other to accept their offer. The model was developed in the PsychSim multi-agent system [9; 10]. PsychSim uses a decision-theoretic framework for quantitative modeling of multiple agents that allows agents to reason about tradeoffs in achieving their goals. PsychSim agents are equipped with a Theory of Mind that allows them to reason about beliefs and behavior of other agents. To realize an agent model for negotiating safe sex in PsychSim, we specified the agent's *states*, *goals*, *goal weights*, *actions*, *action dynamics,* and *beliefs* that define how the agent will behave.

States: provide a description of the world. The states we model are *Offered, Risky, Attractive, Arousal,* and *FeelingSafe. Offered* keeps track of which offer has currently been made. *Risky* is a characteristic of the agent about whether he has a tendency to engage in unsafe sex. *Attractive* is the degree of physical attractiveness. *Arousal* and

FeelingSafe are emotional states that describe the contradictory feelings that are involved with having safe or unsafe sex: to get aroused but also to feel safe.

Actions: change the values of states. The actions of the agents include: *OfferUnsafe*, *offerCondom*, *compliment*, *accept* and *rejectNegotiation*. *OfferUnsafe* and *offerCondom* are actions to offer safe or unsafe sex. *Compliment* is an action where one agent makes a compliment to the other one with the idea to create a better atmosphere between them. If one agent agrees to an offer that he did not make himself, he can use the action *accept*. *RejectNegotiation* can be chosen when one agent wants to end the conversation. Actions change states through action dynamics. For example the action *compliment* changes the values for accepting unsafe sex on *Arousal* and *FeelingSafe*. To influence the partner, the agent who wants to reach an unsafe sex agreement, Adam, compliments Bart and will become more attractive and less risky. This does not mean that he really is safer, but the complimented agent, Bart, will perceive him as a less risky and a more attractive choice than before. This has the consequence that he is more willing to accept an unsafe offer for two reasons: First, he will believe there is a higher reward for *Arousal* which is caused by the increased *Attractive* value and second, the smaller penalty for *FeelingSafe*, caused by the lower *Risky* value. In essence, the compliment changes Bart's view of the payoff, the benefit, and cost, of having sex with Adam.

Goals: states that need to be either maximized or minimized. For example, an agent can want to maximize his *FeelingSafe* or his *Arousal*. Agents can also have multiple goals and preferences or weights over which of these goals are most important. For example, in most of the examples below, Adam weights maximizing *Arousal* 70% and 30% for *Feeling Safe*. Bart's default values are 76% for *Feeling Safe*, 24% for *Arousal*. In the model's decision theoretic framework, the reward the agent receives for maximizing *Arousal* will be proportional to the value of the *Arousal* and the weight the agent gives that goal. Agents can also have goals of maximizing another agent's goals. This goal strongly influences the behavior.

Beliefs: consist of models of all agents (including itself), representing their states, beliefs, goals, and actions. So Adam can have a belief about Bart's goals e.g. his preference for maximizing *FeelingSafe*. Beliefs have a bounded recursive structure: Adam can have a belief about what Bart believes about his goal.

The conversation between agents is structured in steps: one step means both agents take one negotiation turn. The agents are able to think several steps ahead, so they can reason about their and the other one's future actions. How much they think ahead is defined by the *horizon* which can be set to a value individually for the agents. In the case of the experiments conducted with the model, the agents usually have a horizon of two steps per agent in the future (so four conversational turns in total) they can consider for choosing their first action. The recursive assumptions about the mental models of the agents are called the *belief depth* and are per default set to three levels. The mental models of oneself and the other agent can be correct, incorrect or use a probability distribution over possible mental models of the other that is updated during the conversation according to the other agent's actions (using a Bayesian update procedure). However, the default setting is a correct model.

One possible ending of the negotiation is the acceptance of an offer (action *accept*). Then the reward or penalty is added to the goal states *Arousal* and *FeelingSafe*: The more attractive the partner is the more arousing sex is with him. Therefore, a higher value is added to the state *Arousal* when they accept the offer. *FeelingSafe* is dependent on how risky the agent is: If the offer of safe sex is accepted, *FeelingSafe* is increased. However if the offer is unsafe, it will be decreased according to the level of the other one's risk value. This means that a person who is perceived as unsafe will make us feel less safe when we have unsafe sex with him. Another possibility is the action of rejecting the negotiation (*rejectNegotiation*). No reward follows this action, but also no penalty is given which can be the most compelling option.

The described design of the model was chosen for several pedagogical reasons: First of all, we chose the extreme positions for the agents to have the maximum negotiating training. So Bart prefers *FeelingSafe* and Adam prefers *Arousal*. *Arousal* will be most increased when they agree on unsafe sex, whereas the *FeelingSafe* state is maximized for safe sex; unsafe sex even decreases its values. Also the agent with the unsafe sex goal is intended to be hard to negotiate with in order to enhance training effects. Second, the negotiation always reaches an agreement so the user experiences the rest of the game. A third aspect contains the variation of the states *Risky* and *Attractive* and the goal weights: in future versions of the game factors like drinking alcohol will change the preferences for *Arousal* or *FeelingSafe*, their models about the other one and finally, as a result, the actions: They will perceive others as less risky and more attractive, their arousal will go up and their horizon reduces. Therefore, the likelihood for unsafe sex increases.

3   Experiments

Experiments were run to validate the model used in the Solve-It game. A first set of experiments showed the basic behavior of the model. In a standard conversation with one agent who wants safe sex and the other wants unsafe sex, the outcome will be unsafe sex. This is due to the action *compliment* that changes the likelihood of the agent with the goal of safe sex to agree to unsafe sex (an example for the standard conversation can be found in Table 1, lines 1 and 2). First experiments tested the manipulation of the goals: When both agents want unsafe sex they agree on unsafe sex and the same is true for safe sex. So the basic functioning of the model is given.

To explore the behavior of the agents in a more cooperative negotiation, we conducted a second set of experiments where each agent could have an additional goal of maximizing the other's goals, additional to their goals to maximize *Arousal* and *Feeling safe*. We set the value for this goal weight to three different values: 20% as a moderate weight, 60% as a weight that makes helping the other one to achieve his goals more important than the own goals and 80% as an extreme position. Since all combinations with 20% resulted in the standard conversation, they will not be discussed here. For an overview see Table 1.

Results show that Adam, the one who most wants to maximize *Arousal*, keeps negotiating in the same way when he does not care for Bart's goals at all, when he cares for it 60%. Only when he cares for him 80% he behaves differently. A change in Bart's goal weight affects his behavior stronger: 60% of caring for Adam's goals is enough for him to compliment Adam because this changes Adam's values in case of unsafe sex. Adam receives higher values for his *Arousal* then, so Bart helps him even more to maximize this state. When Adam starts, he offers unsafe sex, Bart compliments him, but this time Adam chooses to *rejectNegotiation*, because this increases his value for *Feeling Safe*. If in a human conversation somebody offers unsafe sex, receives a compliment and replies with rejection, he as well makes himself feel safer because he realizes that the other one tries to manipulate him. When Bart cares for Adam 80%, he behaves the same when he starts. But when Adam starts, he just directly accepts: unsafe sex.

When both agents care equally much for each other, for 60% the conversation proceeds as follows: Bart starts with complementing, then Adam compliments, too. They have the same reason for doing so: They want to maximize the other's goal state: Bart wants to maximize Adam's *Arousal* and Adam helps to maximize Bart's *FeelingSafe*. Then Bart offers unsafe sex and Adam agrees. When Adam starts, he instantly offers safe sex (because this helps best to let Bart achieve his goal) and Bart accepts. This is due to the fact that they care more for each other than themselves. With a goal weight of 80% they agree always on unsafe sex. A reason for this is the structure of the goals: In this case both agents care very much for the goals of the other one. So Adam believes that it is Bart's goal to achieve Adam's goal which makes Adam offer again his favorite action. So with 80%, a very high level of caring for the partner, the situation can be compared to not care about the other at all.

Table 1. Overview over results of varying how much they care for each other. Abbreviations used: *OC: offerCondom, OU: offerUnsafe, C: compliment, A: accept, RN: reject negotiations.*

Caring for partner	Outcome	Turn 1	Turn 2	Turn 3	Turn 4
Adam 60%	Unsafe	Bart *OC*	Adam *C*	Bart *OU*	Adam *A*
	Unsafe	Adam *C*	Bart *OU*	Adam *A*	
Adam 80%	Safe	Bart *OC*	Adam *A*		
	Unsafe	Adam *C*	Bart *OU*	Adam *A*	
Bart 60%	Unsafe	Bart *C*	Adam *OU*	Bart *A*	
	Unsafe	Adam *OU*	Bart *C*	Adam *RN*	Bart *A*
Bart 80%	Unsafe	Bart *C*	Adam *OU*	Bart *A*	
	Unsafe	Adam *OU*	Bart *A*		
Both 60%	Unsafe	Bart *C*	Adam *C*	Bart *OU*	Adam *A*
	Safe	Adam *OC*	Bart *A*		
Both 80%	Unsafe	Bart *C*	Adam *OU*	Bart *A*	
	Unsafe	Adam *C*	Bart *C*	Adam *OU*	Bart *A*

In mental models the agents have assumptions about the other one's recent states, beliefs, and goals. The goals are very important in this model because they define which action will be chosen. We ran experiments with three different possible mental models with Adam and Bart: a correct one (so the agent has correct assumptions about the other one's goals), a false one that assumes that the other one has the same goals like himself and a probability distribution over alternative models. The latter is implemented as a probability of 50% for the correct model and 50% for the false model. It adapts the probability of the two models according to the actions of the other agent. All combinations of the three mental model types were evaluated (see Table 2).

False mental models. In the case that Adam has a correct model and Bart has the false one, the standard conversation occurs. However, when Adam's model is wrong and Bart has a correct one, Bart offers condoms. Then Adam offers unsafe, because he thinks that Bart is like himself and will accept this offer immediately. Now Bart does not expect Adam to accept another offer of condoms but to reject the negotiation; therefore he rejects the negotiation himself. Hence, under these conditions they do not reach an agreement, regardless of who starts the conversation. When both agents have a wrong mental model both offer their favorite option and then the first agent does not expect that another offer would lead to success, so he rejects the negotiation. Hence, only when Adam has a correct mental model, an agreement is reached: unsafe sex.

Probability distribution over alternative mental models. When Adam has the correct mental model and Bart uses the probability distribution over possible mental models the standard conversation occurs. When Adam uses the probability distribution or when both use it, a different conversation results: Bart starts with *offerCondom*, which is accepted by Adam. When Adam starts and offers unsafe sex, Bart rejects the negotiation, essentially to avoid being manipulated, for he believes that if he did not do this, Adam would compliment him and he would finally agree to his offer. Unfortunately for Bart, Adam still compliments after this and Bart agrees. If someone in a human conversation asks for unsafe sex and the partner wants to go away he might as well try to change the partner's mind by saying something nice.

The values of 50% for the false model and 50% of the correct model are adapted during the conversations. Even with the low number of only two turns per agent, they reach values up to 70% for the correct model and 30% for the false model. This change of probabilities for the mental models would impact future interactions.

Table 2. Overview over results of varying the mental model of each other. Abbreviations used: *OC: offerCondom, OU: offerUnsafe, C: compliment, A: accept, RN: reject negotiations, PD: probability distribution.*

Mental model	Outcome	Turn 1	Turn 2	Turn 3	Turn 4
Adam correct,	Unsafe	Bart *OC*	Adam *C*	Bart *OU*	Adam *A*
Bart wrong	Unsafe	Adam *C*	Bart *OU*	Adam *A*	
Adam wrong,	No agreement	Bart *OC*	Adam *OU*	Bart *RN*	
Bart correct	No agreement	Adam *OU*	Bart *RN*		
Both wrong	No agreement	Bart *OC*	Adam *OU*	Bart *RN*	
	No agreement	Adam *OU*	Bart *OC*	Adam *RN*	
Adam correct,	Unsafe	Bart *OC*	Adam *C*	Bart *OU*	Adam *A*
Bart *PD*	Unsafe	Adam *C*	Bart *OU*	Adam *A*	
Adam *PD*,	Safe	Bart *OC*	Adam *A*		
Bart correct	Unsafe	Adam *OU*	Bart *RN*	Adam *C*	Bart *A*
Both *PD*	Safe	Bart *OC*	Adam *A*		
	Unsafe	Adam *OU*	Bart *RN*	Adam *C*	Bart *A*

4   Conclusion and Outlook

In order to create game characters that are challenging to negotiate with, we implemented an agent-based model of negotiation with ToM capacities. Computer experiments were run to evaluate the behavior of the agent model. Most experiments conducted revealed an intuitive and logical behavior that shows that the model in general is functioning well.

These various computational experiments are just a first step in evaluating the model. It needs to be also tested for a) their pedagogical appropriateness for the game and b) the subjective impressions of human subjects. As noted earlier, the negotiation dialog paths generated by the model were incorporated in the current version of the Solve-It game. Those behaviors were vetted by the design team as realistic and 50 distinct paths were incorporated into the game. The Solve-It game will be tested and evaluated in large scale longitudinal clinical trial. In addition, we plan to test human subjects directly interacting with the agents in a negotiation to reveal if and how much the agents' behavior is perceived as realistic human behavior.

Various negotiation models use Theory of Mind approaches to make models of negotiations more realistic. Here most approaches use dynamics that are not dependent on emotions. The context of safe sex negotiations is a highly emotional topic that could not be addressed with only rational aspects. The model described in this paper tries to combine handling of emotions with general structures of negotiations. However, the model described only addresses a social negotiation that deals with a safe sex context. Future research could develop a general approach to modeling emotions and social negotiations without a specific context.

Acknowledgments. We thank the National Institute for Mental Health (NIMH) and the German Academic Exchange Service for their support of this project.

References

1. Centers for Disease Control and Prevention. HIV among Gay, Bisexual and Other Men Who Have Sex with Men (MSM) (2010)
2. Noar, S.M., Pierce, L.B., Black, H.G.: Can computer-mediated interventions change theoretical mediators of safer sex? A meta-analysis. Hum. Comm. Res. 36, 261–297 (2010)
3. Bechara, A., Damasio, H., Tranel, D., Damasio, A.R.: Deciding advantageously before knowing the advantageous strategy. Science 275, 1293–1294 (1997)
4. Baron-Cohen, S.: Autism: the empathizing-systemizing (E-S) theory. Annals of the New York Academy of Sciences 1156, 68–80 (2009)
5. Sally, D.: Social maneuvers and theory of mind. Marq. L. Rev. 87, 893–902 (2004)
6. Sycara, K.P.: Persuasive Argumentation in Negotiation. Theo. a. December 28, 203 – 242 (1990)
7. Aylett, R., Louchart, S.: If I were you: double appraisal in affective agents. In: Proc. of the 7th Int. Conf. on Autonomous Agents and Multiagent Systems, pp. 1233–1236 (2008)
8. Kim, J., Hill, R., Durlach, P., Lane, H., Forbell, E., Core, M., Marsella, S., Pynadath, D., Hart, J.: BiLAT: A Game-Based Environment for Practicing Negotiation in a Cultural Context. Int. J. of Art. Int. in Education 19, 289–308 (2009)
9. Marsella, S.C., Pynadath, D.V., Read, S.J.: PsychSim: Agent-based modeling of social interactions and influence. In: Proc. of 6th Int. Conf. on Cognitive Modeling, pp. 243–248 (2004)
10. Pynadath, D.V., Marsella, S.C.: PsychSim: Modeling Theory of Mind with Decision-Theoretic Agents. In: Proc. of the Int. Joint Conf. on Artificial Intelligence, pp. 1181–1186 (2005)

Towards More Comprehensive Listening Behavior: Beyond the Bobble Head

Zhiyang Wang, Jina Lee, and Stacy Marsella

University of Southern California - Institute for Creative Technologies
12015 Waterfront Drive, Playa Vista, CA 90094
zhiyangw@usc.edu, {jlee,marsella}@ict.usc.edu

Abstract. Realizing effective listening behavior in virtual humans has become a key area of research, especially as research has sought to realize more complex social scenarios involving multiple participants and bystanders. A human listener's nonverbal behavior is conditioned by a variety of factors, from current speaker's behavior to the listener's role and desire to participate in the conversation and unfolding comprehension of the speaker. Similarly, we seek to create virtual humans able to provide feedback based on their participatory goals and their partial understanding of, and reaction to, the relevance of what the speaker is saying as the speaker speaks. Based on a survey of existing psychological literature as well as recent technological advances in recognition and partial understanding of natural language, we describe a model of how to integrate these factors into a virtual human that behaves consistently with these goals. We then discuss how the model is implemented into a virtual human architecture and present an evaluation of behaviors used in the model.

Keywords: artificial intelligence, listener feedback, context based feedback, nonverbal behavior.

1 Introduction

Two people are having a heated conversation in a cafe. Around the cafe, various bystanders are listening to the interaction. Some avert their gaze, pretend to do something else, hoping not to become participants in the interaction but nevertheless eavesdropping on the exchange. They are hopelessly drawn to the unfolding scene, glancing at the main protagonists to glean information on the interaction from their dialog and nonverbal behavior, but careful to avoid the mutual gaze that might draw them into the interaction. Meanwhile, the owner of the cafe, wanting to calm the situation, is signaling his intention to join the interaction.

Developing virtual humans that can handle such ranges of participation has become an increasingly important area of research, more so as work has sought to realize more complex dramatic scenarios [16]. Work on listening behavior has tackled various aspects of this challenge. For example, there is work on dyadic interactions between human and *rapport* agents that have an implicit, fixed goal of establishing rapport but often have limited understanding of the content of the speaker's utterance [13]. The agents rather rely on low level analysis of the nonverbal and perceptual features of the

H. Högni Vilhjálmsson et al. (Eds.): IVA 2011, LNAI 6895, pp. 216–227, 2011.

human speaker's behavior that are correlated with listener feedback, such as pauses in the speaker's utterance.

Although effective in establishing rapport, this approach suffers from several limitations. First, such approaches only provide *generic feedback* [3] signaling such factors that the agent is attending. They cannot provide *specific feedback* [3], feedback tied to a deeper understanding of, and reaction to, the personal relevance of what the speaker is saying as the utterance unfolds. Another limitation is the fixed, implicit goal of establishing rapport. In practice, however, people can have very different kinds of stances towards a conversation, including even their lack of interest in understanding the speaker or a desire to leave the conversation. One approach to addressing this limitation is to have the listener's behavior be conditional on attitudinal factors [4]. Finally, the focus for listening behavior has been largely on dyadic conversations, where the listener agent is main and sole addressee, though there have been notable exceptions [18].

In this work, our interest is to realize this richer form of interaction in a multiparty setting where there may be several virtual humans interacting with one or more humans, playing a variety of roles (e.g. main addressee, side-participants, overhearer, bystander, etc.) with varying degrees of participation in, and commitment to, the conversation. The question that interests us is how these characters respond nonverbally according to their current role in the conversation, their desire to participate, their understanding of the speaker's partial utterance, as well as behavioral signals from the speaker.

This raises technical challenges of how to integrate the various factors that influence a listener, including the perception of the speaker's verbal/nonverbal behavior as well as the listener's reactions to the speaker in light of their goals for participation. In this paper, we review the relevant literature on listener feedback and propose a model that tailors behaviors based on how the various roles of participants influence their nonverbal behaviors and how those behaviors can signal their goals to change roles. To provide both generic and specific feedback, the model integrates information from perceptual and comprehension processes. We then discuss how the model is implemented into a virtual human architecture, relying on prior work to provide perceptual processing of the nonverbal and prosodic features of speaker behavior [26] as well as to provide natural language understanding of a speaker's partial utterance [7] and emotional reaction [25] to it. Finally, we present a preliminary evaluation of behavioral signals used in the model and discuss future directions.

2   Related Work

Listener's feedback [28] has been studied both in social science and humanities research on human behavior as well as in technology work on the design of virtual agents. This section discusses the virtual agent work. Literature on human behavior that has informed this work is discussed and referenced in subsequent sections.

Research on listening behavior for virtual agents has largely focused on dyadic interactions between virtual agent and human, where the virtual agent is the main addressee. The Rapport Agent created by Gratch et al. [13] provides listening feedback based on the nonverbal and prosodic features of the speaker's behavior, such as head movements, body postures, and vocal pitch and intensities. They demonstrated that mimicry of the speaker's behavior, including head movements and gaze aversion, improves the human speaker's sense of rapport and speech fluency. Morency et al. [26] learned probabilistic models that predict listener's nonverbal feedback from the human speaker's multimodal output features (e.g., prosody, spoken words and eye gaze).

Because such designs are driven by the speaker's behavior and more importantly do not incorporate the listener's (virtual human) interpretation and reaction to the utterance, they are arguably more important for generic feedback as opposed to specific feedback [3]. To drive listener's specific backchannel behaviors, the virtual agent needs to interpret the utterances and generate feedback based on personal relevance, as the human speaker's utterance is in progress. Research has sought to address this technological challenge in several ways. Jónsdóttir et al. [19] collected human listeners' feedback data, summarized a set of speaker's key phrases in a limited topic domain, and built a system to generate virtual listener's feedbacks when input utterance match those lexical feedback markers (key phrases). Kopp et al. [21] designed an event-based feedback model for their virtual agent Max. The model generates listener's feedback by using multimodal information including the speaker's pauses and lexical information. DeVault et al. [7] used a classifier to classify partial utterances in terms of semantic frames that the agent understands.

In addition to such work on dyadic conversation, there also has been work in multiparty conversation. Jan and Traum [18] involves movement for modeling agents' participation restriction with group conversation. They developed a social force model to control the distance between the agent and the group center. The force would push two agents apart if they were over close to each other, while the virtual bystander may be dragged towards group if they were outside of the circular participation domain.

In contrast to prior work, the focus of this paper is on a model for generating listener nonverbal feedbacks for multiparty conversations that includes both generic and specific feedback, as well as taking into account that there may be a variety of participants with varying roles and goals for their participation.

3   Conversational Roles and Goals

In this section we discuss the relationships between conversation roles and goals which we later use when mapping listener feedback behaviors to in our model. First we define the various conversation roles by adopting the terminology used by Goffman [11]. In a conversation, the core participants are the speaker and nonspeaking participants (ratified participants), which includes the *addressee* ("addressed recipient") and the *side-participants* ("unaddressed recipients"). In addition, unofficial-participants are called *bystanders.* Goffman identifies two types of bystanders: *eavesdroppers,* who purposefully listen to the conversation, and *overhearers,* who accidentally and unintentionally hear the conversation. However, these conversation roles are not static and can change during social interaction [15,27].

We can characterize these various roles from the perspective of the goals that the role normatively presumes. Here we define two types of conversation goals: *participation goal* and *comprehension goal.* Since addressees and side-participants are part of the core conversation participants, they hold positive participation goals and to maintain this status they must act appropriately. However, bystanders (overhearers and eaves-droppers) normatively have a negative participation goal (i.e. they are not or do not want to be perceived as participants) and should act in ways that do not increase their level of participation. The conversation roles can also be further distinguish based on the comprehension goals. Eavesdroppers clearly have stronger intentions to understand the conversation, whereas overhearers do not intend to comprehend the conversation. In contrast, addressees and side participants are expected to have positive comprehension goals and to behave consistently.

We can then summarize the relationships between conversation roles and goals as the following. Addressees have positive participation and comprehension goals; side-participants have positive participation goal and either positive or negative comprehension goal; eavesdroppers have negative participation goal but positive comprehension goal; overhearers have both negative participation and comprehension goals.

Several aspects of this classification must be stressed. First, we assume that all of the agents, regardless of their roles, have freedom to change their participation or comprehension goals. For example, although side-participants are part of the conversation group, they may want to leave the conversation at any time. Second, there is a distinction between having a goal and openly appearing (or signaling) that one has a goal. For instance, eavesdroppers may wish to comprehend the conversation (and thus have a positive comprehension goal), but because they do not want to *participate* in the conversation, it is important to appear so since they could be drawn into the conversation and endanger their role as eavesdroppers. Third, these goals are the norm for the roles. For example, side-participants are presumed to be committed to participate and comprehend the conversation and should act consistently, but in reality they may not be concerned with understanding the context of the conversation. For this reason, it is important to consider the individual's goals for participation and comprehension distinct from the role, since the realization of behaviors may depend on both. In this paper we simplify the goals to have a binary value (positive or negative), but one can also imagine the goals having numerical values to specify the degrees of participation or comprehension.

4   Modeling the Impact of Roles and Goals on Behavior

The literature describes various listening behaviors depending on the conversation roles and goals, which we use to inform the knowledge used in our model. Table 1 categorizes the knowledge currently used in the model. The behaviors are categorized according to the agent's goal to participate in the conversation and its desire to comprehend the speech content. In this section, we discuss that knowledge and in the next section we cover how that knowledge is used by the model.

For addressees, we use gaze and mutual gaze to signal goals of participation and comprehension as well as continued attention [1]. This also helps addressees to get clearer visual and vocal information from the speaker [20]. Addressees also glance at other side-participants to seek social comparison [9] or avert gaze as a signal of cogni-tive overload when comprehending speech [1,12]. In addition, we use various forms of nodding behaviors to signal that the addressee is attending [26], comprehending [5,8] or reacting to the speaker [17] and thereby to signal participation and comprehension.

Table 1. Relationship between conversation goals, roles, and listener feedbacks

Conversation Goals		Conversation Roles	Rule and Behavior
Participating	Not specified comprehending	Addressee or Side-participant	*Attendance*: gaze speaker [1,14] and head nod [26].
			Mimicry: mimic gaze direction: listener mimics speaker's gaze direction when the speaker has gazed away for a long period. Mimic head gesture: Listener repeats speaker's shaking or nodding behavior. [24]
		Switch from Eavesdropper/Overhearer to Addressee/Side-participant	*Enter group*: decrease distance by moving towards the group [18]
		Addressee or Side-participant	*Respond feedback request*: respond to other participant's communication request by gazing at the speaker [17]; Glance at speaker to indicate continued attention and willingness [1]
			Mirror Emotion: adjust its own emotion to group's emotion status [10]
Not Participating	Comprehending	Addressee or Side-participant	*Understand*: head nod [5,8]
			Think: gaze aversion [1]
			Gather Information (addressee/side-participant): glance at speaker to study speaker's facial expressions and direction of gaze [1,20] or generate social comparison behavior [9].
			Confusion: head tilt and frown [5]
			Emotion reaction: different head movement, gaze behavior and facial expression according to different emotion types.
	Not Comprehending	Eavesdropper	*Gather Information(eavesdropper)*: glance at speaker but with faster speed and less magnitude [1] and avoid mutual gaze [2]. Show less reaction [9] .
		Overhearer	*Avoid mutual gaze*: gaze aversion [6,11]
		Switch from Addressee/Side-participant to overhearer	*Leave group*: increase distance by moving away from group [18]

On the other hand, head tilts and frowns are used to signal confusion [5] and various facial expressions are shown to signal emotional reactions to the content of the speech.

Side-participants are also ratified by the speaker and exhibit similar behaviors as addressees. However, they may be less committed to comprehend the current dialog. If side-participants do not care about understanding the speaker's utterance (i.e. comprehension goal is negative) but the goal is to maintain the participation status, they use glances toward the speaker [1,14]. The glances here are not to further comprehend but rather to act as a ratified participant. Mimicking or mirroring the speaker's behavior [10,24] are also exhibited to hold his/her current conversation role.

Eavesdroppers have the goal to understand the conversation but their status as anonymous eavesdroppers may be threatened if they openly signal their comprehension. Thus, they avoid mutual gaze and restrain from showing reactions to the conversation [9]. Furtive glances at the speaker are occasionally used for better comprehension but gaze

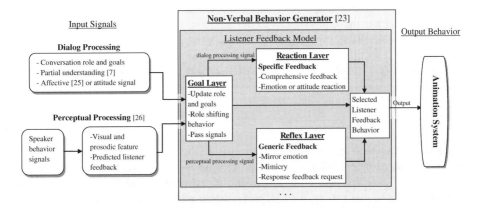

Fig. 1. Architecture of the Listener Feedback Model

is quickly averted to prevent providing visual feedback [2] and signs of attention to the speaker [1,2,20].

Overhearers have neither goals for participation nor comprehension and have fewer concerns about the conversation. Gaze aversion from conversation participants is used to prevent mutual gaze [6,11] since gaze may be considered as a request signal to be included into the current conversation [1]. However, in a highly dynamic conversation, an overhearer may have difficulty avoiding comprehension of, and reactions, to the conversation.

In addition to the behaviors associated with the conversation roles, there are behaviors associated with role shifts. To signal a change in the conversation role, behaviors associated with the current role are avoided and those associated with the new role are adopted. For example, gazing at the speaker and making mutual gaze signal role shifting from a bystander to a side-participant or an addressee [1,11]. To shift from an overhearer to an eavesdropper, increased glances at the speaker is adopted to show desires for better comprehension. When the role shift involves changes in the participation goal, interpersonal distance is also adjusted by either moving toward or away from the group to join or leave the conversation [18].

Finally, note that we have not discussed the varieties of turn-taking behaviors associated with the participant seizing the dialog turn or a speaker relinquishing his role as speaker. Such behaviors are more common components of virtual human systems so we have not discussed them here.

5 The Listener Feedback Model

Based on the listener behaviors categorized in the previous section, we constructed the listener feedback model as a set of feedback rules and incorporated them as an extension to the Nonverbal Behavior Generator [23], the behavior planner of our virtual human system. Figure 1 represents the architecture of our model. In this model, we make a distinction between generic feedback and specific feedback as described in section 1.

Given the agent's conversation roles and goals, the Goal Layer updates this information and propagates the input signals to the Reaction layer or the Reflex layer that is responsible for generating specific feedbacks or generic feedbacks, respectively. Each layer contains a set of listener feedback rules (see Table1) that gets triggered to generate the behaviors. The following sections discuss the details of the input signals and the different layers in the model.

5.1   Inputs

The listener feedback model receives signals from the virtual human system's cognitive module, broadly classified as dialog processing and perceptual processing signals, as shown in Figure 1. The Dialog Processing signal provides (a) the virtual human's current conversational role as well as participation and comprehension goals, (b) incremental partial understanding information and (c) affective or attitude signal. The conversational role and goals are sent by the virtual human's dialogue module at the start of the conversation and are updated as the interaction between participants unfold. The listener's incremental interpretation of partial utterances is realized by DeVault et al.'s classifier [7], which provides a semantic interpretation as well as a measure how confident the agent is of their partial understanding and a measure of whether the agent believes it will understand better if it continues listening. The affective signal comes from the system's emotion model [25], which predicts the agent's emotional state through an appraisal process of the interpretation of the current interaction and its relationship to the environment.

The Perceptual Processing signal is provided by the virtual human's perceptual model which includes information about the *speaker's* behaviors such as the head movements, gaze direction, pitch accents, and speech pauses. It also includes predictions of the listener's backchannel nods, based on the work of Morency et al. [26].

5.2   Layers of the Model

Upon receiving the input signals, the Goal Layer first updates the agent's role and goals and determine whether to generate a role shifting behavior or to pass the incoming signals to the Reaction and Reflex Layers. The role shifting behavior occurs when the agent's updated participation goal differs from the current participation goal. For example, if the agent's current role is *overhearer* (participation goal=negative) and the updated role is *addressee* (participation goal=positive), he will enter the conversation group and generate attendance behavior by gazing at the speaker and nodding. The role shifting behaviors refer to rule*Enter group* and *Leave group* in Table 1.

If the agent's participation goal is unchanged, the input messages are passed to the Reaction and Reflex Layers and corresponding feedback behaviors are generated depending on the comprehension goal. In particular, the dialog processing signals are passed to the Reaction Layer and the perceptual processing signals are passed to the Reflex Layer. In our model, both layers are active, generating feedbacks concurrently. However, one might instead argue for a more complex interaction. For example, once the partial understanding has achieved high confidence, the reaction layer may dominate the reflex layer.

Table 2. Selection of Comprehension Feedback Rules

			Feedback Rules with Different Roles		
	Confidence	maxf	addressee/side-participant	eavesdropper	overhearer
Input	[0.0, 0.5)	0	Confusion	Idle	Idle
		1	Attendance		
	[0.5, 1.0)	0	Partial Understand/ Think/ Idle	Gather Info.(eavesdropper)	
		1	Partial Understand/ Think/ Attendance/ Gather-Info.(addressee/side-participant)	Idle	
	1.0	0	Understand		
		1			

The Reflex Layer generates generic feedback behaviors when the agent's participation goal is positive but the comprehension goal is negative or unknown. It processes the speaker's perceptual information and generates behaviors such as gazing at the speaker or mimicking the speaker's gaze direction and facial expressions, in addition to propagating the listener head nods predicted by the visual module. This layer triggers listener feedback rules *Attendance, Respond feedback request*, and *Mirror Emotion* in Table 1.

The Reaction Layer processes affective or attitudinal information as well as the comprehension information. In this model, the agent's emotional reaction is stronger than the reactions related to the partial understanding of the speaker's utterance, therefore any incoming affective or attitudinal signal will have higher priority than the comprehension information. The affective reactions include behaviors such as smiles for joy and furrowed eyebrows for anger (rule *Emotion reaction*).

The comprehension information contains two parameter values: *confidence* (range [0.0, 1.0]) and *maxf* (0 or 1). The confidence value indicates how confident the agent believes it understands the speaker's utterance and maxf indicates whether the agent believes it will understand the utterance more if it keeps listening. We define three categories of understanding based on the confidence value: confusion ([0.0, 0.5)), partial understanding ([0.5, 1.0)), understand (1.0). The *maxf* value further determines which specific feedback is generated. Table 2 shows how the *confidence* and *maxf* values determine the selection of listener feedback rules.

6   Example

We now go through an example scenario to demonstrate how the listener's nonverbal backchannel behaviors are generated. Note that in the current state the mapping between conversation roles, goals, and feedback behaviors have been implemented in our virtual human system whereas the incoming signals from the external modules have not yet been fully integrated. Therefore, here we emulate the incoming dialog processing and perceptual processing signals to demonstrate the model.

In this example, a human user plays the role of a ranger (Ranger) and tries to convince Utah, the local bartender, to take his place as the new sheriff. Utah is in favor of this offer and initially shows positive reactions, but then becomes concerned about Harmony's reactions, who is the saloon owner. On the other hand, Harmony hears the conversation first as an overhearer and shows negative reactions to Ranger's proposal then switches her role to a side-participant to join the conversation.

Table 3. Feedback Behaviors for the Example Utterance. Here we list the feedback rules for each feedback points. Refer to Table 1 for the specific behaviors. "Idle" indicates idle behavior.

Index	Perceptual (Common)	Dialog (Common)	(Utah)	(Harmony)	Utah Generic	Utah Specific	Harmony Generic	Harmony Specific
①	Predict: nod prob.(0.6)	PU: maxf(0), confidence(1.0)	Role(P,C): A(1,1)	Role(P,C): O(0,0)	Response feedback request	Role shifting: Enter group, Attendance	-	Idle
②	-	PU: maxf(1), confidence(1.0)	-	-	-	Understand	-	Idle
③	-	PU:maxf(0), confidence([0.5,1.0))	-	Role(P,C): E(0,1)	-	Partial Understand/ Think/ Idle	-	Role shifting: Avoid Mutual Gaze
④	-	PU: maxf(1), confidence(1.0)	-	-	-	Understand	-	Idle
⑤	-	PU: maxf(1) confidence(1.0)	Affective: surprise	Affective: surprise	-	Emotion (surprise)	-	Idle
⑥	-	PU: maxf(1) confidence(1.0),	-	Role(P,C): SP(1,1)	-	Understand	-	Role shifting: Enter Group, Attendance
⑦	-	PU: maxf(1) confidence(1.0)	Attitude: like	Attitude: dislike	-	Attitude: (like)	-	Attitude: (dislike)

P-Participation Goal; C-Comprehension Goal; 1-positive; 0-negative; PU-Partial Understanding
A-Addressee; SP-Side Participant; E-Eavesdropper; O-Overhearer.

Below we take an excerpt from the scenario when Ranger offers the job to Utah and describe the input signals and corresponding output behaviors along seven different points in the utterance. We represent the agent's roles and goals as *"Role(participation goal, comprehension goal)."* For example, *"Eavesdropper(0,1)"* denotes that the role is eavesdropper with negative participation goal and positive comprehension goal. Table 3 presents the feedbacks according to different input signals for each agent. The columns are the index for the seven points, input signals and output feedback.

Ranger (Speaker):
"Utah①, it's time for me to move on② and the③ town will need a strong leader④ like yourself⑤ to⑥ maintain law and order⑦."

From Table 3 we can see that even with the same input perceptual and partial understanding signals, the agent's feedbacks are significantly different according to the different conversation roles and goals. This example demonstrates that the feedback model enables the agents with a rich set of reactions that go beyond simply establishing rapport.

7　Behavior Assessments

A key question is whether people can interpret, or decode, the behaviors the model employs, especially the behaviors related to the comprehending goal posited in the model related to the comprehension goal: Gathering Information, Eavesdropping, Thinking, Understand and Confusion. As opposed to the decoding of emotional states which has been extensively studied, there is less evidence that the behaviors we posit for these

Table 4. Behavior Assessments Results

Think ① and ②: gaze aversion with different direction, magnitude, speed and duration.
Gather Information(ratified participant)①: glance between speaker's head and chest; ②: glance between speaker's head and lumbar.

Rule/Behavior	Interpretation					Recog. Rate
	Confusion	Think	Gather-Info.	Eavesdrop	Understand	
Confusion/Head Tilt & Frown	**11**	2	1	0	1	73.33%
Think/Gaze Avert ①	2	**11**	0	0	2	73.33%
Think/Gaze Avert ②	1	**11**	2	1	0	73.33%
Gather-Info(ratified)/Scan①	0	1	**13**	1	0	86.67%
Gather-Info(ratified)/ Scan②	0	4	**10**	0	1	66.67%
Gather-Info(eavesdropper)/ Glance at speaker	0	1	3	**10**	1	66.67%
Understand/Nod	1	0	0	0	**14**	93.33%

states can be effectively decoded. If the behaviors are highly ambiguous to observers, it undermines the rationale for employing the partial understanding component of the model.

To do a preliminary assessment of this, we created seven video clips of virtual listener nonverbal feedback, based on the rules and behaviors listed in the "Comprehending" signal row of Table 1. In each video, there is a hidden speaker (behind the camera) talking to a virtual human in front of the camera who provides nonverbal feedback (e.g. head nods, facial expressions, etc.) to the speaker. Each subject watched all seven videos. The speech played in the background is the same for each video, while the agent's behaviors were different. The speech is gibberish (nonsense content), so the subject is not influenced by the utterance content itself. After watching each video, the subject was given a forced choice questionnaire that asked them to select the best interpretation from a list of the alternative comprehension goals[1]. We recruited 15 subjects to participate in the experiment. Table 4 shows the results. The rows are the rules and behavior exhibited in the video and the columns are the subject's interpretation of the behavior with each cell listing how many subjects picked that interpretation. The hypothesized interpretation is in bold.

The result shows that for every category, the dominant choice was the hypothesized interpretation. However, some behaviors clearly could be improved if our goal was to reduce decoding ambiguity further. Of course, this is an assessment of just one aspect of the design. We discuss additional evaluation goals in the next section.

8   Conclusion and Future Work

In this paper, we have described the Listener Feedback Model for virtual agents in multi-party conversations. The vision behind this model is that the agent will generate both generic feedback and specific feedback conditioned on a variety of factors, including the speaker's behavior, the listener's role and the desire to participate in the conversation as well as the unfolding comprehension of partial utterances. The model has been

---

[1] The forced choice obviously simplifies this decoding task for the observer but the use of gibberish makes it harder.

implemented within the nonverbal behavior generation component of our virtual human system and drives the agent to perform feedback automatically and dynamically.

This work will be extended in several ways. A range of extensions to the model are being considered. In particular, we are interested in incorporating other factors which may influence listener's feedback, such as interpersonal relationship, personality, and culture. There are alternative ways in achieving this; the current listener feedback rules could be further added to and modified according to the varying factors or a data-driven approach (e.g., [22]) could be employed to learn models using different sets of data reflecting variations of those factors. Also, as mentioned earlier, there are alternative approaches to how the reactive and reflex layers interact that need to be assessed.

One pressing empirical question concerns how the specific feedback influences the human-virtual human interaction. There have been studies looking at the impact of the generic feedback of rapport agents, but the kind of specific feedback we are discussing here may have a more profound impact. The feedback might facilitate the interaction, providing the human with important information to guide the interaction. On the other hand, the virtual human's reaction to its partial understanding of the utterance, such as a look of anger, could also conceivably cause pauses or disfluency in the human speaker. This in turn may well throw off speech recognition/natural language understanding, thereby impacting the virtual human's ability to recognize and understand the utterance. Regardless, we expect the feedback to to impact the human user's impression of, and expectations about, the virtual human as well as impact potentially a range of relational factors such as trust. Overall, the design of the virtual human may have to fundamentally change to take into account this finer grain interactivity.

Acknowledgments. The authors would like to thank Dr. Louis-Philippe Morency and Dr. David DeVault for providing technical assistance to this work. This work was sponsored by the U.S. Army Research, Development, and Engineering Command (RDECOM). The content does not necessarily reflect the position or the policy of the Government, and no official endorsement should be inferred.

References

1. Argyle, M., Cook, M.: Gaze and Mutual Gaze. Cambridge University Press, Cambridge (1976)
2. Argyle, M., Lalljee, M., Cook, M.: The effects of visibility on interaction in a dyad. Human Relations 21, 3–17 (1968)
3. Bavelas, J.B., Coates, L., Johnson, T.: Listeners as co-narrators. Journal of Personality and Social Psychology 79, 941–952 (2000)
4. Bevacqua, E., Pammi, S., Hyniewska, S.J., Schröder, M., Pelachaud, C.: Multimodal backchannels for embodied conversational agents. In: Safonova, A. (ed.) IVA 2010. LNCS, vol. 6356, pp. 194–200. Springer, Heidelberg (2010)
5. Brunner, L.: Smiles can be back channels. Journal of Personality and Social Psychology 37(5), 728–734 (1979)
6. Callan, H., Chance, M., Pitcairn, T.: Attention and advertence in human groups. Social Science Inform. 12, 27–41 (1973)
7. DeVault, D., Sagae, K., Traum, D.: Incremental interpretation and prediction of utterance meaning for interactive dialogue. Dialogue & Discourse 2(1), 143–170 (2011)
8. Dittmann, A., Llewellyn, L.: Relationship between vocalizations and head nods as listener responses. Journal of Personality and Social Psychology 9, 79–84 (1968)

9. Ellsworth, P., Friedman, H., Perlick, D., Hoyt, M.: Some effects of gaze on subjects motivated to seek or to avoid social comparison. Journal of Experimental Social Pscyhology 14, 69–87 (1978)

10. Friedman, H.S., Riggio, R.E.: Effect of individual differences in non-verbal expressiveness on transmission of emotion. Journal of Nonverbal Behavior 6(2), 96–104 (1981)

11. Goffman, E.: Forms of Talk. University of Pennsylvania Press, Philadelphia (1981)

12. Goodwin, C.: Conversational organization: interaction between speakers and hearers. Academic Press, NY (1981)

13. Gratch, J., Okhmatovskaia, A., Lamothe, F., Marsella, S.C., Morales, M., van der Werf, R.J., Morency, L.-P.: Virtual rapport. In: Gratch, J., Young, M., Aylett, R.S., Ballin, D., Olivier, P. (eds.) IVA 2006. LNCS (LNAI), vol. 4133, pp. 14–27. Springer, Heidelberg (2006)

14. Gu, E., Badler, N.I.: Visual attention and eye gaze during multiparty conversations with distractions. In: Gratch, J., Young, M., Aylett, R.S., Ballin, D., Olivier, P. (eds.) IVA 2006. LNCS (LNAI), vol. 4133, pp. 193–204. Springer, Heidelberg (2006)

15. Hanks, W.F.: Language and Communicative Practices. Westview Press (1996)

16. Hartholt, A., Gratch, J., Weiss, L., The Gunslinger Team: At the virtual frontier: Introducing gunslinger, a multi-character, mixed-reality, story-driven experience. In: Ruttkay, Z., Kipp, M., Nijholt, A., Vilhjálmsson, H.H. (eds.) IVA 2009. LNCS, vol. 5773, pp. 500–501. Springer, Heidelberg (2009)

17. Ikeda, K.: Triadic exchange pattern in multiparty communication: A case study of conversational narrative among friends. Language and culture 30(2), 53–65 (2009)

18. Jan, D., Traum, D.R.: Dynamic movement and positioning of embodied agents in multiparty conversations. In: Proc. of the 6th Int. Conference on Autonomous Agents and Multiagent Systems, pp. 59–66 (2007)

19. Jonsdottir, G.R., Gratch, J., Fast, E., Thórisson, K.R.: Fluid semantic back-channel feedback in dialogue: Challenges and progress. In: Pelachaud, C., Martin, J.-C., André, E., Chollet, G., Karpouzis, K., Pelé, D. (eds.) IVA 2007. LNCS (LNAI), vol. 4722, pp. 154–160. Springer, Heidelberg (2007)

20. Kendon, A.: Conducting Interaction: Patterns of Behavior in Focused Encounters. Cambridge University Press, Cambridge (1990)

21. Kopp, S., Allwood, J., Grammer, K., Ahlsen, E., Stocksmeier, T.: Modeling embodied feedback with virtual humans. In: Wachsmuth, I., Knoblich, G. (eds.) ZiF Research Group International Workshop. LNCS (LNAI), vol. 4930, pp. 18–37. Springer, Heidelberg (2008)

22. Lee, J., Marsella, S.: Predicting speaker head nods and the effects of affective information. IEEE Transactions on Multimedia 12(6), 552–562 (2010)

23. Lee, J., Marsella, S.C.: Nonverbal behavior generator for embodied conversational agents. In: Gratch, J., Young, M., Aylett, R.S., Ballin, D., Olivier, P. (eds.) IVA 2006. LNCS (LNAI), vol. 4133, pp. 243–255. Springer, Heidelberg (2006)

24. Maatman, R.M., Gratch, J., Marsella, S.C.: Natural behavior of a listening agent. In: Panayiotopoulos, T., Gratch, J., Aylett, R.S., Ballin, D., Olivier, P., Rist, T. (eds.) IVA 2005. LNCS (LNAI), vol. 3661, pp. 25–36. Springer, Heidelberg (2005)

25. Marsella, S., Gratch, J.: EMA: A process model of appraisal dynamics. Cognitive Systems Research 10(1), 70–90 (2009)

26. Morency, L.P., de Kok, I., Gratch, J.: A probabilistic multimodal approach for predicting listener backchannels. In: Prendinger, H., Lester, J.C., Ishizuka, M. (eds.) IVA 2008. LNCS (LNAI), vol. 5208, pp. 70–84. Springer, Heidelberg (2008)

27. Vertegaa, R., der Veer, G.C.V., Vons, H.: Effects of gaze on multiparty mediated communication. In: Proc. of Graphics Interface, pp. 95–102 (2000)

28. Yngve, V.: On getting a word in edgewise. Papers from the 6th Regional Meeting, pp. 567–578 (April 1970)

Backchannels:
Quantity, Type and Timing Matters

Ronald Poppe, Khiet P. Truong, and Dirk Heylen*

Human Media Interaction Group, University of Twente
P.O. Box 217, 7500 AE, Enschede, The Netherlands
{r.w.poppe,k.p.truong,d.k.j.heylen}@utwente.nl

Abstract. In a perception experiment, we systematically varied the quantity, type and timing of backchannels. Participants viewed stimuli of a real speaker side-by-side with an animated listener and rated how human-like they perceived the latter's backchannel behavior. In addition, we obtained measures of appropriateness and optionality for each backchannel from key strokes. This approach allowed us to analyze the influence of each of the factors on entire fragments and on individual backchannels. The originally performed type and timing of a backchannel appeared to be more human-like, compared to a switched type or random timing. In addition, we found that nods are more often appropriate than vocalizations. For quantity, too few or too many backchannels per minute appeared to reduce the quality of the behavior. These findings are important for the design of algorithms for the automatic generation of backchannel behavior for artificial listeners.

1 Introduction

Listening is an important aspect of conversation. In a dialog, the listener actively contributes to the conversation by signalling attention, interest and understanding to the speaker [1]. One particular type of signal is the *backchannel* [2], a short visual (e.g. nod, smile) or vocal (e.g. "uh-huh" or "yeah") signal from the listener that does not interrupt the speaker's speech and is not aimed at taking the turn. There are several types of backchannels [3]. Here, we focus on those with a *continuer* function that convey continued attention but carry no additional affective meaning. From the analysis of human-human conversations, much is known about the *timing* and *type* of such backchannels. We discuss this work in Section 2.

Our goal is to use this knowledge to develop *artificial listeners*, virtual agents that can listen attentively to a human speaker [4]. This requires reliable prediction of backchannel opportunities from observations of the speaker's nonverbal visual and vocal behavior. In addition, appropriate listening behavior needs to

* The research leading to these results has received funding from the European Community's 7th Framework Programme under Grant agreement 211486 (SEMAINE).

H. Högni Vilhjálmsson et al. (Eds.): IVA 2011, LNAI 6895, pp. 228–239, 2011.

be generated, which includes choosing the proper type of backchannel, and making sure that the number and spread of backchannels over a certain period of time is human-like.

Previous work has mainly focused on prediction of backchannel opportunities, initially in telephone-style dialogs [5] and more recently also in face-to-face settings [6]. These works have been evaluated using corpus-based measures such as precision and recall, which are informative of how well the prediction matches the backchannels that are performed in the corpus. However, good approximation of backchannel timings is not a guarantee that the predicted behavior will be *perceived* as human-like. This is partly due to the optionality of backchannels. For example, a predicted backchannel that is not performed by the human listener in the corpus is not necessarily incorrect, and vice versa. Moreover, other factors such as the type of backchannel and the number of backchannels in a period of time are not taken into account in corpus-based research.

To address these issues, Poppe *et al.* [7] have investigated how backchannel behavior, generated using different algorithms, was perceived by human observers. Participants in the perception experiment were shown stimuli of real speakers and animated listeners and were asked to rate how human-like the backchannel behavior appeared to them. Closer analysis revealed some effects of timing, type and quantity of backchannels in short fragments on how they were perceived. However, these factors had not been varied systematically. In addition, they were analyzed at the fragment level, and each fragment typically consisted of multiple backchannels of randomly chosen type.

Therefore, in this research, we conducted a perception experiment where the timing, type and quantity of listener backchannels were varied systematically. Upon viewing a fragment, participants indicated how likely they thought it was that the backchannel behavior had been performed by a human listener. For the three factors under investigation, we briefly explain how we expect each to influence the perception of backchannel behavior. We also present our hypotheses, which we will test in Section 4.

In [7], a significant positive correlation was found between the number of backchannels and the rating of the fragment. In our experiment, we expect to observe the same effect. Our *quantity* hypothesis is therefore formulated as:

Hypothesis 1. *Fragments with higher numbers of backchannels per minute are perceived as more human-like.*

In this study, we consider two types of backchannels: visual (nod) and vocal ("uh-huh"). While both types have the same continuer function, there are differences in timing within the speaker's turn. For example, nods are more often produced during mutual gaze, whereas vocalizations tend to be produced around the end of a segment of speech [8]. We therefore expect that there is no such thing as a general backchannel opportunity, but rather an opportunity for a nod or an opportunity for a vocalization. Although both might partly overlap, in general, we expect that changing the type from that was actually performed would result in lower subjective ratings. The *type* hypothesis is thus:

Hypothesis 2. *Fragments with backchannel types performed by the actual listener are perceived as more human-like compared to fragments in which backchannel types are changed.*

While backchannels are optional, there are many known systematics in the production of a backchannel as a reaction or anticipation of the speaker's verbal and nonverbal behavior. We expect that contingent timings, rather than random timings, will be rated as more human-like. The *timing* hypothesis is therefore:

Hypothesis 3. *Fragments with backchannel timings performed by the actual listener are perceived as more human-like compared to random timings.*

An important addition to the experiment procedure was that participants were not only asked to give a rating per fragment, but also to judge individual backchannels. A common observation in the area of virtual agents is that humans are sensitive to the flaws in animated behavior. With this in mind, we introduced the *yuck* button approach: a button is pressed every time a human observer thinks the behavior displayed is inappropriate. In our experiment, this approach allows us to obtain subjective ratings for both fragments and individual backchannels without additional time requirements. In turn, we can analyze how the rating of individual backchannels influences the perception of an entire fragment.

The paper proceeds with a discussion of related work, followed by a summary of our experiment setup. Results are presented and discussed in Section 4.

2   Related Work

Backchannels, or listener responses, are short visual or vocal signals from the listener to express attention, interest and understanding to the speaker without the aim to take the turn [1,2]. Research into backchannels can be grouped into two directions [9]: the lumping approach and the splitting approach. The former treats backchannels as a single class and is mainly concerned with the timing within a speaker's discourse. The latter approach has investigated specific forms of backchannels and their role in a turn-taking context.

Our goal is to develop artificial listeners, virtual agents that can listen attentively to a human speaker. This requires analysis of the speaker's verbal and nonverbal behavior to identify moments where backchannels might be produced. Research following the lumping approach has investigated the structural properties of backchannels, i.e. the relation between the speaker's behavior and the occurrence of backchannels. Nowadays, the occurrence of backchannels within the speaker's discourse is reasonably well-understood. Dittmann and Llewellyn [10] and Duncan [3] noted that backchannels are often produced after rhythmic units in the speaker's speech, and specifically at the end of grammatical clauses.

Motivated by the goal of automatically identifying backchannel opportunities, recent work has focused on identifying lower-level structural properties of backchannels. Initially, telephone-style conversations have been addressed. Here, the relation between the speaker's speech and the occurrence of listener backchannels was investigated. A region of low or rising pitch [5,11], a high or decreasing energy pattern [12] and a short pause [13] in the speaker's speech have been found to precede backchannels from the listener. More recent work has shifted towards face-to-face conversations. These differ in backchannel behavior due to the additional visual modality that can be used to signal attention. In particular, the relation between gaze and backchannels has been investigated. For example, Kendon [14] and Bavelas [15] observed that backchannels were more likely to occur during a short period of mutual gaze, usually at the end of the speaker's turn.

These low-level structural properties can be extracted in real-time, and have been used to automatically identify backchannel opportunities using rule-based [5,16] and machine learning [6,17,18] algorithms. Typically, these algorithms work with a short time scale, which does not enforce consistent backchannel behavior over time.

Our aim is to develop artificial listeners, that should display active listening behavior that is human-like. In addition to the identification of backchannel opportunities, this requires the generation of human-like backchannel behavior. Attempts in this direction have been taken by Huang *et al.* [19], who generated head nods at moments that had been identified off-line based on multi-modal features. Maatman *et al.* [20] used the rule-based prediction algorithm of Ward and Tsukahara [5] and displayed nods in an online setting. Even though both works considered a face-to-face setting, none of them have addressed the type of backchannel. Poppe *et al.* [7] used either head nods or vocalizations, but the type was chosen randomly.

In the lumping approach, backchannels have been treated as a single class, without distinguishing between the type (e.g. visual and vocal). However, there are systematic differences in the structural properties of backchannels of different types. For example, Dittmann and Llewellyn [21] observed that, on average, a nod is produced 175ms earlier than a vocalization. In addition, Truong *et al.* [8] found that a visual backchannel was more likely to occur during mutual gaze, whereas vocal backchannels were more often produced during a pause in the speaker's speech.

Given these differences in occurrence, it is likely that there is no such thing as a backchannel opportunity, but rather the opportunity for a specific type of backchannel. We therefore expect that a different type of backchannel, produced in the same structural context, will be perceived differently by human observers. Although some researchers have addressed the perception of different types of backchannels [22,23] in isolation, none of them have investigated their perception in a conversational context.

Therefore, in this paper, we investigate how the quantity, type and timing of backchannels influences how human-like the backchannel behavior is perceived by human observers.

3   Experiment Setup

To investigate our hypotheses, we conducted a user experiment where human observers rated fragments from dialogs. We replaced the human listener by a virtual agent, and systematically varied the backchannel behavior. In this section, we describe the setup of the experiment.

3.1   Stimuli

We used dialogs between a speaker and a listener from the Semaine Solid SAL corpus [24], which contains emotionally-colored dialogs between a human listener and a human speaker. Specifically, we selected 12 fragments from [7] with at least two backchannels. The fragments are between 14 and 31 seconds in length.

We showed the speaker and listener side-by-side but replaced the video of the listener by a virtual agent, animated using BML realizer Elckerlyc [25] (see Figure 1). The backchannel behavior performed by this agent was systematically varied along three dimensions: quantity, type and timing. For each dimension, we took the manually annotated backchannels performed by the actual listener as a basis. For the quantity dimension, we defined three conditions. All backchannels were used in the *original* condition. In the *odd* and *even* condition, we selected every second backchannel, starting with the first or second one, respectively. The three conditions contained 46, 26 and 20 backchannels, respectively. As backchannel type, we used a nod, a vocalization ("uh-huh") or a combination of both. We animated either the *original* types, or the *switched* types, with nods replaced by vocalizations, and vocal and bimodal backchannels by nods. For the timing dimension, we used the *original* onsets or *random* onsets. In the latter case, there was at least one second between two onsets. Also, the order of the types of backchannels was left unchanged. The three dimensions were crossed to yield 12 conditions. In addition to the backchannels, we animated the listener's blinks where they occurred in the actual recording.

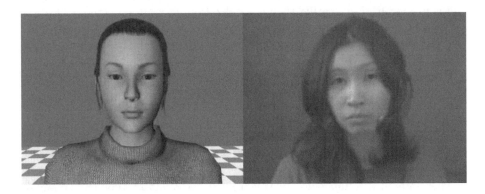

Fig. 1. Example stimulus with artificial listener (left) and actual speaker (right)

3.2   Procedure

The participants were explained they would be participating in an experiment to determine the quality of backchannel behavior. After the briefing, they were shown a set of stimuli. They were instructed to press the yuck button (space bar) every time they thought a listener's backchannel was inappropriate, either in type or timing. Participants could replay the video as often as desired, and adapt their yucks if needed. After watching a video fragment, they were prompted to rate how human-like they perceived the listener's backchannel behavior. They could set a slider that corresponded to a value between 0 and 100.

We divided the 144 condition-fragment combinations into six distinct sets of 24 stimuli. We adopted a Greco-Latin square design to control for order. In addition, this ensured that each participant rated each fragment and condition twice and six participants together rated all possible combinations of both.

3.3   Participants

We recruited 24 colleagues and doctoral students (6 female, 18 male) with a mean age of 32.8 (min 23, max 58). Each of the participants was assigned randomly to a set of stimuli with the lowest number of respondents.

4   Results and Discussion

We collected ratings over fragments, and yucks for individual backchannels. Both are discussed separately in the following sections.

4.1   Fragment Ratings

We analyze how quantity, type and timing of backchannels affects how human-like participants perceived a fragment. We ignore the variable fragment as the number of ratings per fragment-condition combination is limited. We performed a repeated measures ANOVA with order as between-subjects variable and quantity, type and timing as within-subjects variables. There are differences in ratings for different participants. While these do not affect the significance of the observed effects, we will use z-scores of the fragment ratings as our dependent variable unless explicitly stated otherwise.

In Figure 2, the results of un-normalized ratings for quantity, type and timing are shown. Overall, these scores are rather low, which is in line with [7]. We partly attribute this observation to the fact that only backchannels and blinks were animated. The high standard deviations are due to the grouping of ratings from different fragments.

For quantity, we did not find a significant effect ($F(2) = 2.062, p = ns$). We observe in Figure 2(a) that the difference between 46 and 26 backchannels in the *original* and *odd* conditions is minimal. However, there is an interaction effect between quantity and timing ($F(2) = 5.891, p < 0.01$). Specifically, the effect is

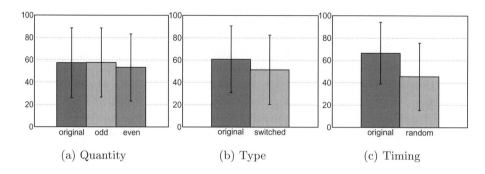

(a) Quantity   (b) Type   (c) Timing

Fig. 2. Average un-normalized fragment ratings per dimension

opposite; the *odd* condition was rated the best with the *original* timings, but lowest with *random* timings. The differences between the quantity conditions for the *random* timings are less pronounced.

In this analysis, we did not account for the duration of the fragment. If we correlate the average ratings per fragment-condition combination with the average number of backchannels per minute, we find no significant effect. We therefore have to reject hypothesis 1 that more backchannels per minute are perceived as more human-like. However, when only the conditions with *original* timing and type are taken into account, the correlation is significant ($r(36) = 0.340, p < 0.05$). Closer analysis reveals that the fragment with the highest number of backchannels per minute (20.18) appears to be an outlier. Leaving this fragment out results in a correlation of $r(35) = 0.537, p < 0.001$. This analysis suggests that too few and too many backchannels will reduce the quality of the backchannel behavior. We expect that a reasonable number of backchannels per minute lies between 6 and 12.

Type proved to be significantly different for the *original* and *switched* conditions ($F(1) = 18.233, p < 0.001$). Apparently, different types of backchannels are performed in different contexts. We therefore accept hypothesis 2 that the original type is rated more human-like. We will investigate this more thoroughly in Section 4.2.

We also found a main effect for timing ($F(1) = 94.684, p < 0.001$). Apparently, participants rated *random* timing lower. This confirms hypothesis 3 that original timings are perceived as more human-like. However, the difference between the two conditions is moderate. The same observation was also made in [7,19] and can be partly attributed to inter-personal differences, the optional nature of backchannels and the fact that, apart from backchannels and blinks, no other behaviors were animated.

While these results reveal differences in perception for different quantity, type and timing conditions, each fragment contains multiple backchannels. In the next section, we will analyze the perception of individual backchannels.

4.2   Individual Backchannel Ratings

For each backchannel, we are interested in how often participants rated it as inappropriate. We obtain this information by linking the yucks to the performed backchannels. In addition, we obtain a measure of optionality for each backchannel using parasocial consensus sampling (PCS), which we explain next.

Parasocial Consensus Sampling. Given that backchannels are often optional and that there are inter-personal differences in backchannel behavior, we are interested in the optionality of specific backchannels. We used PCS [19] as a tool to obtain backchannel opportunities from multiple raters. Specifically, we had nine participants watch the video of the speaker from the fragments that were used in the perception experiment. We asked them to press a button whenever they would perform a backchannel. In total, we obtained 240 responses, which is approximately half the number of actually performed backchannels. Still, we expect that the ratings give a more general idea at which moments backchannels are common, and when they are more optional. Next, we discuss how we linked the PCS and yuck responses to the backchannels generated in the stimuli.

Data Processing. As our aim is to report on the appropriateness of individual backchannels in the stimuli, we need to associate the yucks and the PCS responses to these backchannels. For the yucks, there is a time delay between the stimulus onset and the participants' key press. We analyzed this delay and associated a yuck response with the closest preceding backchannel, provided that the time between them was between 300 and 2500ms.

One would expect that the timings of PCS responses are similar to the actual backchannel onsets. On closer analysis, a PCS response appears to be approximately 200ms later. We use a matching window of 500ms and therefore, we associate a PCS with a backchannel if it is between 300ms before and 800ms after a backchannel onset.

The total number of generated backchannels in all fragments and conditions is 368. Figure 3 shows the frequency of yucks and PCS responses per backchannel. Each fragment-condition combination has been judged by four participants, so the maximum number of yucks per backchannel is four. As the numbers of yuck and PCS responses are a measure of a backchannel's unsuitability and suitability, respectively, it is not surprising that the numbers of these responses are negatively correlated ($r(368) = -0.400, p < 0.001$).

Quantity. For now, we only consider the quantity dimension, and use only the data of the *original* type and timing conditions. As the *odd* and *even* quantity conditions contain a subset of the backchannels in the *original* quantity condition, we expect similar numbers of PCS responses in all conditions. These numbers are 2.35, 2.58 and 2.06, respectively. They are reasonably equal and correlate with the fragment ratings in the previous section.

If quantity would not be an important factor in backchannel behavior, we would expect similar numbers of yucks as well. However, we found the average

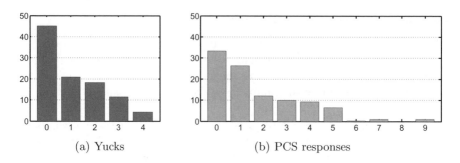

(a) Yucks   (b) PCS responses

Fig. 3. Relative frequency of yucks and PCS responses per backchannel (%)

numbers of yucks per backchannel to be 0.54, 0.19 and 0.25 for the *original, odd* and *even* conditions, respectively. Apparently, more backchannels is not always better. This is somewhat at variance with findings in [7]. Closer analysis reveals that eight out of 25 yucks in the *original* setting originate from the fragment with the highest number of backchannels per minute (20.18). Again, it appears that too few or too many backchannels reduces the perceived quality of the backchannel behavior.

Type. In Section 4.2, we investigated differences between the *original* and *switched* condition as an indication that changing the type of backchannel affects how it is perceived. Given the yucks, we can also analyze whether the type of an individual backchannel matters, disregarding the specific condition. As we expect that the vocal aspect of bimodal backchannels is most salient, we treated these backchannels as vocalizations. The average numbers of yucks for nods and vocalizations are, respectively, 0.32 and 0.88 with *original* timing, and 1.15 and 2.01 with *random* timing (see Figure 4). Over both conditions, the percentage of backchannels that did not receive a yuck was 57.6% and 32.6% for the nods and vocalizations, respectively. We can further narrow down the class with *original* timings and distinguish between the backchannels performed in the *original* and *switched* type conditions. Changing vocalizations and bimodal backchannels to nods caused a slight increase in number of yucks per backchannel, from 0.30 to 0.36. However, changing nods to vocalizations led to an increase from 0.57 to 1.02.

These numbers indicate that a nod is less often perceived as inappropriate. We expect this can at least be partly explained by the fact that nods are communicated over the visual channel, without directly interfering with the main channel of communication. Therefore, it might be that vocalizations are more precisely timed, whereas nods can be performed throughout the speaker's turn. If this would be the case, one would expect higher numbers of PCS responses for a vocalization compared to a nod for the actually performed backchannels. This is indeed the case, with on average 3.20 responses for a vocalization and 1.97 for a nod. These findings are important for the design of backchannel generation algorithms for artificial listeners. High confidence in the backchannel

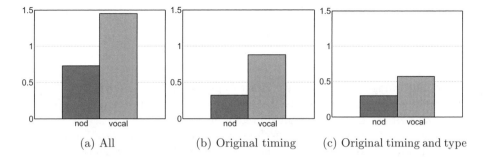

(a) All   (b) Original timing   (c) Original timing and type

Fig. 4. Average number of yucks per nod or vocalization in different conditions

prediction could result in the production of a vocalization, whereas a nod might be produced otherwise.

Timing. The effect of timing on the perception of backchannel behavior can also be observed from the PCS and yuck responses. The average number of PCS responses for a backchannel with *random* timing is 1.03, compared to 2.35 with the *original* timing. Randomly timed backchannels are thus twice less likely to occur. Not surprisingly, the number of yucks in the random condition is much higher than in the original condition, 1.58 versus 0.60. This again shows that timing matters.

5   Conclusion and Future Work

We have conducted a perception experiment where the factors quantity, type and timing of backchannels was varied systematically. Participants in the experiment were shown stimuli of real speakers and animated listeners and were asked to rate how human-like the generated backchannel behavior appeared to them. In addition, we obtained measures of appropriateness and optionality for each backchannel from yuck responses and parasocial consensus sampling (PCS) responses. This approach allowed us to analyze the influence of each of the factors on entire fragments and on individual backchannels.

From the fragment ratings, the number of the backchannels per minute over all conditions was not a significant factor. However, with original timings and type, there was a trend that more backchannels led to a more human-like perception of the fragment. Closer analysis showed that a very high number of backchannels per minute resulted in much lower subjective ratings. In addition, individual backchannels were more often regarded as inappropriate when the rate of backchannels was higher. This was especially true for randomly timed backchannels. In summary, there appears to be a lower and an upper bound on the number of backchannels per minute, around 6 and 12 respectively.

The type of backchannel (originally performed or switched) was a significant factor in the fragment ratings. Apparently, different types of backchannels are performed in different contexts. Analysis of individual backchannels revealed that nods are less often rated as inappropriate, disregarding their timing. This knowledge has implications for the design of backchannel generation algorithms. If the prediction confidence is low, it is probably more appropriate to generate a nod.

For the timing of backchannels, both fragment ratings and yucks indicated that random timings are perceived as less human-like. This again stresses the importance of accurate backchannel prediction algorithms.

While corpus-based research is useful to identify contexts where a specific type of backchannel is more likely, we argue that the models derived from this research should be validated using perception studies. Also, we propose to abandon the concept of a general backchannel opportunity, and focus on predicting specific backchannels with their own structural properties instead.

The combination of PCS and yucks proved to be valuable in the analysis of individual backchannels. In future work, we expect they will continue to be useful tools to unravel the factors involved in designing a human-like backchannel generation algorithm. Specifically, we plan to analyze at which moments backchannels are perceived human-like, and how these moments differ from each other. Our aim is to conduct these studies in online settings as well. In addition, we continue to look for other ways to predict, generate and understand human behavior, its optionality and dependence on social context.

References

1. Bavelas, J.B., Coates, L., Johnson, T.: Listeners as co-narrators. Journal of Personality and Social Psychology 79, 941–952 (2000)
2. Yngve, V.H.: On getting a word in edgewise. Papers from the Sixth Regional Meeting of Chicago Linguistic Society, pp. 567–577. Chicago Linguistic Society (1970)
3. Duncan Jr., S.: On the structure of speaker-auditor interaction during speaking turns. Language in Society 3, 161–180 (1974)
4. Heylen, D., Bevacqua, E., Pelachaud, C., Poggi, I., Gratch, J., Schröder, M.: Generating Listening Behaviour. In: Emotion-Oriented Systems Cognitive Technologies - Part 4, pp. 321–347. Springer, Heidelberg (2011)
5. Ward, N., Tsukahara, W.: Prosodic features which cue back-channel responses in English and Japanese. Journal of Pragmatics 32, 1177–1207 (2000)
6. Morency, L.P., de Kok, I., Gratch, J.: A probabilistic multimodal approach for predicting listener backchannels. Autonomous Agents and Multi-Agent Systems 20, 80–84 (2010)
7. Poppe, R., Truong, K.P., Reidsma, D., Heylen, D.: Backchannel strategies for artificial listeners. In: Safonova, A. (ed.) IVA 2010. LNCS, vol. 6356, pp. 146–158. Springer, Heidelberg (2010)
8. Truong, K.P., Poppe, R., Kok, I., Heylen, D.: A multimodal analysis of vocal and visual backchannels in spontaneous dialogs. In: Proceedings of Interspeech, Florence, Italy (to appear, 2011)
9. Xudong, D.: Listener response. In: The Pragmatics of Interaction, pp. 104–124. John Benjamins Publishing, Amsterdam (2009)

10. Dittmann, A.T., Llewellyn, L.G.: The phonemic clause as a unit of speech decoding. Journal of Personality and Social Psychology 6, 341–349 (1967)
11. Gravano, A., Hirschberg, J.: Backchannel-inviting cues in task-oriented dialogue. In: Proceedings of Interspeech, Brighton, UK, pp. 1019–1022 (2009)
12. Koiso, H., Horiuchi, Y., Tutiya, S., Ichikawa, A., Den, Y.: An analysis of turn-taking and backchannels based on prosodic and syntactic features in japanese map task dialogs. Language and Speech 41, 295–321 (1998)
13. Cathcart, N., Carletta, J., Klein, E.: A shallow model of backchannel continuers in spoken dialogue. In: Proceedings of the Conference of the European chapter of the Association for Computational Linguistics, Budapest, Hungary, vol. 1, pp. 51–58 (2003)
14. Kendon, A.: Some functions of gaze direction in social interaction. Acta Psychologica 26, 22–63 (1967)
15. Bavelas, J.B., Coates, L., Johnson, T.: Listener responses as a collaborative process: The role of gaze. Journal of Communication 52, 566–580 (2002)
16. Truong, K.P., Poppe, R., Heylen, D.: A rule-based backchannel prediction model using pitch and pause information. In: Proceedings of Interspeech, Makuhari, Japan, pp. 490–493 (2010)
17. Noguchi, H., Den, Y.: Prosody-based detection of the context of backchannel responses. In: Proceedings of the International Conference on Spoken Language Processing (ICSLP), Sydney, Australia, pp. 487–490 (1998)
18. Okato, Y., Kato, K., Yamamoto, M., Itahashi, S.: Insertion of interjectory response based on prosodic information. In: Proceedings of the IEEE Workshop Interactive Voice Technology for Telecommunication Applications, Basking Ridge, NJ, pp. 85–88 (1996)
19. Huang, L., Morency, L.-P., Gratch, J.: Learning backchannel prediction model from parasocial consensus sampling: A subjective evaluation. In: Safonova, A. (ed.) IVA 2010. LNCS, vol. 6356, pp. 159–172. Springer, Heidelberg (2010)
20. Maatman, R.M., Gratch, J., Marsella, S.C.: Natural behavior of a listening agent. In: Panayiotopoulos, T., Gratch, J., Aylett, R.S., Ballin, D., Olivier, P., Rist, T. (eds.) IVA 2005. LNCS (LNAI), vol. 3661, pp. 25–36. Springer, Heidelberg (2005)
21. Dittmann, A.T., Llewellyn, L.G.: Relationship between vocalizations and head nods as listener responses. Journal of Personality and Social Psychology 9, 79–84 (1968)
22. Granström, B., House, D., Swerts, M.: Multimodal feedback cues in human-machine interactions. In: Proceedings of the International Conference on Speech Prosody, pp. 11–14. Aix-en-Provence, France (2002)
23. Bevacqua, E., Pammi, S., Hyniewska, S.J., Schröder, M., Pelachaud, C.: Multimodal backchannels for embodied conversational agents. In: Safonova, A. (ed.) IVA 2010. LNCS, vol. 6356, pp. 194–200. Springer, Heidelberg (2010)
24. Valstar, M.F., McKeown, G., Cowie, R., Pantic, M.: The Semaine corpus of emotionally coloured character interactions. In: Proceedings of the International Conference on Multimedia & Expo., Singapore, pp. 1079–1084 (2010)
25. Van Welbergen, H., Reidsma, D., Ruttkay, Z., Zwiers, J.: Elckerlyc - A BML realizer for continuous, multimodal interaction with a virtual human. Journal of Multimodal User Interfaces 3, 271–284 (2010)

Modeling Side Participants and Bystanders: The Importance of Being a Laugh Track

Jina Lee and Stacy Marsella

University of Southern California
Institute for Creative Technologies
12015 Waterfront Drive, Playa Vista, CA 90094, USA
{jlee,marsella}@ict.usc.edu

Abstract. Research in virtual agents has largely ignored the role and behavior of side participants and especially bystanders. Our view is that the behavior of these other participants is critical in multi-party interactions, especially in interactive drama. In this paper, we provide an analysis of nonverbal behaviors associated with these roles. We first review studies of interpersonal relationships and nonverbal behavior. From this review, we construct an analysis framework based on characters' interpersonal relationships, conversational roles, and communicative acts. We then assess this framework by analyzing improv sessions of an old west scenario involving 4 characters. Informed by this analysis, we implemented a general model for participant and bystander behavior.

Keywords: Virtual Agents, Embodied Conversational Agents, Nonverbal Behaviors, Multi-modal Communication.

1 Introduction

Imagine an old cowboy western. The good sheriff is at the bar having a whisky. The evil gunslinger, sworn enemy of the sheriff, enters the bar. All the people initially gaze at the gunslinger, some start to move away wanting to avoid trouble. Others avert their gaze, pretend to do something else, hoping not to be noticed by the gunslinger who runs the town. Such scenes make it clear that much of the drama of a performance is in the reactions provided by the living backdrop of other performers. The performance arts have long acknowledged the important role that audience response plays. In Greek drama, the chorus served in part to provide the context of an ideal audience response for the actual audience. In modern day TV and films, laugh tracks are added to stimulate audience responses. The fact that our responses are mediated by others' responses has also influenced theatrical actors, trained to react to the main action [5] and film editing's use of reaction shots. A variety of psychological theories, such as social comparison theory, social referencing and emotional contagion, similarly argue that the social milieu influences the individual.

With few notable exceptions, research in virtual agents has largely ignored the role of conversation participants other than the speaker and the addressee, perhaps because many virtual agent applications are limited to dyadic interactions.

H. Högni Vilhjálmsson et al. (Eds.): IVA 2011, LNAI 6895, pp. 240–247, 2011.

In this paper, we discuss how to analyze and model the behaviors of not only the core conversation participants, but also the side participants and bystanders that can influence the human observer's reaction to the interaction. We focus on modeling them without requiring a complex cognitive system that forms the goals of the agents.

The approach we take is based on psychological research on interpersonal relational dimensions that inform the pattern of people's interactions. Interpersonal circumplex theories [6,9] argue for two fundamental dimensions, *affiliation* (hostility-friendliness) and *control* (dominance-submissiveness), to explain how different kinds of action elicit predictable responses from others [6]. Interaction partners along the affiliation dimension will elicit similar behaviors (e.g. friendly behaviors evoke friendly behaviors) and those along the control dimension will elicit complementary behaviors (e.g. dominant behaviors evoke submissive behaviors). These dimensions are common to a range of psychological theories and are often used in work of nonverbal behaviors [1,2].

In this paper, we present an analysis framework based on the agents' interpersonal relationships, communicative acts, and conversation roles. We then analyze a set of improv sessions of an old west gunslinger scenario, which includes dramatic behaviors that convey rich interpersonal relationships and emotional reactions, as a testbed to construct mappings to various nonverbal behaviors. This mapping provides us with a model for the behaviors of the participants in the interaction.

2   Analysis Framework

Inspired by interpersonal circumplex theories and techniques in theatrical performances, we first developed an analysis framework to study the behaviors exhibited in a set of improv sessions. Below we provide more details about how we define the analysis framework.

Conversation Roles: We define four conversation roles: speaker, addressee, side participant, and bystander. Speaker and addressee are the core participants of the conversation whereas side participants are the "un-addressed recipients" of the speech at the moment [3][4]. Bystanders are openly present in the environment but do not participate in the conversation.

Interpersonal Relationships: The relationship between characters is described in terms of dominance and friendliness, following theories of interpersonal circumplex [6,9]. In the gunslinger scenario, there are four characters: Rio, Harmony, Utah, and Ranger. Rio is the dominant and hostile character. Harmony is submissive to Rio and 'acts' friendly to him when in truth she dislikes Rio. She is neither dominant nor submissive to Utah and Ranger, but is particularly friendly to Ranger. Similar to Harmony, Utah is submissive to Rio and 'acts' neutral to him in terms of friendliness, but in truth he dislikes Rio. Ranger has neutral relationships with all the characters in terms of dominance and friendliness. Table 1 specifies the interpersonal relationships of the characters.

Table 1. Interpersonal relationship between Gunslinger characters in terms of dominance and affiliation. The symbol in parenthesis represents the masked relationship a character hides from the other character. (D: dominant, S: submissive, H: hostile, F: friendly, N: neutral).

	Rio	Harmony	Utah	Ranger
Rio	-	D/H	D/H	D/H
Harmony	S/F(H)	-	N/N	N/F
Utah	S/N(H)	N/N	-	N/N
Ranger	N/N	N/N	N/N	-

Communicative Acts: Communicative acts are broadly constructed here to include not only the dialogue acts of character utterances but also events that take place which may engender emotional responses from the characters. For example, Rio's entrance into the saloon or even a mere mention of his name may cause strong fear within Utah and Harmony. The following lists the communicative acts defined in the Gunslinger scenario: (S) asks-question-to (A); (S) confirms (A); (S) disconfirms (A); (S) requests (A); (S) accepts-request-of (A); (S) declines-request-of (A); (S) suggests (A); (E)/(C) threatens (C); (E) removes-threat-from (C). (S) and (A) indicate speaker and addressee, (C) indicates character and (E) indicates event. Although we can define a much richer set of communicative acts, here we simplify them to find a commonality and see how the characters' conversation roles or relationships may influence the behaviors given the same communicative act.

3 Analysis and the Behavior Model

To assess the analysis framework described in the previous section, we used it to analyze the Gunslinger improv sessions and mapped each factor of the framework to various nonverbal behaviors exhibited in the videos. We first describe the Gunslinger improv sessions, then the result of the analysis, from which we construct the behavior model.

Gunslinger Improv Sessions: The setting of the Gunslinger Improv sessions is a saloon somewhere in western USA, circa the 1800s. The characters in Gunslinger are extreme stereotypes drawn from the mythology of the Old West: the friendly bartender Utah, the psychotic gunslinger Rio, the fille de joie Harmony and the lawman Ranger. The script begins with Utah and Harmony talking about Rio, who runs the town. The Ranger then enters the bar looking to arrest Rio, unaware of how bad Rio is. Rio stops in the bar on his way to get some smokes in order to tell Harmony that they are leaving town. As Harmony rejects the idea, he shoots up the bar, a nonverbal way of emphasizing that he is the one in control. Upon seeing Ranger's badge, Rio threatens to kill him if he is still in town when he gets back from buying tobacco. Rio exits, leaving Utah, Harmony and Ranger to plot his demise. Upon Rio's return the gunfight ensues.

A troop of 8 actors were recruited and videotaped performing the improvisations based on the script (see Fig. 1 for the improv setting). The actors were

Fig. 1. Improv of Gunslinger scenario   **Fig. 2.** The Gunslinger set

broken up into two groups of four, playing the roles of Rio, Harmony, Utah and the Ranger. The actors in the same group performed once following the script and twice improvising. Each session lasted for about 7-10 minutes. These improv sessions were undertaken to inform the design of a mixed-reality interactive virtual human entertainment experience (see Fig. 2 for the set design) developed at the University of Southern California.

Results of the Analysis and the Behavior Model: Using the analysis framework, we constructed a corpus mapping the factors of the framework to various nonverbal behaviors. Here we focused on gaze, posture shifts, and the dynamics of physical distance between characters (e.g. approach vs. move away). Table 2 shows this mapping exhibited in the video. The following summarizes the results of the video analysis and modifications made to the analysis framework.

First of all, we made several modifications to the list of communicative acts to capture important reactions exhibited by the actors. Communicative act *(S) accepts-request-of (A)* was generalized to *(S) informs (A)* because the analysis showed no differences in the characters' behaviors. On the other hand, we created new communicative acts to handle the cases when characters showed emotional reactions (i.e. (S) expresses-to (A)) and to differentiate different levels of threats exerted by Rio. Finally, we did not observe any cases of communicative act *(S) suggests (A)*.

Foreshadowing behaviors were displayed mainly at the beginning of the Gunslinger scenario. Rio, being dominant and hostile, imposes a large threat to others and tensions are built up or released depending on his actions. For instance, when Rio enters the saloon, his presence engenders fear within other characters, which causes avoidance behaviors such as gazing away or stepping back. When Harmony refuses Rio's order to pack and leave the town with him, Utah shifts his gaze nervously between Rio and Harmony as if to expect something bad to happen. These foreshadowing behaviors informs the audience that Rio is associated with danger and threat.

As expected, the interpersonal relationship was found to affect the behaviors of characters, even when they were not one of the core conversation participants. For example, Harmony showed completely different attitudes toward Ranger and toward Rio (flirtatious vs. submissive). Utah also exhibited different behaviors as a bystander. When Harmony speaks to Ranger, Utah holds a more relaxed

Table 2. Mapping from communicative act, conversation role, and interpersonal relationship to nonverbal behaviors (S: speaker, A: addressee, SP: side participant, B: bystander, D: dominant, S: submissive, H: hostile, F: friendly, N: neutral)

Case	Communicative Act	Conv. Role	Interp. Rel.	Nonverbal Behaviors
1-1	**(S) asks-question-to (A)**	S	N/N	Look at (A)
	(Harmony asks Utah or Ranger)	S	N/F	Look at (A), lean forward, smile
		A	N/N	Look at (S)
		SP	N/N	Look between (S) and (A)
		B	N/N	Quick glances between (S) and (A) occasionally
1-2	**(S) asks-question-to (A)**	S	D/H	Look directly at (A), erect posture
	(Rio asks Utah /Harmony or Ranger)	A	S/N(F), S/F(H)	Look at (S), crouched posture, head down, may step back
	(Rio asks Ranger)	A	N/N	Look at (S)
		B	N/N	Look between (S) and (A) (attention drawn)
		B	S/N(F), S/F(H)	Gaze aversion, occasionally glances between (S) and (A), crouched posture, head down
1-3	**(S) asks-question-to (A)**	S	N/N	Look at (A)
	(Ranger asks Rio)	A	D/H	Look at (S), erect posture
		B	S/N(F), S/F(H)	Gaze aversion, occasionally glances between (S) and (A), may step back, crouched posture, head down
2	**(S) confirms (A)**	S	N/N	Look at (A), head nod(s)
	(Ranger confirms Utah/Harmony)	S	N/F	Look at (A), relaxed posture, smile
	(Harmony confirms Ranger)	A	N/N	Look at (S), may nod after (S)'s speech
		B	N/N	Quick glances between (S) and (A) occasionally
3	**(S) disconfirms (A)**	S	N/N	Look at (A), head shake(s)
	(Ranger disconfirms Utah/Harmony)	A	N/N	Look at (S)
		B	N/N	Quick glances between (S) and (A) occasionally
4-1	**(S) informs (A)**	S	N/N	Look at (A)
	(Harmony, Utah, and Ranger talk to each other)	S	N/F	Look at (A), lean forward, smile (being flirtatious)
		A	N/N	Look at (S)
		B	N/N	Glances between (S) and (A) occasionally, relaxed posture
4-2	**(S) informs (A)**	S	S/F(H)	Look at (A), crouched posture, uneasy smile (masking fear)
	(Harmony or Utah talks to Rio)	S	S/N(H)	Look at (A), crouched posture
		A	D/H	Look at (S), erect posture
		SP	N/N	Look between (S) and (A)
		B	S/N(H), S/F(H)	Crouched posture, gaze aversion, head down, quick glances between (S) and (A)
4-4	**(S) informs (A)**	S	D/H	Look at (S), erect posture
	(Rio talks to Harmony or Utah)	A	S/F(H), S/N(H)	Look at (S), crouched posture
		SP	N/N	Look between (S) and (A)
		B	S/F(H), S/N(H)	Crouched posture, gaze aversion, head down
5-1	**(S) informs-negative-to (A)**	S	N/N	Look at (A)
	(Utah tells Harmony Rio is coming)	A	N/N	Look at (S)
	(Harmony describes Rio to Ranger)	B	N/N	Look between (S) and (A)
5-2	**(S) informs-negative-to (A)**	S	D/H	Glares at (A), erect posture
	(Rio threatens to kill Ranger)	A	N/N	Look at (S), erect posture
		B	S/N(F), S/F(H)	Look between (S) and (A), crouched posture, step back, distressed expression
6-1	**(S) expresses-to (A)**	S	N/N	Look at (A), lean forward, brow frowned, head shakes, disgusted face (nose wrinkle, squinted eyes)
	(Harmony tells Utah not to joke)	A	N/N	Look at (S)
	(Utah tells Ranger about Rio)	B		*(not present in the scenario)*
6-2	**(S) expresses-to (A)**	S	N/F	Eyes open, brow raise, lean forward
	(Harmony is surprised that Ranger haven't heard about Rio)	A	N/N	Look at (S)
		B		*(not present in the scenario)*
7-1	**(S) requests (A)**	S	N/F	Inner brow raise, lean forward (almost begging)
	(Harmony asks Ranger to help get rid of Rio)	A	N/N	Look at (S)
		B	N/N	Look between (S) and (A) (attention drawn)
7-2	**(S) requests (A)**	S	D/H	Straight gaze at (A), pound foot on ground, lean forward (as if attacking)
	(Rio tells Ranger to be quiet)	A	N/N	Look at (S)
		B	S/N(F), S/F(H)	Look between (S) and (A), crouched posture, may step back

Table 2. (*Continued*)

7-3	**(S) requests (A)** *(Rio orders Harmony to pack)*	S	D/H	Straight gaze at (A)
		A	S/F(H)	Look at (A), distressed expression
		SP	N/N	Look between (S) and (A)
		B	S/N(H)	Look between (S) and (A), crouched posture, may step back
7-4	**(S) requests (A)** *(Rio orders Utah to countdown for gunfight)*	S	D/H	Straight gaze at Ranger
		A	S/N(H)	Look at (A), crouched posture, distressed expression
		SP	D/N	Look at (A)
		B	S/F(H)	Look around characters, crouched posture, step back, distressed expression
7-5	**(S) requests (ALL)** *(Rio tells everyone to be prepared when he comes back)*	S	D/H	Look around
		A	S/F(H)S /N(H)	Look at (A), crouched posture, distressed expression
		A	N/N	Look at (S), neutral posture
8	**(S) declines-request-of (A)** *(Harmony refuses to leave with Rio)*	S	S/F(H)	Lean forward, brows raised, crouched posture (as if begging)
		A	D/H	Look at (A), erect posture
		SP	N/N	Look between (S) and (A)
		B	N/N	Look between (S) and (A), crouched posture, distressed expression
9	**(E) threatens-1st (ALL)** *(Rio enters the saloon)*	Utah, Harmony	S/N(F), S/F(H)	Gaze aversion, step back, crouched posture, head down
		Ranger	N/N	Look towards Rio
10	**(E) threatens-2nd (ALL)** *(Rio enters the saloon the second time)*	Utah, Harmony	S/N(F), S/F(H)	Look at Rio, step back, crouched posture, head down
		Ranger	D/N	Look straight at Rio, erected posture, body oriented to Rio
11	**(C) threatens (ALL)** *(Rio shoots gun)*	Utah, Harmony Ranger	S/N(F), S/F(H), N/N	Startled, duck down
12	**(E) heightens-threat** *(Countdown to gunfight)*	Rio, Ranger	D/H, D/N	Erect posture, stare at each other
		Utah	S/N(H)	Look between Rio and Ranger, crouched posture
		Harmony	S/F(H)	Eyes wide open, look between Rio and Ranger, hand to face (panic)
13	**(E) removes-threat-from (ALL)** *(Rio leaves the saloon)*	Utah, Harmony Ranger	S/N(F), S/F(H), N/N	Relaxed posture, mutual gaze among characters
14	**threat-removed-permanently** *(Rio is killed)*	Utah, Harmony	S/N(F), S/F(H)	Mutual gaze among characters, relaxed posture, eyebrow raise, smile
		Ranger	D/N	Mutual gaze among characters, relaxed posture, eyes open

posture, whereas when she speaks to Rio, he crouches his posture, puts his head down, and avoids gaze or quickly glances between Harmony and Rio.

The main difference between listener and bystander behaviors was in the gaze. Addressees mainly looked directly at the speaker (with possibly different postures) but bystanders displayed more gaze aversion or quick glances between the speaker and the addressee using only the eyes (i.e. gaze without revealing gaze). Only when the bystander felt strong fear or surprise did they make more obvious gaze movements between the speaker and the addressee.

Implementation: The mapping shown in Table 2 has been constructed as a set of rules within the Nonverbal Behavior Generator (NVBG) [7], the behavior planner of our virtual human system. For speakers, the communicative act and conversation role further modify the existing nonverbal behavior rules, especially with regards to posture and facial expressions. For non-speakers, new rules were added to generate listener or bystander behaviors. During the system initialization step, the NVBG receives a message specifying the interpersonal relationships of each character and registers this information. Upon receiving an input message including the speaker utterance and communicative acts from the dialogue manager [8], NVBG then detects the agent's conversation role and checks the interpersonal relationship with the speaker or addressee and selects the corresponding nonverbal reaction from the rules.

4   Conclusions and Future Work

In this paper, we presented an analysis framework and a model of side participant and bystander behaviors along with speaker and addressee behaviors based on interpersonal circumplex theories, techniques in theatrical performance, and our own analysis of improvised acting. The model could be used to improve the capability of not only the core conversation characters but also the background characters by generating appropriate reactions that reveal relational factors of the characters. These behaviors can lead to more dramatic impact on human participants and observers.

In the future, we plan to extend our model to include a wider range of interpersonal relationships and communicative acts. The work presented here is based on a limited data and we wish to collect a larger corpus to cover more diverse interpersonal relationships and communicative acts. We also plan to evaluate the model with human participants. Of particular interest is in how the side participant and bystander behaviors impact the user experience including whether they reveal the agents' relational factors, improve the perception of agents, and increase the user's engagement level.

Acknowledgments. This work was sponsored by the U.S. Army Research, Development, and Engineering Command (RDECOM). The content does not necessarily reflect the position or the policy of the Government, and no official endorsement should be inferred.

References

1. Argyle, M.: Bodily communication. Internat. Universities Press, New York (1975)
2. Burgoon, J.K.: Nonverbal Communication: The Unspoken Dialogue. Harper-Collins College Div. (1988)
3. Clark, H.H.: Using Language. Cambridge University Press, Cambridge (1996)
4. Goffman, E.: Footing. Semiotica 25(1/2), 1–29 (1979)
5. Johnson, W.L.: Dramatic expression in opera, and its implications for conversational agents. In: Workshop on Embodied Conversational Characters as Individuals, AA-MAS 2003 (2003)

6. Leary, T.: Interpersonal diagnosis of personality; a functional theory and methodology for personality evaluation. Ronald Press, New York (1957)
7. Lee, J., Marsella, S.: Nonverbal behavior generator for embodied conversational agents. In: Proc. of 6th Int. Conf. on Intelligent Virtual Agents, pp. 243–255 (2006)
8. Leuski, A., Traum, D.: A statistical approach for text processing in virtual humans. In: Proc. of 26th Army Science Conference, Orlando, Florida, USA (December 2008)
9. Wiggins, J.S.: A psychological taxonomy of trait-descriptive terms: The interpersonal domain. Journal of Personality and Social Pscyhology 37, 395–412 (1979)

Appropriate and Inappropriate Timing of Listener Responses from Multiple Perspectives

Iwan de Kok and Dirk Heylen

Human Media Interaction, University of Twente
{i.a.dekok,heylen}@utwente.nl

Abstract. This paper compares two methods to collect multiple perspectives on the appropriate timing of listener responses. Based on the results of the multiple perspectives from both methods a virtual listener produces head nods at appropriate times and times not indicated as appropriate and let a human observer assess the appropriateness of each individual head nod. This way we collected multiple perspectives on inappropriate timing of listener responses. Combining all these perspectives we get a view on the graded optionality and graded inappropriateness of listener responses in certain contexts.

1 Introduction

While interlocutors listen during human-human conversations, they display various behaviors in response to the contributions of the speaker. These behaviors vary from nonverbal behavior such as head nods, shakes and facial expression, to verbal expressions such as 'uh-huh', 'hmm' etcetera. These listener responses [2] serve the function of signalling the state of mind of the listener about the contribution that the behavior is a response to. These signals express whether the contribution has been attended to, understood, agreed upon and/or other attitudinal or affective reactions to it [1]. Our goal is to develop models of these behaviors for embodied conversational agents that can predict when a listener response is due or appropriate. As in human-human conversation, listener responses in conversations between embodied conversational agents and humans have proven to increase the rapport between them [3].

One of the characteristics of listener responses is that they seem to be optional most of the time [7]. When developing models for virtual listening behavior this optionality presents some challenges. To develop a model one needs a clear view of the contexts in which a listener response is appropriate and is inappropriate. Even when a listener response is appropriate in a context, this response may not be mandatory. There is, so to speak, a graded optionality.

In a traditional corpus the distinction between moments where listener responses are mandatory and where listener responses are optional is hard to determine, since only one perspective of one individual is recorded. The closest approximation is to group similar moments and analyze the number of responses in these moments. However, the number of variables that defines a moment is large and thus the amount of data required is large as well.

H. Högni Vilhjálmsson et al. (Eds.): IVA 2011, LNAI 6895, pp. 248–254, 2011.

In the first part of this paper we will compare two recently introduced methods that collect multiple perspectives to deal with this challenge. The first method is described in De Kok and Heylen [5]. It consists of an experimental setup where multiple listeners are recorded in parallel in interaction with the same speaker. The second method was termed by Huang et al. [4] Parasocial Consensus Sampling (PCS). In this method people are invited to look and listen to a video of speaker and pretend that they are the listener. They are instructed to press a key when they feel they should provide a listener response.

The optionality of listener responses has another implication for models of virtual listening behavior. Missed opportunities are less of an issue than listener responses placed at inappropriate times. In a study by Poppe et al. [6] several models for listening behavior were evaluated on how they are perceived by an observer. Authors note that the random model actually performs reasonably well, in some cases as well as other models. In those cases the timing is not perfect and the model missed opportunities, but in some instances no listener responses are placed at clearly inappropriate times.

The collection of multiple perspectives, gives us more instances of contexts in which a response is judged appropriate. However, one still cannot be sure that all the contexts in which no responses is given are inappropriate for a response; where a response would be awkard or disrupt the interaction.

In the second part of the paper we describe a perception experiment in which human observers view an interaction between a recorded speaker and a generated virtual listener. The virtual listener performs head nods which are placed at appropriate times according to the previously collected multiple perspectives, but also at moments where none of the perspectives yielded a responses. The human observers are asked to assess each invidual head nod on its appropriateness, by pressing a key when the observer disapproves of the head nod.

2   Multiple Perspectives on Appropriate Timing

To be able to know whether a listener response is mandatory or optional in a particular situation, one can try to see what different people would do in the same situation. Do all of them respond, or only some? Are there situations in which nobody provides a response? In this paper we compare two methods to acquire responses from multiple people (i.e. from multiple perspectives) to the same context.

Parallel Recording. To record multiple perspectives on listening behavior we invited groups of 4 participants for an experimental session in which 4 mediated face-to-face interactions were recorded. Each participant was once a speaker and three times a listener. The speakers summarized a video they had just seen or they reproduced a recipe they had just studied for 10 minutes. Listeners were instructed to memorize as much as possible about what the speaker was telling. Each listener was unaware of the other two listeners and were recorded in interaction with the same speaker in parallel. The speaker saw one of the listeners, believing that they had a one-on-one conversation with this person.

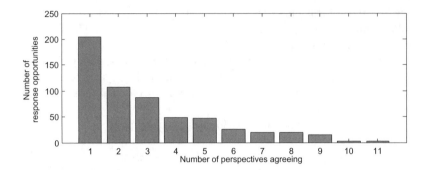

Fig. 1. Histogram illustrating the distribution of the number of perspectives that agree with the response opportunities

This procedure was repeated for eight groups to collect the MultiLis corpus [5]. The 32 Dutch spoken interactions in this corpus have a total duration of 131 minutes and were afterwards annotated on listening behavior. For this paper we use the start times of listener responses from these annotations. From these 32 interaction we used 8 with a total duration of 34 minutes.

Parasocial Consensus Sampling. Huang et al. [4] acquired multiple per-spectives on listening behavior using the method called Parasocial Consensus Sampling (PCS). In this method media is presented to individuals and they are asked to respond as if they were in interaction with this media. Responses were recorded using the keyboard as medium. So the participants were shown a video of a speaker and they were asked to press the spacebar of the keyboard when they would have provided a listener response if they were interacting with that speaker.

To compare this method to the method of parallel recordings, we collected PCS perspectives on the MultiLis corpus. Ten months after the original MultiLis experiments 6 participants were reinvited to collect their PCS perspective for the same interactions in which they were listeners. Three of these participants were in the same session and the other three in another session. Furthermore we invited 10 new participants to collect their PCS perspective. Each participant was assigned to a session and did the 4 interactions in that session.

Comparing the Two Methods. The six participants that took part in both the MultiLis experiment and in the PCS collecting responded in both methods on average 5.75 times per minute. The ten participants that only participated in the PCS collection responded on average 5 times per minute. So in both methods the response rate is comparable.

The responses from the two methods that occur at the same moment are grouped into response opportunities. The response opportunity starts with the first response belonging to that moment and ends with the last response.

In Figure 1 an overview is presented of the 581 response opportunities iden-tified in the 8 interactions by the combination of both methods. It shows that

Table 1. Agreement between the collected PCS perspectives for each participant and the original listeners (measured in F_1 scores). The table is split into two; one for each session of four interactions.

	Original Behavior				Original Behavior		
	Listener	Listener	Listener		Listener	Listener	Listener
PCS	1	2	3	PCS	5	6	7
Lis 1	*0.52*	0.46	0.41	Lis 5	*0.37*	0.29	0.24
Lis 2	0.44	*0.50*	0.48	Lis 6	0.25	*0.36*	*0.43*
Lis 3	0.18	0.21	*0.35*	Lis 7	*0.28*	0.18	0.27
PCS 1	0.42	0.42	0.41	PCS 6	0.24	0.27	0.18
PCS 2	0.27	0.37	0.35	PCS 7	0.18	0.26	0.39
PCS 3	0.39	0.48	0.43	PCS 8	0.30	0.31	0.39
PCS 4	0.24	0.26	<u>0.52</u>	PCS 9	0.27	0.25	0.34
PCS 5	0.41	<u>0.50</u>	0.41	PCS 10	0.25	0.17	0.16

agreement between perspectives is quite small. Most of the response opportunities are agreed upon by a minority of the perspectives. There are only a few response opportunities (76 out of 581) that are agreed upon by a majority of the perspectives (at least 6). It is interesting to note that all response opportunities in which 10 or 11 perspectives agreed and 4 (out of 15) response opportunities where 9 perspectives agreed that a response should be given were from the same interaction. Especially in this interaction the speaker facilitated the opportunities for the listener to respond. In these moments the speaker requested a listener response by nonverbal cues, such as a pause and eye contact until a response was given, more strongly than other speakers.

Next we look at the timing of the original responses versus PCS responses. For this analysis we measured the distance between the start of each individual response and the beginning of the corresponding response opportunity. The mean distance of responses from the original listener is 0.28 seconds and for PCS responses 0.50 seconds. Thus PCS responses are significantly slower than the original responses (ANOVA: $F = 92, p < 0.01$). This delay is probably caused by the fact that they are not as involved in the interaction and need to think about their responses and the delay to perform them by pressing the key, while in interaction they come naturally.

In Table 1 the agreement between the collected PCS perspectives of each participant and each of the original listeners is presented. The agreement was calculated by counting the number of times they responded to the same response opportunity in both methods. From these counts precision (the percentage of responses from A that correspond with B) and recall (the percentage of responses from B that are included in the responses of A) are calculated and combined by taking the weighted harmonic mean into the F_1 measure. Agreement varies from 0.18 to 0.52 in which higher is better.

When one looks horizontally at these numbers one can see the behavior with which of the original listeners their PCS perspective agrees most. For the PCS perspectives of the re-invited listeners this is in 4 out of 6 cases their own listening behavior with F_1 scores ranging from 0.27 to 0.52 (see italic numbers). When one looks vertically at these numbers one can see which of the PCS-ers agreed most with each listeners data. Again in 4 out of 6 cases this is their own PCS perspective with F_1 scores ranging from 0.36 to 0.52 (see underlined numbers). Although it is difficult to make a strong case, it is interesting to see this trend, which points out that there might be some consistency within listeners to produce responses.

Discussion. Figure 1 shows that agreement between perspectives is quite low. This means that one perspective can not capture all the response opportunities that are available in an interaction. Multiple perspectives give a more complete picture of all the possible opportunities to give a response. It tells one even more than that. It also provides one with information about the graded optionality of these opportunities. If all perspectives agree than this opportunity is mandatory, while this is less so for opportunities where only a few perspectives agreed.

Comparison between the two methods to collect these perspectives show that agreement between the real behavior of the listeners and their own PCS perspective is fairly low, but it is in general higher than that of other's PCS perspective. So PCS is able to capture the personal perspective on listening behavior. However due to the optionality of this behavior, differences are still quite large between their actual behavior and their parasocial behavior. It is still unknown if these differences are larger that repeated PCS perspectives from the same individual.

3   Multiple Perspectives on Inappropriate Timing

In the previous section we have shown that the graded optionality of a listener response can be collected by combining multiple perspectives. The question that we face with the multiple perspectives data is whether moments where none of the perspectives has produced a response are really inappropiate times or whether there are still moments that a response is appropriate even though it did not show up with multiple sampling. To answer this we have conducted a perception experiment where participants were shown videos of an actual speaker of our corpus paired with a generated virtual listener.

Procedure. In the experiment we showed participants 8 videos of a real speaker with a generated listener. The participants were told the aim of the experiment was to asses our models for generating listening behavior. The generated listeners perform only head nods. The head nods are partly generated *at* the response opportunities found in the previous sections and partly *between* the response opportunities found. The participant has to assess the appropriateness of each head nod. If the participant judges that the head nod is inappropriately placed he/she was instructed to press the spacebar. The participant had the option to replay the whole interaction again.

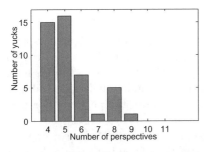 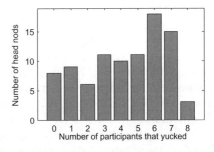

Fig. 2. *Left*: Histogram of the number of yucks corresponding to the number of perspectives agreeing. *Right*: Histogram illustrating the number of participants that pressed the yuck button for the *in-between-head-nods*.

Stimuli. As stimuli we used the 8 speaker videos from the previous analysis. We generated a virtual listener which performs 272 head nods using the Elckerlyc BML Realizer [8]. 182 head nods (the *at-head-nods*) of the listener are generated in the middle of the response opportunities with at least 4 responses. The other 90 head nods (the *in-between-head-nods*) are generated at times where no listener or PCS-er previously provided a response. They were placed in the 90 biggest gaps between the 182 head nods generated at response opportunities.

Results. We invited 8 participants for the experiment (aged 19-30, all male). Participants received the same stimuli, the order was varied among participants.

On average each participant yucked 53 out of 272 head nods, for a total of 424 yucks. *At-head-nods* were yucked 45 times and *in-between-head-nods* were yucked 379 times. There is a significant negative correlation between the number of perspectives agreeing this moment to be a response opportunity and the number of yucks ($r = -0.71, p < 0.01$).

The left histogram in Figure 2 shows the amount of yucks and the amount of perspectives agreeing for the *at-head-nods*. The 45 yucks for *at-head-nods* belong to 31 individual head nods. There are 21 *at-head-nods* that are yucked 1 time, 6 *at-head-nods* yucked 2 times and 4 *at-head-nods* yucked 3 times. We see that most of these *at-head-nods* are agreed upon by a limited number of perspectives, but even with 8 or 9 perspectives agreeing, it is still possible that someone yucks the head nod.

The right histogram in Figure 2 shows of the number of participants that yucked the *in-between-head-nods*. There are 8 *in-between-head-nods* that were never yucked. Most of the *in-between-head-nods* get yucked by at least half of the participants (56 out of 90). Only three *in-between-head-nods* get yucked by every participant. This means that most of the moments which have not been indicated as an appropriate time to give a listener response are indeed inappropriate places to do so. But not according to everyone. Thus, there also seems to be a graded inappropriateness for listener responses. Further analysis of this and similarly collected data should show which contextual cues cause this gradation in inappropriateness.

4   Conclusion

In this paper we have compared two methods of collecting multiple perspectives on the appropriate timing of listener responses. Both methods, parallel recording and Parasocial Consensus Sampling (PCS), are able to collect a similar number of responses. By comparing responses from the same individuals collected in both methods, we have shown that PCS is able to capture the personal perspective of an individual, but exact replication is not achieved. Responses from the PCS method are significantly later than the responses from parallel recordings.

Based on the results of the multiple perspectives from both methods we have generated a virtual listener which gives head nods on appropriate times and times not indicated as appropriate and let a human observer assess each individual head nod. This way we collected multiple perspectives on inappropriate timing of listener responses. We have shown that only a subset of the generated responses not on appropriate times are actually *in*appropriate times to give one.

Combining all these perspectives we get a view on the graded optionality and graded inappropriateness of listener responses in certain contexts, which can be used to develop and evaluate models of listening behavior for embodied conversational agents, but also for other optional behavior.

Acknowledgments. We would like to thank Henry Hoendervangers, Dennis Reidsman and Ronald Poppe for their help.

References

1. Clark, H.H.: Using Language. Cambridge University Press, Cambridge (1996)
2. Dittmann, A.T., Llewellyn, L.G.: Relationship between vocalizations and head nods as listener responses.. Journal of personality and social psychology 9(1), 79–84 (1968)
3. Heylen, D., Bevacqua, E., Pelachaud, C., Poggi, I., Gratch, J., Schröder, M.: Generating Listening Behaviour. Springer, Heidelberg (2011)
4. Huang, L., Morency, L.-P., Gratch, J.: Parasocial Consensus Sampling: Combining Multiple Perspectives to Learn Virtual Human Behavior. In: Proceedings of Autonomous Agents and Multi-Agent Systems, Toronto, Canada (2010)
5. de Kok, I., Heylen, D.: The MultiLis Corpus - Dealing with Individual Differences of Nonverbal Listening Behavior. In: Esposito, A., Esposito, A., Martone, R., Müller, V.C., Scarpetta, G. (eds.) Toward Autonomous, Adaptive, and Context-Aware Multimodal Interfaces: Theoretical and Practical Issues, pp. 374–387 (2011)
6. Poppe, R., Truong, K.P., Reidsma, D., Heylen, D.: Backchannel Strategies for Artificial Listeners. In: Proceedings of Intelligent Virtual Agents, Philadelphia, Pennsylvania, USA, pp. 146–158 (2010)
7. Ward, N., Tsukahara, W.: Prosodic features which cue back-channel responses in English and Japanese. Journal of Pragmatics 32(8), 1177–1207 (2000)
8. Welbergen, H., Reidsma, D., Ruttkay, Z.M., Zwiers, J.: Elckerlyc - A BML Realizer for continuous, multimodal interaction with a Virtual Human. Journal on Multimodal User Interfaces 3(4), 271–284 (2010)

Identifying Utterances Addressed to an Agent in Multiparty Human–Agent Conversations

Naoya Baba[1], Hung-Hsuan Huang[2], and Yukiko I. Nakano[3]

[1] Graduate School of Science and Technology, Seikei University,
Musashino-shi, Tokyo 180-8633 Japan
dm116233@cc.seikei.ac.jp
[2] Department of Information & Communication Science, Ritsumeikan University
huang@fc.ritsumei.ac.jp
[3] Dept. of Computer and Information Science, Seikei University
y.nakano@st.seikei.ac.jp

Abstract. In multiparty human–agent interaction, the agent should be able to properly respond to a user by determining whether the utterance is addressed to the agent or to another person. This study proposes a model for predicting the addressee by using the acoustic information in speech and head orientation as nonverbal information. First, we conducted a Wizard-of-Oz (WOZ) experiment to collect human–agent triadic conversations. Then, we analyzed whether the acoustic features and head orientations were correlated with addressee-hood. Based on the analysis, we propose an addressee prediction model that integrates acoustic and bodily nonverbal information using SVM.

Keywords: Addressee-hood, Multiparty conversation, Head pose, Prosody.

1 Introduction

Various kinds of information kiosk system are used in public places, such as shopping malls, museums, and visitor centers. A typical situation would be a group of people stopping by a kiosk and operating the system to collect information while talking to each other. Thus, to implement information kiosk agents for public places, multiparty conversation functionality facilitating interaction with a group of users is indispensable. When a person talks to the agent, the system needs to respond to the utterance. In contrast, when a person talks to another person, the system should not disturb their conversation. Therefore, conversational agents need to distinguish such side-exchanges between users from utterances addressed to the system.

In previous work [1, 2], it was reported that humans use nonverbal signals like gaze, head nods, and posture to regulate their conversation. In addition to such bodily nonverbal behaviors, this study exploits paralinguistic information in speech to identify the addressee in multiparty human–agent interaction. One intuitive observation is that people speak differently to machines than to other humans by trying to make their speech more easily understood by the artifact.

Thus, to determine when to respond to the users in triadic conversations between two users and an agent, this paper proposes a model for distinguishing utterances addressed to the agent from side-exchanges between users based on bodily and acoustic nonverbal information.

H. Högni Vilhjálmsson et al. (Eds.): IVA 2011, LNAI 6895, pp. 255–261, 2011.
© Springer-Verlag Berlin Heidelberg 2011

To establish this goal, first, we collect human–agent triadic conversations in a WOZ experiment. Then, we analyze how visual cues and acoustic cues correlate with addressee-hood. Based on analyses of these two modalities, we integrate all the information and propose an addressee prediction method using machine-learning techniques.

2 Research Background

Research on human communication has shown that eye gaze plays an important role in turn-taking [2]. Vertegaal [3] reported that gaze is a reliable predictor of addressee-hood. Takemae [4] provided evidence that the speaker's gaze indicates addressee-hood and has a regulatory function in turn-management. In addition to eye gaze information, linguistic information and contextual information are also useful in identifying the addressee in human multiparty conversations [5]. Frampton et al. [6] proposed a model for resolving the English pronoun "you" in human multiparty conversations using linguistic, acoustic, and visual features that were automatically extracted from an automatic speech recognition (ASR) and computer-vision system. They reported a prediction accuracy of 60%.

Related studies were conducted in mixed human–human and human–computer conversations [7-9]. Katzenmaier et al. [10] proposed a method for identifying the addressee in a human–human–robot interaction by combining acoustic and visual cues. For the acoustic cues, they defined some linguistic features obtained from ASR, such as typical phrases and language model, and used them to discriminate the addressee. They reported that the speech addressed to the robot was detected with F-measure of 0.72.

In this study, we employ paralinguistic features as acoustic information because they can be extracted without ASR and are expected to be a more robust measure than linguistic features. We assume that the user's tone of voice may be different depending on whether the person is talking to the agent or talking to another person. We also assume that people will speak slowly to the system in order to be understood.

Thus, to measure the user's speaking manner in talking to the agent, this study focuses on pitch, power, and speech rate as the most important prosodic features [11]; these have already been recognized as useful features in emotion recognition. Considering all these aspects, by integrating bodily and acoustic nonverbal information, this study will employ machine-learning techniques to create a model for distinguishing utterances addressed to the agent from side-exchanges between users.

 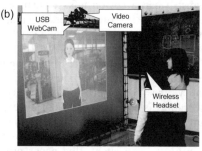

Fig. 1. The setting of the WOZ experiment: (a) the WOZ operating booth, (b) the information-providing agent and the participants

3   Collecting Triadic Human-Agent Conversations

To collect a corpus for analyzing addressee-hood in human–agent multiparty conversations, we conducted a WOZ experiment with two decision-making situations.

3.1   Procedure and Subjects

A pair of subjects was instructed to interact with a life-sized virtual agent on the screen and to collect information to make a decision in a given task. As shown in Fig. 1(b), a pair of subjects stood 1.5 m away from the screen and interacted with a female virtual character. Each pair was instructed to complete two sessions: (1) choosing three lectures to register for the next semester and (2) choosing three sightseeing spots in Kyoto for planning their travel. The order of the tasks was randomized. Both subjects interacted with the agent, thus switching roles as speaker/partner.

Twenty-one pairs (14 male pairs and seven female pairs) of university students participated in the experiment. They came from various departments, and the average age was 20.1 years. In this study, we analyzed the data from 17 pairs (10 male and seven female pairs). In addition, four computer science students were recruited to operate the WOZ agent. The WOZ operators were recommended to make each session end within 10 min, while also trying to help the participants to make decisions as much as they could.

3.2   Collected Data

All sessions were recorded by two video cameras (in front of and behind the subjects). In addition to these regular video cameras, a USB WebCam (960×720 pixels, 30 fps) was set on top of the screen (Fig. 1(b)). Each of the participants was equipped with a wireless headset to record their voice.

Because the interactions between the participants and the agent (WOZ operator) appeared to be smoother in the second session, we only analyzed the data recorded in the second sessions. Thus, we analyzed six lecture registration conversations, and 11 travel-planning conversations. The average length of each conversation was 629 seconds. Since the longer sessions may overly bias the machine-learning results, we only used the first 10 min for longer conversations. The resulting corpus length averaged 524 seconds.

4   Analysis

To analyze the speech and video data collected in section 3, the speech audio was split into utterances as a unit of analysis. The speech was automatically separated using the Julius speech recognition software. When more than 200 ms of silence was observed, it was automatically identified as the end of the current utterance, and the proceeding speech was regarded as a new utterance. Through this process, 1830 utterances were identified and saved as speech audio.

For video data, using the video annotation tool Anvil 4.7.7, we annotated the speaker and the addressee for each utterance, and used these labels as the ground truth. The results of labeling are shown in Table 1. The number of utterances addressed to the agent was 863, and that to the other subject was 967.

Table 1. The number of utterances addressed to the agent and to the other subject (partner)

Addressee / Gender	Agent	Partner	Total
Male pairs	509	522	1031
Female pairs	354	445	799
Total	863	967	1830

4.1   Analysis of Acoustic Information

For acoustic information, we analyzed pitch, power, duration, and speech rate. First, we used the Praat speech analysis tool to extract prosodic information: pitch and power. We wrote a Praat script that measured pitch (F0) and power (intensity) every 0.01 second from each utterance. For speech duration, we just used the length (sec) of each audio file automatically split by Julius ASR. As for the speech rate, a Praat script measured the number of phonemes for each utterance, and this was divided by the speech duration. Thus, the number of phonemes per second was used as the speech rate.

Fig. 2 shows the averages of F0 and power as well as the utterance duration and the speech rate. F0 and power are higher and the duration is longer when talking to the agent as compared to talking to the partner. The speech rate is slower when talking to the agent. All these differences except for F0 for female are statistically significant in t-tests. These results suggest that people talk to the agent with a higher tone of voice and speak more loudly and slowly. We expect that these acoustic cues are useful in judging whether the speaker is directing speech at the agent or at a partner.

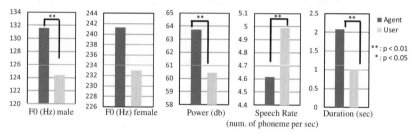

Fig. 2. Results of acoustic analysis

4.2   Analysis of Head Orientation

Automatic Identification of Head Orientation
Video data collected in the experiment were analyzed using face-tracking software, FaceAPI[1], which can measure head position and rotation for x, y, and z coordinates. To automatically recognize the subject's head orientation, we created a decision tree by employing J48 in the Weka data-mining tool. For supervised data, we annotated

---

[1] http://www.seeingmachines.com/product/faceapi/

head orientation for four pairs. For training data, six kinds of head pose data (x, y, and z position and rotation) and measurement confidence scores were used. We distinguished three types of head orientation: forward (looking at the agent), left, and right. Using 10-fold cross validation, we obtained a classification accuracy of 97.2%. Since the model was accurate enough, we used this to automatically label the head orientation for the rest of the video data.

Correlation between Head Orientation and Addressee-Hood
It was assumed that the subjects were looking at the agent when talking to the agent and were looking at the partner when talking to the partner. If the correlation between the head orientation and the addressee is high enough, it would be possible to predict the addressee based only on the head orientation. To measure the correlation between head orientation and addressee-hood, we calculated the agreement between the head orientation label and the addressee label. By looking at the video data frame by frame, we obtained 49170 frames for head orientation data. The number of matching frames between the addressee label and head orientation label was 36867, and the ratio of disagreement was about 25%. This result suggested that although the head orientation was definitely a useful predictor of the addressee, it was not sufficient.

5   Identifying Utterances Addressed to the Agent

5.1   Definition of Features

To consider both acoustic and visual cues for determining the addressee-hood, parameters were selected based on the empirical results in section 4. For the acoustic cues, average pitch (F0), power, duration and speech rate for each utterance were used. In addition, the difference from the average of all the subjects was used for F0 and power.

For the head orientation parameters, the time ratio of looking at the agent/ partner/elsewhere to the duration of utterance, and four types of bigrams of head orientation transition were used. Thus, seven features of head orientation were extracted for each participant, and 14 features in total (from two participants).

5.2   Results of Machine Learning

We set up 20 features (six acoustic features and 14 head orientation features), and applied this training data to an SVM classifier. We used a Weka implementation with a polynomial kernel and a default value for the C parameter ($C = 1$). We created an acoustic model, a head orientation model, and a combination model, and compared the performances of these models.

The prediction results are shown in Table 2. For male subjects, 1031 utterances were used in creating the acoustic model. Head pose data were successfully measured in 825 utterances out of 1031; these were then used in the head orientation model and the combination model. Out of 825 utterances, 415 were addressed to the agent, and 410 were addressed to the partner. Therefore, the majority class baseline was 50.3%. For utterances directed at the agent, F-measures with 10-fold cross-validation were 0.729, 0.782, and 0.807 for the acoustic, head orientation, and combination models, respectively. The combined model outperformed other models in all metrics. Similar results were found in female pairs.

Finally, we integrated the male and female data by adding a gender feature to the original feature set. For the general models, 1830 utterances were used for learning in the acoustic model, and 1237 utterances were used for the head orientation model and the combination model. The performance was slightly worse than the male model in talking to the agent, with an F-measure of 0.799. The prediction accuracy was 80.28%. Since the majority class baseline was 50.3%%, the prediction accuracy was 30 points higher than the baseline.

Table 2. Evaluation of addressee prediction

Model		Number of utterances	Baseline	Accuracy	F-measure	
					Agent	Partner
Male	Acoustic	1031	50.6%	74.49%	0.729	0.759
	Head orientation	825	50.3%	74.4%	0.782	0.691
	Acoustic + Head			80.0%	0.807	0.792
Female	Acoustic	799	55.7%	75.97%	0.693	0.802
	Head orientation	412	50.2%	65.29%	0.709	0.571
	Acoustic + Head			80.1%	0.793	0.808
General	Acoustic	1830	52.8%	75.3%	0.717	0.781
	Head orientation	1237	50.3%	71.62%	0.759	0.656
	Acoustic + Head			80.28%	0.799	0.806

6   Conclusion and Future Work

This study proposed a model for distinguishing utterances addressed to the agent from side-exchanges between users, based on bodily and acoustic nonverbal information. Our model outperformed the previous studies [6, 10] in determining when the user was talking to the agent; however, it would be necessary to consider the task situation when comparing the performances of different experiments. Our method could be improved by adding more features, such as lexical, sentential, and discourse information, but it is also necessary to balance cost with performance. We are implementing this method to determine the addressee in real time and will also integrate the model into a conversational agent system which consists of a discourse model, ASR, text-to-speech (TTS), and an agent animation engine. Then, we will evaluate whether the agent can respond to the user in proper timing.

Acknowledgement. Special thanks to Prof. Toyoaki Nishida and Prof. Igor Pandzic for their useful advice. This work is partially funded by JSPS under a Grant-in-Aid for Scientific Research (S) (19100001).

References

1. Kendon, A.: Some Functions of Gaze Direction in Social Interaction. Acta Psychologica 26, 22–63 (1967)
2. Duncan, S.: Some signals and rules for taking speaking turns in conversations. Journal of Personality and Social Psychology 23(2), 283–292 (1972)

3. Vertegaal, R., et al.: Eye gaze patterns in conversations: there is more the conversational agents than meets the eyes. In: CHI 2001 (2001)
4. Takemae, Y., Otsuka, K., Mukawa, N.: Video cut editing rule based on participants' gaze in multiparty conversation. In: The 11th ACM International Conference on Multimedia (2003)
5. Akker, R.o.d., Traum, D.: A comparison of addressee detection methods for multiparty conversations. In: 13th Workshop on the Semantics and Pragmatics of Dialogue (2009)
6. Frampton, M., et al.: Who is "You"? Combining Linguistic and Gaze Features to Resolve Second-Person References in Dialogue. In: the 12th Conference of the European Chapter of the ACL (2009)
7. Lunsford, R., Oviatt, S.: Human perception of intended addressee during computer-assisted meetings. In: The 8th international Conference on Multimodal interfaces, ICMI 2006 (2006)
8. Bohus, D., Horvitz, E.: Facilitating Multiparty Dialog with Gaze, Gesture, and Speech. In: ICMI-MLMI 2010 (2010)
9. Terken, J., Joris, I., Valk, L.d.: Multimodal Cues for Addressee-hood in Triadic Communication with a Human Information Retrieval Agent. In: International Conference on Multimodal interfaces, ICMI 2007 (2007)
10. Katzenmaier, M., Stiefelhagen, R., Schultz, T.: Identifying the Addressee in HumanHumanRobot Interactions based on Head Pose and Speech. In: international Conference on Multimodal interfaces, ICMI 2004 (2004)
11. Rodriguez, H., Beck, D., Lind, D., Lok, B.: Audio Analysis of Human/Virtual-Human Interaction. In: Prendinger, H., Lester, J.C., Ishizuka, M. (eds.) IVA 2008. LNCS (LNAI), vol. 5208, pp. 154–161. Springer, Heidelberg (2008)

Estimating a User's Conversational Engagement Based on Head Pose Information

Ryota Ooko[1], Ryo Ishii[2], and Yukiko I. Nakano[3]

[1] Graduate School of Science and Technology, Seikei University,
Musashino-shi, Tokyo 180-8633, Japan
dm116212@cć.seikei.ac.jp
[2] Graduate School of Informatics, Kyoto University, Kyoto, Japan/NTT Cyber Space
Laboratories, NTT Corporation, Japan
ishii.ryo@lab.ntt.co.jp
[3] Dept. of Computer and Information Science, Seikei University
y.nakano@st.seikei.ac.jp

Abstract. With the goal of building an intelligent conversational agent that can recognize the user's engagement, this paper proposes a method of judging a user's conversational engagement based on head pose data. First, we analyzed how head pose information is correlated with the user's conversational engagement and found that the amplitude of head movement and rotation have a moderate positive correlation with the level of conversational engagement. We then established an engagement estimation model by applying a decision tree learning algorithm to 19 parameters. The results showed that the proposed model based on head pose information performs quite well.

Keywords: conversational engagement, head pose, eye gaze.

1   Introduction

Studies on virtual agents and communication robots have revealed that conversational engagement is fundamental to communication between human users and humanoid interfaces [1, 2]. By engagement, we refer to "the process by which two (or more) participants establish, maintain, and end their perceived connection," as defined in [3]. If the user is not fully engaged in the conversation, information presented by the system (agent) is not properly conveyed to the user. If the system can monitor the user's attitude toward the conversation and detect whether the user is engaged in the conversation, the system can then adapt its behavior and communication strategy according to the user's attitude.

As a typical nonverbal signal of engagement, in our previous study [4], we focused on eye gaze and investigated the relationship between attentional behavior and conversational engagement. Then, we proposed a method of estimating conversational engagement based on eye gaze information. However, when we implemented our system, we found that the eye gaze information was insufficient. Although an eye

H. Högni Vilhjálmsson et al. (Eds.): IVA 2011, LNAI 6895, pp. 262–268, 2011.

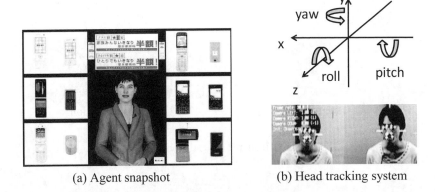

(a) Agent snapshot   (b) Head tracking system

Fig. 1. Equipment used in our experiment

tracker can measure the subject's eye gaze very accurately, it cannot track the subject's pupil if the subject moves her/his head in a wide range. In such cases, the engagement estimation mechanism does not work. Therefore, we need a more robust estimation mechanism while maintaining a high level of accuracy.

To develop a new method that can compensate for the drawbacks of the gaze-based engagement mechanism, this study exploits head pose data that can be measured by a head tracker. A tracker cannot measure the eye gaze, but can measure the movement of the whole head and is quite robust. Thus, focusing on head movement, this study investigates the head position and rotation as well as the amplitude and frequency of head movement. Then, we will propose an engagement estimation method based on the head movement information by applying a decision tree algorithm.

2   Related Work

In previous work on human-agent interaction, Nakano et al. [5] proposed a gaze model for nonverbal grounding in conversational agents using a head tracker. They used a head tracker to estimate the user's gaze direction and implemented an agent that can judge whether the information provided from the agent is grounded based on the estimated gaze information. More recently, Bohus and Horvitz [6] proposed a method of predicting the user's engagement intention in multiparty situations by using a head tracker [7]. They focused on predicting whether the user will be engaged in the conversation but not on judging whether the user is engaged in the ongoing conversation to maintain the communication. In human-robot interaction, Morency et al. [8] and Rich et al. [9] used a head tracker to recognize a user's gaze direction and head nods as a signal of engagement.

In this study, we will investigate the characteristics of head movement by adding more parameters and exploit them to estimate the conversational engagement.

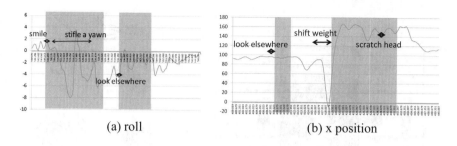

(a) roll   (b) x position

Fig. 2. Example of head motion data

3   Data

As the first step to estimate the user's engagement, we collected a conversational corpus for human-agent communication. A female animated character was displayed on a 120-inch rear-type screen (Fig. 1 (a)), where she acted as a salesperson for a mobile phone store, and six cell phones and advertisements were shown as her background. The subjects stood in front of the agent 1.5 m away from the screen. We employed a Wizard-of-Oz setting where the agent's responses to the user were selected by an experimenter. The agent animation was preset to each response. The details of the experiment are reported in [4]. We collected 10 conversations whose average length was 16 min and built a multimodal corpus consisting of verbal and nonverbal behaviors mentioned below:

Verbal Data: The user's speech was transcribed from the recorded speech audio, and the agent's utterances were extracted from the log of the Wizard-of-Oz system. The total number of the agent's utterances was 951 and that of the user's was 61.

Nonverbal Data: Head pose data were obtained by OMRON's vision-based head tracker, OKAO Vision; the head tracker can measure the position (x, y, z) and rotation (roll, pitch, yaw) of the head (Fig. 1(b)) at 30 fps. For head tracking, two CCD cameras were mounted on top of the screen.

Human judgment of Engagement: We recruited another 10 subjects and asked them to watch the video and mark the time when the subject on the video looked disengaged from the conversation. We used the Anvil video annotation tool to mark the video. The disengagement score was then assigned to each time frame by counting how many subjects marked the frame as disengagement. For example, if all the subjects labeled the frame as disengagement, the disengagement score for the frame was 10. If the score was 0, the subject was believed to be fully engaged in the conversation. Thus, the disengagement score was in the range 0 to 10.[1]

---

[1] Since we used the subject's judgment as disengagement score, we did not calculate inter-coder reliability.

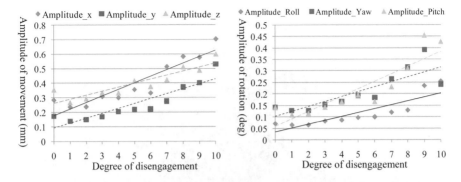

Fig. 3. Correlation between amplitude of head movement and degree of disengagement

4   Analysis of Head Pose Data

This section reports the analysis of the head pose data[2] collected in the previous section. Since the head tracking data were very noisy, the moving average for a 1sec window (30 frames) was calculated to smooth the data. Then, we investigated the head position (x, y, z) and rotation (roll, yaw, pitch). In addition, we identified waves of head movement (such as speech wave forms). For each head movement wave, the amplitude and frequency were calculated.

Fig. 2 shows an example of head motion data. The shadowed area indicates the time for which the disengagement score was higher than 4. As shown in Fig. 2(a), the fluctuations in the roll value became larger in the shadowed areas, and the subject actually stifled a yawn and looked the other way during that time. Likewise, within or right before the shadowed area in Fig. 2(b), the fluctuations in the x position value became larger compared to the other time frames. Looking at the video, we found that at this time, the subject changed his posture, which caused a significant change in his head pose.

4.1   Correlation between Head Pose and Engagement Score

When we plotted the average values for all the parameters with respect to the degree of disengagement, we found a clear correlation between the amplitude and degree of disengagement. Fig. 3 shows the averages for amplitude parameters of seven subjects. The X-axis indicates the degree of disengagement, and the Y-axis indicates the amplitude of head movement. The higher the disengagement score is, the larger the amplitude of movement is in head position and rotation. We found a moderate correlation in Pearson's correlation coefficient (0.45–0.59) between the disengagement score and the amplitude parameters. According to statistical tests using the t-value, all these results were statistically significant ($p < 0.001$). Although we could not find a clear correlation for other parameters, these results suggest that head pose data, specifically the amplitude of head movement and head rotation, may be useful in estimating conversational engagement.

---

[2] In this analysis, we focused on the subject's attitude toward the agent's speech. Therefore, we only analyzed the subject's head movement while listening to the agent.

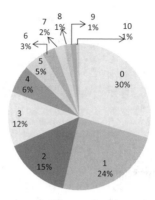

Fig. 4. Distribution of disengagement scores

5   Estimation Model for Conversational Engagement

5.1   Binary Classification

Based on the analysis presented in the previous section, we created a model to estimate the user's conversational engagement. We employed a decision tree learning algorithm J48 in Weka. In addition to 18 parameters (i.e., the position (x, y, z), rotation (roll, pitch, yaw), and amplitude and frequency for each of the previous six parameters), we used the topic change as a feature.[3] This is because the subject's head frequently moved toward the next cell phone (explanation target) displayed on the screen (Fig. 1(a)) when the topic was changed to the next cell phone. In such a case, the subject is actually fully engaged in the conversation. To distinguish head movement during a topic and that occurring at the topic shift, we added the binary parameter "topic change or no topic change" to the set of head movement features.

To set up a threshold for a binary classification of engagement and disengagement, we first investigated the distribution of disengagement scores, which is shown in Fig. 4. Since there was a larger difference between 3 (12%) and 4 (6%) compared to 4 and 5 (5%), we tested whether 3 is a better threshold than 4. The results of 10-fold cross validation are shown in Table 1. The prediction accuracies did not greatly differ between the classification thresholds of 3 or 4; for both engagement and disengagement, the prediction accuracies were over 77%.

Table 1. Results of decision tree learning for binary classification

Disengagement threshold	Accuracy	F-measure	
		Engagement	Disengagement
3	77.2%	0.767	0.777
4	77.8%	0.786	0.77

---

[3] Since only a few topic shifts occurred per conversation, we did not analyze the effect of this parameter in section 4.

5.2   Three-Class Classification

In weaker engagement/disengagement situations, judging the engagement is not very easy even for humans. Therefore, a clear binary classification may be difficult. To avoid this problem, we set up a three-class classification: engagement, disengagement, and neither. Since, as discussed in section 5.1, we found similar results for the thresholds 3 and 4, we classified these two as "neither." If the disengagement score of a given time frame was less than or equal to 2, the frame was classified as "engagement." If the score was greater than or equal to 5, the frame was classified as "disengagement." The results of 10-fold cross validation are shown in Table 2. The prediction accuracy was 88.75%; more importantly, the F-measures were 0.88-0.89 for all the classes. These results indicate that this model can clearly distinguish completely disengaged users from engaged users.

Table 2. Results of three-class classification

Accuracy	F-measure		
	Engagement (score ≤ 2)	Neither ($3 \leq$ score ≤ 4)	Disengagement (score ≥ 5)
88.75%	0.891	0.887	0.884

6   Conclusions and Future Work

This study analyzed the relationship between the head pose and conversational engagement. We found that the amplitude of the head movement has a positive moderate correlation with the level of conversational engagement. Based on the results, we established an engagement estimation method by applying a decision tree learning algorithm to 19 parameters. We defined the engagement judgment as a three-class classification problem and established a model that can classify frames as "completely disengaged," "engaged," and "neither" very well. To improve the model, one possible idea is to employ a regression model to estimate the degree of engagement/disengagement and not just use three classes.

In future research, we plan to integrate the model proposed in this paper into the gaze-based engagement estimation method that we have previously proposed. By combining the gaze and head pose information, the estimation accuracy should be improved. More importantly, we expect that the robustness of the engagement estimation mechanism will be improved. Although an eye tracker can measure gaze information quite accurately, it sometimes cannot measure gaze behavior when the user's head moves by a significant amount. Therefore, by combining these two models, a more accurate and robust estimation mechanism can be realized.

Acknowledgement. This study used OKAO Vision technology provided by OMRON Corporation. This work is partially funded by the JSPS under a Grant-in-Aid for Scientific Research on Innovative Areas (No. 23119721).

References

1. Sidner, C.L., et al.: Explorations in engagement for humans and robots. Artificial Intelligence 166(1-2), 140–164 (2005)
2. Peters, C.: Direction of Attention Perception for Conversation Initiation in Virtual Environments. In: Intelligent Virtual Agents (2005)
3. Sidner, C.L., et al.: Where to Look: A Study of Human-Robot Engagement. In: ACM International Conference on Intelligent User Interfaces, IUI (2004)
4. Nakano, Y.I., Ishii, R.: Estimating User's Engagement from Eye-gaze Behaviors in Human-Agent Conversations. In: 2010 International Conference on Intelligent User Interfaces (IUI 2010), Hong Kong,
5. Nakano, Y.I., et al.: Towards a Model of Face-to-Face Grounding. In: The 41st Annual Meeting of the Association for Computational Linguistics, Sapporo, Japan (ACL 2003) (2003)
6. Bohus, D., Horvitz, E.: Learning to Predict Engagement with a Spoken Dialog System in Open-World Settings. In: SIGdial 2009, London, UK (2009)
7. Kendon, A.: Spatial organization in social encounters: the F-formation system. In: Gumperz, J.J. (ed.) Conducting Interaction: Patterns of behavior in focused encounters. Studies in International Sociolinguistics, Cambridge University Press, Cambridge (1990)
8. Morency, L.-P., et al.: Head gestures for perceptual interfaces: The role of context in improving recognition. Artificial Intelligence 171(8-9), 568–585 (2007)
9. Rich, C., et al.: Recognizing Engagement in Human-Robot Interaction. In: Human-Robot Interaction (2010)

Demonstrating and Testing the BML Compliance of BML Realizers

Herwin van Welbergen[1], Yuyu Xu[2], Marcus Thiebaux[2], Wei-Wen Feng[2], Jingqiao Fu[2], Dennis Reidsma[1], and Ari Shapiro[2]

[1] Human Media Interaction, University of Twente
{h.vanwelbergen@utwente.nl,d.reidsma}@utwente.nl
[2] Institute for Creative Technologies, University of Southern California
shapiro@ict.usc.edu

Abstract. BML realizers are complex software modules that implement a standardized interface –the BML specification language– to steer the behavior of a virtual human. We aim to promote and test the compliance of realizers that implement this interface. To this end we contribute a corpus of example BML scripts and a tool called RealizerTester that can be used to formally test and maintain adherence of realizers to the BML standard. The standardized interface of realizers allowed us to implement RealizerTester as an automatic testing framework that can test *any* realizer. RealizerTester can 1) help in maintaining the stability and extensibility that is crucial for realizers and 2) contribute to the formalization of the emerging BML standard, both by providing test scripts and a formal description of their constraints and by identifying and resolving execution inconsistencies between realizers. We illustrate the testing practices used in the development of two realizers and demonstrate how RealizerTester is integrated with these practices. The scripts in the example corpus were executed on both realizers. This resulted in a video corpus that demonstrates the semantic equivalences and differences in execution of BML scripts by the two realizers.

1 Introduction

The SAIBA framework [5,9] has standardized the architecture of virtual human applications with the aim of making reuse of their software components possible. The SAIBA framework proposes a modular 'planning pipeline' for real-time multimodal motor behavior of virtual humans, with standardized interfaces (using representation languages) between the modules in the pipeline. One of the components in this pipeline is the realizer. A realizer provides an interface to steer the motor behavior of a virtual human: a description of behavior in the Behavior Markup Language (BML) goes 'in', feedback comes 'out'.

Several realizers have been implemented [8,6,4,2,10]. If SAIBA's goal of software reuse is achieved, it will be possible to use such realizers interchangeably with the same BML input. We are interested in measuring and promoting this compatibility between realizers and to provide tools to formally test and maintain adherence to BML standard. To this end, we provide a growing test set of

H. Högni Vilhjálmsson et al. (Eds.): IVA 2011, LNAI 6895, pp. 269–281, 2011.

BML test cases, a corpus of BML scripts and video material of their realization in different (so far, two) realizers: SmartBody [8] and Elckerlyc [10].

By directly comparing BML realizers, we can better determine changes to the BML specification that are necessary due to overly narrow or broad specifications. Overly broad specifications can be detected when realizers provide BML compliant, but semantically very different results. Overly narrow specifications indicate that a specification is not expressive enough, they can be detected when several Realizers implement the same (semantic) functionality, yet require Realizer specific proprietary BML extensions to implement (part of) this functionality.

Since each realizer necessarily implements the same interface, an automatic testing framework can be designed that tests the adherence to the BML/feedback semantics for *any* realizer. We contribute our testing framework RealizerTester[1], which provides exactly this functionality.

2   On BML Versions and Script Creation

Currently, there are two version of the BML specification: a first draft specified after the BML workshop in Vienna in November 2006 (the Vienna draft) and the current draft of BML version 1.0 (draft 1.0). Draft 1.0 is not backward compatible with the Vienna draft. Currently Elckerlyc implements draft 1.0, and SmartBody implements the Vienna draft. It is likely that new versions of BML will be developed[2] and that not all realizers will adapt to these new versions at the same pace. However, test scripts can be constructed that are semantically equivalent (that is, execute behavior that adheres to the same form and timing constraints) for most, if not all, BML behaviors in different versions of BML. This implies that the same test case (albeit not test script) can be used to test realizers that implement different versions of BML.

We aim to construct a test set that contains such semantically equivalent test cases for all BML versions. These tests provides a 'safety net' for migrating a realizer from a previous BML version to the next; the tests that worked for a realizer in the previous version should not break in their updated syntax in a next version of BML.

The process of converting the old tests to a new BML version also helps in the definition of the standard. It can highlight certain cases in which expressivity is lost where this might not be intended. That is: if something can be expressed in a previous version of BML which we cannot express in the new version of BML and this loss of expressivity was not explicitly intended in the new BML version, then their might be something 'wrong' in the definition of the new version.

Most of our current test scripts were originally designed for draft 1.0 and later converted to equivalent Vienna draft scripts. During this conversion process, we have encountered several cases that demonstrate the enhanced expressivity of the newer draft 1.0. For example:

---

[1] RealizerTester is released under the MIT license at
http://sourceforge.net/projects/realizertester/
[2] The BML workshop at this IVA aims to finalize BML 1.0.

- In the Vienna draft it was impossible to specify a realizer-independent posture behavior; draft 1.0 provides the specification of some default lexicalized postures.
- Draft 1.0 provides the specification of a modality (e.g. eyes, neck, torso) in gaze behaviors. The Vienna draft does not allow this. Therefore, SmartBody currently needs to use a custom extension to specify the modality of its gaze behavior.

A small set of scripts was converted from a Vienna draft specification to a draft 1.0 specification. So far we have not encountered any cases in which expressivity of the Vienna draft was lost in draft 1.0.

3   A Corpus of Test Cases and Videos

We provide a growing corpus of BML scripts for the purpose of visual comparison between the execution of a BML script by the different realizers. A matching video corpus illustrates how these scripts are executed in both SmartBody and Elckerlyc. The corpus of BML scripts (and matching video) provides examples of both short monologues and of the execution of isolated behaviors. The companion video and Fig. 1 compare the execution of some of these scripts in SmartBody and Elckerlyc. Here we discuss some preliminary observations on the comparison of such videos.

Script are included for most types of BML behavior. In the scripts used so far, the `speech`, `gaze`, `head` and pointing (part of `gesture`) behaviors look similar in Elckerlyc and SmartBody. A comparison of `face` behaviors, specified through Ekmans FACS [3] gives mixed results, as illustrated in the video. The `posture` behavior could not be compared in a meaningful manner, because the Vienna BML draft does not provide a realizer independent way to specify posture. The `locomotion` behavior is currently not implemented in Elckerlyc and is therefore omitted from the visual comparison corpus for now.

When designing short monologues for the visual comparison corpus, it became clear that existing demonstration scripts of both SmartBody and Elckerlyc rely heavily upon custom behavior elements. One reason for this is the lack of expressivity of the BML standard and specifically the lack of expressivity in the specification of iconic and metaphoric gestures. We recommend, at the very least, to extend the lexicalized set of gestures that can be specified in BML to include more non domain specific gestures. The set of gestures that is already implemented through extensions by current realizers could serve as an inspiration for this. Another reason for the use of custom BML elements is that so far there was no real need for BML compliance of realizers. Some BML elements that are currently implemented using one or more custom BML extensions in Elckerlyc and SmartBody could be implemented in standard BML. This testing and comparison corpus building effort serves as a driving force for this. Already some new core BML behaviors were implemented in both realizers to achieve better BML compliance.

We have created a test corpus containing 19 test scripts in BML draft 1.0, and corresponding test cases that check, e.g., the adherence to the time constraints specified in the scripts. We are currently in the process of converting the test scripts to the Vienna BML draft.

4   Automatic Software Testing of Realizers

Realizers are complex software components. They often form the backbone of several virtual human applications of a research group. Therefore, the stability and extensibility of realizers is crucial. So far, the testing of most of these realizers was limited to *manual*, time consuming inspections of the execution of a selected set of BML scripts [1]. *Automatic* testing can be used to detect errors in realizers and provide a 'safety net' that can, to some extent, ensure that extensions or design cleanups did not introduce a failure in existing functionality. Since the automatic tests do not require manual intervention, they can be run often which ensures that errors are detected early, which makes it easier to fix them.

RealizerTester provides an automatic testing framework for Realizers. We illustrate the use of RealizerTester by describing how it was integrated in the software development process of the Elckerlyc and SmartBody realizers and discuss how it can contribute to the emerging BML standard.

A Behavior Planner communicates with a realizer by sending BML blocks with intended behavior to it and by capturing the feedback provided by the realizer. A BML block defines the form and relative timing (using constraints on its sync points, see also Fig.2) of the behavior that a realizer should display on the embodiment of a virtual human. The realizer is expected to provide the Behavior Planner with feedback on the current state of the BML blocks it is executing: it notifies the Behavior Planner of the start and stop of each BML block (performance start/stop feedback) and on the passing of sync points for each behavior in the block (sync-point progress feedback). Execution failures are sent using warning and exception feedback.

RealizerTester acts as a Behavior Planner: it sends BML blocks to the Realizer Under Test (RUT)[3] and verifies if the feedback received from the RUT satisfies the assertions implied by the BML blocks. This allows automatic testing of the following properties:

1. *Message Flow and Behavior Execution*: RealizerTester can verify if the performance start/stop of each BML block and sync-point progress feedback messages of each behavior was received in the correct order and only once. This implicitly provides some information on whether or not the behaviors were actually executed.
2. *Time Constraint Adherence*: a BML block defines several time constraints upon its behaviors. It can require that a sync point in one behavior occurs simultaneously with a sync point in another behavior, or that a certain sync points should occur before or after another one. These constraints can be tested by inspecting the sync-point progress feedback.

---

[3] After System Under Test used in [7].

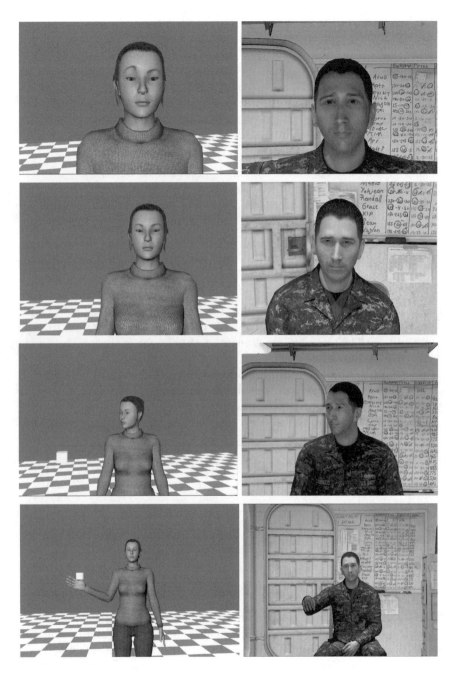

Fig. 1. Execution of some BML behaviors in Elckerlyc (left) and SmartBody(right). From top to bottom: AU 1 (inner eyebrow raise), AU 6 (cheek raiser and lid compressor), gaze, point.

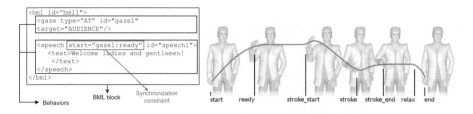

Fig. 2. An example BML script and the sync points of a BML behavior

3. *Error Handling*: The error handling of a realizer can be tested by inspecting its warning and exception feedback. For example, RealizerTester can send BML blocks to the realizer that are invalid or impossible to schedule and then check if the realizer generated the appropriate exception feedback.

4.1 Test Architecture

Each automatic test consists of four phases [7]:

1. *Fixture setup*: The Fixture contains the RUT and everything it depends on to run. During Fixture set up, the RUT is created and put in a state suitable for testing. The necessary functionality to keep track of the feedback sent by the RUT is also hooked up.
2. *Exercise the RUT*: Send BML block(s) to the RUT.
3. *Result verification*: Verify the feedback received from the RUT.
4. *Fixture teardown*: Clean up the fixture.

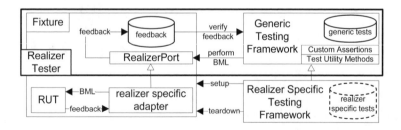

Fig. 3. Testing Architecture

Phase 1 and 4 are realizer specific, phase 2 and 3 are generic. The Generic (realizer independent) Testing Framework contains a set of tests and is responsible for exercising these tests and verifying their results. The Generic Testing Framework exercises the RUT by communicating with it through a RealizerPort. The RealizerPort is a minimal interface for a realizer.

A Realizer Specific Testing Framework is responsible for setting up and tearing down the Fixture before and after each test case. During the setup phase, this framework creates a realizer specific implementation of the RealizerPort and connects it to the RUT. RealizerTester is implemented using the JUnit[4] unit testing framework. Since the Fixture setup and teardown is the same for each test, they are implemented using setup and teardown functions that are called automatically before and after each test respectively.[5] Fig. 3 shows our architecture setup.

4.2   Authoring Test Cases

Test cases are typically set up as follows:

1. Send one or more BML blocks to the RUT, capture all feedback.
2. Wait until the RUT has finished executing all blocks.
3. Verify some assertions on the received feedback.

RealizerTester provides several Test Utility Methods and Custom Assertions [7] to help a test author with this. In the test setup phase, the RUT is coupled to a feedback handler that stores all feedback messages. Most of the Test Utility Methods and Custom Assertions act upon this feedback messages storage. The Custom Assertions in RealizerTester verify various commonly required assertions on the received feedback and provide meaningful error messages if these assertions fail.

Fig. 4 shows an example test case consisting of a BML block (top) and a test function executing the BML block and verifying the assertions implied by the block (bottom). Note that the test case is fully specified using Custom Assertions and Test Utility Methods, which make it very readable.

Many realizers support custom BML behavior elements. Such elements can be tested using test cases in the realizer Specific Framework. The Custom Assertions and Test Utility Methods described above can help in the creation of such test cases.

5   Employing RealizerTester in Elckerlyc

The BML specification is an emerging standard, and at the moment of writing, there are no realizers that fully implement the BML/feedback interface proposed by the SAIBA initiative. Elckerlyc [10] implements several (but not all) BML behaviors and supports BML feedback. This made it a good first test-candidate for RealizerTester. Here we describe our experiences with the integration of Realizer-Tester in Elckerlyc's software development process.

We have implemented an Elckerlyc Specific Testing Framework that sets up a Fixture that uses Elckerlyc as its RUT. Elckerlyc is tested using the 19 test cases provided by RealizerTester. An additional 12 test cases were implemented to test BML behaviors that are specific to Elckerlyc.

---

[4] http://www.junit.org/
[5] Meszaros [7] calls this Implicit Setup and Teardown, functionality for this is available in JUnit.

```
<bml id="bml1">
    <speech id="speech1" start="6">
        <text>Hey punk <sync id="s1" />what do ya want?</text>
    </speech>
    <head id="nod1" action="ROTATION" rotation="X" start="speech1:s1"/>
</bml>

@Test public void testSpeechNodTimedToSync() {
    realizerPort.performBML(readTestFile("testspeech_nodtimedtosync.xml"));
    waitForBMLEndFeedback("bml1");
    assertSyncsInOrder("bml1", "speech1", "start", "ready", "stroke_start",
        "stroke", "s1", "stroke_end", "relax", "end");
    assertAllBMLSyncsInBMLOrder("bml1", "nod1");
    assertBlockStartAndStopFeedbacks("bml1");
    assertRelativeSyncTime("bml1", "speech1", "start", 6);
    assertLinkedSyncs("bml1", "speech1", "s1", "bml1", "nod1", "start");
    assertNoExceptions();
    assertNoWarnings();
}
```

Fig. 4. An example test case. A BML block (top) is sent to a RUT and the test function awaits the end feedback for the block (using the `waitForBMLEndFeedback` Test Utility Method). It then verifies the correctness of the execution using various assertions. The Custom Assertions `assertSyncsInOrder`, `assertAllBMLSyncsInBMLOrder`, and `assertBlockStartAndStopFeedbacks` verify the message flow and behavior execution. They validate respectively that feedback on the syncs points of the `speech1` and `nod1` behavior was received in the correct order, and that the performance start and stop feedback for the block was received once. The BML block specifies that sync point `speech:start` should occur at relative (to the start of the block) time 6, and that sync point `speech1:syncstart1` should occur at the same time as `nod1:start`. The Custom Assertions `assertRelativeSyncTime` and `assertLinkedSyncs` verify these scheduling constraints. Finally, the Custom Assertions `assertNoExceptions` and `assertNoWarnings` verify that the block was executed without failure.

Automatic testing has proven useful in both finding errors in Elckerlyc and making sure that new functionality did not introduce errors. In some cases it was useful to define test cases as acceptance tests for new functionality *before* it was implemented.[6] One such test highlighted deficiencies in Elckerlyc's BML scheduling algorithm. Passing the test (by an update to the scheduling algorithm that fixed these deficiencies) marked the implementation of a certain software requirement.

Automatic testing is more valuable if it is done as often as possible. However, running all test cases on RealizerTester takes some time (roughly 3 minutes on our test set of 31 tests), which might discourage its frequent use by Elckerlyc's

---

[6] This is a common practise in the Test Driven Development software development process [7].

developers. We have solved this issue by running the tests automatically on Elckerlyc's continuous integration server[7] whenever a developer commits changes
to its source repository. If a test fails, the developer responsible for the test failure is automatically notified. The integration server also keeps track of the test
performance over all builds, so it is possible to identify exactly what build introduced an error. RealizerTester helps the Elckerlyc developers in the notification
of errors, but it does not directly help in identifying the exact location of errors,
since it is testing the realizer as a black box. The use of white box testing at
a smaller granularity helps in Elckerlyc's defect localization. To this end, over
1000 unit tests (typically testing one class) and mid-range tests (testing groups
of classes working together) are employed to test Elckerlyc. The unit tests run
fast (in under 10 seconds) so developers run them very often to check the health
of newly created code. The test cases by RealizerTester are used in Elckerlyc to
test how different (unit tested) components work together as a whole, and, if
tests fail, as an indication of locations that require more unit testing.

Automatic testing is useful because it can be done as often as possible without
cost (e.g. in developer/human tester time). However, we have found that manual
inspection is more flexible than the rigid assertion verification employed by automatic tests and that some errors in Elckerlyc can currently only be identified by
manual inspection of the behavior of a virtual human. Therefore we recommend
regular visual inspection in addition to automatic testing.

Most visualization failures that have occurred in Elckerlyc so far are a result of physical simulation errors, resulting in gross movement errors (e.g. the
virtual human falling over, rolling through the scene uncontrollably, showing
large 'hitches' in movement etc.). The occurrence of such failures is often dependent on the specific set of movement combinations and the virtual human
embodiment used. Because of this, there is often a long time span between the
introduction of such failures in the code base and their discovery, which makes
the failures hard to repair. SmartBody's testing framework contributes automatic visual regression testing (discussed in the next section). Integrating such
automatic visual testing in Elckerlyc would be quite helpful to detect these and
other visual regressions in a timely fashion.

6   Testing in SmartBody

SmartBody contributes a test program that provides automatic *visual* regression
testing mentioned above. This test program takes screen snapshots at predefined
moments in an ongoing simulation (e.g. the execution of a BML script). A baseline of such screen snapshots is saved as input for subsequent test simulations.
During a later simulation, another snapshot at the same virtual time in the simulation is taken and then compared pixel by pixel against the baseline image.
If the images differ more than a predefined threshold (see below), then the test
can be marked as failing and examined manually by a tester. To this end, the

---

[7] Elckerlyc uses Jenkins (`http://jenkins-ci.org/`)

test program can provide the tester with an image that shows the baseline image overlayed with the differences from the test snapshot. Fig. 5 shows some examples of such difference images. A similar visual difference regression testing method is used in the graphics industry [11].

By comparing the results of all aspects of the simulation via a graphical image, the tester is better able to determine the impact of various changes to the realizer. When implementing this method, it is important to position the camera where it can detect meaningful differences between the images during a test run. For example, to test head nodding, the camera should be positioned close to and to the side of the virtual human's face. Also, randomness during simulations, such as reliance on real-time clocks, needs to be eliminated in order to generate repeatable results. Different platforms and graphics drivers will also tend to produce similar, but not identical results. This problem can often be mitigated by setting a sufficiently high image comparison threshold. Changes in functionality will often change the results of the test images that are desirable. When this happens, the tester would then create a new set of baseline test images based on the new functionality. Authoring such a graphical test thus involves choosing a certain simulation, defining a set of important times to check for image differences, defining a camera position and setting an image comparison threshold (using the default value often suffices).

SmartBody's test program goes beyond the tests performed by RealizerTester by checking if the correct motion is generated, rather than by checking if the Realizer sends the correct signals. However, unlike RealizerTester, SmartBody's testing system is Realizer specific and limited to provide only regression (and not acceptance) testing functionality. This testing method is thus complementary to testing by RealizerTester.

Therefore, RealizerTester is also used to test SmartBody. To this end, Smart-Body has been extended to allow the feedback messages required by Realizer-Tester, and our (draft 1.0) test scripts have been converted to the Vienna draft BML standard used in SmartBody. Allowing SmartBody to be tested with RealizerTester involved creating a SmartBody Specific Testing Framework and a SmartBody adapter of RealizerPort (see also Section 4.1). This is a relatively simple effort, taking roughly one day of programming. The BML standard only specifies the information that should be contained in the feedback, but does not specify the exact form/syntax of feedback. As a result, much of the implementation effort was spend in parsing SmartBody feedback and converting it to a suitable form for RealizerTester. The process of connecting RealizerTester to a new realizer is similar as connecting any behavior planner to a new realizer. This means that behavior planner developers have to implement error prone and somewhat elaborate feedback parsing for each realizer they connect their behavior planner to. We strongly suggest to incorporate a standard syntax (for example in XML) for feedback in the BML standard to alleviate this issue. By testing SmartBody with RealizerTester, some minor implementation issues in SmartBody were discovered. We did not find any interpretation differences in the constraint satisfaction between SmartBody's and Elckerlyc's realization of

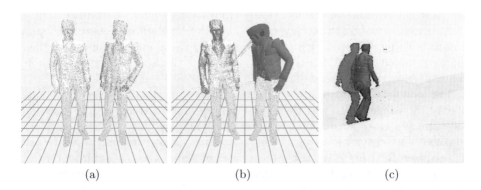

(a)   (b)   (c)

Fig. 5. Fig. 5(a): The simulation run differs from its baseline mostly by subtle differences in the position of the triangular mesh that represents the virtual human's body parts. These differences should not surpass the comparison threshold and should result in a successful test. Fig. 5(b): The character on the right differs from the baseline in the amount of forward lean towards the gaze target. This difference should exceed the comparison threshold and result in a failed test. Fig. 5(c): A test of SmartBody's locomotion system on uneven terrain. The baseline is shown on the right, the results from the new test (with a different parameter configuration for e.g. walking velocity) is shown as a silhouette of the virtual human on the left.

the test scripts. A minor difference in message flow was found. In Elckerlyc, sync-point progress feedback messages are guaranteed to be sent in order (first start, then ready, then stroke_start, then stroke, then stroke_end, then relax, finally end). The performance start messages of a BML block is guaranteed to occur before all sync-point progress feedback messages of the behaviors in the block. The performance stop message of the BML block is guaranteed to occur after all sync-point progress feedback messages are sent. SmartBody does not enforce such a message order; sync-point progress feedback messages and/or performance start/stop feedback messages that occur at the same time are sent in an undefined order.

7   Conclusion and Discussion

We have provided a corpus of BML behaviors and video material of their realization in two realizers and a corpus of BML test cases. We aim to increase the size of these corpora and welcome additions to them, especially from the authors of realizers other than SmartBody and Elckerlyc. The test corpus and the visual comparison movie and script corpus are available online under a creative commons license.[8]

Preliminary inspection of the video corpus shows some expressivity issues in the BML standard, but also shows that several behaviors are executed on the

---

[8] http://sourceforge.net/projects/realizertester/

two different realizers in a semantically equivalent manner. More importantly, the process of creating the corpus created healthy competition between different groups building realizers, each trying to enhance the animation quality of their realizers to out do the other. It also motivated them to move toward more compliance to the BML standard.

The modularity proposed by the SAIBA framework not only allows the reuse of existing realizers with new Behavior Planners, but also reuse of test functionality and test cases for different realizers. The same modularity that allows one to connect a Behavior Planner to any realizer, also allows RealizerTester to test any realizer. RealizerTester and its test cases provides a starting point for a test suite that can test the BML conformance of realizers. Such conformance tests are common for software that interprets XML.[9]

When designing BML test scripts *and* their corresponding test assertions we ran into several cases in which the BML specification lacked detail, was unclear, or was unfinished. For example, the current BML specification does not state whether two posture behaviors (using different body parts) could be active at the same time, if gaze can be a persistent behavior, or how custom sync points in a behavior are to be aligned in relation to its default BML sync points. The process of designing a test set of BML scripts and their corresponding test assertions can significantly contribute to the improvement of the BML standard itself, by highlighting such issues.

Currently each test case consists of an BML script (in a separate XML file) and a test function in RealizerTester. It would be beneficial to merge the test function itself into the BML script, so that new tests can easily be authored without modifying the source code of RealizerTester itself. For many BML scripts (e.g. those that do not deliberately introduce error feedback or change the behavior flow), it should even be possible to automatically generate test assertions directly from the script rather than authoring them by hand.

The BML standard contains several open issues and its interpretation may vary between realizer developers. If adapted by multiple realizers, RealizerTester can contribute to the formalization of the BML standard (by providing BML test scripts and a formal description of their constraints, as expressed in test assertions) and help identify and resolve execution inconsistencies between realizers. A realizer does not need to be fully BML compliant to be tested by RealizerTester; supporting feedback and some BML behaviors is sufficient. We invite the authors and users of realizers to join our realizer testing effort by contributing test cases and hooking up their realizers to RealizerTester.

Acknowledgements. This research has been supported by the GATE project, funded by the Dutch Organization for Scientific Research (NWO).

---

[9] For example, for Collada (`http://www.khronos.org/collada/adopters/`) or XHTML (`http://www.w3.org/MarkUp/Test/`) interpreters.

References

1. Personal communication with the authors of SmartBody, Greta, EMBR, and RealActor (2010)
2. Čereković, A., Pandžić, I.S.: Multimodal behavior realization for embodied conversational agents. In: Multimedia Tools and Applications, pp. 1–22 (2010)
3. Ekman, P., Friesen, W.: Facial Action Coding System: A Technique for the Measurement of Facial Movement. Consulting Psychologists Press, Palo Alto (1978)
4. Heloir, A., Kipp, M.: Real-time animation of interactive agents: Specification and realization. Applied Artificial Intelligence 24(6), 510–529 (2010)
5. Kopp, S., Krenn, B., Marsella, S., Marshall, A.N., Pelachaud, C., Pirker, H., Thórisson, K.R., Vilhjálmsson, H.H.: Towards a common framework for multimodal generation: The behavior markup language. In: Gratch, J., Young, M., Aylett, R.S., Ballin, D., Olivier, P. (eds.) IVA 2006. LNCS (LNAI), vol. 4133, pp. 205–217. Springer, Heidelberg (2006)
6. Mancini, M., Niewiadomski, R., Bevacqua, E., Pelachaud, C.: Greta: a saiba compliant eca system. In: Troisiéme Workshop sur les Agents Conversationnels Animés (2008)
7. Meszaros, G.: xUnit Test Patterns: Refactoring Test Code. Addison-Wesley, Reading (2007)
8. Thiebaux, M., Marshall, A.N., Marsella, S., Kallmann, M.: Smartbody: Behavior realization for embodied conversational agents. In: Autonomous Agents and Multiagent Systems, pp. 151–158 (2008)
9. Vilhjálmsson, H.H., Cantelmo, N., Cassell, J., E. Chafai, N., Kipp, M., Kopp, S., Mancini, M., Marsella, S.C., Marshall, A.N., Pelachaud, C., Ruttkay, Z., Thórisson, K.R., van Welbergen, H., van der Werf, R.J.: The behavior markup language: Recent developments and challenges. In: Pelachaud, C., Martin, J.-C., André, E., Chollet, G., Karpouzis, K., Pelé, D. (eds.) IVA 2007. LNCS (LNAI), vol. 4722, pp. 99–111. Springer, Heidelberg (2007)
10. van Welbergen, H., Reidsma, D., Ruttkay, Z.M., Zwiers, J.: Elckerlyc: A BML realizer for continuous, multimodal interaction with a virtual human. Journal on Multimodal User Interfaces 3(4), 271–284 (2010)
11. Yee, Y.H., Newman, A.: A perceptual metric for production testing. In: ACM SIGGRAPH Sketches, p. 121. ACM, New York (2004)

Robots Meet IVAs: A Mind-Body Interface for Migrating Artificial Intelligent Agents

Michael Kriegel[1], Ruth Aylett[1], Pedro Cuba[2], Marco Vala[2], and Ana Paiva[2]

[1] School Of Mathematical and Computer Sciences
Heriot-Watt University,
EH14 4AS, Edinburgh, Scotland, UK
{michael,ruth}@macs.hw.ac.uk
[2] INESC-ID and IST/UTL
Av. Prof. Cavaco Silva - Taguspark, 2744-016 Porto Salvo, Portugal
pedro.cuba@gaips.inesc-id.pt, {marco.vala,ana.paiva}@inesc-id.pt

Abstract. We describe CMION, an open source architecture for coordinating the various sensors and effectors of an artificial intelligent agent with its mind, i.e. the high level decision making processes. The architecture was designed to work for virtual graphical agents, including those on mobile devices, as well as robots. Its built-in migration feature allows a character to move between these differing embodiments, inhabiting them in turn. We emphasize the importance of modularity for an architecture supporting migration and highlight design decisions promoting modularity in CMION. An applied example of the architecture's use in a migration situation is given.

1 Introduction

Autonomous robots have been researched since the 1970s, but for a long time a functional task-oriented perspective dominated work. Much more recently [11] work has been carried out into social robotics in which the integration of robots into human social environments is the guiding focus. In contrast, work on intelligent graphical agents began much later [3] but interaction with human users has been researched almost from the start, with the development of Embodied Conversational Agents [4] or ECAs.

The LIREC project[1] (Living with Robots and intEractive Characters) is a project investigating long-term interaction that brings these two perspectives together. Its programme combines the development of an innovative technological infrastructure and scientifically-constructed user studies in an attempt to move beyond the novelty effect of both social robots and ECAs to social companions that can play an acceptable long-term role. Both social robots and ECAs are embodied, the former physically and the later virtually. Physical embodiment raises still unsolved engineering problems of power sources, mobility and localization that typically limit the ability of robots to accompany humans as they

---

[1] http://lirec.eu

H. Högni Vilhjálmsson et al. (Eds.): IVA 2011, LNAI 6895, pp. 282–295, 2011.

move from one social environment to another - for example from home to work. Virtual embodiments are much more transportable but by their nature do not support physical task execution (fetch and carry for example).

For this reason, LIREC investigates migration, the ability of a synthetic companion to move from one embodiment to another. This of course raises a new set of research questions, of which the most important is: what exactly migrates? We define this as the companion's identity, by which we mean those features that persist and make it unique and recognizable from the user's perspective.

These features, themselves a research topic [20], may include common attributes of the different embodiments, for example similar facial appearance, but also common aspects of interactional behaviour, such as emotional expressiveness, and a memory of events and interactions that have taken place in multiple embodiments.

The question of what migrates also requires a technological answer. In this paper we consider the impact of migration on the architecture of such a companion. It is clear that a degree of architectural commonality across embodiment platforms is required if migration is to be a generic capability of LIREC companions. Companions may run on a number of different robots, on handheld devices, and fixed graphics installations. Creating a common architectural framework is in our view an innovative enterprise given that most researchers in robotics and ECAs have so far been involved in separate explorations of architectures.

2   An Architecture for Migrating Companions

In this section we first explain our requirements for a social companion's architecture, then extend on those requirements for the specific case of migrating companions and then compare our requirements with related work.

2.1   Basic Requirements

In the context of this paper the term architecture refers to a mind-body interface, i. e. a software framework that links the companion's *mind* (high level deliberative processes working with symbolic representations of the world) with it's *body* (a collection of sensors and actuators for the physical or virtual world).

The most important task of a mind-body architecture is thus the provision of a framework for the bidirectional mapping of information to different levels of abstraction, from raw sensory data to symbolic data and vice versa. For example images from a camera could be mapped by image processing and affect recognition algorithms into symbolic descriptions of what the companion is seeing, e.g. whether a user is present and what affective state the user is currently displaying. The mind processes this information, deliberates and acts upon it, for example it might decide to cheer the user up if they are sad. The architecture then needs to map the symbolic action of cheering up to actual actuator values.

One can identify three layers in such systems where layer 3 is the mind, layer 2 the mind-body interface and layer 1 the body consisting of sensors and effectors. This concept of decomposing an embodied agent into three layers is very common and can be found in the majority of robotics control architectures [13]. Conceptually the same distinction of 3 layers can also be found in the more recent and ongoing efforts of the ECA community to create a common framework for multimodal generation named SAIBA [15]. In the SAIBA context the 3 layers are called Intent Planning, Behaviour Planning and Behaviour Realization.

In three layer architectures typically control of the behaviour of the agent does not exclusively reside on the highest level. Instead the more common and flexible approach is to grant each layer some autonomy. In the case of a robot that means for example that time-critical control loops for processes like obstacle avoidance reside at the lowest level, with the involved perception data never having to travel up to the 2 higher layers. A process taken care of by the middle layer could be for example navigation (path-finding), while the top layer deals with high level task-driven behaviour.

2.2 Additional Requirements for Migrating Companions

Sufficient Level of Abstraction. The separation of mind and body discussed above fits neatly with the concept of migration, which requires a companion's mind to leave one embodiment and enter another one, a process undeniably made easier if mind and body are clearly separated. A mind-body interface for migration that is installed on a certain embodiment must therefore support the dynamic exchange of the mind (layer 3) component.

Once a mind enters a new body it needs to know how to deal with this new body's functions. The mind deals with abstract descriptions of behaviour while the mind-body interface needs to translate them into concrete embodied behaviour that suits the embodiment. For example the mind might simply want to move to a certain destination, but the mode of getting there could be very different depending on the embodiment (e.g. flying, swimming, driving, walking).

Modularity. When designing a scenario involving a companion migrating across multiple embodiments it is of great importance for us to minimize the development effort, especially when some embodiments have things in common. This underlines the need for a highly modular mind-body interface that promotes reusability of components.

Flexible Definition of Identity. We defined migration earlier as a transfer of the companion's identity to a different embodiment and described how this could be achieved by exchanging the companion's mind. While a majority of the identity resides within the mind (e.g. memory, personality, goals, etc) this is clearly not all there is to identity.

There are lower level features that form part of an agent's identity as well that would also be desirable to migrate if they can be used in the new embodiment and the architecture should allow for this. For example, the voice of a companion could be argued to form an important part of its identity. Unless the companion migrates into an embodiment that does not support the use of voices (e.g. a dog robot that can only bark) it would be desirable to migrate the voice in one form or another.

Multiple Platforms. Finally, as mentioned in the introduction to this paper, the LIREC project uses a variety of different companion embodiments, from various mobile and static robots to ECAs and companions on mobile devices. An architecture for LIREC must therefore run on all of these platforms sufficiently well, which is of increased interest on mobiles with limited memory and computing power and on robots that require fast response times for tasks like navigating safely in the physical world.

2.3 Related Work

When examining existing architectures we found most of them not to be generic enough for our purposes and either geared towards robotics (e.g. [2], [12]) or behaviour realization for virtual agents (e.g. [5], [8], [21]). The same applies for the work of Cavazza and colleagues in the COMPANIONS project [6], which shares the exploration of long-term relationships with interactive companions with LIREC, but focuses much more on natural language interaction with ECAs and less on robots. While [17] presents an architecture that was tested with both ECAs and robotic heads, its focus is also on natural language interaction and issues relating to robot bodies that move in and manipulate the physical world are not addressed by it.

Some groups have explored the idea of migration before (e.g. [14], [18]) but the development of a reusable generic architecture seems not to have been the focus in these works. This is not the case of the agent chameleon project which has published details about their architecture for migrating agents [19]. However, rather than a mind-body interface, the agent chameleon architecture is a complete architecture including the deliberative layer. This made it not suitable as an architecture for the LIREC project which employs its own agent mind and implements memory and theory of mind mechanisms within it.

Not so much complete architectures, but nevertheless widely used and promoting our requirement of modularity, are middlewares such as YARP [10] and Player [7] which are both popular in the robotics field and Psyclone [1], which has been applied in the field of ECAs before. In order to not reinvent the wheel we have based our architecture as described in the next section on such a piece of middleware, the agent simulation framework ION [22] and derived from it the name CMION (Competency Management with ION).

3   Technical Overview

The CMION architecture designed for the migrating companions of the LIREC project was written in Java and uses only those features of the Java API that are also supported by the Android mobile OS, making it compatible besides PCs with a wide range of mobile devices. Figure 1 gives a simplified overview of the components in CMION.

Functionalities of an embodiment are encapsulated inside constructs called competencies, which can be thought of as miniature programs that each run in a separate thread and that are directly linked to the sensors and actuators of the embodiment. Competencies can exchange information with each other by writing information onto the blackboard component, which is a hierarchical data storage container, which can contain properties (named data storage slots) and sub containers, which can again contain properties and sub containers. The world model component is another data storage container, whose content is organized in the same way, but in contrast to the blackboard it constitutes an external representation of the knowledge base that the agent mind operates on. Competencies can make changes to the world model which are then propagated to the agent mind and treated as perceptions.

If the agent mind decides to act, the competency manager component maps the action to a predefined competency execution plan consisting of a number of competencies that realize the requested action in the embodiment. The plan also contains specific running parameters for each competency involved and synchronization information regarding the running order and concurrency of the competencies. The structure and information content of a competency execution plan can be roughly compared to behaviours annotated in BML [15]. The competency execution system finally schedules the execution plan by invoking, starting and monitoring the competencies involved in the plan at the right time and with the parameters specified by the plan. Instead of being invoked through the execution system, certain competencies, especially those involved with sensing, can instead also be started immediately when the architecture is loaded and run continuously in the background.

3.1   Communication

By basing the CMION architecture on the ION framework middleware [22] we increased performance, efficiency and modularity. The ION framework was originally designed as a multi-agent simulation environment for virtual worlds that allows to model and simulate the world state of the environment independently

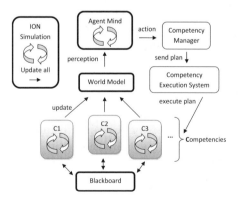

Fig. 1. CMION Architecture Overview

of the realization engine. Based on the observer design pattern it provides a request/event communication model that is synched with a simulation loop. In the case of CMION, every component, i.e. every box in Figure 1 (e.g. the world model, blackboard, agent mind, every competency, etc.) is an ION entity that can raise events, receive requests and register request or event handlers.

The difference between requests and events is subtle: while events are used to broadcast information, requests are directed towards a single entity and the scheduling entity has no guarantee that the receiving entity will actually carry out the request. For this reason it is a good practice for entities to inform others about the result of carrying out requests by using events. Moreover, scheduling entities should not assume success until the respective event is raised. While events are handled one by one, the simulation collects all requests that are scheduled with a certain entity within one update and the request handler processes them all together in a single call. This allows the mediation of conflicts when 2 or more contradicting requests are scheduled within the same update, e.g. when two competencies attempt to write different data onto the same property on the blackboard. All arrows in Figure 1 thus are either ION requests or events. This allows efficient and conflict-free communication between all the components, which is especially important for the competencies and the agent mind which run asynchronously in their own threads.

3.2   Modularity

Modularity is promoted in several ways by CMION. Through the type of inter-component communication provided by the ION framework it becomes very easy to add additional components to the architecture without making any changes to the existing code. Cases where this becomes useful include monitoring and debugging tools that can simply listen to certain events or schedule certain requests. CMION additionally supports this by dynamically loading components specified in an xml file at startup. This means additional components can be developed without recompilation of the architecture. The same also applies to competencies: they are separately compiled from the main architecture, specified in an xml file (the competency library) and dynamically loaded at startup. This allows sharing, adding and swapping competencies. The rules that map actions from the mind to competency execution plans are similarly defined via xml and loaded when the architecture is started.

Modularity is also achieved through object oriented design. Besides the abstract base classes for competencies and the agent mind, we also provide further specialised base classes that allow the remote connection of an agent mind or competency through a tcp socket or the middlewares YARP [10], Psyclone [1] and SAMGAR [9]. Besides greater modularity in the case of robotic embodiments remote connecting a competency can also make sense in order to have the implementation in a language different from Java, possibly resulting in increased performance and reduced reaction time for time critical processes.

4   Migration

Now that we have given an overview of CMION we can proceed in describing how the process of migration works. For migration to be possible several instances of CMION running on several embodiments are needed. Each instance will likely contain a slightly different set of competencies and library of competency execution plans that reflect the abilities of its embodiment. Initially when each CMION instance is started up, its embodiment can either be inhabited or uninhabited.

Inhabited embodiments are considered "'alive"' while uninhabited embodiments are initially empty vessels waiting to be inhabited through a migration. How the agent mind should be initialized for inhabited and uninhabited embodiments respectively depends on the concrete implementation of the agent mind. However it is advisable to design the agent mind so that data and processes are separated. This is the case with our LIREC agent mind, so that when initializing an inhabited embodiment the agent mind data needs to be specified (planning data, personality, previous memory, etc.) whereas it can be left empty when initializing an uninhabited embodiment.

4.1   Outgoing Migration

Migration is implemented as an actuating competency and thus can be initiated by the agent mind like other competencies. How the mind decides to migrate is dependent on the concrete mind implementation and world modelling. It is relatively straightforward to integrate migration into the decision making process of an agent mind. The approach we take in companions developed for LIREC, where we use an agent mind based on a continuous planner, is to model migration as a planning operator that changes certain properties related to embodiment and location. The agent mind will then automatically include migration actions into its plans whenever the current task requires it. Conceptually performing a migration is not supposed to alter an agent's emotional state or personality unless one would conceive a scenario where migrating for some reason is a painful or joyful experience for the agent. Either way for the implementation of migration in CMION this is of no concern as this issue is again dependent on the implementation and configuration of the agent mind used.

When the migration competency in CMION is executed it first looks up the network address of the target embodiment. A network connection is established and if the target embodiment is already inhabited, the migration will obviously fail. Otherwise, the migration competency will raise an ION event stating that a migration is about to occur. It will then wait for one ION simulation update, a time frame during which any component (competencies, agent mind, etc.) in its event handler to the migration event can append data in XML format to migrate to the migration competency. Whether components provide this handler and what data they append depends entirely on their developer and what part of the state of the component is related to the agent's identity.

For companions developed in LIREC we typically append data describing the entire state of the agent mind and the partial state of a few but not most competencies. Since the ION event handlers are processed within the ION simulation thread there is no need to worry that the data might be appended too late and miss the migration. However, there are cases where one might want to gather the data asynchronously, for example because it is expected to take a while and the ION simulation should not stall during this time. For events like this the component can request a migration wait and resolve it later once it has finished gathering data. The migration competency keeps track of all waits requested and will only proceed once all of them have been resolved. It will then package all appended data into one XML document and transfer it to the target embodiment. If the transfer was acknowledged by the receiver as successful the sending embodiment is marked as uninhabited. An agent mind should (as the LIREC agent mind does) handle a successful outgoing migration event and go into a sleeping state.

4.2   Incoming Migration

On the incoming embodiment an event is broadcast that a migration has occurred. Every component that has registered a handler for this event will be able to query whether the received migration XML document contains a section marked as belonging to this component and, if this is the case, receive and parse the data. The embodiment is then marked as inhabited and the previously sleeping agent mind is woken up. It now contains the personality, memory, knowledge base, action repertoire, goals, etc. that previously resided in the source embodiment. This could however present a problem as parts of the knowledge base are a symbolic description of the environment in which the agent is embodied and might be wrong in the new embodiment. For this reason, immediately after loading the migrated state an agent mind should query the world model in the new embodiment, which contains a symbolic description of the new environment and replace the section of its knowledge base containing embodiment specific knowledge with the world model contents.

5   Example Scenario

We now provide a description of a real migration scenario to illustrate the functionality of the CMION architecture. The example is taken from the Spirit Of the Building scenario (see Figure 2), one of the actual companion scenarios developed in LIREC. In this scenario a group of researchers share their office with a robotic companion that assists the team in certain daily tasks. When one day they expect a visitor but are uncertain of his time of arrival they ask their companion to migrate to the screen installed at the building entrance and to wait there for the visitor and greet him. This scenario could continue with the agent migrating to the visitor's phone to guiding him to his destination and then finally migrating back into the robot embodiment. We will only focus on the first migration here.

Fig. 2. The robot and virtual character embodiment of the Spirit Of the Building companion showcase, that the example scenario is derived from

5.1 Technical Realization

Figure 3 shows the state of the 2 embodiments in the example before the task to greet the guest has been activated. The robot embodiment (A) is inhabited and has an active agent mind containing data, while the ECA (B) is uninhabited with an empty inactive mind. Both embodiments have a different set of competencies but share certain of them. Similarly both embodiments have some differences in their execution plans. While the robotic embodiment A can move in physical space, B can't so the way they realize a speech act differs. In both cases the plan specifies the execution of the language generation competency that translates a speech act symbol into an actual utterance followed by a parallel execution of speech synthesis and animation competency to achieve lip synch[2]. In embodiment A however, additionally the robot first needs to move within an acceptable communication distance using the Navigation competency, which can be executed in parallel with the language generation.

The steps that initiate the migration in the robot embodiment would now involve the following:

- The command input competency detects a user's command to greet a guest and passing it to the agent mind via the world model.
- This activates the GreetUser goal in the agent mind.
- The planner in the agent mind knows that a pre-condition for waiting for the user is being embodied in the reception ECA and it also knows that a migration action can change the embodiment.

---

[2] The speech synthesis and animation competencies exchange synchronization data via the black board.

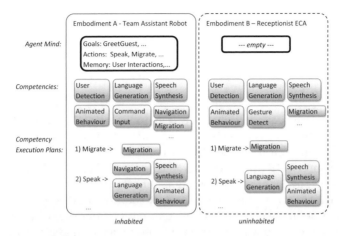

Fig. 3. Initial state of the embodiments

- The agent mind thus sends a migration action with the reception ECA as a target for execution.
- This is mapped by the competency manager to the competency execution plan 1, which passed on to the competency execution system invokes the migration competency.

The migration competency as described before raises an event that a migration is about to occur. The agent mind and some of the competencies append data as shown in Figure 4.

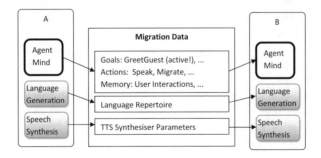

Fig. 4. The data that is being migrated

After the migration, A is uninhabited and B is inhabited. The agent mind's plan to greet the user resumes now on B with the agent waiting. The User Detection competency notifies the agent mind via the world model, when a user has approached the screen. The agent will then ask the user whether they are the expected guest (Speak action). Via the Gesture Detect competency a yes/no answer to this question is obtained. If the answer is yes the scenario then might proceed as outlined earlier.

6   Conclusion

In this paper we have described CMION, a novel architecture that provides a mind-body interface for embodied (robotic or virtual) agents with specific support for migration between different embodiments.

While we motivated migration as a generic method of overcoming the different limitations of physical and virtual embodiments, the scenario discussed above makes it clear that migration is not the only solution. In this scenario, the receptionist could be implemented as a different entity from the team assistant with the two agents communicating rather than one agent migrating. Alternatively, the same agent could have multiple embodiments in several places at once.

The multiple agents solution is not at some implementation level so different from our style of migration. In both cases, there is a transmission of a task, of knowledge, and interaction preferences. However this ducks the issue of agent identity and its realisation. We see maintaining the identity of an agent for the user as a basis for a long-term companion relationship, and argue that this requires more than presenting a similar face and voice (subject to the constraints of the embodiment). Identity involves consistent patterns of behaviour and affect over time, interpretable as personality, and a long-term shared frame of reference that is implemented in our level 3 agent mind as a human-like memory model [16]. The parametrisation of level 3 already referred to allows the dynamic affective state of the agent to be migrated. Work is also being carried out in migrating the agent episodic memory, which given its use of spreading activation across a network of episodes is far from a flat database from which items can be taken and reinserted without altering others in the process. In the future we are planning some long term user evaluation of our companion systems to gain further insight into the users' perception of a companion's identity and its retention after the migration process.

There are both implementational and interactional arguments against an agent with multiple embodiments. Maintaining the consistency of a memory of the type just mentioned would be very challenging. Interactionally, imagine a second research group in the same building with their own companion agent with a distinct personality adapted to that group's preferences. What if on other days this second companion might want to inhabit the reception screen. In order for this to work the screen would need to be vacated if it is not used. One could again counter this argument with an alternative design in which both research groups are actually dealing with the same companion, an omnipresent AI that can interact with both groups simultaneously and in those interactions behave differently for both groups adapting to their preferences. This is reminiscent of many AIs of buildings or spaceships, etc. encountered in Science Fiction but we think realistically this approach has limits in terms of the size such an omnipresent AI could grow to. More than anything else we use migration because it is transparent and easily understood by users and helps them to think of the companion as a social entity rather than just a computer program.

The CMION architecture has been and is being successfully applied in the construction of several migrating social companions in the LIREC project. It is a basis for much longer-term experiments than have typically been carried out with embodied agents. Through this direct link to a wide variety of applications we could establish an iterative development loop where feedback from companion development feeds directly into improvements of CMION.

There are many directions into which this work can be taken further. One could for example add authorization mechanisms that verify whether a companion is allowed to migrate into a certain embodiment. For companions that often move between a number of embodiments one could add a caching mechanism to reduce the amount of data required to transmit. We already commented on the parallels between CMION and the SAIBA framework, but making the architecture fully SAIBA compliant could be a further worthwhile endeavour. By releasing CMION as open source we provide a basis for further research into migrating companions and hope that others will find in it a modular and useful framework to advance the state of migrating companions. The code and documentation for CMION can be found at *http://trac.lirec.org/wiki/SoftwareReleases*.

Acknowledgements. This work was partially supported by the European Commission (EC) and is currently funded by the EU FP7 ICT-215554 project LIREC (Living with Robots and Interactive Companions). The authors are solely responsible for the content of this publication. It does not represent the opinion of the EC, and the EC is not responsible for any use that might be made of data appearing therein.

References

[1] Mindmakers - project psyclone, http://www.mindmakers.org/projects/Psyclone

[2] Albus, J.S., Lumia, R., Fiala, J., Wavering, A.: NASA/NBS standard reference model for telerobot control system architecture (Nasrem). Technical Report 1235, Natl. Inst. Standards and Technology, Gaithersburg, Md (1989)

[3] Aylett, R., Luck, M.: Applying artificial intelligence to virtual reality: Intelligent virtual environments. Applied Artificial Intelligence 14, 3–32 (2000)

[4] Cassell, J., Bickmore, T., Billinghurst, M., Campbell, L., Chang, K., Vilhjálmsson, H., Yan, H.: Embodiment in conversational interfaces: Rea. In: Proceedings of the SIGCHI conference on Human Factors in Computing Systems: the CHI is the Limit, pp. 520–527 (1999), ACM ID: 303150

[5] Cassell, J., Vilhjálmsson, H.H., Bickmore, T.: BEAT: the behavior expression animation toolkit. In: Proceedings of the 28th Annual Conference on Computer Graphics and Interactive Techniques, SIGGRAPH 2001, pp. 477–486 (2001), ACM ID: 383315

[6] Cavazza, M., de la Camara, R.S., Turunen, M.: How was your day?: a companion ECA. In: Proceedings of the 9th International Conference on Autonomous Agents and Multiagent Systems, AAMAS 2010, International Foundation for Autonomous Agents and Multiagent Systems, Toronto, Canada, vol. 1, pp. 1629–1630 (2010), ACM ID: 1838515

[7] Collett, T.H.J., Macdonald, B.A.: Player 2.0: Toward a practical robot programming framework. In: Proc. of the Australasian Conference on Robotics and Automation (ACRA) (2005)

[8] De Carolis, B., Pelachaud, C., Poggi, I., de Rosis, F.: Behavior planning for a reflexive agent. In: Proceedings of the 17th international joint conference on Artificial intelligence, vol. 2, pp. 1059–1064 (2001), ACM ID: 1642236

[9] Du Casse, K., Koay, K.L., Ho, W.C., Dautenhahn, K.: Reducing the cost of robotics software: SAMGAR, a generic modular robotic software communication architecture. In: Int. Conf. on Advanced Robotics 2009, ICAR 2009, pp. 1–6. IEEE, Los Alamitos (2009)

[10] Fitzpatrick, P., Metta, G., Natale, L.: Towards long-lived robot genes. Robot. Auton. Syst. 56(1), 29–45 (2008)

[11] Fong, T., Nourbakhsh, I., Dautenhahn, K.: A survey of socially interactive robots: Concepts, design, and applications. Robotics and Autonomous Systems 42(3-4), 142–166 (2002)

[12] Fritsch, J., Kleinehagenbrock, M., Haasch, A., Wrede, S., Sagerer, G.: A flexible infrastructure for the development of a robot companion with extensible HRI-Capabilities. In: Proceedings of the 2005 IEEE International Conference on Robotics and Automation, ICRA 2005, pp. 3408–3414 (2005)

[13] Gat, E.: On Three-Layer architectures. Artificial Intelligence and Mobile Robots (1998)

[14] Imai, M., Ono, T., Etani, T.: Agent migration: communications between a human and robot. In: IEEE International Conference on System, Man, and Cybernetics (SMC 1999), vol. 4, pp. 1044–1048 (1999)

[15] Kopp, S., Krenn, B., Marsella, S.C., Marshall, A.N., Pelachaud, C., Pirker, H., Thórisson, K.R., Vilhjálmsson, H.H.: Towards a common framework for multimodal generation: The behavior markup language. In: Gratch, J., Young, M., Aylett, R.S., Ballin, D., Olivier, P. (eds.) IVA 2006. LNCS (LNAI), vol. 4133, pp. 205–217. Springer, Heidelberg (2006)

[16] Lim, M.Y., Aylett, R., Ho, W.C., Enz, S., Vargas, P.: A Socially-Aware memory for companion agents. In: Proceedings of the 9th International Conference on Intelligent Virtual Agents, pp. 20–26 (2009), ACM ID: 1612564

[17] Magnenat-Thalmann, N., Kasap, Z., Moussa, M.B.: Communicating with a virtual human or a skin-based robot head. In: ACM SIGGRAPH ASIA 2008 Courses, SIGGRAPH Asia 2008, pp. 55:1–55:7. ACM, Singapore (2008), ACM ID: 1508099

[18] Ogawa, K., Ono, T.: Ubiquitous cognition: mobile environment achieved by migratable agent. In: Proceedings of the 7th international Conference on Human Computer Interaction with Mobile Devices & Services, pp. 337–338 (2005), ACM ID: 1085854

[19] O'Hare, G.M.P., Duffy, B.R., Schön, B., Martin, A.N., Bradley, J.F.: Agent chameleons: Virtual agents real intelligence. In: Rist, T., Aylett, R.S., Ballin, D., Rickel, J. (eds.) IVA 2003. LNCS (LNAI), vol. 2792, pp. 218–225. Springer, Heidelberg (2003)

[20] Syrdal, D.S., Koay, K.L., Walters, M.L., Dautenhahn, K.: The boy-robot should bark!–Children's impressions of agent migration into diverse embodiments. In: Proceedings: New Frontiers of Human-Robot Interaction, a Symposium at AISB (2009)

[21] Thiebaux, M., Marsella, S., Marshall, A.N., Kallmann, M.: Smartbody: Behavior realization for embodied conversational agents. In: Proceedings of the 7th International Joint Conference on Autonomous Agents and Multiagent Systems, vol. 1, pp. 151–158 (2008)

[22] Vala, M., Raimundo, G., Sequeira, P., Cuba, P., Prada, R., Martinho, C., Paiva, A.: ION framework — a simulation environment for worlds with virtual agents. In: Proceedings of the 9th International Conference on Intelligent Virtual Agents, pp. 418–424. Springer, Amsterdam (2009)

Multimodal Plan Representation for Adaptable BML Scheduling

Dennis Reidsma, Herwin van Welbergen, and Job Zwiers

Human Media Interaction, University of Twente
{h.vanwelbergen,d.reidsma,j.zwiers}@utwente.nl

Abstract. In this paper we show how behavior scheduling for Virtual Humans can be viewed as a constraint optimization problem, and how Elckerlyc uses this view to maintain a extensible behavior plan representation that allows one to make micro-adjustments to behaviors while keeping constraints between them intact. These capabilities make it possible to implement tight mutual behavior coordination between a Virtual Human and a user, without requiring to re-schedule every time an adjustment needs to be made.

This paper describes a novel intermediate plan represention for the multimodal behavior of a Virtual Human (VH). A VH displays the verbal and nonverbal behavior that has been specified by higher level communicative intent and behavior planning processes in the context of a dialog or other interaction. Our aim is to achieve capabilities for human-like interpersonal coordination. For this, we need to be able to make on-the-fly adjustments to the behavior being displayed [7,9]. Goodwin describes an example of such adjustments: when a listener utters an *assesment* feedback, the speaker, upon recognizing this, will slightly delay subsequent speech (e.g. by an inhalation or production of a filler) until the listener has completed his assessment [3]. As another example, when a virtual sports coach is performing an exercise along with the user, it needs to continually update the exact timing with which it performs the movements in order to stay synchronized with the user. We have designed our flexible multimodal plan representation specifically for enabling these, and other, on-the-fly adjustments.

The behavior plan representation forms an intermediate level between the scheduling of specified behavior and the surface realization on the embodiment of the VH. The behavior is specified using the Behavior Markup Language (BML) [8], defining the form of the behavior and the constraints on its timing (see Fig. 1). A BML Realizer is responsible for executing the behaviors in such a way that the time constraints specified in the BML blocks are satisfied. Realizer implementations typically handle this by separating the BML scheduling process from the playback process (see also [5]). The scheduling process converts the BML blocks to a multimodal behavior plan that can be directly displayed by the playback process on the embodiment of the VH (see Fig. 2). The flexibility of our plan representation, used in our BML realizer Elckerlyc [13] makes it possible to make on-the-fly adjustments to the plan, during playback, while keeping the constraints on the behaviors intact.

H. Högni Vilhjálmsson et al. (Eds.): IVA 2011, LNAI 6895, pp. 296–308, 2011.

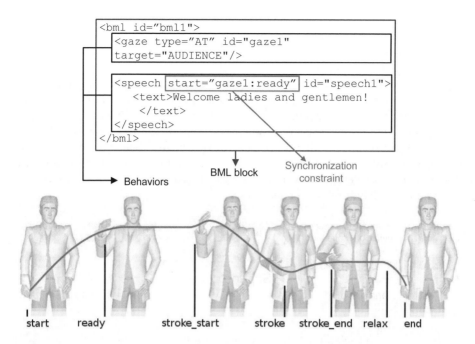

Fig. 1. An example BML script, and the standard phases of a BML behavior; lowermost picture from `http://wiki.mindmakers.org/projects:bml:main`

Our approach requires that we view the scheduling as a constraint optimization problem. Therefore, we will start the paper with an explanation of scheduling in these terms. Both standard constraint optimization techniques and custom BML scheduling algorithms haven been used to solve it. In most BML Realizers scheduling the stream of BML blocks results in a *rigid* multimodal realization plan. Once scheduled, the plan cannot be modified very well – at best, a Realizer allows one to drop (a subset of) the current plan and replace it with a new plan. The more flexible plan representation used in Elckerlyc allows use to interrupt behaviors, change the timing of synchronisation points, add additional behaviors, and change the parameterization of behaviors on-the-fly while keeping the constraints intact. This makes it eminently suitable for VH applications in which a tight mutual coordination between user and VH is required.

1   BML Scheduling as a Constraint Problem

Fig. 2 shows how the scheduling process creates and maintains the intermediate multimodal behavior plan that will be displayed on the VH's embodiment at playback time. A new BML block $u \in \mathbf{u}$ (the collection of all blocks) is sent to the scheduler at time ct (indicated by the vertical white bar). The block u specifies new behaviors $\mathbf{b}$ with sync points $\mathbf{s}$ (such as start, stroke, or end) and their alignment. The scheduling process of a Realizer updates the current multimodal behavior plan on the basis of u. The behaviors are added to the plan subject to a set of timing constraints **c**. Firstly, there are the constraints that are explicitly defined in the BML block specification. Secondly, there are certain implicit constraints that hold for any BML block (e.g., behaviors should start before they end). Thirdly, a specific Realizer can impose additional constraints upon the scheduling, for example motivated by biological capabilities of humans. Finally, Block Level Constraints, as specified by the scheduling attribute in the BML block, define the relation between the start of the to-be-scheduled BML block and the behaviors already present in the current behavior plan (see the difference between the two examples in Fig. 2). The four types of constraints are described in more detail below; due to a lack of space, we refer the reader to [12] for the formal definitions and equations.

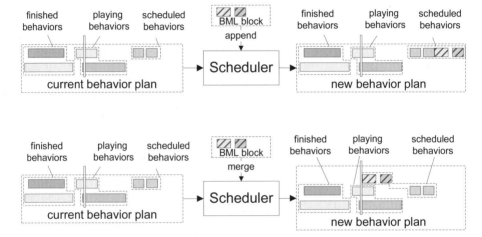

Fig. 2. The scheduling process. The white bar indicates the current time. The new BML block defines how the currently playing and planned behaviors are updated and which new behaviors are inserted, using a scheduling attribute. `append` (top) indicates that the behaviors in the BML block are to be inserted after all behaviors in the current plan. `merge` (bottom) specifies that the behaviors in the BML block are to be started at the current time.

A scheduling function $f : \mathbf{s} \rightarrow \mathbf{t}$ maps sync points s to global time t. The function *blockstart* $: \mathbf{u} \rightarrow \mathbf{t}$ maps blocks u to their global start time t. The goal of scheduling is to find a mapping **f** for all sync points in all behaviors in the block and to determine the start time of the block, in such a way that all constraints are satisfied. Furthermore, a Realizer may specify an additional cost function to select the 'best' solution from the possible solutions, e.g. in terms of amount of stretching of animations, acceleration of body parts, etcetera.

1.1   Explicit Constraints

Explicit time constraints are specified in the BML expression, as a relation between *sync references*. A sync reference consists of either a time value in seconds, denoting an offset from the start of the BML block, or a sync point of one of the behaviors (possibly with an offset). For example, the behavior definition <gaze id="g1" ready="beh1:start+1"> in BML block $bml1$ defines a constraint between the sync refs $[bml1 : g1 : ready + 0]$ and $[bml1 : beh1 : start + 1]$.

A time constraint expresses a time relation between two or more sync references. BML defines two types of time relations:

- *before/after*: sync ref a occurs before (or after) sync ref b.
- *at*: sync refs a and b occur at the same time.

1.2   Implicit Constraints

Apart from the explicit constraints defined in the BML block, several implicit constraints act upon f:

1. Sync points may not occur before the block in which they occur is started.
2. Behaviors should have a nonzero duration.
3. The default BML sync points of each behavior (start, ready, stroke_start, stroke, stroke_end, relax, end) must stay in that order.

1.3   Realizer Specific Constraints

Realizers might impose additional constraints, that are typically behavior specific. They may, for example, be due to a technical limitation. Most Text-To-Speech systems do not allow one to make detailed changes to the timing of the generated speech. Therefore, Realizers typically forbid scheduling solutions that require the stretching of speech behaviors beyond the default timing provided by the TTS system. Constraints may also be theoretically motivated. A Realizer might, e.g., forbid solutions that require a VH to gesture at speeds beyond its physical ability.

1.4   Block Level Constraints

The scheduling attribute associated with a BML Block (see also Fig. 2) defines constraints on the start of the block in relation to the set of current behaviors in the block and the current global time ct. BML defines the following scheduling attributes:

1. merge: start the block at ct.
2. replace: remove all behaviors from the current plan, start the block at ct.
3. append: start the block as soon as possible after all behaviors in the current plan have finished (but not earlier than ct).

2   Existing BML Scheduling Solutions

In this section we describe the scheduling solutions implemented in the BML Realizers SmartBody and EMBR. Both Realizers implement an additional constraint that is not (yet) officially defined in the BML standard: each behavior, and each block, are supposed to start as early as possible, as long as they satisfy all other constraints.

2.1   SmartBody Scheduling

SmartBody's [11] scheduling algorithm assigns an absolute timing for sync points in each behavior by processing behaviors in the order in which they occur within a BML block. Each behavior is scheduled to adhere to its BML block timing constraint and to the timing constraints posed by their predecessors in the BML block. If two time constraints on a behavior require certain phases of that behavior to be stretched or skewed, the scheduler achieves this by stretching or skewing the behavior uniformally, to avoid discontinuities in animation speed. Their scheduling mechanism can result in some time constraints being scheduled into the past (that is, before the start of the BML block). A final normalization pass shifts, where needed, connected clusters of behaviors forward in time to fix this. SmartBody cannot handle before/after constraints yet, but does comply with all explicit constraints and implicit constraints that do not concern before and after constraints.

Because the SmartBody scheduling algorithm schedules behaviors in BML order, the result is dependent on the order in which the behaviors are specified in the BML block. At worst, this may lead to situations in which BML cannot be scheduled in one order while it can be in another. For example, the BML block in Example 1(a) cannot be scheduled because the timing of the nod1 is determined first, and the scheduler attempts to retime speech1 to adhere to this timing. Most speech synthesis systems, including the one used in SmartBody, disallow such retiming. If the behavior order is changed, as in Example 1(b), then speech1 is scheduled first, and nod1 will adhere to the timing imposed by speech1.

That being said, the SmartBody scheduling algorithm is easy to implement and provides rapid scheduling. In practice, most BML scripts are simple and the SmartBody scheduler will find a reasonable scheduling solution for such scripts.

2.2   EMBR

EMBR [4,6] uses a constraint optimization technique to solve the scheduling problem. The EMBR scheduler first solves the absolute value of all BML sync points in speech. A timing constraint solver then solves for the timing of the remaining nonverbal behaviors. Synchronization constraints might require the stretching or skewing of behavior phases as compared to the defaults given in the behavior lexicon. The constraint solver uses the sum of 'errors' (in seconds) of the stretch or skew over all behaviors as its cost function. It thus finds solutions in which the overall stretch/skew is minimized. The EMBR scheduler can schedule BML blocks containing before and after constraints, and favors solutions that result in more natural behavior (for EMBR's measure of the naturalness: minimal overall behavior stretching/skewing).

3   Scheduling and Plan Representation in Elckerlyc

Elckerlyc is a BML Realizer designed specifically for continuous interaction [13] Its multimodal behavior plan can continually be updated: the timing of certain

BML Example 1. Two BML scripts demonstrating SmartBody's order dependent scheduling solution.

(a) BML script that cannot be scheduled using the SmartBody scheduling algorithm.

```
<bml id="bml1">
  <head id="nod1" action="ROTATION" rotation="NOD" start="speech1:start"
  end="speech1:sync1"/>
  <speech id="speech1">
    <text>Yes,<sync id="sync1"> that was great.</text>
  </speech>
</bml>
```

(b) BML script that can be scheduled using the SmartBody scheduling algorithm.

```
<bml id="bml1">
  <speech id="speech1">
    <text>Yes,<sync id="sync1"> that was great.</text>
  </speech>
  <head id="nod1" action="ROTATION" rotation="NOD"
    start="speech1:start" end="speech1:sync1"/>
</bml>
```

synchronisation points can be adjusted, ongoing behaviors can be interrupted using interrupt behaviors, behaviors can be added, and the parametrisation of ongoing behaviors can be changed at playback time.

In order to achieve this flexibility, Elckerlyc needs not only to be able to schedule BML specifications into a multimodal behavior plan that determines the surface realization of the behaviors, but also needs to maintain information about how these surface realizations relate to the original BML specification. This allows the scheduler to figure out which surface realizations need to be changed, when changes to BML behaviors are requested.[1]

Elckerlyc's flexible plan representation allows these modifications, while keeping the constraints on the behavior plan consistent. In this section we describe this plan representation, and the architecture of the scheduling component in Elckerlyc.

3.1 Additional Behavior Plan Constraints in Elckerlyc

Elckerlyc allows a number of additional constraints of different types. The most important ones are described here.

Implicit Constraints: Whitespace. Similar to SmartBody and EMBR, Elckerlyc adds a set of constraints to enforce that there is no 'unnecessary whitespace'

---

[1] The mechanisms for specifying these changes are described in [ANON].

between behaviors. That is, each behavior, as well as each block, is supposed to start as early as possible, as long as it satisfies all other constraints.

Block Level Constraint: Scheduling Types. In addition to the `merge` and `append` scheduling attributes, Elckerlyc provides the `append-after(X)` attribute. Append-after starts a BML block directly after a selected set of behaviors in the current behavior plan (those from all blocks in **X**) are finished.

3.2 Elckerlyc's Plan Representation

Central to Elckerlyc's plan representation is the Peg Board. The sync points of each behavior in the multimodal plan are associated with Time Pegs on the Peg Board. These Time Pegs can be moved, changing the timing of the associated sync points. If two sync points are connected by an 'at' constraint, they share the same Time Peg. This Time Peg can then be moved without violating the 'at' constraint, because this simultaneously changes the actual time of both sync points. Time Pegs provide local timing (that is, as offset from the start of the block), being connected to a BML Block Peg that provides representation of the start time of the corresponding BML block. If the BML Block Peg is moved, all Time Pegs associated with it move along. This allows one to move the block as a whole, keeping the intra-block constraints consistent (see Fig. 3).

A dedicated BML Block management state machine automatically updates the timing of the BML Block Pegs in reaction to behavior plan modifications that occur at runtime, to maintain the BML Block constraints. For example, when a block b_i was scheduled to occur immediately after all behaviors already present in the plan, and the immediately preceding behaviors in the plan are removed from the plan through an `interrupt` behavior, the state machine will automatically move the BML Block Peg of b_i to close the resulting gap.

3.3 Resolving Constraints to Time Pegs

Relative 'at' synchronization constraints that share a sync point (behavior id, sync id pair) should be connected to the same Time Peg. Such 'at' constraints may involve a fixed, nonzero timing offset, for example when a nod is constrained to occur exactly half a second after the stroke of a gesture. Such offsets are maintained by Offset Pegs. An Offset Peg is a Time Peg that is restrained to stay at a fixed offset to its linked Time Peg. If the Offset Peg is moved, its linked Time Peg moves with it and vice-versa. Offset Pegs can also be added by the scheduler for other reasons. For example, if the start sync is not constrained in a behavior, it may be resolved as an Offset Peg. That is: the start sync of the behavior is linked to the closest Time Peg of another sync point within the behavior. If this other Time Peg is moved, the start of the behavior is moved with it. If a behavior is completely unconstrained, a new Time Peg is created and connected to its start sync. BML Example 2 shows how Time Pegs are resolved for an example BML constraint specification.

BML Example 2. Resolving a BML constraint specification to a Time Pegs specification. A Time Peg $tp1$ connects relative 'at' constraints $[[bml1 : speech1 : s1 + 0], [bml1 : nod1 : stroke + 0]]$, and $[[bml1 : speech1 : s1 + 0], [bml1 : point1 : stroke + 0.5]]$. Another Time Peg $tp2$ is created for the 'at' constraint $[[bml1 : point1 : start + 0], [bml1 : walk1 : relax + 0]]$. Since the start time of speech1, nod1, and walk1 is not constrained, they are attached to an Offset Pet linked to the closest other Time Peg in the respective behaviors. The BML Block itself (with id **bml1**) is connected to BML Block Peg **bp1**. All Time Pegs are connected to this Block Peg.

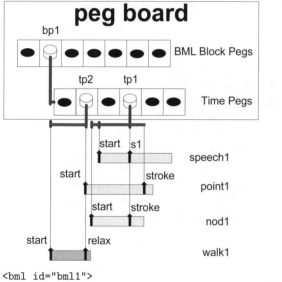

```
<bml id="bml1">
    <speech id="speech1">
      <text>As you can see on <sync id="s1"> this painting, ...</text>
    </speech>
    <gesture id="point1" start="walk1:relax" type="POINT"
    target="painting1" stroke="speech1:s1+0.5"/>
    <head id="nod1" action="ROTATION" rotation="NOD" stroke="speech1:s1"/>
    <locomotion id="walk1" target="painting1"/>
</bml>
```

Each BML Block has its own associated BML Block Peg that defines its global start time. Time Pegs are linked to their associated BML Block Peg. Some behaviors have constraints (and thus Time Pegs) that are linked to external global Pegs, used to synchronize behavior with external events. These are hooked up to a special, unmovable global BML Block Peg at global $t = 0$. See Fig. 3 for a graphical representation of these relations. The actual time of a BML Block Peg is first estimated to be ct (the time at which it is being scheduled). When playback of the Block Peg is started, its time is updated to reflect its actual start time. Since the Time Pegs inside the block are attached to the Block Peg, they will now also adhere to the actual start time of the block.

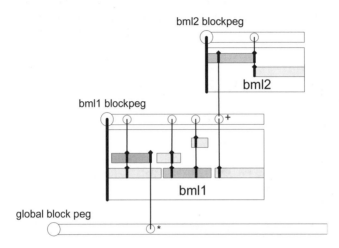

Fig. 3. Each BML block has its associated BML Block Peg. Internal constraints are linked to Time Pegs associated with this BML Block Peg. BML block `bml1` contains a constraint that is linked to an external Time Peg (marked with *). BML block `bml2` is block scheduled with the tight-merge scheduling algorithm. It has a constraint whose timing is defined by a Time Peg from BML block `bml1` (marked with +).

3.4   Scheduling in Elckerlyc

In Elckerlyc, scheduling consists of resolving the constraints in a BML block to Time Pegs (see Section 3.3), and assigning the Time Pegs a first prediction of their execution time. Elckerlyc's main scheduling contribution is in its flexible behavior plan representation described in Section 3.3; Elckerlyc currently uses SmartBody's scheduling algorithm to assign time predictions to the Time Pegs. The architecture of Elckerlyc is set up in such a way that this scheduling algorithm can easily be replaced by other algorithms (e.g. a custom constraint solver such as that of EMBR).

Scheduling Architecture. The Elckerlyc scheduling architecture uses an interplay between different unimodal Engines that provide the central scheduler with detailed information on the possible timing of behaviors, given their BML description and time constraints. Elckerlyc's multimodal plan representation is managed using unimodal plans in each Engine. These unimodal plans contain Timed Plan Units, the timing of which is linked to Time Pegs on the PegBoard. Elckerlyc's Scheduler communicates with these Engines (e.g. Speech Engine, Animation Engine, see also Fig. 4) through their abstract interface (see below). It knows for each BML behavior type which Engine handles it.

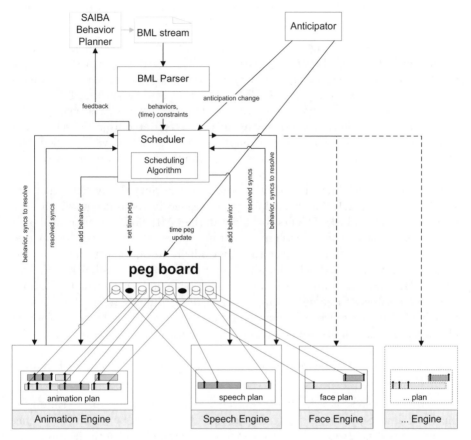

Fig. 4. Elckerlyc's scheduling architecture. The Anticipator is used to adapt the time stamps of Time Pegs based on predictions of the timing of external events, which is useful when the VH should exhibit tight behavior synchronisation with conversation partners.

Interfacing with the Engines Each Engine implements functionality to:

1. Add a BML behavior to its unimodal behavior plan.
2. Resolve unknown time constraints on a behavior, given certain known time constraints.
3. Check which behaviors in the Plan (if any) are currently invalid.

Note that an Engine can be queried for time constraints on behavior without adding it to the plan. This allows a scheduler to try out multiple constraint configurations on each behavior before it commits to a specific behavior plan. Also note that all communication with the Engine is in terms of BML behaviors. It is up to the Engine to map the BML behaviors to Timed Plan Units. The validity check is typically used to check if a valid plan is retained after certain TimePegs have been moved. All implemented Engines check if the order of the TimePegs of each behavior is still correct. Each Engine can also add validity checks specific to its output modality.

Scheduling Algorithm. The scheduler delegates the actual scheduling to a dedicated algorithm, using the strategy pattern [2]. The scheduling algorithm assigns a first prediction of the timing of each Time Pegs to them, given the current multimodal behavior plan and a parsed BML block that is to be scheduled. Elckerlyc is designed in such a way that the scheduling algorithm can easily be changed: the BML parsing and block progress management are separated from the scheduling algorithm, and the Engines provide generic interfaces that provide a scheduling algorithm with the timing of unknown constraints on behaviors, given certain known constraints.

Elckerlyc's scheduling algorithm is based on the SmartBody Scheduler described in Section 2.1. The behaviors are processed in the order in which they occur in the BML block. The first behavior in the BML block is constrained only by its absolute time constraints and constraint references to external behaviors. Subsequent behaviors are timed so that they adhere to time constraints imposed by the already processed behaviors (including those of previous blocks). Elckerlyc's BML Parser lists all constraints on each behavior. Our current scheduler delegates resolving these unknown time constraints directly to the Engine that is dedicated to the given behavior type. Subsequently, the behavior, on which all time time constraints are now resolved, is added to its Plan.

3.5 Managing Adjustments of the Behavior Plan during Behavior Playback

Once a BML block is scheduled, several changes can occur to its timing at playback time. Such changes may, for example, be initiated by a Time Peg being moved for external reasons (e.g., to postpone a speech phrase until the interlocutor finished uttering an assessment feedback, as explained in the introduction), or by other behaviors in the plan being removed. Since the sync points of behaviors are symbolically linked to the Time Pegs, timing updates are handled automatically (stretching or shortening the duration of behaviors when required) and the explicit constraints of Section 1.1 remain satisfied. Plan changes, and constraint satisfaction after plan changes, are achieved in an efficient manner, that is, without requiring a time consuming scheduling action for minor plan adjustments. Interrupting a behavior in a BML block might shorten the length of the block. Since the BML Block management state machine dynamically manages the block end, shortening the block whenever this happens, the whitespace and append constraints automatically remain satisfied.

These and other kinds of microadjustmenst to behavior plans have been experimented with in a number of applications. The latest version of the Reactive Virtual Trainer performs fitness exercises along with the user, adjusting the timing of its performance to that of the user [1]. In experiments on Attentive Speaking, a route guide slightly delays its speech to make room for listener responses from the user [10] (using a Wizard of Oz setup for detecting start and end of listener responses). Other applications and scenarios have been described elsewhere; videos and demonstrations may be found on the Elckerlyc web site and in the open source code release.

More significant updates might require re-scheduling of behaviors, such as when a Time Peg, linked to the start of a behavior, is moved to occur *after* the end of the same behavior. To check for such situations, the Scheduler asks each Engine whether its current plan is still valid (i.e., its constraints are still satisfied). The Scheduler then omits the behaviors that are no longer valid and notifies the SAIBA Behavior Planner using the BML feedback mechanism. It will then be up to the SAIBA Behavior Planner to update the behavior plan (using BML), if desired.

4   Conclusion

We showed in this paper how the BML scheduling process can be viewed as a constraint problem, and how Elckerlyc uses this view to maintain a flexible behavior plan representation that allows one to make micro-adjustments to behaviors while keeping constraints between them intact. In Elckerlyc, scheduling is modeled as an interplay between different unimodal Engines that provide detailed information on the timing of the behaviors that are to be realized. The seperation of concerns between unimodal behavior timing, BML parsing, BML block progress management and multimodal scheduling makes it easy to exchange Elckerlyc's scheduling algorithm by a different one as well as to add new modalities. Thanks to the capability for on-the-fly plan adjustments, Elckerlyc is eminently suitable for Virtual Human applications in which a tight mutual coordination between user and Virtual Human is required.

Acknowledgements. This research has been supported by the GATE project, funded by the Dutch Organization for Scientific Research (NWO).

References

1. Dehling, E.: The Reactive Virtual Trainer. Master's thesis, University of Twente, Enschede, the Netherlands (2011)
2. Gamma, E., Helm, R., Johnson, R., Vlissides, J.: Design Patterns: Elements of Reusable Object-Oriented Software. Addison-Wesley, Reading (1995)
3. Goodwin, C.: Between and within: Alternative sequential treatments of continuers and assessments. Human Studies 9(2-3), 205–217 (1986)

4. Heloir, A., Kipp, M.: Real-time animation of interactive agents: Specification and realization. Applied Artificial Intelligence 24(6), 510–529 (2010)
5. Herman, M., Albus, J.S.: Real-time hierarchical planning for multiple mobile robots. In: Proc. DARPA Knowledge -Based Planning Workshop (Proceedings of the DARPA Knowledge-Based Planning Workshop), pp. 22-1–22-10
6. Kipp, M., Heloir, A., Schröder, M., Gebhard, P.: Realizing multimodal behavior: Closing the gap between behavior planning and embodied agent presentation. In: Proc. IVA, pp. 57–63. Springer, Heidelberg (2010)
7. Kopp, S.: Social resonance and embodied coordination in face-to-face conversation with artificial interlocutors. Speech Communication 52(6), 587–597 (2010), speech and Face-to-Face Communication
8. Kopp, S., Krenn, B., Marsella, S.C., Marshall, A.N., Pelachaud, C., Pirker, H., Thórisson, K.R., Vilhjálmsson, H.H.: Towards a common framework for multimodal generation: The behavior markup language. In: Gratch, J., Young, M., Aylett, R.S., Ballin, D., Olivier, P. (eds.) IVA 2006. LNCS (LNAI), vol. 4133, pp. 205–217. Springer, Heidelberg (2006)
9. Nijholt, A., Reidsma, D., van Welbergen, H., op den Akker, R., Ruttkay, Z.: Mutually coordinated anticipatory multimodal interaction. In: Esposito, A., Bourbakis, N.G., Avouris, N., Hatzilygeroudis, I. (eds.) HH and HM Interaction. LNCS (LNAI), vol. 5042, pp. 70–89. Springer, Heidelberg (2008)
10. Reidsma, D., de Kok, I., Neiberg, D., Pammi, S., van Straalen, B., Truong, K.P., van Welbergen, H.: Continuous interaction with a virtual human. Journal on Multimodal User Interfaces (in press, 2011)
11. Thiebaux, M., Marshall, A.N., Marsella, S.C., Kallmann, M.: Smartbody: Behavior realization for embodied conversational agents. In: Proc. AAMAS, pp. 151–158 (2008)
12. van Welbergen, H.: Specifying, scheduling and realizing multimodal output for continuous interaction with a virtual human. Ph.D. thesis, University of Twente, Enschede, NL (2011)
13. van Welbergen, H., Reidsma, D., Ruttkay, Z.M., Zwiers, J.: Elckerlyc: A BML realizer for continuous, multimodal interaction with a virtual human. Journal on Multimodal User Interfaces 3(4), 271–284 (2010)

Towards the Rapid Development of a Natural Language Understanding Module

Catarina Moreira, Ana Cristina Mendes, Luísa Coheur, and Bruno Martins

Instituto Superior Técnico, INESC-ID
Av. Professor Cavaco Silva, 2744-016 Porto Salvo, Portugal
{catarina.p.moreira,bruno.g.martins}@ist.utl.pt,
{ana.mendes,luisa.coheur}@l2f.inesc-id.pt

Abstract. When developing a conversational agent, there is often an urgent need to have a prototype available in order to test the application with real users. A Wizard of Oz is a possibility, but sometimes the agent should be simply deployed in the environment where it will be used. Here, the agent should be able to capture as many interactions as possible and to understand how people react to failure. In this paper, we focus on the rapid development of a natural language understanding module by non experts. Our approach follows the learning paradigm and sees the process of understanding natural language as a classification problem. We test our module with a conversational agent that answers questions in the art domain. Moreover, we show how our approach can be used by a natural language interface to a cinema database.

1 Introduction

In order to have a clear notion of how people interact with a conversational agent, ideally the agent should be deployed at its final location, so that it can be used by people sharing the characteristics of the final users. This scenario allows the developers of the agent to collect corpora of real interactions. Although the Wizard of Oz technique [7] can also provide these corpora, sometimes it is not a solution if one needs to test the system with many different real users during a long period and/or it is not predictable when the users will be available.

The natural language understanding (NLU) module is one of the most important components in a conversational agent, responsible for interpreting the user requests. The symbolic approach to NLU usually involves a certain level of natural language processing, which includes hand crafted grammars and requires a certain amount of expertise to develop them; by the same token, the statistical approach relies on a large quantity of labeled corpora, which is often not available.

In this paper we hypothesize that a very simple and yet effective NLU module can be built if we model the process of NLU as a classification problem, within the machine learning paradigm. Here, we follow the approach described in [5], although their focus is on frame-based dialogue systems. Our approach is language independent and does not impose any level of expertise to the developer:

H. Högni Vilhjálmsson et al. (Eds.): IVA 2011, LNAI 6895, pp. 309–315, 2011.

he/she simply has to provide the module with a set of possible interactions (the only constraint being the input format) and a dictionary (if needed). Given this input, each interaction is automatically associated with a virtual category and a classification model is learned. The model will map future interactions in the appropriate semantic representation, which can be a logical form, a frame, a sentence, etc. We test our approach in the development of a NLU module for EDGAR(Figure 1) a conversational agent operating in the art domain. Also, we show how the approach can be successfully used to create a NLU module for a natural language interface to a cinema database, JATEDIGO, responsible for mapping the user requests into logical forms that will afterwards be mapped into SQL queries[1].

Fig. 1. Agent Edgar

The paper is organized as follows: in Section 2 we present some related work and in Section 3 we describe our NLU module. Finally, in Section 4 we show our experiments and in Section 5 we conclude and present future work directions.

2   Related Work

NLU is the task of mapping natural language utterances into structures that the machine can deal with: the semantic representation of the utterances. The semantics of a utterance can be a logical form, a frame or a natural language sentence already understood by the machine. The techniques for NLU can be roughly split into two categories: symbolic and sub-symbolic. There are also hybrid techniques, that use characteristics of both categories.

Regarding symbolic NLU, it includes keyword detection, pattern matching and rule-based techniques. For instance, the virtual therapist ELIZA [11] is a classical example of a system based on pattern matching. Many early systems were based on a sophisticated syntax/semantics interface, where each syntactic rule is associated with a semantic rule and logical forms are generated in a

---

[1] All the code used in this work will be made available for research purposes at
  http://qa.l2f.inesc-id.pt/.

bottom-up, compositional process. Variations of this approach are described in [2,6]. Recently, many systems follow the symbolic approach, by using in-house rule-based NLU modules [4,8]. However, some systems use the NLU modules of available dialogue frameworks, like the Let's Go system [10], which uses Olympus[2].

In what concerns sub-symbolic NLU, some systems receive text as input [5] and many are dealing with transcriptions from an Automatic Speech Recognizer [9]. In fact, considering speech understanding, the new trends considers NLU from a machine learning point of view. However, such systems usually need large quantities of labeled data and, in addition, training requires a previous matching of words into their semantic meanings.

3   The Natural Language Understanding Module

The NLU module receives as input a file with possible interactions (the training utterances file), from which several features are extracted. These features are in turn used as input to a classifier. In our implementation, we have used Support Vector Machines (SVM) as the classifier and the features are unigrams. However, in order to refine the results, other features can easily be included. Figure 2 describes the training phase of the NLU module.

Fig. 2. Training the NLU module

Each interaction specified in the training utterances file is a pair, where the first element is a set of utterances that paraphrase each other and that will trigger the same response; the second element is a set of answers that represent possible responses to the previous utterances. That is, each utterance in one interaction represents different manners of expressing the same thing and each answer represents a possible answer to be returned by the system. The DTD of this file is the following:

```
<!ELEMENT corpus (interaction+)>
<!ELEMENT interaction (uterances, answers)>
<!ELEMENT utterances (u+)>
<!ELEMENT answers (a+)>
<!ELEMENT u (#PCDATA)>
<!ELEMENT a (#PCDATA)>
```

---

[2] http://wiki.speech.cs.cmu.edu/olympus/index.php/Olympus

The NLU module also accepts as input a dictionary, containing elements to be replaced with labels that represent broader categories. Thus, and considering that TAG is the label that replaces a compound term $w_1... w_n$ during training, the dictionary is composed of entrances in the format:

TAG $w_1... w_n$ (for example: ACTOR Robert de Niro)

If the dictionary is used, Named Entity Recognition (NER) is performed to replace the terms that occur both in the training utterances file and user utterances. This process uses the LingPipe[3] implementation of the Aho-Corasick algorithm [1], that searches for matches against a dictionary in linear time in terms of the length of the text, independently of the size of the dictionary.

A unique identifier is then given to every paraphrase in each interaction – the interaction category – which will be the target of the training. For instance, since sentences *Há alguma data prevista para a conclusão das obras?* and *As obras vão acabar quando?* ask for the same information (*When will the conservation works finish?*), they are both labeled with the same category, generated during training: agent_7. The resulting file is afterwards used to train the classifier.

After the training phase, the NLU module receives as input a user utterance. If the NE flag is enabled, there is a pre-processing stage, where the NE recognizer tags the named entities in the user utterance before sending it to the classifier. Then the classifier chooses a category for the utterance. Since each category is associated with a specific interaction (and with its respective answers), one answer is randomly chosen and returned to the user. These answers must be provided in a file with the format category answer. Notice that more than one answer can be specified. Figure 3 describes the general pipeline of the NLU module.

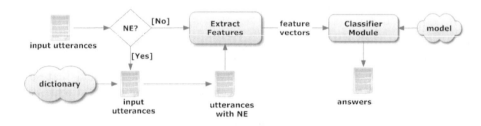

Fig. 3. Pipeline of the NLU module

4   Experiments

This section presents the validation methodology and the obtained results.

---

[3] http://alias-i.com/lingpipe/

4.1   Experimental Setup

In order to test our approach to the rapid development of a NLU module, we first collected a corpus that contains interactions in the art domain: the ART corpus. It was built to train EDGAR, a conversational agent whose task is to engage in inquiry-oriented conversations with users, teaching about the Monserrate Palace. EDGAR answers questions on its domain of knowledge, although it also responds to questions about himself. The ART corpus has 283 utterances with 1471 words, from which 279 are unique. The utterances represent 52 different interactions (thus, having each interaction an average of 5.4 paraphrases).

For our experiments in the cinema domain, we have used the CINEMA corpus, containing 229 questions mapped into 28 different logical forms, each one representing different SQL queries. A dictionary was also build containing actor names and movie titles.

4.2   Results

The focus of the first experiment was to chose a correct answer to a given utterance. This scenario implies the correct association of the utterance to the set of its paraphrases. For instance, considering the previous example sentence *As obras vão acabar quando?*, it should be associated to the category `agent_7` (the category of its paraphrases).

The focus of the second experiment was to map a question into an intermediate representation language (a logical form) [3]. For instance, sentence *Que actriz contracena com Viggo Mortensen no Senhor dos Anéis? (Which actress plays with Viggo Mortensen in The Lord of the Rings?)* should be mapped into the form `WHO_ACTS_WITH_IN(Viggo Mortensen, The Lord of the Rings)`.

Both corpora where randomly split in two parts (70%/30%), being 70% used for training and 30% for testing. This process was repeated 5 times. Results are shown in Table 1.

Table 1. Accuracy results

Corpus	fold 1	fold 2	fold 3	fold 4	fold 5	average
ART	0.78	0.74	0.86	0.87	0.92	0.83
CINEMA	0.87	0.90	0.79	0.77	0.82	0.83

4.3   Discussion

From the analysis of Table 1, we conclude that a simple technique can lead to very interesting results. Specially if we compare the accuracy obtained for the CINEMA corpus with previous results of 75%, which were achieved with recourse to a linguistically rich framework that required several months of skilled labour to build. Indeed, the previous implementation of JATEDIGO was based on a natural language processing chain, responsible for a morpho-syntactic analysis, named entity recognition and rule-based semantic interpretation.

Another conclusion is that one can easily develop an NLU module. In less than one hour we can have the set of interactions needed for training and, from there, the creation of the NLU module for that domain is straightforward. Moreover, new information can be easily added, allowing to retrain the model.

Nevertheless, we are aware of the debilities of our approach. The NLU module is highly dependent of the words used during training and the detection of paraphrases is only successful for utterances that share many words. In addition, as we are just using unigrams as features, no word is being detached within the input utterances, resulting in some errors. For instance, in the second experiment, the sentence *Qual o elenco do filme MOVIE? (Who is part of MOVIE's cast?)* was wrongly mapped into `QT_WHO_MAIN_ACT(MOVIE)`, although very similar sentences existed in the training. A solution for this problem is to add extra weight to some words, something that could be easily added as a feature if these words were identified in a list. Moreover, adding synonyms to the training utterances file could also help.

Another limitation is that the actual model does not comprise any history of the interactions. Also, we should carefully analyze the behavior of the system with the growing of the number of interactions (or logical forms), as the classification process becomes more complex.

5   Conclusions and Future Work

We have presented an approach for the rapid development of a NLU module based on a set of possible interactions. This approach treats the natural language understanding problem as a classification process, where utterances that are paraphrases of each other are given the same category. It receives as input two files, the only constraint being to write them in a given xml format, making it very simple to use, even by non-experts. Moreover, it obtains very promising results. As future work, and although moving from the language independence, we would like to experiment additional features and we would also like to try to automatically enrich the dictionary and the training files with relations extracted from WordNet.

Acknowledgments. This work was supported by FCT (INESC-ID multiannual funding) through the PIDDAC Program funds, and also through the project FALACOMIGO (Projecto em co-promoção, QREN n 13449). Ana Cristina Mendes is supported by a PhD fellowship from Fundação para a Ciência e a Tecnologia (SFRH/BD/43487/2008).

References

1. Aho, A.V., Corasick, M.J.: Efficient string matching: an aid to bibliographic search. Communications of the ACM 18, 333–340 (1975)
2. Allen, J.: Natural language understanding, 2nd edn. Benjamin-Cummings Publishing Co., Inc. (1995)

3. Androutsopoulos, I., Ritchie, G.D., Thanisch, P.: Natural language interfaces to databases–an introduction. Journal of Language Engineering 1(1), 29–81 (1995)
4. Bernsen, N.O., Dybkjær, L.: Domain-Oriented Conversation with H.C. Andersen. In: Proc. of the Workshop on Affective Dialogue Systems, Kloster Irsee, pp. 142–153. Springer, Heidelberg (2004)
5. Bhagat, R., Leuski, A., Hovy, E.: Shallow semantic parsing despite little training data. In: Proc. ACL/SIGPARSE 9th Int. Workshop on Parsing Technologies (2005)
6. Jurafsky, D., Martin, J.H.: Speech and Language Processing, 2nd edn. Prentice-Hall, Englewood Cliffs (2006)
7. Kelley, J.F.: An iterative design methodology for user-friendly natural language office information applications. ACM Transactions on Office Information Systems (1984)
8. Kopp, S., Gesellensetter, L., Krämer, N.C., Wachsmuth, I.: A conversational agent as museum guide – design and evaluation of a real-world application. In: Panayiotopoulos, T., Gratch, J., Aylett, R.S., Ballin, D., Olivier, P., Rist, T. (eds.) IVA 2005. LNCS (LNAI), vol. 3661, pp. 329–343. Springer, Heidelberg (2005)
9. Ortega, L., Galiano, I., Hurtado, L.F., Sanchis, E., Segarra, E.: A statistical segment-based approach for spoken language understanding. In: Proceedings of the 11th Annual Conference of the International Speech Communication Association, pp. 1836–1839 (2010)
10. Raux, A., Bohus, D., Langner, B., Black, A.W., Eskenazi, M.: Doing research on a deployed spoken dialogue system: One year of let's go! experience. In: Proceedings of the 7th Annual Conference of the International Speech Communication Association, pp. 65–68 (2006)
11. Weizenbaum, J.: Eliza - a computer program for the study of natural language communication between man and machine. Communications of the ACM 9(1), 36–45 (1966)

Expressive Multimodal Conversational Acts for SAIBA Agents

Jeremy Riviere[1], Carole Adam[1], Sylvie Pesty[1], Catherine Pelachaud[2],
Nadine Guiraud[3], Dominique Longin[3], and Emiliano Lorini[3]

[1] Grenoble University - LIG, Grenoble, France
{Jeremy.Riviere,Carole.Adam,Sylvie.Pesty}@imag.fr
[2] CNRS - Telecom ParisTech, Paris, France
{catherine.pelachaud}@telecom-paristech.fr
[3] UPS - CNRS, IRIT, Toulouse, France
{nadine.guiraud,emiliano.lorini,dominique.longin}@irit.fr

Abstract. We discuss here the need to define what we call an agent conversational language, a language for Embodied Conversational Agents (ECA) to have conversations with a human. We propose a set of *Expressive Multimodal Conversation Acts (EMCA)*, which is based on the *Expressive Speech Acts* that we introduced in a previous work, enriched with the multimodal expression of the emotions linked to these acts. We have then implemented these *EMCA* for SAIBA-compliant ECA, and specifically for Greta. We were able to use Greta in experiments aimed at assessing the benefits of our language in terms of perceived sincerity and believability of an ECA using it to interact with a human user.

Keywords: ECA, Emotions, Interaction, Dialogue.

1 Introduction

Nowadays, human-computer interactions and agent-agent interactions are omnipresent, making dialogue a major research problem. Therefore, some recent works in the field of human-computer interaction have turned to dialogue annotation [2,1] for understanding dialogue, recognizing its structure and generating dialogues. In parallel, some other works have turned to natural language communication. With the advance of virtual agents, multimodal aspects have become essential in human-agent dialogue. In particular these agents are now able to express (their) emotions, but mainly in a non-verbal manner. We believe that it is important to closely link verbal and non-verbal aspects in order to improve the conversational capabilities of these agents. This is particularly true for what we call *complex emotions* (involving mental representations as cause, self, action ...) that are (in humans) mainly conveyed through language, and are therefore often neglected in current research. In this paper we thus focus on complex emotions such as guilt or reproach and propose a set of *Expressive Multimodal Conversational Act (EMCA)* that allows an ECA to express them in a multimodal manner: verbal and non-verbal.

H. Högni Vilhjálmsson et al. (Eds.): IVA 2011, LNAI 6895, pp. 316–323, 2011.

We ground on the set of *Expressive Speech Acts* that we proposed in [5] and enrich them with the multimodal expression of their intrinsic emotion, thus allowing the automatic generation of the expression of the emotions linked to the act uttered by the agent. We believe that an agent able to not only verbally express sentence but also multimodally express the underlying emotions will be more sincere and believable to the user. To check our claim, we implemented our *MCL* in the standard SAIBA architecture [12], in particular in the Greta agent [10], and then conduced experiments with this agent.

2 Speech Acts to Express *complex emotions*

Starting from the formalization of counterfactual emotions proposed by [7], in [5], we defined *complex emotions* as based on one hand upon the agent counterfactual reasoning and on the other hand upon reasoning about responsibility, skills and social norms. We formalized eight *complex emotions* (rejoicing, gratitude, regret, disappointment, moral satisfaction, admiration, guilt and reproach) in terms of three types of logical operators representing the agent's mental state: beliefs ($Bel_i\varphi$), goals ($Goal_i\varphi$) and ideals ($Ideal_i\varphi$); and one operator for the attribution of responsibility ($Resp_i\varphi$). We then used the operator $Exp_{i,j,H}\varphi$, representing what an agent i expresses to an agent j in front of group H, to define eight *Expressive Speech Acts*, each of which expresses one complex emotion. Each emotion is said to be "intrinsically" attached to each act. The figure 1 shows the set of *Expressive Speech Acts* according to the *complex emotions* they are expressing.

Table 1. *Expressive Speech Acts* expressing *complex emotions*

$Exp_{i,j,H}(...)$	Expressive Speech Acts
$Goal_i\varphi \wedge Bel_i Resp_i\varphi$	$\stackrel{déf}{=} Exp_{i,j,H}(Rejoicing_i\varphi) \stackrel{déf}{=} \mathbf{Rejoice}_{i,j}\varphi$
$Goal_i\varphi \wedge Bel_i Resp_j\varphi$	$\stackrel{déf}{=} Exp_{i,j,H}(Gratitude_{i,j}\varphi) \stackrel{déf}{=} \mathbf{Thank}_{i,j}\varphi$
$Goal_i\neg\varphi \wedge Bel_i Resp_i\varphi$	$\stackrel{déf}{=} Exp_{i,j,H}(Regret_i\varphi) \stackrel{déf}{=} \mathbf{Regret}_{i,j}\varphi$
$Goal_i\neg\varphi \wedge Bel_i Resp_j\varphi$	$\stackrel{déf}{=} Exp_{i,j,H}(Disappointment_{i,j}\varphi) \stackrel{déf}{=} \mathbf{Complain}_{i,j}\varphi$
$Ideal_i\varphi \wedge Bel_i Resp_i\varphi$	$\stackrel{déf}{=} Exp_{i,j,H}(MoralSatisfaction_i\varphi) \stackrel{déf}{=} \mathbf{IsMorallySatisfied}_{i,j}\varphi$
$Ideal_i\varphi \wedge Bel_i Resp_j\varphi$	$\stackrel{déf}{=} Exp_{i,j,H}(Admiration_{i,j}\varphi) \stackrel{déf}{=} \mathbf{Compliment}_{i,j}\varphi$
$Ideal_i\neg\varphi \wedge Bel_i Resp_i\varphi$	$\stackrel{déf}{=} Exp_{i,j,H}(Guilt_i\varphi) \stackrel{déf}{=} \mathbf{FeelGuilty}_{i,j}\varphi$
$Ideal_i\neg\varphi \wedge Bel_i Resp_j\varphi$	$\stackrel{déf}{=} Exp_{i,j,H}(Reproach_{i,j}\varphi) \stackrel{déf}{=} \mathbf{Reproach}_{i,j}\varphi$

Thus, this *Expressive Language* links sharply *complex emotions* and speech acts, meaning you can't compliment somebody without expressing the *complex emotion* of admiration. Indeed, according to the speech act theory, an ECA has to express the intrinsic emotion of the expressive acts to "successfully" perform this act (*conditions of success*). We affirm that the multimodal expression of the *EMCA*'s intrinsic emotions expressed by an ECA increases its perceived sincerity and believability, under the human-ECA dialogue context and the cultural context.

3   Proposition: *EMCA* for SAIBA Agents

Our proposal consists in adding to the *Expressive Speech Acts* we defined the multimodal expression of each act's intrinsic emotion. *Expressive Speech Acts* thus become *Expressive Multimodal Conversational Acts (EMCA)*, containing the emotions intrinsically attached to each act, as well as their multimodal expression. We have implemented these *EMCA* into the SAIBA architecture to allow ECA SAIBA-compliant to express their *complex emotions*. We are only interested here in the expressive category of acts, whose aim is specifically to express emotions.

The SAIBA framework consists of three step process of intention planning, behavior planning and the virtual agent behavior realization. The FML (Function Markup Language [8]) and BML (Behavior Markup Language [12]) languages link the three modules. An xml file (the *lexicon* file) is used by the behavior planning module to convey patterns in multimodal signals before encoding into BML. Such patterns can be emotions, some performatives (like inform, offer or suggest) and other behavior. The *lexicon* file contains the list of these patterns as well as their multimodal expressions, which are mainly defined from psychological theories and video corpus analysis. Thanks to this *lexicon* file the behavior planning thus links the present patterns in the agent's communicative intention and their multimodal signals before encoding into BML and sending to the behavior realization module.

Our work consisted in offering a library of *EMCA* to SAIBA-compliant ECA. These ECA can thus choose the speech act matching with its communicative intention, thanks to the appropriate dialogue processing or reasoning module (which should have a set of rules based on our formalization). We have modified the *lexicon* file, where we have implemented our library of *EMCA*. Every act in the library is associated with its intrinsic emotion (see Section 2): concretely, this emotion is manifested by various multimodal signals that are used in the behavior planning module, and it will thus be expressed by the ECA alongside the conversational act.

For example, let us consider the next turn in a dialogue with the user: *"I am disappointed in your behavior, It's not very nice of you."*. Here, the ECA's intention is to express that the ECA had a certain goal and that the human is responsible for not reaching this goal. In this case, the *EMCA complain*, whose intrinsic emotion is the *complex emotion* of *disappointment*, fits best the ECA's communicative intention. The first module translates this communicative intention in FML-APML[1], and completes it with a BML specification of the agent's utterance, as shown in the example below:

---

[1] Since FML is still under development, we will work here on the FML-APML specification proposed in [8].

<fml-apml>
*<bml> <speech id="s1" language="english" voice="openmary" text="**I am disappointed in your behavior, It's not very nice of you.**"> </bml>*
*<fml> <**performative** id="p1" type="**complain**" > </fml>*
</fml-apml>

In the FML-APML specification, the *performative* tag represents the *EMCA* that is linked with the utterance. The multimodal expression of the emotion associated with each *EMCA*, which was identified in FML by the *performative* tag, is now detailed in the *lexicon* file. For example, here is the *EMCA complain* in the *EMCA* specification general format:

*<behaviorset name ="**complain**">*
<signal id="1" name="faceexp=disappointment" modality="face"/>

Here, the *complex emotion* of disappointment associated to the *EMCA complain* is multimodally expressed by its facial expression (signal 1). The behavior realization Module finally receives all the signals translated in BML, and it adapts them to animation rules and constraints: it checks coherence and absence of conflicts, before animating the verbal and non-verbal behavior of the ECA. So, the ECA has to express the emotion of disappointment to "successfully" complain (*i.e.* to seem sincere and believable to the user in the dialogue and cultural context).

Unlike current works [6,3], we established a link between acts and emotions from both the speech act theory [11] and our *complex emotion* definition. This approach enable a consistency of these acts and should improve the virtual agent's sincerity and credibility. To confirm this hypothesis, we assessed the Greta agent's sincerity and credibility when using our *EMCA* (see next section).

4   *EMCA* Evaluation: Application to Greta

The hypothesis that we want to test is the following: *adding non-verbal signals of the expression of the complex emotions coherent with the verbal signals expressed by an ECA increases its perceived sincerity and believability*. This hypothesis is to be considered through the human-ECA dialogue context, and the cultural context. We ran a first experiment with a subset of our *EMCA* and Greta, a SAIBA-compliant ECA ([10]). We have implemented our library of *EMCA* in the lexicon file of Greta (as described in 3), thus endowing this character with the ability to use our *EMCA*.

4.1   Test Scenario and Protocol

The protocol that we set up allowed us to test our hypothesis for two *EMCA* that express *complex emotions*: *to rejoice*, that expresses *rejoicing*, and *to apologise*, that expresses *regret*[2]. In the setting of a dialogue between a user and a ECA (acted out by Greta) whose aim is to recommend movies, these two *EMCA*

---

[2] *To apologise* is *to regret* something which is against the human's goal.

are expressed by the ECA in three conditions: a congruent condition, a neutral condition and a non-congruent condition. In the congruent condition, the ECA expresses the *EMCA* as it is defined in our language, *i.e.* with the intrinsic emotion matching the corresponding act (the regret emotion with an Apologise utterance, and the rejoicing emotion with a Rejoice utterance). In the neutral condition, the ECA only expresses the utterance without expressing its intrinsic emotion of the act. Finally in the non-congruent condition, the ECA expresses the utterance with the emotion that is the opposite (see table 1) of the intrinsic emotion of the act (an Apologise utterance is expressed with the Rejoicing emotion, while a Rejoice utterance is expressed with a Regret emotion).

In the first stage of the protocol, videos of two scenarios are proposed, each containing the expression by the ECA of one of the two tested *EMCA*. For each scenario, three videos are submitted to the subject (one per condition, i.e altogether six videos) to be evaluated. Both scenarios imply a dialogue with Greta after the user supposedly comes back from the cinema where they saw a movie that had previously been recommended by Greta. In the first scenario, they loved the movie and has just thanked Greta for her good advice. The user is then asked to watch the three videos (in a predefined order that differs for each user), and to evaluate how Greta rejoices. Similarly in the second scenario, the user hated the movie and has just reproached Greta for her bad advice (cf. figure 1). The user is then asked to watch the three videos of the *EMCA to apologize* (also in a predefined order) and to evaluate how Greta apologises.

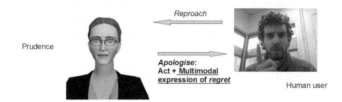

Fig. 1. Apologise *EMCA* in the congruent condition: Greta apologises in reply to user's reproach

The videos are assessed on two criteria: sincerity ("Does Greta seem to express what she thinks?") and believability ("Does the scene played by Greta look plausible?") of the ECA. These criteria can each take four possible values on the same qualitative scale (Not at all - Rather not - Rather - Totally).

The second part of the protocol consists in a questionnaire whose aim is to collect the user's impressions, mainly regarding the impact of the agent, and their subjective feelings. During this part, users can express themselves with their own words.

4.2   Results

23 users selected within students in science between 18 and 26 participated in the first experiment. To perform the statistical tests, we associated a score with

each qualitative value of the sincerity and believability criteria: 1 for "Not at all", 2 for "Rather not", 3 for "Rather", and 4 for "Totally". Since we evaluate 2 characteristics of 2 *EMCA*, we have 4 *dependent variables*: Sinc_Apologize, Believ_Apologize, Sinc_Rejoice, Believ_Rejoice. The only *independent variable* is the condition (congruent, neutral, non-congruent).

The first step was to check that the *dependent variables* follow a normal distribution. Secondly, the analysis of the results told us that the *EMCA* expressed in the congruent condition (C) have the best scores in both sincerity and believability. When Greta apologises under this condition, 65% of participants found Greta "rather" sincere (39%) or "totally" sincere (26%) and 70% of participants found Greta "rather" believable (52%) or "totally" believable (18%). Similarly when Greta rejoices under this condition, 74% of participants found Greta "rather" sincere (52%) or "totally" sincere (22%) and 78% of participants found Greta "rather" believable (52%) or "totally" believable (26%). This tends to confirm our hypothesis; we can thus assume that expressing the coherent emotion (C) with the act makes the ECA more sincere and believable to the user than expressing nothing (N) and expressing the opposite emotion (NC).

We then ran a one-way Analysis of Variance (ANOVA) test on each of our *dependent variables* with respect to the *independent variable*. The hypothesis *H0* we checked through this ANOVA test is the following: "There is no difference between the sincerity means (resp. the believability means) under the condition of congruence for the *EMCA Apologize* and *Rejoice*". *H1* thus says that "there is a difference between the sincerity means (resp. the believability means) under the condition of congruence for the *EMCA Apologize* and *Rejoice*". This ANOVA test allowed us to reject *H0* significantly in both sincerity and believability: for example, it showed a significant effect of the condition of congruence on Greta's sincerity ($F(2.66)=22.80$ $p<0.05$) for the *EMCA Apologize*. A Tukey range test showed us that there is a significant difference between the sincerity (resp. believability) mean in the congruent condition (C) and the sincerity (resp. believability) means in the other conditions for both *EMCA Apologize* and *Rejoice*, while there is no significant difference between the non-congruent condition (NC) and the neutral condition (N) (see for ex. table 2).

Table 2. Tukey range test of the Sinc_Apologize variable: the difference between the congruent condition (C) and the neutral(N) and the non-congruent (NC) conditions is significant

Groups	Difference	Statistic	Probability
C - NC	1.478	$q = 9.290$	0.0000
C - N	1.478	$q = 9.290$	0.0000
NC - N	-0.435	$q = 2.732$	0.1376

Finally, when asked "What do you think about Greta?" during the qualitative interview, a lot of users assessed the Greta's personality. Despite our efforts to avoid this evaluation, Greta's personality Prudence [9] has been described as "austere" and "severe". We do not know how it has influenced the results, but it appears that several users has mentioned the trust notion; Greta's personality and aspect seems to be as important as its expression of coherent emotion to the user, as shown in [4].

5   Conclusions and Perspectives

In this paper we have presented a library of *Expressive Multimodal Conversational Acts*, that make a link between the expression of emotions through language and through other modalities. We formally defined and implemented this set of eight *Expressive MCA* in the SAIBA architecture. Two of them were evaluated through an implementation in Greta, during a first experiment that showed that they contribute to a better perceived sincerity and believability of ECA. A second phase of evaluation will concern all our library in longer dialogue scenarios involving several turns of speech of an ECA and a human user. In order for this library to be useful to other SAIBA-compliant ECA, we intend to complete it with *MCA* from the other categories: assertive (inform, tell ...), directive (ask, offer ...), commissive (promise, assure ...).

Acknowledgments. This work is supported by the French National Research Agency (ANR), project CECIL (*www.irit.fr/CECIL*), grant number ANR-08-CORD-005. We thank the statistician engineer and psychologist Nadine Mandran of the LIG Marvelig unit which is specialized in experimentation protocol.

References

1. Bunt, H.: The dit++ taxonomy for functional dialogue markup. In: Proc. of AMAAS 2009 Workshop "Towards a Standard Markup Language for Embodied Dialogue Acts" (2009)
2. Core, M.G., Allen, J.F.: Coding dialogs with the DAMSL annotation scheme. In: Proc. of the Working Notes of the AAAI Fall Symposium on Communicative Action in Humans and Machines, Cambridge, MA (1997)
3. Gebhard, P., Kipp, M., Klesen, M., Rist, T.: Adding the emotional dimension to scripting character dialogues. In: Rist, T., Aylett, R.S., Ballin, D., Rickel, J. (eds.) IVA 2003. LNCS (LNAI), vol. 2792, pp. 48–56. Springer, Heidelberg (2003)
4. Gong, L.: How social is social responses to computers? the function of the degree of anthropomorphism in computer representations. Comput. Hum. Behav. 24, 1494–1509 (2008)
5. Guiraud, N., Longin, D., Lorini, E., Pesty, S., Riviere, J.: The face of emotions: a logical formalization of expressive speech acts. In: Proc. of AAMAS 2011 (2011)
6. Lee, J., Marsella, S.: Nonverbal behavior generator for embodied conversational agents. In: Gratch, J., Young, M., Aylett, R.S., Ballin, D., Olivier, P. (eds.) IVA 2006. LNCS (LNAI), vol. 4133, pp. 243–255. Springer, Heidelberg (2006)
7. Lorini, E., Schwarzentruber, F.: A logic for reasoning about counterfactual emotions. Artificial Intelligence 175(3-4), 814–847 (2011)

8. Mancini, M., Pelachaud, C.: The fml-apml language. In: Proc. of the Workshop on FML at AAMAS 2008 (2008)
9. McRorie, M., Sneddon, I., de Sevin, E., Bevacqua, E., Pelachaud, C.: A model of personality and emotional traits. In: Ruttkay, Z., Kipp, M., Nijholt, A., Vilhjálmsson, H.H. (eds.) IVA 2009. LNCS, vol. 5773, pp. 27–33. Springer, Heidelberg (2009)
10. Poggi, I., Pelachaud, C., de Rosis, F., Carofiglio, V., Carolis, B.D.: Greta: A believable embodied conversational agent. In: Multimodal Communication in Virtual Environments, pp. 27–45 (2005)
11. Searle, J.R.: Speech acts: an essay in the philosophy of language. Cambridge University Press, London (1969)
12. Vilhjálmsson, H.H., Cantelmo, N., Cassell, J., E. Chafai, N., Kipp, M., Kopp, S., Mancini, M., Marsella, S.C., Marshall, A.N., Pelachaud, C., Ruttkay, Z., Thórisson, K.R., van Welbergen, H., van der Werf, R.J.: The behavior markup language: Recent developments and challenges. In: Pelachaud, C., Martin, J.-C., André, E., Chollet, G., Karpouzis, K., Pelé, D. (eds.) IVA 2007. LNCS (LNAI), vol. 4722, pp. 99–111. Springer, Heidelberg (2007)

Continuous Interaction within the SAIBA Framework

Job Zwiers, Herwin van Welbergen, and Dennis Reidsma

University of Twente, Human Media Interaction
{j.zwiers,h.vanwelbergen,d.reidsma}@utwente.nl

Abstract. We propose extensions to the SAIBA BML language, aiming in particular to specify reactive behavior and continuous interaction. Examples of interaction scenarios are provided that illustrate the usefulness of these extensions. The impact on the SAIBA architecture is discussed.

1 Introduction

Multimodal generation of behavior for Virtual Humans is becoming more sophisticated, aiming to eventually capture the richness of human-human interaction. Not surprisingly, the specification of virtual human behavior and the structure of architectures and frameworks for controlling virtual humans have also become more sophisticated[11,8,3,6,10]. An important initiative has been the proposal of a common reference architecture in the form of the SAIBA framework. (see Figure 1). Several stages in multimodal behavior planning have been identified as well as clearly defined interfaces in the form of XML based languages BML and FML [5,4,12].

Fig. 1. The abstract SAIBA architecture

There is a sound theory behind this modular setup: the agent's communicative intents are first translated into rather abstract communicative signals, and only in a second stage these abstract signals are converted into concrete speech signals and concrete body and face animations. Although this modularization as such is a good idea, the "pipelined" processing of signals is less convincing. It adheres to the well known Sense-Think-Act cycle (STA) of traditional AI. As argued in [1,13] human behavior does not always conform to this pattern, in that not all human behavior stems from intent planning. In particular, bodily behavior is often an immediate and quick reaction on events, either from the environment, or from the behavior of other communicative partners. Such behavior is called *reactive* in [1]. Examples are mimicry and mirroring, where one

H. Högni Vilhjálmsson et al. (Eds.): IVA 2011, LNAI 6895, pp. 324–330, 2011.

human copies behavioral elements, like body pose or gaze direction, from other, observed partners.

Another interesting situation is where one human *predicts* certain events, like in a handshake, where both partners must somehow ensure that their hands arrive at the right place at the right time. This usually requires last minute adaptation to the timing of the appropriate body animation. We refer to this more demanding interaction paradigm as *continuous interaction.*

So we observe that a "pipelined" architecture as indicated in figure 1 is incomplete: in addition to the indicated feedback loops, there are often other interaction/feedback loops involved. As seen in many systems [11,6,1], behavior planning must deal with a reactive behavior loop that bypasses the intent planning stage.

We argue that for continuous interaction one needs an even tighter feedback loop than for reactive behavior: For continuous interaction a Behavior Realizer has to adapt its plans "on the fly" when it must react almost instantly to bodily behavior like head nods, pose shifts, or facial expressions, either observed or predicted for other (virtual or real) humans. The instant reaction times for real humans, as well as the fact that such reactions are largely unconscious, indicate that it is plausible that processing of this type of signals differs from more conscious thinking and planning. We think it is appropriate to maintain an analogous separation of concerns within the agent platform.

Another example of continuous interaction is shown in figure 2 where a feedback loop for sensor date(like tempo and heart rate) is shown.

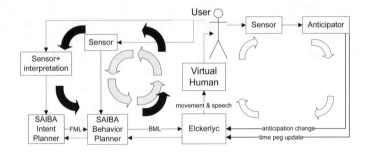

Fig. 2. Continuous Interaction

It reacts on data but also anticipates such data for the near future. What is relevant here is that, again, it bypasses all stages from the SAIBA pipeline and rather affects current, ongoing bodily behavior of the virtual human in a direct way. The idea is rather simple and clear enough, but it is somewhat problematic to deal with within current BML, since the virtual human behavior for making movements in accordance with the tempo has already been planned somewhere in the past. We propose that such alternative interaction mechanisms should be reflected, not just inside the implementation of planners and realizers, but also explicitly at the behavior specification level. Consequently, BML should be extended with appropriate language elements.

We also would like to draw the attention to the SAIBA feedback loops as indicated in Figure 1. Such feedback has more potential than just reporting "errors and problems". In fact, it should be used to communicate important state information from the Behavior Realizer back to Behavior Planner and Intent Planner. Such feedback concerning realizer state is essential for *adaptation* of behavior that is already in the stage of being "executed" or "realized". Typical examples are situations where one communicative partner interrupts another partner. The interrupted agent should not simply continue its current behavior but rather adapt to the situation, for instance by terminating it in a graceful way, or, alternatively, by modifying timing and volume with the aim to "keep the turn". We note that interruption is already part of several BML Realizers, including [10,13]. For the sake of modularity the feedback streams should employ similar mechanisms as the FML and BML streams.

In Figure 2 we see part of the Elckerlyc platform, where several feedback loops are shown, including a loop feeding the Behavior Planner directly from sensor information, for reactive behaviors, and a similar feedback loop feeding the Realizer directly from Anticipators that make predictions directly from sensor information, bypassing Intent Planner and Behavior Planner.

2   Impact on the SAIBA Framework

The continuous interaction paradigm has a profound impact on the SAIBA framework, both on a conceptual level as well as on an implementation level. For instance, when behavior interruption and "on the fly" modification of behavior parameters, including timing, are required then this puts certain demands on the capabilities and implementation of the behavior realizer. But also the "pipelined" nature of the SAIBA framework is challenged. For instance, when a behavior realizer interrupts or even cancels some behavior, then other components such as the behavior planner should be informed. Conceptually one should think in terms of a *behavior plan* that is being constructed "on the fly" and that serves as the *joint* information structure shared by behavior planners [11], reactive behavior planners, behavior realizers, and behavior adapters for continuous interaction.

At first one might think that a behavior plan is merely an implementation aspect, internal to SAIBA components like the Behavior realizer. This is in line with the idea that languages like FML and BML are declarative languages, so a stream of BML behaviors would carry no explicit state information. But for certain continuous interaction mechanisms this in an untenable position. An important example of why this is the case is that of interruption of speech: a behavior planner sending a speech behavior for a single sentence to the behavior realizer cannot prevent the environment, including humans, to interrupt that sentence at a later time. When that happens, continuous interaction demands that there is an instantaneous reaction, for instance by means of sending an interrupt behavior that partially cancels the speech behavior and removes it from the behavior plan, possibly replacing it with some alternate behavior.

The important observation here is that all this implies that behavior planners, and ultimately also intent planners, must be aware of the state (in the form of a behavior plan or otherwise) of the behavior realizer. An intent planner, for instance, can use feedback concerning behavior progress and interrupt information to decide whether some message can be considered to have actually "arrived" at the receiver, or not, and then act accordingly. Based on similar information the dialogue management functionality inside intent planner and behavior planner can make inferences about who has the floor at any moment. (Although "owning the floor" is clearly a higher level concept, it is affected nevertheless by lower level events like interruption, gaze behaviors, etcetera).

It appears that for modeling reactive behavior and continuous interaction, it is better to view major components like various planners and realizers as parallel, loosely coupled, processes (PP), communicating with each other, but not necessarily in a strict pipelined model. For in such architectures it is more natural to include components like action selectors, or components that deal with feedback in a more explicit way. Architecture along these lines have been proposed in [1,13].

2.1   Environment State and Virtual Human State

Another important aspect of the behavior plan is the representation of the state of situated virtual humans themselves. This becomes important whenever the cumulative effect of BML behaviors has a lasting effect on, for instance, the VH body pose or facial expression. State becomes also important when behaviors have an impact on the VH environment, if only by walking from one place to a different physical location. All planners and realizers will have to take this state into account. For example, we must know whether our virtual human is currently looking at some person, or whether his location and body pose are such that some gesture for grabbing some particular object is feasible.

State aspects of bodily behavior cannot be explicitly *specified* in core BML. One possibility to introduce state aspects is to use so called *persistent behaviors* in BML, for instance, to keep a VH in a certain body pose. This is a partial solution, although not without problems. For instance, in [13] there are slightly complicated priority rules for BML behaviors with the effect that persistent behavior can be overruled by other non-persistent behaviors, or that define the cumulative effect of several persistent behaviors.

2.2   The Behavior Plan State

State aspects within the SAIBA framework do not only apply to virtual human state or environment state, but even more so to "Behavior Plan state", shared by the various planners and realizers. As a motivating example consider a classical turntaking scenario, where the Intent Planner has been informed that the human user would like to get the turn. The Intent Planner decides that the virtual human should yield its turn, and seeks to do this in a way that is sensible from a continuous interaction point of view. By this we mean that the behavior realizer should not continue with its currently gesturing behavior and speech behavior, but rather that each of these behaviors could be interrupted or modified in an appropriate way. This requires that the SAIBA Behavior Planner keeps track of the behavior sent to the Realizer and monitors its execution progress. For instance, the gesturing behavior should, depending on the current realization state, be canceled (when it is not yet executing), be ignored (when it is already in a retraction phase, or when it has finished), or be replaced by a "gracefull ending" (when it has started and has not yet entered its retraction phase). In SAIBA based systems that fully implement the feedback mechanism such state-awareness can be achieved using feedback messages sent to the Behavior Planner by the Realizer.

It appears that a shared Behavior Plan is a vital component for specifying continuous interaction. Several existing systems, for instance the Gandalf system [11], do rely on such a shared plan.

2.3   Incremental Scheduling

The Max system [6] is the First ECA-system that simulates the mutual adaptations between the timing of gesture and speech that humans employ to achieve synchrony within *chunks* [7] between the coexpressive elements in those two modalities. Such "chunks" map naturally onto BML blocks.

Gesture movement in the Max system between the successive strokes of two gestures in two *successive* chunks depends on their timing. What is of interest here is that *inter-chunk synchronization* would be specified in the most natural way by introducing synchronization constraints for behaviors from *different* BML blocks. Such inter-block synchronization is cumbersome in core BML, using the start and end of BML blocks as somewhat artificial intermediate synchronization points. It would be more natural to admit inter-block synchronization constraints to be specified *directly*.

2.4   Interactional Synchrony

The current (core) SAIBA framework focusses on behavior for a *single* virtual human. Interaction with the environment, including interaction with other humans, virtual or real, does not affect BML behavior specifications. Such interaction can influence behavior only via coordination on the level of intent planners or possibly on the level of behavior planners. As argued above, this pattern does not suffice for continuous interaction, From the literature there are many examples of interactional synchrony, where observing and predicting external events, possibly stemming from the behavior of other agents, is required. According to Clark [2], joint actions (such as dialogue) can be coordinated because they divide into phases. For example, in a handshake phases include extending the hands, shake, and withdraw. Synchrony requires the coordination of entry and exit times of each phase. In many tasks, interlocutors are unaware of their mutual synchronization [9]. This suggest, again, that such synchronization does not result from conscious intent planning, but rather from more primitive processing that affects behaviors in a direct way. Synchronization, anticipation and prediction of mutual behavior of several (real or virtual) humans is not easily done in current BML. We propose to correct this situation by adding suitable synchronization mechanisms.

3   Recommendations for the SAIBA Framework

We have argued that the current (core) BML language is lacking in various aspects; we therefore propose to augment the language:

First of all there is a need for BML behavior that *interrupts, modifies, or replaces current, ongoing, behavior.*

Second, it will be necessary to *keep track* of the behavior plan state in other modules than just a behavior realizer. To achieve this goal, it is necessary to add communication from Behavior Realizer towards those other modules, for instance in the form of XML based feedback from realizer to planners.

Third, we propose to augment the SAIBA framework with mechanisms for synchronization with, and prediction of, external events, caused by the environment or by "other" humans than the virtual human under control.

Fourth, and finally, it is necessary to define carefully the *semantics* of BML behaviors. For instance, what will be the cumulative effect of various inputs, from behavior planner, reactive behavior insertion, or continuous interaction. The current specification of BML is quite precise when dealing with behavior synchronization inside a BML block. But the relation of behaviors from several independent blocks, or the effect of external agents on behavior is to some extent under exposed in the current BML description.

The current version of our platform [13] addresses several of these points, by offering $\mathbf{BML^T}$ language extensions, and by offering a modular setup where a Behavior Plan is effectively a shared structure.

4   Conclusions and Future Work

We discussed various proposals for extensions to the BML language. The continuous interaction paradigm and its repercussions on the BML language and the BML Realizer enable a lot of interesting use cases, where more advanced social signals play a role than in more classical turn-based dialogue. A challenge is to extend these ideas to multi party interaction, where mutual interaction between members of (small) groups is the goal. An interesting question here is how to deal with synchronization between behavior Plans and BML streams for *different* virtual humans.

Acknowledgements. This research has been supported by the GATE project, funded by the Dutch Organization for Scientific Research (NWO).

References

1. Bevacqua, E., Prepin, E., de Sevin, R., Niewiadomski, R., Pelachaud, C.: Reactive behaviors in saiba architecture. In: Workshop Towards a Standard Markup Language for Embodied Dialogue Acts, held in conjunction with AAMAS 2009 (2009)
2. Clark, H.H.: Using language. Cambridge University Press, Cambridge (1996)
3. Gratch, J., Okhmatovskaia, A., Lamothe, F., Marsella, S.C., Morales, M., van der Werf, R.J., Morency, L.-P.: Virtual rapport. In: Gratch, J., Young, M., Aylett, R.S., Ballin, D., Olivier, P. (eds.) IVA 2006. LNCS (LNAI), vol. 4133, pp. 14–27. Springer, Heidelberg (2006)
4. Heylen, D., Kopp, S., Marsella, S.C., Pelachaud, C., Vilhjálmsson, H.H.: The next step towards a function markup language. In: Prendinger, H., Lester, J.C., Ishizuka, M. (eds.) IVA 2008. LNCS (LNAI), vol. 5208, pp. 270–280. Springer, Heidelberg (2008)
5. Kopp, S., Krenn, B., Marsella, S.C., Marshall, A.N., Pelachaud, C., Pirker, H., Thórisson, K.R., Vilhjálmsson, H.H.: Towards a common framework for multimodal generation: The behavior markup language. In: Gratch, J., Young, M., Aylett, R.S., Ballin, D., Olivier, P. (eds.) IVA 2006. LNCS (LNAI), vol. 4133, pp. 205–217. Springer, Heidelberg (2006)
6. Kopp, S., Stocksmeier, T., Gibbon, D.: Incremental multimodal feedback for conversational agents. In: Pelachaud, C., Martin, J.-C., André, E., Chollet, G., Karpouzis, K., Pelé, D. (eds.) IVA 2007. LNCS (LNAI), vol. 4722, pp. 139–146. Springer, Heidelberg (2007)
7. McNeill, D.: Hand and Mind: What Gestures Reveal about Thought. University of Chicago Press, Chicago (1995)
8. Perlin, K., Goldberg, A.: Improv: a system for scripting interactive actors in virtual worlds. In: SIGGRAPH, pp. 205–216. ACM, New York (1996)
9. Schmidt, R.C., Richardson, M.: Dynamics of interpersonal coordination. In: Fuchs, A., Jirsa, V. (eds.) Coordination: Neural, Behavioral and Social Dynamics. Understanding Complex Systems, vol. 17, pp. 281–308. Springer, Heidelberg (2008)
10. Thiebaux, M., Marshall, A.N., Marsella, S.C., Kallmann, M.: Smartbody: Behavior realization for embodied conversational agents. In: Autonomous Agents and Multiagent Systems, pp. 151–158 (2008)
11. Thórisson, K.R.: Gandalf: an embodied humanoid capable of real-time multimodal dialogue with people. In: Autonomous Sgents, pp. 536–537. ACM, New York (1997)
12. Thórisson, K.R., Vilhjálmsson, H.H.: Functional description of multimodal acts: A proposal. In: Function Markup Language Workshop at AAMAS 2009 (2009)
13. van Welbergen, H., Reidsma, D., Ruttkay, Z.M., Zwiers, J.: Elckerlyc: A BML realizer for continuous, multimodal interaction with a virtual human. Journal on Multimodal User Interfaces 3(4), 271–284 (2010)

A Flexible Dual Task Paradigm for Evaluating an Embodied Conversational Agent: Modality Effects and Reaction Time as an Index of Cognitive Load

Catherine J. Stevens, Guillaume Gibert, Yvonne Leung, and Zhengzhi Zhang

MARCS Auditory Laboratories, University of Western Sydney,
Locked Bag 1797, Penrith, NSW 2751, Australia
{kj.stevens,g.gibert,y.leung,z.zhang}@uws.edu.au

Abstract. A new experimental method based on the dual task paradigm is used to evaluate speech intelligibility of an embodied conversational agent (ECA). The experiment consists of the manipulation of auditory-visual (AV) versus auditory-only (A) presentation of speech. In the dual task, participants perform two tasks concurrently. The secondary task is sensitive to cognitive processing demands of the primary task. In the primary task participants either shadowed words or named the superordinate categories to which words belonged, as the word items were spoken by the ECA under A or AV conditions. Reaction time (RT) on the secondary task–swatting a fly on the ECA face–was affected by the difficulty of the concurrent task. The secondary RT was affected by modality of presentation of the primary task. Using a relatively primitive ECA, RT on the secondary task was significantly slower when shadowing occurred in AV versus A conditions. The benefits of this evaluation system, that returns quantitative behavioural data and self-report ratings, are discussed.

Keywords: Evaluation, Embodied Conversational Agent, Dual Task, Divided Attention, Reaction Time, Shadowing.

1 Introduction

There has been increasing interest and demand for ECA evaluation as more agents and speech, face, and emotion models have been developed. Taxonomies [e.g., 1] and frameworks [e.g., 2] have been proposed often emphasizing the need to distinguish features of user, agent, and task. It is more common now for evaluation of ECAs, or component models such as natural language generation or text to speech (TTS) synthesis systems, to consist of both objective and subjective measures [2-7]. There are still instances, however, where data are collected in the absence of the manipulation of specific variables (comparison conditions) or without a control condition [e.g., 8]. Interpretation of such data without a baseline reference or comparison group is necessarily limited. A promising technique that builds on the collection of both objective and subjective data is the application of an experimental method wherein particular variables of theoretical interest or design relevance are manipulated systematically [e.g., 9, 10].

H. Högni Vilhjálmsson et al. (Eds.): IVA 2011, LNAI 6895, pp. 331–337, 2011.
© Springer-Verlag Berlin Heidelberg 2011

The present study develops a dual task paradigm to gauge indirectly and sensitively the cognitive demand or mental workload imposed by the presence of a very basic ECA model. While improvements to the AV speech, facial expression, and attention models are in progress, the basic model is used to illustrate the logic and flexibility of the dual task paradigm to elicit a range of quantifiable and interpretable behavioural responses and its potential for systematic comparison of different models within or across different ECAs.

1.1   The Architecture and Logic of the Dual Task Paradigm

The dual task paradigm is a useful method to investigate dividing attention across two tasks. The paradigm involves performing two tasks concurrently resulting in impaired behavioural performance on one or both tasks [11]. The general assumption is that attention is finite–either limiting the extent to which two tasks can be carried out at the same time [12] or more flexible with attentional allocation occurring moment to moment depending on task instructions and priorities [11,13,14].

In the present study, participants perform a cognitive word-based primary task and secondary reaction time (RT) task at the same time. The primary task has two levels of difficulty. The easy version involves shadowing or saying aloud the word that was uttered by the ECA–the spoken word being a sensory cue. The more difficult version of the primary task requires the participant to name the superordinate category to which the word belongs–here the spoken word is a semantic cue. With a flexible view of attention, relatively early selection (shadow the word) is possible with a sensory cue but a later mode of selection (categorise the word) is necessary when the word serves as a semantic cue. The secondary task requires a button press response to a visual target on the ECA's face; the target is a small fly. The secondary task is used to measure potential capacity expended on the cognitive task. The rationale is that the greater the capacity allocated to the cognitive task the less capacity available for monitoring the fly and the longer the RTs on the secondary task should be [13]. This is regardless of whether the two tasks involve the same or multiple modalities [14]. Attentional capacity expended is akin to mental workload [15].

We compare the facilitation or impediment on processing achieved by the presence of an ECA producing the primary task sensory or semantic cues. In the auditory-visual (AV) condition, the ECA utters individual words and a participant sees the ECA utter the words. In the auditory only (A) condition, the ECA is present but there are no lip movements, only the voice uttering the individual word items. If the ECA AV model is effective and intelligible then this should facilitate shadowing and we should see equal or reduced RTs on the secondary task in the AV versus A condition. Conversely, if the AV model is ineffective then there will be no difference or poorer secondary task RTs on the AV versus A conditions. The relatively demanding category naming task is included to investigate any interaction between primary task demand and multi- versus uni-modal stimuli on secondary task RTs. A baseline of RTs on the fly swatting task is obtained by presenting the secondary task on its own, serving as a reference from which to measure the capacity (RT) required for the cognitive task. The secondary task RT ordering should be: baseline < shadowing < category naming.

2 Method

2.1 Participants, Stimuli, Equipment, and Procedure

Forty-seven female first year psychology students (M = 20.60 years, SD = 6.42) from the University of Western Sydney (UWS) participated in the study for course credit.

Thirty words from each superordinate category (Cooking, Animal, Seascape) were used as sensory or semantic cues in the shadowing and category-naming version of the primary task, respectively. A one-way analysis of variance (ANOVA) showed that there was no significant difference in word frequency between categories, $F(2,87)=.16$, $p=.90$, η^2_p =.004. Thirty-seven words had one syllable, 51 had two syllables, and two had three syllables. The nine rating scales consisted of five steps labelled from "totally disagree" (1) through to "totally agree" (5).

The ECA was displayed on a Cueword Teleprompter with a colour CCTV video camera and a shotgun microphone for videorecording. Two laptops were connected with a network switch for sending commands from the event manager program on one laptop to another that displayed the ECA and sent the image to the teleprompter. The audio from the ECA was transferred from the laptop to the USB Audio Capture and sent to the headphones and an Ultra Low-noise 8-input 2-Bus Mixer. The mixer also received audio input from the participants and sent the voice of both the ECA (IBM Viavoice) and participants to a DV capture device that transferred all audio input to the recording program. The video camera also sent images directly to the program.

Participants started with the baseline (simple RT only) task while the order of performing the shadowing and category naming tasks was counterbalanced. In the baseline RT task, participants looked at the ECA (static face) and pressed the spacebar as soon as they saw a static fly appearing. RT to the fly was measured from fly onset time. In the shadowing task, participants were instructed to repeat the word that the ECA said (primary task-sensory cue) while concurrently performing the RT (secondary) task. The ECA pronounced 90 words one by one with a 2 s inter-stimulus interval (ISI) between word items. Participants repeated the word as the word was uttered by the ECA. At the same time, they had to press the spacebar whenever they saw a fly appearing on the screen. In the category-naming task (primary task-semantic cue), the ECA pronounced the same 90 words as in the shadowing task and at the same rate of presentation but in a new order. This time, participants were asked to name one of three superordinate categories to which the spoken word belonged while performing the RT task concurrently. In the auditory-only condition, participants looked at a static face version of the ECA with auditory output throughout the experiment. In the auditory-visual condition, a dynamic face of the ECA (with lip movements somewhat correlated with spoken items) was presented in the shadowing and category naming tasks. At the end of the experiment, participants assigned ratings to different qualities of the ECA and the interaction.

3 Results

3.1 Secondary Task

3.1.1 Reaction Time

RTs refer to correct responses on the secondary (fly swatting) task and reported as milliseconds (ms). There was a significant main effect of task, $F(2, 2254)=845.28$, $p<.001$, $\eta^2_p=.43$. Pairwise comparisons showed the ordering of tasks to be as expected: Baseline ($M=429.13$, $SE=3.45$) significantly faster than Shadowing ($M=581.80$, $SE=4.58$), which was significantly faster than Category naming ($M=672.36$, $SE=5.58$). There was a main effect of modality, $F(1, 1127)=22.49$, $p=.001$, $\eta^2_p=.02$ with significantly faster RTs recorded on the secondary task in the A-only condition ($M=546.52$, $SE=0.97$) compared with the AV condition ($M=575.24$, $SE=0.95$); see Figure 1. There was a significant task by condition interaction, $F(2, 2254)=7.11$, $p=.001$, $\eta^2_p=.006$. All levels of task (baseline versus shadowing, baseline versus category, and shadowing versus category) differed significantly from each other in both the Auditory and Auditory-Visual modality conditions, $p<.001$. Modality had the greatest impact on RT during the shadowing task relative to baseline and category naming.

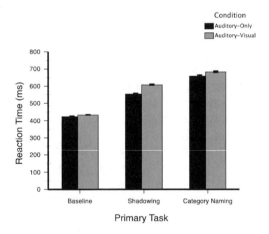

Fig. 1. Mean RT (ms) on the secondary (fly swatting) task shown as a function of Auditory-only and Auditory-Visual conditions and three levels of the primary task

3.1.2 Accuracy

In the secondary (fly swatting) task, it should be the case that accuracy is highest during the baseline condition, followed by shadowing and then the category naming condition. There was a significant main effect of task, $F(2,37)=5.80$, $p=.006$, $\eta^2_p=.24$. Accuracy on the secondary task was significantly higher during the baseline ($M=.99$, $SE=.003$) than the category naming task ($M=.96$, $SE=.009$), $p=.004$ and higher during the shadowing ($M=.99$, $SE=.005$) than the category naming task, $p=.02$. The mean accuracy scores on the secondary task, all > 95%, indicate that participants attended to the primary fly swatting task diligently and accurately. Accuracy on the secondary task did not differ across AV and A conditions.

3.2 Primary Task

3.2.1 Shadowing and Category Naming Latencies

Shadowing latencies were measured from the onset of the word spoken by the ECA to the onset of the shadowing response. The mean shadowing latency in the A condition was 372.52 ms (SD=158.82) and the AV condition was 366.14 ms (SD=151.48); there was no significant difference.

3.2.2 Accuracy

Mean accuracy in response to a sensory cue to shadow the word was .92 (SD=.04) in A and .91 (SE=.03) in the AV condition with no significant difference between these conditions. The overall accuracy exceeding 90% indicates that the individual word items uttered by the ECA were generally intelligible. Category naming (M=.86, SD=.08) was more difficult than shadowing (M=.91, SD=.03), $F(1,38)$=13.68, p=.001, η^2_p=.27. There was no word task x modality interaction.

3.3 Self-report Ratings

Table 1 shows the mode self-report ratings assigned to the nine rating scale items for A and AV conditions. The ratings differ significantly from the midpoint of the scale for both A-only $t(8)$=30.61, p<.001 and for AV conditions $t(8)$=33.16, p<.001; ratings did not differ significantly from each other. There was no effect of modality on mean ratings, A-only (M=3.66, SD=0.36) and AV (M=3.52, SD=0.32).

Table 1. Mode Ratings of ECA and Interaction Quality, Enjoyment and Engagement for auditory-only (A-only) and auditory-visual (AV) conditions; minimum possible rating is 1 ("totally disagree") and maximum possible rating is 5 ("totally agree")

Item	A-Only	AV
I find the Head likeable	4	4
I find the Head engaging	4	4
I find the Head easy to understand	2	2
I find the Head life-like	5	4
I find the Head humorous	3	4
The Head kept my attention	4	4
I would like to interact with the Head again	3	4
I enjoyed interacting with the Head	3	4
I felt as if the Head was speaking just to me	5	5

4 Discussion

The dual task paradigm has been developed as the means to evaluate components of an ECA using the experimental method. Results reveal that the paradigm works. In the present case, where a relatively primitive version of an ECA has been evaluated, the results indicate that the AV speech model does not enhance user perception. Indeed, under some circumstances when task demand is high and the concurrent task relies on speech perception, e.g., shadowing, performance in response to the current AV model impedes RT relative to the auditory only condition. Importantly, performance on the primary task, reflected in shadowing accuracy and latency, are not affected by modality with comparable results in AV and auditory only conditions. Thus, the existing AV model is intelligible, yielding 91-92% shadowing accuracy, but the relatively poor AV integration of spoken word and visemes has a significant processing cost reflected in slower RTs recorded on the secondary task when concurrently shadowing items presented AV compared with presentation of just audio versions of the items. In other words, the poorly integrated visual cues to the spoken items are distracting. The secondary task RT modality x task interaction indicates greater cognitive load or processing cost performing the concurrent task when shadowing (but not category naming) is in response to the AV model. The baseline of RT on the secondary (fly-swatting) task serves as a reference from which we can estimate relative capacity (RT) required for the different levels of the cognitive task. There was no significant effect of modality on baseline RT on the secondary task suggesting that the modality effect observed in shadowing and category naming is not simply overload from the presentation of concurrent visual stimuli.

The evaluation paradigm is a shell into which different modules or systems can be incorporated and systematically and quantitatively compared. The secondary task is sensitive to demands of the primary task and facilitation or impediment from different ECA models or component parts. A comparison with human video has recently been conducted with results currently being analysed.

Acknowledgments. This research is supported by the Thinking Head project and the Australian Research Council and the National Health and Medical Research Council (TS0669874). We thank Stelarc, Damith Herath, and Staci Parlato-Harris.

References

1. Ibister, K., Doyle, P.: Design and evaluation of embodied conversational agents: a proposed taxonomy. In: Proc 1st Intl Joint Conf Autonomous Agents and Multi-Agent System, AAMAS 2002, Bologna, Italy (2002)
2. Catrambone, R., Stasko, J., Xiao, J.: ECA as user interface paradigm: experimental findings within a framework for research. In: Ruttkay, Z., Pelachaud, C. (eds.) From Brows to Trust: Evaluating Embodied Conversational Agents, pp. 239–267. Springer, The Netherlands (2005)
3. Buisine, S., Abrillian, S., Martin, J.-C.: Evaluation of multimodal behaviour of embodied agents. In: Ruttkay, Z., Pelachaud, C. (eds.) From Brows to Trust: Evaluating Embodied Conversational Agents, pp. 217–238. Springer, The Netherlands (2005)

4. Koller, A., Striegnitz, K., Byron, D., Cassell, J., Dale, R., Dalzel-Job, S., Oberlander, J., Moore, J.: Validating the web-based evaluation of NLG systems. In: Proc ACL-IJCNLP, Singapore (2009)
5. Ruttkay, Z., Pelachaud, C. (eds.): From brows to trust: evaluating embodied conversational agents. Kluwer Academic Publishers, Dordrecht (2005)
6. Sharp, H., Rogers, Y., Preece, J.: Interaction design: Beyond human-computer interaction, 2nd edn. John Wiley & Sons, Ltd., Chichester (2007)
7. Stevens, C., Lees, N., Vonwiller, J., Burnham, D.: On-line experimental methods to evaluate text-to-speech (TTS) synthesis: Effects of voice gender and signal quality on intelligibility, naturalness and preference. Computer Speech & Language 19, 129–146 (2005)
8. Kopp, S., Gesellensetter, L., Krämer, N.C., Wachsmuth, I.: A conversational agent as museum guide – design and evaluation of a real-world application. In: Panayiotopoulos, T., Gratch, J., Aylett, R.S., Ballin, D., Olivier, P., Rist, T. (eds.) IVA 2005. LNCS (LNAI), vol. 3661, pp. 329–343. Springer, Heidelberg (2005)
9. Bailly, G., Raidt, S., Elisei, F.: Gaze, conversational agents and face-to-face communication. Speech Comm. 52, 598–612 (2010)
10. Badin, P., Tarabalka, Y., Elisei, F., Bailly, G.: Can you 'read' tongue movements? Evaluation of the contribution of tongue display to speech understanding. Speech Comm. 52, 493–503 (2010)
11. Karatekin, C., Couperus, J.W., Marcus, D.J.: Attention allocation in the dual-task paradigm as measured through behavioral and psychophysiological responses. Psychophysiol. 41, 175–185 (2004)
12. Pashler, H., Johnston, J.C.: Attentional limitations in dual-task performance. In: Pashler, H. (ed.) Attention, pp. 155–189. Psychology Press, East Sussex (1998)
13. Johnston, W.A., Heinz, S.P.: Flexibility and capacity demands of attention. J. Experimental Psychol.: General 107, 420–435 (1978)
14. Wickens, C.D.: Multiple resources and performance prediction. Theoretical Issues in Ergonomic Science 3, 159–177 (2002)
15. Fisk, A.D., Derrick, W.L., Schneider, W.: A methodological assessment and evaluation of dual-task paradigms. Current Psychological Research & Reviews 5, 315–327 (1986)

Did You Notice?
Artificial Team-Mates Take Risks for Players

Tim Merritt[1], Christopher Ong[2], Teong Leong Chuah[2], and Kevin McGee[1]

[1] NUS Graduate School for Integrative Sciences and Engineering
[2] National University of Singapore
{timothy.merritt,cnmoehc,mckevin}@nus.edu.sg, teongleong@gmail.com

Abstract. Artificial agents are increasingly included in digital games, often taking on a role as a team-mate with human players. An interesting area of focus is the differences in player responses to team-mates that are either controlled by another human or a computer. Although there has been research examining social dynamics of team-mates and even some recent research comparing the responses to computer and human team-mates examining blame, credit, enjoyment, and differences in physiological responses of arousal, there does not seem to have been any research looking specifically at the differences in responses to acts of risk-taking on behalf of a team-mate. In order to study this question, a quantitative study was conducted in which 40 participants played a real-time, goal-oriented, cooperative game. The game allows (but does not require) players to perform risky actions that benefit their team-mates – specifically, player's can "draw gunfire" towards themselves (and away from their team-mates). During the study, all participants played the game twice: once with an AI team-mate and once with a "presumed" human team-mate (i.e., an AI team-mate that they believed was a human team-mate). Thus, the team-mate performance and behaviors were identical for both cases – and in both cases, the team-mate "drew gunfire" an equal amount of the time. The main finding reported here is that players are more likely to notice acts of risk-taking by a human team-mate than by an artificial team-mate.

Keywords: media equation, CASA, team-mate, CSCP.

1 Introduction

There is growing effort to develop artificial team-mates for non-game purposes [1,2,3] – and, of course, for team-based games (e.g., sports games, team-based shooters, *RoboCup*, etc). In the context of computer games, interacting socially as a team has been identified as one of the main sources of player enjoyment [4]. Players engage in social interactions with team-mates and derive enjoyment from taking part in or benefitting from acts of loyalty, nurturance, risk-taking, and self-sacrifice [5]. Increasingly, these opportunities include interactions not only with other human team-mates, but with artificial team-mates as well.

An interesting question then is, how do people react to computer team-mates?

H. Högni Vilhjálmsson et al. (Eds.): IVA 2011, LNAI 6895, pp. 338–349, 2011.

Research suggests that people will easily form teams with computers, even if they are only given very minimal cues. By simply explaining to a human player that they are on a team (interdependent) with the computer, the human treats the computer as a team-mate in surprising ways as popularized in *media equation* studies [6].

Responses to human and computer team-mates do not seem to be the same in many situations. Research suggests that playing against a friend results in a more enjoyable game with different physiological responses than when playing against a computer [7]. Research on brain activity during gameplay [8] suggests that players will approach the game experience with human competitors differently than with computer competitors. They identified special brain regions dedicated to understanding the intentions and desires that become active only when interacting with human competitors. In [9] researchers observed the signals in the brain while people interacted with computers and humans who would treat them fairly or unfairly. Their findings suggest that people attach more emotions to interactions with humans who are being unfair vs. computers who are being unfair. In research involving people observing the behaviors of an avatar that performed altruistic acts [10], their findings suggest that the thought processes of the human observer are much more active when they believe the avatar is controlled by a human compared to a computer.

In terms of real-time games, research has also begun to understand some important differences in the way the identity of the team-mate affects the game experience. In one such study examining the emotional and physiological responses to computer or human co-players in cooperative and competitive games [11], findings suggest that when players have a computer as a team-mate or opponent, there is a significant difference in emotional response. The findings suggest that the computer was considered less favorable for competitive games and more desirable in cooperative games, however, the participants rated the experience with human co-players higher on average in all cases. In that study, the cooperative task involved players trading items with each other for a period of two minutes. The researchers noted that the cooperative game used in their study had limitations and did not provide a rich game-like context.

More recently, research has focused on examining the difference in responses to computer and human team-mates. Findings from these studies suggest that in the cooperative game context, players place unfair blame on their computer team-mates and assess the team-mate's skill inaccurately [12], while other findings suggest that, in controlled experiments using only artificial team-mates, when players believe their team-mates are human they prefer them over artificial team-mates and report more enjoyment from the game [13].

2   Research Problem

Although there has been some research that has examined differences in player experience related to demographic factors (experience, gender) and research that examined the differences in player emotions and responses to human and computer team-mates in the cooperative game context [11], within the cooperative

game context, there does not seem to have been any research directly comparing the differences in player perceptions and responses to risk-taking actions by
their human and computer team-mates. The remainder of this paper reports on
a study that provides insights into the question of whether there are differences
in the way players perceive risk-taking on their behalf if a team-mate is artificial
rather than human. Moderating factors such as team-mate gender, player motivations, experience level, etc. are controlled for in game based studies which is
described in more detail in the research protocol.

3   Study

In order to study this question, a quantitative study was conducted in which
40 participants played a real-time, goal-oriented, cooperative game. The game
allows (but does not require) players to perform risky actions that benefit their
team-mates – specifically, player's can "draw gunfire" towards themselves (and
away from their team-mates). During the study, all participants played the game
twice: once with an AI team-mate and once with a "presumed" human team-
mate (i.e., an AI team-mate that they believed was a human team-mate). Thus,
the team-mate performance and behaviors were identical for both cases – and
in both cases, the team-mate "drew gunfire" an equal amount of the time.

3.1   Participants

The 40 participants who took part in the study included 26 female and 14
male students between the ages of 20 and 25 with an average age of 21.7 years.
Participants were briefed on the concept of cooperative game play and were
asked to fill out a small questionnaire and consent form. When asked to rate
their experience and skill level with interactive digital games, the results were
fairly evenly distributed: 10% claimed to be *novice*, 25% claimed to have *little
experience (less than average)*, 45% claimed to have *average experience*, 12.5%
claimed to have *much experience (more than average)*, and 7.5% claimed to be
expert.

3.2   Cooperative Game: Capture the Gunner

The study called for a cooperative game that allows the human participant
to cooperate with a human or with a computer team-mate. The game used was
Capture the Gunner (CTG) as shown in Figure 1, which is simple to understand,
easy to learn and includes a signaling feature to make the intentions for risk-
taking more explicit between team-mates.

The game consists of a human-controlled avatar (a) and a computer-controlled
avatar (b) that, together, must evade bullets and cooperate in order to "capture"
(touch) the gunner (c) which is rotating and firing within its "field of view" (d)
from the middle of the game space. At each level, both players must touch the
gunner (though, not necessarily at the same time); once this occurs, the game

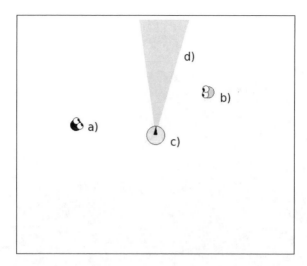

Fig. 1. Capture the Gunner (CTG) game elements: a) human-controlled avatar b) computer-controlled avatar c) gunner d) field of view

proceeds to the next level, with the gunner rotating faster. The game provides opportunities in which the players can assist their team-mate at the expense of placing themselves at greater risk.

Drawing Fire as Self-sacrifice. There are two ways that a player can help their team-mate by attracting attention of the gunner and encouraging the gunner to shift focus from their team-mate and becoming the actively targeted player. These tactics of "drawing fire" include moving into the field of view of the gunner, and additionally, to draw even more attention of the gunner, the player can "yell" by pressing the "W" key while in the field view of the gunner. The "yell" action causes the player's avatar to blink yellow for two seconds to indicate the elevated attempts to draw attention as shown in Figure 2. The AI team-mate is programmed to draw attention in both ways at regular intervals. Game event data is logged for each session including the levels achieved, number of deaths, and actions taken by both team-mates including the number of "yell" events.

Gunner Behavior Algorithm. The gunner, which is the opponent shared by the players, has two actions that it can take – rotation to target the players and firing bullets to strike the players. The behavior algorithm was developed with the aim to be a challenging opponent, somewhat unpredictable by the players, and yet influenced by the player actions. The gunner behavior algorithm is configured to seek out both players equally at the beginning of each level. It rotates until one of the players is in its field of view, at which point it begins firing at that player. Every three seconds, a dice roll is made (not visible to the players), which results in the gunner choosing either to stay with the current

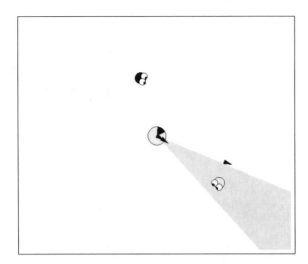

Fig. 2. Avatar blinking yellow to signal "draw fire"

target, or to pursue the other player using odds that begin at 50/50. The players can influence the likelihood of being targeted by positioning their avatar in the field of view of the gunner and activating the "yell" action. With each yell event, the odds shift 10% in favor of targeting the player who has yelled. This shift in odds is not visible to the player, who is told that the yelling action may or may not be effective in drawing the attention of the gunner. The participants are told that by "yelling", they will likely raise the desire for the gunner to target them.

3.3 Conditions

Participants arrived at a private testing room, did not meet any other participants, and were assured that their comments would be kept anonymous and not revealed to other human participants. Each participant was briefed on the game, read a description of the game objectives and explanation of the "yell" feature, which was identified clearly as an additional way of attracting attention of the gunner by taking on additional risk. The participants then watched a short video illustrating the game and the "yell" feature. Participants then played the game for three sessions. The first session was to familiarize the participants with the controls for moving their avatar using the moused and to ensure they understood and could activate the "yell" action. This was followed by two sessions of eight minutes each, one with an AI team-mate and another with a PH ("presumed human") team-mate. The order of these sessions was alternated for each study to minimize the effects of the order of exposure. The PH team-mate was actually controlled by the computer using the same AI algorithm in both sessions, yet the participants were told that there was a human participant who joined through the network controlling the team-mate.

The mild deception was to ensure that any differences in the ways that the participants described or reacted to the team-mate could be attributed to whether they believed the team-mate was computer-based or human. The purpose was not to see whether or how easily humans can be led to believe they are coordinating with other humans (e.g., variant Turing test). Using the same artificial team-mate through-out the study also ensured that the participant's team-mate would perform at a consistent level across all play sessions, the importance of which is noted in [11].

3.4   Measures

Self-report Measures. Participants were asked to rate their subjective experience through simple questionnaires. After each of the 8 minute game sessions, the participants were asked to rate their experience using a 10 point scale (Q1, Q3, Q4). After both sessions had been completed, the participants were asked to make a comparison between both team-mates (Q2).

Q1: Ranking Risk. "How much risk did your team-mate take to help you? (1=Team-mate did not take any risks to help me, 10=Team-mate took many risks to help me)"

After the participants had played with both team-mates, they were asked to reflect on both sessions and then evaluate which team-mate took more risks to help them using a 10 point scale (1-5 favoring the human team-mate / 6-10 favoring the computer team-mate)

Q2: Comparative Risk. "Which team-mate took more risks trying to help you? (1=Human team-mate took more risks to help me, 10=Computer team-mate took more risks to help me)"

Although the main focus of this study is on perceived level of risk-taking, Q3 and Q4 provide support to the inquiry.

Q3: Cooperation. "How well did your team-mate cooperate with you? (1=Team-mate did not cooperate very well at all, 10=Team-mate cooperated very well)"

Q3 focused on the perceived level of cooperation, to ensure that the game feels like a cooperative experience and to note any wide differences across the two team-mate conditions.

Q4: Enjoyment. "How much did you enjoy this game session? (1=I did not enjoy this game session at all, 10=I enjoyed this game session very much)"

Q4 also provided a supporting role in the study and was used to validate that, in fact, the experience was enjoyable – which is expected in the game context. It also served to validate that to some degree, both team-mate conditions resulted in a similar game-like experience.

Game Event Measures. Various game events were logged to a text file during each game session to track in game behaviors, which resulted in two text files per participant, one for each of the two team-mate conditions to allow for later comparisons. These measured events included the following: highest level achieved, number of deaths (participant avatar/agent), number of yell events (participant avatar/agent). The game interface used by the participants indicated the current level, however, the other game statistics were not visible to them to avoid these from possibly influencing the perceptions of their team-mate.

4   Results

The main result of this study is that when participants played with the PH ("presumed human") team-mate, they perceived significantly greater amount of risk taken by the team-mate to help them than when they played with the AI team-mate. In this section, the main finding of identity as a moderator of risk is presented with supporting results about the perception of cooperation and enjoyment.

Before we examined differences in the subjective ratings of the participants toward their team-mates and logged in-game behaviors, statistical analyses were conducted to rule out any confounding effects of the order of exposure to the AI or PH team-mate. There were no significant effects of order for any of the dependent measures including subjective responses and game outcomes. MANOVAs were conducted to detect any possible effect(s) of demographic variables of age, gender, and experience on all the dependent measures, and there were no significant interactions or main effects.

4.1   Effects of Team-Mate Identity on Perception of Risk

Q1 explored the effects of team-mate identity on the perception of risk taken by a team-mate to help the player. Considering the significance of the higher reported level of cooperation in Q1, a paired-sample T-test was conducted with the expectation that a higher level of perceived risk would be present with the PH team-mate. The one-tailed test revealed that when participants played with the PH ("presumed human") team-mate, they perceived significantly greater amount of risk taken by the team-mate to help them (M=8.13, SD=1.285) than when they played with the AI team-mate (M=7.58, SD=1.318), t (39)=1.952, p=0.029.

Q2 further explored the effects of team-mate identity on the perception of risk taken by a team-mate to help the player. When asked to consider both team-mates and compare the amount of risk taken by each to help the participant, 67.5% chose values indicating that the PH took more risks, while 32.5% chose values indication that the AI took more risks.

4.2   Effects of Team-Mate Identity on Perception of Cooperation

The results of Q3 provided insights into the difference in perception of the two team-mate conditions and gave reason to expect that participants would report higher levels of risk-taking by their human team-mates in Q1.

Q3 explored the effects of team-mate identity on the perception of cooperation from the team-mate. Results from a paired-sample T-test revealed that when people played with the PH team-mate, they felt significantly greater cooperation in the game (M=7.88, SD=1.381) than when they played with the AI team-mate (M=7.13, SD=1.522), t (39)=2.940, p=0.005.

4.3   Effects of Team-Mate Identity on Enjoyment

Q4 supports the study by validating that participants reported high levels of enjoyment in both conditions. Q4 explored the effects of team-mate identity on the enjoyment of the game and the results suggest that both conditions were enjoyable with average ratings above 7 on the 10 point scale. The difference in the mean enjoyment level was 0.38, indicating that the human condition was slightly more enjoyable. Results from a paired-sample T-test showed that when people played with the PH team-mate, they felt slightly more enjoyment (M=7.48, SD=1.339) than when they played with the AI team-mate (M=7.10, SD=1.257), t (39)=2.027, p=0.050.

4.4   Effects of Identity on Game Events

Analysis comparing the logged data during both game sessions, revealed that any differences in highest level achieved, number of deaths of participant or team-mate, and number of yell events were not significant. The values for participant signaling, described later in the paper are now briefly summarized.

Signaling Frequency. The amount of signaling by the human participants varied considerably from participant to participant, but the the average difference between the amount of participant signaling when playing with the PH team-mate (M=18.05 SD=39.082) and the AI team-mate (M=16.77 SD=21.526) was not shown to be significant. However, the large difference in the standard deviation reveals that when players had PH team-mates, their signaling behaviors were much more erratic.

5   Discussion

More details are now provided about the fact that people perceived more risk-taking with their "presumed human" team-mates and additional discussion explaining the supporting results of perceived cooperation, reported enjoyment levels, and discussion about the signaling mechanism used in the game.

5.1   Perception of Risk

This study investigated how the perception of team-mate identity (human avatar / artificial agent) in the context of goal-oriented real-time cooperative game play influenced the perception of risk-taking by the team-mate to help the participant. The results showed that the beliefs about the identity of the team-mate influenced the perception of the gaming experiences in a significant way. Participants perceived significantly greater amount of risk taken to help them by the PH ("presumed human") compared to the AI team-mate. These results demonstrate that whether or not a player believes that game characters are controlled by other humans can significantly alter thoughtful evaluations of the cooperative game experience including affiliation related effects of perceived risk-taking and cooperation, as well as overall enjoyment of the game experience. This suggests that human avatars increase the sensitivity to interactions with digital media resulting in the human player noticing or valuing some events to a greater degree. Likewise, it suggests that artificial agents decrease the sensitivity to these interactions, or that some aspects are generally less noticed or valued. In essence, if an artificial team-mate engages in risk-taking in order to help a human player, it is more likely to go unnoticed than if the team-mate is human.

5.2   Cooperation

Cooperation involves coordination toward shared goals. The game context of this study provided the opportunity for players to cooperate in this way – both players had to perform the same primary objective of "touching the gunner." The only instructions given to the participants regarding strategy toward achieving the goals was to avoid the bullets and to "draw gunfire" to help a team-mate by distracting the shared opponent. This activity of "drawing gunfire" is not a primary objective, but the participants had an understanding that the team-mates could cooperate in order to help their team-mate achieve their primary goal. This study recognizes risk-taking as a cooperative behavior and considering the subjective responses by the participants rating the perceived cooperation from both team-mates higher than 7 on the 10-point scale, there seems to be evidence to suggest that the game context of "Capture the Gunner" was in fact regarded as a cooperative experience by the participants. However, the difference between the perception of cooperation favoring humans suggests that people are more likely to perceive that the behaviors of their team-mate are aligned to the group goals when their team-mate is human. This also suggests that designers of artificial team-mate should consider strategies that can make the cooperative behaviors of the agent more explicit in order to overcome the reduced sensitivity in the perception of cooperation.

5.3   Enjoyment

While the findings of this study around risk-taking are compelling on their own, it is important to consider that the context of the user interaction was a cooperative game – the activity should have some measurable amount of enjoyment. Participants were asked to rate their enjoyment of the game sessions primarily to ensure that the task that was used as the instrument of study was in fact enjoyable and therefore, game-like. The results suggest that the game was enjoyable as we expected, however, there was the surprising result that the participants rated their experience with the "presumed human" PH team-mate higher than the AI team-mate even though they were essentially the same.

5.4 Signaling Mechanism

One problematic result presented in the study relates to participant signaling. The logged data shows that the signaling frequency was erratic – some participants signaled incessantly, others moderately, and a large number did not signal at all. This raises questions about why there is such a variance and whether or not this relates to the personalities of the participants, mechanics of the interface, playing style, etc. This study also raises the methodological issues about how to determine when people intend to "draw fire" – our method was to implement a measurable signaling mechanism by having the user press a key on the keyboard, however, it is not clear if this is the most effective way to capture the user intentions. In future studies, other signaling mechanics should be explored to ensure that the user's intentions are easily transferred into the game. The issues that might be raised about the signaling mechanism do not affect the main findings reported in this paper. Our focus was on the perception of risk-taking by a team-mate, and not on the acts of risk-taking by the human participant for their team-mate.

5.5 Limitations of the Study

Although the results of the study are significant and begin to explore the effects of identity on risk-taking with team-mates, there are ways this research can be improved including more rich logging of game events, exploration of other risk-taking contexts, prolonged game sessions, various playing styles of the team-mate, and other variables that might moderate the effect of identity, such as familiarity between team-mates.

The game sessions were not video-recorded and therefore, there are aspects about the individual playing styles that is not gathered through the game event logging. Coding and extracting player behaviors can be very time-consuming and is subject to interpretation by the observer. More sophisticated logging of various events in the game could help strengthen the systematic observance of in-game events including inter-avatar distance, amount of time spent in the field of view of the gunner, proximity to the gunner, etc.

Risk-taking is an act of self-sacrifice that can take many forms in a number of situations. The act of risk-taking was measured in this study through the simple action in measurable "draw gunfire" events, which does not capture other events that might be considered or intended to be risk-taking on behalf of a team-mate, for example, moving out of the way to allow easy passage, assuming more of the work on behalf of a tired team-mate, etc. Other examples of risk-taking should be examined to explore player perceptions and actions in situations related to self-sacrifice on behalf of a team-mate.

Risk-taking on behalf of a team-mate may be an activity that changes over time. While this study involved game session that were substantial in length to begin to see effects of team-mate identity on perceptions of risk-taking, longer-term studies, in which players spend extended periods of time playing the game could explore the effects over time.

The study was conducted with a single algorithm for the AI team-mate in order to keep the game experience consistent across all game sessions. Although the effects were significant using the AI team-mate at the current skill level, it would be worthwhile to examine how team-mates of other skill levels would be perceived.

Finally, this study did not allow the participants to meet or interact with their presumed human team-mates, yet the effects of identity on the perception of risk-taking were observed. Familiarity with the human participant, gender, and personality types would likely influence the ways human players would experience the game and risk-taking behaviors, therefore, in this study, those factors were controlled for and their effects can be explored in future studies.

6   Conclusion and Future Work

What can this study tell us about employing agents in real-time cooperative tasks? In general, the identity of the team-mate (human vs. artificial) seems to influence the player's perception of acts of loyalty (risk-taking) by the team-mate regardless of the actual behaviors of the team-mate. Human team-mates appear to make the cooperative game experience more enjoyable and seem more cooperative than artificial team-mates.

In terms of future work, there are various aspects of team cooperation in the real-time digital game context that deserve more in-depth exploration. There remain open questions about the influence of team-mate identity including other aspects of the subjective game experience and in-game behaviors.

Acknowledgments. This research is supported by the Singapore-MIT GAM-BIT Game Lab research grant "Designing Adaptive Team-mates for Games."

References

1. Van Diggelen, J., Muller, T., Van Den Bosch, K.: Using artificial team members for team training in virtual environments. In: Proceedings of the 10th International Conference on Intelligent Virtual Agents, IVA 2010, pp. 28–34. Springer, Heidelberg (2010)
2. Doherty, S.M.: Human-centered design in synthetic teammates for aviation: The challenge for artificial intelligence. In: Russell, I., Haller, S.M. (eds.) Proceedings of the Sixteenth International Florida Artificial Intelligence Research Society Conference, St. Augustine, Florida, USA, May 12-14, pp. 54–56. AAAI Press, Menlo Park (2003)

3. Babu, S., Grechkin, T., Chihak, B., Ziemer, C., Kearney, J., Cremer, J., Plumert, J.: A virtual peer for investigating social influences on children's bicycling. In: Virtual Reality Conference, VR 2009, pp. 91–98 (March 2009)

4. Sherry, J.L., Lucas, K., Greenberg, B.S., Lachlan, K.: Video game uses and gratifications as predictors of use and game preferences. In: Vorderer, P., Bryant, J. (eds.) Playing Video Games Motives Responses and Consequences, pp. 213–224. Lawrence Erlbaum Associates, Mahwah (2006)

5. Bostan, B.: Player motivations: A psychological perspective. Comput. Entertain. 7 (June 2009)

6. Reeves, B., Nass, C.: The media equation: how people treat computers, television, and new media like real people and places. Cambridge University Press, Cambridge (1996)

7. Mandryk, R.L., Inkpen, K.M., Calvert, T.W.: Using psychophysiological techniques to measure user experience with entertainment technologies. Behaviour & Information Technology 25(2), 141–158 (2006)

8. Gallagher, H.L., Jack, A.I., Roepstorff, A., Frith, C.D.: Imaging the intentional stance in a competitive game. NeuroImage 16(3), 814–821 (2002)

9. Sanfey, A.G., Rilling, J.K., Aronson, J.A., Nystrom, L.E., Cohen, J.D.: The neural basis of economic Decision-Making in the ultimatum game. Science 300(5626), 1755–1758 (2003)

10. Montague, P.R., Chiu, P.H.: For goodness' sake. Nature Neuroscience 10(2), 137–138 (2007)

11. Lim, S., Reeves, B.: Computer agents versus avatars: Responses to interactive game characters controlled by a computer or other player. International Journal of Human-Computer Studies 68(1-2), 57–68 (2010)

12. Merritt, T.R., Tan, K.B., Ong, C., Thomas, A., Chuah, T.L., McGee, K.: Are artificial team-mates scapegoats in computer games. In: Proceedings of the ACM 2011 Conference on Computer Supported Cooperative Work, CSCW 2011, pp. 685–688. ACM Press, New York (2011)

13. Merritt, T.R., McGee, K., Chuah, T.L., Ong, C.: Choosing human team-mates: perceived identity as a moderator of player preference and enjoyment. In: The Proceedings of the 2011 Foundations of Digital Games Conference, pp. 196–203 (2011)

Sharing Emotions and Space – Empathy as a Basis for Cooperative Spatial Interaction

Hana Boukricha, Nhung Nguyen, and Ipke Wachsmuth*

A.I. Group, Faculty of Technology
Bielefeld University
33594 Bielefeld, Germany
{hboukric,nnguyen,ipke}@techfak.uni-bielefeld.de

Abstract. Empathy is believed to play a major role as a basis for humans' cooperative behavior. Recent research shows that humans empathize with each other to different degrees depending on several modulation factors including, among others, their social relationships, their mood, and the situational context. In human spatial interaction, partners share and sustain a space that is equally and exclusively reachable to them, the so-called interaction space. In a cooperative interaction scenario of relocating objects in interaction space, we introduce an approach for triggering and modulating a virtual humans cooperative spatial behavior by its degree of empathy with its interaction partner. That is, spatial distances like object distances as well as distances of arm and body movements while relocating objects in interaction space are modulated by the virtual human's degree of empathy. In this scenario, the virtual human's empathic emotion is generated as a hypothesis about the partner's emotional state as related to the physical effort needed to perform a goal directed spatial behavior.

1 Introduction and Motivation

In human social interaction, empathy plays a major role as a motivational basis of cooperative behavior and as contributing to moral acts like helping, caring, and justice [11]. Recent neuropsychological findings [6] substantiate that empathic brain responses are prone to modulation and thus humans empathize with each other to different degrees. The modulation depends on several factors including, among others, humans' social relationships, their mood, and the situational context. In human spatial cooperation the interactants share and sustain a space that is equally and exclusively reachable to them [13]. In such interaction the partners' reach-spaces, the so called peripersonal spaces, may overlap and establish a shared reach-space defined as their interaction space [19]. Previous works have shown that virtual humans are a suitable testbed to study empathic behavior, e.g., [23] and spatial behavior, e.g., [22]. In this paper, we introduce an approach to trigger and modulate a virtual human's cooperative spatial behavior by its degree of empathy with its interaction partner.

In a spatial interaction scenario of a tower building task, potential field functions are used to control the spatial actions of the virtual human Max [15] in peripersonal

---

* Corresponding author.

H. Högni Vilhjálmsson et al. (Eds.): IVA 2011, LNAI 6895, pp. 350–362, 2011.

and interaction space. Depending on the size and layout of the interaction space, Max can relocate objects to any free location toward or away from locations reachable for its partner [19]. Since in this scenario, Max's cooperative spatial behavior is a helping action that consists of relocating objects toward positions reachable for the partner, the question arises which position within interaction space is chosen to help the partner. In order to deal with this question, Max's helping action is triggered and modulated by its degree of empathy with its partner. That is, spatial distances like object distances as well as distances of arm and body movements while relocating objects toward positions reachable for the partner are modulated by Max's degree of empathy with its partner. Max's empathic behavior consists of three processing steps [5]: First, the *Empathy Mechanism* by which an empathic emotion is generated as a hypothesis about the partner's emotional state as related to the physical effort needed to perform a goal directed spatial behavior. Second, the *Empathy Modulation* by which the empathic emotion is modulated through modulation factors like Max's mood, relationship to the partner, and the situational context. Third, the *Expression of Empathy* by which Max's modulated facial expression and helping action are triggered.

The paper is structured as follows: In Section 2, related work on virtual humans exhibiting empathic and spatial behaviors are outlined. In Section 3, Max's spatial behavior is described. In Section 4, we present the cooperative spatial interaction task. In Section 5, Max's empathic behavior is described. Subsequently in Section 6, we introduce an approach for modulating Max's cooperative spatial behavior. Finally in Section 7, we give a summary of the main aspects underlying our approach and an outlook on future work.

2   Related Work

There are various attempts to endow virtual humans with the ability to empathize. Mc-Quiggan et al. [18] propose an inductive framework for modeling parallel and reactive empathy in virtual agents. Their framework is called *CARE (Companion Assisted Reactive Empathizer)* and is based on learning empirically grounded models of empathy from observing human-agent social interactions. In a virtual training environment, users are able to evaluate the virtual character's empathic reaction allowing it to learn models of empathy from "good" examples. Based on an empirical and theoretical approach Ochs et al. [20] propose a computational model of empathic emotions. The empirical part is based on analyzing human-machine dialogs in order to identify the characteristics of emotional dialog situations. The theoretical part is based on cognitive psychological theories and consists of determining the type and intensity of the empathic emotion. In [24], the empathy model is implemented into an affective agent architecture and the intensity of the empathic emotion is determined by the following modulation factors: *similarity, affective link, mood,* and *personality*. Boukricha and Wachsmuth [5], presented a computational model of empathy. Within this model, the type and intensity of the empathic emotion are modulated by factors like the virtual human's mood and relationship to its interaction partner. In a scenario of interactive affective narratives, Aylett and Louchart [1] use a double appraisal mechanism in order to determine the emotional impact of an action on the other characters. Double appraisal means using a characters' own appraisal mechanisms for reasoning about the emotions of others.

Cooperative behavior of robots and virtual humans in task execution with humans was presented in previous works. In work by Kopp et al. [15] a virtual human performs a construction task with a human partner in a face-to-face virtual reality scenario. The virtual human cooperates with his partner by describing assembly plans and by offering verbal and gestural assistance on request. In another scenario, where a robot is to support human partners in building wooden construction toys, Foster et al. [7] introduced a dialogue system which provides the robot with abilities similar to Max's. In work of Gray et al. [9] a robot performs a button-push task in cooperation with a human partner. The robot uses its own motor-action repertoire to recognize the partner's actions in order to infer the partner's goals and offer help, such as completing a failed action. With a focus on the spatial aspect of actions within cooperative task execution, Nguyen and Wachsmuth [19] presented a model for structuring and controlling a virtual human's spatial behavior and attention in task execution at close distances. Apart of such execution tasks, spatial behavior models have been presented in locomotion scenarios for robots and virtual humans. Pedica and Vilhjálmsson [22] for example controlled virtual humans' spatial group formations in virtual reality environments like games. Sisbot et al. [25] presented their work on robot locomotion planning considering factors like humans' comfort, preferences, and safety.

While significant advances have been made in modeling the empathic, spatial, and cooperative behaviors of virtual humans, triggering and modulating a virtual human's cooperative spatial behavior by its degree of empathy was not addressed so far. In the present work, the virtual human's degree of empathy is affected by factors like its mood, its relationship to the partner, and the situational context. The virtual human's *Empathy Mechanism* is based on using its own appraisal mechanisms for generating an empathic emotion. This process is similar to those mentioned above in [9] and [1].

3   Spatial Behavior

In this section we outline how the space surrounding an individual virtual human and the space in interpersonal interaction is modeled. The surrounding spaces are projected on an assumed 2-D plane on a table in front of the virtual human, in this case Max. Hence, the vertical extent of each space is projected on a lower radial $180°$ 2-D plane. Furthermore, the table size needs to assure sufficient space for object manipulation and for both partners to lean forward and carry out arm movements without too much obstruction.

3.1   Peripersonal and Interaction Space

The work on peripersonal space is motivated by research from biology and cognitive neuroscience. The reach- and lean-forward distances are calculated from Max's body structure [19]. The peripersonal space is divided into subspaces differing in spatial range, extent and frames of reference. In this paper we focus on the *touch space* and the *lean-forward space* (see Figure 1, left). The touch space's boundary is limited to the lengths of the arm limbs. The lean-forward space's boundary is limited to the maximal reaching realm of the upper torso when bending forward. Another agent (human or virtual) entering Max's proximity is assumed to be surrounded by a peripersonal space in the same way as Max. The intersection of their overlapping peripersonal spaces is what was defined in previous work [19] as *interaction space* (see Figure 1, right). This space is equally and exclusively reachable to the interactants, and is the space in which they cooperate.

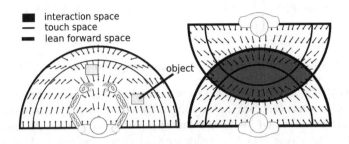

Fig. 1. Left: Subspaces surrounding a virtual human. Lean-forward space as an extension of touch space. Arrows illustrate force vectors in a repulsive artificial potential field, here pointing to the front of the body. Right: Interaction space spanned by two partners.

3.2 Potential Fields

In order to trigger appropriate motor actions with regard to objects at each location in peripersonal and interaction space, we use artificial potential fields [14], a common method for obstacle avoidance and path planning for artificial agents. The peripersonal space is described as a repulsive field. A vector between the center of peripersonal space (i.e. an assumed center of Max's body) and any position P in space is denoted by position vector $\mathbf{p}$. The touch space's field F_{touch} is defined by Equation 1 with tangential directions covering a semicircle in front of Max's torso, defined by Equation 2 and illustrated in Figure 1, left. We calculate the force vector $\mathbf{v}_{touch}(\mathbf{p})$, that is currently affecting $\mathbf{p}$, using Equation 2. The parameter ξ_{peri} denotes a positive scalar which influences the length of the resulting force vector. The force vectors $\mathbf{v}_{touch}(\mathbf{p})$ point to the frontal, sagittal midline of Max's body, described by vector $\mathbf{r}_{perimid}$. This midline defines a default direction in front of Max's body. The field covers all $\mathbf{p}$'s within an angle of $90°$ to both sides of this midline. The regions beyond the radius r_{touch} of touch space are not affected by the potential field, and thus result in a zero force vector. The lean-forward space is located between r_{touch} and a larger radius r_{lean}. It is modeled as an extension of the touch space, thus the potential field F_{touch} can be extended up to r_{lean}. Regions beyond r_{lean} belong to *extrapersonal space*. The interaction space is modeled as an *attractive* potential field. Since interaction space affects the peripersonal spaces of both partners, its radius includes both involved peripersonal potential fields. All forces currently affecting any position P in space have to be summed up to obtain the resulting force. Each time Max perceives an object, the current resulting force vector impacting on the object has to be calculated. Objects outside the interaction space are affected by force vectors within the peripersonal space, describing a path which leads in the direction of the interaction space. With decreasing distance to the center, the strength of the potential field disappears, ending the path.

$$\mathbf{F}_{touch}(\mathbf{p}) = \begin{cases} \xi_{peri}\left(\frac{1}{\|\mathbf{p}\|} - \frac{1}{r_{touch}}\right)\frac{\mathbf{p}}{\|\mathbf{p}\|^3} & \|\mathbf{p}\| \leq r_{touch}, \\ 0 & else \end{cases} \tag{1}$$

$$\mathbf{v}_{touch}(\mathbf{p}) = \begin{cases} -\left(\frac{\pi}{2}\right) * \mathbf{F}_{touch}(\mathbf{p}) & \forall \mathbf{p} \mid \angle(\mathbf{r}_{perimid}, \mathbf{p}) \leq -\left(\frac{\pi}{2}\right), \\ \left(\frac{\pi}{2}\right) * \mathbf{F}_{peri}(\mathbf{p}) & \forall \mathbf{p} \mid \angle(\mathbf{r}_{perimid}, \mathbf{p}) \leq \left(\frac{\pi}{2}\right), \\ 0 & else \end{cases} \tag{2}$$

3.3   Potential Field Parameters for Modulating Spatial Actions and Distances

Potential fields are a suitable method to associate each point in peripersonal space to a specific behavior, in this case motor actions. By superposing several potential fields, behaviors can be combined, allowing for more sophisticated actions like reaching with collision avoidance. Another way to influence Max's spatial behavior is by changing the parameters of the potential field of Max's touch space (see Equation 1). The following parameters are influenced by Max's degree of empathy (see Section 6).

Field strength. The field strength parameter ξ_{peri} in equation 1 determining the lengths of the resulting force vectors controls the velocity of a chosen motor action.

Field radius. The field radius parameter r_{touch} in equation 1 determines the end point of the chosen motor action. The maximum value for r_{touch} is determined by r_{lean}, which results in motor actions within the lean-forward space.

4   Cooperative Building Task

In a virtual reality CAVE-like environment Max and his interaction partner are standing face-to-face at a table in order to solve a cooperative building task with virtual toy blocks. According to Section 3 the partner's overlapping peripersonal spaces form an interaction space.

The goal of the spatial interaction task is to cooperatively build a tower by alternately putting a toy block one upon the other. All tower blocks are labeled with numbers and differ in their size. The numbers ascend with larger size, i.e, the largest block is labeled with the highest number. At the beginning of the game the largest block is placed by default in the center of the partners' interaction space, where they have to place the remaining blocks. The remaining blocks are randomly placed at free locations within the partners' peripersonal spaces. Each partner may get a different number of blocks with respect to a predefined minimum. There are two rules to build a tower: First, the tower blocks can be ordered by their number-labels, e.g., block number two is put on block number three. When all existing blocks are ordered by their numbers, this leads to the highest *ideal* tower. Second, the tower blocks can be ordered by their sizes without matching the direct number order, e.g., block number two is put on block number four, omitting block number three. This leads to a smaller tower. Each partner should place the most appropriate block located in his peripersonal space on the tower. The most appropriate block is defined as the one that best fits the above introduced rules. The tower building task ends when the smallest block is placed on the top of the tower.

The Virtual Human Max has a cognitive architecture composed of a Belief-Desire-Intention (BDI) module [16] and of an emotion simulation module [3]. Based on domain-specific as well as domain-independent appraisal mechanisms, emotional valences are derived in the deliberative component of the BDI module [2] and drive Max's emotion dynamics over time, e.g., achieving a desired goal is rewarded with positive values of emotional valence. The emotion simulation module consists of two components: First, the dynamics/mood component for the calculation of the course of emotions and moods over time and their mutual interaction. Second, the Pleasure-Arousal-Dominance (PAD) space in which primary and secondary emotions are located and their intensity values are calculated. At each point in time, the emotion module outputs values of pleasure, arousal, and one of two possible values of dominance (dominant vs. submissive) as well as intensity values of primary and secondary emotions.

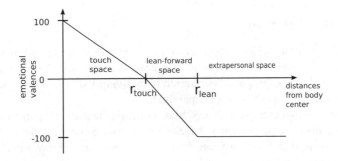

Fig. 2. The cost function maps spatial distances starting from the center of peripersonal space to emotional valences

Max's game moves are performed by means of a sequence of plans defined in his BDI module. In order to place a block on the tower, Max first searches for the most appropriate one. Depending on the block's position, a corresponding emotional valence is triggered according to the cost function illustrated in Figure 2. This cost function associates peripersonal space distances and thus the physical effort of motor actions to emotional valences. The function reflects the effort of Max's reaching movements according to humans' physical effort. With increasing reach distance of objects, more physical effort is needed for humans to reach for them [17].

Blocks located in Max's touch space are easy to reach with less effort and lower cost, thus they are associated with emotional valences ranging in $[0, 100]$ where the value of 100 corresponds to the center of this space. Blocks located in the lean-forward space are reachable but require more effort and higher cost, thus they are associated with emotional valences ranging in $[-100, 0]$ where the value of 0 corresponds to the limiting border of touch space. Blocks located in extrapersonal space are not reachable, thus they are associated with emotional valences with a constant value of -100. If the most appropriate block is not reachable for Max, he searches until he finds the next most appropriate and reachable one. Finally, Max places this block on the tower. This game move is defined as a goal success and is rewarded with a positive emotional valence. Otherwise, if no appropriate reachable block is found Max's turn is missed. This is defined as a goal failure and is rewarded with a negative emotional valence. In this scenario, cooperation consists of helping each other in accomplishing the game move. The helping action is defined as placing the most appropriate block toward a location reachable for the partner. Depending on the position of the placed block, i.e., how near the partner is placing the block to Max, an emotional valence is triggered according to the cost function shown in Figure 2.

5   Empathic Behavior

The work on the virtual human's empathic behavior is motivated by research in psychology and neuropsychology. Max's empathic behavior consists of three processing steps [5]: *Empathy Mechanism*, *Empathy Modulation*, and *Expression of Empathy*.

5.1   Empathy Mechanism

An empathic emotion can be elicited even if it is not felt or expressed by the partner (cf. [20]). Thus, in our spatial interaction scenario, the *Empathy Mechanism* by which an empathic emotion is produced is referred to as *situational role-taking* and is based on Max's *spatial perspective-taking* capabilities.

Spatial perspective-taking consists of Max modeling the partner's peripersonal space by projecting his own peripersonal space to the partner. Simulating the partner's perspective by using own body structure is known as *embodied simulation* [8] and is a hypothesis of how humans understand others. Thus, by means of his spatial perspective-taking capabilities, Max infers the object positions in the partner's simulated peripersonal space.

Situational role-taking (cf. [4]) consists of generating a hypothesis about the partner's emotional state by appraising the partner's situation with the same appraisal mechanisms that Max would use if he were in this situation himself. In our spatial interaction task, during the partner's game turn Max infers the block positions in the partner's peripersonal space by means of his spatial perspective-taking capabilities and generates emotional valences for the partner in the same way as illustrated in Figure 2. These emotional valences drive the hypothesized partner's emotion dynamics which is simulated within Max's emotion simulation module. Thus, the hypothesized partner's emotional state consists of a PAD value and an intensity value of an activated primary emotion and is represented by an additional reference point in Max's emotion simulation module.

The elicitation of an empathic emotion is caused by detecting the occurrence of a desirable or a not desirable event for others [21]. Thus, an empathic emotion is elicited only if the partner's emotional state is positive/negative or rises/fails rapidly with respect to predefined thresholds. That is, with respect to a predefined short time interval T, the difference between inferred PAD values corresponding to the timestamps t_{k-1} and t_k, with $t_k - t_{k-1} <= T$, is calculated as $|PAD_{t_k} - PAD_{t_{k-1}}|$. If this exceeds a predefined saliency threshold TH or if $|PAD_{t_k}|$ exceeds a predefined saliency threshold TH', then the current emotional state PAD_{t_k} and its related primary emotion represent the empathic emotion. Otherwise, no empathic emotion is elicited. The predefined thresholds can be interpreted as representing Max's responsiveness to the partner's situation.

5.2   Empathy Modulation

Based on [6] and [21], the empathic emotion produced by the *Empathy Mechanism* is modulated by the following factors: First, the *empathizer's mood* represented by Max's emotional state. Second, Max relationship to the partner as Max's *liking* toward his partner. Third, the situational context represented by *deservingness* as the degree to which the partner deserves/not deserves the event.

The modulation of the empathic emotion takes place in the PAD space and is realized by applying the following equation each time t an empathic emotion is elicited:

$$empEmo_{t,mod} = ownEmo_t +$$
$$(empEmo_t - ownEmo_t) * \left(\sum_{i=1}^{n} p_{i,t} * w_i\right) / \left(\sum_{i=1}^{n} w_i\right) \tag{3}$$

The value $empEmo_{t,mod}$ represents the modulated empathic emotion. The value $ownEmo_t$ represents Max's emotional state. The value $empEmo_t$ represents the non-modulated empathic emotion resulting from the previous processing step. The values $p_{i,t}$ represent an arbitrary predefined number n of modulation factors that could have values ranging in $[0, 1]$ such as *liking* and *deservingness*. Thus in our scenario, $n = 2$. Based on [21], *liking* and *deservingness* could be represented by values ranging in $[-1, 1]$ from *disliked, not-deserved* to *most-liked, most-deserved*. The value 0 represents neither *liked, deserved* nor *disliked, not-deserved*. In this paper only positive values of *liking* and *deservingness* are considered. Note that positive values of *deservingness* represent deserved positive events and not deserved negative ones.

We define the *degree of empathy* as the distance between $empEmo_{t,mod}$ and $empEmo_t$ (see Figure 3). That is, the closer $empEmo_{t,mod}$ to $empEmo_t$, the higher the *degree of empathy*. The less close $empEmo_{t,mod}$ to $empEmo_t$, the lower the *degree of empathy*.

The impact of the modulation factors on the degree of empathy is as follows: The closer $ownEmo_t$ to $empEmo_t$, the higher the *degree of empathy*. The less close $ownEmo_t$ to $empEmo_t$, the lower the *degree of empathy*. The impact of the modulation factors $p_{i,t}$ is calculated through a weighted mean of their current values at timestamp t. In our scenario, *liking* is defined as having more impact on the *degree of empathy* than *deservingness* and is thus weighted higher. The way how in our scenario the values of *liking* and *deservingness* are determined is introduced in Section 6. The higher the value of $p_{i,t}$'s weighted mean, the higher the *degree of empathy*. The lower the value of $p_{i,t}$'s weighted mean, the lower the *degree of empathy*.

Following [11], the empathic response to the other's emotion can be any emotional reaction compatible with the other's condition. Therefore, $empEmo_{t,mod}$ is facilitated only if its related primary emotion is defined as close enough to that of $empEmo_t$. Otherwise, $empEmo_{t,mod}$ is inhibited. Primary emotions defined as close to $empEmo_t$'s primary emotion should represent emotional reactions that are compatible with the other's situation. 'Closeness' is not defined as Euclidean distance in PAD Space, but by defining thresholds for each of the dimensions individually. The choice of the thresholds is a matter of design and evaluation.

For example, Figure 3 shows Max's PA space of high dominance. At time t_{k-1}, $ownEmo_{t_{k-1}}$ has as related primary emotion *happy*, $empEmo_{t_{k-1}}$ has as related primary emotion *annoyed*, and the weighted mean of $p_{i,t_{k-1}}$ is set to the value 0.4. The resulting $empEmo_{t_{k-1},mod}$ has as related primary emotion *surprised* which is defined as not close enough to *annoyed*. At this stage $empEmo_{t_{k-1},mod}$ is *inhibited* and Max's expression of empathy is not triggered. At time t_k, $ownEmo_{t_k}$ is the neutral state *concentrated*, $empEmo_{t_k}$ has as related primary emotion *angry*, and the weighted mean of p_{i,t_k} is set to the value 0.6. The resulting $empEmo_{t_k,mod}$ has as related primary emotion *annoyed* which is defined as close enough to *angry*. At this stage $empEmo_{t_k,mod}$ is *facilitated* and the next processing step *Expression of Empathy* is triggered.

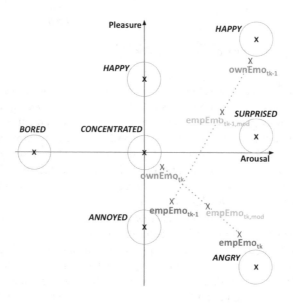

Fig. 3. Max's PA space of high dominance. The primary emotions *happy, surprised, angry, annoyed, bored*, and the neutral state *concentrated* are located at different PA values. The reference points $ownEmo_{t_{k-1}}$ and $ownEmo_{t_k}$ represent Max's emotional state at timestamps t_{k-1} and t_k. The reference points $empEmo_{t_{k-1}}$ and $empEmo_{t_k}$ represent the non-modulated empathic emotion at timestamps t_{k-1} and t_k. The reference points $empEmo_{t_{k-1},mod}$ and $empEmo_{t_k,mod}$ represent the modulated empathic emotion at timestamps t_{k-1} and t_k.

5.3   Expression of Empathy

Max's facial expressions are triggered by the intensity of the primary emotion of the modulated empathic emotion. In our spatial interaction scenario, Max's helping action is triggered only if the partner's pleasure becomes negative. Max can detect changes in the partner's pleasure values by calculating their difference, $P_{t_k} - P_{t_{k-1}}$, at timestamps t_{k-1} and t_k. If $P_{t_k} - P_{t_{k-1}} <= 0$ and $P_{t_k} <= 0$, a helping action is triggered. Max's helping action is modulated by its *degree of empathy*. The calculation of Max's *degree of empathy* as well as its impact on Max's helping action are introduced in the next section.

6   Modulating a Virtual Human's Cooperative Spatial Behavior

The calculation of the modulation factor values *liking*, *deservingness* and *degree of empathy* are introduced in this section. Further, the impact of the *degree of empathy* on Max's helping action is introduced.

Liking. The degree to which Max likes his interaction partner is calculated as the assumed partner's *degree of empathy* with Max. That is, the more the partner empathizes with Max, the more Max likes his partner. Based on the way Max's *degree of empathy* influences his helping actions (see Equation 5), he generates a hypothesis about the partner's *degree of empathy* from the partner's investment of helping actions.

Deservingness. The degree to which the position of an appropriate block needed by the partner is a deserved or not deserved event is calculated as the number of reachable appropriate blocks in Max's touch space divided by the number of all existing appropriate blocks. That is, the more reachable appropriate blocks are in Max's touch space, the higher the value of *deservingness* and vice versa.

Degree of empathy. The *degree of empathy* is defined as the distance between the modulated empathic emotion $empEmo_{t,mod}$ and the non-modulated empathic emotion $empEmo_t$ (see Section 5.2). This is determined by means of the following equation:

$$degEmp_t = 1 - \left\| \frac{empEmo_{t,mod} - empEmo_t}{empEmo_t - min_t} \right\| \tag{4}$$

$empEmo_t$ denotes the maximum value an $empEmo_{t,mod}$ can have (see Figure 3). min_t denotes the minimum value from that $empEmo_{t,mod}$ is *facilitated* (see Section 5.2) and lies on the straight line spanned by $ownEmo_t$ and $empEmo_t$. The degree of empathy $degEmp_t$ has values ranging in $[0, 1]$.

Degree of helping. Each time a helping action is triggered, Max places the most appropriate block to a position where the partner can reach it, i.e., to a position in interaction space illustrated as grey area in Figure 1, right. Interaction space's boundary is determined by two circular arcs spanned by the lean-forward spaces of Max and his partner. We denote the circular arc spanned by Max as $leanArc_{Max}$ and that of his partner as $leanArc_{partner}$. The vectors defined in the following have as origin Max's center of peripersonal space (see Section 3.2). The closest position P_m to the partner where Max can place a block is defined as the intersection of $leanArc_{Max}$ and the line segment spanned by Max's center of peripersonal space and the partner's center of peripersonal space. The position vector of P_m is denoted by $\mathbf{p}_m$. Depending on Max's *degree of empathy* $degEmp$, his helping action is modulated. That is, $degEmp$ determines how near the most appropriate block with vector $\mathbf{p}_b$ is placed toward the partner. With the following equation the new position $\mathbf{p}_{bNew}$ of the block is calculated:

$$\mathbf{p}_{bNew} = \mathbf{p}_b + (degEmp * \mathbf{p}_{help}), \text{ with } \mathbf{p}_{help} = \mathbf{p}_m - \mathbf{p}_b \tag{5}$$

Equation 5 applies only if the block is located within interaction space, otherwise $\mathbf{p}_b$ is set to the intersection point of $leanArc_{partner}$ and the line segment spanned by P_m and

$\mathbf{p}_b$. This assures that *degEmp* only modulates the part of $\mathbf{p}_{help}$ in interaction space that contributes to a helping action. That means, our approach avoids helping actions by which blocks are placed outside interaction space, where the partner still cannot reach them and may judge Max to be non-cooperative. To control the actual placing motion two values of the potential field (see Equation 1) have to be specified: the radius r_{touch} is set to the length of $\mathbf{p}_{bNew}$ and the strength ξ_{peri} is set to *degEmp*. Thus, the distance and velocity of the placing-motion are modulated. Therefore, the higher Max's *degree of empathy*, the faster and nearer to his partner, he places blocks in the partner's periper-sonal space. For example, the maximum value of *degEmp* = 1 leads to a potential field where r_{touch} is set to the maximum value of r_{lean} and ξ_{peri} is set to a predefined max-imum velocity. In this case, Max performs the most *helpful* action by quickly bending the torso to lean forward and placing the block at P_m closest to the partner. The example shows that Max would only perform a motor action associated with more cost, if his *degree of empathy* with the partner is high.

Summarized Task Course. At the beginning of the tower building task Max's values of *liking* and *deservingness* are set to the minimum value of 0. Max's empathy for the partner increases with following factors: with increasing *liking* value, i.e the more the partner helps Max by placing needed blocks closer to Max; with increasing *deserving-ness* value, i.e the more reachable appropriate blocks Max has than the partner; and when the similarity between Max's and the partner's mood becomes higher. The more Max empathizes with the partner, the closer and faster he places needed blocks in front of the partner and thus the more effort he invests in helping him.

7   Conclusion and Future Work

In this paper we presented an approach for triggering and modulating the virtual human Max's helping actions in a cooperative spatial interaction task depending on his *degree of empathy* with his partner. Max's helping action enables his partner to put the most appropriate block on the tower. Thus, the height of the resulting tower implicitly reflects the amount of cooperation in the course of the task. This may be interpreted as follows: The more the partners share their emotions, the more they share their space to help each other. The more Max leans forward to place objects near his partner, the more Max expresses his empathy. This is in agreement with Jones and Wirtz [12], who state that human approach behaviors such as leaning forward, have been shown to convey positive affect, involvement and liking. While this paper focuses more on the technical details of the proposed approach, in future work an evaluation of this approach is planned to investigate how Max's modulated helping actions impact a human partner's engagement in achieving a successful cooperation. Since the more the partner helps Max, the more Max likes his partner, empathizes, and helps him, we expect that in order for the human partner to successfully solve the building task with Max, the human partner will show more engagement in cooperating with and helping Max.

Moreover, a challenging work in the future is to model Max's competitive behavior triggered by his *negative empathy*. This can be realized by modeling the peripersonal space field as an attraction field and by considering negative values for the *liking* and *deservingness* factors. This extension may reveal Max's modulated competitive behavior by placing all blocks from interaction space in his peripersonal space, where only he can access them.

It is conceivable to extend the current model within a more complex scenario of a cooperative city planning game developed in our research group. This scenario consists of a city grid map placed on a table between two interaction partners, thus forming a near-space interaction. The game consists of planning a city by placing buildings on the city grid map where the interaction partners can have joint or interfering goals. Their joint goals are to take the citizens' preferences into account while their interfering goals are to take their own preferences into account when planning the city. The interaction partners' and citizens' preferences consist of security, ecology, and amusement represented by different building types. Again, in this scenario, the virtual human's helping action is defined as relocating the most appropriate, in this case the most preferred object to positions reachable for the partner. The helping action is triggered and modulated by the virtual human's degree of empathy with its partner. A challenge will be to find the best position fitting the degree of empathy even when the determined position is occupied by another object or where the agent is not allowed to place an object during the partner's turn. Individual role-taking [10] will be used in order to find out which object is preferred by the interaction partner. This is defined as the ability to generate a hypothesis about the interaction partner's emotional state by taking, e.g, his preferences, goals, beliefs into account.

Acknowledgments. This research is kindly supported by the Deutsche Forschungsgemeinschaft (DFG) in the Collaborative Research Center 673.

References

1. Aylett, R., Louchart, S.: If i were you: double appraisal in affective agents. In: in Proceedings of 7th International Conference on Autonomous Agents and Multiagent Systems (AAMAS 2008), Estoril, Portugal, pp. 1233–1236 (2008)
2. Becker, C., Lessmann, N., Kopp, S., Wachsmuth, I.: Connecting feelings and thoughts - modeling the interaction of emotion and cognition in embodied agents. In: Seventh International Conference on Cognitive Modeling (ICCM 2006), pp. 32–37. Edizioni Goliardiche (2006)
3. Becker-Asano, C., Wachsmuth, I.: Affective computing with primary and secondary emotions in a virtual human. In: Autonomous Agents and Multi-Agent Systems (2009)
4. Boukricha, H., Becker, C., Wachsmuth, I.: Simulating empathy for the virtual human max. In: 2nd International Workshop on Emotion and Computing, in conj. with the German Conference on Artificial Intelligence (KI 2007, Osnabrück, Germany, pp. 22–27 (2007)
5. Boukricha, H., Wachsmuth, I.: Empathy-based emotional alignment for a virtual human: A three-step approach. German Journal on Artificial Intelligence, Künstl Intell (2011)
6. de Vignemont, F., Singer, T.: The empathic brain: how, when and why? Trends in Cognitive Sciences 10(10), 435–441 (2006)
7. Foster, M.E., Giuliani, M., Isard, A., Matheson, C., Oberlander, J., Knoll, A.: Evaluating description and reference strategies in a cooperative human-robot dialogue system. In: Proceedings of the 21st international joint conference on Artifical intelligence, pp. 1818–1823. Morgan Kaufmann Publishers Inc., San Francisco (2009)
8. Gallese, V.: Embodied simulation: From neurons to phenomenal experience. Phenomenology and the Cognitive Sciences 4(1), 23–48 (2005)

9. Gray, J., Breazeal, C., Berlin, M., Brooks, A., Lieberman, J.: Action parsing and goal inference using self as simulator. In: Proceedings of Fourteenth IEEE Workshop on Robot and Human Interactive Communication (Ro-Man 2005), pp. 202–209. IEEE, Los Alamitos (2005)

10. Higgins, E.T.: Role-taking and social judgment: Alternative developmental perspectives and processes. In: Flavell, J.H., Ross, L. (eds.) Social cognitive development: Frontiers and possible futures, pp. 119–153. Cambridge University Press, Cambridge (1981)

11. Hoffman, M.L.: Empathy and Moral Development. Cambridge University Press, Cambridge (2000)

12. Jones, S.M., Wirtz, J.G.: How does the comforting process work? an empirical test of an appraisal-based model of comforting. Human Communication Research 32(3), 217–243 (2006)

13. Kendon, A.: Conducting Interaction. Cambridge University Press, London (1990)

14. Khatib, O.: Real-time obstacle avoidance for manipulators and mobile robots. Int. J. Rob. Res. 5(1), 90–98 (1986)

15. Kopp, S., Jung, B., Lessmann, N., Wachsmuth, I.: Max – a multimodal assistant in virtual reality construction. KI Zeitschrift (German Journal of Artificial Intelligence), Special Issue on Embodied Conversational Agents 4/03, 11–17 (2003)

16. Lessmann, N., Kopp, S., Wachsmuth, I.: Situated interaction with a virtual human - perception, action, and cognition. In: Rickheit, G., Wachsmuth, I. (eds.) Situated Communication, pp. 287–323. Mouton de Gruyter, Berlin (2006)

17. Mark, L.S., Nemeth, K., Gardner, D., Dainoff, M.J., Paasche, J., Duffy, M., Grandt, K.: Postural dynamics and the preferred critical boundary for visually guided reaching. Journal of Experimental Psychology: Human Perception and Performance 23(5), 1365–1379 (1997)

18. McQuiggan, S., Robison, J.L., Phillips, R., Lester, J.C.: Modeling parallel and reactive empathy in virtual agents: An inductive approach. In: Padgham, Parkes, Müller, Parson (eds.) Proc. of 7th Int. Conf. on Autonomous Agents and Multiagent Systems (AAMAS 2008), Estoril, Portugal, pp. 167–174 (2008)

19. Nguyen, N., Wachsmuth, I.: From body space to interaction space - modeling spatial cooperation for virtual humans. In: Tumer, Yolum, Sonenberg, Stone (eds.) Proc. of the 10th Int. Conf. on Autonomous Agents and Multiagent Systems, AAMAS 2011, pp. 1047–1054 (2011)

20. Ochs, M., Pelachaud, C., Sadek, D.: An empathic virtual dialog agent to improve human-machine interaction. In: Padgham, Parkers, Müller, Parson (eds.) Proc. of 7th Int. Conf. on Autonomous Agents and Multiagent Systems (AAMAS 2008), Estoril, Portugal, pp. 89–96 (2008)

21. Ortony, A., Clore, G.L., Collins, A.: The Cognitive Structure of Emotions. Cambridge University Press, Cambridge (1988)

22. Pedica, C., Vilhjálmsson, H.H.: Spontaneous avatar behavior for human territoriality. In: Ruttkay, Z., Kipp, M., Nijholt, A., Vilhjálmsson, H.H. (eds.) IVA 2009. LNCS, vol. 5773, pp. 344–357. Springer, Heidelberg (2009), http://dx.doi.org/10.1007/978-3-642-04380-2_38

23. Prendinger, H., Ishizuka, M.: The empathic companion: A character-based interface that adresses users' affective states. Applied Artificial Intelligence 19, 267–285 (2005)

24. Rodrigues, S.H., Mascarenhas, S.F., Dias, J., Paiva, A.: I can feel it too!: Emergent empathic reactions between synthetic characters. In: 3rd International Conference on Affective Computing and Intelligent Interaction and Workshops, ACII, Amsterdam, Netherland, IEEE, Los Alamitos (2009)

25. Sisbot, E.A., Marin, L.F., Alami, R., Simeon, T.: A mobile robot that performs human acceptable motion. In: Proc in (IEEE/RSJ) Int. Conf. on Intelligent Robots and Systems (2006)

Perception of Spatial Relations and of Coexistence with Virtual Agents

Mohammad Obaid[1], Radosław Niewiadomski[2], and Catherine Pelachaud[2]

[1] Human Interface Technology Lab New Zealand (HITLab NZ),
University of Canterbury, Christchurch, New Zealand
mohammad.obaid@hitlabnz.org
[2] CNRS-LTCI, Telecom ParisTech, Paris, France
{catherine.pelachaud,niewiado}@telecom-paristech.fr

Abstract. This paper focuses on the user's perception of virtual agents embedded in real and virtual worlds. In particular, we analyze the perception of spatial relations and the perception of coexistence. For this purpose, we measure the user's voice compensation which is one of the human automatic behaviors to their surrounding environment.

The results of our evaluation study reveal that people compensate their voice according to the distance during the interaction with both augmented reality (AR) and virtual reality (VR) based agents. Secondly, in AR-based scenario users perceive stronger the distance between them and the virtual agent. On the other hand, the results do not show any significant differences regarding the notion of coexistence of the user. Finally, we discuss our results in the context of sense of presence in interaction with virtual agent in AR applications.

Keywords: Augmented Reality, Immersive Virtual Reality, Virtual Agents.

1 Introduction

In this paper we address two aspects of the user's perceptual experience when interacting with expressive Augmented Reality (AR)-based agents. In particular, we look at (1) the user's perception of spatial relations with an agent, and (2) the user's perception of coexistence within the environment of an agent. Both aspects directly refer to the notions of "presence". For this purpose we conducted a scenario based user evaluation study that compares the user's responses to an agent in AR and Virtual Reality (VR) environments. The scenario is based on the fact that in human-human communication [1] people speak louder when they believe that they are more distant from each other. Therefore, we expect that the user's reaction is similar in human-agent communication.

When evaluating interaction though different media, such as AR and VR, often the concept of "sense of presence" is used. This concept is usually understood as "subjective experience of being in one place, even when one is physically situated in another" [2]. Thus, it is a subjective state or feeling which includes the

H. Högni Vilhjálmsson et al. (Eds.): IVA 2011, LNAI 6895, pp. 363–369, 2011.

notion of "being there" (for VR environments) or "coexistence in the same space" (for AR environments)[1]. According to Slater et al. [3], a high sense of presence occurs when humans respond to computer-generated data as if they were real. Various forms of human reactions can be then observed from a low level psychological processes (e.g. arousal), by unconscious automatic behaviors (e.g. avoid obstacles) and reflexes, to high-level voluntary (and conscious) behaviors (e.g. speech acts). This extended definition of the sense of presence permits to not only measure subjective impression by post-experiment questionnaires but also to measure more objectively human responses to different environments. Several researchers used behavioral measurements such as skin conductivity [4] or postural responses [5]. In our work we propose to use a Sound Pressure Level (SPL) meter to measure the unconscious adaptation of the volume of the voice when addressing an interlocutor at a long distance. According to Warren [1], people implicitly use "tacit knowledge of the sensory effects of changing distance" and adjust their voice volume based on personal experiences when communicating with distant listeners. Finally, people compensate their voice volume in interaction with a physical speaker but also with an imagined one [6]. Consequently, we expect that this compensation effect will also occur in the interaction with the virtual agent and that people will react to computer-generated data in AR/VR similarly to human-human interaction. We also wonder if embedding the agent in the real world (as in AR) or in the virtual world (as in VR) has an effect on voice compensation.

On the other hand, presenting a virtual agent in an AR environment to the user is a challenging task. In a VR environment, agents are perceived by the user as digital content just as the rest of the surrounding environment. However, embedding virtual agents within a real environment can introduce some visual incoherency to users due to lighting, shadows or occlusions. Consequently, one may expect (e.g. [7,8]) that perception of the coexistence and interaction in AR-based environments can be worse than the classical VR-based one.

2   Experimental Evaluation

Our experiment extends the previous research (e.g [8,7]) by evaluating the perception of the distance of the virtual agent in AR and VR and the user's perception of coexistence in the same environment as of the virtual agent. The hypotheses of the designed experiment are: (H1) The voice compensation for the change in distance occurs in both AR and VR. (H2) Spatial relations and the distance are stronger perceived by the user during the interaction with an AR-based agent. (H3) The perception of coexistence is higher during the interaction with a VR-based agent.

2.1   Design

Scenario: Our scenario exploits spatial relations between the human user and the virtual agent during the interaction. Initially, the virtual agent is standing

---

[1] In the rest of the paper we use the term coexistence for both types of environments.

approximately 15 meters (Point A) from the user. As the agent is setup not to be facing the user, the task of the user is to attract the agent's attention by calling it. After few calls the agent turns around and re-appears in front of the user at a natural communication distance of approx. 1 meter (Point B). The user is then engaged with the agent by asking it to do a simple task (count to three).

Implementation: We used the Greta agent [9] for both conditions. In the AR version (1) the system displays Greta in the real space (see Figure 1b; for the details of the implementation see [9]). Greta initially is standing at the end of a corridor in position (Point A). The user uses a Head Mounted Display (HMD) to interact with Greta. In the VR version (2) the system shows Greta in an immersive 3D environment that is setup to be similar to the AR environment (see Figure 1a). A 3D model of the corridor used in the AR condition is used to simulate the same space as in the AR environment. Greta is initially standing at the end of virtual corridor. In both conditions Greta's body size ratios are all kept the same as much as possible.

2.2   Procedure

Each subject participated in only one out of the two conditions. At the beginning each participant was given a description of their tasks and was told that the character's name that they will be communicating with is Greta, but was not told how loud they need to speak with Greta. Each subject was also asked about his/her level of expertise with the AR (or VR accordingly) and, based on their answer, a short demo was given to participants who are not familiar with the AR (or the VR accordingly) environments. The demo was not related to the content of the experiment.

In the AR condition the procedure starts by positioning the user in the corridor and asking them to wear the HMD. In the VR condition the procedure starts by positioning the user 1.5 meters in front of a three-screen back projection system[2]. Then they were told to put the 3D glasses and headphones on before starting the Greta-corridor 3D scene.

Fig. 1. (a) Greta in the VR condition. (b) Greta in the AR condition.

---

[2] The virtual environment was displayed using a three-screen back projection system with a field of view of 180 degrees. Each screen measured 2.44m x 1.83m.

In both conditions users were told to start communicating with Greta approximately 5 seconds after she appears on their display. This is mainly to get them familiar with the HMD (resp. 3D screen) setup before they start communicating with Greta. The time is also used by the experiment's administrator to start the SPL meter. Users were not aware that there was a SPL meter device near them. They were not allowed to move from their position when interacting with Greta. We used the Wizard-of-Oz approach to operate Greta.

Behavior Measurement: To assess the user's loudness level in both conditions we used a professional Sound Pressure Level meter (SPL) application for iPhone-4. We recorded the peak SPL measurement using A-weighting. Sound pressure level is measured in decibels, dB to the standard reference level of $20\mu Pa$ (this is the threshold of human hearing at 1kHz). The SPL meter application comes pre-calibrated for the typical iPhone-4 built-in headset mic to +7dB. The SPL meter is placed approximately 1 meter away from the user. The measurements of the user's voice were done for two localizations of the agent in both conditions (AR/VR) i.e. at *point A* - when the user tries to call (measurement SPL_A) and at *point B* - when the user asks her to count (measurement SPL_B).

Questionnaire: After the experiment is finished, participants were asked to complete a questionnaire that contains fourteen questions. Twelve questions have a scale from 1-5, where 1 mean strongly disagree and 5 means strongly agree: (Q1) I felt that Greta was really down the corridor. (Q2) I felt as though I was in the same space as Greta. (Q3) I would have liked the experience to continue. (Q4) I felt Greta heard me. (Q6) I felt Greta responded to (resp. understood) my call. (Q7) I felt Greta wanted to start a conversation with me. (Q8) Did you think you had to shout to call for Greta? (Q9) Did you shout to call for Greta? (Q10) Did you feel getting closer to Greta before calling her? (Q11) (resp. (Q12) I felt Greta was far from me in point A (resp. point B). Additionally, two questions (Q13 and Q14) asked the user to estimate how far Greta was in meters at the two points A and B. Users were asked to choose one answer from five: *1m, 3m, 5m, 9m, 15m*. 32 subjects participated in the study. All participants are from New Zealand and are aged between 20 and 63 years old (mean 29.7, SD=9.1). 12 males and 4 females participated in the AR condition with an average age of approximately 32 years. 7 participants have not had any experience with AR in the past. 12 and 4 females participated in the VR condition with an average age of approximately 28 years. 8 participants have not experienced being in an immersive 3D environment in the past.

3   Results

For hypothesis H1, we calculated separately (for each of the conditions AR/VR) the difference between the voice volume at point A and B as well as the difference in perceived distances of the agent (questions Q11-Q14). Table 1 outlines the captured values. In the AR condition, the SPL at point A varied from 54.8 dB to 66.1 dB with a mean value of 60.96 dB, while the SPL at point B varied from

Table 1. The mean values of the users' answers for questions Q11 - Q14 and SPL measurements at point A and B. Standard deviations appear in parentheses.

Condition	SPL_A	SPL_B	Q11	Q12	Q13	Q14
AR	60.96 (3.71)	48.33 (2.70)	4.31 (0.70)	1.5 (0.63)	14.25 (2.05)	1.13 (0.5)
VR	57.92 (4.00)	51.46 (3.66)	4.13 (0.72)	1.69 (0.60)	11.25 (3)	2.38 (1.20)

Table 2. The mean values of the users' answers for questions Q1 - Q10. Standard deviations appear in parentheses. Significant differences in bold.

	Environment		Expertise	
	AR	VR	no	yes
Q1	4.31 (0.70)	4.13 (0.72)	3.93 (0.70)	**4.47** (0.62)
Q2	3.56 (0.96)	3.81 (0.98)	3.27 (0.80)	**4.06** (0.97)
Q3	3.13 (1.02)	3.5 (0.97)	2.80 (1.01)	**3.76** (0.76)
Q4	3.88 (1.02)	**4.44** (0.63)	3.93 (1.03)	4.35 (0.70)
Q5	4.06 (0.93)	4.44 (0.63)	3.87 (0.92)	**4.59** (0.51)
Q6	3.81 (0.91)	**4.25** (0.77)	3.53 (0.83)	**4.47** (0.62)
Q7	2.5 (1.21)	2.31 (0.79)	2.47 (0.74)	2.35 (1.22)
Q8	**2.81** (1.11)	2 (0.73)	2.13 (0.83)	2.63 (1.11)
Q9	**4** (0.82)	2.38 (0.81)	2.67 (0.90)	**3.65** (1.17)
Q10	**2.13** (0.81)	1.56 (0.63)	1.60 (0.90)	3.65 (1.17)

42.8 dB to 53.8 dB with a mean of 48.33 dB. The maximum difference observed for one subject was 17.5 dB and the mean difference was 12.63 dB. The repeated-measure ANOVA test revealed that the SPL difference between points A and B is significant ($F(1,15)= 213$, $p < 0.0001$). Moreover, the post-study questionnaire results show that the mean of the perceived distance between points A and B (obtained from questions Q13 and Q14) is 13.13 meters, while difference between the mean answers for Q11 and Q12 is 2.81 out 5 points in Likert scale. In the VR condition, the SPL at point A varied from 50.2 dB to 63.7 dB with a mean value of 57.92 dB. The SPL at point B varied from 44.3 dB to 57.6 dB with a mean of 51.46 dB. The maximum observed difference was 11.4 dB and the mean difference was 6.46 dB. The repeated-measure ANOVA test revealed that the SPL difference between points A and B is significant ($F(1,15)= 80$, $p < 0.0001$). In the case of the post-study questionnaire, the perceived mean distance between points A and B (Q13 - Q14) is 8.88 meters, while the mean difference between the answers for Q11 and Q12 is 2.44 out 5 points in Likert scale.

Secondly, to check the effect of the Environment variable and the users' Expertise level variable we conducted a 2×2 (*Environment* $\times$ *Expertise*) between subject MANOVA on questions Q1 - Q10. Results show two main effects, one of the Environment [$F(12,17) = 5.147$, Wilks' $\lambda = 0.216$, $p = 0.001$] and one of the Expertise [$F(12,17) = 4.609$, Wilks' $\lambda = 0.235$, $p = 0.002$] and no interaction effect [$F(12,17) = 0.846$, Wilks' $\lambda = 0.625$, $p = 0.609$]. Distinguishing between independent variables, results show an effect of Environment for questions Q4 ($F(1,31) = 4.349$, $p = 0.046$) , Q6 ($F(1,31) = 4.280$, $p = 0.048$), Q8 ($F(1,31) =$

5.875, p = 0.022), Q9 (F(1,31) = 42.813, p=0.0001) and Q10 (F(1,31) = 4.432, p = 0.044). Moreover, an effect of the Expertise was observed on the questions Q1, Q2, Q3, Q5, Q6 and Q9. Table 2 shows the detailed results.

To detect the most important factors we performed PCA on Q1 - Q10, which resulted in two factors. The first factor (GR1) regrouped questions Q1 - Q6. 5 out these 6 appear to be related to the concept of the coexistence. The second factor (GR2) regroups Q7 - Q10. 3 of them (Q8 - Q10) appear to be related to the perception of distance. Question Q7 has the most balanced values (0.485, 0.549) and cannot be easily classified to any of these two concepts. ANOVA test revealed an effect of condition (AR/VR) on group GR2 (F(1,31) = 10.841, p = 0.003). While, no effect was observed for GR1 (F=(1,31) = 1.606, p = 0.215).

4   Discussion

The aim is to study the perception of the distance and the coexistence, which are two very important issues for AR-based applications. According to the obtained results, we confirm hypothesis H1 (regarding the voice compensation) for both environments. The human automatic responses (SPL_A and SPL_B) to the agents located at points A and B are significantly different, while we find that this difference is stronger in the AR condition. The significant difference in the sound level measurements is also supported by the results of Q11 - Q14. Participants consciously perceive the difference in distance between the agent placed at point A and B. Interestingly, the results show that in the AR condition this difference is higher.

Hypothesis H2 focuses on the perception of distance and is addressed by Q8 - Q10 of the post-study questionnaire. The participants' results from those questions receive significantly higher results in AR. Consequently, we can say that hypothesis H2 is confirmed and people perceive the spatial relations stronger in AR.

The results corresponding to hypothesis H3 are ambiguous. We expected that the user's perception of coexistence might be lower in the AR condition. The results for the questions Q4 - "I felt Greta heard me" and Q6 - "I felt Greta understood my call" are lower in the AR condition. One may presume that incoherency between the embedded animation and real image may give the user the impression of not sharing the environment with the virtual agent and thus participants may have the impression that they do not exchange directly the messages with the virtual agent. On the other hand, no significant difference was observed for questions Q1 - "I felt that Greta was really down the corridor" and Q2 - "I felt as though I was in the same space as Greta". Finally, we do not observe any significant difference in the GR1 regrouping questions Q1 - Q6. This makes us think that the "perception of coexistence" with the virtual agent is not lower in the AR environment.

5   Conclusion

In this paper we presented a comparative study of virtual agents in two environments, AR and VR. In the study we used an objective measure of the user's voice loudness level, which is one of the human automatic behaviors to their surrounding environment. Firstly, the results of the evaluation revealed that humans compensate their voice level during the interaction with both AR and VR-based agents. Secondly, users strongly perceive the distance between them and the AR-based virtual agent. On the other hand, the results did not show any significant improvements to the perception of coexistence of the user in the space of the AR-based agent compared with the VR-based agent.

The other interesting conclusion is that we are able to confirm the subjective user impressions by measuring objectively the user's voice loudness level. People use similar mechanism of voice compensation according to the interlocutor's distance when interacting with AR or VR-based agent as when interacting with other human. Voice compensation observed in our experiment is one of the humans' automatic responses towards a virtual entity that do not have any rational motivation as it was already pointed out by several studies [10]. We confirm that people interacting with the virtual agent in AR/VR tend to re-use unconsciously their "natural" behavior patterns learned in "real world" interactions.

References

1. Warren, R.M.: Measurement of sensory intensity. Behavioral and Brain Sciences, 175–189 (1981)
2. Witmer, B.G., Singer, M.J.: Measuring presence in virtual environments: A presence questionnaire. Presence: Teleoper. Virtual Environ. 7, 225–240 (1998)
3. Slater, M., Lotto, B., Arnold, M.M., Sanchez-Vives, M.V.: How we experience immersive virtual environments: the concept of presence and its measurement. Anuario de Psicologa 40, 193–210 (2009)
4. Llobera, J., Spanlang, B., Ruffini, G., Slater, M.: Proxemics with multiple dynamic characters in an immersive virtual environment. ACM Trans. Appl. Percept. 8, 3:1–3:12 (2010)
5. Freeman, J., Avons, S., Meddis, R., Pearson, D.E., Ijsselsteijn, W.: Using behavioral realism to estimate presence: A study of the utility of postural responses to motion stimuli. Presence: Teleoperators and Virtual Environments 9(2), 149–164 (2000)
6. Healey, E.C., Jones, R., Berky, R.: Effects of perceived listeners on speakers? vocal intensity. Journal of Voice: Official Journal of the Voice Foundation 11(1), 67–73 (1997)
7. Dow, S., Mehta, M., Harmon, E., MacIntyre, B., Mateas, M.: Presence and engagement in an interactive drama. In: Proceedings of the SIGCHI Conference CHI 2007, pp. 1475–1484. ACM, New York (2007)
8. Tang, A., Biocca, F., Lim, L.: Comparing differences in presence during social interaction in augmented reality versus virtual reality environments: An exploratory study. In: Raya, M.A., Solaz, B.R. (eds.) Proceedings of PRESENCE 2004, 7th Annual International Workshop on Presence, pp. 204–208 (2004)
9. Niewiadomski, R., Bevacqua, E., Le, Q.A., Obaid, M., Looser, J., Pelachaud, C.: Cross media agent platform. To appear in: Proceedings of Web3D ACM Conference, ACM, New York (2011)
10. Reeves, B., Nass, C.: The media equation: how people treat computers, television, and new media like real people and places. Cambridge University Press, New York (1996)

Failure Detection and Reactive Teaming for Behavior-Based Subsumption

Frederick W.P. Heckel and G. Michael Youngblood

University of North Carolina at Charlotte, Charlotte, NC 28223, USA
{fheckel,youngbld}@uncc.edu

Abstract. Fast, lightweight intelligent controllers make it possible to apply agent-based artificial intelligence to even highly resource-constrained systems. Reactive control methods can provide this capability, and are frequently used in applications such as real-time games and robotics. Unfortunately, reactive controllers may not deal well with errors, as they cannot fall back on a planner to deal with unexpected situations. This limitation makes them more susceptible to certain types of failures than deliberative techniques. In this paper, we describe how four major types of failures can be detected in reactive controllers. We show how this can lead to extensions for behavior-based subsumption which allow more robust single agents, enable inexpensive multi-agent coordination, and improve agent design tools.

1 Introduction

Reactive control methods are extremely useful in resource-constrained systems, such as real-time games and robotics, but they do not always deal well with failures. Without a method to adapt to failure, even small errors in a reactive controller can result in catastrophically incorrect behavior. The types of failures that can limit the applicability of reactive controllers may be due to changes in the agent's capabilities, modifications to the environment, or design oversights. In modern interactive computer games, this can occur frequently when a character is injured or the environment undergoes a major dynamic change. When user-generated content such as custom levels are a factor, even small design oversights may become apparent. Extending reactive architectures to detect and recover from errors would reduce the need to turn to more computationally expensive methods for generating intelligent agents or spend larger amounts of time on testing agents in every feasible situation.

In this paper, we classify four major types of failures that can occur in reactive controllers. These failures can be detected in behavior-based subsumption without major architectural changes. While they are useable with other reactive and behavior-based methods, these extensions are presented in the context of a behavior-based subsumption architecture, and we show that failure detection can provide new capabilities such as dynamic adaptation of subsumption controllers and inexpensive multi-agent coordination.

H. Högni Vilhjálmsson et al. (Eds.): IVA 2011, LNAI 6895, pp. 370–376, 2011.

2   Behavior Monitoring

The behavioral errors that can be generated by a failing reactive agent are as numerous as the number of behaviors that can be expressed in the architecture. Fortunately, the general *types* of errors that are generated by reactive controllers fall into a small number of distinct classes. We have identified four classes of errors: activation failures, capability failures, behavior interaction failures, and environmental failures. Each of these failures can be detected in a well-defined manner, though some are more expensive than others to detect.

For this paper, we assume that we are dealing with two classes of agents: mobile robots and virtual characters. These two types commonly use behavior-based or reactive control, are frequently highly resource-constrained, and use highly crafted controllers. The differences between these types of agents are not insubstantial, as the real-world environment of the robot presents a major challenge in perception. The perceptions of virtual characters are highly restricted by the level of detail present in their environment, but are inherently symbolic and require less processing than the output of sensors carried by intelligent robots.

For this work, we focus on behavior-based subsumption [2]. Our subsumption controller is a prioritized list built from *layers* of behavioral components. A layer has four components: a *trigger*, a *behavior*, a *subsumption policy*, and *state*. Triggers and behaviors are pre-defined software components, and multiple triggers or behaviors can be linked together to create complex behavior. A layer can override, or subsume, any lower-priority layers.

An agent has four major components: a *behavior stack* built from behavior layers, a *perception module*, an *action model*, and *agent state*. The perception module takes raw environmental information, such as game state or sensor output, and translates it into percepts that can be passed to the triggers. The action model accepts requests from the behavior layers, combines simultaneous requests, and builds the commands necessary to execute the requests. Finally, the agent state contains information about the agents capabilities and current status, and is important for reasoning about behaviors and building action requests.

Agent think cycles run asynchronously with the environment (in case of simulations), so at the end of a think cycle, the agent will send commands, which may not be completed by the start of the next think cycle. As commands are executed, the status of the execution process is passed back to the perceptual model to inform the agent whether the commands were successful, failed, or if execution is still pending. Action execution may be low-level application of forces, or use a higher-level interface to request specific actions or motions that will be executed according to the rules of the environment.

In general, triggers in the behavior layers operate on either environmental state information processed by the perception model or on agent state information. Triggers generate a truth value to reflect whether the tested conditions are satisfied. The data that generated the truth value is passed on to the behaviors. Behaviors have access to both sources of information for making decisions. Based on this information, a behavior will generate one or more requests to be processed by the action model. We make a distinction between the process of building behaviors and triggers and the process of constructing agents. This assumes that behaviors exist as pre-programmed modules or have been constructed with a behavior modeling language such as RAPs, Hap, or ABL.

Monitoring for failures adds additional metadata to each layer. This ranges from a simple value added to the behavior state to additional sets of triggers. Behaviors must be capable of returning an error value to convey the success or failure of behavior execution. An important aspect of this metadata is that it can be constructed from existing components. There is no need for major architectural extensions to support new constructs.

Monitoring for failures can be achieved by adding a single layer with a trigger that always returns true. By adding this as the highest priority layer and giving it a subsumption policy that does not override any lower layers, the failure monitoring component is guaranteed to execute. This does require that the architecture is designed with reflection capabilities in mind, as the layer must be able to check the status of all other behavior layers for failures.

2.1   Failure Types

Activation Failures. Activation failures are the simplest types of failures to detect. These failures occur when a component of the controller fails to execute. This indicates that anticipated conditions never occur or that a higher-level behavior is preventing the execution of the layer. Activation failures can be easily detected in both virtual characters and robots, as even in robots they depend entirely on software state without consideration of hardware failures. While they are simple to detect, they may be unreliable if a given behavior is not expected to execute frequently. These failures can be detected by adding an activation history to the layer state.

Capability Failures. Capability failures occur when an agent is not capable of executing a given behavior. These directly correspond to unanticipated changes in agent state; in a virtual character, it may be an item missing from the character's inventory, or an action which is no longer allowed. In robotics, this could correspond to a hardware failure or a partial loss of power. Detection of capability failures can be achieved by adding metadata to behaviors. This metadata can be built from trigger components. While precondition triggers can also be added to the conditions for layer activation, using them to detect failures as metadata eases the agent design task and may provide better information for debugging agent failures.

Environmental Failures. Environmental failures occur when agent capabilities are correct and the behavior executes, but the behavior action fails in the environment. An environmental failure may indicate that the expectations for the behavior are incorrect given the environment (e.g., a lift behavior may fail if objects in the environment are heavier than expected by the behavior) or that another agent has interfered with the execution of the behavior. Environmental failures are detected by the perception model. In virtual environments, we expect the environment to give direct feedback about error conditions, while in real world environments, the perception model will have to do additional work. Detection of environmental failures due to other agents is feasible in real-world environments, but other types of failures may not be easily detected.

Behavior Interaction Failures. Behavior interaction failures are potentially the most difficult failures to detect. This type of failure occurs when a behavior can be executed correctly, does not generate an environmental error, but also does not achieve the expected result. Failures of this type are due to behaviors interacting in a way that causes one behavior to undo or cancel out the effects of another. Detecting behavior interaction failures requires specifying expected pre- and post-conditions for a given behavior. Pre-conditions may be the same as the pre-requisites for the behavior, if the behavior has an effect on agent state. If the behavior affects environmental state, then the triggers for the layer should be used. Post-conditions can be added as additional triggers to check for expected changes in either the agent or environmental state. Detection is complicated if the failure is not instantaneous or the effect of the behavior is intended to be short-term. Some behaviors may already be written to have completion criteria (such as achieving a navigation goal), in which case these completion criteria can be used for the post-conditions.

3   Applying Failure Detection

Augmenting subsumption layers with the information required for failure detection is relatively easy. Pre-requisites and expected results can be described in the same manner as the triggering conditions already used to decide when to activate a behavior. Tracking activation history adds a constant amount of additional state to each layer. The most invasive addition is detection and handling of environmental failures, but most systems will already watch for these error states.

Adding failure detection provides opportunities for major extensions to subsumption. Some of these can be applied to other reactive architectures, such as FSM-based controllers, but we focus on the application of failure detection to subsumption. A major application of failure detection that we have implemented is *reactive teaming*, which uses behavior insertion and removal.

3.1   Behavior Insertion and Removal

For individual agents, failure detection can be used to remove layers that are not functioning correctly. Malfunctioning behaviors can mask correct behaviors that have lower priorities. Consider a virtual guard agent that is designed to walk around its environment and watch for unauthorized agents. In addition, this guard agent has been given a higher priority layer to pick up trash when it sees litter. If the litter-gathering behavior is lower than the patrol behavior, it will be overridden by the movement commands, preventing it from picking up trash, so it must be higher priority. At a certain point, the guard will run out of room to carry the assorted trash it gathers, but without any sort of failure monitoring, it will get stuck trying to pick up the $n + 1^{st}$ piece of trash.

With failure monitoring, the trash gathering layer will be identified as failing by a capability filter; since it has no space in its inventory, it can remove this layer. The patrol behavior will then continue as expected. The same behavior could be achieved by adding an additional trigger to check the inventory space, but if this issue is not anticipated by a novice designer, the failure of the agent to act as expected can be frustrating. If the character also has a *dispose of trash* behavior, which drops the trash when it next sees a trashcan, then eventually the *gather trash* behavior will become available again. Again, capability monitoring can be used; once the agent is capable of performing this behavior again, it can insert the original behavior back into the controller in its previous position.

Behavior insertion and removal can be added to the existing architecture by extending the monitoring layer to not just monitor the behavior stack, but also make modifications.

3.2   Reactive Teaming

Failure detection and behavior insertion and removal make possible the *reactive teaming* approach to multi-agent coordination [1]. Reactive teaming is a computationally inexpensive technique for coordinating between reactive agents. The core mechanism of reactive teaming is *behavior transfer*. Team coordination with this technique occurs between two characters at a time. If the first character, Alice, decides she needs a new behavior to execute, she will make a behavior request to Bob, the second character. Bob will choose a behavior to transfer, and offer it to Alice. Alice then accepts or rejects the behavior from Bob. These transfers occur on a one-to-one basis to reduce complexity; a behavior transfer can occur without involving the entire team. The three major problems to consider are *when* to request a behavior, *which* behavior to transfer, and *where* to place the behavior.

The question of *when* is handled by request strategies. Currently we define four request strategies: *command*, *cooperative*, *failure*, and *greedy*. The *command strategy* allows the creation of team hierarchies through behavior, while the *cooperative* strategy attempts to have one transferred behavior at all times. The *failure* and *greedy* strategies require failure detection. When one of these strategies is used, the character will make requests when one or more behaviors are failing, but *greedy* characters will attempt to resume their original behavior.

Which behavior to choose is handled by transfer strategies. The four defined transfer strategies are *command*, *distribution*, *priority*, and *failure*. The *command* strategy mirrors the command request strategy to allow the creation of team hierarchies. The *distribution* strategy has a target distribution of its behaviors to transfer, while the *priority* strategy focuses on the most important behaviors. The most commonly used transfer strategy is *failure*, which requires failure detection.

Where to place a behavior requires some classification of behavior layers. We classify layers as *self-preservation, task,* and *idle* layers, though additional categories can be used. Failure and greedy behavior requests will specify the category of the layer that needs to be replaced, but command and cooperative requests may be handled with layers from any category.

Multiple steps of reactive teaming require failure detection. Request and transfer strategies may explicitly rely on identifying malfunctioning layers. Characters must also evaluate the capabilities required by a given layer when deciding whether to accept or reject a transferred layer, which can be done using the capability metadata.

The effectiveness of reactive teaming with failure detection can be demonstrated with a case study in our simulation environment. In our scenario, the first agent, Alice, searched the environment for cans. The second agent, Bob, searched the environment for boxes. The goal of the agents is to pick up all of the objects scattered throughout the environment. The environment is initially loaded with many cans placed in the world. After a period, a large number of boxes are added to the environment. With static controllers, each agent will perform only the task initially designed. This means that while Alice is well-occupied for the first part of the scenario, Bob is performing very little work. Two different variations of the scenario were run, one using reactive teaming, and one with static characters.

In the static scenario, Alice was replicated to create 11 characters that searched the environment for cans. Bob was replicated to create 11 characters that searched for boxes. Eleven agents were guaranteed to be idle for the first half of the scenario, when no boxes were in the environment, while in the second half, 11 characters were mostly idle as very few cans were present. The overall team was very inefficient because at any given time, up to half of the characters could not perform a useful task.

The reactive teaming scenario allowed better team utilization. Instead of 11 characters in each role, we used Alice, Bob, and 20 *generic* agents. Generic agents have a base layer, but instead of being designed to perform a task, they are designed to have activation failures. These activation failures lead the agents to use reactive teaming to request behaviors from other characters. Figure 1 shows the number of characters with each behavior vs. time, averaged over 10 trials of 120 seconds each. As the scenario started, each of the 20 agents randomly received either the behavior to pick up cans or the behavior to pick up boxes based on whether they meet Alice or Bob first. Since boxes were nonexistent for the first part of the scenario, the can-gathering agents were quite productive, but the box-gathering agents continued to generate activation failures. The box-gathering agents requested new behaviors, resulting in a surge of can-gathering agents.

As the scenario continued, the boxes were added to the world. With most of the cans gone, the can-gathering agents generated activation failures, causing

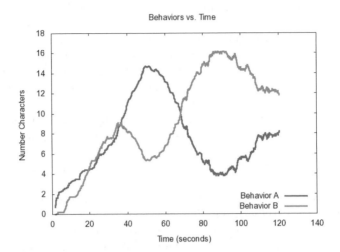

Fig. 1. Reactive teams adapt to environmental changes. Initially, neither behavior is relevant and they spread at the same rate. As Behavior A becomes relevant in the environment, it peaks, and the number of characters with Behavior B decreases. Once Behavior A is no longer relevant, Behavior B takes over.

them to request new behaviors. The number of box-gathering agents then surged, as the majority of agents received the appropriate behavior. Once all but a few objects have been gathered, the distribution of behaviors changed again, as all of the behaviors had become idle.

4   Conclusions

We have presented a framework for adding failure monitoring to behavior-based subsumption architectures. Four classes of errors can be detected without significant changes to the subsumption architecture, and the required metadata also enables dynamic extensions to behavior-based subsumption. Individual agent adaptation and team coordination can be improved through the use of failure detection. Failure detection is currently used to enable the reactive teaming technique for multi-agent coordination.

References

1. Heckel, F.W.P., Youngblood, G.M.: Multi-Agent Coordination Using Dynamic Behavior-Based Subsumption. In: Proceedings, 6th Artificial Intelligence for Interactive Digital Entertainment (AIIDE 2010) (2010)
2. Matarić, M.J.: Behavior-based control: Main properties and implications. In: Proceedings, IEEE International Conference on Robotics and Automation, Workshop on Architectures for Intelligent Control Systems, pp. 46–54 (1992)

Comparing Modes of Information Presentation: Text versus ECA and Single versus Two ECAs⋆

Svetlana Stoyanchev[1], Paul Piwek[1], and Helmut Prendinger[2]

[1] NLG Group, Centre for Research in Computing
The Open University, Walton Hall, Milton Keynes MK7 6AA, UK
{s.stoyanchev,p.piwek}@open.ac.uk
[2] National Institute of Informatics
2-1-2 Hitotsubashi, Chiyoda-ku, Tokyo 101-8430, Japan
helmut@nii.ac.jp

Abstract. In this short paper, we evaluate the prospects of automatic dialogue script generation from text for presentation by a team of Embodied Conversational Agents (ECAs). We describe an experiment comparing user perception and preference between plain text and video ECA presentations modes and between monologue and dialogue presentation styles. Our results show that most users are not indifferent of the presentation mode and the user's preference is guided by the perceived understanding and enjoyment of the presentation.

1 Introduction

As devices for delivering information have become more and more powerful and portable (from SmartPhones and Tablet PCs to the iPad and Kindle), traditional paper-based solutions (including books, leaflets, newspapers, journals) for information presentation are gradually replaced by electronic delivery platforms. Electronic delivery of information opens up new opportunities for presenting information in ways that are more engaging for and adaptive to information consumers.

Traditionally, research in the area of Intelligent Information Presentation has focused on 'some level of internal representation' [13] from which the information is then presented in the most appropriate way. Much of the research on Embodied Conversational Agents (ECAs) for information presentation also relies on this assumption. In the field of Natural Language Generation (NLG), there has recently been a trend away from generation based on manually constructed inputs (usually in a knowledge representation language) to generation from widely available inputs. At least two complementary strands have emerged: data-to-text

---

⋆ The research reported in this paper was carried out as part of the CODA (COherent Dialogue Automatically generated from text) project. The project was funded by the UK's Engineering and Physical Sciences Research Council under Grant EP/G020981/1. The authors would like to thank Ms Sara Winter for preparing the video materials for the experiment.

H. Högni Vilhjálmsson et al. (Eds.): IVA 2011, LNAI 6895, pp. 377–383, 2011.

generation (D2T; e.g., [11]) and text-to-text generation (T2T/paraphrasing, e.g., [4,12]).

In the current paper, we evaluate the prospects of the T2T approach to generate dialogue content for ECA teams. We investigate the efficacy of the resulting presentations by comparing original monologue text with generated dialogue script and also versions of the monologue and dialogue that are performed by one or two ECAs, respectively. Our aim is to compare the perceived quality of the different presentation modes and possible preferences by users for one mode or another.

The remainder of this paper is structured as follows. In the next section, we compare our approach with previous approaches to dialogue script generation and evaluation. Section 3 is at the heart of the current paper. Here we present the results from our user study, comparing monologue versus dialogue and text versus ECAs. Finally, Section 4 contains our conclusions.

2   Related Work

Several empirical studies show that delivering information in the form of a dialogue, as opposed to monologue, can be particularly effective for education [5] and persuasion [17]. However, none of these studies work with automatically generated dialogues. The current study is most similar to [19] where the authors compare presentation of generated information in monologue and dialogue audio mode. The authors generate presentation material from a relational database, in contrast to our approach where we generate dialogues from text.

Whereas most initial work on automatically generating dialogue scripts focused on input in the form of knowledge representations and the use of AI planning techniques [1,18,3], there has also been a parallel strand of research starting from text in monologue form, including Web2Talkshow [6] and the T2D system [8]. Our curent system is most similar to T2D: it also creates dialogue based on the intra and intersential discourse relations in the text, aiming to preserve the information of the input (rather than achieve a comic/humorous effect, as does Web2Talkshow). The main difference with T2D is that our system is based on discourse-to-dialogue mappings which are grounded in a parallel monologue/dialogue corpus. We have described the system [9,14], the corpus [15] and extraction of the mappings [16] elsewhere and also performed a controlled study with four expert judges which showed that the automatically generated dialogue scripts (in text form) have both accuracy (i.e., whether the dialogue preserves the information from the input monologue) and fluency that is not worse than that of human-written dialogues [10]. Our current study aims to determine the potential of using ECAs to present automatically generated dialogues to users.

3   Evaluation and Comparison

We describe an online user study aiming to determine user preference between presentation modalities (video and text) and presentation styles (monologue and dialogue). The experiment participants are presented with four presentation modes: text monologue, text dialogue, video of a single-character monologue, and video of a two-character dialogue.

3.1   Method

Materials. The topic of the presentations is eco-driving. The presentation materials include an adopted version of *What is eco-driving?* [1] and *Game instructions* composed by the video game developers [7].[2]

Table 1. Example of the presentation material

Monologue	Dialogue
It's worth remembering modern cars are designed to set off straight away, so warming your engine is needless and wastes fuel. It also causes engine wear as does keeping the engine running when you're stationary. If you're stuck in traffic it's best to turn your engine off completely as most modern cars are designed to use virtually no extra fuel to re-start.	TEACHER: Warming your engine is needless and wastes fuel. STUDENT: Why is that? TEACHER: It's worth remembering modern cars are designed to set off straight away TEACHER: It also causes engine wear STUDENT: As does keeping the engine running when you 're stationary? TEACHER: Yes. STUDENT: What if you're stuck in traffic? TEACHER: It's best to turn your engine off completely

We created four types of presentations for the materials: plain text monologue (original), text dialogue, single-character video monologue, and two-character video dialogue. To generate dialogues, we first manually parsed the discourse relations of the input monologues [2] and then used our M2D system [10] to generate dialogue. Since we are primarily interested in whether the sequence of dialogue acts proposed by M2D provides suitable content for

Fig. 1. Agents in Video Dialogue Presentation.

ECA video presentations, we corrected manually any syntactic and semantic errors, whilst leaving the dialogue act sequence unchanged. Table 1 shows an example of a snippet from a monologue document and a corresponding dialogue that were presented to the experiment participants. The videos of ECA monologue and dialogue presentations were generated using *xtranormal* MovieMaker.[3]

---

[1] http://www.guardian.co.uk/ford-econetic/driving-lessons
[2] The participants did not play the actual game.
[3] http://www.xtranormal.com/

Non-verbal behaviours were handcrafted using the behaviour authoring tool provided by *xtranormal*. When creating videos, we used the same gestures for the speaking character in both conditions. Figure 1 shows an image from a dialogue presentation.

Questionnaire and Procedure. The participants completed an on-line questionnaire on their personal systems. Each participant viewed four presentations, each in a different modality (video/text) and style (monologue/dialogue). Each presentation took about 2 to 3 minutes to view or read. After each presentation, the participants were asked to report whether they understood the presentation, found it engaging/enoyable/natural/fun. The ratings were made on a 5-point likert scale. The participants were prompted to make a choice for their preferences between each pair of the four presentation modes. The participants were requested not to interrupt while completing the questionnaire. After viewing all of the presentations, the participants were given an option to provide feedback about the presentations.[4]

Participants. We recruited 40 volunteer participants using computational linguistics mailing lists, university mailing lists, and Facebook connections. The participants self-reported language skill as "I can fluently communicate in English".

Design. We designed four groups to control for the presentation mode of a document (see Table 2). Each document was presented in different mode across the four conditions. Each participant viewed exactly one instance of each document in the same order (Doc1, Doc2, Doc3 and Doc4), each in a different presentation mode. The participants were distributed over the groups by adding each new participant to the group with fewest participants so far, resulting in 10 participants per group.

Table 2. Experiment design

	Material	Group A	Group B	Group C	Group D
Doc 1	What is Eco-driving (part 1)	Video Dia.	Video Mono.	Text Dia.	Text Mono.
Doc 2	What is Eco-driving (part 2)	Video Mono.	Text Dia.	Text Mono.	Video Dia.
Doc 3	Game instructions (part 1)	Text Dia.	Text Mono.	Video Dia.	Video Mono.
Doc 4	Game instructions (part 2)	Text Mono.	Video Dia.	Video Mono.	Text Dia.

3.2   Results

Preference. Table 3 shows the results for user preferences between the styles and the modalities. For video presentations, 40% of participants prefer dialogue,

---

[4] The participants were also asked recall questions about the content of the presentations. We are currently analysing the recall results.

45% prefer monologue, and 15% have no preference. For text presentations, the majority of the participants prefer monologue over dialogue (65% over 30%) and only 5% have no preference.

The tendency for the users in both monologue and dialogue modes is to prefer video, however for the dialogue presentations this tendency is stronger than for monologue with 62% of the users preferring video.

Table 3. Experiment results. * indicates statistically significant difference between the two preferences according χ^2 test ($p < .05$).

Compare Preference for Monologue/Dialogue Style			Compare Preference for Text/Video Modality			
modality	Prefer Dialogue	Prefer Monologue	No Pref	style	Prefer Video	Prefer Text	No Pref
Video	40.0%	45.0%	15.0%	Monologue	52.5%	42.5%	5.0%
Text *	30.0%	65.0%	5.0%	Dialogue *	62.5%	30.0%	7.5%

Compare Video Monologue and Dialogue Modes. We compare the scores for the ratings between video monologue and dialogue presentations (see Table 4). The first row of the Table shows the scores for all of the participants. The second row show the scores for only those participants who indicated that they prefer video dialogue over monologue presentation. The third row shows the scores for those preferring video monologue over dialogue.

While the scores between presentation modes for all participants are not significantly different, the participants who preferred dialogue report better understanding and enjoyment for the dialogue than the monologue. On the other hand, those who prefer monologue, report better understanding and enjoyment for the monologue than the dialogue.

Table 4. Ratings for the video dialogue (VD) and video monologue (VM) presentations. Statistically significant difference tested with paired t-test is marked with * for $p < .05$ and ** for $p < .01$.

participants (number)	understand VD/VM	enjoy VD/VM	natural VD/VM	engaging VD/VM	fun VD/VM	see again VD/VM
All (40)	3.83/4.03	3.00/2.95	2.50/2.78	3.00/2.80	2.50/2.35	2.93/2.85
Prefer VD (16)	4.25/3.88**	3.50/2.94*	3.13/2.75	3.63/2.81**	3.13/2.44**	3.81/2.75**
Prefer VM (18)	3.56/4.28	2.67/3.11*	2.06/2.94**	2.67/2.89	2.11/2.44	2.22/3.06**

3.3   Discussion

The results show that majority of the participants have a preference for mode of presentation. While for text presentation majority prefer monologue, for video presentation the participants are almost equally split between monologue and dialogue. Their preference correlates with self-reported understanding and enjoyment. The results suggest that some participants may prefer monologue because they find dialogue less natural. However, those who prefer dialogue, show no statistically significant difference in the naturalness scores between the dialogue and monologue styles suggesting that the preference is personal and subjective.

Presentation quality has a strong effect on the user choice between video and text modality. The participants commented on quality of video/audio as well as of text presentations. 45% of all participants found quality of audio in the presentations *bad* or *very bad*. This may have affected comprehension scores for video and led to a stronger tendency to prefer text over video. One of the participants wrote that *"Maybe if the quality of animation was more Hollywood-like, it would win over the written text."*

4   Conclusions

We compared user preference between two presentation modalities (monologue and dialogue) and two presentation styles (text and dialogue) and found that a majority of users have a preference for one of the two modalities and presentation styles. Additionally, a majority prefers to view dialogues as videos. For text presentations, monologue is preferred over dialogue. Finally, we found that the user's preference is correlated with their perceived understanding of the material and enjoyment of the presentation.

With improved quality of video and audio presentations, we expect that preferences will shift towards video. Since a clear majority of participants prefer a particular presentation mode, ideally an Intelligent Information Presentation system should allow people a choice between the monologue and dialogue modes. This in turn suggests a need for automatic generation of dialogue content for ECAs from text, with text still being one of the most ubiquitous information sources available.

References

1. André, E., Rist, T., van Mulken, S., Klesen, M., Baldes, S.: The automated design of believable dialogues for animated presentation teams. In: Embodied Conversational Agents, pp. 220–255. MIT Press, Cambridge (2000)
2. Carlson, L., Marcu, D.: Discourse tagging reference manual. Technical Report ISI-TR-545, ISI (September 2001)
3. Cavazza, M., Charles, F.: Dialogue Generation in Character-based Interactive Storytelling. In: Proceedings of the AAAI First Annual Artificial Intelligence and Interactive Digital Entertainment Conference, Marina Del Rey, California, USA (2005)
4. Cohn, T., Lapata, M.: Large margin synchronous generation and its application to sentence compression. In: Procs. of EMNLP-CONLL, Prague, pp. 73–82 (2007)
5. Craig, S., Gholson, B., Ventura, M., Graesser, A., and the Tutoring Research Group: Overhearing dialogues and monologues in virtual tutoring sessions. International Journal of Artificial Intelligence in Education 11, 242–253 (2000)

6. Nadamoto, A., Tanaka, K.: Complementing your TV-viewing by web content automatically-transformed into TV-program-type content. In: Proceedings 13th Annual ACM International Conference on Multimedia, pp. 41–50. ACM Press, New York (2005)

7. Nakasone, A., et al.: A 3D Internet based experimental framework for integrating traffic simulation and multi-user immersive driving. In: 4th Int'l Conference on Simulation Tools and Techniques (2011)

8. Piwek, P., Hernault, H., Prendinger, H., Ishizuka, M.: T2D: Generating Dialogues Between Virtual Agents Automatically from Text. In: Pelachaud, C., Martin, J.-C., André, E., Chollet, G., Karpouzis, K., Pelé, D. (eds.) IVA 2007. LNCS (LNAI), vol. 4722, pp. 161–174. Springer, Heidelberg (2007), doi:10.1007/978-3-540-74997-4

9. Piwek, P., Stoyanchev, S.: Generating Expository Dialogue from Monologue: Motivation, Corpus and Preliminary Rules. In: Proc. of NAACL, Los Angeles, USA (2010)

10. Piwek, P., Stoyanchev, S.: Data-Oriented Monologue-to-Dialogue Generation. In: Proc. of ACL/HLT, Portland, USA (2011)

11. Reiter, E.: An Architecture for Data to Text Systems. In: Procs. of ENLG-2007, Schloss Dagstuhl, Germany, pp. 97–104 (2007)

12. Rus, V., Graesser, A., Stent, A., Walker, M., White, M.: Text-to-Text Generation. In: Dale, R., White, M. (eds.) Shared Tasks and Comparative Evaluation in Natural Language Generation: Workshop Report, Arlington, Virginia (2007)

13. Stock, O., Zancanaro, M.: Multimodal Intelligent Information Presentation. Text, Speech and Language Technology, vol. 27. Springer, Heidelberg (2005)

14. Stoyanchev, S., Piwek, P.: The CODA System for Monologue-to-Dialogue Generation. In: Proc. of SIGDIAL, Portland, USA (2011)

15. Stoyanchev, S., Piwek, P.: Constructing the CODA Corpus: a Parallel Corpus of Monologues and Expository Dialogues. In: Proc. of LREC, Malta (2010)

16. Stoyanchev, S., Piwek, P.: Harvesting re-usable high-level rules for expository dialogue generation. In: Proc. of INLG, Trim, Ireland (2010)

17. Suzuki, S.V., Yamada, S.: Persuasion through overheard communication by lifelike agents. In: Procs of the 2004 IEEE/WIC/ACM International Conference on Intelligent Agent Technology, Beijing (September 2004)

18. Deemter, K.v., Krenn, B., Piwek, P., Klesen, M., Schroeder, M., Baumann, S.: Fully Generated Scripted Dialogue for Embodied Agents. Artificial Intelligence Journal 172(10), 1219–1244 (2008)

19. Williams, S., Piwek, P., Power, R.: Generating Monologue and Dialogue to Present Personalised Medical Information to Patients. In: Procs ENLG 2007, Schloss Dagstuhl, Germany, pp. 167–170 (2007)

Empirical Evaluation of Computational Emotional Contagion Models

Jason Tsai[1], Emma Bowring[2], Stacy Marsella[3], and Milind Tambe[1]

[1] University of Southern California, Los Angeles, CA 90089
{jasontts,tambe} @usc.edu
[2] University of the Pacific, Stockton, CA 95211
ebowring@pacific.edu
[3] USC Institute for Creative Technologies, Playa Vista, CA 90094
marsella@ict.usc.edu

Abstract. In social psychology, emotional contagion describes the widely observed phenomenon of one person's emotions being influenced by surrounding people's emotions. While the overall effect is agreed upon, the underlying mechanism of the spread of emotions has seen little quantification and application to computational agents despite extensive evidence of its impacts in everyday life.

In this paper, we examine computational models of emotional contagion by implementing two models ([2] and [8]) that draw from two separate lines of contagion research: thermodynamics-based and epidemiological-based. We first perform sensitivity tests on each model in an evacuation simulation, ESCAPES, showing both models to be reasonably robust to parameter variations with certain exceptions. We then compare their ability to reproduce a real crowd panic scene in simulation, showing that the thermodynamics-style model ([2]) produces superior results due to the ill-suited contagion mechanism at the core of epidemiological models. We also identify that a graduated effect of fear and proximity-based contagion effects are key to producing the superior results. We then reproduce the methodology on a second video, showing that the same results hold, implying generality of the conclusions reached in the first scene.

1 Introduction

Emotional contagion, the tendency for one's emotions to reflect the emotions of others, has been shown to arise in a wide range of scenarios in everyday life [10]. Its effects are felt every time someone cheerfully walks into the room with a big smile and brightens up everyone's day. Extensive work has been done in researching emotional contagion's role in occupations that require an employee to promote certain emotions in clients via displayed emotions, such as bill collectors promoting anxiety or flight attendants creating good cheer [9,15]. Less often, but with far more severe implications, it is also felt during the spread of fear and anxiety that surrounds any crowd-based disaster.

Virtual agents designed for these domains must also incorporate the effects of emotional contagion. For example, virtual patients in clinical training applications must incorporate not only the linguistic response of a real patient to a clinician's questions [11] but also a real patient's emotional response to a clinician's demeanor that results

H. Högni Vilhjálmsson et al. (Eds.): IVA 2011, LNAI 6895, pp. 384–397, 2011.

from emotional contagion. Similarly, an evacuation training simulation must include not only emotional contagion between simulated agents and its impact on escape behavior, but also exhibit emotions accurately to the user to mimic the contagion effects in a true evacuation [18]. With the growing awareness of the powerful impact that emotion has on human behavior, the contagion of these emotions can no longer be marginalized in virtual agents and must be accurately modeled and incorporated.

Recent work has sought to quantify the qualitative findings of social psychology into useable models, primarily drawing from two bodies of research on similar phenomena. Researchers at VU University introduced one of these in [2] (ASCRIBE) that used a deterministic, interaction-based model derived directly from a social psychology theory of emotional contagion [1]. This model is a prototypical example of the heat dissipation phenomena studied in thermodynamics wherein neighboring substances will transfer energy to each other at rates unique to each substance (i.e., specific heat). In contrast, Durupinar [8] used a probabilistic threshold model wherein successive interactions with emotionally 'infected' people raises the chance of infection with an emotion. This model is a standard one from the extensive epidemiology literature that models the spread of diseases [6,12,14], the research in diffusion of innovations [16], and social contagion work [17].

Although both models come from studies of contagion phenomena, they use fundamentally different mechanisms. While work could proceed using both approaches by extending existing models to accurately reproduce increasingly complex situations, it remains unclear which contagion paradigm should be used in emotional contagion. Perhaps a new mechanism should be designed, but the lack of data in this domain makes evaluation very difficult. We not only empirically compare these two paradigms but begin to identify the key features that should be added to the underlying contagion mechanisms to further improve their fidelity in reproducing human emotional contagion.

We begin by using the ESCAPES evacuation simulation [18] to explore the impact of replacing the original ESCAPES model with these two models on predicted outcomes, showing substantial differences in their predictions, motivating the need for an accurate model of emotional contagion in this context. Even in simulation, we are able to identify key differences that indicate epidemiological / social contagion models are less suited to modeling emotional contagion. Next, we attempt to reproduce real video footage of a panic situation using each of the models, showing the ASCRIBE model to indeed be superior to both the Durupinar model and the original ESCAPES model, beating out the Durupinar model by 14% *per agent per frame* during the 15s scene. To identify which of the key features causes the differences in the results, we test hybrid models to conclude that while adding a 'decay' feature (as found in the Durupinar model) to the ASCRIBE model does not improve it, removing proximity effects and fear's graduated effect on speed substantially worsen the model. Finally, we perform the same evaluation on a second video and show the ASCRIBE model to again be superior, outperforming the Durupinar model by 12% per agent per frame during the *four-second* scene.

2 Related Work

Seminal works in social psychology first began the discussion around emotional contagion. In particular, Hatfield et al. [10] first codified the observed phenomena that were just beginning to receive researcher attention. Follow-up work by the co-authors as well as in related fields such as [1,9,15] in managerial and occupational sciences continued to detail the effects of the phenomenon in new domains. Recently, there have been works beginning to quantify emotional contagion and explore cross-cultural variations in attributes that affect emotional contagion [7,13].

From a computational perspective, the previously mentioned work from VU University and Durupinar are two of the most recent models of emotional contagion upon which a few follow-up works have been based [3]. As mentioned in Section 1, the AS-CRIBE model resembles heat dissipation models found in basic physics wherein each substance has its own heat dissipation rate and heat absorption rate. The Durupinar model draws inspiration from a long line of contagion models [6,12] that was popularized in the diffusion of innovations [16] literature and has also seen heavy use in other types of social (e.g., belief, behavior, idea) contagion [17].

Although not the focal point, the ESCAPES evacuation simulation [18] serves as the test bed for our models of emotional contagion, so we describe it briefly here. ESCAPES focuses on the features identified by experts that particularly effect airport evacuations, including first time visitors' incomplete knowledge of the area, the presence of families, and the presence and effects of authority figures [5]. ESCAPES also models fear's impact on behavior as an increase in speed of more fearful agents, mimicking their attempt to escape quickly [4]. Finally, ESCAPES uses a basic model of emotional contagion, wherein agents inherit the highest fear level of neighboring agents. We use ESCAPES to evaluate the spread of emotion through the crowd, illustrating substantial differences in the contagion process when using different models of emotional contagion.

3   ASCRIBE Model

Introduced in 2009 by researchers at VU University [2] and built upon in multiple works including [3], the ASCRIBE model iterates through all agents and deterministically calculates new emotional levels based on a set of individual and pairwise parameters that we describe here. The mechanism used resembles heat dissipation modeling in physics, wherein each material has a specific heat capacity, which can be likened to a person's susceptibility to other people's emotions in emotional contagion. As such, the model moves a crowd towards a weighted-average of the group's emotional levels, just as heat will dissipate until adjacent temperatures are the same, barring generative heat sources.

The model defines 5 parameters for every pairwise interaction based on theory put forth in [1]: level of sender's emotion q_S, level of receiver's emotion q_R, sender's expressiveness ϵ_S, receiver's openness δ_R, and the channel strength between S and R α_{SR}. All values are numbers in the interval $[0, 1]$. At each time step, each agent calculates the average emotional transfer from all relevant agents. Specifically, the differential equations for emotional contagion in a group G of agents is:

$$dq_R/dt = \gamma_R(q_R^* - q_R)$$

for all $R \in G$, where γ_R is the overall strength at which emotions from all other group members are received, defined by $\gamma_R = \Sigma_{S \in G \setminus \{R\}} \gamma_{SR}$. q_R^* is the weighted combination of emotions from the other agents, defined with a weight factor:

$$w_{SR} = \epsilon_S \alpha_{SR} / \Sigma_{C \in G \backslash \{R\}} \epsilon_C \alpha_{CR}$$

$$q_R^* = \Sigma_{S \in G \backslash \{R\}} w_{SR} q_S$$

Specifically, from a sender S to a receiver R, the strength of the emotion q_S received would be $\gamma_{SR} = \epsilon_S \cdot \alpha_{SR} \cdot \delta_R$. [2] details the mathematical formulation, but the emotional level of an agent converges towards a weighted average of the group's emotional level. The speed at which this convergence occurs as well as the weighting depend on the parameter settings for the channel strength, expressiveness, and openness for each agent as well as, of course, their individual emotional levels.

The latest version of the model [3], extends the original emotional contagion model and includes beliefs and intentions and belief/intention contagion as well. However, as our goal is to empirically evaluate emotional contagion models and the latest work extends far beyond simply emotional contagion, we leave its validation to future work. Thus, we do not use the extended model but instead modify the initial model by incorporating a proximity effect as done in [3].

4   Durupinar Model

Durupinar [8] uses a probabilistic threshold model based on epidemiological models of disease contagion. While many types of epidemiological models exist [6,12,14,17], Durupinar implements a version with only *susceptible* and *infected* states (as opposed to recovered, innoculated, etc. states). The epidemiological model's applicability to emotional contagion was not discussed in [6], from which Durupinar drew, but its use by Durupinar assumes similarity between disease spread and emotion spread that we criticize in this work.

Each agent begins with a randomized threshold drawn from a pre-determined log-normal distribution. At each time step, for each agent, a random agent is chosen from the relevant population group. If the agent is infected, it generates a random dose drawn from a pre-determined log-normal distribution and passes it to the original agent. If the agent is not infected, then a dose of 0.0 is generated. Each agent maintains a running history of the last K doses received. If the cumulative total of all doses in the agent's history exceeds his threshold, the agent enters the infected state. This causes the emotion level to be set to 1.0 with an exponential decay towards 0.0, at which point the agent re-enters the susceptible state. A non-zero emotion level indicates that the agent has the emotion, but the actual value does not hold meaning other than to track the decay. The random dose and threshold are generated from log-normal distributions with user-specified averages and standard deviations and K is a static global variable.

5   Simulation Experiments

The ASCRIBE model and the Durupinar model use very different mechanisms to recreate emotional contagion. Thus, we evaluate the impact of these differences in two ways, beginning first with simulation. We ran the evacuation simulation, ESCAPES, using each model to perform sensitivity analysis as well as identify any qualitative trends that

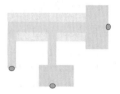

Fig. 1. Evacuation scenario

might support or discredit either one of the models. We can also evaluate the model's robustness to errors in parameter estimation, which is extremely important in emotional and crowd modeling which usually lack high fidelity, fine-grain data.

For all the experiments discussed in this section, the same map was used (spatial layout can be seen in Figure 1) and 30 trials were run for each setting. It features 2 large spaces, each with an exit (marked with dots), connected by hallways which are lined with smaller spaces that represent shops. 15 seconds into the simulation, an event occurs at the center of the scenario, inciting fear and a need to evacuate that is communicated by authority figures to pedestrians. For initial fear levels, we define a 'seeing distance', σ_d. Agents within this distance of an event will immediately have a fear level of 0.75 in the ASCRIBE model and 1.0 in the Durupinar model, since the Durupinar model does not feature a continuous measure of fear. We also define a 'hearing distance', ω_d, within which the agent will receive 0.1 in the ASCRIBE model and 1.0 in the Durupinar model. The scenario features 100 normal pedestrians, including 10 families of 4 each, as well as 10 authority figures that patrol the scenario. In Sections 5.1 and 5.2 we evaluate model robustness and then identify qualitative differences in Section 5.3.

5.1 ASCRIBE Model

In examining the contagion effect, the parameters of interest in the ASCRIBE model were the individual expressiveness settings and individual openness settings. The channel strength is set to 1 if an agent is nearby and 0 otherwise, as done in [3]. Given that we had a whole population of agents, we elected to use randomly drawn values for expressiveness and openness based on a normal distribution. We explored variations of the averages and standard deviations (SD) used, but surprisingly, none yield substantial changes in the outcome of the simulation from both a contagion perspective (i.e., how the fear spread) and a safety analysis. The only exception was, unsurprisingly, when the receiver openness or sender expressiveness parameters varied tightly around a very low mean, leaving many agents with 0.0 openness or expressiveness. This caused the majority of agents to remain at their initial fear level which was vastly different from the mean convergence behavior seen in the other settings.

Figure 2a plots the percentage of people with low fear (≤ 0.1) on the y-axis and the time step on the x-axis, while Figure 2b shows the same results for high- fear people. In both figures, openness varied from 0.1 to 0.9 in increments of 0.2 while keeping a SD of 0.1 and sender expressiveness was fixed with an average of 0.5 with a SD of 0.1. In Figure 2a, when an event first occurs, those near it become fearful and slowly

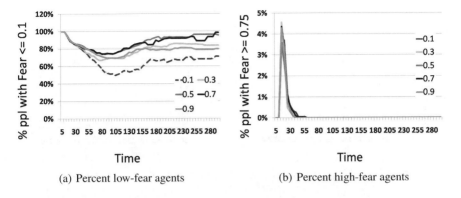

(a) Percent low-fear agents   (b) Percent high-fear agents

Fig. 2. Variations in Openness

raise nearby peoples' fear as they move towards exits, causing a steady decline in the percentage of people with fear less than 0.1 that only rises again as fearful agents make their way out of the simulation. Note how the dotted line (0.1) dips much lower than the other lines, showing the exception mentioned above. In Figure 2b, agents near the event have their fear raised very high, but as they encounter zero-fear agents, their fear levels are brought down below 0.75 and never again rise higher since no new events occur. The tightness of the lines implies that the trend is robust to variations in the average receiver openness except at very low settings. Similar tightness of lines was observed in variations of sender expressiveness, with the same exception.

We also conducted experiments exploring the second-order effects on safety, as measured by the ESCAPES system. In particular we examined the evacuation rates of pedestrians as well as the number of collisions experienced on average. Neither set of results showed significant variation through the parameter space, indicating the results' robustness to parameter variation.

5.2   Durupinar Model

Sensitivity analysis of the Durupinar model is considerably more delicate than the AS-CRIBE model, because although there are only 5 key parameters for the whole population (as compared to 2 per individual plus 1 for each pair for the ASCRIBE model) they are very fragilely related. Thus, we begin with experimentally chosen default values and vary each parameter to identify key sensitivities. In particular, we begin with a baseline of K of 4, dose average of 2, dose standard deviation of 0.5, threshold average of 7, and threshold standard deviation of 2.

Figure 3a shows the percentage of no-fear pedestrians ($= 0$) on the y-axis and time steps on the x-axis, with each line representing a different setting of K. Figure 3b shows the percentage of newly fearful pedestrians (defined as ≥ 0.75) during the same variations of K. Unsurprisingly, altering any one of the parameters' averages *or* standard deviations individually alters the magnitude of the contagion effect, but not the overall trends. The exceptions are at values far from the baseline. For example, at extremely low values for K or dose distribution average and at extremely high values for

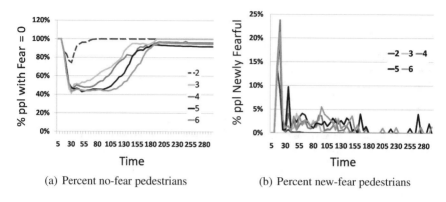

(a) Percent no-fear pedestrians   (b) Percent new-fear pedestrians

Fig. 3. Variations of K

threshold distribution average, when very few agents become fearful at all, as seen in the dotted $K = 2$ line in Figure 3a. This implies that the model remains robust to parameter changes with respect to the contagion trends that emerge as long as parameter values are chosen within a tolerance of the baseline. Similar results were found for variations of threshold and dose strength averages and standard deviations.

We again explored the second-order impacts of parameter variations on the safety of the evacuation by measuring the evacuation rates and average number of collisions of pedestrians in the simulation. As in the ASCRIBE experiments, we again found no significant variation as long as the parameters varied across the non-trivial parameter space.

5.3 Key Differences

In Sections 5.1 and 5.2 we have shown the ASCRIBE model to be robust to parameter variations (except at the extreme of zero) and the Durupinar model to be robust if we stay within a tolerance of a baseline. In conducting these simulation tests and taking a closer look at the contagion effect, we already find that a number of key differences can be identified between the two models. One difference can be seen by comparing Figures 2b and 3b, where the spikes occurring throughout the graph indicate that Durupinar model produces newly fearful agents throughout the life of the simulation, *regardless of the nature of the event*, and the ASCRIBE model only exhibits a spike due to the impact of the event. Under the Durupinar model, fear can be transferred indefinitely under certain parameter settings. In the ASCRIBE model, encounters with agents who are less fearful will slowly erode the average fear level, eventually reaching zero after sufficiently many agents have been encountered.

Also, combining the binary fear metric with a speed modifier, as done in ESCAPES, results in only extremes of movement speeds. While one could argue that this is a result of the simulation, the model itself cannot incorporate any gradation of effect. For example, even if we directly map the fear level (as it decays) to the speed modifier, an agent that is near zero-fear (and is hence traveling slowly) can infect another agent who will then dart off at maximal speed since he begins at maximal fear, as evidenced by the spikes in Figure 3b. This may occur as a result of physiological or informational changes, but no evidence suggests this would occur from emotional contagion alone. A more fundamental alteration is needed to change this aspect of epidemiological / social contagion models for convincing application to emotional contagion.

Finally, as mentioned, the Durupinar model does not include a proximity of effect, whereas the ASCRIBE model does. This obviously means that the Durupinar model could potentially cause contagion of emotions to agents randomly throughout the world of the simulation, a very unrealistic effect, as emotional contagion requires *some* form of interaction by definition. As seen in a comparison between Figures 2a and 3a, the Durupinar model induces more fearful agents far more rapidly than the ASCRIBE model does because its contagion calculation incorporates the entire population immediately.

6   Scene Reproduction

Now we discuss the validation method used to evaluate the models of emotional contagion, first used in [3]. In their work, VU University researchers used a 15-second portion of a crowd panic scene in Amsterdam caused by a screaming person[1] as their dataset for validating their general mental state contagion model. In processing the data, the researchers traced the locations of 35 people scattered through the crowd through the 15 seconds, converted these into top-down coordinates and built a simulator to reproduce the paths of the people in simulation. The operating hypothesis was that a simulator without their mental state contagion model would not be able to reproduce the scene as accurately as a simulator with it. To test this hypothesis, the researchers tuned parameters associated with each agent's maximum speed, a global parameter specifying a 'sight range' within which agents could 'see' the event, and an initial desire to remain in place. The tuning was done via hill-climbing to minimize the error produced by the simulator, testing each parameter and moving a single parameter at a time in the direction of highest error reduction until a local optimum was reached. Error was defined as the sum of the average distances from each simulated agent to the corresponding real people's locations over the life of the simulation. Then, they incorporated the mental state contagion model, tuning a parameter associated with the proximity of contagion and showed that lower error was achieved with this addition.

We replicate their methodology using the ESCAPES simulator, setting 3 exit locations towards which agents proceed when the simulation starts. The locations were chosen to roughly mimic the real situation, leading to most agents moving in the same direction as the people did. Some agents did not move precisely in the simulated direction as a result of obstructions that we did not model and a person very close to the screaming person that barely moved. The primary task was to match the crowd's location over time, first without contagion effects and then with each contagion model in turn. Since people's directions did not vary based on the emotion, the contagion model could only impact the speed of each agent.

The speed of an agent, without incorporating contagion effects, is based on the emotional level multiplied by the maximum speed multiplied by a distance-based modifier. The distance-based modifier is σ_s if the agent is within sight range and ω_s if the agent is

---

[1] http://youtu.be/0cEQp8OQj2Y

only within hearing distance. We include these tunable speed modifiers so that the simulation is robust to the choice of initial fear levels, which is particularly helpful given the lack of data surrounding how to set the initial fear levels.

For each contagion model, we use the default settings discussed in Section 5, with the exception of the ASCRIBE model's channel strength, which we set to 1.0 or 0.0 depending on the proximity of other agents, as was done in [3]. In the ASCRIBE model, we follow [3] and fix Receiver Openness and Sender Expressiveness each to 0.5 *for every agent*, but allow the proximity parameter to be tuned. In the Durupinar model, we set the dose history to 6, the mean and standard deviation of the dose strength distribution to 2 and 0.5, and the mean and standard deviation of the threshold distribution to 7 and 2. The ESCAPES contagion model, used as a baseline for comparison, only requires tuning of the proximity parameter as it simply brings all agents to the highest level of fear found in surrounding agents. In an attempt to not only identify which model is more appropriate but also to discern key features from unsupported augmentations, we used each model as given, then turned on/off implementations of 'decay', emotional level impacting speed, and proximity effects. For each parameter setting, 30 trials were run.

6.1   Amsterdam Crowd

We first use the Amsterdam crowd scene featured in [3]. In their results, VU University researchers found that the inclusion of contagion effects achieved significantly less error in reproducing the movement of a selection of 35 agents from the crowd scene. Examination of the dataset revealed that 60-70% of the error in each of the models' results can be attributed to 12 agents near the explosion. We show the error breakdown in Figure 4. Two other categories of error are shown as well: faraway agents, and the agent closest to the yelling. The agent closest to the yelling barely moved in the video, which is a situation that the cognitive model of ESCAPES does not naturally simulate. Hence, all models produce large errors quite unrelated to the underlying emotional contagion model. The faraway agents, by contrast, move extremely little, making it easy to fit any model to them by simply forcing those agents to remain completely still. Thus, the largest portion of the error, that caused by the agents near the event (except the closest agent) also provides the most potential for the emotional contagion models to differ.

The results from the different variations of each model is listed in Table 1. Table 1a shows the results for the base models as defined previously, illustrating OVERALL error (for all 35 agents) as well as the error associated with the most substantial group of agents, the 12 NEAR the event, excepting the closest agent. Table 1b shows the

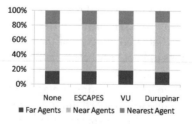

Fig. 4. Error attribution

Table 1. Average error (in pixels) per agent per frame

(a) Base models

	Overall	Near			Overall	Near			Overall	Near			Overall	Near
None	0.375	0.699	ESCAPES		0.375	0.698	ASCRIBE		0.362	0.663	Durupinar		0.383	0.758

(b) ESCAPES	(c) ASCRIBE model	(d) Durupinar model

Model	Overall	Near	Variation	Overall	Near	Model	Overall	Near
Base	0.375	0.698	Base	0.362	0.663	Base	0.383	0.758
Decay	0.379	0.703	Decay	0.363	0.687	No Decay	0.387	0.771
No Speed	0.381	0.721	No Speed	0.387	0.767	Speed	0.388	0.784
No Prox	0.385	0.721	No Prox	0.414	0.797	Prox	0.380	0.754

variations associated with the original ESCAPES formulation. The second line of the table indicates that a 'decay' feature was added to the base model. The third line indicates that we turned on/off the effect that different levels of fear have on speed. When off, this means that any level of fear causes agents to travel at maximum speed. When on, the speed of travel is proportional to the fear level. Finally, the fourth row represents whether the contagion effect was moderated with a tuned proximity effect. Tables 1c and 1d show the analogous set of variations for the ASCRIBE and Durupinar models.

No results from the ESCAPES contagion formulation were statistically significantly better than the No Contagion case, as measured with a one-tailed t-test. This indicates that the ESCAPES contagion model does not add anything in the context of this dataset. In sharp contrast, all results for ASCRIBE and Durupinar were statistically significantly different from the No Contagion case, although in the case of Durupinar, they were significantly *worse* ($p < 0.001$). As found in [3], the ASCRIBE model's formulation provided substantial improvements in the simulation's ability to reproduce this scene (14% superior to Durupinar for NEAR agents in the Base cases for the 15s clip).

For ESCAPES, no feature change offered statistically significantly different results from the base case, implying that in this formulation, for this data set, adding 'decay' did not help and the presence of 'speed' and 'proximity' features did not add value to the model either. In the ASCRIBE model, adding 'decay', removing 'speed', and removing 'proximity' all had statistically significantly negative impacts on the results ($p < 0.001$). This implies that the 'speed' and 'proximity' features were crucial to generating the positive result in the Base case and adding 'decay' does not improve it. Finally, removing 'decay' produced significantly worse results in the Durupinar model, and the other two variations did not produce statistically different results.

These results imply that the ASCRIBE model's contagion mechanism and current formulation provides the highest fidelity in modeling this dataset versus other variations and models tested. To properly frame the magnitude of improvement, consider a crowd being modeled for five minutes. In real terms, the 14% average difference between ASCRIBE and Durupinar amounts to over *two meters* of error over the 12 NEAR agents in a *single frame*. 'Small' errors like this in the first 15s can easily snowball into a completely different crowd structure after five minutes, suggesting much larger implications to this 14% improvement.

(a) Amsterdam video

(b) Greece video

Fig. 5. Amsterdam and Greece video screenshots

Table 2. Average error (in pixels) per agent during the simulation

(a) Base models		(b) ESCAPES		(c) ASCRIBE		(d) Durupinar	
Model	Error	Model	Error	Variation	Error	Model	Error
None	1.635	Base	1.478	Base	1.478	Base	1.656
ESCAPES	1.478	Decay	1.474	Decay	1.466	No Decay	1.653
ASCRIBE	1.478	No Speed	1.567	No Speed	1.653	Speed	1.669
Durupinar	1.656	No Prox	1.658	No Prox	1.660	Prox	1.654

6.2   Greece Crowd

Since one dataset could be particularly well-suited to the ASCRIBE model, we elected to perform the same process on a second video from recent protests in Greece[2], where officers fired tear gas into the middle of a small crowd. The clip used was from 0:16 to 0:20, from which 24 frames were extracted for analysis. 10 figures throughout the crowd were traced for the duration of the clip. Conversion of the pixel coordinates into top-down coordinates was done by first estimating true axes in the top-down view by tracing the sidewalk and steps that were perpendicular to the sidewalk. Then, the distance to each of the axes was calculated (where 'distance' is measured from the point to the axis, parallel to the other axis) and used as the new coordinates.

Even in such a short video clip with such a small crowd that we are able to match extremely well, the emotional contagion models still showed significant differences. Surprisingly, the original ESCAPES model performs extremely well, matching the AS-CRIBE model's accuracy. However, as before, we see the Durupinar model again performing substantially worse than all other models, implying some generality of the previous result. In fact, this scene is an even stronger testament than the previous one, as the ASCRIBE model performs 12% better than Durupinar in the Base case per agent per frame during only a *four-second* clip as opposed to the 15s Amsterdam clip. For both the original ESCAPES model and the ASCRIBE model, removing fear's impact

---

[2] http://www.youtube.com/watch?v=NsoDwM_KKfo

on speed and the proximity effect statistically significantly worsen's the model's accuracy ($p < 0.001$). Surprisingly, the ASCRIBE model benefits from the addition of a decay component ($p < 0.001$), implying that a decay effect may be context-dependent.

7 Conclusions

In this work, we have made the first attempt to compare existing models of emotional contagion and identify key attributes of appropriate models using real data. The AS-CRIBE model produced a 14% improvement *per agent per frame* over the Durupinar model in a 15s clip and a 12% improvement in only a *four-second* clip. After attempts to transform the Durupinar model into one more similar to the ASCRIBE model with little success. This suggests that the primary cause of the statistically significantly worse performance found with the epidemiological / social contagion model is in the mechanism of contagion itself, which is probabilistic and uses a binary representation of the effect. Although the ASCRIBE model requires setting $(N^2 + N)$ parameters to model N agents, even when we do away with them by fixing openness/receptiveness and only formulaically varying channel strength, the model produces superior results, implying that the underlying heat dissipation-style mechanism is better-suited to the phenomenon. In actual crowd modeling, simulators could use population averages for the parameters, as found in recent work [7,13] (instead of arbitrarily setting them at 0.5), resulting in a simplified model with one or two global parameters similar to 'specific heat capacities' for people's emotional transfer strength and one formulaic descriptor of proximity's impact. This leaves a simple, data-driven model of emotional contagion with empirical evidence supporting its superior performance.

As we deepen our understanding of how quickly and how strongly emotional contagion occurs, we can greatly improve the fidelity of simulations designed to reproduce and predict human behavior in emotionally-charged situations. In addition, this work serves as a first step towards honing in on the key factors that influence the speed and strength of emotional contagion. Armed with this knowledge, the design of virtual agents can more accurately mimic human responses to emotional situations in their interactions with other agents as well as humans. For example, virtual patients that understand questions and respond properly [11] will also react to the user's smiles, nods and other facial/vocal features to train clinicians to control the emotional contagion they inevitably cause. Virtual agents in emergency response simulations will not only be able to exhibit appropriate behaviors for a trainee to view and interact with, but also have a more accurate emotional effect on the user that will prepare him/her for the psychological strains that will inevitably arise. Only with the comprehensive quantitative understanding of emotional contagion that we have begun developing here will we be able to produce truly interactive, human-like agents.

Acknowledgement. We would like to acknowledge the generosity of the VU University group that we have cited extensively in this work for sharing their experience and resources pertaining to the video evaluation. This research was sponsored in part by the U.S. Army Research, Development, and Engineering Command (RDECOM)

Simulation Training and Technology Center (STTC). The content or information pre-sented does not necessarily reflect the position or the policy of the Government, and no official endorsement should be inferred. This research was also supported by the United States Department of Homeland Security through the National Center for Risk and Economic Analysis of Terrorism Events (CREATE) under award number 2008-ST-104-000013. However, any opinions, findings, and conclusions or recommendations in this document are those of the authors and do not necessarily reflect views of the United States Department of Homeland Security, or the University of Southern California, or CREATE.

References

1. Barsade, S.G., Gibson, D.E.: Group Emotion: A View from Top and Bottom. In: Gruenfeld, D., Mannix, E., Neale, M. (eds.) Research on Managing on Groups and Teams, pp. 81–102. JAI Press, Stamford (1998)
2. Bosse, T., Duell, R., Memon, Z.A., Treur, J., Wal, C.N.V.D.: A Multi-Agent Model for Mu-tual Absorption of Emotions. In: European Council on Modeling and Simulation, ECMS 2009, pp. 212–218 (2009)
3. Bosse, T., Hoogendoorn, M., Klein, M., Treur, J., van der Wal, N.: Agent-Based Analysis of Patterns in Crowd Behaviour Involving Contagion of Mental States. In: IEA/AIE 2011, Springer, Heidelberg (2011)
4. Brown, J.S., Martin, R.C., Morrow, M.W.: Self-punitive behavior in the rat: Facilitative ef-fects of punishment on resistance to extinction. Journal of Comparative and Physiological Psychology 57(1), 127–133 (1964)
5. Diamond, J., McVay, M., Zavala, M.W.: Quick, Safe, Secure: Addressing Human Behavior During Evacuations at LAX. Master's thesis, UCLA Dept of Public Policy (June 2010)
6. Dodds, P., Watts, D.J.: A generalized model of social and biological contagion. Journal of Theoretical Biology 232(4), 587–604 (2005)
7. Doherty, W.: The Emotional Contagion Scale: A Measure of Individual Differences. Journal of Nonverbal Behavior 21(2) (1997)
8. Durupinar, F.: From Audiences to Mobs: Crowd Simulation with Psychological Factors. PhD dissertation, Bilkent University, Dept. Comp. Eng (July 2010)
9. Grandey, A.A.: Emotional regulation in the workplace: A new way to conceptualize emo-tional labor. Journal of Occupational Health Psychology 5(1), 95–110 (2000)
10. Hatfield, E., Cacioppo, J.T., Rapson, R.L.: Emotional Contagion. Cambridge University Press, Cambridge (1994)
11. Kenny, P., Parsons, T.D., Gratch, J., Rizzo, A.A.: Evaluation of Justina: A Virtual Patient with PTSD. In: Prendinger, H., Lester, J.C., Ishizuka, M. (eds.) IVA 2008. LNCS (LNAI), vol. 5208, pp. 394–408. Springer, Heidelberg (2008)
12. Kermack, W.O., McKendrick, A.G.: A contribution to the mathematical theory of epidemics. Proceedings of The Royal Society of London. Series A, Containing Papers of A Mathemati-cal and Physical Character (1905-1934) 115, 700–721 (1927)
13. Lundqvist, L.-O.: Factor Structure of the Greek Version of the Emotional Contagion Scale and its Measurement Invariance Across Gender and Cultural Groups. Journal of Individual Differences 29(3), 121–129 (2008)
14. Murray, J.D.: Mathematical Biology, 3rd edn. Springer, New York (2002)
15. Pugh, S.D.: Service with a smile: Emotional contagion in the service encounter. Academy of Management Journal 44(5), 1018–1027 (2001)

16. Rogers, E.M.: Diffusion of Innovations. The Free Press, New York (1962)
17. Schelling, T.C.: Hockey helmets, concealed weapons, and daylight saving: a study of binary choices with externalities. Journal of Conflict Resolution 17, 381–428 (1973)
18. Tsai, J., Fridman, N., Bowring, E., Brown, M., Epstein, S., Kaminka, G., Marsella, S., Ogden, A., Rika, I., Sheel, A., Taylor, M.E., Wang, X., Zilka, A., Tambe, M.: ESCAPES: Evacuation Simulation with Children, Authorities, Parents, Emotions, and Social Comparison. In: AAMAS 2011, pp. 457–464. ACM Press, New York (2011)

Don't Scratch! Self-adaptors Reflect Emotional Stability

Michael Neff[1], Nicholas Toothman[1], Robeson Bowmani[2], Jean E. Fox Tree[2], and Marilyn A. Walker[2]

[1] University of California, Davis
{mpneff,njtoothman}@ucdavis.edu
[2] University of California, Santa Cruz
{rbowmani,foxtree}@ucsc.edu, maw@soe.ucsc.edu

Abstract. A key goal in agent research is to be able to generate multimodal characters that can reflect a particular personality. The Big Five model of personality provides a framework for codifying personality variation. This paper reviews findings in the psychology literature to understand how the Big Five trait of *emotional stability* correlates with changes in verbal and nonverbal behavior. Agent behavior was modified based on these findings and a perceptual study was completed to determine if these changes lead to the controllable perception of emotional stability in virtual agents. The results reveal how language variation and the use of self-adaptors can be used to increase or decrease the perceived emotional stability of an agent. Self-adaptors are movements that often involve self-touch, such as scratching or bending one's fingers backwards in an unnatural brace. These results provide guidance on how agent designers can create particular characters, including indicating that for particular personality types, it is important to also produce typically non-communicative gestural behavior, such as the self-adaptors studied.

Keywords: Personality, gesture, conversational and nonverbal behavior, evaluation.

1 Introduction

Animated Intelligent Virtual Agents are a key component for many emerging applications, ranging from virtual worlds to interactive story systems to educational games. As with previous media such as books and film, for these agents to be effective, they must convey the richness of traditional characters, showing clear personality and mood. Yet it remains an open challenge as to how to imbue an agent with these qualities and how to organize the underlying range of expressive variation. The "Big Five" or "OCEAN" model of personality represents an appealing organizing framework [5,23,22,26]. The model has emerged as a standard in psychology, with research over the last fifty years systematically documenting correlatons between a wide range of behaviors and the Big Five traits (extraversion, neuroticism/emotional stability, agreeableness, conscientiousness, openness to experience) [24,30,33].

H. Högni Vilhjálmsson et al. (Eds.): IVA 2011, LNAI 6895, pp. 398–411, 2011.

Table 1. Example adjectives associated with the extremes of the Big Five traits of Emotional Stability and Agreeableness

Big Five Trait	High	Low
Emotional stability	calm, even-tempered, reliable, peaceful, confident	neurotic, anxious, depressed, self-conscious, oversensitive, vulnerable
Agreeableness	trustworthy, friendly, considerate, generous, helpful, altruistic	unfriendly, selfish, suspicious, uncooperative, malicious

This work examines how both an agent's verbal and nonverbal behavior can be altered to control the perception of one of the Big Five traits, *Emotional Stability*. As a control, we test whether the same parameters affect the perception of *Agreeableness*. Emotional stability (EMS) ranges between two extremes, *Emotionally Stable* and *Neurotic*. Emotional stability—or neuroticism—is the second most studied personality trait after extraversion; it is part of most existing frameworks of personality, such as the Big Five and the PEN model [30,12]. The trait adjectives associated with both emotional stability and agreeableness are shown in Table 1. Neurotics tend to be anxious, negative and oversensitive, while emotionally stable people are calm and even-tempered. Eysenck et. al (1985) suggest that this dimension is related to activation thresholds in the nervous system, i.e. neurotics turn more easily into a 'fight-or-flight' state when facing danger, resulting in an increase in heart beat, muscular tension, and level of sweating [12]. Previous findings such as these suggest parameters for controlling the perception of neuroticism. For example, neuroticism findings suggest a CONTENT POLARITY parameter for selecting negative content, as well as a REPETITIONS parameter [33,40]. Neurotics are also more likely to engage in self touch [43] and less likely to gesture towards others [3].

We begin by first reviewing and summarizing previous work on how neuroticism is expressed. Section 2 summarizes these findings and describes how they are mapped to agent behavior in order to produce multimodal animation clips. These animations are then used in a perceptual study to evaluate if the variations are sufficient to control the perception of emotional stability in virtual agents (Section 3). As detailed in Section 4, key results include that: (1) generated utterances previously validated only as written text also effectively capture variation in emotional stability when used in a multimodal agent; and (2) that there is a significant relationship between the use of self-adaptors, such as head scratches, and the perception of neuroticism. A detailed discussion of the results is presented in Section 5, along with a comparison to recent related work.

2   Nonverbal and Verbal Expression of Personality

For nonverbal expression of emotional stability, we systematically organize findings relating gesture, posture and hand-movement to emotional stability. For verbal expression, we build on Mairesse & Walker's personality models for the expression of EMS through linguistic reflexes alone, but introduce linguistic parameters related to the voice, speaking rate, and pause length [22].

2.1   Nonverbal Expression of Emotional Stability

Emotional stability provides particular challenges for findings related to non-verbal communication. While the literature describes numerous characteristics regarding general body language for neurotic, nervous, and anxious personality types, it offers little detail or operationalization of the exact variations in motion for low and high dimensional values.

Gesture Behavior. The psychology literature provided qualitative descriptions of how EMS modifies nonverbal communication, but little in the way of quantitative measurements. In order to form a cohesive model of gesture behavior, we classified the results and our postulates into three categories based on the aspect of nonverbal communication they govern: gesture direction, gesture form, and timing. Argyle [3] notes that high levels of neuroticism results in fewer other-directed gestures, or gestures that are directed at a target that is not the person performing the gesture.

Gesture form touches on discoveries in both psychology and linguistics. Furnham describes a reduction in fluency, a higher proportion of silence to speech, and the presence of speech discontinuities in anxious speakers [14]. Cappella and Palmer investigate the relationship between speech and gesture, noting that the two aspects of communication are strongly synchronized, despite being conveyed separately through body language and verbal utterance [7]. This work allowed us to consider two properties for low EMS types: pauses in speech synchronize with pauses in gesture, and speech discontinuities might be accompanied by gesture discontinuities (repetition or stuttering motion, filled pauses, etc.). Other descriptions, including higher levels of tension and irregularity of motor activities, aided in the synthesis of gesture form control [41].

Finally, we determined that it was important to control the **timing** in conversation, e.g. how the gesture planning framework should control the speed of gestures and other forms of body language for an EMS level. Campbell and Rushton observed that people with a high level of anxiety made longer pauses before responding than participants with a normal emotional stability level [6]. Daly cites early work that verifies the presence of speech disturbances in individuals with transient anxiety, in addition to conflicting results on whether individuals with anxiety spend less time talking, or generate fewer utterances [9]. Given the disruption of fluency described by Furnham, we decided to use pauses in speech and gesture as a form of discontinuity for both verbal and nonverbal communication.

Self-adaptors. Hand gestures can be classified into two categories: signaling, where the performer intends to transmit a message using motion, and non-signaling, where the motion of the hand is not intended to convey a particular meaning [43]. Signaling gestures could include a point directed at a target, or a chopping motion to emphasize a key phrase whereas a non-signaling gesture could be a scratch on the body, or the massaging of a sore neck. Waxer [43] concluded that individuals with low EMS scores produced more non-signaling hand motion, also called self-adaptors, during speech. Other research supports this [3,11], even showing a negative association between outward-directed gestures and self-adaptors [6]. These findings indicate both the importance of self-adaptors in conveying a personality with a particular EMS level - as well as that behavior not intended as communicative can still be interpreted by others as an indicator of personality. Because of the pervasive evidence on self-adaptors, we sought to extend the existing gesture planning framework to generate these motions.

We found no literature that explicitly described when and how such self-adaptors should be realized, so we made its planning system independent of the existing hand gesture system. If a hand is not being used for a gesture, it can be used for a self-adaptor. Figure 1 displays a left-handed neck scratch that occurs during a right-handed conversational gesture. Based on comments collected during Waxer's experiments, we focused on self-adaptors involving scratching a body part, tapping nervously, unnatural bracing of the hands, rubbing the face or head in soreness or fatigue, and adjusting the hair. These represent a subset of possible self-adaptors.

Body Language. After hand gestures and self-adaptors, the two aspects of body language most commonly described to vary with EMS were posture and head movement. Feyereisen and de Lannoy observe more changes in posture for individuals with low EMS ratings, but do not explain how or when such changes occur [13]. Waxer's results suggest that individuals with low anxiety move the upper body more freely than individuals with high anxiety, though the differences were not significant. Wallbott notes the presence of a more "collapsed" posture for low EMS individuals [42]. Campbell and Rushton observed greater forward lean in individuals who tested high for anxiety, which could possibly be a property of the posture collapse observed by Wallbott [6]. With respect to these observations, we controlled the variance in posture for low EMS by increasing the frequency and speed of weight shifts and torso swivels in order to generate posture changes that seem forced or uncomfortable.

Fig. 1. A neck scratch self-adaptor occurring simultaneously with a gesture using motion planning for an emotionally stable personality type

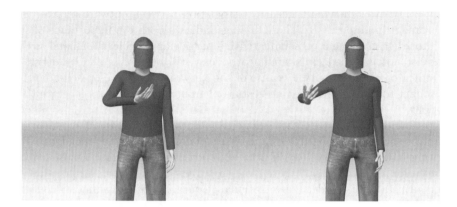

Fig. 2. A comparison between low EMS (left) and high EMS (right) motion for the same utterance

There are significant previous findings on the impact of EMS on gaze and head motion [13,6,9]. However, controlling eye motion is beyond the scope of this work. Worth noting, the literature consistently suggests that increased gaze aversion and decreased head height are features of low EMS.

Motion Generation. In order to map the findings from the literature to character motion, we divided the variation in nonverbal behavior into two categories: the use of self-adaptors and a set of variations related to gesture performance. *Self-adaptor use* was either active or not. If active, self-adaptors were added to the motion from a list including: scratches (face, chin, neck), rubs (forehead), asymmetric shrugs (twitch), and an unnatural brace in which the one hand pushes the other hand's fingers back in an uncomfortable way. These were timed to occur quickly, consistent with a sense of unease.

Gesture Performance involved variations in both gesture and collarbone use. Reflecting a tendency to make fewer outward or other directed gestures, the path of low EMS gestures were adjusted to move inward, across the body whereas they moved outward in the high EMS case. The gestures were also made smaller. Abrupt downward beats were added to the low EMS gestures, reflecting reported increased irregularity. Posture adjustments for low EMS included bringing the collarbones up and in, bringing the elbows in and making more rapid posture shifts. These reflected a less relaxed posture and more rapid posture changes. Figure 2 illustrates differences in gesture placement and posture.

2.2   Verbal Expression of Emotional Stability

Our experiments use the PERSONAGE generator with rule-based models of emotional stability for verbal realization. We utilize utterances that were found in previous work on text-based perception [22] to reliably be perceived as either low EMS or high EMS. Table 2 summarizes the linguistic cues for emotional stability and the hypothesized personality models, and Table 3 provides example utterances generated using the personality models. Here, we explore for the first

Table 2. Summary of language cues for emotional stability, with corresponding generation parameters. See Mairesse & Walker (2010) for more detail.

Neurotic findings	Stable findings	Parameters	NeuroEmot	
Content planning:				
Problem talk,	Pleasure talk, agreement,	CONTENT POLARITY	low	high
dissatisfaction	compliment	REPETITION POLARITY	low	high
		CONCESSION POLARITY	low	high
Direct claim	Inferred claim	POSITIVE CONTENT FIRST	high	low
High verbal productivity	Low verbal productivity	VERBOSITY	high	low
Many lexical repetitions	Few lexical repetitions	REPETITIONS	high	low
Polarised content	Neutral content	POLARIZATION	high	low
Stressed	Calm	REQUEST CONFIRMATION	low	high
		INITIAL REJECTION	high	low
Syntactic Structural Template selection:				
Many self-references	Few self-references	SELF-REFERENCES	high	low
Problem talk	Pleasure talk	TEMPLATE POLARITY	low	high
Aggregation:				
Low use of 'punct *which*'	High use of 'punct *which*'	RELATIVE CLAUSE	low	high
Many conjunctions	Few conjunctions	MERGE	high	low
Few short silent pauses	Many short silent pauses	CONJUNCTION	low	high
Low use of 'punct *so*'	High use of 'punct *so*'	JUSTIFY - SO CUE WORD	low	high
Low use of clause final *also*	High use of clause final *also*	INFER - ALSO CUE WORD	low	high
Many inclusive words (e.g. *with*, *and*)	Few inclusive words	WITH CUE WORD	high	low
High use of final *though*	Low use of final *though*	CONCEDE - BUT/THOUGH CUE WORD	high	low
Many long silent pauses	Few long silent pauses	PERIOD	high	low
Many 'non-ah' disfluencies	Few 'non-ah' disfluencies	RESTATE - OBJECT ELLIPSIS	high	low
Pragmatic marker insertion:				
Many pronouns, few articles	Few pronouns, many articles	SUBJECT IMPLICITNESS	low	high
		PRONOMINALIZATION	high	low
Few tentative words	Many tentative words	SOFTENER HEDGES	low	high
Many self-reference	Few self-references	·I THINK THAT	high	low
Many filled pauses (apprehensive)	Few filled pauses	FILLED PAUSES:	high	low
		· ERR, I MEAN, MMHM, LIKE		
More aquiescence	Few aquiescence	ACKNOWLEDGMENTS	high	low
Many self references	Few self references	·I SEE	high	low
High use of 'punct *well*'	Low use of 'punct *well*'	·WELL	high	low
Exaggeration	Realism	EMPHASIZER HEDGES	high	low
Many rhetorical interrogatives	Few rhetorical interrogatives	TAG QUESTION	high	low
Frustration	Less frustration	EXPLETIVES	high	low
Many 'non-ah' disfluencies	Few 'non-ah' disfluencies	STUTTERING	high	low
Lexical choice:				
Many frequent words	Few frequent words	LEXICON FREQUENCY	high	low
Exaggeration	Realism	VERB STRENGTH	high	low
Speech:				
Many long pauses (+2 sec.)	Few long pauses	TTS PAUSE INSERTION	high	low
Short response time	Long response time	TTS RESPONSE DELAY	high	low
High speech rate	Low speech rate	TTS SPEECH RATE	high	low
Loud	Quiet	TTS LOUDNESS	high	low

time parameters related to speech synthesis, also motivated by findings from previous studies. These are shown under the heading **Speech** in Table 2. For example, pauses are a significant feature that are incorporated as part of speech synthesis by inserting longer pauses in the low EMS vocal track.

Note that in Table 3 that some parameters are illustrated in the primarily negative and neutral content selection mechanisms, with negative content repeated

Table 3. PERSONAGE outputs for the **emotional stability** personality model. Score is the average of user judgments on a scale from 1 = very low and 7 = very high.

#	Content plan	End	PERSONAGE's output	Score
L1	recommend(V)	low	Ok, although Vinnie's Pizza has awful ambience, its price is 13 dollars. Even if the waiters are bad, I mean, the food is just nice somewhat, the food is quite decent. It's located in Manhattan. There could be worse places, alright?	2.2
L2	compare(LR,PP)	low	Obviously, ok, I might recommend Le Rivage and Pintaile's Pizza. Actually, I suppose Pintaile's Pizza's price is 14 dollars. Err... on the other hand, Le Rivage's price is 40 dollars.	2.3
H1	compare(A,M)	high	Did you say Acacia and Marinella? I imagine you would appreciate them, you see? It seems to me that Marinella provides kind of satisfactory food, also it's an italian place mate, but Acacia offers sort of acceptable food, you know.	6.0
H2	recommend(E)	high	You want to know more about Edgar's Cafe? Basically, I think that Edgar's Cafe, which has rather decent food, is kind of the best restaurant.	5.5

and foregrounded in utterances L1 and L2. The high STUTTERING parameter is also seen in utterance L2. Weaver [44] shows that neuroticism is associated with frustration and acquiescence, which we model respectively with high EXPLETIVES and ACKNOWLEDGMENTS parameter values (e.g. *okay, although* in utterance L1). We hypothesize that neurotics are more likely to exaggerate, based on the impulsiveness facet of that trait, so we associate it with high EMPHASIZER HEDGES parameters (e.g. *obviously, actually* in utterance L2). Neuroticism is conveyed through a high VERBOSITY parameter value, e.g. utterance L1 describes 5 restaurant attributes, whereas utterance H2 only mentions the claim and one attribute.

3   Experimental Design

For the purpose of evaluating their impact on EMS, the variations found in the pyschology literature were coalesced into three factors: gesture performance (incl. changes to posture and communicative gesture), whether self-adaptors were present, and linguistic variation in text and speech production.

We used PERSONAGE to generate utterances of restaurant recommendations for high and low EMS personalities as shown in Table 3. The Loquendo TTS was used to produce audio for each utterance and annotated with respect to theme and rheme. Gesture strokes were aligned with the rheme.

Software based on [25,28] was used to generate the accompanying animation clips. Both the communicative gestures and self-adaptors were generated by editing sampled motion data and these can be controlled independently. The same background body motion was used in all clips, but posture shifts were time warped in the low EMS case to make them more rapid.

Four clips were generated for each utterance, with the variations of "low" and "high" gesture performance and "self-adaptors" or "no self-adaptors", yielding a total of 16 clips. The same gesture placement was used for each variant of an utterance. When self-adaptors were active, between one and three were added to the test utterance, based on the length of the utterance and the presence of appropriate locations for the behavior. The same adaptors were always used for a given utterance and the sequence was not otherwise changed.

The avatar's face was blocked with a mask to avoid judgements based on his facial expression, or lack thereof, while still allowing the general motion and position of the head to remain visible.

3.1 Experiment Execution

We recruited 30 participants for a web-based experiment (12 female, 18 male; 18 between age 18 and 30, 9 between 31 and 50, 3 over 50; 20 spoke English as their first language). Prior to taking the survey, participants were shown a training video consisting of four of the clips in order to familiarize them with the experiment's material. Example clips are included in the accompanying video.

A clip could be viewed as many times as desired, but returning to previous clips was not permitted. After watching each clip, participants were asked to rate the avatar's levels of emotional stability and agreeableness using the questions representing these traits taken from the Ten-Item Personality Inventory. This instrument was shown to be psychometrically superior to a "single item per trait" questionnaire [16]. Although the agreeableness dimension of the Big Five model was not a targeted part of the experiment, we included it in order to measure the impact of our system on unintended personality features. The ratings began with the statement "I perceive the speaker as...", followed by 7-point Likert scale ratings for: "Anxious, Easily Upset," "Calm, Emotionally Stable," "Critical, Quarrelsome," "Sympathetic, Warm", and "Natural". The first two ratings represent low EMS and high EMS measurements, respectively. The third and fourth ratings represent low agreeableness and high agreeableness. For analysis, the reverse-scored item for each personality type was flipped (e.g. a low EMS score of 2 corresponds to a high EMS score of 6) and averaged with the positive rating to provide a final score. Naturalness ratings were included to see if changes in agent behavior affected how natural the resulting clip appeared.

Our hypotheses were:

- **H1:** The linguistic manifestations of emotional stability will affect perceived emotional stability when used in a multimodal agent.
- **H2:** The use of self-adaptors will be perceived as less emotionally stable
- **H3:** The changes in gesture performance will affect perceived emotional stability
- **H4:** There will be no correlation between agreeableness and the three variations.

4   Results

We ran a repeated measures ANOVA with the factors "self-adaptors" (on, off), "EMS linguistic parameters" (low, high), and "gesture performance" (low, high) and dependent variables our ratings of Emotional Stability, Agreeableness, and

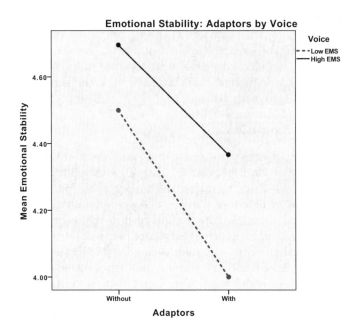

Fig. 3. The effect of linguistic variation and the use of adaptors on the perception of emotional stability

Naturalness. Our principal novel finding is that the presence of self-adaptors made agents appear less emotionally stable, 4.18 (.11 SE) with adaptors to 4.60 (.12 SE) without, on a scale from 1 (less stable) to 7 (most stable), F(1, 29) = 11.50, p = .002, confirming Hypothesis 2. At the same time, adaptors had no effect on agreeableness ratings, 4.16 (.12 SE) with adaptors to 4.26 (.11 SE) without, F(1, 29) = .62, p = .44. Importantly, agents were rated as equally natural with and without adaptors, 3.51 (.18 SE) to 3.51 (.22 SE), F(1, 29) = .002, p = .97.

Linguistic parameters affected ratings as expected. The low and high stability utterances as spoken by the male avatar were judged to be equally natural, 3.43 (.23 SE) low to 3.60 (.20 SE) high, F(1, 29) = .85, p = .37. The high stability spoken utterances were judged to be more stable, 4.25 (.11 SE) low to 4.53 (.12 SE) high, F(1, 29) = 5.44, p = .03. This confirms Hypothesis 1. The high stability utterances were also judged to be more agreeable, 4.05 (.11 SE) low to 4.37 (.11 SE) high, F(1, 29) = 8.32, p = .007. In addition, the lack of interaction suggests an additive effect between (1) presence of linguistic parameters and (2) presence of low EMS adaptors, such that either one changes perception to be of lower EMS and more so with both, as shown in Figure 3.

There was no effect of non-adaptor gestures on naturalness ratings (3.52, .19 SE, low to 3.50, .20 SE, high, F(1, 29) = .12, p = .73), emotionality ratings (4.37, .12 SE, low to 4.42, .09 SE, high, F(1, 29) = .42, p = .52), or agreeableness ratings (4.22, .10 SE, low to 4.20, .10 SE, high, F(1, 29) = .05, p = .83). These findings disconfirm Hypothesis 3.

The perception of agreeableness seems to have no simple relation with the presence of self-adaptors or non-adaptor gestures, but high measures of agreeableness correlate with high EMS voices. This disconfirms Hypothesis 4.

Across all variables, there were only two interactions, for the agreeableness variable: adaptors X gesture performance, $F(1, 29) = 4.64$, $p = .04$, and adaptors X gesture performance X voice, $F(1, 29) = 5.12$, $p = .03$. The adaptors X gesture performance interaction suggests that adaptors do not make a difference for low EMS gesture performance for agreeableness. For high EMS gesture performance, having adaptors made agents appear less agreeable. Inspection of the three-way interaction suggests that low EMS gesture performance plus adaptors made agents appear more agreeable when presented with a low EMS voice, but less agreeable when presented with a high EMS voice.

5   Discussion and Conclusion

This paper summarizes findings on verbal and nonverbal manifestations of emotional stability from the psychology literature and reports results of an experiment analyzing the perception of EMS when these findings are mapped to a virtual agent. This work is part of a broader effort to establish empirical principles for modifying agent behavior in order to control the perception of personality.

Our work builds on recent work on gesture form and performance in interactive contexts, across many different settings and contextual and cultural assumptions. While we do not consider at all the effect of culture on agent gesture, it is clear that there are culturally-defined preferences for expressive behaviors. Thus it is possible that the expression of an agent's personality is subject to a cultural filter, or may even be culturally defined [36,20,4,35]. Related work on gesture [39,37,34] has addressed how high level characteristics of an agent, such as culture or age, and of the situation (listener, physical context) affect the choice and the performance of gestural and postural behaviors. Recent work has shown the importance of an agent displaying emotion [29] and we expect personality plays a similarly important role. This represents one aspect of a very significant effort to design emotion and personality models for agents (e.g.[2,17,10,38,32,1,15,31]).

There has been considerable previous work developing methods for procedurally varying the expressive qualities of character motion (e.g. [8,18,27]). While establishing useful tools, these approaches do not define what variations are necessary to obtain a particular personality. The idea of mapping motion variations to traits in the Big Five model was suggested by Badler et al. [5] in connection with their Laban Movement Analysis-based EMOTE system. Our work establishes mappings between changes in motion generation, language and perceived personality and validates the mappings experimentally.

Recently, Neff et al. [26] examined the combined effect of linguistic and nonverbal expression of personality for the Extraversion trait of the Big Five. Previously, Isbister & Nass [19] presented the only other work we are aware of to explore the combined gestural and linguistic expression of personality, also focusing on extraversion. They used fixed poses to accompany hand scripted utterances, rather than a multimodal agent. Kipp et al. [21] demonstrated that gesture units consisting of multiple gestures performed better than singleton gestures on a variety of criteria such as naturalness and friendliness and found singleton gestures appeared more nervous. Our work is the first we are aware of to address the combined verbal and nonverbal expression of emotional stability.

Our results demonstrate that the inclusion of self-adaptors significantly impacts the perception of neuroticism. This provides clear evidence that noncommunicative gesture movements contribute significantly to particular aspects of personality, suggesting that future agent architectures should be extended to support self-adaptor production, which may occur simultaneously with communicative gestures. In addition, our results demonstrate that linguistic variations that work for written text, along with appropriate speech variations such as increased pauses for low EMS, transfer successfully to the agent domain.

We suspect that we did not get a significant result for "gesture performance" because the differences between the two variations were too subtle. The literature offers limited guidance on the exact form and degree of variation and we may need to arrive at better definitions for descriptors like "fluency" in terms of low-level gesture parameters. Including more disruptions in the low EMS gestures and more erratic body behavior seems likely to yield stronger results. Gesture placement rules may also need to differ with variation in this dimension.

It is interesting to note that linguistically, emotional stability and agreeableness are highly correlated, while the nonverbal factors in the experiment had no effect on perceived agreeableness for our agent. This may signify an area of interest that future work should return to in order to unify the perception of agents through both verbal and nonverbal means.

The three way interaction for agreeableness suggests that consistent expression in which each factor (linguistic, performance and adaptor use) is aligned may have a positive impact on agreeableness. This also seems worth further investigation.

A significant challenge faced in this work concerned limitations on what the literature was capable of advising in terms of detailed reproduction of body language to match human EMS varation. The qualitative descriptions often seen in the literature provide a reasonable mental picture for a human reader, but lack the specificity to directly translate into parameters for agent behavior. Nevertheless, the results of this experiment provide meaningful guidance on how to refine our model and will hopefully inspire future work that will further define the key aspects of physical motion that express particular personality types, both for virtual agents and human interaction.

Acknowledgements. Thanks to Jonathan Graham for building the character models used in this work, to all the experiment participants and the anonymous reviewers for their useful feedback. Financial support for this research was provided in part by NSF grants 0845529 and 0856084 and a software donation from Autodesk.

References

1. André, E., Klesen, M., Gebhard, P., Allen, S., Rist, T.: Integrating models of personality and emotions into lifelike characters. Affective interactions, 150–165 (2000)
2. Andre, E., Rehm, M., Minker, W., Bühler, D.: Endowing spoken language dialogue systems with emotional intelligence. Affective Dialogue Systems, 178–187 (2004)
3. Argyle, M.: Bodily communication. Taylor & Francis, Abington (1988)
4. Aylett, R., Vannini, N., Andre, E., Paiva, A., Enz, S., Hall, L.: But that was in another country: agents and intercultural empathy. In: Proceedings of The 8th International Conference on Autonomous Agents and Multiagent Systems-, vol. 1, pp. 329–336. International Foundation for Autonomous Agents and Multiagent Systems (2009)
5. Badler, N., Allbeck, J., Zhao, L., Byun, M.: Representing and parameterizing agent behaviors. In: Proc. of Computer Animation, pp. 133–143. IEEE, Los Alamitos (2002)
6. Campbell, A., Rushton, J.: Bodily communication and personality. The British Journal of Social and Clinical Psychology 17(1), 31–36 (1978)
7. Cappella, J., Palmer, M.: The structure and organization of verbal and non-verbal behavior: Data for models of production. In: Giles, H., Robinson, W. (eds.) Handbook of Language and Social Psychology, pp. 141–161. Wiley, Chichester (1990)
8. Chi, D.M., Costa, M., Zhao, L., Badler, N.I.: The EMOTE model for effort and shape. In: Proc. SIGGRAPH 2000, pp. 173–182 (2000)
9. Daly, S.: Behavioural correlates of social anxiety. British Journal of Social and Clinical Psychology 17, 117–120 (1978)
10. Dias, J., Paiva, A.C.R.: Feeling and reasoning: A computational model for emotional characters. In: Bento, C., Cardoso, A., Dias, G. (eds.) EPIA 2005. LNCS (LNAI), vol. 3808, pp. 127–140. Springer, Heidelberg (2005)
11. Ekman, P., Friesen, W.V.: Hand movements. Journal of Communication 22, 353–374 (1972)
12. Eysenck, S.B.G., Eysenck, H.J., Barrett, P.: A revised version of the psychoticism scale. Personality and Individual Differences 6(1), 21–29 (1985)
13. Feyereisen, P., de Lannoy, J.: Gestures and Speech: Psychological Investigations. Cambridge University Press, Cambridge (1991)
14. Furnham, A.: Language and personality. In: Giles, H., Robinson, W. (eds.) Handbook of Language and Social Psychology, pp. 73–95. Wiley, Chichester (1990)
15. Gebhard, P.: Alma: a layered model of affect. In: Proceedings of the fourth international joint conference on Autonomous agents and multiagent systems, pp. 29–36. ACM Press, New York (2005)
16. Gosling, S.D., Rentfrow, P.J., Swann, W.B.: A very brief measure of the big five personality domains. Journal of Research in Personality 37, 504–528 (2003)
17. Gratch, J., Rickel, J., André, E., Cassell, J., Petajan, E., Badler, N.: Creating interactive virtual humans: Some assembly required. IEEE Intelligent Systems 17(4), 54–63 (2002)
18. Hartmann, B., Mancini, M., Pelachaud, C.: Implementing expressive gesture synthesis for embodied conversational agents. In: Gibet, S., Courty, N., Kamp, J.-F. (eds.) GW 2005. LNCS (LNAI), vol. 3881, pp. 188–199. Springer, Heidelberg (2006)
19. Isbister, K., Nass, C.: Consistency of personality in interactive characters: Verbal cues, non-verbal cues, and user characteristics. International Journal of Human Computer Studies 53(2), 251–268 (2000)

20. Johnson, W., Marsella, S., Mote, N., Viljhálmsson, H., Narayanan, S., Choi, S.: Tactical language training system: Supporting the rapid acquisition of foreign language and cultural skills. In: Proc. of InSTIL/ICALLNLP and Speech Technologies in Advanced Language Learning Systems (2004)

21. Kipp, M., Neff, M., Kipp, K., Albrecht, I.: Towards natural gesture synthesis: Evaluating gesture units in a data-driven approach to gesture synthesis. In: Pelachaud, C., Martin, J.-C., André, E., Chollet, G., Karpouzis, K., Pelé, D. (eds.) IVA 2007. LNCS (LNAI), vol. 4722, pp. 15–28. Springer, Heidelberg (2007)

22. Mairesse, F., Walker, M.: Towards personality-based user adaptation: psychologically informed stylistic language generation. User Modeling and User-Adapted Interaction, 1–52 (2010)

23. Mairesse, F., Walker, M.A.: Controlling user perceptions of linguistic style: Trainable generation of personality traits. Computational Linguistics (2011)

24. Mehl, M.R., Gosling, S.D., Pennebaker, J.W.: Personality in its natural habitat: Manifestations and implicit folk theories of personality in daily life. Journal of Personality and Social Psychology 90, 862–877 (2006)

25. Neff, M., Kim, Y.: Interactive editing of motion style using drives and correlations. In: Proceedings of the 2009 ACM SIGGRAPH/Eurographics Symposium on Computer Animation, pp. 103–112. ACM, New York (2009)

26. Neff, M., Wang, Y., Abbott, R., Walker, M.: Evaluating the effect of gesture and language on personality perception in conversational agents. In: Intelligent Virtual Agents, pp. 222–235. Springer, Heidelberg (2010)

27. Neff, M., Fiume, E.: AER: Aesthetic Exploration and Refinement for expressive character animation. In: Proc. ACM SIGGRAPH / Eurographics Symposium on Computer Animation 2005, pp. 161–170 (2005)

28. Neff, M., Kipp, M., Albrecht, I., Seidel, H.P.: Gesture modeling and animation based on a probabilistic re-creation of speaker style. ACM Transactions on Graphics 27(1), 5:1–5:24 (2008)

29. Niewiadomski, R., Demeure, V., Pelachaud, C.: Warmth, competence, believability and virtual agents. In: Intelligent Virtual Agents, pp. 272–285. Springer, Heidelberg (2010)

30. Norman, W.T.: Toward an adequate taxonomy of personality attributes: Replicated factor structure in peer nomination personality rating. Journal of Abnormal and Social Psychology 66, 574–583 (1963)

31. Ochs, M., Niewiadomski, R., Pelachaud, C., Sadek, D.: Intelligent expressions of emotions. In: Affective Computing and Intelligent Interaction, pp. 707–714 (2005)

32. Ortony, A.: On making believable emotional agents believable. Emotions in Humans and Artifacts, 189 (2002)

33. Pennebaker, J.W., King, L.A.: Linguistic styles: Language use as an individual difference. Journal of Personality and Social Psychology 77, 1296–1312 (1999)

34. Poggi, I.: Mind markers. The Semantics and Pragmatics of Everyday Gestures. Berlin Verlag Arno Spitz (2001)

35. Poggi, I.: Symbolic gestures: The case of the italian gestionary. Gesture 2(1), 71–98 (2002)

36. Rehm, M., André, E., Bee, N., Endrass, B., Wissner, M., Nakano, Y., Nishida, T., Huang, H.: The cube-g approach–coaching culture-specific nonverbal behavior by virtual agents. In: Organizing and Learning Through Gaming and Simulation: Proceedings of Isaga 2007, p. 313 (2007)

37. Rehm, M., Nakano, Y., André, E., Nishida, T.: Culture-specific first meeting encounters between virtual agents. In: Prendinger, H., Lester, J.C., Ishizuka, M. (eds.) IVA 2008. LNCS (LNAI), vol. 5208, pp. 223–236. Springer, Heidelberg (2008)

38. Reilly, W.: Believable social and emotional agents. Ph.D. thesis, CMU (1996)
39. Ruttkay, Z., Pelachaud, C., Poggi, I., Noot, H.: Exercises in style for virtual humans. Animating Expressive Characters for Social Interaction, 143 (2008)
40. Scherer, K.R.: Vocal indicators of stress. In: Darby, J. (ed.) Speech Evaluation in Psychiatry, pp. 171–187. Grune & Stratton, New York (1981)
41. Takala, M.: Studies of psychomotor personality tests, 1-. Suomalainen Tiedeakatemia (1953)
42. Wallbott, H.G.: Bodily expression of emotion. European Journal of Social Psychology 28, 879–896 (1998)
43. Waxer, P.: Nonverbal cues for anxiety: An examination of emotional leakage. Journal of Abnormal Psychology 86(3), 306–314 (1977)
44. Weaver, J.B.: Personality and self-perceptions about communication. In: McCroksey, J.C., Daly, J.A., Martin, M.M., Beatty, M.J. (eds.) Communication and Personality: Trait Perspectives, ch. 4, pp. 95–118. Hampton Press (1998)

Exploration on Context-Sensitive Affect Sensing in an Intelligent Agent

Li Zhang

School of Computing, Teesside University, Middlesbrough, TS1 3BA, UK
l.zhang@tees.ac.uk

Abstract. Virtual drama systems generally promote users' experience on learning/training. It is even challenging to produce intelligent conversational agents which are capable of engaging in drama performance and responding to human users' emotion and language effectively and intelligently. In our previous work, we developed an intelligent agent embedded in a text-based improvisational virtual drama system to interact with human users and detect affect from their text input. The detection was solely based on the interpretation of each turn-taking input. In this paper, we further equip the AI agent with the capabilities of the inferences of the improvisational mood of individual characters and emotions embedded in communication context to further verify the affect drawn solely from the analysis of each turn-taking input itself. Evaluations results on context-based affect interpretation are also provided. Our work shows great potentials in employing emotions embedded in the characters and interaction context to provide personalized learning/training experience.

Keywords: Affect detection, drama improvisation, and a conversational agent.

1 Introduction

Improvised drama and role-play are widely used in education, counselling and conflict resolution. Various researchers have explored virtual, computer-based frameworks for such activities, leading to virtual drama systems in which virtual characters interact under the partial control, at least, of human actors. Such research also allows the room for the inclusion of intelligent automation and inspires the production of intelligent agents which are capable of conducting drama performance, interpreting social relationships, context, general mood and emotion, sensing or reasonably predicating others' inter-conversion, identifying its role and participating intelligently in open-ended improvisational interaction. Our springboard prototype also provided a similar text-based virtual improvisational framework and allowed human users to be creative at their role-play under the improvisation of loose scenarios including Crohn's disease and school bullying[1]. Human actors controlled virtual characters on a virtual stage, with textual "speeches" displayed as text bubbles typed by the actor operating the character. One director and up to five actors were

---

[1] The bully, Mayid, is picking on a new schoolmate, Lisa. Elise and Dave (Lisa's friends), and Mrs Parton (the school teacher) are trying to stop the bullying.

H. Högni Vilhjálmsson et al. (Eds.): IVA 2011, LNAI 6895, pp. 412–418, 2011.

involved in one improvisational session. The human director monitored the drama performance constantly and may intervene e.g. if characters lacked of appropriate emotions. In order to reduce the burden of the director, we developed an affect detection component embedded in an intelligent agent, which played a minor role in the improvisation and interacted with human characters. The affect detection component interpreted 25 emotions from users' text input. However the affect detection conducted mainly focused on the analysis of each turn-taking input (i.e. the input contributed by each character at one time) without any contextual inference [1].

Since open-ended natural language input could be ambiguous, sometimes interaction context is required in order to further justify the affect implied by the speaking character. Emotion research conducted by Hareli and Rafaeli [2] also discussed how emotions evolve within one individual given various stimuli and how emotions of an individual influence the emotions, thoughts and behaviours of others. Therefore in this paper, we discuss contextual affect sensing integrated with emotion modeling of personal and social context to justify the affect conveyed in emotional ambiguous input.

2 Related Work

Although merely detecting affect is limited compared to extracting the full meaning of characters' utterances, we found that in many cases this is sufficient for the purposes of stimulating the improvisation. Moreover, textual affect sensing has also become a rising research branch. ConceptNet [3] is a toolkit to provide practical textual reasoning for affect sensing for six basic emotions, text summarization and topic extraction. Shaikh et al. [4] provided sentence-level textual affect sensing to recognize evaluations (positive/negative). They adopted a rule-based domain-independent approach, but have not made attempts to recognize different affective states from open-ended text input. Also Ptaszynski et al. [5] developed a context-based affect detection component with the integration of a web-mining technique to detect affect from users' input and verify the contextual appropriateness of the detected emotions. The detected results made an AI agent either sympathize with the player or disapprove the user's expression by the provision of persuasion. However, their system targeted conversations only between an AI agent and one human user, which greatly reduced the complexity of the modeling of the interaction context.

Much research has also been done on creating affective virtual characters in interactive systems. Gratch and Marsella [6] presented an integrated model of appraisal and coping, to reason about emotions and to provide social intelligence for virtual agents. Endrass, Rehm and André [7] carried out study on the culture-related differences in the domain of small talk behaviour. Their agents were equipped with the capabilities of generating culture specific dialogs. There is much other work in a similar vein. Our work focuses on the following aspects: (1) real-time affect sensing for basic and complex emotions in improvisational role-play situations; (2) affect interpretation based on context; and (3) affect detection across scenarios.

3 The Affect Sensing Processing

From the inspection of recorded transcripts, we noticed that the language used is often complex and idiosyncratic. It is almost invariably ungrammatical and borrows heavily from the language of chat-rooms. Most importantly, the language also contains a large number of weak cues to the affect that is being expressed. These cues may be contradictory or they may work together to enable a stronger interpretation of the affective state. In order to build a reliable and robust analyser of affect it is necessary to undertake several diverse forms of analysis and to enable these to work together to build stronger interpretations. It thus guides not only our previous research but also our current developments. For example, previously we undertook several analyses of any given utterance. These would each build representations which may be used by other components and would construct (possibly weak) hypotheses about the affective state conveyed in the input. In our current study, we integrate contextual information to further derive the affect embedded in the communication context to justify the affect annotation concluded purely based on the analysis of each individual input.

Research of Hareli and Rafaeli [2] also discussed how emotions evolve within individuals and how people react emotionally to emotional expressions of other individuals in organizations. E.g., an 'angry' team leader makes his/her teammates 'scared' and the leader feels 'embarrassed' later on. This inspires our work to find out how emotions evolve within individual characters and in social context. Therefore in this section, we discuss cognitive emotion simulation for personal and social context, and our approach developed based on these aspects to interpret affect from emotionally ambiguous input, especially affect justification of the previously detected 'neutral' expressions based on the analysis of individual turn-taking input.

3.1   Emotion Modeling and Prediction in Personal Communication Context

Lopez et al. [8] suggested that context profiles for affect detection included social and personal contexts. In our study, personal context may be regarded as one's own emotion inclination or improvisational mood in communication context. We believe that one's own emotional states have a chain reaction effect, i.e. the previous emotional status may influence later emotional experience. We make attempts to include such effects into emotion modeling. Bayesian networks are used to simulate such personal causal emotion context. In a Bayesian network, if we regard the first, second and third emotions experienced by a particular user respectively as A, B and C, we assume that the second emotion B is dependent on the first emotion A. Further, we assume that the third emotion C is dependent on both the first and second emotions A and B. In our application, given two or more most recent emotions a user experiences, we may predict the most probable emotion this user implies in the current input using a Bayesian network.

Briefly, a Bayesian network employs a probabilistic graphical model to represent causality relationship and conditional (in)dependencies between domain variables. It has a set of directed arcs linking pairs of nodes: an arc from a node X to a node Y means that X (parent emotion) has a direct influence on Y (successive child emotion). Such causal modeling between variables reflects the chain effect of emotional experience. It uses the conditional probabilities (e.g. P[B|A], P[C|A,B]) to reflect such influence between prior emotional experiences to successive emotional expressions.

In our contextual affect analysis, we mainly consider the following 10 emotions due to their high occurrences in the annotated transcripts, including 'neutral', 'happy', 'approval', 'grateful', 'caring', 'disapproval', 'sad', 'scared', 'threatening', and 'angry'. Any combination of the above emotional states could be used as prior emotional experience of the user. Also each conditional probability for each potential emotion given two prior affects (such as P[approval| A,B]) will be calculated. The affect with the highest probability is selected as the most probable emotion the user conveys in the current input. We construct a Bayesian network for each character to sense his/her improvisational mood. At the training stage, two human judges marked up 3 example transcripts of the school bullying scenario. 450 example inputs with agreed annotations are used for the training of Bayesian networks while the disagreed annotations are discarded. For each character, we extract three sequences of emotions from the improvisation of the 3 example transcripts to produce prior conditional probabilities. We take a frequency approach to determine the conditional probabilities for each Bayesian network. When an affect is annotated for a turn-taking input, we increment a counter for that expressed emotion given the two preceding emotions. For each character, a conditional probability table is produced based on the training data.

For the prediction of an emotion mostly likely implied in the current input at the testing stage, the two preceding emotions are used to determine which row to consider in the probability matrix, and select the column with the highest probability as the final output. The emotional sequences used for testing have also been used to further update and enrich the training samples. An example algorithm of the Bayesian affect sensing is provided in the following. For the initial run of the algorithm, emotions A, B and C are initialized with the most recent three affects detected for each character purely based on the analysis of individual input.

Pseudo-code for affect prediction using a Bayesian network

```
Function Bayesian_Affect_Prediction {
1. Verify the contextual appropriateness of the affect C
   predicted by the Bayesian reasoning;
2. Produce the row index, i, for any given combination of the
   two preceding emotional states A & B in the matrix;
3. Indicate the column index, j, for the recommended affect
   C;
4. Increment counters: N_AB[i] and N_CAB[i][j];
5. Update two preceding emotions by: Emotion A = Emotion B;
   Emotion B = The newly recommended affect C;
6. Produce the new row index, k, for any given combination of
   the updated two preceding emotional states A & B;
7. Calculate probabilities (P[C|A,B]= N_CAB[k][column]/N_AB[k])
   for the predicted emotional state C being any of the 10
   emotions;
8. Select and return the affect with the highest probability
   as the predicted affect C;}
```

We extract the following example from the school bullying scenario. Based on the affect detection purely from the analysis of each individual input, we assigned an emotional label for each input. We use the sequence of emotions expressed by Mayid to illustrate how the contextual affect sensing using Bayesian networks performs.

1. Mayid: u probably 2 ugly 2 look at [angry]
2. Dave: Oi that no laughing matter [angry]
3. Lisa: Mayid u aren't very nice [disapproval]

4. Mrs Parton: don't be horrible mayid [disapproval]
5. Mayid: shit it lisa [angry]
6. Elise: don't tell lisa to shut up [disapproval]
7. Mayid: or else!! u'll end up beaten up [threatening]
8. Dave: mayid behave ur self [disapproval]
9. Lisa: threatening people won't get u anywhere [disapproval]
10. Mrs Parton: mayid u don't want another detection do u [threatening]
11. Mayid: Lisa, u need ur brain checking. Oh yeah i forgot, u aint got one. [neutral] -> [angry]

Affect annotation based on the analysis of each turn-taking input derives 'angry', 'angry' and 'threatening' respectively for Mayid's 1st, 5th and 7th inputs. 'Neutral' is detected for Mayid's last input, 11th input. In our application, the context-based affect sensing will be activated if 'neutral' is detected based on the analysis of the users' input itself. As mentioned earlier, the Bayesian affect sensing algorithm uses the most recent three emotions experienced by Mayid to initialize the emotions A, B & C, i.e. respectively initialized as 'angry', 'angry', and 'threatening'. We increment both the counter of the frequencies of N_{angry_angry} and the counter of the occurrences of $N_{angry\_angry\_threatening}$. Then the system updates the two preceding emotions by shifting the emotion B to A and replacing B with C, i.e. the two updated preceding emotions A & B are respectively 'angry' and 'threatening'. Then conditional probabilities, P[C| angry, threatening] are calculated for the predicted emotion C. The affect with the highest probability is regarded as the most probable emotion implied in the 11th Mayid's input. The algorithm indicates 'anger' is implied in this input. Since the above processing is iterative, the contextual appropriateness of the detected affect 'angry' is further verified by the social context inference using neural networks.

In this way, the AI agent is capable of predicting the improvisational mood of each character throughout the improvisation. We provide detailed evaluation results for the performances of the improvisational mood modeling in the evaluation section. However, since the Bayesian inference gathers frequencies of emotional sequences throughout improvisations in a global manner, it relies heavily on the probability produced based on such frequencies for prediction and ignores the responding to local emotional indications. Thus it may lead to detection errors. In the following section, we discuss a local social affect interpreter using neural network-based inference to provide another justification channel for contextual affect analysis.

3.2 Affect Sensing from Local Social Communication Context

In order to sense emotional implication in the local context, our approach is developed as follows. In one improvisational session, up to 5 human actors are involved in. Thus emotions contributed respectively by the 5 human characters in the most related context are employed to inference the evaluation implication (positive, neutral and negative) in the interaction context. A supervised neural network based on backpropagation learning is used to perform the affect interpretation task. It employs three layers with 5 nodes in the input layer and 3 nodes respectively in the hidden and output layers. The 5 nodes in the input layer indicate emotions embedded in the most recent utterances contributed by each character. The 3 outputs represent the predicted positive, neutral and negative implication in this interaction context.

At the training stage, we used 5 transcripts of the school bullying scenario to generate the 150 training emotional contexts. Two human judges are used to provide positive/negative annotations of these interaction contexts. After the neural network is trained to reach a reasonable average error rate (< 0.05), it is used to predict positive/negative/neutral implication in the test interaction contexts. We demonstrate how the neural net based reasoning performs using the above example shown in section 3.1. The Bayesian net recommended 'anger' implied in the 11th input from Mayid previously. Now we use the neural net based affect interpretation to verify the contextual appropriateness of the previously recommended affect, 'angry'. First we retrieve the emotions embedded in the most recent utterances contributed by each character and obtain the following input sequence: [disapproval (6th), threatening (7th), disapproval (8th), disapproval (9th) and threatening (10th)]. The neural net predicts this interaction context is most likely to embed 'negative' with a prediction probability 0.633. Thus 'anger' predicted by the Bayesian inference in the 11th input is verified as the appropriate emotion embedded in a consistent 'negative' interaction context.

Generally affect inference from local social interactions based on neural networks verifies the personal context emotion prediction using the Bayesian reasoning. Moreover, we use 4 transcripts of the school bullying scenario for the evaluation of the neural network-based reasoning and discussion details are presented in section 4.

4   Evaluations and Conclusions

We carried out user testing with 220 secondary school students in the UK schools. Improvisational transcripts were automatically recorded to allow further evaluation. We produce a new set of results for the evaluation of the updated affect detection component with contextual affect interpretation based on the analysis of some recorded transcripts of the school bullying scenario. Generally two human judges marked up the affect of 400 turn-taking user inputs from the recorded 4 transcripts of this scenario (different from those used for the training of Bayesian and neural networks). In order to verify the efficiency of the new developments, we provide Cohen's Kappa inter-agreements for the AI agent's performance with and without the new developments for the detection of the most commonly used 10 affective states. The agreement for human judge A/B is merely 0.45. Since 10 emotions were used for annotation and the annotators may not experience the exact emotions as the testing subjects did, it led to the low inter-agreement between judges. The inter-agreements between human judge A/B and the AI agent with the new developments are respectively 0.43 and 0.35, while the results between judge A/B and the agent without the new developments are only respectively 0.39 and 0.30.

We also provide evaluation results of the improvisational mood modeling using the Bayesian networks for the 3 leading characters in the school bullying scenario based on the analysis of the 4 testing transcripts. We converted the recognized affective states into binary evaluation values and obtained the following accuracy rates by comparing with the annotation of one human judge: Mayid: positive (52%), neutral (27%) and negative (94%); Lisa: positive (46%), neutral (35%) and negative (73%); and Elise: positive (55%), neutral (33%) and negative (86%). Generally negative emotions are well detected across testing subjects. Since in the school bullying scenario, the big bully tends to make other characters suffer, the improvisation tends to be filled with negative expressions. Although positive and neutral expressions are recognized less well, the percentages of the inputs indicating positive and neutral expressions based on the human judges' interpretation are respectively approximate 30% and 25%. Thus although there is room for improvements, the performances of affect sensing from positive and neutral expressions are acceptable.

Moreover, we also provide Cohen's Kappa for the performance of the affect sensing in social interaction context using neural networks. The same judges are employed to mark up the emotional implications in the 110 interaction contexts extracted from the selected 4 example transcripts. The inter-agreement between judges is 0.91, while the results between judges and the neural net based reasoning are respectively 0.71 and 0.70. The results indicate that evaluation implication embedded in the social context is well recovered using neural network inference.

Overall, we have made initial developments of an AI agent with emotion and social intelligence, which employs communication context for affect interpretation using Bayesian and supervised neural networks. Although the AI agent could be challenged by the rich diverse variations of the language phenomena and other improvisational complex context situations, we believe these areas are very crucial for development of effective intelligent user interfaces and our processing has made promising initial steps towards these areas. We also intend to develop context-aware processing to interpret metaphors esp. for those which do not violate semantic preferences.

References

1. Zhang, L.: Exploitation of Contextual Affect Sensing and Dynamic Relationship Interpretation. ACM Computer in Entertainment 8(3) (2010)
2. Hareli, S., Rafaeli, A.: Emotion cycles: On the social influence of emotion in organizations. Research in Organizational Behavior 28, 35–59 (2008)
3. Liu, H., Singh, P.: ConceptNet: A practical commonsense reasoning toolkit. BT Technology Journal 22 (2004)
4. Shaikh, M.A.M., Prendinger, H., Mitsuru, I.: Assessing sentiment of text by semantic dependency and contextual valence analysis. In: Paiva, A.C.R., Prada, R., Picard, R.W. (eds.) ACII 2007. LNCS, vol. 4738, pp. 191–202. Springer, Heidelberg (2007)
5. Ptaszynski, M., Dybala, P., Shi, W., Rzepka, R., Araki, K.: Towards Context Aware Emotional Intelligence in Machines: Computing Contextual Appropriateness of Affective States. In: Proceeding of IJCAI 2009 (2009)
6. Gratch, J., Marsella, S.: A Domain-Independent Framework for Modeling Emotion. Journal of Cognitive Systems Research 5(4), 269–306 (2004)
7. Endrass, B., Rehm, M., André, E.: Planning Small Talk Behavior with Cultural Influences for Multiagent Systems. Computer Speech and Lan-guage 25(2), 158–174 (2011)
8. Lopez, J.M., Gil, R., Garcia, R., Cearreta, I., Garay, N.: Towards an Ontology for Describing Emotions. In: Proceedings of the 1st world summit on The Knowledge Society: Emerging Technologies and Information Systems for the Knowledge Society (2008)

To Date or Not to Date? A Minimalist Affect-Modulated Control Architecture for Dating Virtual Characters

Michal Bída, Cyril Brom, and Markéta Popelová

Charles University in Prague, Faculty of Mathematics and Physics,
Department of Software and Computer Science Education
Malostranské nám. 2/25, Prague, Czech Republic
michal.bida@gmail.com, brom@ksvi.mff.cuni.cz,
PopelovaM@seznam.cz

Abstract. As part of our broader initiative on promoting the education in the field of IVA control mechanisms at high schools and universities, we have created a micro-game Cinema Date, which introduces students challenges posed by controlling 3D virtual characters and expressing their emotional state. The game features two virtual teenagers dating on their way to the cinema. The player can influence the course of the date by influencing behavior of the boy. Existing IVA architectures did not satisfy our requirements on the architecture being reasonably simple, yet capturing affect-modulated behavior, transition behavior and future-directed intentions. Here, we present the game, focusing on the minimalist control architecture of its main characters.

1 Introduction

With the field of intelligent virtual agents (IVAs) maturing, a limited number of tools supporting education of students entering the field is becoming increasingly problematic. To our knowledge, out of many agent-authoring tools only Storytelling ALICE [1] and NetLogo [2] address the issue of education explicitly. However, Alice is oriented on teaching primary and middle school children the programming basics and uses 3D virtual reality as a means rather than an educational object, and NetLogo, while being an excellent entry-level tool for building simple agents and running social simulations, is not well suited for building 3D agents with complex behavior.

To fill the gap, we adopted a long-lasting aim to develop educational applications suitable for advanced high-school and university students for improving their skills in programming high-level behavior of 3D IVAs. Our main project, Pogamut [3], a tool enabling a rapid development of IVAs based in worlds of first person shooter action games, has been already adopted as an educational platform at several universities. Despite generally positive comments [4], Pogamut has a limitation: it is oriented on action game AI. Thus, under the umbrella name Emohawk, we are now coming with a new set of tools featuring a less violent content and addressing more issues connected with development of IVAs, including, e.g., emotion modeling. Two such tools have been already finished and released: StoryFactory [5], an application supporting teaching high-school and non-programming university students (e.g., new media art)

H. Högni Vilhjálmsson et al. (Eds.): IVA 2011, LNAI 6895, pp. 419–425, 2011.

basics of 3D animations by developing machinimas, and SteeringTool [6], a simulation for teaching the topic of IVA navigation. Meanwhile, as a prequel to the Emohawk package, we have developed a micro-game Cinema Date to draw attention of students to several key IVA issues. The focus of this paper is this game.

In the present version of the game, a simple narrative is played out by two IVAs: Barbara and Thomas. The player observes the narrative from the third-person perspective (Fig. 1). At the beginning of the story, the characters agree to go to the cinema, and during their approximately two minutes long walk there, the player has the opportunity to influence the behavior of the boy towards the girl. In case of no player input, the characters will be engaged in a casual dating conversation; however, the player can make the characters to argue with each other by making Thomas acting strangely. The story has two possible ends: either the characters make it to the cinema together or Barbara breaks up with Thomas, which is the player's goal. The exact course of the story is emergent and depends on the player's actions, the characters' current state and a limited random element. Note that the story will actually have four variants in the final version of the game: a player will be allowed to choose on behalf of which character to play and whether the game goal is negative or positive (i.e., to reconcile an initial tension between the characters).

The IVAs act in a virtual city we developed for UnrealEngine2Runtime. For affect simulation, we use the ALMA model [7] and recognize about 50 events triggering eight OCC [8] emotions. Characters exhibit eight different complex behaviors that are triggered by about 20 reactive rules. The behaviors are expressed by means of about 200 mo-caped animations, 50 emoticons and colored bubbles around characters heads expressing the characters' overall feeling. Examples of actions include: joke, compliment, insult, slap, apology, question, speaking, laugh, kiss, touch, bump, etc. The player can make Thomas a) to perform a positive or a negative action to Barbara, b) to increase or decrease his distance from Barbara, c) to change the angle in which he is following her, and d) to switch between a normal walking and a "silly" walking style. Barbara's reaction depends on her emotional state and the action of Thomas, e.g., when Thomas starts walking silly, Barbara may ask him to stop it. Her action may also trigger a reaction of Thomas, resulting in a short sequence of actions between the characters (with the player triggering the chain with the first action).

When specifying this scenario, we had several goals in mind. We wanted to show students that IVAs are fun and life-like, to immerse them in a VR environment and to motivate them to play with the scenario and explore its possibilities. Though the game is short, its state space is already large. From the pedagogical standpoint, we wanted to highlight the distinction between an *autonomous* agent and a user controlled 3D VR puppet (with which students become familiarized using StoryFactory tool). Additionally, the game, when supplemented with a teacher's explanation, introduces students the issues of IVA navigation, emotion modeling and reactive behavior.

Our major technical issue was the development of the IVAs' control architecture, balancing its complexity so that we can describe intended behavior but not burden the designer during development with the architecture's superfluous features or wasting computational resources in run-time due to the architecture's superfluity. Additionally, the architecture should serve well for demonstrative purposes regarding novices to the IVA field. Different architectures suit different purposes, as highlighted by the empirical study [9].

We required the architecture 1) to allow us to define the overall story shape yet to generate behavior in an emergent manner within the story boundaries. We further needed to handle: 2) reactive behavior with transitions (to swiftly change behavior and depict a transition behavior), 3) affective behavior (to portray emotions), 4) occasional future-directed intentions (to make the overall behavior more persistent), 5) a limited user interaction, 6) synchronizing the characters. Solutions friendly from the designer's perspective and operating in a timely fashion, such as finite-state machines (FSMs), behavior trees [10] or the reactive planner POSH [11], are insufficient due to Requirement (4) and partly (2), (3) and (6). Advantages of complex solutions, e.g. [12, 13, 14], addressing issues beyond our needs, such as equipping agents with general planning abilities and/or making them plausible emotionally and cognitively, comes at a price: increased design time and/or slower real-time computation. Complex reactive approaches that work in a timely fashion, such as ABL language [15], can still overburden the designer. Additionally, these solutions may be too complex for entry-level demonstration.

Thus, we have developed our own control architecture for IVAs: an affect-modulated action selection mechanism working with transition behaviors, future-directed intentions, and with a very simple "drama manager" for synchronizing the characters and making high-level adjustments to the story in real-time. Technically, our mechanism can be conceived as an extension to classical finite state-machines and simple rule-based systems. Its strength lies in adding several features without which would the development of stories of the Cinema Date's complexity be problematic.

The goal of the rest of this paper is to present this architecture. It is detailed in Section 2. Section 3 discusses the architecture's strengths, limitations, and scalability.

Fig. 1. Cinema Date examples. Upper left: an overview of the city. Upper right: Thomas performs "silly" walking. Lower left: Characters argue. Lower right: Thomas is angry.

2   Control Architecture of Cinema Date's Characters

The architecture features 2 kinds of procedural entities, actions and behaviors, and 3 control modules: reactive factories making top-level decisions, an appraisal module appraising events, and a user interaction module handling the user input (for Thomas).

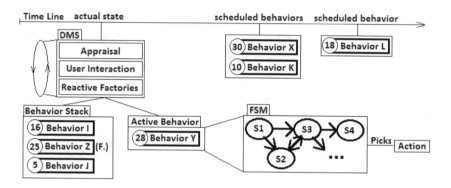

Fig. 2. Control architecture of a single agent. Priorities are given in circles. (F.) represents a frozen behavior. The drama manager is not portrayed here. See text for further explanation.

Actions. Actions are used to capture atomic behavior. Everything our IVAs can do is represented by an action. An example is slapping the other character or laughing (in these cases, the respective action runs an animation and shows an emoticon). Every action goes through an initialization, an execution and a clean up phase.

Behaviors. A behavior organizes actions to sequences to achieve the behavior's goal, which can be, for instance, "to lead the other agent to a certain place". Every behavior has a fixed priority and can be *succeeded* or *failed* with respect to its goal. An agent can have only one behavior *active* at a time.

So far, the notion of behavior is similar to how behaviors are used in other simple control architectures. However, to fulfill Requirement (2) on transitions, we augmented behaviors so that every behavior can pass through the following stages during its lifetime:

- *Init.* This stage executes preparations for the behavior if necessary.
- *Execution.* This is the main state of the behavior life cycle and it executes the normal course of the behavior.
- *Freezing.* It may happen that a behavior with a higher priority (HPB) should take control over the agent and the currently active behavior (CAB) should be interrupted. Before that happens, the CAB's freezing phase is executed, which allows us to specify the initial part of the behavioral transition if needed.
- *Resuming.* If frozen before, this stage is executed first after de-frosting.
- *Finishing.* When the behavior succeeds or fails, clean up actions or a transition to the next behavior can be executed here before the behavior is discarded.

A transition behavior can be executed when a) a CAB is interrupted by a HPB, b) a CAB ends and a frozen behavior is resumed, or c) a CAB ends and a new behavior is initialized. In each case, the transition behavior has an outgoing and an incoming part, which can be implemented in respective stages of the two behaviors. The two parts can be linked smoothly since the two behaviors are informed about each other.

In order to represent decision making, a FSM is embedded in each stage of every behavior. FSMs in execution stages are complex ones, other FSMs are usually simple.

Behaviors competing for execution at a particular moment are represented on the behavioral stack. Behaviors scheduled for execution in future, i.e., future-directed intentions, are linked with the time-line (Fig. 2).

Decision Making System (DMS). The DMS works in a cycle. Every cycle, three control modules evaluate the events in the environment (Fig. 2). The appraisal module (AM) matches events using reactive rules, appraises them by OCC variables, sends them to the ALMA model as an input and processes the ALMA output emotions. Reactive factories module (RF) use rules to monitor the agent and the environment state and generates new behaviors either on the behavior stack or the time-line, or it removes a behavior from there. The user interaction module (UM) changes (based on the user input) Thomas' parameters, e.g. distance between him and Barbara when he is following her, and generates or removes new behaviors similarly to the UM. After the modules finish their job, the DMS checks the time-line and moves all behaviors scheduled for the current time to the behavior stack (if there are such behaviors). Then, one behavior that will execute a next action is chosen using the following rules (only the first applicable rule is employed):

1. If the CAB has just completed its finishing stage, it is discarded and the behavior with the highest priority is selected as the next CAB from the stack and the execution thread is passed on to it (to its init or resuming stage).
2. If the CAB is in any stage except the execution one, the control is given to it.
3. A behavior with the highest priority is selected from the stack. If it is the CAB, the control is given to it. If it is a different behavior, the CAB's freezing stage starts.

Affect and behavior. The AM processes output ALMA OCC emotions to generate one dimensional value for representing social affect between the two characters. We call this value ranging from -1 to 1 "a feeling". It resembles the pleasure dimension from dimensional theory of emotions, but in our scenario it is valenced to a character. This value is taken into account in individual behaviors and reactive rules in the RF, and it determines the color of the bubbles around the characters' heads.

Representing the story. The architecture offers a designer four key elements for representing a plot (Req. 1). First, the designer starts with capturing the basic story shape by using the time-line for scheduling behaviors with known time of execution, e.g., the designer can set behaviors for Barbara a) to lead Thomas to the cinema at the beginning of the story and b) to call her mother in the middle of the walk. Second, the designer defines a set of reactive factories to monitor the agent or environmental state and generate/remove behaviors accordingly. This mechanism enables two things: executing reactions on some events, e.g., by adding the "kiss girl" behavior after she made a compliment twice and the boy's feeling is high enough, and executing story-important behaviors that do not have a fixed, in advance known time of execution, e.g., "turn right" after the character arrives at a particular crossing. The former may also trigger a short sequence of follow-up behaviors. This mechanism also allows for generating (removing) future-directed intentions such as if the girl complains that a particular boy's action was silly, the boy will do the same action on purpose half a minute later again. Third, the designer has the same opportunity to add/remove a behavior from within another behavior. Fourth, the architecture features a simple drama manager that allows for synchronizing agents and changing the overall story shape by removing all behaviors from the stack and/or the time-line of both characters at important story points, such as when the couple breaks up (however, we did not use the drama manager extensively).

3   Discussion and Future Work

In this paper we have presented a control architecture for dating characters from a micro-game Cinema Date, a motivational prequel to our larger educational package Emohawk. The architecture is a compromise between simple mechanisms, such as finite-state machines, and complex solutions like ABL language. It goes beyond the simple mechanisms in that it enables easily i) modulating behaviors by emotions, ii) representing transition behaviors, iii) representing future-directed intentions, and iv) synchronizing the characters centrally and adjusting the whole story at important plot points. All of these are important requirements even for short plots featuring several IVAs that express emotions.

Technically, the game served as a case-study project on which we verified that the architecture works well for plots of our complexity. The design time is rather short, though deep testing of the characters' resulting behavior is, of course, needed due to partly emergent nature of the plot. Features (i) – (iii) of the architecture are exploited extensively in the game. The drama manager (iv) has not been employed to its full potential: arguably, it would be needed more urgently in a longer plot with several branches. At the time of writing this paper, we already know the architecture can be scaled well for a similarly long scenario with three characters and more than 15 different behaviors (which we already implemented as an extension to the Cinema Date plot). Scaling it for four characters and longer and branching plots, where the drama manager is expected to be used extensively, is a work in progress. A possible limitation of the architecture for some projects is that it does not feature concurrent behaviors. It also does not employ now popular hierarchical behavioral representation, except the fact that all of our behaviors comprise a FSM (cf. hierarchical FSM and behavior trees). We found the hierarchical approach unnecessary for our purpose.

The game also stands on its own as an educational simulation for quick introduction to the issues of IVA navigation, emotion modeling and reactive behavior. Preliminary evaluation of the game with 5 lecturers/teaching assistants with IVA background suggested that i) the game has indeed a large educational potential as judged by the lecturers subjectively, ii) the lecturers perceived well the internal emotional state of the character, but iii) the game goal can be achieved too easily. Though the easy game-play was intentional, we are currently considering making it more challenging. An evaluation on target subjects is planned, but we first want to have the four variants of the game-play mentioned in Introduction.

The project can be downloaded at: http://amis.mff.cuni.cz/emohawk/.

Acknowledgments. The research related to this application was supported by the Ministry of Education of the Czech Republic (Res. Project MSM0021620838), by a project P103/10/1287 (GACR), by a student grant GA UK No. 0449/2010/

A-INF/MFF, and partially supported by SVV project number 263 314. The name "Emohawk" is inspired by Emohawk: Polymorph II, an episode of Red Dward VI (BBC). The graphical content was created by I. Diosi and Z. Krulich using Mayang's Free Textures library: http://mayang.com/textures/. We thank to J. Gemrot, R. Kadlec, J. Tomek, R. Pibil, and three anonymous referees for their comments on the paper.

References

1. Kelleher, C.: Motivating Programming: Using storytelling to make computer programming attractive to middle school girls. PhD thesis. Carnegie Mellon University, School of Computer Science, Technical Report CMU-CS-06-171 (2006)

2. Wilensky, U.: NetLogo. Center for Connected Learning and Computer-Based Modeling, Northwestern University (1999),
   http://ccl.northwestern.edu/netlogo/ (6.6.2011)

3. Gemrot, J., Kadlec, R., Bída, M., Burkert, O., Píbil, R., Havlíček, J., Zemčák, L., Šimlovič, J., Vansa, R., Štolba, M., Plch, T., Brom, C.: Pogamut 3 Can Assist Developers in Building AI (Not Only) for Their Videogame Agents. In: Dignum, F., Bradshaw, J., Silverman, B., van Doesburg, W. (eds.) Agents for Games and Simulations. LNCS, vol. 5920, pp. 1–15. Springer, Heidelberg (2009), http://pogamut.cuni.cz (6.6.2011)

4. Brom, C., Gemrot, J., Burkert, O., Kadlec, R., Bída, M.: 3D Immersion in Virtual Agents Education. In: Spierling, U., Szilas, N. (eds.) ICIDS 2008. LNCS, vol. 5334, pp. 59–70. Springer, Heidelberg (2008)

5. Artifical Minds for Intelligent Systems (AMIS): StoryFactory – a tool for creating machinimas in UnrealEngine2RuntimeDemo (in Czech), http://storyfactory.cz/ (6.6.2011)

6. Popelova, M.: Knihovna steering technik pro virtualni agenty. Bachelor thesis. Charles University in Prague (in czech) (2011), http://amis.mff.cuni.cz/emohawk/ (6.6.2011)

7. Gebhard, P.: ALMA - A Layered Model of Affect. In: Proceedings of the Fourth International Joint Conference on Autonomous Agents and Multiagent Systems (AAMAS 2005), Utrecht, pp. 29–36 (2005), http://www.dfki.de/~gebhard/alma/ (6.6.2011)

8. Ortony, A., Clore, G.L., Collins, A.: The cognitive structure of emotions. Cambridge University Press, Cambridge (1988)

9. Gemrot, J., Brom, C., Bryson, J., Bida, M.: How to compare usability of techniques for the specification of virtual agents' behavior? An experimental pilot study with human subjects. In: Proc. Agents for Education, Games, and Simulation, AAMAS Workshop (2011)

10. Rabin, S. (ed.): AI Game Programming Wisdom I-IV, Charles River Media (2002-8)

11. Bryson, J.J.: Inteligence by design: Principles of Modularity and Coordination for Engineering Complex Adaptive Agent. PhD thesis, MIT, Department of EECS, Cambridge, MA (2001)

12. Aylett, R.S., Louchart, S., Dias, J., Paiva, A.C.R., Vala, M.: FearNot! - An Experiment in Emergent Narrative. In: Panayiotopoulos, T., Gratch, J., Aylett, R.S., Ballin, D., Olivier, P., Rist, T. (eds.) IVA 2005. LNCS (LNAI), vol. 3661, pp. 305–316. Springer, Heidelberg (2005)

13. Lim, M., Dias, Y., Aylett, J., Paiva, R., Creating, A.: Creating adaptive affective autonomous NPCs. In: Autonomous Agents and Multi-Agent Systems, pp. 1–25. Springer, Heidelberg (2010)

14. Porteous, J., Cavazza, M., Charles, F.: Applying planning to interactive storytelling: Narrative control using state constraints. ACM Trans. Intell. Syst. Technol. 1(2) (2010)

15. Mateas M.: Interactive Drama, Art and Artificial Intelligence. PhD thesis. Department of Computer Science, Carnegie Mellon University (2002)

Interactive Characters for Cultural Training of Small Military Units

Priti Aggarwal, Kevin Feeley, Fabrizio Morbini, Ron Artstein, Anton Leuski,
David Traum, and Julia Kim

Institute for Creative Technologies, University of Southern California,
12015 Waterfront Drive, Playa Vista CA 90094-2536, USA

CHAOS, the Combat Hunter Action and Observation Simulation, is an immersive simulation training environment which gives small military units the experience of interacting with local Afghan villagers during a patrol. It is a physical build-out of a housing compound in a mock Afghan village, with several life-size reactive and interactive animated Pashto-speaking virtual characters. The exercise requires an infantry squad to locate and interview a character named Omar, communicating through a live human interpreter and attending to proper protocol regarding Omar's family. Character animation and behavior is based on extensive interviews with Afghan experts to provide a realistic setting of the intended locale. The system combines virtual human technology, story engineering, and physical set building to provide a compelling training environment that can handle a full squad, requiring trainees to integrate tasks such as working with an interpreter, dealing with non-English speakers from another culture, and assessing information and disposition to make decisions in a mission context.

The simulation is part of the Future Immersive Training Environment Joint Capabilities Technology Demonstration (FITE JCTD), located in a reproduction of an Afghan village at Camp Pendleton, California. It is an enclosed area consisting of a forecourt and a house with two rooms. As a unit enters the compound it encounters Farhan, a boy playing in the forecourt, projected life-size on a screen at the edge of the compound. Farhan receives signals from a radio frequency locator system which tracks the position of trainees

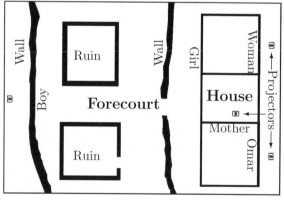

throughout the FITE installation; as soon as Farhan senses the squad's presence he runs away, providing a distraction from the main mission. A flat screen monitor positioned as the window of the women's residence shows a girl named Tasleem, who scuttles inside when the squad approaches the house; if the squad makes the mistake of entering the women's room then Nasira, an adult woman, admonishes them and gestures to them to leave. All three characters are merely reactive, responding only to the presence of trainees in their vicinity.

H. Högni Vilhjálmsson et al. (Eds.): IVA 2011, LNAI 6895, pp. 426–427, 2011.

The main interaction takes place in the men's residence in the house. Two characters are projected at life size on screens on adjacent walls: Omar, the head of the household, and Asala, Omar's mother. The characters only speak and understand Pashto, a local language of Afghanistan and Pakistan. The trainees interact with the characters through a live human interpreter, who translates the English questions into Pashto and then translates the characters' responses back into English. The interpreter's speech is transformed into Pashto text with customized acoustic, language, and dictionary models using the OtoSense speech recognition engine. The characters are driven by NPCEditor [2], an engine that selects appropriate character responses to Natural Language input based on a statistical learned mapping between input and output utterances. NPCEditor is trained using English and Pashto text in both the questions and responses. The characters can respond automatically to the input speech, or run in semi-automatic mode, where an operator can override the system's selected responses.

To allow a coherent interaction in the face of noisy speech recognition, the characters follow a structured story-driven interaction similar to the Gunslinger architecture [1]. The interaction consists of four "beats", intended to progressively raise the stress level of the trainees and get them out of their comfort zone. Advancement from one beat to the next can happen either in response to a question by the squad, or at the character's initiative if the squad fails to move the interview in the desired direction. The first beat is small talk and greetings. Conflict emerges in the second beat, when the squad tries to find information about a generator that Omar controls while he tries to get the squad to help with the generator's maintenance. Tensions rise in the third beat when the mother gets involved, interrupting the conversation and shouting at both the trainees and her son. Resolution is reached in the fourth beat; at this point a signal is sent to operators at mission control, who radio the squad with their next assignment.

We developed and tested the system with nine infantry squads at Camp Pendleton. This demonstrated that a mixed-reality, multiple character environment can successfully engage a small military unit, allowing them to practice tactical questioning and decision-making skills in a safe, consistent, and controlled environment that realistically depicts situations they will encounter in deployment. Innovations in this system include Pashto language interaction, combining virtual characters with a live human interpreter, use of story for scaffolding the interaction, and integration with a locator system to drive multiple virtual characters to engage (and distract) a whole military unit in a single exercise.

References

1. Hartholt, A., Gratch, J., Weiss, L., The Gunslinger Team: At the Virtual Frontier: Introducing Gunslinger, a Multi-Character, Mixed-Reality, Story-Driven Experience. In: Ruttkay, Z., Kipp, M., Nijholt, A., Vilhjálmsson, H.H. (eds.) IVA 2009. LNCS, vol. 5773, pp. 500–501. Springer, Heidelberg (2009)
2. Leuski, A., Traum, D.: Practical language processing for virtual humans. In: Proceedings of the Twenty-Second Innovative Applications of Artificial Intelligence Conference (IAAI 2010), July 2010, pp. 1740–1747. AAAI Press, Atlanta (2010)

The BML Sequencer:
A Tool for Authoring Multi-character Animations

Priti Aggarwal and David Traum

Institute for Creative Technologies, University of Southern California, 12015
Waterfront Drive, Playa Vista CA 90094-2536, USA

The BML sequencer is a tool to allow artists to create SmartBody compliant BML [4] animation sequences for multiple virtual humans. SmartBody [3] allows for complex behavior realization, synchronizing speech recordings with non-verbal behaviors by using the Behavior Markup Language (BML) [4]. However, there remain two problems for using BML and smartbody to achieve the vision that an artist has for animating the character: the authoring problem and multi-party behavior syncronization. The BML Sequencer addresses both.

BML is not so easy for non-programmer artists to write, understand and validate. Tools like NVBG [1] can automatically generate non-verbal behavior using rules based on the words and syntactic and discourse patterns present. However these behaviors may not adequately reflect the artist's vision. The BML Sequencer allows an artist to select, schedule, and modify animations and compile the resulting animation schedules to BML and view the resulting behavior on an agent animated by Smartbody. The BML sequencer tool has a simple user interface allowing artists to rapidly realize their vision for expressive multi-character behavior by facilitating easy creation, viewing, fine-tuning and testing of complex animation sequences for a spoken audio clip, ensuring BML compliant output sequences to be used by a BML realizer such as SmartBody and supporting animation of multiple characters on one schedule. Three animation channels are provided: **Body Animations, Facial Animations,** and **Gazes.** For each, the artist can select the character to be animated, choose from a menu of animation types, and choose timing and duration.

SmartBody only allows animations for a single agent within a bml schedule. We developed a protocol for animations of other characters, using the "sbm:event" message to trigger a supplementary BML request for the subordinate behavior to another agent. This enabled us to schedule animations for multiple characters simultaneously for each utterance without becoming familiar with the underlying BML syntax. The test options "Play" and "Play All" enable the user to validate each individual animation or the entire sequence, allowing effective debugging, polishing and refining the sequences. The tool can also be used during run-time of the system, retrieving a BML schedule when presented with an FML behavior request for a specific utterance, using the same protocol as NVBG in the virtual human toolkit.[1]

---

[1] http://vhtoolkit.ict.usc.edu/index.php/

H. Högni Vilhjálmsson et al. (Eds.): IVA 2011, LNAI 6895, pp. 428–430, 2011.

The InterFaces project,[2] a collaboration between the USC Institute for Creative Technologies (ICT) and the Museum of Science, Boston (MOS) successfully engages the visitor in an interactive exchange with virtual museum guides, Ada and Grace. The Twins domain include a finite but large set of utterances (mainly responses to questions). The initial set included 330, which was later expanded to 436. The tool used by an animator who was not previously familiar with the BML sequencing tool or BML specifications. The artist was able to understand and start using the tool effectively in less than 4 hours and do very good first pass on all 320 lines in 7 working days (ten minutes per utterance). Another animator, also was not familiar with the tool or BML specification, took over and polished the lines and added 116 more utterances in 5 days.

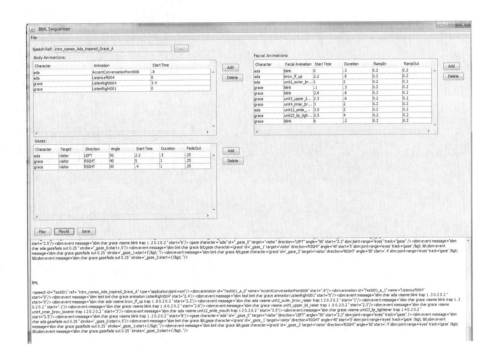

References

1. Lee, J., Marsella, S.: Nonverbal behavior generator for embodied conversational agents. In: Proceedings of Intelligent Virtual Agents (2006)
2. Swartout, W., Traum, D., Artstein, R., Noren, D., Debevec, P., Bronnenkant, K., Williams, J., Leuski, A., Narayanan, S., Piepol, D., Lane, C., Morie, J., Aggarwal, P., Liewer, M., Chiang, J.Y., Gerten, J., Chu, S., White, K.: Ada and grace: Toward realistic and engaging virtual museum guides. In: Intelligent Virtual Agents, pp. 286–300. Springer, Heidelberg (2010)

3. Thiebaux, M., Marshall, A., Marsella, S., Kallmann, M.: Smartbody: Behavior re-
alization for embodied conversational agents. In: Proceedings of AAMAS (2008)
4. Vilhjálmsson, H.H., Cantelmo, N., Cassell, J., E. Chafai, N., Kipp, M., Kopp, S.,
Mancini, M., Marsella, S.C., Marshall, A.N., Pelachaud, C., Ruttkay, Z., Thórisson,
K.R., van Welbergen, H., van der Werf, R.J.: The behavior markup language: Recent
developments and challenges. In: Pelachaud, C., Martin, J.-C., André, E., Chollet,
G., Karpouzis, K., Pelé, D. (eds.) IVA 2007. LNCS (LNAI), vol. 4722, pp. 99–111.
Springer, Heidelberg (2007)

Intelligent Virtual Environment Development with the REVE Platform: An Overview

George Anastassakis and Themis Panayiotopoulos

Knowledge Engineering Lab, Department of Informatics, University of Piraeus
{anastas,themisp}@unipi.gr

Abstract. The development of intelligent virtual environments is a demanding process due to their increased complexity and the need for integration of diverse technologies. Substantial efforts are made to address the issue in a targeted fashion, in terms of virtual space representation, virtual object semantics and functionality, and intelligent virtual agent perception and action. However, the field lacks methodologies that address the issue uniformly and provide for reusability, maintainability and extendibility. In this paper we present an overview of our own efforts in that direction, which build upon the REVE representation for intelligent virtual environments and the REVE platform.

After at least two decades of research and attempts for practical applications, the potential of intelligent virtual environments (IVEs) [1] for contribution to numerous areas, such as entertainment, education and simulation, has become apparent. However, it has become equally apparent that IVE development is not a straightforward task: IVEs are highly complex systems that rely on tight and efficient cooperation of different components serving different needs. The majority of related work addresses the issue selectively, focusing on individual aspects such as the representation of 3D spaces, perception and behaviour, while relying on ad hoc methods for the necessary integration into complete systems. In this paper, we present a brief overview of our own efforts towards systematization of IVE development, that is, a methodology which builds upon the *REVE representation for intelligent virtual environments* [2] and a set of fully-implemented, Java-based software tools collectively referred to as the *REVE platform* [3].

Our methodology introduces a *conceptual IVE design*, that is, a generalized, high-level view of all IVEs, regardless of purpose and implementation, as systems of specific components. The central component is the *virtual world store* whose purpose is to store, and enable access to, virtual world data. The *initialization* component is responsible for initializing the system given appropriate source data. The *rendering* component sequentially generates instances of the virtual world over time. An arbitrary number of *virtual agent behaviour* components interact with the virtual world through virtual bodies, thus introducing the element of autonomous behaviour into the system. The *interface* component enables presentation of the virtual world to human users on various levels (visual, auditory, etc.)

In accordance with the REVE representation, our methodology considers virtual worlds as sets of virtual objects encoded as *items*. Items consist of *item aspects*, each containing data about a certain aspect of the virtual object. All items have a *physical*

H. Högni Vilhjálmsson et al. (Eds.): IVA 2011, LNAI 6895, pp. 431–432, 2011.

aspect, an *access aspect* and a *semantic aspect*, while items encoding virtual bodies additionally have an *activity aspect* and a *perception aspect*.

The physical aspect is defined as an abstract scenegraph. As such, it can host, and benefit from, different scenegraph implementations, while enabling transparent, implementation-independent access to the data it manages by node and field name. It contains a sequence of automatically-generated nodes that encode physical properties fundamental to all objects – location, orientation and bounding-box dimensions – while the rest of its content is object-dependent and is retrieved from compatible external sources, such as X3D files. The access aspect contains *accesspoints*, which are parts of the virtual object's physical structure where functionality is available. Each accesspoint has a number of *functions*, which are means to affect the virtual object in a certain dictated by the function's *function class*. The semantic aspect encodes perceivable information about the virtual object in a symbolic form. Its content is partially standard and partially defined by application designers, so that encoding both fundamental properties (location, orientation, bounding-box dimensions, functionality, and, in case of virtual bodies, action and perception abilities) as well as object-specific ones is possible. The activity aspect encodes a virtual body's action abilities as a set of *effectors*, each containing a number of *actions*. An action is a specific function execution pattern that can be executed upon an item using functions in one of the item's accesspoints if specific, application-dependent *activity restrictions* (such as an *effective distance* between the effector and the accesspoint) are satisfied. The *perception aspect* encodes a virtual body's perception abilities as a set of *sensors*, each capable of accessing the semantic aspect content of all *perceivable items* in the virtual body's surroundings according to specific, application-dependent *perceptual restrictions* (such a *field-of-sense*).

Our methodology relies largely on the *REVE Worlds* system, a Java-based application that manages virtual worlds, renders them in real-time, presents them to users and enables external behaviour-generation applications to connect on the fly over TCP/IP. To define virtual worlds as sets of virtual objects in an implementation-independent fashion, application designers can use the XML-based *Virtual Environment Representation Language* (*VERL*). On the agent side, the Java-based *Simple API for REVE Agents* (*SARA*) offers multiple levels of reusable functionality.

So far, we have used the REVE platform as a basis for collaborative research on two occasions and as an educational aid in Artificial Intelligence- and Virtual Reality-related course modules and dissertations in the Department of Informatics, University of Piraeus. With the systematized development of reusable, maintainable, extendible IVEs as our goal, we are constantly improving and extending our methodology.

References

1. Aylett, R., Luck, M.: Applying Artificial Intelligence to Virtual Reality: Intelligent Virtual Environments. Applied Artificial Intelligence 14(N1), 3–32 (1999)
2. Anastassakis, G.: Representation and Operation of Virtual Environments. PhD Thesis, University of Piraeus, Greece (2010)
3. Anastassakis, G.: REVEnet (2011), http://kelnet.cs.unipi.gr/reve

Users's Expectations of IVA Recall and Forgetting

Karla Bransky and Debbie Richards

Computing Department, Macquarie University, North Ryde, NSW, 2109, Australia
deborah.richards@mq.edu.au

Abstract. To understand the role that memory plays we have collected data from three online experimental sessions in which participants interact with our virtual real-estate agent in both a recall and forget mode. We found that partial forgetting and even total loss of recall of an item, whether domain or social-based, was more believable and less frustrating than incorrect recall.

Keywords: Intelligent virtual agents, memory, remembering, forgetting.

1 Introduction

We have conducted a study into the kinds of things that users expect VCs to remember, and how users react to agents that exhibit memory from contexts wider than their design role, specifically the recall of social or personal details about the user. The study involved implementing and testing various levels of recall ability in a virtual real-estate agent in a series of three controlled experiments conducted over a three week period.

2 Experimental Environment, Design and Procedure

To achieve the goals of the project we have implemented a web-based study where participants played the role of a prospective buyer interacting with a virtual real-estate agent over three distinct experimental sessions. The VC was developed using Haptek PeoplePutty. The experiment was based on a 'Repeated Measures' design with two within subject factors (Recall/Forget, stimuli order) and one between subjects factor (stimuli order). Participants took part in three experimental online sessions lasting around 30 minutes each with at least 4 days between each session. The first session (S1) allowed the agent to get to know the participant and gathered biographical data (age, gender, education, English proficiency, experience with buying/renting, and attitude to real-estate agents, technology and computer games). In the second session (S2) and third session (S3) the agent displayed different kinds of recall and forgetting. Participants were asked to list what was remembered/forgotten and evaluate the interactions they had with the agent using a 4-point forced choice likert scale to indicate if

H. Högni Vilhjálmsson et al. (Eds.): IVA 2011, LNAI 6895, pp. 433–434, 2011.

the agent remembered/forgot them, naturalness and in-contextness of the recollection, level of enjoyment, believability, trust and preference for human or VC. The third session also had questions regarding accuracy of recall, noticed differences and empathy exhibited by the VC. In each session casual conversation occurred to provide content in later experimental sessions.

3   Results of Comparison of Results across Sessions

The three sessions were completed by 7 males and 5 females with mean age 28.4, median age of 24.5. All participants were confident with using computers and liked technology, English was the first language for 9, 7 liked playing computer games, 9 did not like real estate agents though only 7 had experience with real estate agents. We performed two-tailed paired t-tests between each likert item that occurred in Session 1 and other sessions for each condition. Statistically significant results were found for the enjoy item only ($p=0.037$) for S1 and S2, indicating that participants enjoyment of the interaction was affected by the agent displaying recall, as expected. The same test for S1 and S3 revealed a significant difference between the results for the remembering agent for both believability (0.009) and enjoyment (0.009). These results strongly indicate that over time memory does contribute to believability and enjoyment.

We conducted two-tailed paired t-tests for recall and forget for each item between session 2 and 3. There were no significant differences in the recall comparisons. In the forget comparison, at the 95% confidence level there was a significant difference of 0.023 between the naturalness of the recall in session 2 and 3. Again this supports that the forgetting was more natural in S3 than S2. Also there was a significant difference between how forgetful the agent was of 0.022, and again in how trustworthy the agent was (0.019). So exhibiting partial loss of recall in S3 over incorrect recall in S2 also contributed to the decrease in how forgetful the agent seemed, as well as increasing the user's trust in the agent in the forget condition. Additionally, the significant difference for the order of the forget condition was seen when we combined the results for forget in the first dialog for S2 and S3, and similarly when the forget condition was received second in both sessions. The p-value was 0.02, admittedly less significant than the previous measure for just session 2, but this may be as a result of regression threat; a movement towards the mean common in longitudinal studies.

4   Conclusion

In conclusion, we found that IVAs should exhibit recall about the user which demonstrates some level of caring and interest in the user. Memory exhibited must be natural and in context or believabilty, enjoyment and trust, necessary for long term interactions, will be negatively affected. Naturalness and believability include forgetting which should be exhibited as partial loss and what is partially recalled should be explicitly stated. The agent needs sufficient intelligence (sensitivity and adaptivity) to be able to adjust their behaviour through the conversation like (most) people do.

Validity of a Virtual Negotiation Training

Joost Broekens, Maaike Harbers, Willem-Paul Brinkman, Catholijn Jonker, Karel Van den Bosch, and John-Jules Meyer

Delft University of Technology, Utrecht University, TNO Human Factors Soesterberg

Abstract. In this paper we present a rigorously setup VR negotiation training, including an intelligent virtual agent able to express emotion and to give explanations of its behavior. We discuss the measures we took to ensure the validity of the VR training. We also present a small scale experiment showing convergent validity of the VR training.

1 Introduction

Virtual training systems are reported to be an effective means to train people for complex, dynamic tasks like negotiation or crisis management. Intelligent virtual agents that express emotion and that give explanations about their behavior can be used in such training [4,3,10]. Here we focus on measures taken to ensure the validity of a VR negotiation training we developed and present preliminary experimental results on the convergent validity of the training.

2 Validity of the Virtual Reality Training System

The learning goals of the negotiation training are to help people understand the importance of issues (e.g. height of salary) versus interests (e.g. enough money to make a world trip), and to train people to ask about interests to find compatible issues to get to a win-win deal with the IVA. These goals are confirmed to be important by negotiation literature [5] as well as by 8 case studies we did as a requirement analysis for the VR training.

The training content was based on the issues and underlying interests that arose in the 8 case studies. The training involves a negotiation about terms of employment with a human playing the employer and a virtual agent playing the candidate employee. A win-win solution appears only when the trainee explored the agent's interests. No agreement is reached when the trainee did not do so.

The virtual agent communicates in natural speech, recorded by a professional voice actor. In negotiation support, emotions play an important role [1]. The virtual agent expresses three basic emotions as feedback to the trainee's selected response option. Happiness signals a - for the IVA - positive outcome of a chosen option, sadness signals a potentially bad outcome, anger signals an actual bad outcome. These expressions were uniquely identifiable [2], and their meaning is compatible with cognitive appraisal theory [9], and operant conditioning. To support users in their learning, the IVA is able to explain its own behavior.

H. Högni Vilhjálmsson et al. (Eds.): IVA 2011, LNAI 6895, pp. 435–436, 2011.

Explanations aim to help trainees to better understand and learn from training sessions [8,6]. Our explanation method is grounded in our previous work [7].

The virtual training and scenario were reviewed and approved by a professional negotiator not involved in the design and development of the VR training. All of these measures bolster the validity of the VR training.

We performed an experiment (n=18, 12m, 6f, avg age=27, sd=4.0) to test if self-reported negotiation skill relates to better training performance (convergent validity). Subjects rated (5-point scale) self-reported negotiation skill, negotiation liking, negotiation frequency, and negotiation perseverance. Then, all subjects played the scenario as well as possible. We counted how often the subject made the IVA happy, sad and angry, and recorded the outcome utility of the deal (u=[0,8]). We found a significant correlation between self-reported negotiation frequency and sad IVA reactions (r(18)=-0.5, p=-0.036), and correlations between frequency and utility (r(18)=0.44, p=0.066) and between frequency and happy reactions (r(18)=0.418, p=0.085) approached significance. These findings indicate convergent validity.

3   Conclusion

We have described the validity of a VR negotiation training. We plan to investigate the actual effect of the training combined with instruction, exploration, and reflection, and the specific effects of emotion expressions and explanations.

References

1. Broekens, J., Jonker, C., Meyer, J.-J.: Affective negotiation support systems. Journal of Ambient Intelligence and Smart Environments 2, 121–144 (2010)
2. Broekens, J., Qu, C., Brinkman, W.-P.: Factors influencing user perception of affective facial expressions in virtual characters (submitted)
3. Cassell, J., Bickmore, T.: Negotiated collusion: Modeling social language and its relationship effects in intelligent agents. User Modeling and User-Adapted Interaction 13(1), 89–132 (2003)
4. Core, M., Traum, T., Lane, H., Swartout, W., Gratch, J., Van Lent, M.: Teaching negotiation skills through practice and reflection with virtual humans. Simulation 82(11), 685–701 (2006)
5. Fisher, W.U.,, R., Patton, B.: Getting to yes: negotiating agreement without giving in. Houghton Mifflin Harcourt (1991)
6. Gomboc, D., Solomon, S., Core, M.G., Lane, H.C., van Lent, M.: Design recommendations to support automated explanation and tutoring. In: Proc. of BRIMS 2005, Universal City, CA (2005)
7. M. Harbers, J. Broekens, v. d. Bosch, K., Meyer, J.-J.: Guidelines for developing explainable cognitive models. In: Proceedings of ICCM 2010, pp. 85–90 (2010)
8. Johnson, L.: Agents that learn to explain themselves. In: Proceedings of the Conference on AI, pp. 1257–1263 (1994)
9. Ortony, A., Clore, G.L., Collins, A.: The Cognitive Structure of Emotions. Cambridge University Press, Cambridge (1988)
10. Reilly, W.S., Bates, J.: Natural negotiation for believable agents. Technical report (1995)

A Software Framework for Individualized Agent Behavior

Ionut Damian, Birgit Endrass, Nikolaus Bee, and Elisabeth André

Human Centered Multimedia, Institute of Computer Science,
Augsburg University, 86159 Augsburg, Germany

1 Introduction and Motivation

Inter-agent interactions play an important part in virtual simulations of social behavior. Such interactions help visualize and analyze theoretical findings and assumptions in key sociological domains. However, most computer applications that simulate agent behavior lack the flexibility and adaptability researchers need to visualize theoretical concepts. This shortcoming can also be observed in modern computer games. For example, while most online games allow the player to customize his or her character, this customization is only aesthetical, such as hair color or outfit. These games do not allow the customization of the way the player's character behaves, for example how it gazes, how fast it gesticulates or what position it will take during an interaction. Strong and intelligent parametrization of the virtual agents is a solution to this problem. Each agent can have its own set of preferred gazing techniques, positions during an interaction and execute gestures in a specific way. Placing these custom agents together in a scene would then create a realistic and diverse virtual environment.

2 The System

An implementation of the above mentioned approach represents the Advanced Agent Animation (AAA) framework[1]. This framework is able to reproduce complex yet customizable agent interactions, using a powerful action parametrization system covering all important aspects of an agent interaction: body location, body orientation, gestures, gazing and movement. The generation of the low-level behavior of agents is automated and the framework enables the user or external systems to control the high-level behavior.

Formation System. To represent inter-agent interactions, the system uses F-formations [2]. Agents can join together to form formations. While in a formation, an agent will always try to satisfy its preferences for interpersonal distance and orientation. Possible conflicts between agents' interpersonal distance constraints are explicitly handled by the system.

The framework automatically generates the low-level behavior of positioning and orienting agents during an interaction. This can be customized by altering

---

[1] http://hcm-lab.de/projects/aaa/

H. Högni Vilhjálmsson et al. (Eds.): IVA 2011, LNAI 6895, pp. 437–438, 2011.

an agent's parameters for interpersonal distance, willpower, deviation from the default orientation, and preferred formation type.

Animation System. The animation management system is responsible for the loading, management and playback of animations. The system is capable of dealing with indeterministic animation playback requests. For this it employs a powerful animation blending system which is able to realistically start the playback of an animation even if other animations are already being rendered on the agent. The expressivity [1] of each animation can be customized with the help of the parameters: fluidity, stroke repetitions, playback speed and spatial extent.

Movement System. Agents can be placed inside a virtual scene and are able to locomote through the scene and orient themselves to face specific objects or coordinates. Each time an agent moves from one point in the scene to another, a movement action is performed. The movement actions can be customized with the help of the parameters: walking speed and movement animation.

Gazing System. The virtual agents are able to move their head and eyes to gaze towards specific targets, may these be points in space, objects or other agents. The system automatically generates gazing actions for an agent when it shows interest in another agent's action. The user or external systems can also request gazing actions. These can be customized with the help of the parameters: morphing speed and gaze duration.

3   Conclusion

This paper presented an approach to individualizing interactions between virtual agents by describing a software framework for generating non-verbal behavior of virtual agents. The major strength of the framework is the high customizability of the behavior generation processes. It is plausible that such a feature can support user immersion in video games by giving users the opportunity to create avatars with which they can identify themselves more easily.

Acknowledgments. This work has been funded in part by the European Commission under the grant agreement DynaLearn (FP7-ICT-231526).

References

1. Hartmann, B., Mancini, M., Pelachaud, C.: Implementing expressive gesture synthesis for embodied conversational agents. Science 3881, 188–199 (2005)
2. Kendon, A.: Conducting Interaction: Patterns of behavior in focused encounters. Cambridge University Press, Cambridge (1990)

The Mona Lisa Gaze Effect as
an Objective Metric for Perceived Cospatiality

Jens Edlund, Samer Al Moubayed, and Jonas Beskow

KTH Speech, Music and Hearing, Stockholm, Sweden
{edlund,sameram,beskow}@speech.kth.se

Abstract. We propose to utilize the Mona Lisa gaze effect for an objective and repeatable measure of the extent to which a viewer perceives an object as cospatial. Preliminary results suggest that the metric behaves as expected.

Keywords: Copresence, Face-to-face interaction.

Face-to-face interaction evolved between humans present in the same physical space (cospatial) and time (cotemporal; not discussed further here). This copresence is essential for face-to-face interaction. Cospatiality concerns interaction between people and ECAs as well, and a potential design goal for ECAs is that they be perceived by persons interacting with them as cospatial. In some ECA implementations, the virtual and physical spaces are implicitly connected via a conduit such as a monitor, which acts as a window onto virtual space. In others, designers attempt to blend virtual and physical space to create a mixed reality. In immersive virtual realities the viewer is pulled from physical space into the virtual reality, and in the holographic projections of science fiction (e.g. the holodeck of Star Trek), virtual characters and objects are moved from virtual to physical space. Some ECAs are clearly perceived as being cospatial: Pepper's ghost displays (e.g. Disney's Haunted Mansion ghosts) give a very strong notion of being present in the room. Others, like traditional paintings, clearly display characters a different space than that of the viewer. There is a range of less obvious examples in-between. The Robot receptionist at CMU [1] features a talking head displayed on a monitor, but the monitor itself moves to face the person it is targeting. One interpretation is that the entire monitor is to be taken for a head – then clearly present in physical space. The image on the monitor, on the other hand, can be interpreted as a head residing in a virtual space. [2] has capabilities that suggest to the user that it is present in the room, such as using gaze to address one out of two persons standing in front of it, while the graphical representation is that of a traditional ECA, suggesting that the character is present in virtual space. In general, any ECA that is represented in virtual space while behaving as if it were present in physical space risks being ambiguous. It is likely that the more properties suggesting that the ECA is present in the room, the more likely it is to be perceived as cospatial. But there is no obvious metric to measure to what extent a viewer perceives cospatiality, short of asking viewers post-interaction, which is notoriously unreliable [3].

In [4], we presented an interpretation of the well-documented Mona Lisa gaze effect in which gaze in 2D images is interpreted accurately, although in relative terms

H. Högni Vilhjálmsson et al. (Eds.): IVA 2011, LNAI 6895, pp. 439–440, 2011.

from the perspective of the viewer, whereas gaze projected on a 3D surface – an object in physical space – is interpreted accurately in absolute terms. We propose to capitalize on this to achieve an objective and repeatable measure of the extent to which a viewer perceives an object and the viewer as being cospatial. Given a set of observer judgments of gaze direction, we can score these against the intended gaze target in both relative and absolute terms. A match against the target in relative terms would indicate that the gaze is interpreted as being situated in a virtual space, and not cospatial. A match in absolute terms would indicate that the gaze is interpreted as cospatial. If neither a relative nor an absolute interpretation yields a match with the intended target, we may conclude that the gaze direction was generally difficult to perceive. [4] also presents an experiment paradigm for acquiring large amounts of gaze direction judgments with relative ease.

In the following preliminary experiments, the relative-absolute score range has been normalized so that a perfect relative score (lowest cospatiality) gives -1 and a perfect absolute score (full cospatiality) gives a score of 1. The first experiment tests two varieties of an animated talking head [4]: the first is displayed on a 2D monitor, and we expect of low cospatiality. The second projects the face of the talking head on a 3D model of a head, creating the impression of a physical head in the room. We expect this to be considerably more cospatial. For cospatiality, the 2D monitor scores -0.15 and the 3D head model 0.49, corresponding to expectations. The second experiment utilizes the same monitor, but a back projected mask for the second case. A group of five engaged in dialogue with the ECA, and we noted carefully who answered each question, taking this as an indication of perceived gaze direction. Scores for cospatiality was 1.0 for the back projected mask and 0.75 for the 2D monitor. The first number is as expected, and indicates that the mask is very successful. The second number is lower than the first, which is as expected, yet it is relatively high. We interpret this as an effect of the situation: when engaging in an actual dialogue with the talking head, people are more inclined to think of it as present in the room. This interpretation would require more cognitive effort, as people are overriding the initial interpretation. The 2D case shows significantly longer response times, which is consistent with this interpretation. As a final sanity test, we ran an experiment in which a live person gazed at different subjects. The result, again, was a full 1.0 for cospatiality, which is exactly as expected.

References

[1] Michalowski, M.P., Sabanovic, S., Simmons, R.: A spatial model of engagement for a social robot. In: Proc. of the 9th International Workshop on Advanced Motion Control (AMC 2006), pp. 762–767 (2006)

[2] Bohus, D., Horvitz, E.: Facilitating multiparty dialog with gaze, gesture, and speech. In: Proc. ICMI 2010, Beijing, China (2010)

[3] Nisbett, R.E., Wilson, T.D.: Telling more than we know: Verbal reports on mental processes. Psychological Review 84(3), 231–259 (1977)

[4] Al Moubayed, S., Edlund, J., Beskow, J.: Taming Mona Lisa: communicating gaze faithfully in 2D and 3D facial projections. ACM Transactions on Interactive Intelligent Systems (in press)

Bots in Our Midst: Communicating with Automated Agents in Online Virtual Worlds

Doron Friedman, Beatrice Hasler, Anat Brovman, and Peleg Tuchman

The Advanced Virtuality Lab
Sammy Ofer School of Communications
Herzliya, Israel
doronf@idc.ac.il

These days we spend an increasing amount of our time online communicating with automated digital entities. Millions of people spend time in multi-user online games and virtual worlds, where they not only play but also engage in various social activities together. Of particular interest is Second Life (SL): it is a generic platform that enables a virtual world constructed completely by its citizens. The study presented here was conducted in collaboration between AVL and a scholar of online religion (Prof. Gregory Price Grieve of the Department of Religious Studies, University of North Carolina). In this paper we discuss the methodology of using research bots for surveying a virtual world, and the lessons learned regarding the communicative responses to such entities. Bots in virtual worlds, such as SL, are avatars that are controlled by software rather than by a human operator. Our AVL bots have already taken part in other studies [1], and are available for other researchers upon request. In this study we compare the responses to the bot with responses to a human interrogator asking a single question about their RL religion. We coded participants' responses in two ways: affective coding and functional-semiotic coding. For affective analysis, responses were coded using the categories "neutral", "positive", and "negative". The functional-semiotic classification was analyzed using Jakobson's functional-semiotic mode [2,3] which distinguishes among six communicative functions: the referential function is assigned to the context, the emotive function is assigned to addresser (the participant, in our case), the conative function is assigned to addressee (the bot, in our case), the poetic function is assigned to the message, the phatic function is assigned to the contact, and the meta-lingual function is assigned to the code. The bot received 1227 replies from 954 (out of 2480 contacted) avatars; we note that this sample is comparable to the number of subjects in the previously-reported largest-scale case study performed in SL (N = 2094) [4]. Although in our case the number of valid responses is smaller, our method has the advantage of approaching participants in a highly-random fashion, whereas the majority of the subject recruiting to the Bell et al. study [4] was made in traditional channels (mailing list and classified ads), and the number of valid responses obtained by a random placement of kiosks in-world was much smaller (N = 75) than the number of valid responses obtained from randomly approaching participants in world in our case (N = 954). The response rate to the human experimenter was significantly higher (66%) than the response rate to the bot (35%). The human experimenter received slightly more negative responses overall as compared with the bot. The

H. Högni Vilhjálmsson et al. (Eds.): IVA 2011, LNAI 6895, pp. 441–442, 2011.
© Springer-Verlag Berlin Heidelberg 2011

specific pattern of result depends on the way we do the analysis, but the overall trend is consistent. If we take all responses to the human experimenter into account, then the human received significantly more negative responses (N=82, M=74.8, SD=33.0) than the bot (N=767, M=14.1, SD=33.6) and significantly less neutral responses (N=82, M=7.1, SD=22.4) than the bot (N=767, M=67.0, SD=44.3).

The results indicate that communication with the bot involved all functions of the model suggested by Jakobson. The most salient function operated by the respondents was the referential function, i.e., answering the question (66.7%). Surprisingly, the phatic function came second and was also quite frequent (20.5%). The responses to the human were also mostly referential (53.1%) followed by phatic (23.5%). We see that the difference in communicative functions is not dramatically different. However, the number of referential responses to the bot was significantly higher than to the human ($\chi2$ (1) = 16.0, p < .001), whereas the numbers of phatic and meta-lingual responses to the human were significantly larger than to the bot ($\chi2$ (1) = 15.14, p < .001 and $\chi2$ (1) = 10.40, p = .001, correspondingly).Our results in this preliminary study indicate that participants responded more negatively to the human interrogator than to the bot. One interpretation would attribute that to the fact that participants do not expect the bot to understand the negative responses. Yet another interpretation is that this indicates that people are not negatively inclined towards bots, but rather some of them do not want to be solicited for filling in surveys. We note that the semiotic functions operated towards the bot and the human interrogator seemed relatively similar in distribution, as compared with a "baseline" of public human chat in SL. This is evident by the significantly higher percentage of emotive and phatic messages and the significantly lower percentage of referential messages in public chat. This indicates that the responses to the interrogator were more informative and "down to the point" than public chat, thus validating the semiotic analysis. The responses to the bot were also more informative than to the human interrogator, as indicated by the higher percentage of the referential responses and the lower percentage of phatic and meta-lingual responses. However, we find that the most interesting lesson from this analysis is that while communicating with a bot in IM (private chat), addressers operate all functions of communication. We were surprised that the referential function only takes 66% of the messages, and that a third of the messages were attempts to communicate with the bot beyond the referential function.

References

1. Friedman, D., Steed, A., Slater, M.: Spatial Social Behavior in Second Life. Paper presented at the Proc. Intelligent Virtual Agents (September 2007)
2. Jakobson, R.: Closing Statement: Linguistic ands Poetics. In: Sebeok, T.A. (ed.) Style in Language. The MIT Press, Cambridge (1960)
3. Jakobson, R.: Language in Relation to other Communication Systems. In: Selected Writings, 2, Word and Language, pp. 697–708. Monto, The Hague-Paris (1971)
4. Bell, M.W., Castronova, E., Wagner, G.G.: Surveying the Virtual World: A Large Scale Survey in Second Life Using the Virtual Data Collection Interface (VDCI) (2009)

Realistic Eye Models Taking into Account Pupil Dilation and Corneal Reflection

Guillaume Gibert

MARCS Auditory Laboratories, University of Western Sydney,
Locked Bag 1797, Penrith NSW 2751, Australia
g.gibert@uws.edu.au

1 Introduction

The eye is a complex organ and gaze is only one of its features. Even if the pupil's primary role is to regulate the amount of light entering the eye in response to different lighting conditions, pupil dilation/constriction may be due to top-down processes. For example, the Task-Evoked Pupillary response [1] could be elicited by spontaneous thoughts or emotions. When interacting with an avatar, the importance of avatar pupil dilation/constriction together with blink rate has been studied recently in a lie detection task. The inclusion of these eye features driven from real data increased the rate of truth/lie detection compared with the same stimuli without these eyes characteristics [2]. Another eye component is the cornea which is a transparent tissue that covers the iris. On its surface, a reflection of the world surrounding the person appears: this effect is called corneal reflection. A vast amount of observable environmental information can be recovered from the corneal reflection of a single eye [3]. Only recently, anatomically accurate eye models have been implemented that clone the video of an eye taking into account this reflection [4] but not tested embedded in an avatar interacting with humans.

2 Eye Model

Each eye model was composed of an eyeball, a pupil, an iris and a cornea. A webcam was mounted on top of the screen displaying the avatar and facing the human partner. Images were grabbed at 30 Hz and then cropped around the gaze point (on the left and right side for the left and right corneas, respectively). These cropped images were then warped onto the cornea surfaces (see Fig. 1.).

The pupil diameter of the avatar can be accurately controlled. The average intensity of the grayscale cornea images was computed and used to control the variation of the pupil size via an adapted version of the model of pupil light reflex proposed by Pamplona and colleagues [5]. In addition, the hippus (i.e. a low frequency variation of the apparent pupil diameter) was also implemented in our model. This phenomenon refers to a spontaneous and bilateral synchronous oscillation of the pupil diameter under steady conditions of illumination. In the present model, it was implemented as a constant oscillation of the pupil diameter with a frequency equal to 1.4Hz.

H. Högni Vilhjálmsson et al. (Eds.): IVA 2011, LNAI 6895, pp. 443–444, 2011.

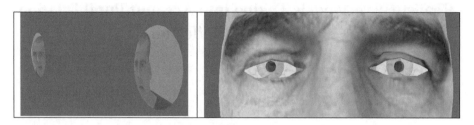

Fig. 1. The corneal reflection phenomenon: a reflection of the world surrounding the avatar appears on the cornea of each eye; in this example, the reflected image is of the avatar's human partner

Pupil dilation/constriction and corneal reflection may increase the sense of presence of the avatar during face to face communication.

Acknowledgements. This work was supported by the Thinking Head project a *Special Initiative* scheme of the Australian Research Council and the National Health and Medical Research Council (TS0669874).

References

1. Blackwell, R.D., Hensel, J.S., Sternthal, B.: Pupil dilation: What does it measure? Journal of Advertising Research 10, 15–18 (1970)
2. Steptoe, W., Steed, A., Rovira, A., Rae, J.: Lie Tracking: Social Presence, Truth and Deception in Avatar-Mediated Telecommunication. In: Chi2010: Proceedings of the 28th Annual Chi Conference on Human Factors in Computing Systems, vol. 1-4, pp. 1039–1048 (2010)
3. Nishino, K., Nayar, S.K.: Corneal imaging system: Environment from eyes. International Journal of Computer Vision 70, 23–40 (2006)
4. François, G., Gautron, P., Breton, G., Bouatouch, K.: Anatomically accurate modeling and rendering of the human eye. ACM SIGGRAPH 2007 Sketches, SIGGRAPH 2007 (2007)
5. Pamplona, V.F., Oliveira, M.M., Baranoski, G.V.G.: Photorealistic models for pupil light reflex and iridal pattern deformation. ACM Transactions on Graphics 28 (2009)

Control of Speech-Related Facial Movements of an Avatar from Video

Guillaume Gibert and Catherine J. Stevens

MARCS Auditory Laboratories, University of Western Sydney,
Locked Bag 1797, Penrith NSW 2751, Australia
{g.gibert,kj.stevens}@uws.edu.au

1 Introduction

Several puppetry techniques have been recently proposed to transfer emotional facial expressions to an avatar from a user's video stream. Correspondence functions between landmarks extracted from tracking and MPEG-4 Facial Animation Parameters driving the 3D avatar's facial expressions [1] have been proposed. More recently, Saragih and colleagues [2] proposed a real-time puppetry method using only a single image of the avatar and user.

While facial expression generation may not be sensitive to small tracking errors, generation of *speech*-related facial movement would be severely impaired leading to auditory-visual integration issues. Indeed, speech is in essence a multimodal phenomenon. Compelling examples of multimodal integration are the McGurk effects [3] which are automatic perceptual phenomena appearing under incoherent multimodal information. Inaccurate transfer of facial motion can modify the sounds perceived.

The present paper describes a new method to mimic directly the user's speech facial movements from a video or a webcam.

2 Training Phase

An Australian English speaker uttered 3 times a series of non-words with a Vowel-Consonant-Vowel structure. The initial and final vowels of the non-words were identical and chosen between /a/, /i/ and /u/ (extreme lips movements) and the consonants were selected from Australian English consonants. This dataset provided the basis for building a complete articulatory model for speech production. A video was recorded consisting of a front view of a human speaker uttering the non-words against a white background. One subset of images was manually segmented i.e. the position of 68 landmarks were selected by hand for each image. An Active Shape Model (ASM) using the toolbox STASM [4] was trained on this set of images. An articulatory model was built using the method proposed by [5]. The contribution of the speech articulators (lips and jaw) was iteratively subtracted. The procedure extracted 5 articulatory parameters: one for the jaw, 3 for the lips and one for the eyebrow. Cropped images around the inner mouth area were created from the landmark positions. The DCT coefficients were computed for the red component of each image. A manual transcription was conducted between these selected images and

H. Högni Vilhjálmsson et al. (Eds.): IVA 2011, LNAI 6895, pp. 445–446, 2011.
© Springer-Verlag Berlin Heidelberg 2011

the 5 articulatory parameters driving the tongue: jaw height, tongue body, tongue dorsum, tongue tip vertical and tongue tip horizontal. The least squares solution was then determined for the linear correspondence between the DCT coefficients and the articulatory parameter values.

3　Video Puppetry

The video puppetry animation consisted of several steps: an image was grabbed from the video stream and then cropped around the face using a face detector (Viola-Jones algorithm), then the ASM searched the best landmark positions for this image and the jaw and lip articulatory parameters were determined; finally the tongue articulatory parameters were then estimated from the DCT coefficients of the cropped images around the oral cavity area.

Acknowledgements. We thank James Heathers for manually segmenting the images. This work was supported by the Thinking Head project, a *Special Initiative* scheme of the Australian Research Council and the National Health and Medical Research Council (TS0669874).

References

1. Baptista Queiroz, R., Braun, A., Moreira, J., Cohen, M., Musse, S.R., Thielo, M.R., Samadani, R.: Reflecting User Faces in Avatars. In: Allbeck, J., et al. (eds.) IVA 2010. LNCS, vol. 6356, pp. 420–426. Springer, Heidelberg (2010)
2. Saragih, J.M., Lucey, S., Cohn, J.F.: Real-time avatar animation from a single image. Automatic Face and Gesture Recognition. Santa Barbara, CA (2011)
3. McGurk, H., MacDonald, J.: Hearing lips and seeing voices. Nature 264, 746–748 (1976)
4. Milborrow, S., Nicolls, F.: Locating Facial Features with an Extended Active Shape Model. In: European Conference on Computer Vision, Marseille, France, pp. 504–513 (2008)
5. Reveret, L., Bailly, G., Badin, P.: MOTHER: A new generation of talking heads providing a flexible articulatory control for video-realistic speech animation. In: 6th Int. Conference of Spoken Language Processing, ICSLP 2000, Beijing, China (2000)

Teaching Her, Him ... or Hir?
Challenges for a Cross-Cultural Study

Magnus Haake[1], Annika Silvervarg[2], Betty Tärning[3], and Agneta Gulz[2]

[1] Dept. of Design Sciences, Lund University, Sweden
[2] Dept. of Computer and Information Science, Linköping University, Sweden
[3] Cognitive Science, Lund University, Sweden
magnus.haake@design.lth.se, {annika.silvervarg,
agneta.gulz}@liu.se, betty.tarning@lucs.lu.se

This paper discusses some cultural considerations that we stand before in developing and exploiting an agent based educational software for use by Swedish and American students, age 11-14. The reported cultural challenges arise in software development, study designs, and decisions on actual pedagogical use in the two cultural settings.

The software in the study is an educational game for basic mathematics [1] using Teachable Agents (*TAs*), an educational technology based on *learning by teaching*. In brief, a TA is a computer agent that is taught or trained by a student, where AI techniques guide the agent's behaviour based on what it is taught [2]. The TA in the math game both asks the student to explain game related math questions and enters a chat-like conversation on a broader set of topics. An important rationale behind the latter, more socially oriented conversation, is to enable additional pedagogical interventions regarding, among others, math attitude, math self-efficacy. The two conversational modes are linked by the persona of the agent: 11-year old, going to school, learning math in the game, having various interests such as music and film.

The actual cross-cultural study takes place within a larger 3-year project. One project theme concerns the pedagogical effect of a *visually androgynous* TA as compared to a *visually gender stereotypical* TA. Gender stereotypes have been shown to have a considerable impact within STEM education, where manipulations of these stereotypes influence students' learning outcomes as well as attitudes. A previous study [3] with ambassador or presenter agents targeted Swedish high school students and university educations. A more gender neutral female ambassador agent evoked considerably more positive utterances on females within the computer engineering domain than did a more stereotypically feminine female agent. As to female students' declared interest in choosing a computer engineering university education, the two female ambassador agents had an equally positive effect. An overall research goal is – besides contributing knowledge about the importance of cultural contexts for the design of learning games – to show how more gender neutral or ambigous characters can have positive effects: in short terms by not associating students with a category standing for weakness or incompetence and in longer terms by not reproducing such stereotypes over time. The now planned study has some similarities with the former in that both mathematics and computer engineering are male domains according to cultural images or stereotypes, and that both projects target student attitudes. However, the agent in the present case is not an ambassador or presenter but instead a digital tutee, somewhat younger than the student. Thus, phenomena like role

H. Högni Vilhjálmsson et al. (Eds.): IVA 2011, LNAI 6895, pp. 447–448, 2011.

modelling may be less pronounced or work differently. At the same time, the character – and specifically its gender – is not without effects. Observations on younger children (age 9-10) using the same software with more obviously gendered agents shows that some of the boys may protest when their TA is a girl and may insist that they cannot teach her much since she is female and thus not very capable.

Another important difference is that the former study made use of *relatively gender neutral*, yet clearly female or male characters, whereas the present study makes use of a visually *androgynous* character. With this, the present study approaches two issues: (i) "How does an androgynous vs. a gender stereotypical character affect students' attitudes towards their TA as their tutee?" and (ii) "How does an androgynous vs. a gender stereotypical character affect the chat conversation and the students' attitudes towards it?".

In the present study all participants interact and chat with two different TAs, one a girl or a boy character and the other visually androgynous, yet assigned a gender (the same as that of the other TA that they interact with).

Before study off-set, it is essential to ensure that the androgynous character is perceived as such *by the students that are to use the software*. For Swedish students this test has been carried out with a total of 38 students, with 17 of the students holding the character to look more like a female than a male, 10 holding it to look more like a male than a female, and 11 stating that they could not chose one before the other. Furthermore, the three TA characters must not differ in any substantial way as to attractiveness, which also has been pre-validated for the Swedish target group. However, before conducting studies in the US, similar pre-validations have to be carried out with US students as it is uncertain whether the result will diverge or not. It is possible that the characters have to be redesigned to for use in the US study, since the goal is to explore the pedagogical effects of androgynous TA characters in the two cultures – not to evaluate the effects of a specific set of characters.

This goal is aligned with an *overall goal* of achieving pedagogically powerful software for different cultural settings, and a conviction that this requires far more than working this out for one cultural setting and then "translate" the software for another. Most obviously, the TA conversation, including anecdotes with cultural references, talk of school, etc. cannot simply be "translated". But neither can, as discussed above, visual aspects.

Furthermore, when conducting studies and drawing conclusions on how software can be used to achieve pedagogical goals, still other cultural differences must be taken into account. In this case, the stricter curriculum in the US requires the use of other study designs than would have been needed for a project within Sweden only.

References

1. Pareto, L., Schwartz, D., Svensson, L.: Learning by Guiding a Teachable Agent to Play an Educational Game. In: Proc. of AIED 2009, pp. 662–664. IOS Press, Amsterdam (2009)
2. Blair, K., Schwartz, D., Biswas, G., Leelawong, K.: Pedagogical Agents for Learning by Teaching. Educational Technology Special Issue 47, 56–61 (2007)
3. Gulz, A., Haake, M.: Challenging Gender Stereotypes using Virtual Pedagogical Characters. In: Goodman, S., Booth, S., Kirkup, G. (eds.) Gender Issues in Learning and Working with IT: Social Constructs and Cultural Contexts, pp. 113–132. IGI Global, Hershey (2010)

Examining Learners' Emotional Responses to Virtual Pedagogical Agents' Tutoring Strategies

Jason Harley, François Bouchet, and Roger Azevedo

McGill University, Department of Educational and Counselling Psychology,
Laboratory for the Study of Metacognition and Advanced Learning Technologies
3700 McTavish Street, Room 614, Montréal, Québec, H3A 1Y2, Canada
jason.harley@mail.mcgill.ca,
{francois.bouchet,roger.azevedo}@mcgill.ca

Keywords: Pedagogical agent, affect, emotion, intelligent tutoring systems, tutoring strategies, goal-setting, self-regulated learning.

1 Introduction

Given the preponderance of emotions in academic settings, particularly those related to achievement emotions [1] and the strides in both affect and affectively-embodied and sensitive virtual pedagogical agents (VPAs) [2], there has been a surge in research exploring the roles and possibilities that VPAs can play in facilitating learners' experience of positive emotions. This paper contributes to this ever-growing body of work by laying out recommendations for VPA tutorial strategies. In this study, we measured basic, universal, and discrete emotions identified by Ekman and Friesen [3]: happiness, sadness, anger, surprise, disgust and fear, in addition to neutral. These emotions can also be conceptualized into a valence dichotomy, where happiness is positively-valenced, surprise and neutral are non-valenced and the rest are negatively-valenced emotions. The second theoretical lens we used was Pekrun's Control-Value Theory of Achievement Emotions [1], which postulates that students' sense of control and attribution of value toward the achievement activity will influence their emotions and subsequently their learning outcomes.

In this study we examined the impact of two tutorial approaches on students' embodiment of discrete, basic emotions. These approaches were deployed in two separate conditions: (1) a prompt only (PO) condition, where the VPA prompted students to set three sub-goals, be mindful of their overall learning goal and either accepted or rejected students' proposed sub-goals and (2) a feedback (FB) condition, in which participants were additionally given information related to the relevancy and proximity of their proposed sub-goal to one or more of the seven ideal sub-goals. Our research question for this study was to determine what the proportional embodiment of discrete and valenced emotional states was during the sub-goal setting portion of participants' learning episode with MetaTutor, a multi-agent adaptive hypermedia learning environment for science learning [4]. We hypothesized, due to the lower affordance of control in the PO condition and achievement task-specific value being held constant across both conditions, that students would embody a greater proportion of negatively-valenced emotions in the PO than the FB condition.

H. Högni Vilhjálmsson et al. (Eds.): IVA 2011, LNAI 6895, pp. 449–450, 2011.
© Springer-Verlag Berlin Heidelberg 2011

2 Methodology

Participants included 18 undergraduate students (78% female) from 2 large public universities in North America. Participants were randomly assigned to one of three experimental conditions, where, for the purposes of this study, they interacted with a VPA which deployed one of the two aforementioned tutorial approaches for the goal-setting phase of the learning session with MetaTutor. In this study we used *FaceReader*[TM] 3.1, a software program developed by Noldus that analyzes participants' facial expressions, using an artificial neural network and thousands of models of faces and facial expressions to identify meaningful configurations of facial action units. The configuration of these facial action units, which are based on Ekman and Friesen's FACS system [3], is used to draw theoretically based inferences about the emotional states of participants.

3 Results and Conclusions

We performed two 2x3 Factorial Repeated Measures MANOVAs, one for each of the sets of emotions (discrete and valenced). Our preliminary analysis revealed that the VPA's tutorial strategy exerted a significant main effect upon participants' negatively-valenced emotions (F (1,16) = 8.10, p < .05). Our analysis of the discrete emotions revealed that the VPA's tutorial strategy exerted a significant main effect upon participants' embodiment of anger during the goal-setting episode (F (1,16) = 5.21, p < .05). Taken together, these results provide preliminary support for the existence of significant differences in the emotions participants embody at both the valenced and discrete emotional level in response to different VPA tutorial strategies. This study contributes to the development and design of affectively-competent VPAs by highlighting the importance and influence of meaningful and contextualized feedback on students' emotions. More broadly, these results demonstrate the importance of evaluating VPA tutorial strategies.

Acknowledgements. Funding for this study was provided by a sub-contract (DRL 1008282) from the National Science Foundation to the third author.

References

1. Pekrun, R.: The Control-Value Theory of Achievement Emotions: Assumptions, Corollaries, and Implications for Educational Research and Practice. Educational Psychology Review 18, 315–341 (2006)
2. Calvo, R.A., D'Mello, S.: Affect Detection: An Interdisciplinary Review of Models, Methods, and Their Applications. IEEE Trans. on Affective Computing. 1, 18–37 (2010)
3. Ekman, P., Friesen, W.: Facial action coding system: A technique for the measurement of facial movement. Consulting Psychologists Press, Palo Alto (1978)
4. Azevedo, R., Johnson, A., Burkett, C., Fike, A., Lintean, M., Cai, Z., Rus, V.: The Role of prompting and feedback in facilitating students' learning about science with MetaTutor. In: Pirrone, R., Azevedo, R., Biswas, G. (eds.) Proc. of the AAAI Fall Symposium on Cognitive and Metacognitive Educational Systems, pp. 11–16. Association for the Advancement of Artificial Intelligence (AAAI) Press, Menlo Park (2010)

Source Orientation in Communication with a Conversational Agent

Yugo Hayashi[1], Hung-Hsuan Huang[1], Victor V. Kryssanov[1], Akira Urao[2],
Kazuhisa Miwa[3], and Hitoshi Ogawa[1]

[1] Ritsumeikan University, Japan
[2] Suzuka National College of Technology, Japan
[3] Nagoya University, Japan

Do people directly interact with a computer as an independent social actor during simple conversations, or do they orient to the unseen programmer behind the program or an imagined person operating from another room? In the former case the CAS (Computers As Source) model would be valid, while in the latter it would be the CAM (Computers As Media) model that describes the interaction [1]. This study specifically attempts to address the following research questions: (a) Whether the CAM model adequately describes bi-directional communication, and (b) Whether the CAS model adequately describes one-directional communication when the representation of the agent is unfamiliar to the user. Two factors were thus investigated: (1) directions of communication (bi-directional vs. one-directional), and (2) familiarity of the agent's representation to the user (familiar vs. unfamiliar).

An experiment was conducted by a 2(bi-directional vs. one-directional) x 2 (familiar vs. unfamiliar) mixture factorial design. A collaborative problem solving task originally proposed in [2] was used to investigate bi-directional communication. In this task, two participants are engaged in a rule discovery game and discuss their ideas about the solution through a text-based chat. To investigate one-directional communication, a similar task was designed with two adjustments made: (1) participants are presented not just one but several decision-making problems called 'trolley problems', and (2) participants are not allowed to discuss their ideas.

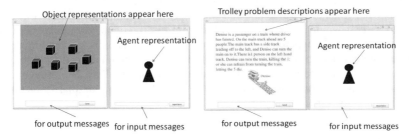

Fig. 1. Examples of the bi-directional and one-directional communication task interfaces

Two types of animated characters were created to investigate influences of the conversational agent representation's familiarity (see Fig. 2). Under the Familiar condition, an avatar of one of the authors, who conducted the experiment, was used. Participants in this group were instructed to use a social network service (SNS) for

H. Högni Vilhjálmsson et al. (Eds.): IVA 2011, LNAI 6895, pp. 451–452, 2011.

four months prior to the experiment. They were required to read, on a weekly basis, updates written on the experimenter's page, which included the avatar. The simple conversational computer agent used in the experiments is a typical rule-based system. This system has an ability to meaningfully respond to sentences input by the user, based on pre-defined rules.

Familiar condition   Unfamiliar condition

Fig. 2. Avatars of the animated characters used in the study

To explore the CAS and CAM models, exactly the same as described in [1] procedure was used. Two conditions were set as the independent variables: the "computer condition" and the "programmer condition". Participants in the computer condition were told that they would interact with a computer labeled on the screen 'Computer'. In the programmer condition, participants were told that they would interact with a human programmer through the interface labeled 'Programmer'. Any differences of the dependent variables across the two conditions were interpreted in support of the CAS model, while the absence of such differences was interpreted in support of the CAM model. Dependent variables were answers to a questionnaire about psychological characteristics of communication collected from each participant after completion of the communication task. The questionnaire included 16 questions, each with possible answers defined on a five-point semantic differential scale.

In the one-directional task, results obtained for the unfamiliar condition group suggest that communication characteristics, such as 'ease loneliness', 'feel close', 'discuss private issues', 'ability to express', 'purpose of claim is clear', were significant factors by a 2 x 2 ANOVA ($F_{(1,25)}= 5.032$, $p<.05$; $F_{(1,25)}= 5.556$, $p<.05$; $F_{(1,25)}= 5.644$, $p<.05$; $F_{(1,25)}= 7.646$, $p<.01$; $F_{(1,25)}= 7.998$, $p<.01$, respectively). In the bi-directional task, there were no significant factors detected.

These experimental results showed that: (a) communication based on CAM appeared as if it would be based on CAS during bi-directional communication, and (b) communication apparently based on CAS emerged in one-directional communication when the avatar of the agent used was unfamiliar to the participants. These results provide new interpretations for the cognitive behavior in human-agent interaction: source orientation depends on the interplay of the familiarity factor and the communication direction factor.

References

1. Sundar, S., Nass, C.: Source orientation in human-computer interaction: Programmer, networker, or independent social actor? Communication Research 27(6), 683–703 (2000)
2. Hayashi, Y., Miwa, K.: Prior experience and communication media in establishing common ground during collaboration. In: Proceedings of the 31th Annual Conference of the Cognitive Science Society, pp. 526–531 (2009)

Checkpoint Exercise: Training with Virtual Actors in Virtual Worlds

Dusan Jan, Eric Chance, Dinesh Rajpurohit, David DeVault, Anton Leuski,
Jacki Morie, and David Traum*

Institute for Creative Technologies

Abstract. We have implemented a checkpoint exercise in Second Life
where the user interacts with several computer avatars in a team based
activity. We describe the experience and the implementation of our solution and show some evaluation results.

1 Introduction

In this work we examine the application of autonomous avatars that can play
roles that involve interaction with the trainees in a complex situation such as
a checkpoint operation. In addition to controlling civilians in the simulation we
explore the use of virtual human technology to control virtual teammates. In this
way the trainee can go through the training even when the whole team required
to perform the exercise is not available.

We have developed the training exercise in Second Life. Our main reasons for
choosing this platform were the availability of libraries that allow programmatic
control of avatars and the fact that Second Life has a large user base. There has
been previous work on conversational agents in Second Life, but those usually
just involved a single avatar. We expand on the architecture of Staff Duty Officer
Moleno [1] to facilitate the requirements of the checkpoint exercise. The main
differences are that we control a larger number of avatars that have to coordinate
with each other and exhibit a wide range of behaviors. As such we have developed
a more robust behavior control system that provides flexibility and modularity in
control. In addition the controlled civilians can play various roles in the exercise
similar to live role-players. For this purpose we're using a director component
that assigns roles and coordinates the different autonomous avatars in a way
similar to that used in interactive drama. The conversation management keeps
track of the active conversations and handles the processing of user input. The
understanding of user input works at the surface text with NPCEditor [2] as the
classifier, which uses cross-language information retrieval techniques to learn the
best output for any input from a training set of linked questions and answers.

---

* This work was sponsored by the U.S. Army Research, Development, and Engineering
  Command (RDECOM), and the content does not necessarily reflect the position or
  the policy of the Government, and no official endorsement should be inferred.

H. Högni Vilhjálmsson et al. (Eds.): IVA 2011, LNAI 6895, pp. 453–454, 2011.

2   Checkpoint Exercise

The checkpoint exercise involves a team of two soldier avatars, stationed at a checkpoint outside of a Middle Eastern desert village. In the current setup one of the avatars is controlled by the human trainee, the other – by a virtual human (Grunt Rumble). Potentially the second avatar can also be controlled by a human player. Multiple indigenous villagers (avatar agents) approach the checkpoint to enter the village. The task of the team is to make sure that no illegal or dangerous goods make it into the village. The teammates take turns inspecting the village visitors, examining their possessions and identifications. They can question the visitors about their business in the village. If a visitor's story raises suspicions, the team may decide to seek confirmation by sending one of the members into the village to investigate. The team can either allow the visitor into the village or detain him based on the outcome of the interview and investigation.

We had several goals in the design process. We wanted an activity where the users could learn procedural skills and required some distribution of tasks to make the role of the teammate meaningful. We also wanted an activity that involved many avatars. Finally, we wanted the experience to be fun for the users.

The entire creation of the activity from conceptualization to implementation was done in about two months. We initially planned for nine different story vignettes, each with two possible outcomes (chosen at random) that could be revealed after investigation, but we only implemented two of them due to time constraints. The two stories involved a total of twelve unique avatars.

3   Evaluation and Future Work

For evaluation purposes we had 15 participants go through the exercise. Most expressed that they liked the free-form nature of the experience where they were able to decide who performs what task and to move around the world and ask any questions they wanted. Some also expressed that they liked it because it gave them an idea of what a checkpoint inspection feels like. A few participants commented that understanding problems were more acceptable from villagers than from the teammate. We also entered our application in the Federal Virtual Worlds Challenge where we won second place in the "Patterns of Life" category.

Our current focus is the development of dynamic content and language capabilities within the checkpoint scenario. In particular, we are working to equip our characters with an ability to communicate what they know about their dynamic virtual environment.

References

1. Jan, D., Roque, A., Leuski, A., Morie, J., Traum, D.: A virtual tour guide for virtual worlds. In: Intelligent Virtual Agents, pp. 372–378. Springer, Heidelberg (2009)
2. Leuski, A., Traum, D.R.: Npceditor: A tool for building question-answering characters. In: Proceedings of The Seventh International Conference on Language Resources and Evaluation, LREC' (2010)

Modeling Nonverbal Behavior of a Virtual Counselor during Intimate Self-disclosure

Sin-Hwa Kang[1], Candy Sidner[2], Jonathan Gratch[1], Ron Artstein[1], Lixing Huang[1], and Louis-Philippe Morency[1]

[1] Institute for Creative Technologies, University of Southern California, USA
[2] Dept of Computer Science, Worcester Polytechnic Institute, USA
{kang,gratch,artstein,lhuang,morency}@ict.usc.edu,
sidner@wpi.edu

1 Introduction

Humans often share personal information with others in order to create social connections. Sharing personal information is especially important in counseling interactions [2]. Research studying the relationship between intimate self-disclosure and human behavior critically informs the development of virtual agents that create rapport with human interaction partners. One significant example of this application is using virtual agents as counselors in psychotherapeutic situations. The capability of expressing different intimacy levels is key to a successful virtual counselor to reciprocally induce disclosure in clients. Nonverbal behavior is considered critical for indicating intimacy [1] and is important when designing a social virtual agent such as a counselor. One key research question is how to properly express intimate self-disclosure. In this study, our main goal is to find what types of interviewees' nonverbal behavior is associated with different intimacy levels of verbal self-disclosure. Thus, we investigated humans' nonverbal behavior associated to self-disclosure during interview setting (with intimate topics).

The video sequences analyzed in our paper were recorded during the Kang & Gratch [3] study that showed a virtual agents' behavior to promote users' self-disclosure. The original study design [3] was an interview interaction between two humans communicating via a computer. In the interview interaction, the interviewee was asked to answer ten questions asked by an interviewer that required gradually increasing levels of intimate self-disclosure. We annotated six nonverbal cues: eye gazes, head nods, head shakes, head tilts, pauses (silence) and smiles. The choice of six nonverbal behaviors was motivated by a literature review and a pre-analysis by an expert in nonverbal communication. These six nonverbal behaviors were identified as having the most potential. While nonverbal behavior was annotated for both answers and questions, the analysis presented in this paper focuses on annotations of just the answers. We define two types of features for each annotated nonverbal behavior: *Normalized Duration*: Percentage of the time the nonverbal behavior was active during the answer; *Normalized Count*: Number of time a nonverbal behavior occurs divided by the length of the answer (in seconds). We normalized the duration and count features to remove any confounding effect caused by a big difference of the total lengths between interviewees' answers. The association between interviewees' answer intimacy and their nonverbal behavior was analyzed by categorizing three levels of intimacy: Low Intimacy (N = 92), Medium Intimacy (N = 91), and High

H. Högni Vilhjálmsson et al. (Eds.): IVA 2011, LNAI 6895, pp. 455–457, 2011.
© Springer-Verlag Berlin Heidelberg 2011

Intimacy (N = 177). The Low Intimacy included "no intimacy (0)" and "lower intimacy (1)." The Medium Intimacy included "intermediate intimacy (2)." The High Intimacy included "higher intimacy (3)."

2 Results and Conclusion

Using one way ANOVA, we explored patterns in the six nonverbal behaviors associated with three intimacy levels of self-disclosure. The results show that individual features (e.g., head nods or tilts) and co-occurrence features (e.g., head tilt occurring during a pause) are associated with intimate self-disclosure (see Figure 1 & 2). We found that head tilts and pauses are strong nonverbal cues that convey high intimacy. There was no statistically significant difference for the gaze feature, but, in general, interviewees looked at an interviewer more when they gave less intimate answers. We, however, found that interviewees showed more eye gaze accompanying head nods while interviewees were giving less intimate information about themselves. These outcomes imply that head nods may be a strong cue representing low intimacy in communication. Finally, head shakes and smiles were not affected significantly by intimacy levels of interviewees' self-disclosure.

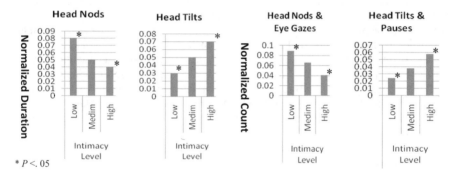

Fig. 1. Mean difference of normalized duration for head nods and head tilts

Fig. 2. Mean difference of normalized count for two co-occurrence patterns

Our study of nonverbal behavior in association with intimate self-disclosure provides future directions for designing virtual agents who talk about themselves in counseling interactions. Based on the outcomes of our current study, we argue that virtual counselors should show head nods and eye gazes for less intimate self-disclosure and head tilts and pauses for highly intimate self-disclosure. We believe that virtual counselors' intimate self-disclosure accompanying with appropriate nonverbal behavior will enable human clients to like their counselors more and create better rapport with them.

Acknowledgement. This study was funded by the National Science Foundation (grants # IIS-0916858 and HCC-0917321) and the U.S. Army Research, Development, and Engineering Command. The content does not necessarily reflect the position or the policy of the Government, and no official endorsement should be inferred.

References

1. Edinger, J., Patterson, M.: Nonverbal Involvement and Social Control. Psychological Bulletin 93(1), 30–56 (1983)
2. Farber, B.: Self-Disclosure in Psychotherapy. Guilford, New York (2006)
3. Kang, S., Gratch, J.: Virtual Humans Elicit Socially Anxious Interactants' Verbal Self-Disclosure. Journal of Computer Animation and Virtual Worlds 21(3-4), 473–482 (2010)

The Effects of Virtual Agent Humor and Gaze Behavior on Human-Virtual Agent Proxemics

Peter Khooshabeh[1], Sudeep Gandhe[1], Cade McCall[2], Jonathan Gratch[1],
Jim Blascovich[3], and David Traum[1]

[1] USC Institute for Creative Technologies, 12015 E. Waterfront, Los Angeles, CA 90094
[2] MPI Cognitive and Brain Sciences
[3] UCSB Department of Psychology, Santa Barbara, CA 93106
{Khooshabeh,Gandhe,Gratch,Traum}@ict.usc.edu,
McCall.Cade@gmail.com, blasocovi@psych.ucsb.edu

Abstract. We study whether a virtual agent that delivers humor through verbal behavior can affect an individual's proxemic behavior towards the agent. Participants interacted with a virtual agent through natural language and, in a separate task, performed an embodied interpersonal interaction task in a virtual environment. The study used minimum distance as the dependent measure. Humor generated by the virtual agent through a text chat did not have any significant effects on the proxemic task. This is likely due to the experimental constraint of only allowing participants to interact with a disembodied agent through a textual chat dialogue.

Keywords: Humor, proxemics, natural dialogue management, persuasion, social influence, culture.

People follow implicit social norms that determine nonverbal behaviors during interpersonal interactions. Proxemics, which refers to physical distancing, is one form of nonverbal behavior. Here we studied whether a funny virtual agent would be approached more closely by individuals in embodied interaction with it. If a virtual agent is humorous, will listeners stay closer during an interpersonal interaction?

Undergraduate psychology students (N=54) participated for course credit. Four participants were excluded from the proxemics analysis due to technical errors during data capture in the walking task. The definition of proxemic distance was how close individuals got to the virtual agent just before passing him to read the number on his back.

The study employed a mixed two factor design with agent humor (humor vs. no humor) as a between-subjects factor and proxemics agent type (idle, gazing, & inanimate object) as a within subjects factor. The inanimate object was used as a control, and the other two types were animated agents. In the idle type, the agent did not look at participants; whereas the gaze agent looked at them.

About 55% of the participants said that the virtual agent was humorous, which suggests that the manipulation was not strong. However, independent coders of the conversation logs all rated the humorous virtual agent as funnier so this serves as a manipulation check [1]. After completing a dialogue with the humorous or

H. Högni Vilhjálmsson et al. (Eds.): IVA 2011, LNAI 6895, pp. 458–459, 2011.
© Springer-Verlag Berlin Heidelberg 2011

non-humorous agent, participants walked toward each of the three different proxemic agents in succession, according to a randomized schedule, in order to read a number displayed on the agents' back. For the inanimate object proxemics task, there were two parallel tables that participants had to walk through in order to read a number on a far table that was perpendicular. This was a control condition that geometrically constrained individuals to walk slowly in the virtual world in order to pass through the two tables. Vizard rendered the environment (WorldViz, LLC) and participants wore an nVisor SX60 head-mounted display that was enabled with motion and inertial tracking (6 DOF Precision Position Tracker and InterSense InertiaCube 2).

The procedure in the proxemic task began with participants told to remain stationary at a fixed start location, at which time they wore a tracking backpack and HMD. Once they put on the equipment, participants were instructed that they would see Bradley, the virtual agent with whom they chatted, or some tables. Their task was to read a number that was on the back of the agent or on a table.

A repeated measures ANOVA on the minimum proxemic distance measure showed a main effect of the *proxemics agent type*, F (2, 90) = 72.6, $p < .001$, $\eta^2 = .62$. There was no significant interaction between agent type and humor conditions. Participants got closer to the inanimate object, a table, ($M = .22$ meters, $SD = .21$) compared to the idle ($M = .91$ m, $SD = .38$) and gaze agent ($M = .96$ m, $SD = .39$).

The results suggest that an ostensibly humorous virtual agent did not have an effect on individuals' proxemic behavior using a chat-based interaction technique. We pursued a purely linguistic medium to manipulate humor and did not use an embodied conversational agent so as not to confound the experimental design with other factors [1]. When participants interacted with the virtual agent, they saw a static image that represented the agent. It is possible that when participants performed the proxemics task they might not have associated that virtual human with the agent with whom they interacted (although they were explicitly told that it was the same agent). In current research, we put participants in more situated and immersive interactive experimental settings. For example, participants will use spoken language to communicate with an embodied conversational agent.

Acknowledgments. Peter Khooshabeh was supported by a postdoctoral fellowship from the Army Research Laboratory.

Reference

1. Khooshabeh, P., McCall, C., Gandhe, S., Gratch, J., Blascovich, J.: Does it matter if a computer jokes. In: Proceedings of the 2011 Annual Conference Extended Abstracts on Human Factors in Computing Systems - CHI EA 2011, Vancouver, BC, Canada, pp. 77–86 (2011)

CLARION as a Cognitive Framework for Intelligent Virtual Agents

Michael F. Lynch, Ron Sun, and Nicholas Wilson

Rensselaer Polytechnic Institute
Troy, New York, USA
{lynchm2,rsun,wilson3}@rpi.edu
http://www.cogsci.rpi.edu/

Abstract. This paper examines the CLARION cognitive architecture as a framework for constructing IVAs. CLARION is a unified, comprehensive theory of the mind based on a hybrid architecture able to represent both implicit and explicit knowledge. We examine several features of CLARION as they relate to the construction of IVAs.

Keywords: CLARION, cognitive architecture, IVA.

1 Introduction to CLARION

This paper introduces CLARION, a full hybrid cognitive architecture (both rule- and neural net-based) developed by Ron Sun and colleagues [4] [5] [6]. CLARION incorporates several capabilities which we suggest may be of value in the construction of intelligent virtual agents (IVAs). CLARION has been used successfully in multi-agent simulations in social psychology [3] and personality [6].

CLARION may be better suited to emergent narrative approaches in which agents are given initial personalities and behavioral suites and are thereafter allowed to interact with other agents (and the player) without supervision from a "drama manager" or similar component. This suggests applicability in interactive narratives where characters and the player engage in ongoing relationships that evolve over time, for example, in soap opera stories and for major NPCs, like mentor and sidekick characters.

We look now at several capabilities of CLARION that may be of interest for IVA applications.

Chunk structure. CLARION is more useful for modeling higher-level cognitive processes than for lower-level processes such as visual perception. Inputs, outputs and internal representations are modeled both as "chunks" (named collections of "dimension/value pairs') and as nodes in neural nets. CLARION generates actions, in the form of chunks, which are abstract command structures handled by downstream lower-level processes. These can represent simultaneous action outputs along several dimensions: verbalizations, tone-of-voice, gesture, posture, gaze, interpersonal distance, and physical actions. These outputs could then be mapped to an intermediate representation like BML [1] [2].

H. Högni Vilhjálmsson et al. (Eds.): IVA 2011, LNAI 6895, pp. 460–461, 2011.
© Springer-Verlag Berlin Heidelberg 2011

The Motivation Subsystem. The Motivation Subsystem handles the agent's drive states (in the lower level) and performs overall goal setting (in the upper level). The role of the MS is to provide the context for driving the rest of the agent's behaviors; it is supervisory in nature and establishes what goals the agent will attempt to pursue moment by moment, and can, in turn, suspend a goal, retarget the current goal, or abandon the current goal.

Personality Modeling. Sun and Wilson [6] have modeled personality as characteristic vector "profiles" of the settings of the vector of drives. In this view, traditional measures of personality are epiphenomena of more fundamentally rooted drive thresholds. For example, extraversion in an agent is seen as it having relatively low thresholds for drives like "need for affiliation," coupled with a rich set of learned behaviors through which it can satisfy those drives.

Episodic Memory. Episodes are stored in CLARION as a series of time-stamped events. From an accumulation of related episodic events, CLARION can extract knowledge (rules) while permitting the gradual decay (forgetting) of the details of the events themselves. The episodic memory subsystem could thus be purposed for so-called "autobiographic" memory, which can aid character believability (Dias, Ho et al. 2007), among other potential story-based uses.

The Meta-Cognitive Subsystem. The Meta-Cognitive Subsystem (MCS) is engaged in on-going monitoring, regulating and coordination of the activities occurring within the other subsystems.

2   Conclusions

This brief introduction (poster session) presented CLARION, a comprehensive hybrid cognitive architecture that may be of use in the construction of IVAs.

References

1. The Behavior Markup Language Project,
   http://wiki.mindmakers.org/projects:BML:main
2. Dias, J., Ho, T., Vogt, N., Beeckman, A., Paiva, A.: André () I Know What I Did Last Summer: Autobiographic Memory in Synthetic Characters. In: Paiva, A.C.R., Prada, R., Picard, R.W. (eds.) ACII 2007. LNCS, vol. 4738, Springer, Heidelberg (2007)
3. Sun, R.: Cognitive Science Meets Multi-Agent Systems: A Prolegomenon. Philosophical Psychology 14(1), 5–28 (2001)
4. Sun, R.: A Detailed Specification of CLARION 5.0. Technical report (2003)
5. Sun, R.: Motivational representations within a computational cognitive architecture. Cognitive Computation 1, 91–103 (2009)
6. Sun, R., Wilson, N.: Motivational processes within the perception-action cycle. In: Cutsuridis, V., Hussain, A., Taylor, J.G. (eds.) Perception-Action Cycle: Models, Architectures, and Hardware, Springer, New York (2010)

Towards a Design Approach for Integrating BDI Agents in Virtual Environments

Joost van Oijen and Frank Dignum

University of Utrecht
PO Box 80.089, 3508 TB Utrecht, the Netherlands
{oijen,dignum}@cs.uu.nl

Keywords: Intelligent Virtual Agents, BDI Agents, Virtual Environments.

1 Introduction

Employing agent technology for virtual character behavior in games and simulations enforces a distributed IVA design where the agent is part of the cognitive layer, situated in a multi-agent system, and its embodiment makes up the physical layer, situated in a game engine. Creating the mind-body connection is not straightforward since one has to bridge the conceptual gap present between agent and game engine technology. In this paper we present key conceptual design issues that have to be tackled within this connection in order to ensure an IVA's ability to express certain aspects of natural behavior in real-time.

2 Design Issues

Figure 1 shows a small scenario which we'll use to illustrate the design issues. It concerns an agent dealing with a fire alarm. Achieving the scenario as described, the agent requires high-level decision making as offered by the BDI-paradigm including plan execution, detecting plan failure, adopting new goals based on new situations and recognizing when to stop pursuing goals when they are no longer relevant. Within this small scenario, a few important design issues can be identified which are described below.

The first issue concerns the **level of abstraction** for the agent's sense and act interface. An agent can reason efficiently in a human-like manner when it is able to sense its environment at a strategic abstraction level based on meaningful concepts (e.g. *door* or *fire*). Though, this is generally not the level at which information is represented in a game engine and one is required to bridge the gap in representational levels. A similar issue holds true for acting. An agent can act efficiently when it can perform more high-level actions conveying a specific meaning or function (e.g. *open door* or *grab fire extinguisher*). This will delegate a certain level of control to the game engine and prevents an agent from micromanaging every detail of behavior realization.

The second issue concerns **real-time perceptual attention** which is an important ability for an agent to behave more naturally. Referring to the example

H. Högni Vilhjálmsson et al. (Eds.): IVA 2011, LNAI 6895, pp. 462–463, 2011.

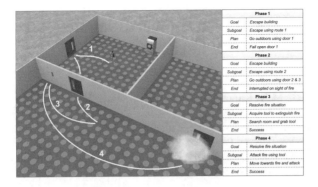

Fig. 1. Example Scenario

scenario, an agent in search for a fire extinguisher would not need to pay attention to all other types of objects in the room. Receiving too much irrelevant sensory information could slow down its deliberation cycle and may lead to slow reaction times. An agent should have the ability to control the flow of sensory information preventing it from reasoning about irrelevant information on one hand but still let it be susceptible for unexpected changes in the environment on the other hand (e.g. *react to a fire alarm*).

The third issue concerns **embodiment control**. First of all, an agent should be able to perform multimodal behavior in a visually fluent manner that seems natural for human behavior. This requires a certain level of anticipation on future actions to perform, allowing seamless transitions from one action to the next, preventing unnatural or 'robotic' movements (e.g. *move to door* followed by *open door*). Further, an agent should be able to interrupt planned or active actions in order to naturally transit to newly dispatched actions (e.g. start searching for a fire extinguisher after noticing the fire). Last, since actions can be designed at a more functional level, the meaning of an action's success or failure becomes less obvious. Being able to perceive a *reason* for failure within the context of an action's execution allows an agent to make intelligent decisions on future actions or plans (e.g. *open door* failed because it is locked).

3 Conclusions

In the scope of a broader effort to develop a structured solution for connecting multi-agent systems to game engines, a middleware framework has been designed for connecting an IVA's cognitive and physical layer focusing on the previously identified design issues. A more technical overview can be found in [1].

Reference

1. van Oijen, J., Vanhée, L., Dignum, F.: CIGA: A Middleware for Intelligent Agents in Virtual Environments. In: Proceedings of the 3rd International Workshop on Agents for Education, Games and Simulations, AAMAS 2011 (2011)

Animating a Conversational Agent
with User Expressivity

M.K. Rajagopal[1], P. Horain[1], and C. Pelachaud[2]

[1] Institut Telecom, Telecom SudParis, 9 rue Charles Fourier, 91011 Évry Cedex, France
[2] CNRS Telecom ParisTech, 37-39 rue Dareau, 75014 Paris, France
{Manoj_kumar.Rajagopal,Patrick.Horain}@Telecom-sudparis.eu,
Catherine.Pelachaud@telecom-paristech.fr

Abstract. Our objective is to animate an embodied conversational agent (ECA) with communicative gestures rendered with the expressivity of a real human user it represents. We describe an approach to estimate a subset of expressivity parameters defined in the literature (namely spatial and temporal extent) from captured motion trajectories. We first validate this estimation against synthesis motion and then show results with real human motion. The estimated expressivity is then sent to the animation engine of an ECA that becomes a personalized autonomous representative of that user.

1 Introduction

In day-to-day life, people express gestures with their own natural variations. These variations are consistent with individuals across gesture, so we call them "expressivity". We considered the expressivity parameters defined by Hartmann et al. [1] that are based on the wrist movement in 3D space, irrespective of joint angles (shoulder, elbow, etc.) information. In this work, we estimate spatial extent (SPC) and temporal extent (TMP) of the Hartmann's et al. [1] expressivity parameters from captured user motion and then animate an ECA to render the captured expressivity.

2 Estimating Expressivity Parameters and Its Validation

Generally a gesture is formed from a set of key poses of wrist positions p having SPC and TMP as 0.0 called "basic gesture". From the wrist positions of human communicative gestures, we compute the 3D distance between the wrists and the sacroiliac vertebra. This distance should be mapped to SPC from -1 to +1. The wrist position p' of captured communicative gestures of a person is varied by a factor of SPC from basic gesture wrist positions p. (i.e.) $p' = [SPC] \, p$. For zero SPC value, the wrist position p' is same as p. When value of p is known, the SPC is determined by back substituting p in the above equation.

TMP is measured using wrist speed. Wrist speed in whole motion is determined from the instant speed of the wrist among each poses. Distance covered between consecutive poses defines instant speed of the motion. From the example trajectories

H. Högni Vilhjálmsson et al. (Eds.): IVA 2011, LNAI 6895, pp. 464–465, 2011.
© Springer-Verlag Berlin Heidelberg 2011

we considered, instant speed among each pose is sorted with descending order and the range of 5 to 5.5% of upper quantile gives 99% correlation with TMP values. The 99% correlated upper quantile value is mapped to TMP ranging from -1.0 to +1.0 through linear regressions.

We tested the estimated method against synthesized motion with known SPC and TMP values for validating of our process. The absolute mean error of estimated SPC with respect to ground truth SPC is 0.13. Similarly absolute mean error for estimated TMP with respect to actual TMP value is 0.15. This error value shows our method is working well for estimating expressivity parameters.

3 Experiments

We used motion data captured by computer vision from two video lectures (hereafter named V1 and V2) using software developed by Gómez Jáuregui et al., [2] and it outputs the upper body joint angles. 3D wrist positions are obtained from upper body joint angles using forward kinematics [3]. Experiment yields SPC as 0.8 for V1 and 0.6 for V2 and TMP as -1.0 for V1 and -0.7 for V2. These estimated values are given as input to the Greta [4] and the conversational agent is animated.

4 Conclusion

By estimating the SPC and TMP from motion by a real user, we can then animate the conversational agent to render the expressivity captured from a real user. This animation can be played virtually when the user is not available to control his avatar. Rendering the expressivity parameters allows generating personalized animations, so that the viewer can have the feeling of interacting with an expressive virtual human.

References

1. Hartmann, B., Mancini, M., Pelachaud, C.: Implementing Expressive Gesture Synthesis for Embodied Conversational Agents. In: Gibet, S., Courty, N., Kamp, J.-F. (eds.) GW 2005. LNCS (LNAI), vol. 3881, pp. 188–199. Springer, Heidelberg (2006)
2. Gómez Jáuregui, D., Horain, P., Rajagopal, M., Karri, S.: Real-Time Particle Filtering with Heuristics for 3D Motion Capture by Monocular Vision. In: Multimedia Signal Processing, Saint-Malo, France, pp. 139–144 (2010)
3. Craig, J.: Forward Kinematics. In: Introduction to Robotics: Mechanics and Control, 3rd edn. Prentice-Hall, Englewood Cliffs (1986)
4. Pelachaud, C.: GRETA,
   http://perso.telecom-paristech.fr/~pelachau/Greta/

Expressing Emotions on Robotic Companions with Limited Facial Expression Capabilities

Tiago Ribeiro[1], Iolanda Leite[1], Jan Kedziersski[2], Adam Oleksy[2], and Ana Paiva[1]

[1] INESC-ID, Instituto Superior Técnico, Universidade Técnica de Lisboa, Portugal
[2] Institute of Computer Engineering, Control and Robotics
Wrocaw University of Technology, Wroclaw, Poland
{tiago.ribeiro,iolanda.leite,ana.paiva}@gaips.inesc-id.pt,
{adam.oleksy,robert.muszynski}@pwr.wroc.pl

Abstract. Facing the challenge of accurately expressing emotions with robots and characters with limited expressive capabilities, we developed an abstraction model for generating emotional expressions based on the atomic features that enable human beings to recognize emotions in other humans' faces. The model is also augmented by animation theory from movies and puppetry. A small evaluation of the expressions showed that some expressions were well recognized, in particular *Anger* and *Sadness*.

Keywords: Non-Verbal Communication, Expressive Behavior, Animation, Robotic Companion, Facial Expression.

1 Motivation

Non-verbal expression of emotions serves very important functions in human social relationships, for example, to convey information about ourselves, to regulate social interactions (e.g. turn-taking and proximity) and express intimacy and emotional closeness [1], and thus is also a very important mechanism in human-agent interaction[3]. In this paper, we present an approach to the problem of expressing emotions in robotic companions with limited facial expression capabilities, in a way that they are correctly perceived by users. Our approach is based on both FACS [2] theory and cartoon animation principles. The work of Ekman and Friesen [2] describes, in terms of action units of the face, how humans universally express the six basic emotions: surprise, disgust, fear, anger, happiness and sadness, along with psychological and physical descriptions of their reflection in the human being. In robotic embodiments the expression of emotions is limited because, in most platforms, there is a lack of features that are present in the human face. Thus, we took inspiration from some of the twelve principles of animation [4]: *exaggeration, slow in/out, arcs* and *timing*, in order to better transmit emotions. We also made use of the *Tex Avery expression* [5], in which eyes pop out of a character's face, for use in a robot that supports it.

H. Högni Vilhjálmsson et al. (Eds.): IVA 2011, LNAI 6895, pp. 466–467, 2011.

2   Expressing Emotions in Robotic Companions through Facial Animation

We developed a model of expressions based on a simplification of FACS coding system[2]. Abstract definitions of expressions were created from FACS, by analysing which are the necessary features in facial expression that humans use to understand emotions. We then map each expressive feature of the robot (e.g., eyebrows) to a feature from our model, thus mapping the abstract definitions into concrete expressions for each specific robot. Cartoon practices are finally introduced to refine the model with regard to each robot's expressive capabilities.

3   Evaluation and Discussion

We implemented our model on the EMYS robot and performed a preliminary evaluation with six children, using soft and strong intensities for each of the six emotions, illustrated in Figure 1. Our results showed that Anger and Sadness were easily recognized, with Disgust being confused with Anger, and the other three confused all between them. These results were used to refine the expressions for a large-scale online evaluation. We also plan on implementing and evaluating the same model on the iCat[1] robot, in order to validate our abstraction.

Fig. 1. The six basic emotions expressed on EMYS, using our model

Acknowledgments. This work was supported by the EU FP7 ICT-215554 project LIREC (LIving with Robots and intEractive Companions).

References

1. Patterson, M.: Functions of non-verbal behaviour in social interaction. In: Handbook of Language and Social Psychology, pp. 101–120 (1990)
2. Ekman, P., Friesen, W.V.: Unmasking the face: A guide to recognizing emotions from facial clues. Prentice-Hall, Englewood Cliffs (1975) ISBN: 1-88353-636-7
3. Breazeal, C.: Role of expressive behaviour for robots that learn from people. Philos. Trans. of the Royal Society of London. Series B, Biological Sciences (2009)
4. Thomas, F., Johnston, O.: Disney Animation: The Illusion of Life. Abbeville Press, New York (1981) ISBN: 0-78686-070-7
5. Canemaker, J.: Tex Avery: The MGM Years, 1942-1955. Turner Press, Atlanta (1996) ISBN: 1-57036-291-2

---

[1] http://www.hitech-projects.com/icat/

A BML Based Embodied Conversational Agent for a Personality Detection Program

Guillermo Solano Méndez and Dennis Reidsma

Human Media Interaction, University of Twente
Drienerlolaan 5,7522 NB Enschede, The Netherlands
pepitogrillo37@gmail.com

Keywords: BML realizer, gaze, dialogue, Elckerlyc, Psychometer.

1 Introduction

This paper presents a project in which an Embodied Conversational Agent (ECA) attemtps to detect the personality of the user by asking him (or her) a series of questions. The project uses the Elckerlyc platform, a Behavior Markup Language (BML) compliant behavior realizer for ECAs [1]. BML allows the design and implementation of verbal and nonverbal behaviors in an abstract way, without reference to the ECA model in question. This means the designer only needs to decide "what" kind of behaviors should be performed by the ECA and to specify "when" these behaviors should be performed, without needing to know how the realization engine actually displays these behaviors on the ECA's embodiment.

The aim of this research was to extend the Psychometer [2], a text based dialogue system for personality detection, with a virtual embodiment that uses gaze behavior and facial expressions. The Psychometer asks the user questions, adapted from an existing questionnaire, until it has enough answers to classify the user's personality according to the well-known Big Five theory of personality traits.

2 System

The system presented here captures the output of the Psychometer program and connects it to the ECA controlled by Elckerlyc. To create appropriate gazing behavior we adapted an existing gazing algorithm [3] to the different conversational states of the Psychometer ("greeting", "asking", "listening", "farewell" and "user invalid input"). For each state, the appropriate sequence of behaviors is triggered. The gazing algorithm makes a strong distinction between long and short utterances, based on the idea that a speaker who starts a longer utterance tends to look away in order to concentrate, avoiding distraction and sending to the listener the message that he does not want to be interrupted. In addition, at the end of a turn and/or the end of a phrase, speakers tend to seek eye contact with the listener (looking up) to monitor their reaction.

More than fifty gazing behaviors and twenty-three facial expressions (and combinations of them) have been included in a repository, along with some

H. Högni Vilhjálmsson et al. (Eds.): IVA 2011, LNAI 6895, pp. 468–469, 2011.
© Springer-Verlag Berlin Heidelberg 2011

pseudo-random methods to introduce variety during the generation of behaviors. The gaze behaviors and facial expressions are selected as function of the dialogue state. For example, when the user enters an invalid input, the reaction of the ECA ranges from surprise for getting an unexpected answer to anger if the user repeatedly enters incorrect input.

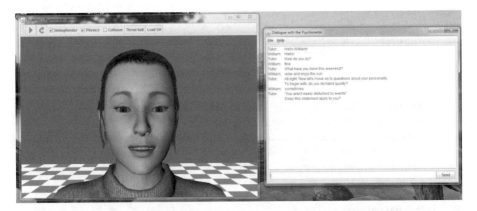

Fig. 1. Example of the ECA performing a behavior (left) during the dialogue

3 Evaluation

The system was evaluated by ten students using AttrakDiff (www.attrakdiff.de), complemented with a more focused questionnaire and open discussion. In general, the participants found the ECA natural and interesting, giving the system an average rating of 4.1 out of 5. The AttrakDiff evaluation classified the project as very attractive. Critical comments by the participants mostly involved dialogue aspects and not so much the nonverbal behavior of the ECA. A point of improvement mentioned by several participants was the visual integration of the ECA with the dialogue system (currently shown in separate windows).

Acknowledgements. The work presented here was supported by the Elckerlyc project. Many thanks go to the project members who helped me so much!

References

1. van Welbergen, H., Reidsma, D., Ruttkay, Z.M., Zwiers, J.: Elckerlyc - A BML Realizer for continuous, multimodal interaction with a Virtual Human. Journal on Multimodal User Interfaces 3(4), 271–284 (2010)
2. Bodewitz, M.: Detecting the Student Personality. MSc Thesis, Faculty of Computer Science, University of Twente (2004)
3. Heylen, D., van Es, I., Nijholt, A., van Dijk, B.: Controlling the Gaze of Conversational Agents. In: van Kuppevelt, et al. (eds.) Natural, Intelligent and Effective Interaction in Multimodal Dialogue Systems, pp. 245–262. Kluwer, Dordrecht (2005)

Flipper: An Information State Component for Spoken Dialogue Systems

Mark ter Maat and Dirk Heylen

Human Media Interaction, University of Twente
PO Box 217, 7500 AE Enschede, The Netherlands
{maatm,heylen}@ewi.utwente.nl

Abstract. This paper introduces Flipper, an specification language and interpreter for Information State Update rules that can be used for developing spoken dialogue systems and embodied conversational agents. The system uses XML-templates to modify the information state and to select behaviours to perform.

1   Introduction

One of the main challenges in creating multi-model dialogue systems is how to respond on the perceived input. Several models have been proposed to make such decisions. For example, one could use a Finite State Machine (e.g. in the agent MACK [1]), or one could use statistical approaches to find the best match (e.g. in the agent Hassan [2]). Another approach presented in the literature is the Information State approach [3]. In this approach, all dialogue information is stored in one structured data-structure called the `Information State` (IS), and `update rules` are used to modify this information and to select behaviour to perform.

This paper introduces Flipper, an implementation of an Information State based template system for dialogue systems. With this system, it is possible to create an information state and templates — written in XML — that either modify the values in the IS or select a certain behaviour to perform.

2   Flipper

Flipper[1] is an Information State update system based on XML-tem-plates, and was developed for the SEMAINE project[2]. The rationale behind the rule system of Flipper is to have a flexible set of easily definable templates which specify exactly what kind of behaviour to perform under which circumstances. Each template has a set of preconditions that all need to be true to fire that template. These preconditions check certain conditions in the IS, usually by comparing

---

[1] http://sourceforge.net/projects/hmiflipper/
[2] http://www.semaine-project.eu

H. Högni Vilhjálmsson et al. (Eds.): IVA 2011, LNAI 6895, pp. 470–472, 2011.

values ($=$, $<$, $>$, etc), optionally with several simple arithmetic operations. Data in the IS can be structured by putting it in lists or records.

The second part of the templates contains the effects of the template. These can be modifications to the IS (remove, add or change variables), custom Java-functions, or certain behaviour to perform with optional parameters.

Here is an example template:

```
<template id="RespondToSmile1" name="A response to a smile">
 <preconditions>
  <compare value1="$face.nrOfSmiles" comparator="greater_than" value2="1" />
  <compare value1="$speakingIntention" value2="want_turn" />
 </preconditions>
 <effects>
  <update name="$nrResponses" value="$Agent.totalResponses + 1" />
  <update name="$responses._addlast" value="#Response129" />
 </effects>
 <behaviour class="ResponsePerformer" quality="0.5" />
  <argument name="response_id" value="#Response129" />
 </behaviour>
</template>
```

This template checks if there was a smile and if the agent wants the turn. If so, then the total number of the agent's responses is incremented by one, and the agent's response (#129) is put in a list of performed responses and is send to the ResponsePerformer (a custom Java class that has to be written for each project, since Flipper does not know how to perform a certain behaviour).

The result of the complete checking procedure is a list of templates that have all their preconditions met. In further processing, the first step is to execute all templates that do not result in actual behaviour but only update the IS. After that, a selection algorithm determines which of the templates that do result in actual behaviour will be executed, based on a quality-value that is specified in the template itself. The selected behaviour is then performed.

When incorporating Flipper into a new project, some things have to be done. First of all, an Information State has to be created, which should be filled with data from the input components. Secondly, the templates have to be written, which process this data, make interpretations, and decide how to behave. Finally, the component has to be written that forwards the data in the behaviour element in the templates to the output component of the system.

3   Conclusion

We described Flipper, an Information state based system for dialogue systems that uses XML-templates to modify the information state and select behaviour to perform. We have briefly explained how it works and shown a small example of a template. So far, Flipper has been used in several projects, for example in Semaine and in a demonstration system of the Sera project[3].

---

[3] http://project-sera.eu/

References

1. Cassell, J., Stocky, T., Bickmore, T., Gao, Y., Nakano, Y., Ryokai, K., Vaucelle, C., Vilhjálmsson, H.: MACK: Media lab Autonomous Conversational Kiosk. In: Proceedings of Imagina 2002 (2002)
2. Traum, D., Roque, A., Leuski, A., Georgiou, P., Gerten, J., Martinovski, B., Narayanan, S., Robinson, S., Vaswani, A.: Hassan: A Virtual Human for Tactical Questioning. In: 8th SIGdial Workshop on Discourse and Dialogue, pp. 71–74 (2007)
3. Traum, D.R., Bos, J., Cooper, R., Larsson, S., Lewin, I., Matheson, C., Poesio, M.: A model of dialogue moves and information state revision. Tech. rep., Deliverable D2.1, Trindi-project (1999)

Dynamic Planning for Agents in Games Using Social Norms and Emotions

Palli R. Thrainsson, Arnkell Logi Petursson, and Hannes Högni Vilhjálmsson

Center for Analysis and Design of Intelligent Agents, School of Computer Science,
Reykjavik University, Menntavegur 1, IS-101 Reykjavik, Iceland

Abstract. In realistic social game environments, agents need to exhibit
a certain level of social awareness to maintain the illusion of life and to
provide important interaction cues. Previously we have reported on an
engine that imbues game agents with socially reactive behavior based
on a continuous steering framework and a model of human territoriality.
However, some social action requires deliberation and planning. In this
paper we describe an addition to our engine that provides dynamic social
planning on top of the reactive layer. We propose a novel approach that
considers both the emotional and social impact of events and actions on
the agent. An implementation demonstrates the approach.

This work fits within a larger research effort to make game characters more visually convincing in social game environments. A significant piece of the puzzle
was to make the agents aware of their social surroundings and have them continuously react according to fundamental rules of human territoriality. This is
something we have built into a social engine middleware for games [1]. However,
a purely reactive framework is not capable of producing complex social action
sequences that realize higher level social goals. Even seemingly simple goals such
as ordering a drink would require the planning of a sequence of social steps such
as establishing contact with a bartender and politely thanking for the drink at
the end (Fig. 1). Not only is planning required, but it also needs to be dynamic
because the social environment is constantly changing. What would happen if a
friend greeted you in the middle of your drink order? To address this, we have
added a BDI system, called JADEX [2] that has been augmented with a dynamic
planner[3], to the social engine.

Social planning occurs in the context of a particular social environment where
certain behavior is expected, which we call social norms. But the agent performing the planning also brings to it a personal emotional context, which may affect
some of its choices. In fact, emotion can take quite a central role in social planning, as in FearNot! [4] and the Mission Rehearsal Exercise (MRE) [5]. MRE
uses the Emotion and Adaptation (EMA) [6] computational model based on
Appraisal Theory by Lazarus [7]. EMA continuously appraises how the dynamic
environment affects the agent resulting in emotional and coping responses.

H. Högni Vilhjálmsson et al. (Eds.): IVA 2011, LNAI 6895, pp. 473–474, 2011.
© Springer-Verlag Berlin Heidelberg 2011

Inspired in particular by the EMA model, but wanting to increase the influence of social norms on action selection, we coupled the planner with a more general appraisal module that appraises events and possible responses both in terms of emotional and social impact on the agent. These are treated as two separate dimensions, along which action choices are ordered. The social impact essentially represents adherence to social norms. A final choice may be influcened by a personality trait that for example favours social order over emotionality. If an emotion becomes strong enough, a negative social consequence may get overlooked. This approach creates a cycle where events come from the environment, the appraisal module suggests and rates responses and the planner decides what actions should be taken using the provided appraisal.

Fig. 1. Drink being ordered only after social contact is initiated

As a concrete example, consider agent A, with the goal of ordering a drink. It comes up with a socially accepted plan and starts executing it. On the way to the bar, agent B greets it. A may choose to alter its plans to meet a social obligation to greet B back, while still pursuing the drink. But A may appraise the situation differently if it doesn't like B, in which case A's emotions may cause it to ignore B. That might come at a high social cost though.

References

1. Pedica, C., Vilhjálmsson, H.H.: Spontaneous avatar behavior for human territoriality. In: Ruttkay, Z., Kipp, M., Nijholt, A., Vilhjálmsson, H.H. (eds.) IVA 2009. LNCS, vol. 5773, pp. 344–357. Springer, Heidelberg (2009)
2. Pokahr, A., Braubach, L., Lamersdorf, W.: Jadex: A BDI reasoning engine. In: Weiss, G., et al. (eds.), vol. 15, pp. 149–174. Springer, US (2005b)
3. Walczak, A., Braubach, L., Pokahr, A., Lamersdorf, W.: Augmenting BDI agents with deliberative planning techniques. In: Bordini, R.H., Dastani, M.M., Dix, J., El Fallah Seghrouchni, A. (eds.) PROMAS 2006. LNCS (LNAI), vol. 4411, pp. 113–127. Springer, Heidelberg (2007)
4. Aylett, R., Dias, J.: Paiva, Ana.: An Affectively Driven Planner for Synthetic Characters. In: Long, D., Smith, S.F., Borrajo, D., McCluskey, L. (eds.) ICAPS 2006, pp. 2–10. AAAI Press, Menlo Park (2006)
5. Hill, R.W., Gratch, J., Marsella, S., Rickel, J., Swartout, W., Traum, D.: Virtual humans in the mission rehearsal exercise system. KI Special Issue on Embodied Conversational Agents 03(4), 5–10 (2003)
6. Marsella, S.C., Gratch, J.: EMA: A process model of appraisal dynamics. Cognitive Systems Research 10(1), 70–90 (2009) (Modeling the Cognitive Antecedents and Consequences of Emotion)
7. Lazarus, R.S.: Emotion and adaptation. Oxford, New York (1991)

Are Intelligent Pedagogical Agents Effective in Fostering Students' Note-Taking While Learning with a Multi-agent Adaptive Hypermedia Environment?

Gregory Trevors, Melissa Duffy, and Roger Azevedo

Laboratory for the Study of Metacognition and Advanced Learning Technologies,
McGill Univeristy, Montreal, Canada

Abstract. The effectiveness of intelligent virtual pedagogical agents (IVAs) at fostering adaptive note-taking strategies in a hypermedia learning environment was examined. Sixty college students participated in experimental learning sessions with four IVAs. Results revealed the presence of IVAs significantly decreased measurements of quantity and quality of notes. Recommendations are discussed for improving agent design in supporting adaptive note-taking behaviours.

Keywords: Pedagogical Agents, Note-taking, Product and Process Data.

1 Experiment and System Design

Intelligent virtual agents (IVAs) have been touted as the panacea in facilitating students' learning with various computer-based learning environments [1]. There are, however, many unresolved questions related to their effectiveness in assisting students to regulate strategies associated with learning complex topics. The current study investigated the effects of IVAs designed to promote learning skills on various dimensions of students' note-taking.

A sample of 60 students from a large, public research university completed a pretest on the human circulatory system and then engaged in the two-hour learning session within MetaTutor, a multi-agent adaptive hypermedia learning environment, which provides 41 pages of text and static diagrams on the human circulatory system. Participants were randomly assigned to one of two agent conditions. In the Agent condition, learners received prompts from pedagogical agents to engage in a specific self-regulated learning strategy and feedback on its use, which were tailored to learners' individual interactions with the system. In the No Agent condition, learners received neither prompts nor feedback and thus acted as a control.

Three categories of adaptive rules trigger agent action: user initiated actions, timed-triggered, and user-system interactions. An example of the latter, after navigating too quickly away from a page with relevant content (e.g. < 7 seconds) an agent will prompt users to evaluate their own understanding of the current content and then administer a short quiz. Users receive feedback based on the accuracy of their subjective self-evaluations of comprehension vis-à-vis their objective quiz results (e.g. agent speaks: "It seems you might not know this content as well as you expected").

H. Högni Vilhjálmsson et al. (Eds.): IVA 2011, LNAI 6895, pp. 475–476, 2011.

Note-taking is typically user initiated, but an agent will prompt students to take notes as one of several learning strategies randomly selected based on a timed rule. Beyond prompting, there are no instructional supports or feedback on note-taking. Importantly, other timed rules that support learning skills will take precedence over learner actions, including note-taking; the screen will fade, leaving only the rule-relevant interface operational. Thus, the effectiveness of agents' prompting for note-taking and possible benefit or interference of other agent actions was examined in relation to qualities of students' notes in order to ascertain agent design guidelines.

Frequency and duration of note-taking episodes were recorded as quantitative measures. Notes were parsed using naturalistic segments (e.g. the use of periods) as another quantitative unit of analysis, and it was determined if a segment of notes qualitatively represented either *reproduction* (i.e. verbatim copying or paraphrasing the content) or *elaboration*, which involved the addition of new semantic information (i.e. using text-based or prior knowledge-based inferencing).

2   Results and Conclusions

To test the effects of IVAs on note-taking behaviours, a MANCOVA was conducted between the two experimental conditions, controlling for the effects of prior knowledge, on five dependent variables of note-taking: frequency, duration, number of unique segments (quantities), and instances of content reproduction and elaboration (qualities). A significant multivariate difference was obtained, $F(4, 46) = 3.04$, $p < .05$, $\eta^2 = .21$. Univariate analyses showed significant differences between duration, number of segments, and instances of content reproduction (p's $< .05$), but no significant difference for frequency of note-taking ($p > .1$). For instances of content elaboration there was a marginally significant difference, $F(1, 49) = 3.47$, $p = .07$, $\eta^2 = .07$. These results demonstrate that the presence of agents decreased the duration, number of segments, and content reproduction in notes while students still initiated an equivalent number of note-taking episodes. Also, the reductive effect of agents on instances of content elaboration was not as large as on content reproduction ($\eta^2 = .07$ vs. .11, respectively), suggesting perhaps that elaborative note-taking was slightly more robust. However, this interpretation remains speculative pending further study. Overall, IVAs were not found to foster adaptive note-taking strategies.

Findings from this research will help to guide instructional design of IVAs. This includes having agents model the appropriate sophisticated cognitive strategies and detect in real-time qualities of learners' note-taking content, thus equipping computer-based learning environments with additional scaffolding for skilled learning.

Reference

1. Azevedo, R., Behnagh, R., Duffy, M., Harley, J., Trevors, G.: Metacognition and self-regulated learning with advanced learning technologies. In: Jonassen, D., Land, S. (eds.) Theoretical Foundations of Student-Centered Learning Environments, 2nd edn., Erlbaum, Mahwah, NJ (in press)

Toward a Conversational Virtual Instructor of Ballroom Dance

Masaki Uejou, Hung-Hsuan Huang, Jooho Lee, and Kyoji Kawagoe

College of Information Science & Engineering, Ritsumeikan University, Japan
huang@fc.ritsumei.ac.jp

In learning/training activity of physical tasks such as sport, aerobic exercise, rehabilitation, or dance, it usually involves an instructor and one or more learners. Since it is hard for the instructor to propagate his(her) knowledge to the learners merely by oral instructions, the instructor usually has to demonstrate exemplary movements, figures out the movements which are error-prone to the learner. The learner observes the instructor's movements, mimics them. In the whole activity, each of them observes the interaction partner's body movements, talks to the partner and may intercept the partner's action.

The learning activity of physical tasks is supposed to be more effective if it is more interactive, mutual-adaptive, and more personalized. An exclusively personal instructor who is aways available is therefore desirable for effective training; however, this is often impractical due to financial, temporal, or location constrains. Embodied conversational agents are thus suitable candidates for such tasks. The agents (virtual instructor) can be available at anytime and everywhere. More than that, they never feel tired due to long-time service or loose patience on awkward learners. The users (learner) can practice the tasks for unlimited times at their favorite place whenever. They also do not need to mind requesting the instructor to repeat the exemplary movements and never feel embarrassed to practice when they are still unskillful. In order to enable highly interactive instruction dialogs, it requires the measurement of the similarity of user's movement and the control of agent's multi-modal communicative actions in fine granularity both temporally and spatially. This paper presents an ongoing project aiming in realizing such a virtual instructor for ballroom dance training.

Using virtual characters for instruction task is not a brand new idea. Chua et al. [2] proposed a training system of Tai Chi, the learner wears a HMD where one or more instructors are projected to. The authors tried five kinds of instructor/learner layouts, e.g. one instructor standing in front of the learner, four instructors surrounding the learner, etc. The learner's movements are motion captured and compared to template movements based on Euclidean distance. Nakamura et al. proposed [3] a dance training system using demonstration video instead of an agent projected on a screen . The authors compared learners' performance between a fixed screen and a moving screen synchronized to the dance movements. Chan et. al. [1] evaluated the effects of three different ways of feedback to the learner's performance in a dance training system: an avatar of highlighted limbs where the learner did badly, a slow motion replay, and numeric scores. However, these present systems merely use CG characters for demonstrating exemplar motions but have no thought for utilizing the character as a "virtual instructor" teaching the learner like how a human instructor does. This project then focuses on the verbal and nonverbal information exchanges between the instructor and the learner in finer granularity.

H. Högni Vilhjálmsson et al. (Eds.): IVA 2011, LNAI 6895, pp. 477–478, 2011.

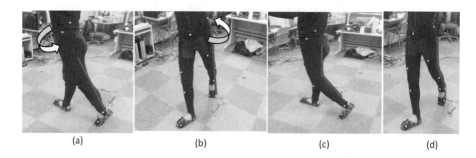

(a)   (b)   (c)   (d)

Fig. 1. (a)(b): a good example of poise. the dancer fully extends his hip and his two legs and keeps his back straight at good position. (c)(d): a bad example of poise where the dancer's could not extend his legs sufficiently.

Ballroom dance is becoming a world-wide competitive sport. There are two styles of Ballroom dance, "international standard" and "Latin American. " The moving of feet servers as an important role in Ballroom dance. In Latin American style, the way of walking is scrubbing tiptoe or foot every time. When the dancer walks in that way, we say that he is making a "poise" (Fig. 1). The training of poise is the only task of current prototype. The learner stands in front of a large screen where a virtual instructor demonstrating motion-captured animation is projected.

The project is still in its very early stage. Automatic real-time segmentation on the motion of both the instructor and the learner is being developed based on detecting local minimums of speed and the extension of the movements. These segments will be treated as the smallest unit for replaying exemplar movements and the evaluation on the learner's movements. The similarity evaluating method is based on AMSS[4]. Also, an human-human experiment for collecting instructive dialog corpus is being planned at the same time. The multi-modal information-exchange between the human instructor and learner will be detailedly analyzed and implemented into the dialogue management mechanism of the agent.

References

1. Chan, J.C., Leung, H., Tang, J.K., Komura, T.: A virtual reality dance training system using motion capture technology. IEEE Transactions on Learning Technologies PP(99) (2010)
2. Chua, P.T., Crivella, R., Daly, B., Hu, N., Schaaf, R., Ventura, D., Camill, T., Hodgins, J., Pausch, R.: Trainning for physical tasks in virtual environments: Tai chi. In: IEEE Virtual Reality, VR 2003 (2003)
3. Nakamura, A., Tabata, S., Ueda, T., Kiyofuji, S., Kuno, Y.: Dance training system with active vibro-devices and a mobile image display. In: IEEE/RSJ International Conference on Intelligent Robots and Systems, IROS 2005 (2005)
4. Nakamura, T., Makio, K., Uehara, K.: Discovering and translating skills from motion data. Tech. Rep. CS24-2006-3, Department of Computer and Systems Engineering, Kobe University, Japan (2006)

Author Index

Adam, Carole   316
Aggarwal, Priti   426, 428
Al Moubayed, Samer   439
Anastassakis, George   431
André, Elisabeth   1, 437
Artstein, Ron   426, 455
Aylett, Ruth   282
Azevedo, Roger   449, 475

Baba, Naoya   255
Barange, Mukesh   93
Bee, Nikolaus   437
Beskow, Jonas   439
Bickmore, Timothy   55, 106
Bída, Michal   419
Blanco, Gabriel   148
Blascovich, Jim   458
Bouchet, François   449
Boukricha, Hana   350
Bowmani, Robeson   398
Bowring, Emma   384
Bransky, Karla   433
Brinkman, Willem-Paul   435
Brisson, António   35
Broekens, Joost   435
Brom, Cyril   419
Brovman, Anat   441
Buschmeier, Hendrik   169

Carstensdottir, Elin   48
Chance, Eric   453
Chevaillier, Pierre   93
Chiu, Chung-Cheng   127
Chuah, Teong Leong   338
Coheur, Luísa   309
Core, Mark   100
Cuba, Pedro   282

Damian, Ionut   437
de Kok, Iwan   248
DeLeon, Christopher   42
De Loor, Pierre   93
DeVault, David   453
Dignum, Frank   462

Dohogne, Peter   42
Duffy, Melissa   475

Edlund, Jens   439
Endrass, Birgit   1, 437

Feeley, Kevin   426
Feng, Wei-Wen   269
Fox Tree, Jean E.   398
Friedman, Doron   28, 441
Fu, Jingqiao   269

Gandhe, Sudeep   458
Gibert, Guillaume   331, 443, 445
Gratch, Jonathan   68, 80, 455, 458
Guiraud, Nadine   316
Gulz, Agneta   447
Gudmundsdottir, Kristin   48

Haake, Magnus   447
Harbers, Maaike   435
Harley, Jason   449
Hasler, Beatrice   441
Hayashi, Yugo   451
Heckel, Frederick W.P.   202, 370
Heloir, Alexis   113
Heylen, Dirk   228, 248, 470
Hoffmann, Laura   183
Horain, P.   464
Huang, Hung-Hsuan   255, 451, 477
Huang, Lixing   68, 455
Huang, Yazhou   155

Ishii, Ryo   262

Jan, Dusan   100, 453
Jonker, Catholijn   435

Kallmann, Marcelo   155
Kang, Sin-Hwa   80, 455
Kawagoe, Kyoji   477
Kedzierssski, Jan   466
Khooshabeh, Peter   458
Kim, Julia   426
Kipp, Michael   113

Klatt, Jennifer   183, 209
Klüwer, Tina   14
Kopp, Stefan   169, 195
Krämer, Nicole C.   80, 183, 209
Kriegel, Michael   282
Kryssanov, Victor V.   451
Kulms, Philipp   80

Lee, Jina   216, 240
Lee, Jooho   477
Lehtonen, Klaus   162
Leite, Iolanda   466
Leung, Yvonne   331
Leuski, Anton   426, 453
Lipi, Afia Akhter   1
Longin, Dominique   316
Lorini, Emiliano   316
Louis, Vincent   93
Lynch, Michael F.   460

Magerko, Brian   35, 42
Maisel, Éric   93
Marsella, Stacy   127, 209, 216, 240, 384
Martins, Bruno   309
Matlock, Teenie   155
Matthews, Justin L.   155
McCall, Cade   458
McGee, Kevin   338
Mendes, Ana Cristina   309
Méndez, Guillermo Solano   468
Merritt, Tim   338
Meyer, John-Jules   435
Miwa, Kazuhisa   451
Morbini, Fabrizio   426
Moreira, Catarina   309
Morency, Louis-Philippe   68, 455
Morie, Jacki   453

Nakano, Yukiko I.   1, 255, 262
Neff, Michael   398
Nguyen, Nhung   350
Nguyen, Quan   113
Niewiadomski, Radosław   363

Obaid, Mohammad   363
Ogawa, Hitoshi   451
Oleksy, Adam   466
Olney, Andrew M.   141
Ong, Christopher   338
Ooko, Ryota   262

Paiva, Ana   35, 148, 282, 466
Panayiotopoulos, Themis   431
Pelachaud, Catherine   316, 363, 464
Person, Natalie   141
Pesty, Sylvie   316
Petursson, Arnkell Logi   473
Pfeifer, Laura   55
Piwek, Paul   377
Popelová, Markéta   419
Poppe, Ronald   228
Prendinger, Helmut   377
Pugliese, Roberto   162

Querrec, Ronan   93

Rajagopal, M.K.   464
Rajpurohit, Dinesh   453
Rehm, Matthias   1
Reidsma, Dennis   269, 296, 324, 468
Ribeiro, Tiago   466
Richards, Debbie   433
Riviere, Jeremy   316
Roque, Antonio   100

Schulman, Daniel   55, 106
Shapiro, Ari   269
Sidner, Candy   455
Silvervarg, Annika   447
Snaider, Javier   141
Soler, Julien   93
Stevens, Catherine J.   331, 445
Stoyanchev, Svetlana   377
Sun, Ron   460

Tambe, Milind   384
Tärning, Betty   447
ter Maat, Mark   470
Thiebaux, Marcus   269
Thrainsson, Palli R.   473
Toothman, Nicholas   398
Traum, David   100, 426, 428, 453, 458
Trevors, Gregory   475
Trinh, Thanh-Hai   93
Truong, Khiet P.   228
Tsai, Jason   384
Tuchman, Peleg   28, 441

Uejou, Masaki   477
Urao, Akira   451

Vala, Marco   148, 282
Valgardsson, Gunnar   48

Van den Bosch, Karel   435
van Oijen, Joost   462
van Welbergen, Herwin   269, 296, 324
Vilhjálmsson, Hannes Högni   48, 473
von der Pütten, Astrid M.   183

Wachsmuth, Ipke   350
Walker, Marilyn A.   398
Wang, Zhiyang   216
Wilson, Nicholas   460

Xu, Yuyu   269

Yaghoubzadeh, Ramin   195
Youngblood, G. Michael   202, 370

Zhang, Li   412
Zhang, Zhengzhi   331
Zwiers, Job   296, 324